DUBLIN UNIVERSITY CALENDAR
1966-7

A

Dublin University Calendar

1966-7

1966

HODGES FIGGIS AND CO. LTD

DUBLIN

Arms of the College

Azure, a Bible closed, clasps to the dexter, between in chief, on the dexter, a lion passant, on the sinister, a harp, all or, and in base a castle with two towers domed, each surmounted by a banner flotant from the sides, argent, the dexter flag charged with a cross, the sinister with a saltire, gules.

This book, which has been set in 10 and 11 point Bembo solid, has been printed in the Republic of Ireland by Hely Thom, Limited, Dublin.

CONTENTS

Contents

Contents

ALMANACK

DATES OF ACADEMIC TERMS AND
ARTS LECTURES

MICHAELMAS TERM 1966

Term begins	Tuesday 20 September
Term ends	Monday 12 December
Arts lectures begin	Monday 24 October
Arts lectures end	Saturday 10 December

HILARY TERM 1967

Term begins	Saturday 7 January
Term ends	Tuesday 7 March
Arts lectures begin	Monday 16 January
Arts lectures end	Saturday 4 March

TRINITY TERM 1967

Term begins	Saturday 1 April
Term ends	Wednesday 12 July
Arts lectures begin	Monday 10 April
Arts lectures end	Saturday 27 May

MICHAELMAS TERM 1967

Term begins	Wednesday 20 September
Term ends	Tuesday 12 December
Arts lectures begin	Monday 23 October
Arts lectures end	Saturday 9 December

DAYS OF PUBLIC COMMENCEMENTS[1]

MICHAELMAS TERM 1966	Thursday 10 November
	Thursday 8 December
TRINITY TERM 1967	Thursday 11 May
	Tuesday 11 July
MICHAELMAS TERM 1967	Thursday 9 November
	Thursday 7 December

DATES OF MOVABLE FEASTS

	1967	1968	1969
Easter Day	26 March	14 April	6 April
Whitsunday	14 May	2 June	25 May
Trinity Sunday	21 May	9 June	2 June
Advent Sunday	3 December	1 December	30 November

For services in the Chapel see CHAPEL OF TRINITY COLLEGE.

[1]The dates in 1967 are subject to approval by the Senate.

SEPTEMBER 1966

Thursday	1	**Last day for payment of Junior Freshman fees**
Friday	2	
Saturday	3	

Sunday	4	*13th Sunday after Trinity*
Monday	5	
Tuesday	6	
Wednesday	7	
Thursday	8	
Friday	9	
Saturday	10	

Sunday	11	*14th Sunday after Trinity. Ember Week*
Monday	12	
Tuesday	13	
Wednesday	14	
Thursday	15	
Friday	16	
Saturday	17	

Sunday	18	*15th Sunday after Trinity*
Monday	19	
Tuesday	20	Michaelmas term begins
		Matriculation examination
		Moderatorship honor and prize examinations begin
		Engineering school entrance examination
		Supplemental engineering examinations (including B.A.I. degree)
		Supplemental examinations in Junior Freshman preliminary science year and in agriculture (all classes)
		Supplemental pre-registration examination

September 1966

Wednesday 21	*St Matthew*
Thursday 22	Supplemental first and second medical examinations
	Supplemental second dental examination
Friday 23	
Saturday 24	

Sunday 25	*16th Sunday after Trinity*
Monday 26	Supplemental divinity examinations
	Examination for the Diploma in Biblical Studies
Tuesday 27	
Wednesday 28	Supplemental Junior Freshman examination in general studies and for Church of Ireland Training College students
Thursday 29	*St Michael and all Angels*
Friday 30	Supplemental first dental examination

October 1966

Saturday 1	**Annual fees due (excluding Junior Freshmen)**

Sunday 2	*17th Sunday after Trinity*
Monday 3	Supplemental B.A. degree and Junior Sophister examinations in general studies
Tuesday 4	
Wednesday 5	
Thursday 6	Second special supplemental examination for B.Comm. degree
	Supplemental Freshmen and Senior Sophister examinations in business studies and social studies
Friday 7	
Saturday 8	

Sunday 9	*18th Sunday after Trinity*
Monday 10	Medical lectures begin

October 1966

Tuesday 11	Post-graduate lectures, School of Education, begin
Wednesday 12	
Thursday 13	
Friday 14	
Saturday 15	

Sunday 16	*19th Sunday after Trinity*
Monday 17	Divinity term begins
	Engineering lectures (except first year) begin
Tuesday 18	*St Luke*
	Registration for all students entering the College
Wednesday 19	**Registration for all students entering the College**
Thursday 20	
Friday 21	General essay for rising Junior Freshmen in general studies and in professional schools
	Supplemental final dental examination (A)
Saturday 22	Catechetical examinations (all classes)

Sunday 23	*20th Sunday after Trinity*
Monday 24	**Undergraduate lectures in arts and science begin**
	Agriculture lectures begin
	Business studies and social studies lectures begin
	Engineering lectures (first year) begin
	Law School lectures begin
	Pre-medical lectures begin
Tuesday 25	
Wednesday 26	
Thursday 27	
Friday 28	*St Simon and St Jude*
Saturday 29	Catechetical lectures begin

Sunday 30	*21st Sunday after Trinity*
Monday 31	

November 1966

Tuesday	1	*All Saints*
		Last day for return of registration cards, all students
Wednesday	2	
Thursday	3	Supplemental final dental examination (B)
		Supplemental final medical examination, part IV
Friday	4	Meeting of General Studies School Committee
Saturday	5	

Sunday	6	*22nd Sunday after Trinity*
Monday	7	
Tuesday	8	
Wednesday	9	
Thursday	10	**Autumn Commencements** 2 p.m.
Friday	11	Supplemental final medical examination, part V
Saturday	12	

Sunday	13	*23rd Sunday after Trinity*
Monday	14	Divinity School Council meets
Tuesday	15	Last day for tardy payment of fees without fine (excluding Junior Freshmen)
Wednesday	16	
Thursday	17	
Friday	18	Supplemental final medical examination, part III
Saturday	19	Last day for giving notice for optional honor and special prize examinations in Hilary term.

Sunday	20	*24th Sunday after Trinity*
Monday	21	
Tuesday	22	
Wednesday	23	
Thursday	24	
Friday	25	
Saturday	26	

Sunday	27	*1st Sunday in Advent*

November 1966

Monday 28
Tuesday 29
Wednesday 30   *St Andrew*

December 1966

Thursday 1
Friday 2   Supplemental final medical examination, part I
Saturday 3   Law School lectures end

Sunday 4   *2nd Sunday in Advent*
Monday 5   Law School term examinations
                Choral Society Concert
Tuesday 6   Supplemental B.D. degree examination
                Choral Society concert
Wednesday 7
Thursday 8   **Winter Commencements** 11.30 a.m. and 3.30 p.m.
Friday 9   Divinity term ends
Saturday 10   **Undergraduate lectures in arts and science end**
                Agriculture lectures end
                Business studies and social studies lectures end
                Catechetical lectures end
                Engineering lectures end
                Pre-medical and medical lectures end

Sunday 11   *3rd Sunday in Advent. Ember Week*
Monday 12   Michaelmas term ends
                LL.B. degree examinations
                Supplemental general essay for Junior Freshmen in general
                    studies and in professional schools
Tuesday 13
Wednesday 14
Thursday 15
Friday 16
Saturday 17

DECEMBER 1966

Sunday 18   *4th Sunday in Advent*
Monday 19
Tuesday 20
Wednesday 21   *St Thomas*
Thursday 22
Friday 23
Saturday 24

Sunday 25   *Christmas Day*
Monday 26   *St Stephen*
Tuesday 27   *St John*
Wednesday 28   *Innocents' Day*
Thursday 29
Friday 30
Saturday 31

JANUARY 1967

Sunday 1   1st *Sunday after Christmas.*   *Circumcision*
Monday 2
Tuesday 3
Wednesday 4
Thursday 5
Friday 6   *Epiphany*
Saturday 7   Hilary term begins

Sunday 8   1st *Sunday after the Epiphany*
Monday 9   Divinity term begins
     Engineering lectures (except first year) begin
     Honor and prize examinations begin
     Pre-medical and medical lectures begin
Tuesday 10   Post-graduate lectures, School of Education, begin
Wednesday 11
Thursday 12

JANUARY 1967

Friday 13	Final medical examination, part II
Saturday 14	Catechetical examinations (all classes)

Sunday 15	*2nd Sunday after the Epiphany*
Monday 16	**Undergraduate lectures in arts and science begin**
	Agriculture lectures begin
	Business studies and social studies lectures begin
	Engineering lectures (first year) begin
	Law School lectures begin
Tuesday 17	
Wednesday 18	
Thursday 19	
Friday 20	
Saturday 21	Catechetical lectures begin

Sunday 22	*Septuagesima*
Monday 23	Second supplemental general essay for Junior Freshmen in general studies and in professional schools
Tuesday 24	
Wednesday 25	*Conversion of St Paul*
Thursday 26	
Friday 27	
Saturday 28	

Sunday 29	*Sexagesima*
Monday 30	
Tuesday 31	

FEBRUARY 1967

Wednesday 1	
Thursday 2	*Purification of the Blessed Virgin Mary*
Friday 3	
Saturday 4	

FEBRUARY 1967

Sunday	5	*Quinquagesima*
Monday	6	
Tuesday	7	
Wednesday	8	*Ash Wednesday*
Thursday	9	
Friday	10	
Saturday	11	**Last day for giving notice for optional honor, foundation scholarship and prize examinations in Trinity term**

Sunday	12	*1st Sunday in Lent. Ember Week*
Monday	13	Divinity School Council meets
Tuesday	14	
Wednesday	15	
Thursday	16	
Friday	17	
Saturday	18	

Sunday	19	*2nd Sunday in Lent*
Monday	20	
Tuesday	21	
Wednesday	22	**University Senate meets:** graces for honorary degrees, and other business
Thursday	23	Second dental examination
Friday	24	*St Matthias*
Saturday	25	Law School lectures end

Sunday	26	*3rd Sunday in Lent*
Monday	27	Law School examinations
Tuesday	28	B.D. degree examination

MARCH 1967

Wednesday	1	Choral Society concert
Thursday	2	Choral Society concert
		First medical examination

MARCH 1967

Friday 3
Saturday 4   **Undergraduate lectures in arts and science end**
           Agriculture lectures end
           Business studies and social studies lectures end
           Catechetical lectures end
           Divinity term ends
           Engineering lectures end
           Pre-medical and medical lectures end

Sunday 5   *4th Sunday in Lent*
Monday 6
Tuesday 7   Hilary term ends
Wednesday 8
Thursday 9
· Friday 10
Saturday 11

Sunday 12   *5th Sunday in Lent*
Monday 13
Tuesday 14
Wednesday 15
Thursday 16
Friday 17   *St Patrick*
Saturday 18

Sunday 19   *6th Sunday in Lent*
Monday 20
Tuesday 21
Wednesday 22
Thursday 23
Friday 24   *Good Friday*
Saturday 25   *Annunciation of the Blessed Virgin Mary*

Sunday 26   *Easter Day*
Monday 27   *Monday in Easter Week*

MARCH 1967

Tuesday 28
Wednesday 29
Thursday 30
Friday 31

APRIL 1967

Saturday 1   Trinity term begins

Sunday 2   *1st Sunday after Easter*
Monday 3   **Foundation scholarship examination**
         Pre-medical and medical lectures begin
Tuesday 4   Post-graduate lectures, School of Education, begin
Wednesday 5
Thursday 6
Friday 7
Saturday 8   Catechetical examinations (all classes)

Sunday 9   *2nd Sunday after Easter*
Monday 10   **Undergraduate lectures in arts and science begin**
         Agriculture lectures begin
         Business studies and social studies lectures begin
         Divinity term begins
         Engineering lectures begin
         Law School lectures begin
Tuesday 11
Wednesday 12
Thursday 13
Friday 14
Saturday 15   Catechetical lectures begin

Sunday 16   *3rd Sunday after Easter*
Monday 17
Tuesday 18
Wednesday 19   Engineering examination (third year, part I)
Thursday 20

April 1967

Friday 21   Supplemental final medical examination, part II
Saturday 22

Sunday 23   *4th Sunday after Easter*
Monday 24   **Entrance scholarship and exhibition examination**
Tuesday 25   *St Mark*
Wednesday 26
Thursday 27
Friday 28
Saturday 29

Sunday 30   *Rogation Sunday*

May 1967

Monday   1   *St Philip and St James*
Tuesday   2
Wednesday   3
Thursday   4   *Ascension Day*
Friday   5   Matriculation examination
Saturday   6   **Last day for giving notice for prize examinations in Michaelmas term**

Sunday   7   *Sunday after Ascension Day*
Monday   8
Tuesday   9
Wednesday 10
Thursday 11   **First Summer Commencements** 2 p.m.
Friday 12
Saturday 13

Sunday 14   *Whitsunday.   Ember Week*
Monday 15   *Monday in Whitsun Week*
Tuesday 16   *Tuesday Whitsun Week*

MAY 1967

Wednesday 17	
Thursday 18	
Friday 19	**Trinity Week begins**
Saturday 20	Law School lectures end

Sunday 21	*Trinity Sunday*
Monday 22	*Trinity Monday*
	Election to Fellowship and Scholarship
Tuesday 23	Final medical examination, part III
Wednesday 24	College races
	Final medical examination, part IV
Thursday 25	Choral Society concert
Friday 26	Final medical examination, part V
Saturday 27	**Undergraduate lectures in arts and science end**
	Agriculture lectures end
	Business studies and social studies lectures end
	Catechetical lectures end
	Engineering lectures end

Sunday 28	*1st Sunday after Trinity*
Monday 29	B.A.I. degree examination
	Business studies and social studies examinations
	Law School annual examinations
Tuesday 30	
Wednesday 31	

JUNE 1967

Thursday 1	B.A. degree examination in general studies
	Examination for the Higher Diploma in Education
Friday 2	
Saturday 3	Divinity term ends

Sunday 4	*2nd Sunday after Trinity*
Monday 5	*June Monday*

JUNE 1967

Tuesday	6	Junior Sophister examination in genera lstudies
		Annual examinations in agriculture
		Annual examinations preliminary science year
		Engineering examinations (except B.A.I. degree
Wednesday	7	
Thursday	8	
Friday	9	*St Columba*
		Final medical examination, part I
Saturday	10	Pre-medical and medical lectures end

Sunday	11	*3rd Sunday after Trinity. St Barnabas*
Monday	12	Pre-registration examination
Tuesday	13	
Wednesday	14	Junior Freshman examination in general studies and for Church of Ireland Training College students
Thursday	15	
Friday	16	Business studies examinations for Graduate course in Administration
		First dental examination
		Second medical examination
Saturday	17	

Sunday	18	*4th Sunday after Trinity*
Monday	19	Divinity School Council meets
		Senior Freshman examination in general studies and for Church of Ireland Training College students
		Final dental examination
		LL.B. degree examinations
		Examination for Mus.D. (five days)
Tuesday	20	Examination for Mus.B. (Part II)
Wednesday	21	Examinations for Mus.B. (Parts I and III)
Thursday	22	Examinations for Mus.B. (Parts I and III)
Friday	23	Examination for Mus.B. (Part III)
Saturday	24	*St John the Baptist*

Sunday	25	*5th Sunday after Trinity*
Monday	26	

June 1967

Tuesday 27   Examination for the Diploma in the History of European Painting

Wednesday 28

Thursday 29   *St Peter*

Friday 30

July 1967

Saturday 1

Sunday 2   *6th Sunday after Trinity*

Monday 3

Tuesday 4   International Summer School begins

Wednesday 5

Thursday 6

Friday 7

Saturday 8

Sunday 9   *7th Sunday after Trinity*

Monday 10   Library closed to readers

Tuesday 11   **Second Summer Commencements** 11.30 a.m. and 3.30 p.m.

Wednesday 12   Trinity term ends

Thursday 13

Friday 14

Saturday 15

Sunday 16   *8th Sunday after Trinity*

Monday 17

Tuesday 18

Wednesday 19

Thursday 20

Friday 21

Saturday 22

Sunday 23   *9th Sunday after Trinity*

Monday 24   Library re-opens to readers

July 1967

Tuesday 25
Wednesday 26   *St James*
Thursday 27
Friday 28
Saturday 29

Sunday 30   *10th Sunday after Trinity*
Monday 31

August 1967

Tuesday 1
Wednesday 2
Thursday 3
Friday 4
Saturday 5

Sunday 6   *11th Sunday after Trinity.   Transfiguration*
Monday 7
Tuesday 8
Wednesday 9
Thursday 10
Friday 11
Saturday 12

Sunday 13   *12th Sunday after Trinity*
Monday 14
Tuesday 15
Wednesday 16
Thursday 17
Friday 18
Saturday 19

August 1967

Sunday 20	*13th Sunday after Trinity*
Monday 21	
Tuesday 22	
Wednesday 23	
Thursday 24	*St Bartholomew*
Friday 25	
Saturday 26	

Sunday 27	*14th Sunday after Trinity*
Monday 28	
Tuesday 29	
Wednesday 30	
Thursday 31	

September 1967

Friday 1	**Last day for payment of Junior Freshman fees**
Saturday 2	

Sunday 3	*15th Sunday after Trinity*
Monday 4	
Tuesday 5	
Wednesday 6	
Thursday 7	
Friday 8	
Saturday 9	

Sunday 10	*16th Sunday after Trinity*
Monday 11	
Tuesday 12	
Wednesday 13	
Thursday 14	
Friday 15	
Saturday 16	

September 1967

Sunday 17	*17th Sunday after Trinity. Ember Week*
Monday 18	
Tuesday 19	
Wednesday 20	Michaelmas term begins
	Matriculation examination
	Moderatorship honor and prize examinations
	Engineering School entrance examination
	Supplemental engineering examinations (including B.A.I. degree)
	Supplemental examinations in Junior Freshman preliminary science year and in agriculture (Freshmen years)
	Supplemental pre-registration examination
Thursday 21	*St Matthew*
	Supplemental first medical examination
Friday 22	Supplemental second medical examination
Saturday 23	

Sunday 24	*18th Sunday after Trinity*
Monday 25	Supplemental Divinity examinations
	Examination for the Diploma in Biblical Studies
	Supplemental second dental examination
Tuesday 26	
Wednesday 27	
Thursday 28	Supplemental Junior Freshman examination in general studies and for Church of Ireland Training College students
Friday 29	*St Michael and all Angels*
	Supplemental first dental examination
Saturday 30	

October 1967

Sunday 1	*19th Sunday after Trinity*
Monday 2	**Annual fees due (excluding Junior Freshmen)**
	Supplemental B.A. degree examination
Tuesday 3	

October 1967

Wednesday 4

Thursday 5   Supplemental examinations in business studies and social studies

Friday 6

Saturday 7

Sunday 8   *20th Sunday after Trinity*

Monday 9   Medical lectures begin

Tuesday 10

Wednesday 11

Thursday 12

Friday 13

Saturday 14

Sunday 15   *21st Sunday after Trinity*

Monday 16   Divinity term begins

Engineering lectures (except first year) begin

Tuesday 17   **Registration for all students entering the College**

Post-graduate lectures, School of Education, begin

Wednesday 18   *St Luke*

Registration for all students entering the College

Thursday 19

Friday 20   General essay for rising Junior Freshmen in general studies and in professional schools

Saturday 21   Catechetical examinations (all classes)

Sunday 22   *22nd Sunday after Trinity*

Monday 23   **Undergraduate lectures in arts and science begin**

Agriculture lectures begin

Business studies and social studies lectures begin

Engineering lectures (first year) begin

Law School lectures begin

Pre-medical lectures begin

Tuesday 24

Wednesday 25

xxviii

OCTOBER 1967

Thursday 26
Friday 27
Saturday 28   *St Simon and St Jude*
Catechetical lectures begin

Sunday 29   *23rd Sunday after Trinity*
Monday 30
Tuesday 31   **Last day for return of registration cards, all students (except new entrants)**

NOVEMBER 1967

Wednesday 1   *All Saints*
Thursday 2   Supplemental final medical examination, part IV
Friday 3   Meeting of General Studies School Committee
Saturday 4

Sunday 5   *24th Sunday after Trinity*
Monday 6
Tuesday 7
Wednesday 8
Thursday 9   **Autumn Commencements** 2 p.m.
Friday 10   Supplemental final medical examination, part V
Saturday 11

Sunday 12   *25th Sunday after Trinity*
Monday 13   Divinity School Council meets
Tuesday 14
Wednesday 15
Thursday 16   Supplemental final dental examination
Friday 17   Supplemental medical examination, part III
Saturday 18   Last day for giving notice for optional honor and special prize examinations in Hilary term

November 1967

Sunday 19   *26th Sunday after Trinity*
Monday 20
Tuesday 21
Wednesday 22
Thursday 23
Friday 24
Saturday 25

Sunday 26   *27th Sunday after Trinity*
Monday 27
Tuesday 28
Wednesday 29
Thursday 30   *St Andrew*

December 1967

Friday 1   Supplemental final medical examination, part I
Saturday 2   Law School lectures end

Sunday 3   *1st Sunday in Advent*
Monday 4   Law School term examinations
       LL.B. degree examinations (provisional)
       Choral Society concert
Tuesday 5   Supplemental B.D. degree examination
       Choral Society concert
Wednesday 6
Thursday 7   **Winter Commencements** 11.30 a.m. and 3.30 p.m.
Friday 8
Saturday 9   Undergraduate lectures in arts and science end
       Agriculture lectures end
       Business studies and social studies lectures end
       Catechetical lectures end
       Divinity term ends
       Engineering lectures end
       Pre-medical and medical lectures end

December 1967

Sunday 10	*2nd Sunday in Advent*	
Monday 11	Law School term examinations	
Tuesday 12	Michaelmas term ends	
	Supplemental general essay for Junior Freshmen in general studies and in professional schools	
Wednesday 13		
Thursday 14		
Friday 15		
Saturday 16		

Sunday 17	*3rd Sunday in Advent. Ember Week*	
Monday 18		
Tuesday 19		
Wednesday 20		
Thursday 21	*St Thomas*	
Friday 22		
Saturday 23		

Sunday 24	*4th Sunday in Advent*	
Monday 25	*Christmas Day*	
Tuesday 26	*St Stephen*	
Wednesday 27	*St John*	
Thursday 28	*Innocents' Day*	
Friday 29		
Saturday 30		

Sunday 31	*1st Sunday after Christmas*

Note

Letters concerning the general academic business of the College should be addressed to the Secretary to the College, Trinity College, Dublin. Telephone number of the College: Dublin 72941.

The *Calendar* is issued annually in early October, price fifteen shillings (seventeen shillings and threepence, post-free). Copies may be obtained from the publishers, Hodges Figgis and Co. Ltd., Dawson Street, Dublin 2, or from the university booksellers.

The Board of Trinity College is not bound by errors in, or omissions from, the *Calendar*.

While every effort will be made to give due notice of major changes the Board of Trinity College reserves the right to suspend, alter or initiate courses, examinations and regulations at any time.

INTRODUCTION

A HISTORY OF TRINITY COLLEGE

CONSTITUTION OF THE COLLEGE AND UNIVERSITY

BUILDINGS OF TRINITY COLLEGE

B

The history of Trinity College can be conveniently divided into three epochs—a century or so during which the foundations were laid, a period of colourful expansion extending over the eighteenth century, and a century and a half of strenuous adaptation to a rapidly changing world.

Trinity was founded just before the Tudor monarchy had completed the task of extending its authority over the whole of Ireland. The idea of an Irish university had been in the air for some time, and in 1591 a small group of Dublin citizens obtained a charter from Queen Elizabeth incorporating Trinity College *juxta Dublin*. The Corporation of Dublin granted to the new foundation the lands and dilapidated buildings of the monastery of All Hallows, lying about a quarter of a mile south-east of the city walls. Two years later a few Fellows and students began to work in the new college, which then consisted of one small square. During the next fifty years the community increased. Endowments, including considerable landed estates, were secured, new fellowships were founded, the books which formed the beginning of the great library were acquired, a curriculum was devised and statutes were framed.

The second half-century of the College's history was a time of turmoil, marked in Ireland by an interregnum and two civil wars. In 1641 the Provost fled, and two years later the College had to pawn its plate; some Fellows were expelled by the Commonwealth authorities, others were excluded at the Restoration, and in 1689 all the Fellows and students were expelled when the College was turned into a barrack for the soldiers of James II. But the seventeenth century was also an age of ardent learning; and Trinity men such as Ussher, a kindly polymath, Marsh, the orientalist, Dodwell, the historian, Stearne, who founded the Irish College of Physicians, and Molyneux, the correspondent of Locke, were typical of the adventurous and wide-ranging scholarship of their day.

The eighteenth century was for the most part a peaceful era in Ireland, and Trinity shared its calm, though at the beginning of the period a few Jacobites and at its end a very small group of political radicals seriously perturbed the college authorities. During this century Trinity was the university of the Protestant ascendancy. Parliament, meeting on the other side of College Green, viewed it benevolently and made generous grants for building. The first building of the new age was the Library, begun in 1712; then followed the Printing House and the Dining Hall; and during the second half of the century Parliament Square slowly emerged. The great building drive was completed in the early nineteenth century by Botany Bay, the square which derives its name in part from the herb garden it once contained.

These buildings expressed the ordered vigour of the College's life. Unlike the English universities Trinity took its duties seriously. The Fellows were hard-worked, both as teachers and administrators. The curriculum was kept up-to-date, there were quarterly examinations at which prizes were granted to successful candidates, and the fellowship examination was a Homeric contest. Most of the outstanding Irishmen of the eighteenth century, including Swift, Berkeley, Burke, Goldsmith, Grattan and Tone, were Trinity graduates, and the influence of their university is discernible in their writings and speeches.

Three of the eighteenth-century provosts were outstanding. Richard Baldwin (1717-58) was a strong disciplinarian who strove to prevent the boisterous high spirits that characterised contemporary Anglo-Irish society from playing havoc with academic peace. His successor, Francis Andrews (1758-74), was a member of parliament and a widely travelled and popular man of the world, whose taste and social ambitions are reflected in the Provost's House, erected in 1759. He provided in his will for the foundation of a chair of astronomy and an observatory. He was succeeded by Hely-Hutchinson (1774-94), a barrister and an enlightened if self-interested politician. Eager to widen the curriculum, he was responsible for the foundation of chairs of modern languages, and he pushed forward the eighteenth-century building programme. His sometimes not over-scrupulous approach to college problems involved him in wrangles with many of the Fellows, and his provostship is the Dublin equivalent of Bentley's stormy and litigious mastership of Trinity, Cambridge.

So far as Trinity was concerned, the nineteenth century only began when Bartholomew Lloyd became Provost in 1831. A determined if conciliatory reformer, his provostship was marked by a number of important changes, of which the most significant was the introduction of the modern system of honor studies in 1833. Until then there had been only one course for the degree of B.A., the ordinary or general course in arts embracing classics, mathematics, a little science and some philosophy. It became possible for an undergraduate to specialise when in 1834 examinations for degrees with honors, or moderatorships, were established in mathematics, in ethics and logics, and in classics. In 1851 a moderatorship in experimental science was added; this at first included physics, chemistry and mineralogy, and was later expanded to comprise geology, zoology and botany. In 1871 it was divided into two, moderatorships being given in natural science and in experimental science. This arrangement was maintained till 1955, when the two groups were again combined in a moderatorship in natural sciences. In 1856 a moderatorship was founded in history and English literature, which continued till 1873, when separate moderatorships were instituted in history and political science and in modern literature. The introduction of these moderatorship examinations was accompanied by the development of honor courses and of a system of 'honor privileges' which eventually enabled honor students to substitute honor for ordinary lectures, and honor for all ordinary examinations except the Final Freshman examination, or 'Little-go'. The abolition in 1959 of Little-go for honor students has completed the separation of the honor from the ordinary curriculum. At the same time, the ordinary course in arts has been radically reconstructed.

The nineteenth century was also marked by important developments in the professional schools. Divinity had been taught from the foundation of the College, and in the nineteenth century its teaching was systematised. The Law School was reorganised after the middle of the century. Medical teaching had been given in the College since 1711, but it was only after the establishment of the School on a sound basis by legislation in 1800 and under the inspiration of Macartney, the brilliant and quarrelsome anatomist, that it was in a position to play its full part, with such teachers as Graves and Stokes, in the great age of Dublin medicine. The Engineering School was established in 1842 and was one of the first of its kind in the British Isles. In the early twentieth century professorships of education (1905) and of agriculture (1906) were founded and the School of Commerce was established in 1925.

This expansion of the College's activities had an outward sign in the buildings erected since 1800. Just after the middle of the century, the New Square was completed by the erection of the Museum Building; and new buildings at the east end of the College Park expressed the increasing importance of the natural sciences and of medicine in the life of the College.

Between 1830 and 1900 twenty new chairs were founded, and Trinity scholarship displayed to the full the versatility, the industry and the self-confidence of the Victorian age. The Trinity tradition, which, even in an age of increasing specialisation, favoured a wide range of interests, had a stimulating effect on members of the College. Towards the end of the nineteenth century the School of Classics could boast not only of classical scholars like Palmer and Purser, but also of men such as Tyrrell and Mahaffy, whose interests ranged from ancient

Egypt to Georgian Ireland, and Bury, whose Byzantine studies straddled the classical and modern eras. In mathematics and science there were Rowan Hamilton, Humphrey Lloyd, Salmon, Fitzgerald and Joly. In English there was Dowden, a sensitive critic and an irascible politician, and in economics Ingram, the most outstanding of the Irish positivists.

It would be a mistake to picture these men and their colleagues as working in an undisturbed academic calm. Momentous changes were taking place in Ireland, and these were reflected in the controversies that raged round the government's Irish university policy. Between 1873 and 1908 schemes were proposed by the government of the day which would have made the College a member of a federated university, in which several other Irish academic bodies would have been included. These schemes were strenuously and effectively resisted by Trinity as threats to its independence. On the other hand the College progressively abandoned the exclusive religious character that, in common with Oxford and Cambridge, it had hitherto borne. As early as 1793 Roman Catholics had been permitted to enter and to take degrees in Trinity. In 1854 non-foundation scholarships, open to candidates of all denominations, were instituted. In 1873 all religious tests, except those connected with the Divinity School, were abolished.

In the government of the College the last century has witnessed far-reaching changes. The creation in 1874 of the University Council, a representative body, gave control over the shaping of courses and appointments to the teaching departments. From 1900, as can be seen from the evidence given before the royal commission of 1906, the composition of the Board was being strongly criticised by important sections of college opinion, and in 1911 the constitution was modified by the addition of two representatives of the Junior Fellows and two representatives of the non-fellow Professors to the Board. The representation of the Junior Fellows was increased to four members in 1958. At the same time the statutes were altered to require that half of the professors should be Fellows.

Strange to say, one innovation of far-reaching significance aroused relatively little controversy. In 1904 women were admitted to the University and by 1914 they already amounted to sixteen per cent of the students on the college books. In 1908 a women's hall of residence, Trinity Hall, was founded. In 1934 the first woman professor was appointed and women continue to play an increasing part in many spheres of college life.

The Great War of 1914-18 marks in more than one way the end of an epoch for Trinity College. When conditions again became settled

5

Ireland had undergone a constitutional revolution and the College found itself in a divided Ireland outside the United Kingdom. Moreover, at a time when the newer universities in the British Isles were growing in strength and prestige, Trinity College found itself lacking in the resources required to maintain its position in the new age. In 1920 a royal commission recommended that the College needed both a large capital grant and an annual subsidy. But the change of regime occurred before its recommendations could be implemented, and it was not until 1947 that the College secured an annual grant from the state. The grant was substantial and since then has been increased, so that by now it represents about fifty per cent of the College's income.

In recent years numbers have risen well above what had come to be considered the norm. In 1962 they stood at 3,000 as compared with 1,500 in 1939. The increase in numbers has brought greater diversity, many of the undergraduates coming from Great Britain and from overseas. This change in the composition of the student body has been accompanied by a similar change in the composition of the academic staff. Until the nineteen-thirties, the great majority of the holders of academic posts in Trinity College were doubly indigenous, being Irishmen and Dublin University graduates. But since 1945 many of those appointed to the staff have come from other universities, British and Irish. Probably this is one of the factors which accounts for the accelerated pace of change, which has been a striking characteristic of the period since the end of the war—change reflected in an increase of the representative element on the Board, in a radical recasting of the arts curriculum, in the erection of new buildings and the adaptation of old buildings to new needs, in the establishment of new departmental libraries, in the improvement of college rooms, and in the provision of new amenities for undergraduates.

CONSTITUTION OF THE COLLEGE
AND UNIVERSITY

The relation between Trinity College and the University of Dublin

The relation between Trinity College and the University of Dublin is peculiar, and in many respects anomalous. For most practical purposes the two bodies are, very reasonably, regarded as identical, but much of the academic terminology of Dublin presupposes a distinction between the two.

The simplest way of regarding the relationship is by supposing that both the University and the College are formally similar to their counterparts at Oxford and Cambridge, but that there happens to be only one college within the University. Since Trinity College, Dublin, was, at the time of its foundation, and the enactment of its first statutes, frankly modelled on Trinity College, Cambridge, it is natural that many similarities in organisation, constitution and terminology should exist. Some further support is lent to this interpretation by the fact that the project of founding a second college within the University has been more than once seriously considered. The terminology of today is also in harmony with it; bodies such as the Senate and Council, and officers such as the Chancellor and Proctors, who are concerned with the conferring of degrees and the fixing of courses required for them, are considered to pertain to the University, while the Provost, Fellows and Scholars, and bodies or officers concerned with the teaching or domestic arrangements are considered to pertain to the College.

This precision is, however, relatively modern, and in the late eighteenth and early nineteenth centuries such phrases as 'Fellow of Dublin University' and 'The University of Trinity College' are often found, even in official documents. It is possible, therefore, to adopt an alternative interpretation: that the institution founded by Queen Elizabeth was essentially a college, designed no doubt to form part of a university, and vested as an interim measure with some of the powers and functions of a university; but that, since no other colleges were in fact founded, this temporary dual nature became permanent, and thus the same body has continued to fill the dual role of college and university. In support of this view it may be mentioned that, although the Senate of the University was formally incorporated in 1858, the University of Dublin is not itself a corporate body.

The curious phrase *mater universitatis* which is used to describe the

College in the foundation charter can be claimed in support of either interpretation. It would appear that the founders and early rulers of the College were concerned only to see that the essential collegiate and university functions were, in some manner or another, performed from the start, and that they would have shown little interest in the fine distinctions debated by their successors.

The Chancellor, Pro-Chancellors and Visitors

The Chancellor is the head of the University, as distinct from the College, and has custody of the common seal of the Senate. He presides over Commencements and other meetings of the Senate; but he may from time to time depute this or any other of his duties to one of the Pro-Chancellors. If none of the Pro-Chancellors is able to act the appointment of a Pro-Chancellor for the occasion (usually the other Visitor or a senior member of the College) is made by the Board.

The Chancellor (or in his absence one of the Pro-Chancellors) and one other person appointed for the purpose act as Visitors to the College and University; they form, in this capacity, the ultimate court of appeal within the University, whether in disciplinary matters or in the interpretation of the statutes, and their consent is required for changes in the statutes and certain other legislative enactments by the Board.

The Chancellor is appointed for life by the Senate from a list of three names submitted to them by the Board. The Pro-Chancellors, who are not more than three in number, are elected by the Senate from nominations approved by the Chancellor; they take precedence in the University next after the Chancellor and in order of their election. Pro-Chancellors hold office until they reach the age of 70 years. The other Visitor (who is very often a judge) is appointed by the President of Ireland, on the advice of the Government, from a panel of two persons nominated to them by the Senate.

The Provost

The Provost is appointed by the Government and holds office for life. He is head of the College, and in the words of the statutes is 'invested with higher authority than any other person in the control both of the members and of the business of the College.' He convenes and presides at meetings of the Board

In University affairs, also, the Provost occupies a special place. He summons and presides at meetings of the Council, and is a member of the Caput of the Senate.

The Fellows

The Fellows are elected by the Board, the election usually taking

8

place on Trinity Monday. The average rate of election was until lately one or two Fellows a year, but in recent years the number has been larger, and the Board has discretion to arrange in any year for the election of any number that it thinks fit, or of none. Fellowships are open only to men.

There are at present two normal modes of election:

1. If the Board decides that it is desirable to elect to Fellowship a particular person holding a teaching post other than that of Professor in the University of Dublin, or a graduate of the University holding an academic or similar post elsewhere, it may invite him to submit his published and unpublished work for examination. If the report of the examiners is favourable, and if at least three-fifths of the Fellows assent, he is elected Fellow forthwith.

2. The Board has also power to elect any Professor of the University to Fellowship if a majority of the Fellows assent; and it is bound to arrange elections in such a way that not less than half the total number of Professors is included in the body of Fellows.

Fellows were originally elected for a period of seven years. From 1637 to 1959, the appointment was for life. Fellows elected in or after 1959 must retire at the age of 70, and are thereafter given the title of Fellow Emeritus.

There is no upper limit fixed by the statutes to the number of Fellows, but a statute directs that it shall not be allowed to fall permanently below 36.

Fellows are entitled, in addition to their salary, to chambers and commons free of charge.

In the early days of the College almost the whole of the work of teaching, examining and administration was undertaken by the Fellows. During the eighteenth and nineteenth centuries the Professors not holding Fellowships took over an increasing proportion of the teaching and examining, and in the present century the large increase in the number of lecturers means that the Fellows no longer discharge the major part of this work. A large part of the administration, however, remains in their hands. Rather more than half the Fellows hold Professorships; of the remainder most are either Tutors (see below) or hold one of the administrative offices.

The Fellows are divided into two classes, Senior and Junior. The Senior Fellows are seven in number, and all sit *ex officio* on the Board. (Up to 1911 the Board consisted of the Provost and Senior Fellows alone.) They consist normally of the seven most senior on the roll of Fellows, but succession to the body is not strictly automatic. When a vacancy occurs, by death or resignation, the Provost and remaining Senior

Constitution of the College and University

Fellows meet to co-opt a successor; and although the Provost is bound to propose the most senior of the Junior Fellows, he can be passed over if he is not considered by the electors 'worthy' of co-option[1].

The Junior Fellows have the right to elect four of their number to represent them on the Board (see below). They also meet regularly to discuss matters of current interest in the College and University.

The Professors

Most of the Professors are nominated by the University Council, and appointed by the consent of the Board. A number of them, however, are elected by other bodies; Erasmus Smith's Professors of Oratory and of Natural and Experimental Philosophy are elected by the Governors of Erasmus Smith's schools; the Professors of Irish and of Pastoral Theology are nominated by persons specified in the trusts under which these chairs were endowed; the Reid Professor of Penal Legislation is elected by the Board on the results of an examination; the Professors in the Divinity School (other than the Professor of Pastoral Theology) are appointed by the Divinity School Council; and the University Professors of Anatomy, Chemistry and Botany are appointed by the Provost and Senior Fellows.

Each Professor is responsible for the teaching, examining and research in the sphere of knowledge to which his chair pertains.

A number of the Professors are also Fellows. Those Professors who are not Fellows have the right to elect two representatives on the Board (see below).

The retiring age for Professors is 70.

Readers, Lecturers and other members of the teaching staff

Members of the teaching staff not holding Professorships are Readers, Senior Lecturers[2], Lecturers, Junior Lecturers, Assistants or Demonstrators. Assistants and Demonstrators are usually appointed for one or two years only.

The retiring age for all these offices is 70.

The Board

The Board is the principal governing body, both of the College and of the University, and its consent is required for all enactments, changes or

---

[1] Only two instances are on record of the co-option of a Junior Fellow other than the most senior. In 1800 the most senior of the Junior Fellows was declared ineligible by a disciplinary censure of the Visitors; in 1938 the most senior did not wish to be co-opted.

[2] In the School of Veterinary Medicine only.

appointments of any consequence. In matters of property and finance, discipline, domestic arrangements, administration, and relation with outside bodies the authority of the Board is, subject to the Statutes, absolute. In strictly academic affairs, *i.e.* those relating to teaching, examinations, degrees and appointments of academic staff, it can act only in conjunction with the University Council, Divinity School Council or Senate of the University.

It consists of the following members:

1. The Provost.
2. The seven Senior Fellows.
3. The Bursar, the Senior Lecturer and the Registrar, whether they be Senior or Junior Fellows.
4. Four representatives elected by the Junior Fellows from among themselves.
5. Two representatives elected by those Professors who are not Fellows. They may be chosen either from among themselves, or from among the Junior Fellows.

The representatives of the Junior Fellows and non-Fellow Professors are elected each for a term of two years, and at the end of this term are eligible for re-election.

The following standing committees are appointed annually by the Board: the Finance Committee; the Library Committee; the Advisory Committee on Honorary Degrees; the Development Committee.

The Board normally meets on alternate Wednesdays in term at 10.15 a.m., and also at such other times as the pressure of business may necessitate. Any matter to be placed on the agenda of a Board meeting must be communicated to the Secretary to the College not later than noon on the Monday immediately preceding the meeting.

The Body Corporate

The Body Corporate of the College consists of the Provost, Fellows and Scholars on the Foundation, together with the two representatives on the Board of the Professors who are not Fellows.

The Administrative Officers

The annual statutory officers—the Vice-Provost, Bursar, Registrar, Senior Lecturer, Catechist, Proctors, Deans, Senior Tutor and Registrar of Chambers—are elected in June from among the Fellows.

The Vice-Provost is appointed from among the Senior Fellows, the Provost having a statutory right of veto on the appointment. He discharges all the functions of the Provost during the absence or illness of the latter, and in the interval between the death or resignation of one

Provost and the appointment of the next. He also hears the declaration of persons to be admitted as readers to the College Library.

The Bursar advises the Board on general financial policy.

The Registrar acts as secretary to the Senate. He coordinates the work of the various committees and legislative bodies, and deals with administrative matters of a general nature which do not fall within the province of one of the other officers.

The Senior Lecturer directs the educational system of the College and supervises all matters relating to lectures and examinations, such as the arrangement of time-tables, the publication of examination results, the recording of each student's academic progress, and the application to individual cases of the rules governing credit for courses or examinations.

The Catechist, who must be a Senior Fellow, supervises lectures and examinations (compulsory in earlier days, now voluntary) in religious knowledge for students of the Church of Ireland and the Presbyterian Church.

The Proctors are in charge of procedure at Commencements, for which they prepare the lists, and at which they present the candidates for their degrees. The Junior Proctor is responsible for candidates for the B.A. degree; the Senior Proctor for all others.

The Senior Dean, who must be a Senior Fellow, shares with the Junior Dean responsibility for discipline in the College, and he acts for the Provost in assigning the use of rooms in the College to students and to College societies.

The Junior Dean is responsible for the maintenance of discipline among the students, and assists the Provost, Senior Dean and Bursar in various ways in the domestic administration of the College. He usually holds the office of Registrar of Chambers, and in this capacity assists the Provost in the assignment of chambers and is responsible for the collection of rents and other charges.

The Senior Tutor conducts all correspondence relating to matriculation, and he is responsible for the admission to the College of students duly qualified. He assigns to a Tutor every undergraduate on his entrance to the College, and he transfers to other Tutors the pupils of an outgoing Tutor. He presides over meetings of the Tutors.

In addition to the above officers, who are elected annually, the Board elects a number of other administrative officers from among the academic staff, either for a longer period of years, or without any fixed term of office. These include the Public Orator (who presents in Latin addresses the candidates for honorary degrees), the Tutors, the Dean of the Faculty of Physic, the Dean of the School of Dental Science, the Dean of Graduate Studies and registrars of various schools and courses.

Of these, the Tutors are appointed by the Board from among the academic staff for a term of five years, which may be renewed. The Tutor stands *in loco parentis* to his pupils, and advises them on their academic course, the nature of the regulations by which they are bound, and other matters as may be required. He also represents them before the college authorities.

The Secretary, the Treasurer, the Librarian and a number of other administrative officers are not recruited from the academic staff. The Secretary has responsibility for the general administration and records of the College, and acts as secretary to the Board. The Treasurer is in charge of all financial transactions of the College, including investment and management of property, and he acts as secretary to the Finance Committee.

The Senate of the University

The main function of the Senate is to confer the degrees of the University. No degree, whether honorary or ordinary, can be conferred without its consent. Such consent is also required for the institution of new degrees and for changes in the requirements of standing or seniority for admission to the various degrees. The Senate has no voice, however, in arranging the courses of study or the examinations required for degrees.

Although it possesses a power of veto in the matters specified above, the Senate has no power of initiative, since no business can be brought before it which has not previously been approved by the Board. Its functions are, therefore, for the most part formal and ceremonial.

The Senate consists of about three hundred members, all doctors or masters of the University. Members of the staff of the College or University who hold a doctor's or a master's degree are enrolled as members of the Senate during their tenure of office. The following are also inscribed on the roll of the Senate without payment of any fee: former Fellows of the College; present or former representatives of the University in parliament and graduates who were awarded a Studentship, or a gold medal at Moderatorship, or two Moderatorships of the first or second class (provided in all cases that such persons hold a doctor's or master's degree of the University). Any other doctor or master of the University can become a member of the Senate on payment of a fee.

Three members of the Senate, who together constitute its Caput, have each an individual veto over the conferring of any degree. They are (1) the Chancellor (or in his absence one of the Pro-Chancellors), who presides over all meetings of the Senate (2) the Provost (3) the Senior Master Non-regent. This officer is elected annually by the Senate; in recent years, it has been the practice to elect the most senior of the Junior Fellows who does not hold any major administrative office.

The Senate meets four times a year for the conferring of degrees; such meetings are called Commencements. Two are held in Michaelmas term and two in Trinity term. Another stated meeting is held on the last Wednesday in February to consider the list of persons on whom it is proposed to confer honorary degrees. Other meetings are held as required.

The proceedings at Commencements are conducted in Latin; at the other meetings they are conducted in English.

The University Council

The University Council is in charge of the academic functioning of the University. It nominates to all professorships, readerships, lecturerships and other academic posts, apart from a few to which nomination is made, for historical reasons, by other bodies; it determines, usually on the advice of the appropriate school committee, details of courses and examinations in all subjects other than divinity; and it regulates the conditions for graduate research and study. The assent of the Board is required to all *Acta* of the Council but this can be taken for granted unless the proposals imply increased expenditure.

The Council consists of twenty-two members.

Twelve members are elected from amongst their own number by the professors and other heads of departments, who are divided for this purpose into four electoral bodies representing four major fields of scholarship: literature and the arts; the social sciences; the natural sciences and engineering; the medical sciences. Each body elects annually a member who sits for three years.

Four members of Council are elected by those members of the academic staff who are neither professors nor heads of departments (one of the four being specifically designated as a representative of the tutors). These also hold office for three years.

The Senate of the University elects two members who hold office for two years.

The remaining four seats are filled *ex officio* by the Provost, Senior Lecturer, Registrar and Senior Tutor. The Senior Lecturer acts as secretary of the Council.

The following standing committees are appointed annually by the

14

Council: the Academic Appeals Committee; the Appointments and Promotions Committee; the Curricula Committee; the Graduate Studies Committee.

The Council normally meets on alternate Wednesdays in term at 10.15 a.m. Any matter to be placed on the agenda of a Council meeting must be communicated to the Secretary to the College not later than noon on the Thursday immediately preceding the meeting.

The Divinity School Council

The Divinity School Council has charge of all appointments in the Divinity School, and of all regulations governing the teaching and examinations in it. It also has charge of the catechetical teaching and examinations for Church of Ireland students. The consent of the Board is required for all its enactments; but the Board cannot refuse to appoint to a teaching post in the Divinity School the nominee of the Divinity School Council unless it is prepared to justify its refusal before the Chancellor.

The Divinity School Council consists of twelve members, all of whom must be members of the Church of Ireland. They are as follows:

1. The Provost, who acts as chairman. If the Provost is not a member of the Church of Ireland, the Vice-Provost or some other deputy sits and presides in his stead.

2. Five members appointed by the Board.

3. The Regius Professor, Archbishop King's Professor, and one other member of the teaching staff of the Divinity School.

4. Three bishops of the Church of Ireland.

The Divinity School Council holds one stated meeting each term, on a date published in advance in the *Calendar*. Business to be considered by the Divinity School Council should be communicated to the secretary of the council.

The School Committees

For various branches of study in the University school committees have been established. These committees meet as required, to consider revision of courses or of regulations relating to lectures or examinations in the subject concerned, and the application of these regulations to individual cases; they are also consulted from time to time by the Board or Council on the wider matters of educational policy. Some executive power has been delegated to them, but most of their recommendations must be confirmed by the Council or Senior Lecturer.

Order of precedence in the College

The order of precedence in the College, as laid down by the statutes, is as follows:

Constitution of the College and University

1. The Provost
2. The Vice-Provost
3. The Senior Fellows, in the order of their co-option
4. The Junior Fellows, in the order of their election
5. The Regius Professors of Divinity, Laws, Physic and Surgery, in that order
6. The other Professors, in the order of their election
7. Doctors, in the order specified in the statutes
8. Bachelors in Divinity
9. Masters, in the order specified in the statutes
10. Bachelors, in the order specified in the statutes
11. Scholars on the Foundation
12. Non-foundation Scholars
13. Pensioners (*i.e.* undergraduates who are not Scholars or Sizars)
14. Sizars

BUILDINGS OF TRINITY COLLEGE

The original college buildings, erected in the last years of the sixteenth century, consisted of a single small quadrangle. Of this no trace now remains, though a stone panel, carved with the arms of Queen Elizabeth and now preserved in the Library, is believed to be that which stood over the gate.

In the latter part of the seventeenth century and the early years of the eighteenth century Trinity College was rebuilt on the scale of one of the smaller colleges at Oxford or Cambridge, with two squares chiefly in red brick. Of these buildings the range known as the Rubrics is the only one to survive today.

The final rebuilding, which, thanks to generous grants from the Irish parliament, was on a much larger scale, began with the erection of the Library in 1712. This was followed by the Printing House. Then came the Dining Hall, and later the other buildings of the Front Square, which was completed in 1798. The nineteenth century saw the completion of Botany Bay, and the building of the New Square and of the main block of laboratories in the College Park. The Physical Laboratory and the School of Botany, the Moyne Institute, the new Library and a few smaller buildings have been added in this century.

The West Front

The West Front, like all the principal buildings of the College, is built of Wicklow granite, with the columns, pilasters, window-cases and other decorative features in Portland stone. It is 300 feet long and 65 feet high. It was designed by Henry Keene and John Sanderson of London, and was built between 1752 and 1759. The large room over the gateway is known as the Regent House from its use in earlier times for the disputations (over which a junior graduate presided as 'regent') which formed a necessary preliminary to a degree. During much of the nineteenth century it housed the College Museum; it is now used principally as an auxiliary reading-room and library for students.

The Public Theatre

The Public Theatre, more usually known as the Examination Hall, was intended primarily for public meetings of the University. It is used for Commencements and other meetings of the Senate, as well as for examinations, concerts and public meetings. It was designed by Sir William Chambers, and was begun about 1777 and completed in 1791.

17

The stucco work in the interior is, at least in part, the work of Michael Stapleton. Against the west wall stands a large monument in marble, granite and porphyry, executed in Rome by Christopher Hewetson: it commemorates Provost Baldwin (d. 1758), who bequeathed his substantial fortune to the College. The case of the organ in the gallery came from the former chapel. There is a tradition that it belonged to an organ, built in the Spanish Netherlands, which was taken as a prize by the English fleet at the battle of Vigo Bay in 1702, and was presented to the College by the Duke of Ormonde, when he came to Ireland as Lord-Lieutenant in 1703. The chandelier of gilt wood is from the Irish House of Commons; it was given to the College when the Irish Parliament was abolished by the Act of Union.

The Chapel

The Chapel, also designed by Chambers, was completed in 1798. The wooden stalls and panelling, and the stucco work of the ceiling are good examples of Dublin craftsmanship of the period. The altar-rails, floor-tiles and painted windows are nineteenth-century work. The windows commemorate Archbishop Ussher, Bishop Berkeley and Richard Graves. In the ante-chapel are memorial tablets to a number of nineteenth and twentieth-century Fellows.

By the easterly wall of the Chapel is a small enclosure in which are buried some Fellows of the College who died in the seventeenth and eighteenth centuries.

The Dining Hall

The Dining Hall was designed by Richard Cassels (otherwise Cassel or Castle). It was begun in 1743 and finished, after various difficulties, in 1761. The large room over the vestibule, formerly used as a museum and later as a debating-room for the College Historical Society, has been since 1843 the Common Room for the academic staff. A small addition was made in 1891 on the west side of the building to give further accommodation for the Common Room.

The Library

The Library was designed by Sir Thomas Burgh, Chief Engineer and Surveyor-General of Fortifications in Ireland. Its building was begun in 1712 and it was opened in 1732. The lowest storey, built of local calp limestone, was originally an open arcade which was, however, divided longitudinally by a central wall. It was enclosed in 1892 to give further storage space for books. The two upper stories were originally faced with sandstone; this weathered badly and was replaced early in the nineteenth century by the present granite ashlar.

The Long Room on the first floor measures 209 by 40 feet and is perhaps the largest single-chamber library in Europe. Originally it had a flat plaster ceiling; this was removed in 1859 and replaced by wooden barrel-vaulting which considerably increased the height of the room. At the same time the roof, which had originally been of low enough pitch to be hidden by the balustrade, was rebuilt in its present form.

The stained-glass window in the Fagel Library (east of the Long Room) commemorates Charles Graves, Fellow 1836-66. At the foot of the main staircase is a memorial to John Brinkley, Professor of Astronomy 1790-1827.

The reading-room, which has underground connexion with the main library, was opened in 1937. It contains a memorial tablet to the Rev. Michael Moore, who saved the Library from destruction when the College was occupied by Jacobite troops in 1689. The Hall of Honour, which forms the entrance to the reading-room, was completed in 1928; on its walls are engraved the names of those members of the College who fell in the war of 1914-18. Its cost was largely met by public subscription.

The new library building, which will be completed in 1967, will provide greatly improved reading-room facilities and accommodation for the library staff as well as storage space for books. The design, by Paul Koralek, was selected from over two hundred entries which were submitted to an international competition held in 1960. Half the cost was met by gifts and subscriptions to a public appeal, the other half by a grant from the Government.

The Manuscript Room

The manuscripts of the Library are housed in a small building in the Fellows' Garden which was built in 1838. It was designed by Frederick Darley as a magnetical observatory and was used for some time for this purpose; any metal used in its original construction was copper or brass.

The Provost's House

The Provost's House is the only Dublin stone-built mansion of the eighteenth century which is still used as a residence. It was built in 1759-60 by John Smyth. The main block is, in its external features, very closely modelled on a house (now demolished) in Upper Burlington Street, London, designed for General Wade in 1723 by the Earl of Cork and Burlington. The wings and the interior plans are original.

The most striking features of the interior are the large hall and staircase with boldly rusticated walls, and the richly decorated saloon, 50 feet long, which occupies the whole of the west front of the first floor.

Some additions were made to the house by Provost Hely-Hutchinson.

The Graduates' Memorial Building

This building, which divides Library Square from Botany Bay, was erected in 1899-1902. Its cost was largely met by subscriptions from graduates of the University to provide a memorial of the tercentenary. It contains the premises of certain student societies, a hall for lectures, meetings and debates, and numerous sets of chambers.

The Campanile

When the chapel previous to the present one was demolished there was nowhere to accommodate the great bell of the College, which was cast in Gloucester in 1744. The Campanile was built in 1853 to fill this need; it was the gift of Lord John George Beresford, Archbishop of Armagh and Chancellor of the University. The architect was Charles Lanyon. Besides the great bell it houses the smaller 'Provost's bell', which may have hung in the monastery of All Hallows on the site which the College now occupies.

The seated figures on the Campanile represent Divinity, Law, Medicine and Science; the keystones of the arches are masks of Homer, Socrates, Plato and Demosthenes.

Botany Bay

The ranges of chambers which form the north and east sides of the northern square (nicknamed Botany Bay because it had formerly contained a herb-garden) were begun about 1790, but work was suspended for some years on account of the serious fall in student numbers in the decade 1795-1805, and the buildings were not completed till 1816. They are built of calp limestone.

On the west side of Botany Bay are the baths, which were built and endowed in 1924 by the first Earl of Iveagh, Chancellor of the University.

The Rubrics

The range of buildings known as the Rubrics which separates the New Square from Library Square, was built within a few years of 1700. The front is of brick, the back of calp rubble faced with stucco. The top storey was remodelled about 1891, the former attics with dormer windows being replaced by larger rooms with windows surmounted by Dutch gables.

The New Square

The south side of the New Square is occupied by the Museum Building, which houses the Departments of Engineering, Geology and Geography, as well as the Lecky Library and some general lecture rooms. It was designed by Thomas Deane and Benjamin Woodward, and was built in 1853-7. It is inspired mainly by the Byzantine architecture of Venice, and is, perhaps, the first building to have been designed explicitly in accordance with the principles advocated by Ruskin. The most notable features are the plant and animal carvings on the exterior (the work of the O'Shea brothers from Cork), and the lofty hall and staircase, in which the marble and other decorative stones are (except for two columns of English serpentine) of Irish origin. The rooms, as originally designed, were remarkably high, and many of them have been divided horizontally in recent years.

The Printing House, a small building with a Doric portico, standing at the north-west corner of the square, was designed by Cassels in 1734. It was a gift of John Stearne, Bishop of Clogher and Vice-Chancellor of the University. It was enlarged by the College in 1844.

The granite ranges of chambers and lecture-rooms on the north and east sides of the square were built in 1838-44.

The Scientific Laboratories

The principal block of scientific laboratories, near the east end of the College Park, was built in stages between the years 1875 and 1887. It accommodates the offices and lecture-rooms of the School of Physic, and the Departments of Chemistry, Anatomy, Zoology, Physiology, Experimental Surgery and Pharmacology.

To the south of the main block is the School of Pathology, built in 1898, and the Moyne Institute of Preventive Medicine, in which are housed the Departments of Bacteriology and Social Medicine. The Moyne Institute, designed by Desmond Fitzgerald and opened in 1953, was the gift of Grania, Marchioness of Normanby, as a memorial of her father, the first Baron Moyne.

To the north of the main block are the Physical Laboratory and the School of Botany, built in 1906-7. Their cost was met by the first Earl of Iveagh. To the east is the Department of Biochemistry, built in 1966. Part of its cost was met by a grant from the Wellcome Foundation.

Buildings of Trinity College

The Engineering workshop and laboratory stands on the north side of the College Park. It was built in 1902, and extended in 1954.

The Dixon Hall

The Dixon Hall, which is used for examinations, lectures and film-shows, was designed by W. G. Hicks and was built in 1938. It commemorates A. F. Dixon, for many years Professor of Anatomy and Dean of the Faculty of Physic.

UNIVERSITY AND COLLEGE OFFICERS

Chancellor of the University
Frederick Henry Boland, LL.D., LL.D. (*h.c.* N.U.I.)

Pro-Chancellors of the University
The Right Hon. The Earl of Rosse, LL.D. (*h.c.*)
The Right Hon. the Lord Moyne, LL.D. (*h.c.*)
George Alexander Duncan, M.A., LL.B.

Visitors of the College
The Chancellor (or in his absence one of the Pro-Chancellors)
The Hon. Theodore Conyngham Kingsmill Moore, LL.D.

Provost of the College
Albert Joseph McConnell, M.A., M.SC., SC.D., DOTTORE D'UNIVERSITÀ (ROME),
D.SC. (*h.c.* Q.U.B.), SC.D. (*h.c.* COLUMBIA)

FELLOWS OF THE COLLEGE[1]

Senior Fellows

Arthur Aston Luce, M.A., LITT.D., D.D., D.LIT. (*h.c.* Q.U.B.)
Joseph Johnston, M.A. (DUBL., OXON.)
Francis La Touche Godfrey, M.A., *Senior Dean and Catechist*
Herbert William Parke, M.A. (DUBL., OXON.), LITT.D., *Vice-Provost*
George Alexander Duncan, M.A., LL.B.
Ernest Thomas Sinton Walton, M.A., M.SC., PH.D. (CANTAB.), D.SC. (*h.c.* Q.U.B.)
William Bedell Stanford, M.A., LITT.D.

Junior Fellows

Donald Ernest Wilson Wormell, M.A. (DUBL., CANTAB.), PH.D. (YALE), *Senior Lecturer*
Theodore William Moody, M.A., PH.D. (LOND.), D.LIT. (*h.c.* Q.U.B.)
Robert Allen Quain O'Meara, M.A., SC.D., M.D., D.P.H., F.R.C.P.I.
George Francis Mitchell, M.A., M.SC.
Ernest Gordon Quin, M.A., *Senior Proctor*
Edmund James Joseph Furlong, M.A.
Aleyn Hunter Gregg, M.A., M.SC. (Q.U.B.), PH.D. (LOND.)
John Victor Luce, M.A. (DUBL., OXON.), *Senior Tutor*
David Allardice Webb, M.A. (DUBL., CANTAB.), PH.D. (DUBL., CANTAB.), SC.D.
William Fitzroy Pyle, M.A., PH.D.
Robert Brendan McDowell, M.A., PH.D., *Junior Dean and Registrar of Chambers*
David Charles Pepper, M.A., B.SC. (LOND.), PH.D. (CANTAB.)
Frederick Basil Chubb, M.A. (DUBL., OXON.), D.PHIL. (OXON.), *Bursar*
Cyril Francis George Delaney, M.A., PH.D.
William James Louden Ryan, M.A., PH.D.
Edward Calverley Riley, M.A. (DUBL., OXON.)
John Hewitt Jellett Poole, M.A., M.A.I., SC.D.
Jacob Weingreen, M.A., PH.D.
Émile Jules François Arnould, M.A. (DUBL., LOND.), PH.D., D.LIT. (LOND.), D. ÈS LETTRES (PARIS)
Wesley Cocker, M.A., SC.D., PH.D. (MANCHESTER), D.SC. (MANCHESTER)
William John Edward Jessop, B.A., M.SC., M.D., M.R.C.P., F.R.C.P.I.
David William Greene, M.A.
William Wright, M.A., B.SC. (GLASGOW), PH.D. (ABERDEEN), SC.D.
Thomas Brian Hamilton McMurry, M.A., PH.D.
Cecil Alexander Erskine, M.A., PH.D.
Frederick Stanley Stewart, B.A., M.D., F.R.C.P.I.

[1] Where not otherwise indicated, the degrees stated have been conferred by the University of Dublin. (This convention is not adhered to in the case of the honorary fellows.)

William Arthur Watts, M.A.
George William Percy Dawson, M.A. (DUBL., CANTAB.), B.SC. (LOND.)
John Noel Rowland Grainger, B.A., M.SC., PH.D. (LOND.)
Francis Gerard Augustine Winder, M.A., M.SC. (N.U.I.)
David Ian Dickson Howie, M.A., B.SC. (ST ANDREWS), PH.D. (ST ANDREWS),
  Registrar
James Kirkwood Walton, M.A., B.LITT., *Junior Proctor*
Brendan Kevin Patrick Scaife, B.SC. (ENG.) (LOND.), PH.D. (LOND.)
Percival Davis McCormack, M.A., M.SC., PH.D.
David Andrew Thornley, M.A., PH.D.
James Thomson Baxter, M.A., PH.D., M.R.C.V.S.
Peter Barry Brontë Gatenby, B.A., M.D., F.R.C.P.I., F.R.C.P.
Brian Spencer, M.A., B.SC. (LIVERPOOL), PH.D. (LIVERPOOL)
Derek William Forrest, M.A. (OXON.), PH.D. (LOND.)
Brian Hughes Murdoch, M.A., PH.D. (PRINCETON), A.M. (PRINCETON)
James Michael Francis Lydon, M.A. (DUBL., N.U.I.), PH.D. (LOND.)
William Thomas Elliott McCaughey, M.D.,. (Q.U.B.), M.C.PATH.
Charles Christopher Creagh O'Morchoe M.A., M.D.
Peter Frederick Smith-Keary, B.A., PH.D.
John Gerald Simms, M.A. (DUBL., OXON.). PH.D.

Honorary Fellows

Sir William David Ross, K.B.E., M.A., D.LITT., LL.D. (*h.c.* EDINBURGH,
  MANCHESTER), LITT.D. (*h.c.*), L.H.D. (*h.c.* COLUMBIA), F.B.A., Provost of Oriel
  College, Oxford, 1929–1948
Sir George Norman Clark, M.A., D.LITT., LL.D. (*h.c.* ABERDEEN), LIT.D. (*h.c.*
  UTRECHT), D.LITT. (*h.c.* DURHAM, SHEFFIELD, HULL, COLUMBIA), LITT.D. (DUBL.,
  CANTAB.), F.B.A., Provost of Oriel College, Oxford, 1948–1957
Walter Fitzwilliam Starkie, C.M.G., C.B.E., M.A., LITT.D.
John Lighton Synge, M.A., SC.D., F.R.S.
Adams Andrew McConnell, M.A., M.B., M.CH. (*h.c.*), F.R.C.S.I., HON. F.R.C.S.
Ernest Sheldon Friel, B.A., M.DENT.SC., SC.D., F.D.S.
George Henry Phillips Hewson, M.A., MUS.D., F.R.C.O.

PROFESSORS, READERS, LECTURERS AND OTHER OFFICERS[1]

Mathematics

---

[1] Corrected to 24 August, 1966. The dates given after the titles of certain offices are those when the posts, or posts with which they are continuous, were founded. For further details the *Trinity College record volume* (1951) may be consulted.
The names of part-time members of the staff are marked with an asterisk.

Lecturers in Classics

1.10.65   Alfred Edward Hinds, M.A.
1.10.65   Valerie Ann Hilda Rodgers, B.A. (LOND.), M.A.

Mental and moral science

PHILOSOPHY
Professor of Moral Philosophy (1837)
23.6.49   Edmund James Joseph Furlong, M.A.   1959
Berkeley Professor of Metaphysics[1]
9.12.53   Arthur Aston Luce, M.A., LITT.D., D.D., D.LIT. (*h.c.* Q.U.B.)
Lecturer in the History of Philosophy
30.6.37   Francis La Touche Godfrey, M.A.
Lecturers in Mental and Moral Science
4.6.50   William Vincent Denard, M.A., B.LITT.
1.10.65   Norman Coles, B.A. (OXON.), B.PHIL. (OXON.)
1.10.66   William Edward Walmsley St George Charlton, M.A. (OXON.),
           B.PHIL. (OXON.)
1.10.66   John Charles Addison Gaskin, M.A. (OXON.), B.LITT. (OXON.)
Visiting Professor of Psychology
1.10.66   Lloyd Joseph Borstelmann, M.A., PH.D. (CALIFORNIA)

PSYCHOLOGY
Reader in Psychology
21.9.62   Derek William Forrest, M.A. (OXON.), PH.D. (LOND.)
Junior Lecturers in Psychology
1.10.64   Richard Stevens, M.A. (EDIN.)
1.10.65   Lionel Joseph Valentine Baker, B.SC. (LOND.)
1.10.66   Desmond Poole, B.A.

Natural sciences

BACTERIOLOGY
See SCHOOL OF PHYSIC below.
BIOCHEMISTRY
See SCHOOL OF PHYSIC below.
BOTANY
University Professor of Botany (1711)
1.1.66   William Arthur Watts, M.A.
Professor of Systematic Botany
1.1.66   David Allardice Webb, M.A. (DUBL., CANTAB.),   1956
           PH.D. (DUBL., CANTAB.), SC.D.

Lecturers in Botany
1.10.64   Dorothy Margarita Lösel, M.A., B.SC. (GLASGOW), PH.D. (GLASGOW)
1.10.66   Colin Hedley Dickinson, B.SC. (NOTTINGHAM), PH.D. (NOTTINGHAM)

[1] Founded 1953 for present holder only.

University and college officers

CHEMISTRY

Professor of General Chemistry (1922)
1.10.46 Wesley Cocker, M.A., SC.D., PH.D. (MANCHESTER),   1953
D.SC. (MANCHESTER), F.R.I.C.

University Professor of Chemistry (1711)
21.4.48 Wesley Cocker, M.A., SC.D., PH.D., D.SC., F.R.I.C.   1962

Professor of Physical Chemistry
21.6.61 David Charles Pepper, M.A., B.SC. (LOND.), PH.D. (CANTAB.)

Reader in Organic Chemistry
1.10.66 Thomas Brian Hamilton McMurry, M.A., PH.D.

Lecturers in Chemistry
1.10.47 Edward Robertson Stuart, M.A., B.SC. (ST ANDREWS), F.R.I.C.
21.9.55 William John Davis, M.A., M.SC. (Q.U.B.), PH.D. (Q.U.B.)
21.9.62 George Anthony Lonergan, M.A., B.SC. (N.U.I.), PH.D. (N.U.I.)
1.10.65 Peter Howard Boyle, M.A., PH.D.
1.10.65 Gerald Roy Brown, B.A., PH.D.

Junior Lecturers in Chemistry
1.10.64 William Barber Simpson, B.SC. (ABERDEEN), PH.D. (ABERDEEN)
1.10.66 Mary Silvey Carson, B.A.

Demonstrators in Chemistry
21.9.64 Joseph Smith, B.SC. (LOND.)
1.10.65 Edward Thomas Walshe, B.SC. (N.U.I.)
1.10.66 David Plunkett Hanna, B.A.

Imperial Chemical Industries Research Fellow
21.9.64 Patrick Shannon, B.SC. (ST ANDREWS), D.PHIL. (OXON.)

GENETICS

Reader in charge of the Department of Genetics
21.12.59 George William Percy Dawson, M.A. (DUBL., CANTAB.),
B.SC. (LOND.)

Lecturer in Genetics
21.9.63 Peter Frederick Smith-Keary, B.A., PH.D.

Research Associates in Genetics
27.11.63 Edward Patrick Cunningham, M.AGR.SC. (N.U.I.), PH.D. (CORNELL)
16.9.65 Gyula Ficsor, B.SC. (COLORADO), PH.D. (MISSOURI)
1.10.65 Adrienne Jessop, B.A., PH.D. (BIRMINGHAM)
1.10.65 Shahla Riyasaty, B.A., M.SC.

Demonstrator in Genetics
1.10.65 *Thomas Gilbert Barham Howe, B.A.

GEOGRAPHY

Professor of Geography
1.10.66 Joseph Pedlow Haughton, M.A., M.SC.

Lecturers in Geography

21.9.57   John Harwood Andrews, M.A. (CANTAB.), PH.D. (LOND.)
21.9.57   Gordon Leslie Davies, M.A. (DUBL., MANCHESTER)
21.9.64   Frederick Herman Andreasen Aalen, M.A., M.SC., B.A. (DUNELM.)
1.10.66   Desmond Alfred Gillmor, M.A., PH.D.

Junior Lecturers in Geography

1.10.64   Eric Acheson Colhoun, B.A. (Q.U.B.), M.SC. (WISCONSIN)
1.10.64   Paul Worthing Williams, B.A. (DUNELM), PH.D. (CANTAB.)

GEOLOGY

Professor of Geology and Mineralogy (1844)

1.10.66   Charles Hepworth Holland, B.SC. (MANCHESTER), PH.D. (LOND.)

Professor of Quaternary Studies[1]

3.12.65   George Francis Mitchell, M.A., M.SC.

Lecturer in Geology

1.10.65   Christopher John Stillman, B.SC. (LEEDS), PH.D. (LEEDS)

Junior Lecturers in Geology

1.1.62   William Edward Adrian Phillips, B.A. (CANTAB.), PH.D.
21.9.63   Michael John Clarke, M.A. (DUBL.), B.SC. (BIRMINGHAM)

Research Assistant in Geology

1.7.65   John Harrison, B.SC. (EXETER)

GEOPHYSICS

Professor of Geophysics[2]

8.5.34   John Hewitt Jellett Poole, M.A., M.A.I., SC.D.

PHYSICS

Erasmus Smith's Professor of Natural and Experimental Philosophy (1724)

21.9.47   Ernest Thomas Sinton Walton, M.A., M.SC., PH.D. (CANTAB.), D.SC. (*h.c.* Q.U.B.)   1951

Professor of Experimental Physics

1.10.66   Cyril Francis George Delaney, M.A., PH.D.

Lecturers in Experimental Physics

29.6.29   John Hewitt Jellett Poole, M.A., M.A.I., SC.D.
20.5.39   Aleyn Hunter Gregg, M.A., M.SC. (Q.U.B.), PH.D. (LOND.)
1.1.48   Robert Blair Elliott, B.A., M.SC. (BIRMINGHAM)
1.10.65   Ian Ross McAulay, B.A., PH.D.

Demonstrator in Physics

1.10.65   Desmond James Reid, B.A.

[1] Founded for present holder only.
[2] Founded 1934 for present holder only.

University and college officers

ZOOLOGY

Professor of Zoology and Comparative Anatomy
21.9.59   John Noel Rowland Grainger, B.A., M.SC., PH.D. (LOND.)

Lecturers in Zoology
21.9.56   David Ian Dickson Howie, M.A., B.SC. (ST ANDREWS),
        PH.D. (ST ANDREWS)
21.9.63   Reginald Derek Goodhue, M.A., B.SC. (LOND.), PH.D. (LOND.)
21.9.64   Bryan Llewellyn Powell, B.SC. (WALES), M.A., PH.D.

Junior Lecturer in Zoology
1.10.65   Frank Jeal, B.A. (OXON.)

Modern languages

ENGLISH

Professor of English Literature (1867)
[Vacant]

Reader in English
23.6.51   William Fitzroy Pyle, M.A., PH.D.

Lecturers in English Literature
30.6.37   Robert Butler Digby French, M.A.
21.9.61   James Kirkwood Walton, M.A., B.LITT.
1.10.66   Timothy Brendan Kennelly, M.A.

Lecturer in English Language
21.9.64   Joseph Donovan Pheifer, M.A. (DUBL., OXON.), B.LITT. (OXON.)

Junior Lecturers in English Literature
20.3.64   Geoffrey Thurley, B.A. (CANTAB.)
1.10.66   Mary Harden Rodgers, B.A.
1.10.66   Eileán Ní Chuilleanáin, M.A. (N.U.I.)

FRENCH

Professor of French
5.12.45   Émile Jules François Arnould, M.A. (DUBL., LOND.),
        PH.D., D.LIT. (LOND.), D. ÈS LETTRES (PARIS)
21.9.52   *Assistant*: Meta Evelyn North, M.A.   1955

Reader in French
10.1.46   Owen Lancelot Sheehy Skeffington, M.A., PH.D.

Lecturers in French
1.1.65   Barbara Wright, M.A., LL.B., PH.D. (CANTAB.)
1.10.65   Hugh Edwin Shields, M.A.
1.10.66   Christopher John Charles Thacker, M.A. (OXON.), DIP. ED. (OXON.),
        PH.D. (INDIANA)

Junior Lecturers in French
21.9.61 Geneviève Rollin, M.A.
1.10.65 Jean-Paul Pittion, L. ÈS LETTRES (E.N.S. PARIS),
DIP. ÉT. SUP. (E.N.S. PARIS)

French Assistants (4)

GERMAN
Professor of German (1776)
1.10.65 Lionel Hugh Christopher Thomas, M.A. (DUBL., OXON.), PH.D.
(LEEDS)

Visiting Professor of German
1.10.66 Leroy Robert Shaw, A.B., M.A., PH.D. (CALIFORNIA)

Lecturers in German
21.9.61 Franz Adolph Gustav Lösel, M.A., DR PHIL. (FRANKFURT AM MAIN)
21.9.63 Mary Ita O'Boyle, M.A. (DUBL., N.U.I.), B.LITT. (OXON.)
1.10.66 Maurice Michael Raraty, B.A. (KEELE), M.A. (DUBL.),
PH.D. (SHEFFIELD)

German Assistants (2)

IRISH
Professor of Irish (1840)
21.9.55 David William Greene, M.A.   1962

Reader in Celtic Languages
21.12.55 Ernest Gordon Quin, M.A.

Lecturer in Modern Irish
18.1.56 Máirtín Ó Cadhain, M.A.

Lecturer in Irish
21.9.63 Terence Patrick McCaughey, M.A. (CANTAB.), B.D. (EDIN.)

Junior Lecturer in Irish
21.9.56 May Haughton Risk, M.A., PH.D.

ITALIAN
Reader in charge of the Department of Italian
[Vacant]

Lecturers in Italian
1.11.44 Eduardo Tomacelli, M.A., D. GIURISPRUDENZA (NAPLES)
1.10.65 Corinna Salvadori Lonergan, M.A. (DUBL., N.U.I.)

Italian Assistant (1)

PHONETICS AND LINGUISTICS
Lecturer in Phonetics and Linguistics
25.6.41 Ernest Gordon Quin, M.A.

31

University and college officers

RUSSIAN
Lecturers in Russian

21.9.62	Winifred Helen Baird MacBride, M.A. (DUBL., GLASGOW, EDIN.)
1.10.49	Margaret Mary McMackin, M.A. (Q.U.B.)

SPANISH
Professor of Spanish

1.10.65   Edward Calverley Riley, M.A. (DUBL., OXON.)

Lecturer in Spanish

1.1.66   Kenneth William John Adams, M.A. (DUBL., LOND.)

Junior Lecturers in Spanish

21.12.63   Eamonn Joseph Rodgers, B.A. (Q.U.B.), M.A. (DUBL.)

1.10.66   Judith Mary Bull, B.A. (LOND.)

Spanish Assistants (2)

Ancient and modern literature

See CLASSICS and MODERN LANGUAGES.

Hebrew and semitic languages

Erasmus Smith's Professor of Hebrew (1724)

23.2.37   Jacob Weingreen, M.A., PH.D.   1958

Lecturer in Hebrew

12.10.32   *Joshua Baker, M.A., LL.B., PH.D.

Lecturer in Arabic

3.12.41   Jacob Weingreen, M.A., PH.D.

Lecturer in Sanskrit and Comparative Philology

23.6.34   Ernest Gordon Quin, M.A.

Lecturer in Hebrew and Semitic Languages

1.10.65   Ernest Wilson Nicholson, M.A., PH.D. (GLASGOW)

History and political science

MODERN HISTORY
Professor of Modern History (1762)

1.10.39   Theodore William Moody, M.A., PH.D. (LOND.), D.LIT.
(h.c. Q.U.B.)   1959

Erasmus Smith's Professor of Oratory and History (1724)

1.10.39   Theodore William Moody, M.A., PH.D. (LOND.), D.LIT.
(h.c. Q.U.B.)   1954

Reader in Modern History

21.1.62   Robert Brendan McDowell, M.A., PH.D.

Lecturers in Modern History

21.9.64   John Gerald Simms, M.A. (DUBL., OXON.), PH.D.

1.10.65   Louis Michael Cullen, M.A. (N.U.I.), PH.D. (LOND.)

Junior Lecturers in Modern History

1.10.65   Aidan Clarke, M.A., PH.D.

1.10.65   David John Sturdy, B.A. (HULL)

Assistant in History

1.11.65   John Winston Cox, B.A.

MEDIEVAL HISTORY

Lecky Professor of History (1913)

23.6.51   Annette Jocelyn Otway-Ruthven, M.A., PH.D. (CANTAB.)   1956

Lecturer in Medieval History

21.9.62   James Francis Michael Lydon, M.A. (DUBL., N.U.I.), PH.D. (LOND.)

Junior Lecturer in Medieval History

1.10.64   Christine Elizabeth Meek, M.A. (OXON.)

POLITICAL SCIENCE

Professor of Political Science

16.3.60   Frederick Basil Chubb, M.A. (DUBL., OXON.), D.PHIL. (OXON.)

Lecturers in Political Science

21.9.62   David Andrew Thornley, M.A., PH.D.

1.10.66   Neil Patrick Keatinge, B.A., M.SC. (ECON.) (LOND.)

Economics and political science

Professor of Political Economy (1832)

7.2.34   George Alexander Duncan, M.A., LL.B.   1959

Professor of Applied Economics[1]

5.7.39   Joseph Johnston, M.A. (DUBL., OXON.)

Professor of Industrial Economics

21.5.61   William James Louden Ryan, M.A., PH.D.

Lecturers in Economics

21.9.63   Alan Anderson Tait, M.A. (DUBL., EDIN.)

21.9.64   Catherine Brock, M.A. (DUBL., OXON.), B.LITT. (OXON.)

1.10.65   James William McGilvray, M.A. (DUBL., EDIN.)

1.10.65   Martin O'Donoghue, B.A., B.COMM.

1.10.65   John Connor, B.A., B.COMM.

Junior Lecturer in Economics

1.10.65   Patrick Matthew David Lyons, B.A.

Assistant in Economics

1.10.65   John Patrick Feeney, B.A.

Professor of Political Science

16.3.60   Frederick Basil Chubb, M.A. (DUBL., OXON.), D.PHIL. (OXON.)

[1] Founded 1939 for present holder only.

University and college officers

Lecturers in Political Science
21.9.62   David Andrew Thornley, M.A., PH.D.
1.10.66   Neil Patrick Keatinge, B.A., M.SC. (ECON.) (LOND.)

Legal Science

See LAW.

Divinity

Regius Professor of Divinity (1607, ? 1600)
21.8.63   Hugh Frederic Woodhouse, M.A., D.D.

Archbishop King's Professor of Divinity (1718)
21.9.57   Frederick Ercolo Vokes, M.A. (CANTAB.), B.D. (CANTAB.)

Professor of Pastoral Theology (1888)
1.9.64   *John Simpson Brown, M.A. (DUBL., CANTAB.), B.D.

Lecturer on the Bible (1898)
28.6.39   *Raymond Gordon Finney Jenkins, M.A., B.D.   1964

Junior Lecturer in Divinity
1.10.66   John Raymond Bartlett, M.A. (OXON.), B.LITT. (OXON.)

Law

Regius Professor of Laws (1668)
1.10.66   *Charles Bueno McKenna, M.A., M.SC., LL.D.

Reid Professor of Penal Legislation, Constitutional and
Criminal Law, and the Law of Evidence (1888)
1.10.65   *John Sydney Richard Cole, B.A.

Lecturers in Law
21.9.64   Eldon Young Exshaw, M.A., LL.B.
1.10.65   *Matthew Russell, M.A., LL.B.
1.10.66   Abdul Kader Asmal, B.A. (SOUTH AFRICA), M.A. (DUBL.),
             LL.M. (LOND.)
1.10.66   Thomas Cedric Jones, M.A. (DUBL.), LL.B. (LOND.), B.C.L. (OXON.)

Lecturer in Roman Law (1920)
22.6.32   *Charles Beuno McKenna, M.A., M.SC., LL.D.

Registrar of the Law School
1.10.64   Eldon Young Exshaw, M.A., LL.B.

Physic

DEAN OF THE FACULTY OF PHYSIC
20.4.59   William John Edward Jessop, B.A., M.SC., M.D., M.R.C.P., F.R.C.P.I.

VICE-DEAN OF THE FACULTY OF PHYSIC
20.4.59   David Smyth Torrens, M.A., M.B.

First appointment		Last appointment

ANATOMY

Professor of Human Anatomy and Embryology (1922)
3.12.47 — Cecil Alexander Erskine, M.A., PH.D., M.R.C.P.I. — 1954

University Professor of Anatomy and Chirurgery
1.8.47 — Cecil Alexander Erskine, M.A., PH.D., M.R.C.P.I.

University Anatomist (1716)
[Vacant]

Lecturer in Human Anatomy
18.5.49 — Blanche Weekes, M.A., M.D., M.SC.

Junior Lecturer in Anatomy
1.10.66 — Peter Clive Masterman Loly, B.A., M.B.

Demonstrators in Anatomy
1.10.66 — Niall Mercer Heney, B.A., M.B.
1.10.66 — John Patrick Werge Varian, B.A., M.B.

Lecturer in Applied Anatomy (1919)
[Vacant]

PHYSIOLOGY

Professor of Physiology (1922)
12.2.36 — David Smyth Torrens, M.A., M.B.

Lecturers in Physiology
21.9.63 — Patricia Jean O'Morchoe, B.A., M.B.
1.1.66 — Charles Christopher Creagh O'Morchoe, M.A., M.D.

Junior Research Lecturer in Physiology
1.8.66 — Paul McNeil Hill, M.A., M.B.

Lecturer in Applied Physiology
30.5.42 — *Robert Wilson, M.A., M.D., F.R.C.P.I.

Demonstrators in Physiology
1.10.66 — Brigid Teresa McKenna, B.A., M.B.
1.10.66 — Grahame Elmslie Blundell, B.A., M.B.

BIOCHEMISTRY

Professor of Biochemistry
21.12.60 — Brian Spencer, M.A., B.SC. (LIVERPOOL), PH.D. (LIVERPOOL)

Reader in Biochemistry
1.10.66 — Francis Gerard Augustine Winder, M.A., M.SC. (N.U.I.)

Lecturers in Biochemistry
21.9.62 — Bruno Angelo Orsi, B.SC. (READING), PH.D. (READING)
21.9.63 — John Rowland Baker, B.SC. (READING), PH.D. (READING)

Research Lecturer in Biochemistry
1.9.65 — Maxwell Howard Richards Lewis, B.SC. (WALES), PH.D.

35

University and college officers

Junior Lecturers in Biochemistry
1.10.64 Michael Joseph Carroll, B.SC. (LONDON), PH.D.
1.10.65 John Martin Scott, B.SC., PH.D. (N.U.I.)
Research Associate in Biochemistry
6.11.63 Paris Panayotou, B.A., M.B.
Lecturer in Clinical Biochemistry
1.5.66 Patrick Joseph Leonard, M.SC. (N.U.I.), PH.D. (SHEFFIELD)

PHARMACOLOGY

Professor of Pharmacology
1.10.66 Cedric William Malcolm Wilson, B.SC. (EDIN.), M.D. (EDIN.),
PH.D. (EDIN.)
Lecturer in Pharmacology
1.11.65 Philip Leo Chambers, B.SC. (SHEFFIELD)
Lecturer in Veterinary Pharmacology
6.4.64 David Michael Pugh, B.V.SC. (BRISTOL), M.SC. (BRISTOL), M.R.C.V.S.
Lecturer in Endocrine Pharmacology
17.5.61 *Augustine Sharpe Darragh, M.A., M.D.
Junior Research Lecturers in Pharmacology
1.10.65 Dymphna Christiana Smyth, B.SC. (N.U.I.)
1.10.65 Fidelma O'Donoghue, B.SC. (N.U.I.)
Research Lecturer in Clinical Pharmacology
1.5.66 Michael Gerard Cecil Kelly, M.A., M.B.
Junior Research Lecturers in Clinical Pharmacology
20.10.65 James Magrath, M.B. (N.U.I.), M.R.C.O.G.
1.10.66 John Henry Dill Black, B.A., M.B., M.R.C.P.I.

PATHOLOGY

Professor of Pathology (1895)
1.11.64 William Thomas Elliott McCaughey, M.D. (Q.U.B.), M.C. PATH.
Reader in Pathology
1.8.65 Dermot O'Brien Hourihane, M.D. (N.U.I.), M.R.C.P.I.
Lecturers in Pathology
[Vacant]
Pathologists
1.4.65 Geraldine Mary McCarthy, B.SC. (N.U.I.), M.B. (N.U.I.)
1.11.65 Cintra Savitri Moosai-Maharaj, M.B.
Clinical Tutors in Pathology
*Niall Gerard Gallagher, B.SC. (N.U.I.), M.D. (N.U.I.), M.C. PATH.
*Nicholas Jaswon, M.A., M.D.
*Betty Eileen Wallace, M.A., M.D.
Reader in Haematology
1.1.66 Ian Jesse Temperley, M.A., M.D., M.R.C.P.I., M.C. PATH.

EXPERIMENTAL MEDICINE
Professor of Experimental Medicine[1]

25.2.43 Robert Allen Quain O'Meara, M.A., SC.D., M.D.,   1955
         D.P.H., F.R.C.P.I.

Lecturer in Experimental Medicine

21.4.63 William Austin Boggust, M.A., PH.D., M.SC. (DUNELM.)

Research Associate in Experimental Medicine

1.10.65 Margaret Ann Carmel Bermingham, M.SC. (N.U.I.)

BACTERIOLOGY AND PREVENTIVE MEDICINE
Professor of Bacteriology and Preventive Medicine (1919)

1.10.50 Frederick Stanley Stewart, B.A., M.D., F.R.C.P.I., F.C. PATH.   1958

1.9.65 *Assistants* Malcolm Richard Boyd, M.A.

1.1.66   Mary Margaret McLoughlin, B.SC. (N.U.I.)

Lecturer in Applied Bacteriology

21.12.49 Joseph Deryck McKeever, M.A., M.D.

Lecturer in Bacteriology

21.9.58 William Spence Lee Roberts, M.A., PH.D.

Senior Bacteriologist

1.1.66 Harriett Mary Pomeroy, M.A.

Lecturer in Clinical Bacteriology

1.10.66 Betty Eileen Wallace, M.A., M.D.

Bacteriologist

1.1.66 Rosemary Hone, B.A., M.B.

Research Associate in Bacteriology

1.10.66 Gilbert Thomas Lancelot Archer, B.A., M.B., C.B., F.R.C.P.I.

SOCIAL MEDICINE
Professor of Social Medicine

11.12.52 William John Edward Jessop, B.A., M.SC., M.D., M.R.C.P.,   1958
          F.R.C.P.I.

Lecturer in Social Medicine
[Vacant]

Lecturer in Industrial Medicine

1.10.53 *Robert Brian Pringle, M.B. (CANTAB.), B.CHIR. (CANTAB.),
         F.R.C.P.I.

Lecturer in Teratology

21.9.61 *Victoria McCall Coffey, M.A., PH.D., L.R.C.P. and S.I., D.P.H.

Lecturer in Chemotherapy

9.11.55 *Vincent Christopher Barry, D.SC. (N.U.I.), F.R.I.C.

Lecturer in Public Health

23.5.56 *James Austin Harbison, M.D. (N.U.I.), D.P.H., M.P.H. (HARVARD)

Lecturer in House Planning and Sanitary Construction

3.2.37 *Andrew Ian Norton Roberts, M.A., B.A. (CANTAB.), B.A.I.

[1] Founded 1942 for present holder only.

37

First
appointment

Last
appointment

MEDICINE
Regius Professor of Physic (1637)

10.12.56 *Victor Millington Synge, B.A., M.D., D.P.H., F.R.C.P.I., F.R.C.P.
Professor of Clinical Medicine

21.12.60 Peter Barry Brontë Gatenby, B.A., M.D., F.R.C.P.I., F.R.C.P.
Lecturers in Medicine

21.9.61 *Brendan Edward OBrien, B.A., M.D., F.R.C.P.I.

1.10.64 Donald George Weir, B.A., M.D., M.R.C.P.I.
Lecturer in Dermatology

21.5.62 *David Michael Mitchell, M A., M.D., F.R.C.P.I.
Lecturers in Psychological Medicine

21.2.48 *Henry Jocelyn Eustace, B.A. M.B., D.P.M.

1.10.59 *Thomas McCracken, B.A. (Q'U.B.), M.B. (N.U.I.), D.P.M.

21.2.48 *John Norman Parker Moore, B.A., M.D., D.P.M., F.R.C.P.I.
Lecturer in Infectious Diseases
[Vacant]
Lecturer in Cardiology

21.7.63 *Gerard Francis Gearty, M.B. (N.U.I.), M.SC. (N.U.I.), M.R.C.P.I.
Research Associate in Medicine

19.5.65 *Terence Telford Chapman, B.A., M.D.
Clinical Tutors in Medicine
*Herbert Fitzroy Devine, M.B. (N.U.I.)
*William Stanley Jagoe, M.D.
*John Gilbert Kirker, M.B., F.R.C.P.I.
*Carmel Teresita Mary Long, M.B. (N.U.I.)
*Stephen Szanto, M.SC. (BUDAPEST), M.D. (BUDAPEST), M.R.C.P.I.
*Francis Joseph Timoney, M.B. (N.U.I.), M.R.C.P.I.

PAEDIATRICS
Professor of Paediatrics

21.9.60 Robert Elsworth Steen, B.A., M.D., F.R.C.P.I., F.R.C.P.G. (*Hon.*)
Lecturers in Paediatrics

21.9.60 *Eric Edwin Doyle, F.R.C.P.I., D.P.H., D.C.H.

21.9.60 *John Peter Raymond Rees, M.B., F.R.C.P.I., D.C.H.
Lecturer in Child Health
*Catherine Mary O'Brien, B.SC. (N.U.I.), M.D. (N.U.I.), D.P.H.
Clinical Tutor in Paediatrics

1.1.66 Sheikh Mohammad Basheer, L.R.C.P. and S.I., L.M. (DUBL.)
D.OBST.R.C.O.G. (LOND.), D.C.H. (R.C.S. and P.I.)

MIDWIFERY AND GYNAECOLOGY
Professor of Midwifery and Gynaecology

1.10.53 *John Browne Fleming, M.A., M.D., M.A.O., F.R.C.P.I., F.R.C.O.G.
Assistants: *Hugo McVey, B.A., M.D., M.A.O., F.R.C.P.I., M.R.C.O.G. 1957
*Alan Drury Harling Browne, B.A., M.D., M.A.O., 1957
F.R.C.P.I., F.R.C.O.G.

Clinical Tutor in Midwifery and Gynaecology
★Edwin William Lillie, M.D., M.A.O., M.R.C.O.G.

SURGERY
Regius Professor of Surgery (1852)
[Vacant]
Professor of Clinical Surgery
21.12.60 Robert Francis Jack Henry, B.A., M.B., F.R.C.S.I.
Assistant: ★Stanley Thomas McCollum, M.A., M.B., F.R.C.S.I., F.R.C.S.
Lecturers in Clinical Surgery
25.11.59 ★William George Fegan, B.A., M.CH., F.R.C.S.I.
25.11.59 ★Thomas O'Neill, M.D. (N.U.I.), M.CH. (N.U.I.), F.R.C.S.
Honorary Professor of Orthopaedic Surgery
14.12.50 ★Arthur Chance, B.A., M.D., M.CH., F.R.C.S.I.
Lecturer in Laryngology and Otology
22.11.50 ★Robert Rowan Woods, B.A., M.B., F.R.C.S.I.
Lecturer in Ophthalmology
1.1.60 ★Louis Emil Joseph Werner, B.A., M.B., D.O.M.S.
Lecturer in Thoracic Surgery
1.1.60 ★Keith Meares Shaw, B.A., M.D., F.R.C.S.I.
Lecturers in Urological Surgery
1.11.64 ★Daniel Francis Victor Lane, M.B., M.CH., F.R.C.S.I.
1.11.64 ★James Dermot O'Flynn, M.B. (N.U.I.), M.CH. (N.U.I.), F.R.C.S.ED.
Clinical Tutors in Surgery
★David John FitzPatrick, B.A., M.B., D.OBST. R.C.O.G.
★David Amyrald Armstrong Lane, B.A., M.B., F.R.C.S.I., F.R.C.S.
★Patrick John Logan, M.B. (N.U.I.), F.R.C.S.I.
★James Copeland Milliken, M.A., M.D., F.R.C.S.ED.

MEDICAL JURISPRUDENCE
Lecturer in Medical Jurisprudence (1888)
27.2.35 ★John Alexander Wallace, B.A., M.B., B.SC., F.R.C.P.I.

RADIOLOGY
Lecturer in Radiology
21.4.43 ★Charles Lewers McDonogh, M.A., M.D., D.P.H., F.F.R.

ANAESTHETICS
Lecturer in Anaesthetics (1910)
[Vacant]

KING'S PROFESSORS
King's Professor of Materia Medica and Pharmacy (1749)
[Vacant]
King's Professor of Midwifery (1827)
11.3.53 ★Andrew Hope Davidson, B.A., M.D., F.R.C.P.I., F.R.C.O.G.

University and college officers

CLINICAL TEACHERS

*Richard Samuel William Baker, B.A., M.D., F.R.C.P.I.
*Norman Jackson, B.A., M.B.
*Nigel Alexander Kinnear, M.A., M.B., F.R.C.S.I.
*Charles Heber MacMahon, M.A., M.B., F.R.C.P.I.
*Edward Allen Martin, M.D., F.R.C.P.I., M.R.C.P.
*Brian Mayne, B.A., M.D., F.R.C.P.I.
*Douglas Wellington Montgomery, M.A., M.D., F.R.C.S.I.
*Edward Brandon Stephens, B.A., M.B., F.R.C.S.I.
*John Colvan de Renzy Sugars, B.A., M.B., F.R.C.S.I.
*John Alexander Wallace, B.A., B.SC., M.B., F.R.C.P.I.
*Robert Wilson, M.A., M.D., F.R.C.P.I.

Dental science

DEAN OF THE SCHOOL OF DENTAL SCIENCE

10.2.65   *Rodney Beresford Dockrell, M.A., M.B., M.DENT.SC., F.F.D.R.C.S.I., F.D.S.R.C.S.ENG.

CONSERVATIVE DENTISTRY
Professor of Conservative Dentistry

1.10.64   *Norman Patrick Butler, M.D.S. (N.U.I.), F.F.D.R.C.S.I., F.D.S.R.C.S.ENG.

Lecturer in Operative Technique

1.10.64   *Patrick Joseph Creaven, B.DENT.SC., D.D.S. (TORONTO)

ORAL MEDICINE AND PATHOLOGY
Professor of Oral Medicine and Pathology

1.10.64   *Francis Joseph Dunkin, B.D.S. (N.U.I.), M.B. (N.U.I.), F.F.D.R.C.S.I.

Lecturer in Oral Medicine

13.9.65   *Peter Leo Heslin, M.B. (N.U.I.), B.D.S. (N.U.I.), F.F.D.R.C.S.I., F.D.S.R.C.S.ENG.

ORTHODONTICS
Professor of Orthodontics

1.10.64   *Rodney Beresford Dockrell, M.A., M.B., M.DENT.SC., F.F.D.R.C.S.I., F.D.S.R.C.S.ENG.

Lecturer in Orthodontics

1.10.64   *Vincent Bernard Morris, B.D.S. (N.U.I.), D.ORTH., F.F.D.R.C.S.I., F.D.S.R.C.S.ENG.

Lecturer in Periodontology

13.9.65   *Fergal Nally, L.R.C.P. and S.I., L.D.S.R.C.S.I., F.D.S.R.C.S.ENG.

ORAL SURGERY
Professor of Oral Surgery

1.10.64   *Ian Arthur Findlay, B.D.S. (Q.U.B.), PH.D. (Q.U.B.), L.D.S.R.C.S.ED., F.F.D.R.C.S.I., F.D.S.R.C.S.ENG.

DENTAL PROSTHETICS
Professor of Prosthetic Dentistry

19.7.65   *Wilfrid Alan Lawson, B.D.S. (BIRMINGHAM), M.S. (MICHIGAN) F.F.D.R.C.S.I., F.D.S.R.C.S.ENG.

Lecturer in Denta, Prosthetics

4.7.45 ★Andrew Ganly, M.A., B.DENT.SC., F.F.D.R.C.S.I.

DENTAL ANATOMY
Lecturer in Dental Anatomy

1.2.65 ★James Edward Keith, L.D.S., L.R.C.P. and S.I., F.F.D.R.C.S.I.

MEDICINE
Lecturer in Medicine to Dental Students

23.5.45 ★Brendan Edward OBrien, B.A., M.D., F.R.C.P.I.

SURGERY
Lecturer in Surgery to Dental Students

1.7.53 ★Stanley Thomas McCollum, M.A., M.B., F.R.C.S.I., F.R.C.S.

DENTAL JURISPRUDENCE AND ETHICS
Lecturer in Medical Jurisprudence

27.2.35 ★John Alexander Wallace, B.A., M.B., B.SC., F.R.C.P.I.

Veterinary medicine

DIRECTOR OF THE SCHOOL OF VETERINARY MEDICINE

13.2.63 James Thomson Baxter, M.A., PH.D., M.R.C.V.S.

PRE-CLINICAL SCIENCES
Professor in Pre-Clinical Veterinary Sciences

1.1.60 John Armytage Nicholson, M.A. (DUBL., CANTAB.),
M.VET.SC. (N.U.I.), PH.D. (CANTAB.), M.R.C.V.S.
Senior Lecturer in Anatomy

1.1.60 Justin Pascal Keating, M.A., B.SC. (LOND.), M.V.B. (N.U.I.), M.R.C.V.S.
Lecturer in Veterinary Anatomy

21.12.61 John Ailba Evans, M.A., B.SC. (N.U.I.), M.V.B. (N.U.I.), M.R.C.V.S.,
M.I.C.I.
Reader in Biochemistry

1.1.60 Francis Gerard Augustine Winder, M.A., M.SC. (N.U.I.)
Lecturer in Pharmacology

6.4.64 David Michael Pugh, B.V.SC. (BRISTOL), M.SC. (BRISTOL), M.R.C V.S.
Lecturer in Veterinary Physiology

1.12.66 Cornelius Patrick Ahern, B.A., M.V.B., M.R.C.V.S.

CLINICAL SCIENCES
Professor in Clinical Veterinary Sciences

1.10.66 Robert Pearson Lee, M.R.C.V.S.
Senior Lecturer in Parasitology

1.1.60 Charles Hatch, M.A., M.S. (IOWA), M.R.C.V.S.
Senior Lecturer in Veterinary Pathology and Bacteriology

1.1.60 Michael Anthony Gallaher, M.A., M.SC., M.R.C.V.S.
Lecturer in Pathology

21.9.60 Muhammad Irfan, M.A., B.V.SC. (PUNJAB), PH.D. (LOND.), M.R.C.V.S.

University and college officers

Lecturer in Bacteriology
21.4.62 Said Ahmad Yasin, M.A., M.SC., PH.D., M.R.C.V.S.

CLINICAL PRACTICES
Professor in Clinical Veterinary Practices
1.3.60 James Thomson Baxter, M.A., PH.D., M.R.C.V.S.
Senior Lecturer in Surgery
1.6.66 Louis Norman Gleeson, DR.MED.VET. (BERNE), M.D. (ZURICH),
L.M.S.S.A. (LOND.), M.R.C.V.S.
Lecturer in Surgery
1.11.64 John James Sharpe, B.A., M.V.B., M.R.C.V.S.
Lecturer in Obstetrics and Reproductive Diseases
21.9.60 William Richard Nunn, M.A., B.SC. (VET.), M.R.C.V.S.
Lecturer in Veterinary Medicine
1.10.66 Kenneth Percy Baker, PH.D., M.R.C.V.S.
Lecturer in Animal Husbandry
21.1.62 John Alexander Milton, M.A., B.SC. (AGRIC.) (ABERDEEN), M.R.C.V.S.
Lecturer in Animal Nutrition
1.10.64 Ian Hubert Bath, B.SC. (Q.U.B.), B.AGR. (Q.U.B.), PH.D. (READING),
F.R.I.C.
Research Assistant in Veterinary Medicine
1.11.64 Patrick Joseph Kavanagh, B.A., M.V.B., M.R.C.V.S.

Engineering
Professor of Engineering (1842)
21.9.57 William Wright, M.A., B.SC. (GLASGOW), PH.D. (ABERDEEN), SC.D.,
M.I.C.E., M.INST.PROD.E., M.I.C.E.I., F.R.S.E.
Reader in Civil Engineering
21.1.62 Gerald FitzGibbon, M.A., M.A.I., A.M.I.C.E., M.I.C.E.I.
Lecturers in Civil Engineering
5.5.48 Reginald William Kirwan, M.A., M.A.I., PH.D., A.M.I.C.E., A.M.I.C.E.I.
21.9.63 Ronald Charles Cox, M.A., M.A.I., PH.D., A.M.I.C.E., A.M.I.C.E.I.
Lecturers in Mechanical Engineering
21.12.55 Dermot O'Clery, M.A., M.A.I., M.I.MECH.E., M.I.C.E.I.
21.9.59 *William Eccles, M.A., M.SC. (MANCHESTER), M.I.MECH.E.,
M.INST.PROD.E., A.M.I.E.E.
21.12.61 William Garrett Stanley Scaife, M.A., B.SC. (ENG.) (LOND.),
A.M.I.E.E., A.M.I.MECH.E.
Lecturer in Electrical Engineering
21.9.61 Percival Davis McCormack, M.A., M.SC., PH.D.
Reader in Electronic Engineering
1.10.66 Brendan Kevin Patrick Scaife, M.A., B.SC. (ENG.) (LOND.),
PH.D. (LOND.), A.M.I.E.E., F.INST.P.
Demonstrator in Electronic Engineering
[Vacant]

Lecturer in Town and Country Planning
*Norman Ernest Jones, B.A., B.A.I., M.I.C.E.I., M T.P.I.

Registrar of the Engineering School
21.9.57   William Wright, M.A., B.SC. (GLASGOW) PH D. (ABERDEEN), SC.D.,
      M.I.C.E., M.INST.PROD.E., M.I.C.E.I., F.R.S.E.

Graduate school of engineering studies

Director
20.9.63   William Wright, M.A., B.SC. (GLASGOW), PH.D. (ABERDEEN), SC.D
      M.I.C.E., M.INST.PROD.E., M.I.C.E.I., F.R.S.E.

Lecturer in Electrical Engineering
20.9.63   Percival Davis McCormack, M.A., M.SC., PH.D.

Reader in Electronic Engineering
1.10.66   Brendan Kevin Patrick Scaife, M.A., B.SC. (ENG.) (LOND.)
      PH.D. (LOND.), A.M.I.E.E., F.INST.P.

Lecturers in Computer Science
20.9.63   *John James Moriarty, B.E. (N.U.I.)
20.9.64   *John Bosco Cantwell, B.E. (N.U.I.), M.SC.
20.9.65   John Gabriel Byrne, M.A., B.A.I., PH.D., D.I.C.

Junior Lecturer in Computer Science
1.10.66   Neville Robert Harris, B.A., B.A.I., M.S. (ILLINOIS)

Registrar of the Graduate School of Engineering Studies
20.9.63   William Garrett Stanley Scaife, M.A., B.SC. (ENG.) (LOND.).
      A.M.I.E.E., A.M.I.MECH.E.

Agriculture; Forestry

Registrar of the Schools of Agriculture and Forestry
22.6.64   William John Davis, M.A., M.SC. (Q.U.B.), PH.D. (Q.U.B.)
      For other members of staff, see SCHOOLS OF AGRICULTURE
      AND FORESTRY.

Music

Professor of Music (1764)
21.9.62   *Brian Patrick Boydell, B.A. (DUBL., CANTAB.), MUS.D.

Registrar of the School of Music
21.9.62   *Brian Patrick Boydell, B.A., (DUBL., CANTAB.), MUS.D.

Visual Arts

Director of Studies in Visual Arts
1.2.66   Anne Olivia Crookshank, B.A. (DUBL.), M.A. (LOND.)

Education

Professor of Education (1905)
1.10.66   John Valentine Rice, B.A., B.SC. (N.U.I.), B.D. (MANUT.),
      ED.M., ED.D. (HARVARD)
      Assistant: Anita Carlotte Little, M.A.

University and college officers

Lecturer in Education
21.9.62　Philip Clive Williams, B.SC. (ECON.) (LOND.),
　　　　　M.A. (ED.) (WALES), M.A., PH.D.

Junior Lecturer in Education
1.10.66　Susan Mary Parkes, B.A.

Registrar of the School of Education
1.10.66　John Valentine Rice, B.A., B.SC. (N.U.I.), B.D. (MANUT.),
　　　　　ED.M., ED.D. (HARVARD).

Business and Social Studies

BUSINESS STUDIES

Professor of Industrial Economics
21.5.61　William James Louden Ryan, M.A., PH.D.

Lecturer in Management
21.5.59　Amory Allfrey Pakenham-Walsh, M.A., J.DIP.M.A.
　　　　　(DUBL., OXON.), F.A.C.C.A., F.C.W.A.

Lecturer in Accounting
21.9.62　Mostafa Hamdy Bahgat Abd El-Motaal, M.A., B.COM. (CAIRO),
　　　　　M.COM. (BIRMINGHAM), A.C.A.

Lecturer in Management
1.10.64　Frank Stephen Drechsler, M.E. (N.U.I.), M.A.S.E.

Lecturer in Administration
21.9.62　★William Murray, M.A. (EDIN.), B.COM. (EDIN.), C.A.

Lecturer in Marketing
23.9.64　★Bernard Prendiville, M.SC. (MANCHESTER)

Lecturer in Psychology
1.10.64　★Laurence Blaise Joseph Healy, B.COMM. (N.U.I.), M.S. (PURDUE)

Junior Lecturer in Economics
1.7.64　Charles Mulvey, M.A. (ABERDEEN)

SOCIAL STUDIES

Professor of Political Science
21.9.61　Frederick Basil Chubb, M.A. (DUBL., OXON.), D.PHIL. (OXON.)

Lecturer in Political Science
21.9.62　David Andrew Thornley, M.A., PH.D.

Director of Practical Training
21.9.59　Mary Sinclair Lynch, M.A. (DUBL., ABERDEEN)
1.2.51　*Assistant:* Vivienne Honor Darling, M.A.

Lecturer in Social Administration
21.9.64　John Anthony Coughlan, M.A. (DUBL., N.U.I.)

Lecturer in Child Care
6.3.65　★Anna Maria Thompson, A.A.P.S.W.

First
appointment

Last
appointment

Lecturers in the Church of Ireland Training College

Mathematics
5.7.47   Victor William Graham, M.A.
English and Irish
[Vacant]
History
12.1.49   *Albert Edward Stokes, M.A., B.D.
Geography
21.9.60   Frederick Herman Andreasen Aalen, M.A., M.SC., B.A. (DUNELM.)

Special Lecturers for 1966

Donnellan Lecturer (1794)
Kenneth Jackson, M.A., LITT.D.
Godfrey Day Memorial Lecturer (1939)
Leslie Wilfred Brown, M.TH., D.D.
O'Donnell Lecturer in Celtic History and Literature (1957)
Louis Michael Cullen, M.A., PH.D.

Other university and college officers[1]

VICE-PROVOST
1.10.52   Herbert William Parke, M.A. (DUBL., OXON.), LITT.D.

BURSAR
21.3.64   Frederick Basil Chubb, M.A. (DUBL., OXON.), D.PHIL. (OXON.)

TREASURER
1.3.62   Franz Carl Walter Winkelmann, M.A., A.C.A.
Accountant
21.9.59   William George Booker, M.A.
External Auditors
Craig, Gardner and Company

REGISTRAR
13.7.66   David Ian Dickson Howie, M.A., B.SC. (ST. ANDREWS),
        PH.D. (ST. ANDREWS)

SECRETARY
1.1.66   Gerald Henry Henzell Giltrap, M.A.
Administrative Assistant
[Vacant]

SENIOR LECTURER
20.9.64   Donald Ernest Wilson Wormell, M.A. (DUBL., CANTAB.),
        PH.D. (YALE)
Clerk of Examinations
1.6.58   Winifred Margaret Matthews, B.A.

[1] Some of these have been already stated. They are here repeated for convenience.

45

University and college officers

SENIOR PROCTOR
13.7.66   Ernest Gordon Quin, M.A.

JUNIOR PROCTOR
13.7.66   James Kirkwood Walton, M.A., B.LITT.

CATECHIST
1.10.57   Francis La Touche Godfrey, M.A.
Catechists (Presbyterian Church)
9.5.45   *George Brian Greer McConnell, M.A., B.A. (Q.U.B.)
1.10.61   *William Taylor McDowell, B.A., B.D. (EDINBURGH)

SENIOR DEAN
1.10.53   Francis La Touche Godfrey, M.A.

JUNIOR DEAN
1.10.56   Robert Brendan McDowell, M.A., PH.D.

CURATOR OF THE LIBRARY
12.7.65   Herbert William Parke, M.A. (DUBL., OXON.), LITT.D.

LIBRARIAN
12.7.65   Francis John Embleton Hurst, M.A. (DUBL., OXON.), A.L.A.
Deputy-Librarian
1.4.66   William Wolfgang Dieneman, M.A. (DUBL., OXON.), A.L.A.
Assistant Librarian
William O'Sullivan, M.A. (*Keeper of Manuscripts*)
Senior Library Assistants
William Elliott Mackey, M.A. (*Acquisitions Librarian*)
Hazel Marie Hornsby, M.A. (DUBL., OXON.), B.D., PH.D., A.L.A.
   (*Chief Cataloguer*)
Margaret Gertrude Chubb, M.A., B.A. (LOND.) (*Information Librarian*)
Margaret Harte, M.A., B.SC. (N.U.I.) (*Science Librarian*)
Mary Pollard, M.A., A.L.A. (*Rare Books Librarian*)
Deirdre Enid Rosaleen Hamill, M.A., A.L.A. (*Reading Rooms
   Superintendent*)
Veronica Margaret Ruth Morrow, M.A. (*Periodicals Librarian*)
Eileen Mary Ismay Roche, B.A. (*College Lending Librarian*)
Library Assistants
Bertha Gladys Bower, M.A.
Francis Byrne, M.A. (N.U.I.)
Claire Thérèse Maria Dowling, B.A. (N.U.I.), DIP.IN LIB. (N.U.I.)
Ursula Maeve Doyle, M.A. (N.U.I.), DIP. IN LIB. (N.U.I.)
Padraigin FitzGerald, B.A. (N.U.I.), DIP. IN LIB. (N.U.I.)
Mary Margaret Flynn, B.A. (N.U.I.)
*Monica Henchy, M.A. (N.U.I.), DIP. IN LIB. (N.U.I.)
Frances Killingley, M.A., A.L.A.
Mary Catherine Melvin, DIP. IN LIB. (N.U.I.)
Hilary Ann Pyle, B.A., M.LITT. (CANTAB.)

Clerical Staff

Teresa O'Doherty (*Secretary to the Librarian and Senior Catalogue Clerk*)

Elizabeth Mary Keatinge (*Supervisor of the Long Room Shop*)

Sheila Astbury

Dorothy Lefroy Chisnall

Joan Lesley Forsyth

Pauline Lynda Elizabeth Horton

Florence Joynt

Ann Creagh Langford

Mairead Looby

Mary Quinn (née Davis)

Jean Ross

Mary Stanley

SENIOR TUTOR

20.9.64 John Victor Luce, M.A.

Admissions Officer

1.11.63 Helen Middleton Watson, M.A.

TUTORS (*with tutorial numbers*)

46 Frederick Herman Andreasen Aalen, M.A., M.SC.

27 John Harwood Andrews, M.A., PH.D.

37 Catherine Brock, M.A., B.LITT.

38 Norman Coles, B.A., B.PHIL.

39 John Anthony Coughlan, M.A.

40 Lawrence John Crane, M.A., B.SC., PH.D.

28 Gordon Leslie Davies, M.A.

24 William Vincent Denard, M.A., B.LITT.

17 Robert Blair Elliott, B.A., M.SC.

35 Eldon Young Exshaw, M.A., LL.B.

22 Gerald FitzGibbon, M.A., M.A.I.

16 Robert Butler Digby French, M.A.

2 Aleyn Hunter Gregg, M.A., M.SC., PH.D.

42 Alfred Edward Hinds, M.A.

48 Thomas Cedric Jones, M.A., LL.B., B.C.L.

49 Timothy Brendan Kennelly, M.A.

19 Franz Adolph Gustav Lösel, M.A., DR.PHIL.

20 James Francis Michael Lydon, M.A., PH.D.

30 Mary Sinclair Lynch, M.A.

45 William Richard Nunn, M.A., B.SC.

36 Mary Ita O'Boyle, M.A., B.LITT.

34 Bryan Llewellyn Powell, B.SC., M.A., PH.D.

50 William Garrett Stanley Scaife, M.A., B.SC.

43 John Gerald Simms, M.A., PH.D.

23 Edward Robertson Stuart, M.A., B.SC.

47

University and college officers

32   Alan Anderson Tait, M.A.

29   David Andrew Thornley, M.A., PH.D.

25   Blanche Weekes, M.A., M.D., M.SC.

26   Francis Gerard Augustine Winder, M.A., M.SC.

44   Barbara Wright, M.A., LL.B., PH.D.

DEAN OF WOMEN STUDENTS
21.9.59   Anne Elizabeth Rogers Denard, M.A.

WARDEN OF TRINITY HALL
1.9.65   Leila Mary McCutcheon
Vice-Warden

1.1.61   Vivienne Honor Darling, M.A.

DEANS OF RESIDENCE
Dean of Residence for Church of Ireland Students

1.10.60   Ernon Cope Todd Perdue, M.A., B.D.
Assistant

1.10.66   Peter Hiscock, B.A. (OXON.)
Dean of Residence for Presbyterian Students

5.7.47   *George Brian Greer McConnell, M.A., B.A. (Q.U.B.)
Dean of Residence for Methodist Students

1.7.63   *Arthur Desmond Gilliland, B.A. (Q.U.B.)

DEAN OF GRADUATE STUDIES
1.11.64   David Ian Dickson Howie, M.A., B.SC. (ST ANDREWS), PH.D. (ST ANDREWS)

REGISTRARS AND SECRETARIES OF SCHOOLS, COMMITTEES AND COURSES[1]
Registrar of the Senate

1.10.66   David Ian Dickson Howie, M.A., B.SC. (ST ANDREWS), PH.D. (ST. ANDREWS)
Secretary of the University Council

20.9.64   Donald Ernest Wilson Wormell, M.A. (DUBL., CANTAB.), PH.D. (YALE)
Registrar of the School of Natural Sciences

21.9.58   William John Davis, M.A., M.SC. (Q.U.B.), PH.D. (Q.U.B.)
Secretary of the School of Modern Languages

12.7.63   Joseph Donovan Pheifer, M.A. (DUBL., OXON.), B.LITT. (OXON.)
Registrar of the Dublin University International Summer School
[Vacant]

OTHER ADMINISTRATIVE AND EXECUTIVE OFFICERS
Public Orator (1879)

12.3.52   Donald Ernest Wilson Wormell, M.A. (DUBL., CANTAB.), PH.D. (YALE)

[1]For the various professional schools, these officers are listed under the headings 'Law,' 'Physic', etc., respectively above.

48

Registrar of Chambers
21.9.56 Robert Brendan McDowell, M.A., PH.D.

Warden of Residences
21.9.59 Margaret Eleanor MacManus, M.A.

Agent
3.11.58 John Mainwaring Walsh, M.A.

Buildings Officer
15.6.64 Raymond Simpson

Steward
1.10.64 David William Greene, M.A.

Student Records Officer
21.12.64 Dermot John Mary Sherlock, B.A., B.COMM.

Appointments Officer
7.11.57 Dermot Norman Kenneway Eaton Montgomery, B.A.

Assistant Appointments Officer
19.7.65 William Neville Keery, B.A.

Recorder of Alumni and University Electors
7.11.57 Dermot Norman Kenneway Eaton Montgomery, B.A.

Director of the Botanic Garden
1.1.66 William Arthur Watts, M.A.

Manager of the Kells Ingram Farm
1.1.64 Noel Hayes, B.A., AGR.B.

Medical Officers
1.10.64 *Brendan Edward O Brien, B.A., M.D., F.R.C.P.I.
1.10.64 *John Alexander Wallace, B.A., M.B., B.SC., F.R.C.P.I.
1.10.64 *Helen Sophie Watson, M.A., M.B., F.F.A.R.C.S.I.

Nurse
19.10.64 Anna Alicia O'Doherty, S.R.N.

Law Agent and Keeper of the Records
9.12.48 *Dermot McGillycuddy, M.A.

Consulting Architect
11.6.38 *Andrew Ian Norton Roberts, M.A., B.A. (CANTAB.), B.A..

Editor of HELMATHENA
10.10.62 Edmund James Joseph Furlong, M.A.

Editor of TRINITY
26.1.49 Robert Butler Digby French, M.A.

Editor of the CALENDAR
1.1.66 Gerald Henry Henzell Giltrap, M.A.

Reader in the College Chapel
20.9.65 Ernon Cope Todd Perdue, M.A., B.D.

Organist and Choir-Master
1.1.61 *William Sydney Greig, MUS.B.

University and college officers

Gentlemen of the Choir

*Ewart Grace   *William Young

*Arthur Moyse   *Lionel Walker

Secretarial Staff

Wendy Louise Ashmore
Barbara Jane Baker
Joyce Edith Sybil Bannister
Teresa Gabriel Brennan
Aileen Mary Campbell, B.A.
Madeleine Carroll
Daphne Stopford Carter
Mary Clarke
Esmé Florence Helen Colley
Beatrix Vance Conlan
Geraldine Counahan
Rosemary Lees Darley, B.A.
Sybil Edith Doreen Davis, M.A.
Corinne Elizabeth Dennison
Doreen Kathleen Dunlop
Phyllis Mary Elizabeth Ford
Ann Gallagher
Mairead Maura Garvan
Jane Gibson
Sheila Patricia Goff
Merle Olivia Hanna, M.A.
Phyllis Marion Hannaford
Patricia Ann Horan
Catherine Mary Hughes
Hilary Margaret Hughes
Margaret Mary Hurley
Margaret Larminie, M.A.
Peter Joseph Gabriel McKenna
Alice Mary Miley
Mildred Joyce Moore
Pamela Morgan
Dorothy Murphy
Anita Newell
Angela Attracta Noone
Carmel O'Donnell
Judy Elizabeth O'Farrell
Gabrielle Ann O'Reilly
Marina Ann Pearson
Myrtle Katherine Peters
Elizabeth Proud

Heather Ann Rosemary Parker-Reeves
Aileen Mary Rowe
Marie Sheridan
Harriette Mary Sinton
Claire Anne Smythe
Ellie Margaret Star, M.A.
Jean Ward
Deirdre Honor Wilson

Treasurer's Staff
Olive Muriel Ashe
Dermot Joseph Boucher, A.C.A.
Margaret Clancy
Barbara Ivy Lillian Crawford
Nancy Cullen
Doris Rachel Dolan
Ann Forde
Jennifer Gill
Louie Rose Mossop Griffin
Colette Hanley
Maureen Winifred Hare
Hilary Hayward
Marilyn Heneghan
Ruth Hughes
Barbara Frazer Mackinnon
Jennifer Margaret Murdock
Mary Josephine O'Donnell
Margaret Mary Taggart

Chief Steward
18.10.49 Alexander McCartney

Lady Superintendent of the Kitchen
1.4.66 Elizabeth Catherine Pickering

Lady Housekeeper
12.1.55 Katherine McClure

Booksellers
Hodges Figgis and Co., Ltd
Fred Hanna, Ltd
Greene's Library
Browne and Nolan, Ltd
Association for Promoting Christian Knowledge
Eason and Son, Ltd

Robemakers
Messrs. Bryson

51

University and college officers

MATHEMATICS
Pure	M. Kennedy, M.SC., PH.D., University College, Dublin.
Applied	Professor A. Dalgarno, B.SC., PH.D., Queen's University, Belfast.

CLASSICS
Latin	Professor D. R. Dudley, M.A., F.S.A., University of Birmingham.
Greek	Professor J. J. Tierney, M.A., University College, Dublin.

MENTAL AND MORAL SCIENCE	Professor J. L. Evans, M.A., D.PHIL., University College of South Wales.
Psychology	Professor S. G. Lee, M.A., PH.D., University of Leicester.

NATURAL SCIENCES
Bacteriology	Professor K. E. Cooper, PH.D., M.R.C.S., L.R.C.P., University of Bristol.
Biochemistry	Professor K. S. Dodgson, PH.D., D.SC., University College of South Wales.
Botany	Professor D. H. Valentine, M.A., PH.D., F.L.S., University of Durham.
Organic chemistry	Professor A. J. Birch, M.SC., D.PHIL., F.R.S., University of Manchester.
Physical and inorganic chemistry	Professor C. E. H. Bawn, B.SC., PH.D., F.R.S., University of Liverpool.
Genetics	Professor G. Pontecorvo, DR.AGR., PH.D., F.R.S., University of Glasgow.
Geography	Professor M. J. Wise, M.C., B.A., PH.D., London School of Economics.
Geology	Professor Sir William Pugh, D.SC., F.R.S., Imperial College, London.
Physics	Professor S. K. Runcorn, M.A., SC.D., PH.D., F.I.P., F.R.S., University of Newcastle-upon-Tyne.
Zoology	Professor J. M. Dodd, B.SC., PH.D., University of Leeds.

MODERN LANGUAGES AND LITERATURE
English	Professor A. R. Humphreys, M.A., A.M., University of Leicester.
French	Professor L. P. Roche, M.A., D.U. POITIERS, University College, Dublin.
German	Professor K. Brooke, M.A., University of Keele.

Irish	Professor T. de Bhaldraithe, M.A., PH.D., University College, Dublin.
Italian	Professor T. G. Griffith, M.A., B.LITT., University of Hull.
Spanish	Professor A. H. Terry, M.A., Queen's University, Belfast.
CELTIC LANGUAGES	Professor P. MacCana, PH.D., University College, Dublin.
SEMITIC LANGUAGES	Professor B. J. Roberts, D.D., University College of North Wales.
HISTORY	
Modern	Professor C. L. Mowat, M.A., PH.D., University College of North Wales.
Medieval	Professor H. Rothwell, B.A., PH.D., University of Southampton.
ECONOMICS	Professor D. Walker, M.A., University of Exeter.
STATISTICS	Professor J. D. Sargan, M.A., University of London.
POLITICAL SCIENCE	Professor P. W. Campbell, M.A., University of Reading.
LEGAL SCIENCE	Professor D. Seaborne Davies, M.A., LL.B., University of Liverpool.
PHYSIC	
Anatomy	Professor G. M. Irvine, M.D., Royal College of Surgeons in Ireland.
Physiology	Professor H. P. Gilding, M.A., M.D., University of Birmingham.
Biochemistry	Professor R. A. Morton, PH.D., D.SC., F.R.S., University of Liverpool.
Materia medica, pharmacology and therapeutics	Professor O. L. Wade, M.D., F.R.C.P., Queen's University, Belfast.
Pathology	Professor J. H. Biggart, C.B.E., M.D., D.SC., F.R.C.P., Queen's University, Belfast.
Bacteriology	Professor P. J. Collard, M.D., M.R.C.P., University of Manchester.
Midwifery and gynaecology	Professor C. H. G. Macafee, D.SC., F.R.C.S., F.R.C.O.G., Queen's University, Belfast.
	C. K. Vartan, F.R.C.S., F.R.C.O.G., University of London.
	A. P. Barry, M.D., M.A.O., F.R.C.O.G., National Maternity Hospital.
Medicine	D. Hunter, M.D., F.R.C.P., University of London.

University and college officers

Medical jurisprudence	T. K. Marshall, M.D., Institute of Pathology, Belfast.
Paediatrics	Professor Sir A. A. Moncrieff, C.B.E., M.D., F.R.C.P., University of London.
Social medicine	Professor D. B. Bradshaw, M.A., M.B., Public Health Department, Leeds.
Surgery	H. Reid, M.D., F.R.C.S., Wales.
DENTAL SCIENCE	J. H. Scott, M.D., D.SC., L.D.S., Queen's University, Belfast.
	Professor A. Wilson, M.D., PH.D., F.R.F.P.S., University of Liverpool.
	R. Storer, M.SC., F.D.S.R.C.S., University of Liverpool.
	Professor A. I. Darling, D.D.SC., F.D.S.R.C.S., University of Bristol.
VETERINARY MEDICINE	
Animal husbandry	Professor J. S. S. Inglis, B.SC. (AGRIC.), M.R.C.V.S., University of Glasgow.
Animal management	[Vacant]
Anatomy	R. A. Greene, M.A., B.SC., PH.D., M.R.C.V.S., University of Cambridge.
Physiology	Professor F. R. Bell, B.SC., PH.D., F.R.C.V.S., Royal Veterinary College, London.
Biochemistry	Professor R. A. Morton, PH.D., D.SC., F.R.S., University of Liverpool.
Histology and embryology	G. K. Benson, B.SC., PH.D., University of Liverpool.
Veterinary pharmacology	J. Sanford, B.V.SC., PH.D., M.R.C.V.S., University of Glasgow.
Parasitology	E. L. Taylor, D.V.SC., F.R.C.V.S.
Pathology	Professor P. E. Mullaney, University College, Dublin.
Bacteriology	S. J. Edwards, D.SC., F.R.C.V.S., Institute for Research on Animal Diseases.
Clinical veterinary medicine	R. F. W. Goodwin, M.A., PH.D., M.R.C.V.S., University of Cambridge.
Veterinary state and preventive medicine	Professor A. Robertson, M.A., PH.D., M.R.C.V.S., University of Edinburgh.
Veterinary surgery	W. MacLennan, M.R.C.V.S., University of Edinburgh.
Veterinary obstetrics and reproductive diseases	R. B. Walker, M.A., M.R.C.V.S., University of Cambridge.

ENGINEERING

Civil Professor J. K. T. L. Nash, M.A., M.A.I., C.ENG., M.I.C.E.
King's College, London.

Electrical Professor J. H. Calderwood, M.ENG., PH.D., C.ENG.,
M.I.E.E., F.INST.P.,
University of Salford.

Mechanical Professor J. L. M. Morrison, C.B.E., D.S.C., C.ENG.,
M.I.MECH.E.,
University of Bristol.

MUSIC Professor I. Keys, D.MUS., F.R.C.O.,
University of Nottingham.

EDUCATION Kathleen M. Evans, M.A., B.SC.,
University College of South Wales.

SOCIAL STUDIES Vivienne O. Laughton, B.A.,
University of Glasgow.

REPRESENTATION OF THE UNIVERSITY
IN SEANAD ÉIREANN

By the provisions of the Seanad Electoral (University Members) Act, 1937, the University of Dublin became a constituency for the election of three members of Seanad Éireann.

The above Act prescribes that every person who is a citizen of Ireland, is not subject to any legal incapacity and has received a degree (other than an honorary degree) in the University of Dublin, or has obtained a foundation scholarship or, if a woman, has obtained a non-foundation scholarship in the said University and (in any case) has attained the age of twenty-one years, shall be entitled to be registered as an elector in the Register of Electors for the University of Dublin constituency.

The Register of Electors is published annually on 1 June. Any person who is not entered on the electors' list, and claims to be entitled to be so entered, and all graduates and scholars who fulfil the above-mentioned conditions, may obtain forms of claim to be registered as university electors from the Seanad Electoral Officer, 1 Trinity College, to whom all correspondence should be addressed.

Representatives of the University in Seanad Éireann

William John Edward Jessop, B.A., M.SC., M.D., F.R.C.P.I.   Elected 1965
Owen Lancelot Sheehy Skeffington, M.A., PH.D.   ,,   ,,
William Bedell Stanford, M.A., LITT.D.   ,,   ,,

BOARD, COUNCILS
AND COMMITTEES

BOARD OF TRINITY COLLEGE

UNIVERSITY COUNCIL

DIVINITY SCHOOL COUNCIL

STANDING COMMITTEES

SCHOOL COMMITTEES

Board, Councils and Committees

---

[1] For constitution, see CONSTITUTION OF THE COLLEGE AND UNIVERSITY.

UNIVERSITY COUNCIL

Ex-officio members
  The Provost
  The Senior Lecturer, *Secretary*
  The Senior Tutor
  The Registrar

Representatives of Class I
  Brian Patrick Boydell, B.A., MUS.D. (*retires 1967*)
  David William Greene, M.A. (*retires 1968*)
  Émile Jules François Arnould, M.A., D.LIT. (*retires 1969*)

Representatives of Class II
  Derek William Forrest, M.A., PH.D. (*retires 1967*)
  Annette Jocelyn Otway-Ruthven, M.A., PH.D., (*retires 1968*)
  William James Louden Ryan, M.A., PH.D. (*retires 1969*)

Representatives of Class III
  George William Percy Dawson, M.A., B.SC. (*retires 1967*)
  David Charles Pepper, M.A., PH.D. (*retires 1968*)
  William Wright, M.A., SC.D. (*retires 1969*)

Representatives of Class IV
  William John Edward Jessop, M.SC., M.D. (*retires 1967*)
  James Thomson Baxter, M.A., PH.D. (*retires 1968*)
  Peter Barry Brontë Gatenby, B.A., M.D. (*retires 1969*)

Representatives of Class V
  Mary Sinclair Lynch, M.A. (*retires 1967*)
  George Anthony Lonergan, M.A., PH.D. (*retires 1967*)
  David Andrew Thornley, M.A., PH.D. (*retires 1968*)
  William John Davis, M.A., PH.D. (*retires 1969*)

Representatives of Class VI
  Ralph Wallace Reynolds, M.A., PH.D. (*retires 1967*)
  Hektor Rex Cathcart, M.A., PH.D. (*retires 1968*)

DIVINITY SCHOOL COUNCIL

The Vice-Provost, *Chairman*

Members nominated by the Board (retire 1967)
Arthur Aston Luce, D.D.
Francis La Touche Godfrey, M.A.
Edward Christopher Micks, M.A., LL.B.
William Bedell Stanford, M.A., LITT.D.
Edmund James Joseph Furlong, M.A.

Members of the teaching staff
The Regius Professor of Divinity
Archbishop King's Professor of Divinity, *Secretary*
Raymond Gordon Finney Jenkins, M.A., B.D. *(retires 1967)*

*Three Bishops of the Church of Ireland elected by the House of Bishops
(retire 1969)*

Dates of Council meetings
Meetings of the Council are held on the third Monday in November, February,
and June. In the years 1966–7 the dates will be 14 November 1966, 13 February
1967, 19 June 1967, 13 November 1967.

STANDING COMMITTEES OF THE BOARD

DEVELOPMENT COMMITTEE

The Provost	W. J. E. Jessop, M.SC., M.D.
The Bursar, *Secretary*	W. A. Watts, M.A.
The Registrar	The Secretary
The Senior Lecturer	The Treasurer
D. W. Greene, M.A.	

FINANCE COMMITTEE

The Provost	Catherine Brock, M.A., B.LITT.
The Bursar	T. B. H. McMurry, M.A., PH.D.
The Registrar	B. H. Murdoch, M.A., PH.D.
The Treasurer, *Secretary*	B. Spencer, B.SC., PH.D.

Board, Councils and Committees

ADVISORY COMMITTEE ON HONORARY DEGREES

The Vice-Provost
The Registrar
The Public Orator

Annette J. Otway-Ruthven, M.A., PH.D.
D. C. Pepper, M.A., PH.D.

LIBRARY COMMITTEE

The Curator, *Chairman*
The Librarian, *Secretary*
G. L. Davies, M.A.
W. J. Davis, M.A., PH.D.

W. J. L. Ryan, M.A., PH.D.
B. Spencer, B.SC., PH.D.
L. H. C. Thomas, M.A., PH.D.

STANDING COMMITTEES OF THE UNIVERSITY COUNCIL

ACADEMIC APPEALS COMMITTEE

The Provost
The Senior Lecturer
The Senior Tutor

J. F. M. Lydon, M.A., PH.D.
D. W. Forrest, M.A., PH.D.
R. B. D. French, M.A.

APPOINTMENTS AND PROMOTIONS COMMITTEE

The Provost
The Senior Lecturer
The Registrar

C. F. G. Delaney, M.A., PH.D.
J. F. M. Lydon, M.A., PH.D.
W. B. Stanford, M.A., LITT.D.

CURRICULA COMMITTEE

The Vice-Provost
The Senior Lecturer
D. W. Greene, M.A.
G. W. P. Dawson, M.A., B.SC.

D. W. Forrest, M.A., PH.D.
W. J. E. Jessop, M.SC., M.D.
E. R. Stuart, M.A., B.SC.
D. A. Thornley, M.A., PH.D.

GRADUATE STUDIES COMMITTEE

The Dean of Graduate Studies
F. B. Chubb, M.A., D.PHIL.
P. B. B. Gatenby, M.D.
G. F. Mitchell, M.A., M.SC.
H. W. Parke, M.A., LITT.D.
D. C. Pepper, M.A., PH.D.

B. Spencer, B.SC., PH.D.
L. H. C. Thomas, M.A., PH.D.
H. F. Woodhouse, M.A., D.D.
W. Wright, M.A., SC.D.
The Treasurer

SCHOOL COMMITTEES

All members of the teaching staff in any School are members of the School Committee, whether or not their names are recorded below, except in the case of the following School Committees: Natural Sciences, General Studies, Physic, Dental Science, Veterinary Medicine, Engineering, Agriculture and Forestry, Business and Social Studies.

Degrees are given only after the names of members from Magee University College. Degrees of other members are to be found above, under UNIVERSITY AND COLLEGE OFFICERS.

Persons who are not members of the staff of the University or of Magee University College are marked with an asterisk.

MATHEMATICS

B. H. Murdoch, *Chairman*
P. S. Florides, *Secretary*
L. J. Crane
C. F. G. Delaney
V. W. Graham
W. G. Guthrie, M.A., PH.D.
T. G. Murphy

D. C. Pepper
D. J. Simms
T. D. Spearman
E. T. S. Walton
T. T. West
W. Wright

Quorum 4

CLASSICS

H. W. Parke, *Chairman*
J. V. Luce, *Secretary*
A. E. Hinds, *Deputy Secretary*
F. La T. Godfrey
Valerie A. H. Rodgers
J. Johnston
F. J. Lelièvre, M.A.

A. A. Luce
E. G. Quin
L. J. D. Richardson
W. B. Stanford
D. E. W. Wormell

Quorum 4

MENTAL AND MORAL SCIENCE

The Provost
E. J. Furlong, *Chairman*
W. V. Denard, *Secretary*
L. J. V. Baker
W. E. W. St G. Charlton
N. Coles
D. W. Forrest
F. C. A. Gaskin

F. La T. Godfrey
A. A. Luce
J. V. Luce
H. F. Nicholl, M.A., M.LITT.
A. D. Poole
R. Stevens

Quorum 4

Board, Councils and Committees

GENERAL STUDIES

The Senior Lecturer (Greek and Latin), *Chairman & Secretary*
W. F. Pyle (English)
O. L. S. Skeffington (French)
F. A. G. Lösel (German)
J. Weingreen (Hebrew)
T. P. McCaughey (Irish)
Corinna S. Lonergan (Italian)
Winifred H. B. MacBride (Russian)
E. C. Riley (Spanish)
J. F. M. Lydon (History)
B. P. Boydell (Music)
Anne O. Crookshank (Visual Arts)
J. P. Haughton (Geography)
A. A. Tait (Economics)
B. H. Murdoch (Mathematics)
E. J. Furlong (Philosophy)
D. W. Forrest (Psychology)
F. J. E. Hurst (Library)
Quorum 7

LAW

C. B. McKenna, *Chairman*
E. Y. Exshaw, *Secretary*
A. K. Asmal
J. S. R. Cole
T. C. Jones
M. Russell
Quorum 4

PHYSIC

V. M. Synge, *Chairman*
W. J. E. Jessop, *Secretary*
W. Cocker
A. H. Davidson
C. A. Erskine
J. B. Fleming
P. B. B. Gatenby
J. N. R. Grainger
R. F. J. Henry
W. T. E. McCaughey
R. A. Q. O'Meara
B. Spencer
R. E. Steen
F. S. Stewart
D. S. Torrens
J. A. Wallace
E. T. S. Walton
W. A. Watts
C. W. M. Wilson
Quorum 7

DENTAL SCIENCE

R. B. Dockrell, *Secretary*
N. P. Butler
F. J. Dunkin
I. A. Findlay
P. B. B. Gatenby
J. N. R. Grainger
R. F. J. Henry
W. J. E. Jessop
W. A. Lawson
B. Spencer
C. W. M. Wilson
Quorum 4

65

D

Board, Councils and Committees

VETERINARY MEDICINE

J. T. Baxter, *Secretary*
M. A. Gallaher
C. Hatch
W. J. E. Jessop
W. T. E. McCaughey
J. A. Milton
G. F. Mitchell

J. A. Nicholson
R. A. Q. O'Meara
D. M. Pugh
B. Spencer
F. S. Stewart
D. S. Torrens
Quorum 4

ENGINEERING

W. Wright, *Chairman*
G. FitzGibbon, *Secretary*
W. Cocker
*L. D. G. Collen
R. C. Cox
W. Eccles
V. W. Graham
R. W. Kirwan

P. D. McCormack
D. O'Clery
J. H. J. Poole
B. K. P. Scaife
W. G. S. Scaife
E. R. Stuart
E. T. S. Walton
Quorum 4

AGRICULTURE AND FORESTRY

E. T. S. Walton, *Chairman*
W. J. Davis, *Secretary*
W. Cocker
J. N. R. Grainger
N. Hayes
J. Johnston
*L. G. Carr Lett

J. A. Milton
G. F. Mitchell
A. A. Pakenham-Walsh
W. A. Watts
W. Wright
Quorum 4

MUSIC

B. P. Boydell, *Chairman & Secretary*
T. W. Moody
D. O'Sullivan
H. W. Parke

A. A. Tait
D. A. Webb
The external examiner
Quorum 3

EDUCATION

J. V. Rice, *Chairman & Secretary*
D. W. Forrest
E. J. J. Furlong
Anita C. Little

Susan M. Parkes
P. C. Williams
Quorum 3

66

BUSINESS AND SOCIAL STUDIES

W. J. E. Jessop, *Chairman*
Mary S. Lynch, *Secretary*
L. J. V. Baker
Catherine Brock
Agnes B. Cassidy
F. B. Chubb
J. A. Coughlan
L. M. Cullen
Vivienne H. Darling
F. S. Drechsler
M. H. B. Abd El-Motaal
D. W. Forrest
E. J. J. Furlong
J. W. Garmany, M.A., B.LITT.
J. C. A. Gaskin
D. A. Gillmor
L. B. J. Healy

*M. J. Killeen
P. M. D. Lyons
J. W. McGilvray
C. Mulvey
W. Murray
M. O'Donoghue
Patricia J. O'Morchoe
H. W. Parke
M. Russell
W. J. L. Ryan
*J. H. Sedgwick
R. Stevens
A. A. Tait
Anna M. Thompson
D. A. Thornley
A. A. Pakenham-Walsh
Quorum 4

GENERAL INFORMATION, DEGREES, ADMISSION, COLLEGE CHARGES AND GENERAL REGULATIONS

GENERAL INFORMATION FOR STUDENTS

DEGREES, LICENCES AND DIPLOMAS

ADMISSION REQUIREMENTS

COLLEGE CHARGES

GENERAL REGULATIONS FOR STUDENTS

GENERAL INFORMATION FOR STUDENTS

Enquiries

All initial enquiries should be addressed to the Admissions Office, Trinity College. Subsequent correspondence is dealt with by the following officers of the College:

Admission: The Senior Tutor
Fee concessions: The Senior Tutor
Residence in the College (men): The Registrar of Chambers
Trinity Hall (women): The Warden of Trinity Hall
Lodgings: The Warden of Residences
Careers: The Appointments Officer
Graduate Study and Research: The Dean of Graduate Studies

The references below are to sections of the *Calendar*. Booklets containing the following sections may be obtained free of charge from the Admissions Office: ALMANACK, ADMISSION REQUIREMENTS, COLLEGE CHARGES, GENERAL REGULATIONS FOR STUDENTS, GRADUATE STUDIES AND HIGHER DEGREES, ENTRANCE AWARDS, FINANCIAL ASSISTANCE, RESEARCH AWARDS AND MODERATORSHIP PRIZES. The various courses are similarly available.

Courses available

Students in the College may take

(1) a course for an honor or an ordinary degree in arts (which includes natural sciences), or

(2) a course for a degree in one of the professional schools, or

(3) a course for a diploma in an arts, science, or a professional subject, or

(4) a course or research leading to a higher degree.

For details of these courses see below.

A certain number of students are permitted to attend lectures for one year or one term.

Admission

For details, see ADMISSION REQUIREMENTS.

The college tutors

When a student comes on the college books he is assigned to one of the college tutors. In making the choice his academic course and any preference he may have expressed are taken into account. A student's tutor is a member of the teaching staff who takes a personal interest in his academic career, and is willing to advise him on courses, lectures to attend, examinations, fees, discipline and other matters. For the list of tutors, see COLLEGE TUTORS. A student may communicate with a tutor and be provisionally accepted by him before he comes on the college books.

Women students may obtain advice on lectures, examinations, rules, regulations and other college matters from the Dean of Women Students as well as from the tutors. Her office in 6 Trinity College is open daily during term except at week-ends and college holidays.

Courses for the degree of Bachelor in Arts

The ordinary and the honor courses for the B.A. degree are normally of four years' duration. The ordinary degree of B.A. is awarded on the course in general studies, and also on the course in natural sciences. Honor courses are available in mathematics, classics, mental and moral science, philosophy and psychology, natural sciences, modern languages and literature (including English), ancient and modern literature, early and modern Irish, Celtic languages, Hebrew and semitic languages, history and political science, economics and political science, legal science.

Diplomas in arts and science

Diplomas may be obtained in the history of European painting and in science.

Courses for professional degrees and diplomas

Degree courses are available in divinity, law, physic, dental science, veterinary medicine, engineering, agriculture, forestry, music, business studies, social studies; and diploma courses in education, social studies, physiotherapy, biblical studies, gynaecology and obstetrics, psychological medicine.

Academic year and terms

The academic year begins on 20 September. It is divided into three terms, Michaelmas term (20 September–12 December), Hilary term (7 January–7 March), Trinity term (1 April–12 July). The period in each of these terms during which lectures are given is called lecture term. Arts lecture terms are of seven weeks' duration. Professional lecture terms are usually longer. The dates of all lecture terms are given in the ALMANACK.

Terminology defined

During the first year of the arts course a student is called a Junior

General information for students

Freshman, during the second year a Senior Freshman, during the third a Junior Sophister, and during the fourth a Senior Sophister. After this, he becomes a Candidate Bachelor, until he has received the B.A. degree, when he becomes a Bachelor. Three years after passing the B.A. degree examination a graduate becomes entitled to take the degree of M.A.

The expression 'rising Junior Freshman' is used to describe a student who has been granted admission to the Junior Freshman class of the coming Michaelmas term, and whose name has been placed on the college books. A rising Senior Freshman is a student who has credit for the Junior Freshman year but has not entered upon the Senior Freshman year; and similarly in the Sophister years.

Time-tables

LECTURES IN ARTS AND IN PROFESSIONAL SUBJECTS

Time-tables for the ensuing term's lectures in arts are published on the college notice-boards during the preceding vacation.

Time-tables for divinity, law, medicine and other professional lectures are published by the schools concerned on the school notice-boards, at the beginning either of each term or of the academic year.

EXAMINATIONS AT ENTRANCE

Time-tables for the matriculation examination are published on the college notice-boards three weeks beforehand, and those for the examination for entrance scholarships and exhibitions are published six weeks beforehand. These examinations usually begin at 9.30 a.m.

ORDINARY EXAMINATIONS IN ARTS

Ordinary examinations in arts begin on the days stated in the ALMANACK. Time-tables are published about two weeks before the examinations. These examinations usually begin at 9.30 a.m.

HONOR EXAMINATIONS IN ARTS

Honor examinations in arts are usually held at the beginning of term during the two or three weeks before lectures begin. Time-tables are published at the end of the preceding lecture term. The usual hours are 9.30 a.m. to 12.30 p.m., and 2 p.m. to 5 p.m. For further details the regulations for the various honor courses should be consulted.

EXAMINATIONS IN PROFESSIONAL SUBJECTS

Examinations in professional subjects begin on the days stated in the ALMANACK. Time-tables are published by the schools concerned.

NOTE

The dates for examinations, lectures, etc., given in the ALMANACK and elsewhere in the *Calendar* may be altered at any time by order of the Board. Notice of any such alterations is published on the college notice-boards.

College holidays

On the following days (which may fall within the academic terms) no lectures, demonstrations or examinations are held: St Patrick's Day, Good Friday, Easter Monday, Whit Monday, Trinity Monday and after 1 p.m. on the Wednesday of Trinity Week.

Academicals

Students wear academicals at all arts lectures and all arts examinations after matriculation.

Chapel of Trinity College

For details of services see GENERAL REGULATIONS FOR STUDENTS.

Libraries

In addition to the College Library the following libraries are available for students: the Lecky Library, from which books may be borrowed by honor students in history, economics, political science, business and social studies, and legal science; the Regent House Library, for students taking modern languages or the course in general studies; various departmental libraries.

Health

A student health service is in operation with consulting rooms in 11 College. A nurse is in attendance during the day and the doctors to the service attend at stated times or in cases of need at the student's residence. Hospital care is provided. Further information is given under STUDENT HEALTH SERVICE.

Residence for men

College rooms are arranged in sets where one, two, or three occupants may reside. They are of two types: (1) fully-furnished rooms, and (2) rooms with essential furniture only provided by the College. Most single rooms are fully-furnished bed-sitting rooms. A student usually makes his own breakfast and sometimes his own lunch. He can, however, have his mid-day meal at the college buffet and he dines on commons at least five nights in the week.

Men who do not live in the College or at home are required to live in lodgings approved by the College. See GENERAL REGULATIONS FOR STUDENTS.

Residence for women

Women students not resident in their own homes must reside either at

General information for students

Trinity Hall or in one of the lodgings approved by the College. See
GENERAL REGULATIONS FOR STUDENTS. Luncheons may be obtained in
the College.

Societies and athletic clubs

For details of the various societies and athletic clubs available, see
SOCIETIES AND CLUBS. Provision is made for football, cricket, hockey,
tennis, athletics and other sports within the college precincts.

Appointments Office

An appointments office is available to assist students. See under that
heading.

Costs

For fees see COLLEGE CHARGES. Students are expected to make themselves familiar with the regulations for payment of fees. The charges
for rooms are stated in GENERAL REGULATIONS FOR STUDENTS.

A student living in College will normally need about £8 a week
for an average period of 30 weeks' residence a year, to cover rent,
food, service, books, heating, but not fees or personal expenses.

Fee concessions

In cases of need, duly substantiated, the College grants fee concessions
varying from £30 to £60 per annum to Irish students, or remits the
surcharge on fees of non-Irish students one of whose parents is a
graduate of the University of Dublin. Various private benefactions are
also available. See FINANCIAL ASSISTANCE.

Prizes

See ENTRANCE AWARDS, RESEARCH AWARDS AND MODERATORSHIP PRIZES
and other items under the heading PRIZES AND OTHER AWARDS.

Graduate study

Students suitably qualified may engage in research work or follow
courses of instruction leading to higher degrees in arts and in professional subjects. Research awards are available to graduates of the University of Dublin. See GRADUATE STUDIES AND HIGHER DEGREES.

Examination papers

The examination papers set in each calendar year are published in the
following Hilary term. They are arranged in booklets according to
courses in arts and professional subjects and may be obtained from
the university booksellers, or from the University Press, for 2s. 7d.
each, postage 9d. extra.

DEGREES, LICENCES AND DIPLOMAS

I DEGREES OBTAINABLE

1. Degrees are obtainable as follows:

Arts
> Bachelor in Arts (B.A.)
> Master in Arts (M.A.)

Science
> Master in Science (M.Sc.)
> Doctor in Science (Sc.D.)

Philosophy
> Doctor in Philosophy (Ph.D.)

Letters
> Master in Letters (M.Litt.)
> Doctor in Letters (Litt.D.)

Divinity
> Bachelor in Divinity (B.D.)
> Doctor in Divinity (D.D.)

Law
> Bachelor in Laws (LL.B.)
> Doctor in Laws (LL.D.)

Physic
> Bachelor in Medicine (M.B.)
> Doctor in Medicine (M.D.)
> Bachelor in Surgery (B.Ch.)
> Master in Surgery (M.Ch.)
> Bachelor in Obstetrics (B.A.O.)
> Master in Obstetrics (M.A.O.)

Dental Science
> Bachelor in Dental Science (B.Dent.Sc.)
> Master in Dental Science (M.Dent.Sc.)

Veterinary Medicine
> Bachelor in Veterinary Medicine (M.V.B.)
> Master in Veterinary Medicine (M.V.M.)

Degrees, licences and diplomas

Engineering

    Bachelor in Engineering (B.A.I.)
    Master in Engineering (M.A.I.)

Agriculture

    Bachelor in Agriculture (Agr.B.)
    Master in Agriculture (Agr.M.)
    Bachelor in Agriculture (Forestry) (Agr. (Forest.) B.)
    Master in Agriculture (Forestry) (Agr. (Forest.) M.)

Music

    Bachelor in Music (Mus.B.)
    Doctor in Music (Mus.D.)

Business Studies

    Bachelor in Business Studies (B.B.S.)

Administration

    Master in Administrative Studies (M.S.A.)

Social Studies

    Bachelor in Social Studies (B.S.S.)

II REGULATIONS GOVERNING THE AWARD OF DEGREES

Bachelors

Bachelors in Arts

2. See HONOR COURSES IN ARTS, General regulations, and ORDINARY COURSE IN ARTS.

Bachelors in professional subjects

3. In the case of the following professional subjects—physic, dental science, engineering—candidates for the bachelor's degree must be bachelors in arts of the University. Special requirements for the B.A. degree are laid down for such students. See ARTS REQUIREMENTS FOR PROFESSIONAL STUDENTS.

Both the B.A. degree and the professional degree must be conferred at the same Commencements, except that the B.A. degree may be conferred upon a student in physic, dental science or veterinary medicine who has fulfilled all the arts requirements for professional students and has satisfactorily completed the third year in his professional course.

Students in agriculture and forestry and in business and social studies who have satisfactorily completed their professional course and have fulfilled all the arts requirements for professional students may have both the B.A. degree and their professional degree conferred at the same Commencements.

4. *B.D.* Candidates for the degree of Bachelor in Divinity must be graduates of the University of Dublin, or of a recognized university. See DEGREES IN DIVINITY.

5. *LL.B.* Candidates for the degree of Bachelor in Laws must be Bachelors in Arts or Masters in Letters, or Doctors in Philosophy of the University. See SCHOOL OF LAW.

6. *Mus.B.* Candidates for the degree of Bachelor in Music need not hold any other degree of the University. See SCHOOL OF MUSIC.

Masters
Masters in Arts
7. A Bachelor in Arts of the University of at least three years' standing may proceed to the degree of Master in Arts. Candidates may present themselves for this degree only at the Winter or Second Summer Commencements.

Masters in Science and Letters
8. See GRADUATE STUDIES AND HIGHER DEGREES.

Masters in professional subjects
9. See the regulations of the respective professional schools.

Doctors
Doctors in Science, Philosophy and Letters
10. See GRADUATE STUDIES AND HIGHER DEGREES.

Doctors in professional subjects
11. See the regulations of the respective professional schools.

Degrees awarded in special cases
Degrees honoris causa
12. A meeting of the Senate for the consideration of names proposed for honorary degrees is held on the last Wednesday in February. Attention is called to this meeting a week before by a notice at the front gate of the College.

Degrees jure dignitatis
13. Subject to such regulations as may from time to time be made by the Board, with the approval of the Senate, the Board may, at its discretion, at any time submit to the Senate a grace for conferring a doctorate in divinity or laws, *jure dignitatis*, upon any graduate of the

University who has been appointed to such public position as may seem to the Board sufficiently distinguished; provided always that every such grace must receive the approval of not less than two-thirds of the members of the Board present when it is proposed. After admission to the said degree *jure dignitatis* the person admitted is eligible for membership of the Senate on fulfilling the prescribed conditions.

Degrees jure officii

14. The Board may submit to the Senate a grace for conferring *jure officii*, the degree of Master in Arts upon any fellow, professor, lecturer or other officer of the University or College or of any related institution work in which is accepted in part fulfilment of the requirements for the degree of bachelor in any faculty, provided that:

(i) Graces for admission of fellows, professors, heads of departments and the holders of the offices of secretary, treasurer and deputy librarian may be proposed at the Annual Business Meeting next after their admission to office.

(ii) Graces for admission of other full-time academic staff of the status of lecturer or higher, serving in the College or a related institution may be proposed at the Annual Business Meeting fourth after their admission to office.

(iii) Graces for admission of other officers and staff of the University and College who have given notable service during a period of not less than ten years may be proposed at the Annual Business Meeting eleventh after their admission to office.

Degrees ad eundem gradum

15. Graduates of the Universities of Oxford and Cambridge may, if the Board think fit, be admitted *ad eundem gradum* to all degrees which they have received in either of these universities. When the rules of the University of Dublin governing a degree thus sought prescribe the holding of a degree in arts as a condition necessary for its conferment, applications from graduates in arts of Oxford or Cambridge will alone be considered.

16. Applications should be made to the Senior Proctor, to whom the necessary certificates of graduation must be submitted, with a college testimonial as to character, and a statement of the reasons why the degree is sought.

17. The fees payable are the same as those for Dublin graduates, with the following sums in addition: for B.A., £25; for LL.B., £8; for M.B., B.Ch. and B.A.O. together, £15; for all other bachelors'

and all masters' and doctors' degrees, £10. All fees are paid to the Accountant.

18. Candidates who have paid the fee for a degree *ad eundem* may present themselves for the examination for a higher degree before the *ad eundem* degree has been conferred, on payment of the regular examination fee; and, if the candidate be successful, the higher and lower degrees may be conferred at the same Commencements.

19. For the purpose of ascertaining the date at which a higher degree may be taken, the candidate is reckoned as having taken the lower degree *ad eundem* on the date at which he obtained the corresponding degree in his own university.

Degrees in absentia

20. A student of the University may be allowed, although not present in the Senate, to proceed to his degree upon the following conditions:

(i) The academic qualifications required for degrees to be conferred *in absentia* are the same as those required for degrees conferred in person.

(ii) The requirements as to fitness of character are also the same as those required for degrees conferred in person, *viz.*, that before passing any grace for a degree *in absentia* the Board shall require such evidence as it may deem necessary to secure that no unworthy candidate is presented to the Senate.

(iii) Subject to the foregoing, the Board may pass a grace for a degree *in absentia* (a) for any candidate resident without the British Isles, or (b) in special cases for any candidate resident within the British Isles who submits reasons for non-attendance in person which seem to the Board to be sufficiently urgent. An additional fee of £3 is payable for a degree, or degrees (provided they are taken at the same Commencements), conferred *in absentia*; and all applications should reach the Senior Proctor at least a fortnight before the date of Commencements.

21. A candidate who is prevented from attending in person because of a college examination in which he is concerned may be excused payment of the additional fee if he applies to the Senior Proctor at least a fortnight before the date of Commencements.

III CONFERRING OF DEGREES AND LICENCES
General procedure at Commencements

22. Degrees are publicly conferred by the Chancellor, or his deputy, in the Senate or Congregation of the University, at the ceremony known as Commencements.

Degrees, licences and diplomas

23. When the results of a degree examination have been promulgated, successful candidates at that examination who seek to have the degree conferred on them at a particular Commencements must give notice on the prescribed form to the Proctor concerned, and pay the appropriate fee to the Accountant, so as to be received by these officers not later than the morning of the seventh day before that Commencements. Candidates who seek the degree of Bachelor in Arts and who propose to appear at Commencements give notice to the Junior Proctor; candidates who seek to receive that degree *in absentia* and candidates for all other degrees give notice to the Senior Proctor.

24. The grace of the House for a degree in any faculty, having first been granted by the Board, must pass the Caput before it can be proposed to the rest of the Senate and each member of the Caput has a negative voice. If no member of the Caput objects, the Proctor, in a prescribed form of words, supplicates the Congregation for their public grace; and, having collected their suffrages, declares the assent or dissent of the House accordingly; if the *placets* be the majority, the candidates for degrees are presented to the Senate by the Regius Professor of the faculty in which the degree is to be taken, or by one of the Proctors; they then advance in order before the Chancellor, who confers the degree according to a formula fixed by the university statutes, after which the candidates subscribe their names in the Register. Except in special cases, see DEGREES IN ABSENTIA above, candidates for degrees must appear at Commencements and have the degrees for which they are qualified publicly conferred on them.

Detailed procedure at Commencements

25. The Chancellor announces the opening of the Comitia. At the Winter Commencements the Senior Master non-regent is elected on the proposition of the Chancellor and the Provost; and the two Proctors and the Registrar make the statutory affirmation, if they have not already done so.

26. The Senior Proctor supplicates for the Licences in Medicine, Surgery, and Obstetrics, and in Engineering. The Junior Proctor supplicates for the degree of Bachelor in Arts. The Senior Proctor supplicates for the other ordinary degrees.

27. The Senior Lecturer introduces the moderators to the Chancellor, who gives them their medals or certificates. The moderators are presented to the Senate by the Junior Proctor, and admitted by the Chancellor. The Senior Lecturer introduces the respondents to the Chancellor, who presents them with their certificates. The respondents are presented by the Junior Proctor, and admitted.

28. Licences in Medicine, Surgery, and Obstetrics, and in Engineering are conferred.

29. Candidates for honorary degrees are presented by the Public Orator, and admitted.

30. Candidates for degrees *jure dignitatis* are presented by the Regius Professor of Divinity or the Regius Professor of Laws, and admitted.

31. Candidates for ordinary degrees are presented and admitted. Candidates are presented by the Proctors or by the professors of their respective faculties. In presenting the candidates the following order is observed:

Bachelors in Music who are not graduates in arts
Doctors in Music who are not graduates in arts
Bachelors in Arts
Bachelors in Social Studies
Bachelors in Business Studies
Bachelors in Veterinary Medicine
Bachelors in Agriculture
Bachelors in Agriculture (Forestry)
Bachelors in Dental Science
Bachelors in Music who are graduates in arts
Bachelors in Engineering
Bachelors in Obstetrics
Bachelors in Surgery
Bachelors in Medicine
Bachelors in Laws

Masters in Administrative Studies
Masters in Letters
Masters in Veterinary Medicine
Masters in Science
Masters in Agriculture
Masters in Agriculture (Forestry)
Masters in Dental Science
Masters in Engineering
Masters in Obstetrics
Masters in Surgery
Masters in Arts
Bachelors in Divinity
Doctors in Philosophy
Doctors in Music who are graduates in arts
Doctors in Science
Doctors in Letters
Doctors in Medicine
Doctors in Laws
Doctors in Divinity

NOTE

32. Candidates (women and clergymen excepted) must wear evening dress. Each candidate must wear the hood and gown of the degree he is qualified to receive. See HOODS AND GOWNS below. Candidates for doctors' and masters' degrees should present themselves in the anteroom to the Board Room ten minutes before the beginning of the ceremony. Candidates for bachelors' degrees and licences take their seats in the Public Theatre at the same time.

Commencements are normally held at 2 p.m., except in the case of the Winter Commencements and the Second Summer Commencements, when the arrangements are as follows: all candidates for bachelors' degrees, except the degree of B.D., and for licences, have their degrees or licences conferred at a ceremony beginning at 11.30 a.m.; all other candidates have their degrees conferred at a ceremony beginning at 3.30 p.m.

IV FEES

33.

	Bachelors	£	Masters	£	Doctors	£
Arts	B.A.	10	M.A.	10		
Science			M.Sc.	15	Sc.D.	25
Philosophy					Ph.D.	15
Letters			M.Litt.	15	Litt.D.	25
Divinity	B.D.	10			D.D.	21
Law	LL.B.	12			LL.D.	25
Medicine	M.B.				M.D.	25
Surgery	B.Ch.	30	M.Ch.	25		
Obstetrics	B.A.O.		M.A.O.	25		
Dental science	B.Dent.Sc.	30	M.Dent.Sc.	25		
Veterinary medicine	M.V.B.	25	M.V.M.	25		
Engineering	B.A.I.	10	M.A.I.	25		
Agriculture	Agr.B.	10	Agr.M.	25		
Forestry	Agr. (Forest.) B.	10	Agr. (Forest.) M.	25		
Music	Mus.B.	10			Mus.D.	25
Business Studies	B.B.S.	10				
Administration			M.S.A.	25		
Social Studies	B.S.S.	10				

34. The Accountant receives all the above fees.

No grace for a degree is presented to the Senate unless the candidate has paid the fees due and has given notice in accordance with §23.

35. Testimoniums of degrees are presented to candidates for degrees at Commencements, and are sent as soon as possible after Commencements to candidates who have received degrees *in absentia*.

Application for a duplicate degree testimonium, marked 'Duplicate', may be made to the Senior Proctor on payment to the Accountant of a fee of £2. Such a duplicate testimonium may be issued provided the applicant declares in writing that to the best of his belief his testimonium has been destroyed, or has been lost for more than twelve months, or (the degree having been conferred *in absentia*) did not reach him through the post; and that if the original testimonium is found he will return the duplicate to the Senior Proctor. Duplicate testimoniums are not issued during the vacation.

V HOODS AND GOWNS

Hoods

36. Where an edging of a different colour from the lining is not prescribed, the hood is edged with the same colour as the lining. The material is silk unless otherwise specified.

Bachelors

Arts	B.A.	Black, lined with white fur
Divinity	B.D.	Black, lined with fine black silk
Law	LL.B.	Black, lined with white
Medicine	M.B.	Black, lined with crimson
Surgery	B.Ch.	Black, lined with white, edged with blue
Obstetrics	B.A.O.	Black, lined with olive
Dental science	B.Dent.Sc.	Myrtle green, lined with black watered silk, edged with crimson
Veterinary medicine	M.V.B.	Black, lined with maroon, edged with olive green
Engineering	B.A.I.	Black, lined with green
Agriculture	Agr.B.	Black, lined with brown
Forestry	Agr. (Forest.) B.	Black, lined with brown, edged with green
Music	Mus.B.	Pale blue, lined with white fur
Business Studies	B.B.S.	Black, lined with gold (silk or poplin lining)
Social Studies	B.S.S.	Black, lined with gold (silk or poplin lining), edged with white

Masters

Arts	M.A.	Black, lined with blue
Science	M.Sc.	White, lined with myrtle green
Letters	M.Litt.	White, lined with blue
Surgery	M.Ch.	Crimson, lined with white, edged with blue
Obstetrics	M.A.O.	Black, lined with purple
Dental Science	M.Dent.Sc.	Myrtle green, lined with pale blue, edged with crimson
Veterinary medicine	M.V.M.	White, lined with maroon
Engineering	M.A.I.	White, lined with green
Agriculture	Agr.M.	White, lined with brown
Forestry	Agr. (Forest.) M.	White, lined with brown, edged with green
Administration	M.S.A.	White, lined with gold

Degrees, licences and diplomas

Doctors

Science	Sc.D.	Scarlet cloth, lined with myrtle green
Philosophy	Ph.D.	Scarlet cloth, lined with yellow
Letters	Litt.D.	Scarlet cloth, lined with blue
Divinity	D.D.	Scarlet cloth, lined with black
Law	LL.D.	Scarlet cloth, lined with pink
Medicine	M.D.	Scarlet cloth, lined with crimson
Music	Mus.D.	White flowered silk, lined with rose satin

Gowns

37.

Bachelors and Masters	Black cloth, silk, or poplin
Doctors	
Sc.D.	Scarlet cloth, faced with myrtle green silk
Ph.D.	Scarlet cloth, faced with yellow silk
Litt.D.	Scarlet cloth, faced with blue silk
D.D.	Scarlet cloth, faced with black velvet
LL.D.	Scarlet cloth, faced with pink silk
M.D.	Scarlet cloth, faced with crimson silk
Mus.D.	White flowered silk, faced with rose satin

VI LICENCES

38. Licences may be obtained in

Medicine   Surgery
Obstetrics   Engineering

VII DIPLOMAS

39. Diplomas may be obtained in

History of European painting   Physiotherapy
Biblical studies   Education
Gynaecology and obstetrics   Social studies
Psychological medicine   Entomology

For the regulations governing the award of the various licences and diplomas, see under the respective subjects.

ADMISSION REQUIREMENTS

Every Irish applicant who satisfies the requirements will be assured of a place in the University. Entry to particular schools may from time to time be restricted by limitations of space, but every effort will be made to place Irish applicants in the schools of their choice. Irish applicants are those whose home residences are within the thirty-two counties of Ireland, or who have received their secondary education at Irish schools.

Except in certain schools, places are also available for applicants from outside Ireland. Preference will be given to those who are of Irish birth or parentage, or who are children of graduates of this University.

All who wish to enter the University to read for primary degrees must obtain admission from the Senior Tutor according to the rules set out in Part A. The mode of admission for those intending to take diploma courses and for other non-graduating students is indicated in Part B, and for students proceeding to higher degrees in Part C.

A. ADMISSION OF CANDIDATES FOR PRIMARY DEGREES

I GENERAL REGULATIONS

Application for admission

1. Written enquiries concerning admission should be addressed to the Admissions Office, and should if possible indicate the course or courses in which the prospective applicant is interested. Owing to their great number, letters of initial enquiry are not preserved, and relevant information contained in them must be repeated on forms of application. Application forms are obtainable from the Admissions Office. Personal enquiries about admission should be made in the Assistant Registrar's Office, where application forms and booklets are obtainable.

Irish applicants should send in their application forms, duly completed, before 1 January of the year in which they wish to enter, but applications may be accepted from them until 1 September. They are strongly urged to apply as early as possible. Other applicants must send in their application forms, duly completed, before 1 January, and must pay an application fee of £3. Their applications will not be considered unless this fee has been received, together with all necessary details, by this date. Candidates should note that their applications

Admission requirements

for admission may be submitted before the examination requirements for matriculation have been fully satisfied, provided they intend to take appropriate examinations.

Entry is possible only at the beginning of the academic year, in October. No person shall be admitted as a matriculated student of the University who is under the age of 17 years on 15 October of the year in which he enters.

General admission requirements

2. To be considered for admission as an undergraduate member of the University a candidate must be supported by evidence of (*a*) character and academic suitability, preferably from the head of the school last attended, (*b*) good physical and mental health, and (*c*) a satisfactory level of general education. Students from outside Ireland and Great Britain should also, unless they are officially sponsored, name a referee, preferably one resident in Ireland or Great Britain.

3. As evidence of a satisfactory level of general education a candidate must either (i) pass the matriculation examination in full, or (ii) qualify for complete exemption from it, or (iii) qualify for partial exemption, and pass the matriculation examination in part as directed by the Senior Tutor. These qualifications, whether gained at the matriculation examination, or at one of the approved certificate examinations listed below, or partly at a certificate examination and partly at the matriculation examination, must in any event be gained *at not more than three sittings*; that is, a candidate must be able to show that he has satisfied the full examination requirements by passing at the appropriate level in all the necessary subjects on not more than three separate occasions of presenting himself at examinations.

The matriculation examination

4. This examination is held only in Trinity College. It takes place twice a year, starting usually in late May and late September.

The subjects of the matriculation examination are English composition, mathematics, additional mathematics, physics, chemistry, biology, geography, geology, history, English literature, French, German, Greek, Hebrew, Irish, Italian, Latin, Russian, Spanish. In all subjects except English composition there are four passing grades, D (65 per cent and over), P_1 (60–64 per cent), P_2 (50–59 per cent), and P_3 (40–49 per cent). To pass the examination in full a candidate must

(*a*) pass in English composition; and

(*b*) pass in five further subjects, viz. either

    (i) Latin and four others, of which at least one must not be a language, or

    (ii) mathematics and four others, which must include at least one language other than English; and

  (c) pass with a mark of not less than P_2 in two or more of these five further subjects.

To be permitted to take certain honor or professional courses a candidate may have to satisfy certain additional requirements. For these, see sections II and III below.

Exemption from the matriculation examination

5. (*a*) *Complete exemption.* Holders of approved certificates in a range of subjects conforming to those required to pass the matriculation examination in full may, if the Senior Tutor is satisfied with the standard attained, be granted complete exemption from the matriculation examination and qualify to be considered for admission.

(*b*) *Partial exemption.* Holders of approved certificates whose qualifications are deficient may be granted exemption in one or more subjects, and may make good their deficiencies with appropriate passes at the matriculation examination. Alternatively, they may seek to qualify for complete exemption from the matriculation examination, as stated above, completing the matriculation requirements by passing at the other approved certificate examinations.

A candidate's claim for exemption, whether complete or partial, must be authenticated by a certified statement or statements, to the satisfaction of the Senior Tutor, of the marks or grades of the relevant examination results.

Certificate qualifications which include subjects other than those forming part of the matriculation examination will be considered, and the Senior Tutor will decide upon their suitability in individual cases after the completed applications have been received. An overseas student who passes an approved examination in his own language (with credit, in the case of a School Certificate examination) is exempted from the matriculation examination in a modern language; but he must satisfy the Senior Tutor that he has an adequate knowledge of English, both spoken and written.

Approved certificates are

    (i) the Leaving Certificate of the Department of Education, Ireland, normally with honours in at least two subjects;

    (ii) the Northern Ireland General Certificate of Education, with

87

Admission requirements

passes at advanced level in at least two subjects gained at one sitting;

(iii) other General Certificates of Education issued by recognized examining authorities, if they include passes at advanced level in at least two subjects, gained with good marks at a single sitting. Passes with credit at a School Certificate examination, supplemented by Higher School Certificate principal level or G.C.E. advanced level passes in at least two subjects, gained with good grades at a single sitting, are also approved. A Certificate of Fitness issued by the Scottish Universities Board qualifies the holder for exemption if he has passed with good marks at the higher standard in at least three subjects, including English, at a single sitting;

(iv) the matriculation certificates of certain universities, if these certificates have been gained with good marks in at least two subjects at one sitting.

Matriculation fee

6. A matriculation fee of £8 is payable. If a candidate proposes to take the University's matriculation examination in whole or in part, the fee must be paid by a fixed date before the examination (see below, under MATRICULATION EXAMINATION); if a candidate seeks complete exemption from the matriculation examination, as provided above, the matriculation fee is payable when the Senior Tutor has signified that he is prepared to grant such exemption and offers the candidate a place in the University. The payment should be sent direct to the Bank of Ireland, College Green, Dublin 2. Payment should be made by draft, cheque, money order or postal order made payable to TRINITY COLLEGE, DUBLIN, NO. 2 ACCOUNT, and must be accompanied by the appropriate fee payment form. The matriculation fee cannot be refunded except in very special circumstances and at the discretion of the Senior Tutor.

Acceptance of places

7. Applicants will be informed by the Senior Tutor whether or not their applications are successful. To indicate his acceptance of a place a successful applicant must by 1 September at the latest either pay the ensuing year's fees appropriate to his course of study, together with the capitation fee of £12, or produce evidence that they will be paid by a grant-making authority. Places not so accepted by that date will be re-allocated to deferred applicants, who must indicate acceptance in the same manner within a fortnight of allocation.

II SPECIAL REQUIREMENTS OF HONOR SCHOOLS

8. Candidates wishing to enter certain honor schools must have matriculation qualifications in the subjects listed in the following table.

SCHOOL	SUBJECT
Celtic languages	Latin
Early and modern Irish	Latin
Economics and political science	Mathematics
Legal science	Latin
History and political science	Latin; also one of French, German, Irish, Italian, Spanish
Modern languages and literature	Latin

9. A candidate for admission to an honor school should obtain high qualifications (good marks at the matriculation examination; honours in the Leaving Certificate; high advanced level grades) in at least two subjects including as a rule the subject or subjects he wishes to study, where these are part of a normal school curriculum. Where they are not, high qualifications in other subjects may make him eligible to be considered. Applicants should note the following points in relation to certain specific schools.

Ancient and modern literature. A candidate must be well qualified in Latin; the requirements concerning a modern language are as stated below for the school of modern languages and literature.

Mental and moral science. Preference is given to candidates with matriculation qualifications in mathematics and either Latin or Greek.

History and political science. Students from Africa or Asia whose mother tongue is not English must present Latin but need not present one of the other languages listed above.

Modern languages and literature. (*a*) Students wishing to read French, German or Irish must possess an adequate knowledge of both the spoken and written language. Italian or Spanish may be studied without previous knowledge of the language, but satisfactory evidence of general linguistic ability is required. In all departments of the school of modern languages and literature applications are judged on evidence furnished of general intellectual ability and of aptitude for linguistic and literary study. (*b*) Students wishing to take the course in English literature and language alone must normally have obtained good passes in the matriculation examination (or an approved certificate examination at honor or advanced level) in English and in one of the languages French, German, Irish, Italian, Spanish, Latin, Greek. For either (*a*) or (*b*) a pass in Latin at the matriculation examination, or its recognised equivalent, is an essential requirement.

Admission requirements

Natural sciences. Preference is given to applicants who have passed with good marks at the matriculation examination, or obtained honours at the Leaving Certificate, or passed with high grades at advanced level in a General Certificate of Education examination, in two of the following subjects: chemistry, physics, mathematics, additional mathematics, biology[1], botany, geography, geology, zoology. Applicants who do not have qualifications in scientific subjects, but have a high level of attainment in other subjects, may be considered, if places are available.

III SPECIAL REQUIREMENTS OF PROFESSIONAL SCHOOLS

10. Candidates wishing to enter certain professional schools must have matriculation qualifications in the subjects listed in the following table.

SCHOOL	SUBJECT
Law (course for LL.B. degree)	Latin
Medicine, dental science and veterinary medicine	Mathematics or physics

11. Applicants should note the following points in relation to certain specific schools.

Agriculture and forestry. The special requirements of these schools are the same as those of the honor school of natural sciences, for which see above. It should be noted that at present only Irish candidates can be considered for these schools.

Business Studies. Entrants should have a matriculation qualification in mathematics. Applications will, however, be considered from candidates with good qualifications in other subjects.

Divinity. A student may not enter the divinity school until he is of at least Junior Sophister standing in arts. For details, see the regulations of the school.

Engineering. The school of engineering holds a special entrance examination in mathematics. This is held in the College usually in September or October. Suitably qualified candidates may be exempted from it.

Medicine, dental science, veterinary medicine. A candidate for admission to any one of these schools, who holds a matriculation qualification in physics but not in mathematics, must possess a matriculation qualification in Latin in order to satisfy the general requirements for admission to the University.

Social Studies. All candidates for admission to this school are required to attend for interview.

---

[1] Biology may not be offered with botany or zoology.

IV MATRICULATION EXAMINATION

12. The matriculation examination is held twice a year. Forthcoming examinations will begin on the following dates: 5 May 1967, 20 September 1967. A detailed time-table is sent to candidates a fortnight before the examination.

To take the earlier examination application must be made before 15 April, and to take the later examination application must be made before 1 September. By the appropriate date intending candidates must have completed and sent to the Senior Tutor a matriculation examination form, and must have paid to the Bank of Ireland, College Green, Dublin 2, the non-returnable matriculation fee of £8, accompanied by a completed fee-payment form. Examination forms and fee-payment forms are obtainable from the Admissions Office. The matriculation fee is payable on each occasion on which a candidate is permitted to take the examination, whether he takes it in whole or in part.

13. Candidates who pass the examination in whole are given a matriculation certificate. Candidates who, having been exempted in certain subjects, complete the matriculation requirements by gaining appropriate passes in three or more subjects at the matriculation examination, are given a certificate to that effect.

14. Candidates may present themselves in any subject or subjects in which the examination is held, and they receive credit for any subject or subjects in which they satisfy the examiners. But matriculation certificates are granted only as stated in the preceding paragraph.

15. Candidates presenting themselves for the examination as a whole and seeking to qualify in more than six subjects may submit an additional language, or an additional non-linguistic subject, or both, but may not submit more than eight subjects in all; English literature is regarded, for the purposes of this regulation, as a non-linguistic subject. If they pass the examination as a whole, all the subjects in which they are successful are recorded on their certificates.

16. Entrance scholarships and (for students of narrow means) sizarships are awarded each year on the results of a special examination held in Trinity Term. Awards are also made on the results of the midsummer matriculation examination, provided that sufficient merit is shown. For particulars see ENTRANCE AWARDS.

17. Except in English composition (one hour), and in geography where there is also a two-hour practical examination, one three-hour paper is set in each subject. In French, German, Hebrew, Irish, Italian, Russian and Spanish there is also a *viva voce* examination. The paper

Admission requirements

in these languages counts for 70 per cent of the total marks and the *viva voce* examination for 30 per cent.

18. The courses prescribed for 1967 are as follows.

English composition

Candidates are required to write an essay on one of a number of topics proposed.

English literature

Shakespeare, *Julius Caesar*; Goldsmith, *She stoops to conquer*; poems of Milton, Gray, Wordsworth, Shelley, Keats and Tennyson as in *Oxford book of English verse* or Palgrave, *Golden treasury* (World's Classics); Pope, *The rape of the lock*; Yeats, the first four poems of *The tower*: 'Sailing to Byzantium', 'The tower', 'Meditations in time of civil war', 'Nineteen hundred and nineteen'; Jane Austen, *Pride and prejudice*; Conrad, *Heart of darkness*; a representative selection of essays by Addison, Lamb and R. L. Stevenson as, *e.g.*, in *A book of English essays*, ed. W. E. Williams (Penguin).

In 1967 candidates will be examined in the following: Shakespeare, *Julius Caesar, Macbeth*; Goldsmith, *She stoops to conquer*; Synge, *Riders to the sea*; poems of Shakespeare, Milton, Marvell, Burns, Wordsworth, Shelley, Keats, Tennyson and Browning as in *Oxford book of English verse* or Palgrave, *Golden treasury* (World's Classics); Milton, *Paradise lost*, books 1, 2; Yeats, the first four poems of *The tower*: 'Sailing to Byzantium', 'The tower', 'Meditations in time of civil war', 'Nineteen hundred and nineteen'; Swift, *Gulliver's travels*; Maria Edgeworth, *Castle Rackrent*; Stephens, *The crock of gold*; a representative selection of essays by Bacon, Addison, Goldsmith, Lamb and Hazlitt as, e.g., in *A book of English essays*, ed. W. E. Williams (Penguin). Candidates will also be expected to show a general knowledge of the development of English literature since 1550.

Languages

LATIN

The paper comprises (i) passages for translation from the prescribed texts, (ii) passages for unseen translation, (iii) passages for translation from English into Latin, (iv) questions on grammar, history, literature and mythology.

The course for 1966 is Virgil, *Aeneid*, 6; Cicero, *De amicitia*.

The course for 1967 is Virgil, *Aeneid*, 1; Cicero *De amicitia*.

Candidates are required to offer *one* prescribed book only.

GREEK

The paper comprises (i) passages for translation from the prescribed texts, (ii) passages for unseen translation, (iii) questions on grammar and literature, (iv) an optional passage for translation from English into Greek, which may be attempted in place of one of the passages in (i) or (ii).

The course for 1966 is Homer, *Iliad*, 10; Xenophon, *Anabasis*, 3.

The course for 1967 is Homer, *Odyssey*, 6; Xenophon, *Anabasis*, 3.

Candidates are required to offer *one* prescribed book only.

HEBREW

The paper comprises (i) Hebrew grammar, (ii) passages for translation from the prescribed texts, (iii) passages for unseen translation, (iv) passages for translation from English into Hebrew.

There is a *viva voce* examination on the prescribed course.

Prescribed texts: *Genesis*, chs 39–48, *Psalms* 1–10.

OTHER LANGUAGES

The paper comprises a choice of topics for free composition, an unseen passage for translation into English, a passage for translation into the language selected, and a question on the prescribed books. The *viva voce* examination is primarily designed to test the candidate's familiarity with, and ability in, the spoken language.

French: Beaumarchais, *Le barbier de Séville* (Blackwell) or Racine, *Andromaque*; Mérimée, *Colomba* (Harrap) or Daudet, *Le petit Chose*. Mérimée, *Colomba*, will remain an option for the 1967 examinations.

German: Hochwälder, *Das heilige Experiment* (Harrap), or Grillparzer, *Der Traum ein Leben*.

Irish: Sayers, *Peig*; *Filíocht na nGael*, ed. Ó Cannain, poems 9–19, 35, 43–7, 84–94, 130–2, 143–5, 193, 213, 229, 240.

Italian: G. Deladda, *Canne al vento* (Manchester).

Russian: Turgeniev, *Mumu*, or Pushkin, *Pikovaya Dama*.

Spanish: *Cuentos de autores contemporáneos* (Harrap).

History

Outlines of the history of *either* Great Britain and Ireland, 1815–1914, *or* Europe and Ireland, 1815–1914.

Geography

Physical geography. Structure of the earth, denudational processes, land forms. Elementary meteorology, atmospheric and oceanic circulation, climates of the earth. Distribution and inter-relationships of the major soil groups and vegetational formations.

Human geography. World distribution of major agricultural and industrial activities and related settlement forms. World population growth and distribution.

Regional geography. Western Europe: France, Germany, Holland, Belgium, Luxembourg, Norway, Sweden, Denmark and the British Isles, and one of the two following regions: South America or Monsoon Asia.

Practical examination. Interpretation of an Irish half-inch, or British one-inch, Ordnance Survey topographic map.

Mathematics

ARITHMETIC

The positive and negative integers. Prime numbers. The number of primes is infinite. Factorisation of integers into products of prime numbers, its uniqueness

Admission requirements

apart from the order of the factors. The rational numbers. Binary notation, transformation from base 10 to base 2 and vice versa. Mathematical induction.

SET THEORY

Idea of a set; notation; union, intersection, complement, subset, null set, universal set. A *relation* as a set of ordered pairs. Idea of a function and of a sequence.

ALGEBRA

Linear equations and inequalities. Quadratic equations. Factorisation. Remainder Theorem. Finite arithmetic and geometric progressions. Permutations and combinations. Binomial Theorem with positive integral exponent.

TRIGONOMETRY

Radian measure of angles. Definitions of the trigonometric functions for all possible real values of the independent variable, the graphs of the trigonometric functions; periodicity; simple identities; compound angle formulae; sine and cosine rules for triangles and simple applications. Idea of complex number.

GEOMETRY

The substance of Euclid, Books I–IV, and of Propositions 1, 2, 3, 4, 5, 6, 8, 9, 10, 11, 12, 13, 14, 19 of Books VI, but proof of VI 1 for commensurables only. Inversion. Elementary analytical geometry of the straight line. Mensuration of simple areas and solids including cone and sphere.

ANALYSIS

Distinction between rational and irrational numbers. The real number system. Idea of a limit of a sequence of real numbers and of a function. Simple infinite series, including geometric series. Continuity. Indices and logarithms. The derivative of a function; the derivative of polynomials and of simple rational functions; easy applications.

STATISTICS

Introduction to Statistics. Elementary idea of frequency distribution; graphical representation; very simple treatment of mean and standard deviation. Easy applications.

Additional mathematics

Syllabus A[1]

The material prescribed for the matriculation examination in mathematics and in addition:

SET THEORY

Fuller treatment of sets. Finite, enumerable and non-enumerable sets. Proof that the set of real numbers is not enumerable.

ALGEBRA

Theory of equations. Determinants. Approximation to the roots of equations.

TRIGONOMETRY

Solution of trigonometrical equations. The inverse trigonometrical functions

---

[1] *Syllabus A* and *Syllabus B* are separate subjects. A candidate may take both, but not more than two of the three mathematical subjects available shall count towards the award of matriculation.

and their graphs. Further treatment of complex numbers. De Moivre's Theorem with simple applications.

GEOMETRY

Ceva's Theorem. Menelaus' Theorem. Cross ratio, harmonic ranges and pencils, coaxal circles, poles and polars. Cartesian and polar coordinates. Elementary analytical geometry of the conic sections.

ANALYSIS

Inverse functions. Fuller treatment of infinite series, simple tests for convergence. Differential calculus, differentiation of sums, products, quotients and of algebraic, trigonometrical exponential and logarithmic functions; chain rule. Introduction to the integral calculus. Integrals of easy algebraic, trigonometrical, exponential and logarithmic functions. Applications of the calculus to the determination of tangents, maxima and minima, areas and volumes.

Syllabus B[1]

The material prescribed for the matriculation examination in mathematics and in addition:

CALCULUS

Derivatives of simple algebraic and trigonometrical functions, product, quotient and chain rules. Integration as the inverse of differentiation. Areas. Centroids of simple bodies.

GEOMETRY

Coordinate Geometry of circle, and parabola in simplest form. Parametric equations. Polar coordinates.

PROBABILITY AND VECTORS

Elementary operations with plane vectors including scalar product. Elementary probability and statistical inference.

MECHANICS

Basic concepts: space, time, mass, force as a vector; resolution and composition of forces; moments, centroids; laws of statics; friction; Newton's laws; motion with constant acceleration; work, kinetic and potential energy and linear momentum; conservation laws; Newton's law of impact; motion in a circle; simple harmonic motion and the pendulum; Hooke's law.

Biology

A

Characteristics of plants and animals. Modes of nutrition; diet.
Structure and constituents of the cell; mitosis.
Bacteria; carbon and nitrogen cycles; food chains.
Organic evolution.

B

Morphology of a herbaceous plant, without microscopic detail; character-

---

[1] *Syllabus A* and *Syllabus B* are separate subjects. A candidate may take both, but not more than two of the three mathematical subjects available shall count towards the award of matriculation.

Admission requirements

istic features in summer and winter of the common trees of the countryside; adaptive variation in root, stem and leaf structure.

The parts of a flower and their functions, as exemplified by one monocotyledon and one dicotyledon; the nature of the composite flower-head.

Pollination; development of seed and fruit; the principal types of fruit, and their dispersal; structure and germination of seeds.

Photosynthesis; gaseous exchange; soil; absorption and transpiration; mineral nutrition; aerobic and anaerobic respiration; growth and movement in plants.

Structure and reproduction of *Spirogyra, Fucus, Mucor.*

C

Elementary morphology and physiology of a mammal[1].

Elementary anatomy, life-history and habits of a fish[1], a frog[1] and a bird.

Morphology and physiology of *Amoeba, Paramoecium, Hydra.*

External features of the cockroach; life-history and economic importance of the cockroach, butterfly, house-fly, clothes-moth, honey-bee.

Development of a frog from fertilisation to metamorphosis.

Chemistry

GENERAL AND PHYSICAL CHEMISTRY

Atomic theory; the electron, proton, neutron; atomic structure; atomic number; isotopes; periodic classification, and atomic structure of the first twenty elements.

Types of bonds; simple ionic crystals; the shapes of simple molecules with reference to orbitals and hybridisation.

The gas laws; kinetic theory of gases and simple applications.

Determination of chemical equivalents, atomic weights, molecular weights in the gas phase and in solution; osmotic pressures.

Chemical reactions; chemical equilibrium; dissociation equilibria treated qualitatively; acids and bases; pH and indicators; electrolysis.

Oxidation and reduction as electron transfers; oxidation number.

First law of thermodynamics; heats of reaction and formation.

Standard solutions and volumetric analysis using acids and alkalis, iodine, permanganate and silver nitrate. Principles of gravimetric analysis.

INORGANIC CHEMISTRY

Oxygen, air, oxides, ozone; hydrogen, water, hydrogen peroxide; carbon, its oxides, carbonates; nitrogen, including its fixation, ammonia and its salts, oxides of nitrogen, nitric acid, nitrites, nitrates; phosphorus, its oxides and chlorides, phosphoric acid; sulphur, hydrogen sulphide, oxides of sulphur, sulphuric acid, sulphites, sulphates; the halogens, halogen acids, oxy-acids of the halogens; the simple physical and chemical properties of sodium, potassium, copper, silver, magnesium, calcium, zinc, aluminium, iron, lead, and the preparation and the properties of their common oxides and salts.

ORGANIC CHEMISTRY

Empirical and molecular formulae; chemistry of alkanes, alkenes, alkynes,

[1] These should be studied by demonstration-dissection.

alcohols, aldehydes and ketones, carboxylic acids and their derivatives, treated in such a way as to show the properties of the functional groups; geometrical isomerism; optical isomerism derived from one and two asymmetric centres; glucose, fructose, sucrose, starch; benzene, aniline, benzaldehyde, toluene, nuclear and side chain substitution.

Geology

The characteristic features, occurrence, origin and economic importance of the common minerals (crystallography, and optical properties in thin section, not required) and the common rocks (microscope studies not required). The nature and preservation of fossils, their role as rock-formers and indicators of geological age and palaeoecology (biological studies of fossils not required).

The action of erosional agencies (atmospheric, fluvial, marine, aeolian and glacial) on the rocks of the earth's surface and the resulting land forms. Cycles of erosion. The localised effect of crustal movement (joints, cleavage, folds, faults, etc.). The principles of stratigraphy.

Further details of the course may be obtained from the Professor of Geology.

Physics

MECHANICS

Displacement, velocity and acceleration. Vectors and scalars. Addition and resolution of vectors. Newton's laws. Mass, force and weight. Moments, momentum, work and energy. Circular motion. Simple harmonic motion. Conservation laws. Gravitation.

HEAT

Gas thermometer. Absolute scale of temperature. Gas laws. Mechanical equivalent of heat. Kinetic theory and its application to pressure and temperature of a gas. Brownian movement. Avogadro's constant.

WAVE MOTION

Transverse and longitudinal waves. Frequency, wavelength, velocity, amplitude and energy. Simple interference and diffraction of waves.

SOUND

Wave nature. Transmission, reflection, refraction. Velocity in various media. Pitch, loudness and tone.

LIGHT

Transmission, reflection and refraction. Velocity. Formation of images by mirrors and lenses. Simple telescope and spectroscope. Ultraviolet and infrared light. Wave nature. Elementary interference and diffraction. Electromagnetic spectrum.

MAGNETISM

Properties of magnets. Magnetic poles and fields. Dipole moment. Couple on dipole in a magnetic field. Terrestrial magnetism.

ELECTRICITY

Law of force between charges. Conductors and insulators. Electroscopes.

E

Admission requirements

Induction of charges. Electric fields and potential. Condensers. Energy of charged bodies.

Voltaic cells. Magnetic field due to a current. Unit current and potential difference. Heating effect. Relation between potential difference and current for various conductors. Ohm's law and resistance. Production of magnetic fields. Force on a conductor carrying a current in a magnetic field. Moving coil galvanometers and meters. Electrolysis. Faraday's laws and their explanation. Electromagnetic induction. Alternating currents.

MODERN PHYSICS

Descriptive account of atomic and nuclear structure. Isotopes. Radioactivity. Emission of alpha, beta and gamma rays. Radioactive decay. The neutron. Examples of nuclear reactions. Artificial radioactivity.

Elementary treatment of thermionic and photoelectric effects. Production of X-rays. Ionisation and fluorescence by X-rays. Mass energy conservation. Compton effect and pair production.

B. ADMISSION OF CANDIDATES FOR DIPLOMAS AND OF OTHER NON-GRADUATING STUDENTS

I CANDIDATES FOR DIPLOMAS

19. Candidates for diplomas must apply for admission to the registrars of the schools concerned. Candidates for the Higher Diploma in Education must hold a university degree or other qualification recognised by the Teachers' Registration Council of Ireland. Candidates for the Diploma in Social Studies, the Diploma in Physiotherapy, and the Diploma in Biblical Studies, must satisfy the admission requirements of the University. Evidence of character must be supplied to the satisfaction of the appropriate school committee. For particulars of the various diplomas see the regulations of the respective schools.

II STUDENTS OF THE KING'S INNS AND SOLICITORS' APPRENTICES

20. Students of the King's Inns and solicitors' apprentices may take part of their professional course in the Law School of Trinity College. The conditions of admission are set out under LAW SCHOOL.

III ONE-YEAR AND ONE-TERM STUDENTS

21. Students of other universities who desire to work for an academic year in Trinity College must apply for permission to the Senior Tutor. Applications must be supported by a recommendation from the principal of the university to which the applicant belongs, and by an official statement of his academic record. Approved candidates are

assigned to a tutor and are entitled to attend lectures (but not usually tutorials) and to take an ordinary or honor examination, if available, on the same conditions as full-course students. If they intend to take an examination, notice must be given to the Senior Lecturer's office at least three weeks before the end of the preceding lecture term specifying the examination and the subjects to be taken. For the fees payable by one-year students see COLLEGE CHARGES.

22. Students of other universities, and other sufficiently qualified students, who desire to work for one term in Trinity College must apply for permission to the Senior Tutor. Applications must be supported by a recommendation from the principal of the university to which the applicant belongs, or (if he is not a member of a university) of the educational institution he last attended. Approved candidates are entitled to attend lectures on the same conditions as full-course students, but not to take examinations. The Senior Tutor may also admit suitably qualified applicants to attend specific courses of lectures. For the fees payable see COLLEGE CHARGES.

A one-term student who has shown satisfactory progress may apply to the Senior Tutor for permission to work in the College for one further term but no longer.

C. ADMISSION OF CANDIDATES FOR HIGHER DEGREES

23. Candidates for the degrees of Master in Letters, Doctor in Philosophy, Doctor in Letters, Master in Science, and Doctor in Science and higher degrees in professional subjects must apply for registration to the Dean of Graduate Studies. Those who are not graduates of the University of Dublin are required to pay the matriculation fee. See GRADUATE STUDIES AND HIGHER DEGREES.

D. RE-ADMISSION

24. Students who for any reason have gone off the books can be re-admitted to the College in a subsequent academic year only at the discretion of the Senior Tutor. Students who for reasons of ill-health have gone off the books can be re-admitted even in the current academic year only at the discretion of the Senior Tutor, who may require them to produce a satisfactory certificate from a medical referee nominated by the Senior Tutor. A special application form for re-admission is obtainable from the Senior Tutor's office.

COLLEGE CHARGES

*N.B. The Board of Trinity College, Dublin, is not bound
by any error in, or omission from, the following regulations.*

I GENERAL REGULATIONS

1. The charges for any academic course, examination or other service
are those stated in the *Dublin University Calendar* for the current year.

The Board of Trinity College, Dublin, reserves its right to alter its
scales of charges at any time. Revised scales of charges will apply,
from the date appointed by the Board, to all students pursuing any
course the charges for which have been revised, whether or not such
students have entered upon the course before the appointed date.

2. All charges become due on the dates specified in the *Calendar* for
the current year, and must be paid to the Bank of Ireland or the
appointed officer of the College on or before that date. Tardy payment,
subject to fine, may be accepted under conditions specified in each case.

*N.B. The College sends out reminders in September to students on the
books, advising them that the date for payment of annual fees is imminent.
Non-receipt of such a reminder is not a valid excuse for failure to pay fees
at the proper time.*

3. Arrangements have been made whereby the Bank of Ireland will
receive at its head office, College Green, Dublin, payment of all college
charges, by post or personal payment, subject to §4 below, and all
payments should be sent to or presented at the Bank, with the exception
of the following charges which are payable to the Accountant:

B.A. and other degree conferring fees

Chamber deposits (through the Registry of Chambers)

Occasional and extraordinary charges

4. Payment should be made by crossed draft, cheque, money order,
or postal order, drawn payable to TRINITY COLLEGE, DUBLIN, NO. 2
ACCOUNT, for the exact amount due, and accompanied by a duly completed fee-payment form, obtainable in the College or at the Bank.

5. A student who holds an educational grant and wishes the College
to apply to his educational authority for payment of his fees must
complete and return to the Senior Tutor a form to this effect.

6. Students whose home residences are outside Ireland (thirty-two
counties) pay a surcharge of fifty per cent on all annual college fees,
on other tuition fees and on laboratory fees. The fifty per cent surcharge

is also payable in the case of a student whose home residence is in Ireland but whose fees are paid by an authority outside Ireland.

7. A student required to repeat the academic exercises of a year must repeat the fee of that year.

8. A student granted any exemption from attendance at lectures pays the same fees as he would pay if attending lectures.

Matriculation fee

9. Every candidate for admission to the University must pay a matriculation or registration fee of £8. If the candidate intends to take the matriculation examination of the University, in full or in part, the fee is payable by a fixed date before the examination; see ADMISSION REQUIREMENTS. If he does not intend to take the matriculation examination, the fee is payable as soon as the Senior Tutor informs the candidate that he is granted admission to the University. The matriculation fee cannot be refunded except in very special circumstances and at the discretion of the Senior Tutor.

Payment of first College fees

10. Students entering the College for the first time must by 1 September (or if offered a place after that, within fourteen days of being informed of admission) pay the annual fees appropriate to the course to which they are admitted, or produce evidence that they will be paid by a grant-making authority. In cases where students are admitted after the beginning of the academic year no reduction in fees is granted.

11. All overseas students, that is students from outside Ireland and Great Britain, must lodge the sum of £50 as caution money, to be refunded, on the written request of their tutors to the Treasurer, when they complete their course or leave the University, less any sums that may be owing to the University. The lodgment is made through the Bank of Ireland, at the same time as the first annual fee is paid.

12. The annual capitation fee (see section III below) must be paid at the same time as the annual College fee.

Payment of subsequent fees

13. Students not entering the College for the first time, unless they are permitted by special regulations to do otherwise, should pay the annual fee, together with the annual capitation fee (see section III below) and laboratory fees if applicable, on or before 1 October in each year. Tardy payment may be accepted up to 15 November, without fine;

College charges

up to 21 November, subject to a fine of £1; up to 28 November, subject to a fine of £3; and up to 5 December, subject to a fine of £5.

Replacement fee

14. If, on the expiry of the limit for tardy payment stated in §13 above, an undergraduate's appropriate fees have not been paid, his name may be replaced on the college books for the current or any subsequent academic year only on payment of a replacement fee of £10, together with the fees due. Before paying, a student should consult his tutor. He must apply for re-admission to the Senior Tutor.

15. A student who has kept the Junior Freshman year and proceeded regularly thereafter without dropping a class, and who, with the prior approval of the Senior Lecturer and the head of the department concerned, goes off the books to study elsewhere for a full academic year is exempt from the replacement fee, if the period of his absence does not exceed one year.

Refund of fees

16. The Board accepts no obligation to refund any fee, or any part of any fee, paid in respect of any exercise to be performed in the University. Refunds may, however, be made as stated in §§17, 18 below.

17. If a student having paid the annual fee due on 1 October fails in an examination held in Michaelmas term on which his class depends, and in consequence discontinues his course, the fee is refunded. If he is permitted to repeat the year, the fee so paid is retained in full as an annual fee for the year repeated.

18. The Fee Concessions Committee may also authorise the Treasurer to make refunds as follows:

(a) where a college or professional school annual or terminal fee has been paid, and the student has not attended any instruction or examination, the fee may be refunded subject to a deduction of £5;

(b) where a student discontinues his studies in the course of an academic year one-half of the relevant fee may be refunded.

Requests for refunds under (a) or (b) above should be addressed to the Treasurer, through the student's tutor. In case (a) the application must reach the Treasurer within one month after payment of the fee, and in case (b) before 1 March. No other applications will be considered. The Treasurer will not authorise a refund unless he is satisfied that good reasons have been established. A refund in respect of the first annual fee will be made only in exceptional circumstances. The Treasurer will refer doubtful cases to the Fee Concessions Committee.

II FEE CONCESSIONS

19. In cases of hardship, the College grants fee concessions to Irish students or remits the surcharge on fees of non-Irish students one of whose parents is a graduate of the University of Dublin. Applications for fee concessions must be made to the Senior Tutor before 1 June, on forms obtainable from the Senior Tutor. Applications will be considered from prospective candidates for admission, as well as from students whose names are on the books of the College Postgraduate students may also apply.

20. There are also funds, endowed by private benefactors, from which assistance can be obtained. Full information is given in the *Calendar*, under FINANCIAL ASSISTANCE.

III CAPITATION FEE

21. All students on the college books paying the full annual fee in arts, in a professional school, for the Diploma in Social Studies, for the Testimonium in Divinity or as students registered for a higher degree must (apart from the exceptions noted in §23 below) pay a capitation fee each year *together with their annual fee*. The capitation fee is £12; £9 is administered by a representative standing committee of the clubs and societies and £3 is devoted to the provision of a student health service.

Students registered for higher degrees pay £9, £6 of which is for the clubs and societies and £3 for the student health service.

In the case of Veterinary students attending the Veterinary College, the capitation fee of £12 includes their subscription of £3 to the Students' Union Fund at the Veterinary College.

22. In those cases (see §§17 and 18) where a student's whole annual fee is refunded the capitation fee is also refunded.

23. Magee University College students attending lectures in Trinity College during only one term in the year, Church of Ireland Training College students, students excused from all lectures during the three terms of the academic year, and students registered for higher degrees who are certified by the Dean of Graduate Studies to be pursuing their studies at another university or institution, are not required to pay the capitation fee. If a student in any of these excepted categories wishes to use the facilities of the college clubs and societies, he, or she, must pay a capitation fee of £6.

IV UNDERGRADUATE FEES IN ARTS

24. The fees stated in this section are those payable by a student

College charges

taking the course in general studies or one of the honor courses in arts (including the honor course in natural sciences).

25. A matriculation fee of £8 is payable on admission to the University (see §9).

26. The annual college fee payable by a student resident in Ireland (thirty-two counties) is £80; the annual college fee payable by a student not resident in Ireland is £120.

All students, except as provided in §23, also pay the annual capitation fee of £12.

Fees for laboratory instruction

27. An undergraduate taking a course in natural sciences pays, in addition to the annual college fee, a laboratory fee. The fee is £30 per annum for a student resident in Ireland, £45 per annum for a student not resident in Ireland.

28. This fee must be paid together with the annual college fee, and is subject to the same provisions in respect of tardy payment, but only one fine is chargeable on account of tardy payment of either or both of these fees (if paid together).

29. Where an undergraduate loses his class or discontinues the subjects of his course the same rules concerning refund of fees apply as in the case of college fees.

Abridgement of courses

30. A student exempted from part of the undergraduate course pays the fee for the class that he joins.

31. A student who is admitted as a Senior Freshman to the course in general studies, or to one of the honor courses in arts (including the honor course in natural sciences), in accordance with the regulations for the various courses, pays an examination fee of £8 when sending in notice of intention to present himself for the Junior Freshman examination in each case, and if successful in the examination pays the fee for the class that he joins.

B.A. degree examination fee

32. Candidates for the B.A. degree examination must pay a degree examination fee of £8 twenty-one clear days before the last day of the preceding lecture term. Where a moderatorship examination is divided into two or more parts, this rule applies to the final part only.

33. A candidate for the B.A. degree in general studies who fails to pass the degree examination in Trinity term of his Senior Sophister year may present himself at the supplemental degree examination in

the immediately following Michaelmas term, without further payment. If a student is allowed to present himself on a subsequent occasion for the B.A. degree examination or for a supplemental moderatorship examination, a degree examination fee of £10 must be paid.

B.A. degree conferring fee
34. The fee for conferring of the B.A. degree is £10.

V UNDERGRADUATE FEES IN PROFESSIONAL SCHOOLS

35. The fees stated in this section are those payable by an undergraduate student in one of the following schools: agriculture and forestry, business and social studies, dental science, engineering, medicine, veterinary medicine.

The general regulations stated above, in section I, apply to the professional schools.

36. The fees payable by candidates for the LL.B. degree are stated in the regulations of the SCHOOL OF LAW; those payable by candidates for the Mus.B. degree are stated in the regulations of the SCHOOL OF MUSIC.

37. Fees payable for supplemental examinations, in the schools of agriculture and forestry (first two years), business and social studies, engineering, and veterinary medicine are as follows: £2 for one subject, £5 for more than one subject. The fee for supplemental examinations in the medical school is £5. See the regulations of the various schools.

Agriculture and forestry
38. The fees payable for the courses leading to the degrees of Bachelor in Agriculture or Bachelor in Agriculture (Forestry) are as follows: £

Students resident in Ireland: annual college fee 110
farm tuition fee 20

In the third and fourth years £90 of the annual fee is payable to University College, Dublin, and £20 to Trinity College. £

Students not resident in Ireland: annual college fee 165
farm tuition fee 30

In the third and fourth years £135 of the annual fee is payable to University College, Dublin, and £30 to Trinity College.

The farm tuition fee is payable only for the Senior Freshman year.

All students also pay the following fees: £
Matriculation fee 8
Annual capitation fee 12
Agr.B. degree conferring fee 10

College charges

A student taking an arts course, leading to the B.A. degree, pays the B.A. degree examination fee of £8, and the B.A. degree conferring fee of £10.

Business and social studies

39. Students taking the course for the B.B.S. degree or for the B.S.S. degree pay fees as follows:

	£
Matriculation fee	8
Students resident in Ireland: annual college fee	90
Students not resident in Ireland: annual college fee	135
Annual capitation fee	12
B.B.S. degree or B.S.S. degree conferring fee	10

Dental science

40. Students taking the course for the B.Dent.Sc. degree pay fees as follows:

Students resident in Ireland:	£
pre-dental, first and second dental years	110 per annum
third, fourth and fifth dental years	160 per annum
Students not resident in Ireland:	
pre-dental, first and second dental years	165 per annum
third, fourth and fifth dental years	240 per annum

Each of the fees listed above is a consolidated fee, and includes fees due to the College for instruction in medical, dental and arts subjects, and hospital fees.

All students also pay the following fees:

	£
Matriculation fee	8
Registration fee (at beginning of first dental year)	6
Annual capitation fee	12
B.A. degree examination fee	8
B.A. degree conferring fee	10
B.Dent.Sc. degree conferring fee	30

41. A medical graduate admitted to the School pays, if he is resident in Ireland, consolidated fees (including hospital fees) of £35 for the second dental year and £160 for each succeeding dental year. If he is not resident in Ireland, he pays a surcharge of fifty per cent on each of these fees. If he is not a graduate of the University of Dublin he must also pay the dental registration fee of £6.

Engineering

42. Students taking the course for the B.A.I. degree pay fees as follows:

	£
Matriculation fee	8
Students resident in Ireland: annual college fee	110
Students not resident in Ireland: annual college fee	165
Annual capitation fee	12
B.A. degree examination fee	8
B.A. degree conferring fee	10
B.A.I. degree conferring fee	10

43. The fee for the Licence in Engineering, granted to a student who has passed the B.A.I. degree examination but has failed to pass the B.A. degree examination, is £2.

Medicine (School of Physic)

44. Students taking the course for the M.B., B.Ch., and B.A.O. degrees pay fees as follows:

Students resident in Ireland:	£
pre-medical year consolidated fee	110
annual consolidated fee (five years)	110
Students not resident in Ireland:	
pre-medical year consolidated fee	165
annual consolidated fee (five years)	165

The consolidated fees include fees due to the College for instruction in medical and arts subjects, and hospital fees. The hospital fees include fees for the general and special clinical courses, but not the booking fees charged by some hospitals.

All students also pay the following fees:	£
Matriculation fee	8
Registration fee (at beginning of first medical year)	6
Annual capitation fee	12
B.A. degree examination fee	8
B.A. degree conferring fee	10
M.B., B.Ch., B.A.O. degree conferring fees, together	30

Extern students in the School of Physic, *i.e.* students permitted to attend lectures and classes in the School but not proceeding to degrees or licences of the University, pay the following fees: £110 per year if they attend for one or more years, £35 per term if they attend for less than a year. The fifty per cent surcharge for students not resident in Ireland applies to these fees; see §6 above.

107

College charges

45. The fee for the Licences in medicine, surgery and obstetrics, granted to a student who has satisfied the requirements of the courses in medicine, surgery and obstetrics, and who has completed the arts requirements for medical students, but has not passed the B.A. degree examination, is £14.

Veterinary medicine

46. Students taking the course for the M.V.B. degree pay fees as follows:

	£
Students resident in Ireland:	
pre-veterinary year	110
annual college fee (four years)	110
Students not resident in Ireland:	
pre-veterinary year	165
annual college fee (four years)	165

All students also pay the following fees:	£
Matriculation fee	8
Annual capitation fee	12
B.A. degree examination fee	8
B.A. degree conferring fee	10
M.V.B. degree conferring fee	25

47. An entrance fee of £1 is payable on admission to the Veterinary College, at the beginning of the first veterinary year. A subscription of £3 is payable to the Students' Union Fund at the Veterinary College for each of the four veterinary years; this subscription is paid by Trinity College on behalf of its veterinary students using the proceeds of their capitation fees for the purpose.

VI FEES FOR DIPLOMA COURSES

Diploma in Social Studies

48. A student taking the course for the Diploma in Social Studies pays fees as follows:

	£
Matriculation fee	8
Students resident in Ireland: annual fee	60
Students not resident in Ireland: annual fee	90
Annual capitation fee	12

Testimonium in Divinity

49. An undergraduate divinity student pays the college fees appropriate to the degree course he is taking. He does not pay any special fee for the divinity course.

Graduate students and candidate bachelors pay a fee of £60 per annum, payment being made in the same manner as the annual college fee. The surcharge of fifty per cent, payable by students whose home residences are not in Ireland, applies to this fee.

Both undergraduates and graduates pay the annual capitation fee of £12.

A student permitted to take a supplemental final examination for the Divinity Testimonium under §9 of the Divinity School regulations, who has not paid the annual college fee, pays a fee of £2 for each paper taken.

Other diplomas

50. The fees payable by candidates for the diplomas in biblical studies, gynaecology and obstetrics, physiotherapy, psychological medicine and for the higher diploma in education are stated in the *Calendar* under the regulations for the various diplomas.

VII FEES PAYABLE BY STUDENTS ADMITTED FOR ONE ACADEMIC YEAR OR FOR ONE TERM

51. Students admitted for one year or for one term in accordance with ADMISSION REQUIREMENTS, Part B, section III, pay fees as follows.

Students admitted for one year pay the matriculation fee, the annual college fee appropriate to the course to which they are admitted, and the capitation fee of £12. If they receive laboratory instruction they also pay a laboratory fee of £30 for the year. The fifty per cent surcharge for students from outside Ireland applies to the annual college fee and the laboratory fee. The fees must be paid before 1 September. Overseas students admitted for one year must also lodge before 1 September the sum of £50 as caution-money (see §11 above).

Students admitted for one term pay a term fee of £30, and if they receive laboratory instruction, a laboratory fee of £10 for the term. A student may be admitted to attend one specific course of lectures for a term on payment of a fee of £5; to attend more than one course of lectures a student must register as and pay the fees prescribed for a one-term student. All fees mentioned in this paragraph must be paid before 1 September for Michaelmas term, before 1 January for Hilary term, and before 1 April for Trinity term.

52. For fees payable by extern students in the School of Physic, see §44 above.

VIII POSTGRADUATE FEES

53. The fees payable by candidates for higher degrees are summarised below.

College charges

54. Graduate students who are registered by, and are pursuing studies at, other recognised centres in Ireland may, with the agreement of the centre concerned and the head of the appropriate department in Trinity College, attend classes in Trinity College. Such students pay a fee of £30 per term, and a further fee of £10 per term if working in a laboratory.

IX SUMMARY OF FEES FOR HIGHER DEGREES

		£
M.Litt. and M.Sc.[1]	matriculation (where applicable)	8
	first year[2]	80
	subsequent years: annual	5
	laboratory, first year	30
	laboratory, per term (after first year)	10
	computer course (consolidated course fee[2])	110
	annual capitation fee	9
	examination	10
	degree	15
Ph.D.[1]	matriculation (where applicable)	8
	first and second years, per annum[2]	80
	subsequent years: annual	5
	laboratory, per annum (first and second years)	30
	laboratory, per term (after first two years)	10
	annual capitation fee	9
	examination	15
Litt.D. and Sc.D.	application	20
	degree	25
B.D.	matriculation fee (where applicable)	8
	qualifying examination	1
	examination (per division, and thesis)	1
	theological exhibition candidates	6
	degree	10
D.D.	examination	21
	degree	21

[1] Full-time members of the University staff are exempt from all fees except the examination fee.

[2] The surcharge on tuition fees for students from outside Ireland does not apply to these fees.

		£
L.LD.	examination	20
	degree	25
M.D.	examination	25
	degree	25
M.Ch.	examination	25
	degree	25
M.A.O. and	examination	25
M.Dent.Sc.	degree	25
M.V.M. and M.A.I.	examination	25
	degree	25
Agr.M. and	examination	25
Agr. (Forest.) M.	degree	25
Mus.D.	exercise	10
	examination	20
	degree	25
M.S.A.	registration fee (where applicable)	10
	course fee (student without a contract of employment, resident in Ireland)	130
	course fee (student with a contract of employment, resident in Ireland)	210
	course fee (student without a contract of employment, not resident in Ireland)	195
	course fee (student with a contract of employment, not resident in Ireland)	315
	annual capitation fee	9
	diploma or degree fee	25
Postgraduate students not registered for higher degrees	term	30
	laboratory, per term	10
	annual capitation fee	9

GENERAL REGULATIONS FOR STUDENTS

I DISCIPLINE AND ACADEMIC PROGRESS

Registration

1. Every rising Junior Freshman, and every other student entering the College for the first time, is required to attend for registration in the Examination Hall on a stated day, or days, during the week preceding the beginning of arts lectures in Michaelmas term. Information about this will be sent to successful applicants by the Senior Tutor, when he offers them a place.

2. Every student, other than a student entering the College for the first time, must, before a prescribed date in Michaelmas term, complete a registration card and return it to the Student Records Office.

3. Every student must, within one week, notify the Student Records Office, on a prescribed card, of any change of address or of course occurring after he has registered.

4. A fine of £5 will be imposed for
   (a) late registration (i.e. for 1966–67, after 1 November 1966)
   (b) failure to notify change of address within one week of such change
   (c) failure to notify change of course/subject within one week of the Senior Tutor's or Senior Lecturer's authorisation.

Change of course or address cards must be delivered to the Student Records Office or posted in the box marked REGISTRATION CARDS in the hallway of East Theatre.

A student who has not registered by the last day of Michaelmas term, unless admitted subsequently, will not be eligible to present himself for any College examination.

5. Women students entering the College for the first time are expected, if they intend to reside with their parents or guardians while students, to seek an interview with the Dean of Women Students during the long vacation; other women students should do so at their first opportunity, and at latest by the end of the first week of arts lecture term.

Attendance

6. All students are required to be in attendance at the College during lecture term throughout the period of their course, unless in special

circumstances they have been exempted for one or more terms by the Senior Lecturer.

7. All students must have entered into residence in or near Dublin and must begin attendance at the College not later than the first day of lecture term, and may not go out of residence before the last day of lecture term, unless they have previously obtained permission from the Senior Lecturer through their tutors.

General discipline

8. The general discipline of all students is in the hands of the Senior and Junior Deans, and women students are under the immediate supervision of the Dean of Women Students.

9. Students are required to wear academic gowns at all arts lectures and examinations, and on other formal occasions.

10. Women, whether students or visitors, may not enter the rooms of students resident in College before midday, and must leave the College precincts not later than midnight.

Academic progress

11. The Board of the College reserves the right to exclude from the College at any time any student whose conduct is unsatisfactory, or, on the recommendation of the University Council, any student whose academic progress is unsatisfactory.

12. A student must pursue his undergraduate course continuously, unless he is permitted by the Senior Lecturer to interrupt it for a stated period. During this period he is not required to keep his name on the college books.

13. A student who for any reason has allowed his name to go off the books can be re-admitted to the College in a subsequent academic year only at the discretion of the Senior Tutor. A student who for reasons of ill-health has allowed his name to go off the books can be re-admitted, even in the current academic year, only at the discretion of the Senior Tutor, who may require a satisfactory certificate from a medical referee nominated by him. A special application form for re-admission is obtainable from the Senior Tutor's office.

14. A student may not repeat any academic year more than once and may not repeat more than two academic years, except by special permission of the University Council.

Conduct during examinations

15. Candidates for examinations are forbidden to bring any books or notes with them into the hall in which the examination is held. A

candidate found in an examination hall in possession of such material will be dismissed from the examination. Candidates in an examination found copying from, or exchanging information with, other candidates, or in any way using information improperly obtained, will be expelled from the College.

Attendance on divine service

16. SERVICES IN THE COLLEGE CHAPEL IN ARTS LECTURE TERM

Sunday	8.30 a.m.	Holy Communion
	10.15 a.m.	Morning Prayer
	7.30 p.m.	Evening Prayer (8.30 p.m. in Trinity Term)
Monday	9.30 a.m.	Morning Prayer
	6.45 p.m.	Evening Prayer
Tuesday	9.30 a.m.	Morning Prayer
	6.45 p.m.	Evening Prayer
Wednesday	1.05 p.m.	Holy Communion
	9.30 a.m.	Morning Prayer
	5.10 p.m.	Choral Evensong
	10.00 p.m.	Compline
Thursday	9.30 a.m.	Morning Prayer
	6.45 p.m.	Evening Prayer
Friday	9.30 a.m.	Litany
	6.45 p.m.	Evening Prayer
Saturday	9.30 a.m.	Morning Prayer
	6.45 p.m.	Evening Prayer
	10.00 p.m.	Compline

The Holy Communion is also celebrated at 5.10 p.m. on Saints' Days and Holy Days when these fall on a week day.

During the other weeks of statutory term services are held as announced on the College Chapel notice-board.

At the 10.15 a.m. University Service on Sunday mornings men students must wear surplices or gowns, and women students must wear gowns. Gowns are worn at all other services.

17. A student may be deprived of his rooms for non-attendance at the public worship of the Church of which he is a member.

II RESIDENCE IN GENERAL

1. The regulations are administered by the Warden of Residences in consultation with the Committee consisting of:

The Treasurer (Chairman), the Senior Dean, the Junior Dean, the Dean of Women Students, the Warden of Trinity Hall, Mary S. Lynch,

M.A., F. G. A. Winder, M.SC., B. E. O'Brien, M.D., the Warden of Residences (Secretary).

2. Students not residing with their parents, near relatives or guardians, are required to reside either in College, if men, or in Trinity Hall, if women, or in approved lodgings.

3. Approved lodgings fall into three categories:
   (a) accommodation in which breakfast and an evening meal are provided on week-days, and all meals are provided on Sundays;
   (b) accommodation in which breakfast only is provided on week-days, all meals are provided on Sundays, and some facilities are provided for cooking;
   (c) apartments and flats.

Students of Freshman standing or students below the age of twenty-one are not allowed to reside in accommodation of type (c).

4. Students may obtain lodgings through the Warden of Residences, or may seek lodgings in accordance with the provisions of §3. In the latter case the accommodation must be approved by the Warden of Residences before the student takes up residence. No student may change lodgings without the prior consent of the Warden of Residences.

5. Men students and women students, other than a husband and wife, are not permitted to reside in the same house.

6. Flats are approved only if the landlord or landlady or other responsible person resides on the premises.

7. A student is not permitted to take up single occupancy of a flat.

8. Students may apply through their tutors to the Warden of Residences for exemption, in exceptional cases, from the preceding regulations.

9. All students who fail to observe these regulations will be severely penalised.

10. Upon admission to the University all women students must complete the form entitled APPLICATION FOR RESIDENCE FOR WOMEN STUDENTS and return it to the Dean of Women Students. Women students seeking to reside at Trinity Hall or in approved lodgings must also return a completed medical form to the Dean of Women Students.

III RESIDENCE IN THE COLLEGE
Application for rooms

1. Chambers in the College are granted by the Provost, through the Registrar of Chambers. They are of two types, (1) fully-furnished rooms, and (2) rooms with essential furniture only. Single, double and treble sets of rooms are available, but nearly all single rooms are fully-furnished bed-sitting rooms.

General regulations for students

2. A student seeking rooms must have his name on the college books; if he is a rising Junior Freshman he must have paid his Junior Freshman fee, that is, the fee payable for the academic year begininng in the following October.

3. The student makes application through his tutor or through the Registry of Chambers. The largest number of sets falls vacant in October, and their prospective occupants are informed in July or later in the long vacation. Applications received before June stand the best chance of success, but those received later in the summer or early autumn may also be successful. Casual vacancies may occur at any time of the year, and applicants interested in taking up sets should keep in touch with the Registry of Chambers.

Deposits

4. Every student granted rooms must pay a deposit of £25 to the Registrar of Chambers within a fortnight of their being granted; otherwise his right to the rooms lapses. Having paid his deposit he should collect the key of his rooms from the Registry of Chambers when taking up residence. The deposit is returned when he vacates, after he has paid all outstanding charges and surrendered his key.

Rents

5. Occupants of fully-furnished rooms pay a rent of £30 each quarter except for the July to September quarter, during which the rent is £3 per week of occupancy (see §14 below). Occupants of other rooms pay a rent of £20, covering the full quarterly period, for each of the four quarters in the year. Rents charged for rooms include the hire of furniture, consumption of electricity for lighting only and meter rents. Rents are payable in advance (see §12 below).

If for any reason a vacancy exists in a double or treble set, the remaining occupant or occupants may be permitted to undertake responsibility for the entire rent for the set if, with the concurrence of the Registrar of Chambers, he wishes, or they wish, to leave the vacancy unfilled.

Sub-letting and guests

6. A student may not permit anyone other than a student on the books of the College to reside in his rooms. With the permission of the Registrar of Chambers another student on the books of the College may be permitted to reside (a) as a guest, or (b), in the absence of the student in whose name the rooms are registered, as a sub-tenant. If a student allows any unauthorised person to share or occupy his rooms, the rooms are immediately declared vacant.

Tenure

7. Foundation and non-foundation scholars may retain their rooms while they continue to pursue their studies in the College.

8. Other students may as a rule retain their rooms for two years, provided that their names remain on the college books. The normal practice is as follows:

(a) If a student comes into residence in the course of Michaelmas term, or in the preceding long vacation, he is due to vacate on 30 September two years later, and he receives notice to quit before 1 May;

(b) If a student comes into residence at any other time during the year, he is due to vacate on 30 September following completion of two years' tenure, and he receives notice to quit before 1 May;

(c) If a student who is due to vacate on 30 September intends to present himself for an honor or moderatorship examination in October, he may retain his rooms until immediately after the examination, provided that he informs the Registrar of Chambers before 1 June that he wishes to avail himself of this concession.

9. A student who has received notice to quit under Rule 8 (a) or (b) may before 1 June apply in writing to the Provost (through the Senior Dean) for special leave to retain his rooms after he is due to vacate. Such an extension of the normal period of residence is sparingly granted, and only in exceptional circumstances exceeds one year.

10. A student who wishes to relinquish his rooms must give three months' notice to the Registrar of Chambers. If he fails to give the required notice he will be charged rent for such period (not exceeding three months) as is required to fill his place.

Charges for servants

11. Servants are paid by the College, and they are engaged on the understanding that they are not to look for additional payments from students, except that if a student has been permitted by the Registrar of Chambers to receive a guest, he may pay a reasonable gratuity to his servant.

Quarterly accounts

12. Quarterly accounts include rent, commons charges, gas and dilapidations, and may include fines. The rent charged is normally one quarter's rent in advance, together with any weekly rent incurred in respect of the July to September quarter by students occupying fully-furnished rooms. Gas is charged according to consumption. No charges are made for consumption of electricity for lighting, routine wear and

tear, or for periodic re-decoration. All queries concerning charges should be addressed to the Accountant.

The first quarterly account is furnished at the end of the first quarter's residence. No accounts are furnished in respect of deposits or the first quarter's rent in advance, which are payable when rooms are allocated and when residence is taken up respectively. If the first quarter's rent in advance is not paid within one week of taking up residence, the same scale of fines applies as applies to late payment of quarterly accounts (see next paragraph).

Quarterly accounts are sent out shortly after the end of each quarter, *i.e.* after 30 September, 31 December, 31 March, 30 June, and are ordinarily sent to a student's home address. If a student wishes his account to be sent elsewhere, he must notify the Accountant. Accounts should be paid to the Accountant, Trinity College, Dublin 2, within 21 days of their date of issue at the latest. No reminders are sent out. A fine of £1 per week late is imposed, up to a limit of four weeks; if the rent and fines are still unpaid at the end of this time, the student forfeits his rooms.

13. A student in whose name rooms stand registered at the beginning of any quarter is liable for all rent in respect of his rooms, unless he has given due notice to the Registrar of Chambers and surrendered his key.

14. If for any reason a student is absent from his rooms he must nevertheless pay a full quarter's rent, except in the case of fully-furnished rooms in the third quarter (July to September) when a rent of £3 per week or part of a week in which the student is in residence is charged. A student occupying fully-furnished rooms should return his key to the Registry of Chambers whenever he goes out of residence during the third quarter; if he fails to do so, he is charged rent as if he were in residence.

Tenants of fully-furnished rooms may be asked to surrender their rooms for a period or periods during the July to September quarter in order to accommodate conferences. They will be given one month's notice to surrender their rooms and must, if they have received such notice, leave their rooms in a tidy condition. If a student leaves his rooms in such a condition that a conference tenant cannot readily be accommodated, he will be charged rent for the period that the room is not available or fined a sum which will compensate for time lost by the cleaning staff. Students who do not wish to be dispossessed during the July/September quarter should appeal to the Registrar of Chambers who will give strong weight to a student's wish to avoid disturbance while working for an examination, or, as an alternative, will try to find other accommodation in College.

15. A student who fails to vacate his rooms on or before the date appointed is liable to forfeiture of his deposit, or of such portion of it as the Registrar of Chambers may determine.

16. Students who are the sons of Fellows of the College are granted priority in the allocation of rooms. They pay two-thirds of the normal rent if occupying fully-furnished rooms, and one-half of the normal rent if occupying other rooms. In all other respects they must conform to the regulations regarding Commons and tenure which are binding on students in general.

Transfer fee

17. If a student wishes to change his rooms, he must apply to the Registrar of Chambers for permission to do so. If permission is granted he is charged a transfer fee of £1, and his rent is adjusted according to the date on which he exchanges his key.

Discipline

18. All students resident in the College, below the standing of B.A., may be required to attend night roll, which is called at ten o'clock. Exemption from attendance at night roll may be granted on the ground of diligence and seniority. The extent of this indulgence is decided by the Junior Dean, subject to the approval of the Provost and the Senior Dean.

Students are not permitted to leave the College after attending night roll.

19. No student may leave the College after midnight without a written order from the Provost or the Junior Dean.

20. A student wishing to have a guest in rooms overnight must apply in advance to the Junior Dean for permission.

21. No student may entertain women in his rooms before midday. A student in residence who wishes to hold a party in his rooms must obtain the Junior Dean's permission three days in advance.

COMMONS[1]

Long and Short Commons

22. There are three portions of the year known as periods of 'short commons'. They coincide with the three arts lecture terms. A short commons period begins on the first day of arts lectures and lasts for

---

[1] Commons regulations for the academic year 1966-7 will be reviewed by the Board in Michaelmas term 1966.

seven full weeks. During these weeks commons is normally served in two evening sittings every day except Friday, Saturday and Sunday. On Fridays there is one evening sitting; on Saturdays and Sundays commons is served at lunch time. The remainder of the year is known as the period of 'long commons'. During University Term long commons is normally served at one evening sitting on Mondays to Fridays, and at lunch time on Saturdays and Sundays. During the vacations long commons is served at lunch time.

All commons regulations are subject to revision at short notice should the Board consider it necessary.

Students holding rooms

23. Every student holding rooms in College must dine on short commons, unless expressly excused by the Provost. He must arrange his attendances at commons at the Registry of Chambers shortly before the beginning of arts lecture term for the periods of short commons, at the beginning of each week in the period of long commons, or immediately upon arrival if he takes up residence during a commons period.

24. Commons bookings are made by means of a docket system. Each docket costs 6s. and covers one dinner. The dockets are distinguished by number and colour, in order to identify the day and sitting to which they refer, and they are valid only for that day and sitting. They cannot be exchanged at the Registry of Chambers, nor can any refunds be made.

25. For the period of short commons a student holding rooms is charged £8 8s. in his quarterly account (i.e. 6s. per day for four days of the week, for seven weeks) and this entitles him to attend on four occasions each week. The Registry of Chambers will issue to him, on request, dockets enabling him to dine on four selected days each week (the same days in each week). The charge will be made whether he is actually in residence or not, but a medical student who is temporarily resident in a general or maternity hospital is exempt from payment during the period of such residence.

26. During the period of long commons the week is reckoned as beginning on Monday. A student in residence is charged 6s. for each commons docket issued to him when he makes his weekly booking. During this period students may arrange and pay for part-weeks, in the weeks when they move into or out of residence.

27. Throughout the year, students holding rooms can purchase commons dockets additional to those required by these regulations, at the Registry of Chambers, for 6s. each.

28. Scholars and Sizars receive their commons free of charge, but must arrange their attendances in the same way as resident students. Their dockets are marked to distinguish their status and may not be used by any other students. If, having received his docket for any sitting of commons, a Scholar or Sizar finds that he is unable to attend, he must return his docket to the Registry of Chambers not later than 11a.m. on the day to which it applies.

29. Non-resident students (men only) whose names are on the college books may dine on commons, provided that there is room for them. They should apply to the Registry of Chambers not later than 11 a.m. on the day on which they wish to dine, and can purchase any dockets for commons that have not been taken up by residents, at 6s. each. No money so paid will be refunded.

Students not holding rooms

30. A student residing normally at a distance from Dublin, who comes to the College for examinations, may in special circumstances be allowed by the Junior Dean to put his name on commons for the days of his examination at the rate of 6s. per day.

31. A limited number of non-resident students, whose names are on the college books and who have engagements in the College, may dine on commons on any day of the week, except on Saturday or Sunday. Such students must obtain the permission of the Junior Dean, and pay the Registry of Chambers at the rate of 6s. per day for each day on which they wish to dine. Arrangements with the Registry of Chambers must be made before 11 a.m. on Saturday in respect of any day in the following week and the exact sum be paid at that time. No money so paid will be refunded, should a student be unable to dine on any day which he has named.

IV RESIDENCE IN TRINITY HALL

In the year 1908 the house and grounds, now known as Trinity Hall, were acquired by the University and established as the official residence for those women students who do not reside with their parents or guardians. The adjoining house and grounds were purchased in 1910 by John Purser Griffith, M.I.C.E., and Mrs. Griffith, and presented to the University in memory of Frederick Purser, M.A., F.T.C.D. A further five acres were acquired in 1966. In the grounds the Dublin University Women's Hockey and Tennis clubs have their fields and courts; and Trinity Hall thus serves as a centre for the use of all women students, whether resident or non-resident.

General regulations for students

Trinity Hall which is two and a half miles from the centre of Dublin has direct omnibus connections with Trinity College by two routes and is within easy cycling distance of the College.

Application for Residence

1. Application for residence in Trinity Hall should be made to the Warden of Trinity Hall through the Dean of Women Students, 6 Trinity College, Dublin 2. There is a waiting list for Trinity Hall and candidates for admission are strongly advised to return their completed application and medical forms (see II: §10 above) to the Dean of Women Students as early as possible. It must be emphasised, however, that places are not awarded solely on the basis of date of application.

2. Vacancies for October are filled in the preceding July. Vacancies occurring during the academic year are normally filled from the waiting list. The Warden of Trinity Hall communicates her decision direct to all applicants.

Fees

1. Fees for residence in Trinity Hall are £6 per week (excluding week-day lunches). The term fee is £42 and is payable in advance, not later than the second Tuesday of each arts lecture term. Personal expenses, such as laundry, are not included in these fees. A fine of £3 is levied for tardy payment.

2. Cheques should be drawn in favour of Trinity College, Dublin, Trinity Hall Account, and are payable to the Warden.

3. Students to whom places have been allocated must pay a non-returnable deposit of £10 on account of the first term fee. If the deposit is not forwarded to the Warden within fourteen days of acceptance of a place in Trinity Hall, the allocation lapses.

Regulations for Residents in Trinity Hall

1. The internal management and discipline of the Hall are in the hands of the Warden and students must conform to all house rules laid down by her.

2. Students whose conduct is unsatisfactory or who do not make due progress in their studies may be required to leave the Hall. The Trinity Hall Committee decides such cases.

3. Students are expected to be in residence throughout the seven weeks of arts lecture terms.

4. Students are required to give one term's notice of their intention to leave the Hall. Such notice must be given to the Warden in writing not later than the first day of arts lecture term; in default of such notice a term's fee will be charged.

5. The Warden must be notified of any changes in a candidate's condition of health subsequent to the completion of the medical form.

6. The Student Health Service is available to all students but residents should note that all cases of illness must be reported to the Warden immediately.

7. Unless a student's parent or guardian has nominated a doctor, the Hall's medical adviser (who works in conjunction with the Student Health Service), or a doctor selected by him or by the Warden, will attend the student when necessary.

8. The Hall is closed at midnight each night. Late leave may be granted for University dances, and for other approved dances and private parties, if application is made to the Warden. Keys are granted to Non-Foundation Scholars and to Sophisters at the Warden's discretion.

9. Minors wishing to stay overnight with friends must have the written permission of their parents or guardian; and all students must ask the Warden's leave at least 24 hours in advance.

10. Visitors must leave the Hall by mid-night.

11. Students will be held responsible for any damage done to their rooms or furniture.

12. The authorities of the Hall and College do not accept responsibility for losses of student's property.

ORDINARY COURSE FOR THE DEGREE OF BACHELOR IN ARTS

COURSE IN GENERAL STUDIES

Note

Students should also see GENERAL REGULATIONS FOR STUDENTS, Discipline and academic progress.

COURSE IN GENERAL STUDIES

REGULATIONS

General requirements

1. A student seeking the degree of B.A. in general studies is required to study a group of subjects selected as in §§4, 5, 6. He must be admitted to the School of General Studies by the Senior Tutor, by whom also his choice of subjects must be approved. A student who wishes to read any of the following subjects, French, German, Irish, Latin, mathematics, must have a matriculation qualification in that subject. Italian, Spanish and Russian may be studied without previous knowledge of the language, but satisfactory evidence of general linguistic ability is required[1].

2. To rise with his class, a student taking the course must (a) attend satisfactorily the lectures given in each of his three subjects each term, (b) perform the exercises (essay, tutorial or practical work) prescribed for each year, and (c) pass the annual examination in each subject. See §§7, 8, 10, 11, 21 for qualifications of this rule. The exercises of the Junior Freshman year include at least one English essay on a general subject, failure in which involves failure in the year as a whole.

3. A student who in any year has failed to satisfy any one or more of the requirements in §2 will not, except as provided in §§7-11, receive credit for the year. If he wishes to proceed in general studies and if he is entitled to do so (see GENERAL REGULATIONS, I, §14), he must repeat attendance on the courses taken during the unsuccessful year, unless exempted by the Senior Lecturer in accordance with §10, or unless he is a Junior Freshman, in which case, with the Senior Lecturer's permission, he may revise his choice of subjects. He must also perform the exercises and pass the annual examination of the year he is repeating.

4. At least two of the three subjects taken in the Junior Freshman year must be studied throughout the four undergraduate years. A student may change one of his three subjects as a Junior Freshman or as a Senior Freshman, with the permission of the Senior Lecturer, in consultation with the head of department to which the new subject relates. No change of subject may be made after the end of the Senior

---

[1] Subject to the above requirements, limitation on a student's freedom of choice, except as provided in §6, will be imposed only where it is made necessary by pressure of numbers. Students are advised to make early application to the Senior Tutor.

Course in general studies

Freshman year, unless the subject is one of those given as a unit in the Sophister years. See also §§13,14.

5. All applications for change of subjects of study must be made to the Senior Lecturer not later than one week before the beginning of lectures in Hilary Term.

Subjects of study

6. The subjects in which courses are given are as follows:

GROUP A

English, French, German, Greek, Hebrew, Irish, Italian, Latin, Russian, Spanish.

GROUP B

History, fine arts I (music), fine arts II (visual arts), geography, economics.

GROUP C

Pure mathematics, applied mathematics, philosophy, psychology.

GROUP D

Biblical studies I: Old Testament, Biblical studies II: New Testament.

Not more than two subjects may be chosen from any one group. Courses are given in fine arts I in either the Freshman or the Sophister years and in fine arts II in the Sophister years. The courses in fine arts I may be followed either by the courses in fine arts II or by Sophister courses in English (provided that the student's other two subjects are not also in Group A) or in history. The courses in fine arts II may be taken in continuation of any Freshman course, provided that the student's other two subjects are not also in Group B. Students taking Biblical studies I: Old Testament may not take Hebrew in Group A and students taking Biblical studies II: New Testament may not take Greek in Group A.

Students taking one or two modern languages other than English must spend not less than two months as undergraduates in the country of each language in order to fulfil the requirements of their course; students of Irish must spend at least the same length of time in the Gaeltacht. This requirement can be waived only in exceptional circumstances and with the prior approval of the Department concerned.

Absence from lectures or examinations

7. A student who in any term has been unable, through illness or other unavoidable cause, to attend the prescribed lectures satisfactorily, may be granted credit for the term by the Senior Lecturer, but must perform such supplementary exercises as the Senior Lecturer may require.

8. A student unavoidably absent from any part of an annual examination may be allowed a special examination by the Senior Lecturer, and for this a fee of £5 is charged.

A student who is taken ill before an examination and wishes to apply for a special examination must submit a medical certificate covering the period of the illness.

A student who is taken ill during an examination and wishes to apply for a special examination must withdraw at once from the examination and submit a medical certificate covering the period of the illness.

9. When a student is absent from lectures through illness he must supply the Senior Lecturer with a medical certificate.

10. In special circumstances exemption from attendance for one or more terms may be granted by the Senior Lecturer; application for such exemption must be made in advance. A student thus exempted must perform such exercises as the Senior Lecturer may require. If these exercises are specially provided, a fee is usually charged.

Abridgement of course

11. A student may be admitted to the course in general studies as a Senior Freshman if, in the opinion of the Senior Tutor, he is qualified by his knowledge and attainment to be so, or if he passes the Junior Freshman examination in June, with sufficient merit, in the subjects that he proposes to study. Such a student must take the same three subjects in his Sophister years as in his Senior Freshman year (except as provided in §6). He must pay an examination fee when sending in notice of intention to present himself for the Junior Freshman examination. See COLLEGE CHARGES.

Transference from honor or professional courses

12. A student may, on the recommendation of his school committee, be permitted by the General Studies Committee to transfer from an honor or professional course to the course in general studies, and will be credited with so much of the latter course as the General Studies Committee, having regard to the student's performance as a whole, shall determine. A student seeking to transfer to the Junior Freshman year of the course in general studies must first apply, through his tutor, to the Senior Tutor for permission to apply to the General Studies Committee. See HONOR COURSES IN ARTS, General regulations, §3.

Transference to honor courses

13. A student may be permitted by the Senior Lecturer to transfer to an honor course, on the recommendation of the school committee

F

Course in general studies

concerned; except that permission to transfer to the Junior Freshman year of an honor course may be given only by the Senior Tutor, to whom application must be made through the student's tutor. See HONOR COURSES IN ARTS, General regulations, §10.

Students from other universities

14. A student admitted to the University as a Senior Freshman, in virtue of courses studied at other universities or colleges, must take the same three subjects in his Sophister years as in his Senior Freshman year (except as provided in §6). No student may enter the School of General Studies as a Senior Sophister, except by special permission of the General Studies Committee.

Examinations

15. At the end of each Freshman year and of the Junior Sophister year a student must pass an examination in the subjects studied during the year. This annual examination is held in June; there is a supplemental examination for Junior Freshmen in September/October. A student in General Studies intending to present himself for a supplemental examination must pay a fee of £5 before 1 September, and a professional student taking a supplemental examination in Arts must pay a fee of £2 before 1 September.

16. At each annual examination a three-hour paper is set in each subject. In some subjects there are additional tests as follows: in Greek and Latin, a two-hour paper; in French, German, Hebrew, Irish, Italian, Russian and Spanish, a *viva voce* examination; in fine arts I, a practical test.

17. The B.A. degree examination is held in June of the Senior Sophister year. A candidate who has failed to pass this examination, or who has been unavoidably absent from any part of it, may present himself at a supplemental examination in October. If he fails to pass this supplemental examination he may be permitted by the Senior Lecturer, on the recommendation of the court of examiners, to repeat his Senior Sophister year and to present himself again for the degree examination or the supplemental degree examination. For fees payable for the degree examination see COLLEGE CHARGES.

18. At the B.A. degree examination candidates are examined in each of the three subjects studied during their Sophister years.

In all subjects two three-hour papers are set. These may include questions on any part of the course, but special emphasis is given to the courses of the Sophister years.

In some subjects there are additional tests as follows: in Greek and Latin, a two-hour paper; in French, German, Hebrew, Irish, Italian,

Russian and Spanish, a *viva voce* examination; in geography and fine arts I, a practical test; in psychology, a practical project.

19. A student unavoidably absent from any part of a supplemental degree examination may be permitted by the Senior Lecturer to present himself at the next following degree examination.

20. In special circumstances a student who has completed the course in general studies may, with the approval of the General Studies Committee, be permitted by the Senior Lecturer to defer his degree examination for one year.

21. At all examinations a student must satisfy the examiners in each of his three subjects, except that, at the Senior Freshman, Junior Sophister and B.A. degree examinations, the court of examiners may allow a deficiency in one subject to be compensated by the answering in the other two. The principle of compensation does not apply to the Junior Freshman year, but a candidate who fails in the June examination will not be required to present himself in the supplemental examination in any subject in which he has gained a pass mark.

22. At all examinations in modern languages candidates must satisfy the examiners in writing and speaking the language concerned.

23. The names of candidates who pass the B.A. degree examination are published in three classes according to merit. Specially meritorious candidates are called respondents and receive honorary testimoniums.

Prizes

24. The Jellett prizes for general answering, of £11 and £7 respectively, are awarded on the results of the Senior Freshman examination in June.

25. A premium of £10 is awarded to the student who answers best in Irish at the Senior Freshman examination in June. See also COSTELLO PRIZES.

26. The King Edward prize of £10 is awarded to the student who answers best at the B.A. degree examination in June.

II COURSES
GROUP A
English

Junior Freshmen

(A) Literature to 1640. Selected works by Chaucer, More, Spenser, Marlowe, Shakespeare, Donne, Herbert.

(B) Introduction to twentieth-century literature. Selected works by Joyce, Lawrence, Forster, Fitzgerald, Yeats, Eliot, Beckett.

(C) The English language.

Course in general studies

Senior Freshmen

(A) Literature 1640–1800. Selected works by Milton, Dryden, Pope, Defoe, Swift, Johnson, Fielding, Congreve, Farquhar, Gray, Goldsmith, Sheridan.

(B) Twentieth-century drama. Selected works by Shaw, Synge, Yeats, O'Casey, O'Neill, Auden and Isherwood, Johnston, Miller.

Junior Sophisters

(A) Nineteenth-century poetry.

(B) The twentieth-century novel.

Senior Sophisters

(A) Nineteenth-century prose (including the novel).

(B) Twentieth-century poetry.

French

Students beginning this course must possess a good French-English dictionary (the smaller edition of Mansion in two volumes is specially recommended); H. Ferrar, *A French reference grammar* (Oxford); Roe and Lough, *French prose composition* (Longmans); Ledésert and Smith, *La France* (Harrap); *Oxford book of French verse*.

Junior Freshmen

Corneille, *Le Cid*; Molière, *Don Juan*; Racine, *Phèdre*; Madame de Sévigné, *Lettres* (Classiques Larousse); Maupassant, *Fifteen tales* (Cambridge); Camus, *L'étranger* (Methuen); Ledésert and Smith, op. cit., pts 1 and 2; L. Cazamian, *A history of French literature*, pts IV and X (Oxford Paperbacks).

Senior Freshmen

Prévost, *Manon Lescaut*; Voltaire, *Candide*; Rousseau, *Discours*; *Lettres sur les spectacles* (Classiques Larousse); Hugo, *Hernani*; poetry of Hugo, Lamartine, Vigny, Musset; Armstrong, *The phonetics of French*; Ledésert and Smith, op. cit., pts 3–6; L. Cazamian, *A history of French literature*, pts V, VI and VII.

Junior Sophisters

Balzac, *Le père Goriot*; Flaubert, *Madame Bovary*; Zola, *Germinal*; Fromentin, *Dominique* (Blackwell); Proust, *Combray* (Harrap); Gide, *Les caves du Vatican*; poetry of Baudelaire, Verlaine, Rimbaud, Mallarmé, Apollinaire, Claudel, Valéry; L. Cazamian, *A history of French literature*, pts VIII and IX.

Senior Sophisters

Prose: selections from Montaigne, Pascal. (Classiques Larousse).

Verse: poets already studied together with Villon, Ronsard, Du Bellay, Malherbe, La Fontaine, Boileau.

Drama: Molière, *Le misanthrope*; Racine, *Athalie*; Beaumarchais, *Le mariage de Figaro* (Blackwell); Giraudoux, *La guerre de Troie n'aura pas lieu*; Anouilh, *Antigone* (Harrap).

German

Students following this course must acquire a good German-English and English-German dictionary (e.g. *A German and English Dictionary* ed. Betteridge, Cassell) and J. G. Robertson, *A history of German literature* (new edition revised by Edna Purdie).

Junior Freshmen

E. P. Dickins, *German for advanced students* (Oxford); *German tales of our time*, ed. Forster (Harrap); Halm, *Die Marzipan-Lise*, ed. Thomas (Nelson); Grillparzer, *König Ottokars Glück und Ende*, ed. Thomas (Blackwell); Tieck, *Der blonde Eckbert*, Brentano, *Geschichte vom braven Kasperl und dem schönen Annerl*, both ed. Atkinson (Blackwell).

Senior Freshmen

Hoffmann, *Der goldene Topf*; Storm, *Der Schimmelreiter*; Hebbel, *Maria Magdalena*, ed. Brychan Rees (Blackwell); Grillparzer, *Des Meeres und der Liebe Wellen*, ed. Yates (Blackwell); G. Hauptmann, *Bahnwärter Thiel, Fasching* (ed. Stirk).

Junior and Senior Sophisters

Course A and Course B are given in alternate years.

COURSE A (1965–6)

Goethe, *Faust*, bk 1; *Fifteen German poets*, ed. S. H. Steinberg (London); Carossa, *Eine Kindheit*, ed. Bithell (Blackwell); Lessing, *Minna von Barnhelm*; Kafka, *Short Stories*, ed. J. M. S. Pasley (Clarendon); *Germany: a companion to German studies*, ed. Bithell (Methuen), chapters on German history; Büchner, *Dantons Tod*.

COURSE B (1966–7)

Schiller, *Wallenstein*, ed. Witte (Blackwell); Thomas Mann, *Two stories*, ed. Witte (Nelson); Eichendorff, *Aus dem Leben eines Taugenichts*; Schiller, *Maria Stuart*; Goethe, *Iphigenie auf Tauris*; Keller, *Die Leute von Seldwyla*, pt 1.

Greek

Junior Freshmen[1]

An introductory course in the language, based on G. Thomson, *The Greek language* (Cambridge, 1960), and J. A. Nairn, *Greek through reading* (London, 1952).

Special instruction at a more advanced level will be provided for students who have satisfied the matriculation requirements in Greek.

Senior Freshmen[1]

Xenophon, selected passages from *Hellenica*; Homer, *Odyssey*, 6, 9; Plato, *Crito*.

Greek composition and unseen translation; Greek literary and political history.

[1] Intending divinity students may take a course in Hellenistic Greek. See TESTIMONIUM IN DIVINITY.

Course in general studies

Junior and Senior Sophisters

Course A and Course B are given in alternate years.

COURSE A (1966–7)

Greek philosophy, with special attention to Plato, *Apology*, and Aristotle, *Ethics*, 1, 2.

Greek drama, with special attention to Aeschylus, *Prometheus Vinctus*; Sophocles, *Ajax*; Euripides, *Medea*; Aristophanes, *Clouds*.

Greek composition and unseen translation.

COURSE B (1967–8)

Greek history, with special attention to Homer, *Iliad* 1, 9; Herodotus, 8, chs 1–99; Thucydides, 7.

Greek oratory, with special attention to Demosthenes, *Philippics* 1, 3.

Greek composition and unseen translation.

Hebrew

Junior Freshmen

The history of Israel to the foundation of the monarchy.

The historical and archaeological background to the Pentateuch.

Hebrew grammar; *Genesis*, chs 1–4, 12–15 and *Joshua*, chs 1–5.

Senior Freshmen

The history of Israel to the fall of Samaria.

Introduction to Biblical archaeology.

1 *Samuel*, chs 1–11; *Amos*, chs 1–4; *Psalms* 90–9.

Junior Sophisters

The history of Israel to the return of the exiles.

Introduction to the literature of the Old Testament.

1966–7: 2 *Kings*, chs 1–13; *Isaiah*, chs 40–50; *Psalms*, 100–106.

1967–8: 2 *Samuel*, chs 1–12; *Amos*, chs 5–9; *Psalms*, 120–134.

Senior Sophisters

The history of Israel of the Maccabees.

The religion of Israel from Moses to the exile.

1966–7: 2 *Kings*, chs 14–25; *Isaiah*, chs 1–12; *Proverbs*, chs 1–10.

1967–8: 2 *Samuel*, chs 13–22; *Jeremiah*, chs 1–8; *Job*, chs 1–7.

Irish

Junior Freshmen

Scothscéalta Phádraic Uí Chonaire, ed. de Bhaldraithe; Ó Flaithearta, *Dúil*; Ó Cadhain, *Idir shúgradh agus dáiríre*; Corkery, *The hidden Ireland*.

Senior Freshmen

Máire, *Rann na Feirste*; Mac Grianna, *Mo bhealach féin*; *Stories from Keating's history of Ireland*, ed. Bergin.

Junior and Senior Sophisters

Course A and Course B are given in alternate years.

COURSE A (1965-6)

Measgra dánta, ed. O'Rahilly, pt 1; *Bruidhean chaorthainn*, ed. Mac Piarais; *Irish syllabic poetry*, ed. Knott; *Desiderius*, ed. O'Rahilly; *Dánta grádha*, ed. O'Rahilly; *Eachtra Uilliam*, ed. O'Rahilly; R. Flower, *The Irish tradition*.

COURSE B (1966-7)

Ó Laoghaire, *Séadna*; Ó Cuív, *Irish dialects and Irish-speaking districts*; Ó Cuív, *The Irish of Muskerry*; Ó Criomhthain, *An t-oileánach*; Mac an tSaoi, *Margadh na saoire*; Ó Súilleabháin, *Fiche blian ag fás*; Ó Ríordáin, *Eirbeall spideoige*; Ó Direáin, *Ó Morna*.

Italian

Junior Freshmen

D. Lennie and M. Grego, *Italian for you* (Longmans); Butler and Reynolds, *Tredici novelle moderne* (Cambridge); Poems by Ungaretti, Montale and Quasimodo in *The Penguin Book of Italian Verse*.

Senior Freshmen

C. Goldoni, *La locandiera* (Biblioteca Universale Rizzoli); V. Alfieri, *Saul* (Sansoni); G. Leopardi, *I canti*, ed. Straccali (Sansoni); A. Manzoni, *I promessi sposi* (Biblioteca Universale Rizzoli); Poems by Parini, Monti, Foscolo, Manzoni, Giusti, Carducci, Pascoli and D'Annunzio in *Oxford book of Italian verse* (2nd edition, 1952); A. Peers, *Extracts for translation (with Italian notes)* (Harrap).

Junior and Senior Sophisters

Course A and Course B are given in alternate years.

COURSE A (1965-6)

N. Machiavelli, *Il principe*, ed. Russo (Sansoni); L. Ariosto, *Orlando furioso*, ed. Zingarelli (Hoepli) selected passages; G. Della Casa, *Il Galateo* (Le Monnier); T. Tasso, *Gerusalemme liberata* (Biblioteca Universale Rizzoli). Poems by Boiardo, Lorenzo de' Medici, Michelangelo Buonarroti, Vittoria Colonna, Berni, Gaspara Stampa and Torquato Tasso in *Oxford book of Italian verse*.

COURSE B (1966-7)

Dante, *La divina commedia*, vol. 1; *Inferno*, ed. Casini-Barbi (Sansoni); F. Petrarca, *Rime scelte*, ed. Steiner-Piccioni (Classici italiani commentati); G. Boccaccio, *Il decameron*, ed. Russo (Sansoni). Poems by Jacopone, Guinizelli, Angiolieri, Cavalcanti, Dante and Cino da Pistoia in *Oxford book of Italian verse*.

Latin

Junior Freshmen

Introduction to Latin literature. Prescribed reading: *Fifty Latin lyrics* (Longmans); selections from Livy, 1, 2; Cicero, *Pro Archia*; Ovid, *Metamorphoses*, 1; Virgil, *Aeneid*, 4.

Latin composition and unseen translation.

Course in general studies

Literature of the Republic. Comedy, with special attention to Terence, *Phormio*. History and oratory, with special attention to Sallust, *Catiline* and Cicero, *In Catilinam*, 1, 2. Didactic poetry, with special attention to Lucretius, 3, 5.

Latin composition and unseen translation.

Junior and Senior Sophisters

Course A and Course B are given in alternate years.

COURSE A (1966–7)

Satire, with selections from Horace, *Epistles*, 1, and Juvenal.
History, with special attention to Tacitus, *Histories*, 1, and *Agricola*.
Epigram, with selections from Catullus and Martial (Carrington).
Latin composition and unseen translation.

COURSE B (1967–8)

Amatory poetry, with special attention to Virgil, *Eclogues* and Propertius, 1.
Letter writing, with selections from Cicero and Pliny (Methuen).
Epic, with special attention to Virgil, *Aeneid*, 2, 6.
Latin composition and unseen translation.

Russian

Junior Freshmen

An introductory course in the language.

Senior Freshmen

Students of this and higher classes will require good dictionaries. Strongly recommended are: Smirnitskiy, *Russian-English dictionary*; Muller, *English-Russian dictionary*; Ozhegov, *Dictionary of the Russian language*.

Russian literature to 1837. Special attention will be given to the work of Pushkin.

Junior Sophisters

Russian literature in the nineteenth century. Special attention will be given to the work of Lermontov, Gogol, Turgenev, Tolstoy, Dostoevskiy and Chekhov.

Senior Sophisters

Russian literature from Symbolism to the present day.
A course in Russian history will be given during the Sophister years.

Spanish

Junior Freshmen

H. Ramsden, *An essential course in modern Spanish* (Harrap); García Lorca, *Yerma, La casa de Bernarda Alba*; poems by Bécquer, Unamuno, Darío, *Penguin book of Spanish verse* (revised edition); B. Pérez Galdós, *Misericordia*; W. C. Atkinson, *A history of Spain and Portugal* (Pelican).

Course in general studies

Unamuno, *Niebla, San Manuel Bueno, Mártir*; Baroja, *El mundo es ansí*; Pérez de Ayala, *Luna de Miel, Luna de Hiel*; García Lorca, *Romancero gitano*; Cela, *La familia de Pascual Duarte, Viaje a la Alcarria*; poems by Jiménez, Salinas, Guillén, Alberti in *Penguin book of Spanish verse* (revised edition); A. Machado, *Campos de Castilla*.

Junior and Senior Sophisters

Course A and Course B are given in alternate years.

COURSE A (1965–6)

Lope de Vega, *Fuenteovejuna* (Bell), *El caballero de Olmedo*; Tirso de Molina, *El Burlador de Sevilla, El vergonzoso en palacio*; Calderón, *El gran teatro del mundo* (Clasicos Castellanos, *Autos sacramentales*, vol 1), *El alcalde de Zalamea* (Manchester), *La vida es sueño* (Manchester); poems of Garcilaso, Luis de León, Lope de Vega, Góngora, Quevedo, in *Oxford book of Spanish verse*.

COURSE B (1966–7)

Cervantes, *Don Quixote*, pt 1, *Rinconete y Cortadillo*; *El celoso extremeño*; *Lazarillo de Tormes* (Manchester); Quevedo, *El buscón*; *Romances anónimos* and *Poesía de tipo tradicional*, in *Oxford book of Spanish verse*, pp. 59–74 and 443–60.

GROUP B

History

Freshmen

Junior Freshmen take any one of the following courses, and Senior Freshmen any other.

COURSE A

History of Britain, 400–1485.

COURSE B

History of Ireland, 400–1494.

COURSE C

History of Britain, 1485–1939.

COURSE D

History of Ireland, 1494–1939.

Junior Sophisters

History of Europe, 1713–1939.

Senior Sophisters

History of the U.S.A. to 1939.

Fine arts I (music)

Only students who have a reasonable knowledge of musical notation will be accepted for the courses in fine arts I.

Facilities are provided in the library of the School of Music for the study of scores and recorded examples of the music relevant to the courses.

Course in general studies

Junior Freshmen and Junior Sophisters

The history of European music from about 1400 to about 1750, related to other art forms and to the social conditions of each period. Music before 1400 is included as a general background in so far as it has relevance to the period under more detailed study.

A practical class is held each week, devoted to aural training and participation in selected examples of music from the period under study. Students will be trained in the recognition of styles, simple forms, instrumentation and elementary harmonic progressions. They are expected to develop an elementary knowledge of harmony and some ability in simple musical dictation and the construction of melodies. A practical test, covering this part of the course, is held in conjunction with the examinations.

A study period is held each week, during which recorded examples of the music relevant to the history course are played.

Senior Freshmen and Senior Sophisters

The history of music in Europe and America from about 1750 to the present day, including a knowledge of contemporary Irish music.

A practical class, on the lines indicated for Junior Freshmen and Junior Sophisters above, forms part of the course. A practical test is held in conjunction with the examinations.

A study period as described above will be available in conjunction with this course.

Senior Sophisters taking the B.A. degree examination in fine arts I will be given two three hour papers. These may include questions relating to the Junior and Senior courses but special emphasis will be given to the Senior Sophister course.

Fine arts II (visual arts)

Junior Sophisters

I   A brief survey of painting, sculpture and architecture in Western Europe from Classical times to the nineteenth century.
The Italian Renaissance.

Senior Sophisters

Art in Northern Europe 1400–1600
Art in Ireland.
The twentieth century.

II   Though the main stress of the course will be on painting, sculpture and architecture will be considered throughout.

Geography

Junior Freshmen

The content and purpose of geography. Climatology and biogeography with relevant practical work. Introduction to map interpretation.

Senior Freshmen

Geomorphology. Australasia. Tropical agriculture. Practical work in geology and geomorphology.

Junior Sophisters

Economic, political and social geography. The United States of America. Map interpretation, statistical maps and map projections.

Senior Sophisters

Western Europe. Great Britain and Ireland. Advanced interpretation of British and European Ordnance Survey maps. Work in the field.

Field courses, usually of one week's duration, are held during the Easter vacation. Students must have attended at least one of these courses before presenting themselves at the B.A. degree examination.

Economics

Junior Freshmen

INTRODUCTORY ECONOMICS I

National income: meaning, measurement, growth and distribution. Consumption, investment and the multiplier. Full employment policy, deflation and inflation. Demand and supply, monopoly and imperfect competition. Monopoly and public policy.

Senior Freshmen

INTRODUCTORY ECONOMICS II

Factors of production, wages, interest, rent and profits. The price mechanism. Elementary theory of international trade. The economic role of the State.

Junior Sophisters

THE IRISH ECONOMY

Structure and evolution of the Irish economy and contemporary problems of adaptation and development.

Senior Sophisters

CURRENT ECONOMIC PROBLEMS

An examination of contemporary problems in the fields of public finance, international trade and finance, economic growth and development.

GROUP C

Pure mathematics

Junior Freshmen

The elements of higher arithmetic, combinatorial analysis and probability theory.

Further geometry and trigonometry.

Polynomials, algebraic equations, rational functions, mathematical induction, binomial theorem for a positive integer exponent. The summation of series. Approximation. Concept of a function; limiting processes and continuity. Elements of the differential and integral calculus, with applications to extremal problems, curve-tracing, and ordinary differential equations.

Course in general studies

Senior Freshmen

Further calculus: Leibnitz's theorem, tangents and normals to curves. Mean value theorems, Taylor's theorem; techniques of integration, the determination of plane areas, volumes of revolution and centres of gravity.

Introduction to complex numbers.

Spherical trigonometry; elements of coordinate geometry.

The algebra of determinants.

Junior Sophisters

Curvature, area and mass, moments of inertia. Rectification of curves, areas of surfaces of revolution. Reduction formulae in integration.

Functions of several variables. Partial differentiation.

Approximate methods. Extrema.

Coordinate geometry in two and three dimensions.

Complex numbers continued.

Systems of linear equations and matrix algebra.

Vector analysis.

Senior Sophisters

Ordinary differential equations, solution in series. Euler's homogeneous equations. Partial differential equations of physics; solution by separation of variables. Fourier series. Simple properties of Legendre, Hermite and Laguerre polynomials.

Relaxation for special problems.

Bessel and Legendre functions. Functions of a complex variable; simple conformal mapping and contour integration. Further vector analysis.

Applied Mathematics

Junior Freshmen

A general introductory course.

Senior Freshmen

Plane statics of particles and rigid bodies. Centres of gravity. Friction.

Motion of a particle in a plane: projectiles, simple and circular harmonic motion.

Newton's laws of motion and gravitation. Work, energy, conservation of energy and momentum.

Bending moments and shearing force.

Junior Sophisters

Plane dynamics of a particle and rigid body, including theory of vibrations and central forces. Elementary theory of elasticity. Elementary hydrodynamics, including Bernoulli's theorem.

Senior Sophisters

Rigid body dynamics in three dimensions. General dynamical methods. The vibrating string. Two-dimensional hydrodynamics.

Introduction to numerical methods and programming.

Philosophy

Junior Freshmen

Theory of knowledge. Prescribed reading: Descartes, *Meditations*; Berkeley, *Principles of human knowledge*.

Logic I.

Senior Freshmen

Logic II.

Metaphysics and theory of knowledge. Prescribed reading: Hume, *Enquiry concerning human understanding*; Kant, *Prolegomena to any future metaphysics*; Russell, *Problems of philosophy*, chs 1–3, 6–9.

Junior Sophisters

Ethics. Prescribed reading: Plato, *Republic*, bks 1–4; Aristotle, *Nicomachean ethics*, bks 1–4, 10; Butler, *Sermons*, 1–3; Hume, *Enquiry concerning the principles of morals*; Kant, *Fundamental principles of the metaphysic of ethics*; Moore, *Ethics*, chs 3–4; Ayer, *Language, truth and logic*, chs 1, 2, 6; Hare, *The language of morals*, pts 1–2; Lewis, *Morals and revelation*, chs 3–5.

Senior Sophisters

Recent philosophy. Prescribed reading: G. Ryle and others, *The revolution in philosophy*.

Problems in philosophy: causation, memory and imagination; free-will, mind and body; topics in philosophical theology.

Psychology

Each year of the course is accompanied by laboratory demonstrations and practical work. A course in elementary statistics is also provided.

Junior Freshmen

Introduction to the study of behaviour. Instinctive behaviour. Learning and motivation. Remembering.

Senior Freshmen

Biological foundations of psychology; evolution of *homo sapiens*. Comparative and developmental psychology. Physiological psychology.

Junior Sophisters

Perception and learning theory.

Senior Sophisters

The Senior Sophister course will bring together topics dealt within previous years and consider their specific application to personality.

Course in general studies

Biblical studies I: Old Testament

Junior Freshmen

Hebrew grammar; *Genesis*, chs 1–4, 12–15; *Joshua*, chs 1–5.

Senior Freshmen

1 Samuel, chs 1–11; *Amos*, chs 1–4; *Psalms* 90–99.
The history, literature and religion of Israel until the Exile.

Junior Sophisters

1966–67: *2 Kings*, chs 1–13; *Isaiah*, chs 40–50; *Psalms* 100–106.
1967–68: *2 Samuel*, chs 1–12; *Amos*, chs 5–9; *Psalms* 120–134.
The history, literature and religion of the Jews from the Exile to 70 A.D.

Senior Sophisters

1966–67: *2 Kings*, chs 14–25; *Isaiah*, chs 1–12; *Proverbs*, chs 1–10.
1967–68: *2 Samuel*, chs 13–22; *Jeremiah*, chs 1–8; *Job*, chs 1–7.
Biblical archaeology.

Biblical studies II: New Testament

Junior Freshmen

A course on New Testament Greek based on J. W. Wenham, *Elements of New Testament Greek* (Cambridge), with appropriate readings from the New Testament.

Senior Freshmen

Gospel according to St Luke, exposition and commentary, with chapters 1–12 in Greek.
The history, literature and thought of the Four Gospels.

Junior Sophisters

Epistle to the Romans in Greek with exposition and commentary.
The history, literature and thought of the New Testament apart from the Gospels.

Senior Sophisters

Selected writings from the Old Testament Apocrypha and New Testament in Greek as follows: *Wisdom of Solomon, Gospel according to St John, First Epistle of St Peter, First Epistle of St John, Epistle of St James.*

Each of the courses in Biblical studies may be taken separately. Normally, however, they are taken together.

HONOR COURSES FOR THE DEGREE OF BACHELOR IN ARTS

Note

Students should also see GENERAL REGULATIONS FOR
STUDENTS, Discipline and academic progress.

HONOR COURSES IN ARTS

GENERAL REGULATIONS

General requirements

1. Honor courses are offered in I Mathematics, II Classics, III Mental and moral science, IV Philosophy and psychology, V Natural sciences, VI Modern languages and literature, VII Ancient and modern literature, VIII Early and modern Irish, IX Celtic languages, X Hebrew and semitic languages, XI History and political science, XII Economics and political science, XIII Legal science. A student seeking the degree of B.A. with honors (moderatorship) must first be admitted to the appropriate school or schools and follow the course prescribed in each of his four undergraduate years. See also §§10, 11.

2. To rise with his class, a student must (*a*) attend satisfactorily the lectures given in the subjects of his course each term, (*b*) perform the prescribed exercises (essay, tutorial or practical work), and (*c*) pass, in accordance with the regulations of his school, the prescribed examinations. If he is reading the honor course in natural sciences he must also, in order to rise from the Junior Sophister to the Senior Sophister class, satisfy his school committee that he is qualified to proceed in the subject in which he proposes to present himself for moderatorship.

Repetition of year; transference to general studies

3. A student who in any year has failed to satisfy any one or more of the conditions defined in §2 will not, except as provided in §§5-9, receive credit for the year. If he wishes to proceed as an undergraduate, and if he is entitled to do so (see GENERAL REGULATIONS, I, §14), he must either repeat the year in his honor course or transfer to the course in general studies, and in either case he may do so only with the permission of the appropriate authority. The committee of his school may permit him to repeat the year or may exclude him from the school. As an alternative to repeating the year he may, on the recommendation of the school committee, be permitted by the General Studies Committee to transfer to the course in general studies. If he is excluded from the school, he may similarly be permitted by the General Studies Committee to transfer to the course in general studies. A student thus transferring to the course in general studies will be credited with so much of that course as the General Studies Committee, having regard

to his performance as a whole shall determine, subject to the provision
that permission to apply for transfer to the Junior Freshman year of the
course in general studies must be granted by the Senior Tutor (see
COURSE IN GENERAL STUDIES, §12).

4. A student required to repeat a year in an honor course must
repeat attendance on the honor lectures taken during the unsuccessful
year unless exempted by the Senior Lecturer in accordance with §8.
He must also perform the exercises and pass the examinations of the
year he is repeating.

Absence from lectures or examinations

5. A student who in any term has been unable, through illness or
other unavoidable cause, to attend the prescribed lectures satisfactorily,
may be granted credit for the term by the Senior Lecturer, but must
perform such supplementary exercises as the Senior Lecturer may
require.

6. A student unavoidably absent from any part of an honor examination, may, on the recommendation of his school committee, be
allowed a special examination by the Senior Lecturer, and for this a
fee of £5 is charged.

A student who is taken ill before an examination and wishes to
apply for a special examination must submit a medical certificate
covering the period of the illness.

A student who is taken ill during an examination and wishes to
apply for a special examination must withdraw at once from the
examination and submit a medical certificate covering the period of
the illness.

7. When a student is absent from lectures through illness he must
supply the Senior Lecturer with a medical certificate.

8. In special circumstances exemption from attendance for one or
more terms may be granted by the Senior Lecturer on the recommendation of the school committee concerned; application for such
exemption must be made in advance. A student thus exempted must
perform such exercises as the Senior Lecturer, on the recommendation
of the school committee, may require. If these exercises are specially
provided, a fee is usually charged.

Abridgement of course

9. In all honor schools a student may be admitted as a Senior Freshman if, in the opinion of the School Committee or the Admission
Committee concerned, he is qualified by his knowledge and attainment
to be so, or if he passes the Junior Freshman honor examination with

sufficient merit. Such a student must pay a fee before presenting himself for this examination. See COLLEGE CHARGES.

Transference from general studies and from one honor course to another

10. A student reading the course in general studies may be permitted by the Senior Lecturer to transfer to an honor course, on the recommendation of the school committee concerned, except that permission to transfer to the Junior Freshman year of an honor course may be given only by the Senior Tutor, to whom application must be made through the student's tutor. A student may be permitted by the Senior Lecturer, on the recommendation of the school committees concerned, to transfer from one honor course to another, with the same proviso in respect of the Junior Freshman year.

Students from other universities

11. A student exempted from part of the undergraduate course in virtue of courses kept at other universities or colleges may be allowed to take an honor course only by permission of the school committee concerned.

Honor examinations

12. Honor examinations are held in each of the Freshman years and in the Junior Sophister year. A student is required to pass at least one honor examination in each of these three years; in some schools a student is required to pass more than one such examination in a year.

13. Credit for a Trinity Senior Freshman honor examination may be obtained by satisfactory performance in the examination for foundation scholarships. In certain schools credit for a Michaelmas Senior Freshman honor examination may be granted on the recommendation of the appropriate school committee to a student who has been elected to foundation or non-foundation scholarship in the preceding term.

14. Honor examinations are usually held during the two or three weeks immediately preceding lecture terms.

A student intending to present himself at an honor examination which is not a compulsory examination of his course must give notice to the Senior Lecturer at least twenty-one days before the end of the preceding lecture term.

15. The names of successful candidates in honor examinations are published in three ranks according to merit.

147

16. The examination for the degree of B.A. with honors is called the moderatorship examination. In most schools, it is divided into two or three parts, a Senior Freshman or a Junior Sophister honor examination counting as the first part. The final part of the examination, or (where it is undivided) the examination as a whole, is taken in the autumn following the completion of the Senior Sophister year, except in certain schools in which it is taken in June. For fees payable for the moderatorship examination see COLLEGE CHARGES.

17. A student unavoidably absent from any part of a moderatorship examination at the end of his Senior Sophister year may be permitted to present himself for a supplemental moderatorship in the same subject, on conditions laid down by the Senior Lecturer and the school committee concerned.

18. In special circumstances a student who has completed an honor course may, with the approval of his school committee, be permitted by the Senior Lecturer to defer his moderatorship examination for one year.

19. The successful candidates in the several schools are called moderators, and their names are placed according to merit in three classes, first, second and third. The names of candidates in the second class are further grouped in two divisions, first and second. Gold medals are awarded by the Board to candidates who have shown exceptional merit.

20. A student who has failed to obtain a moderatorship may nevertheless be allowed the B.A. degree on his answering at the examination provided that a special recommendation to that effect is made to the Senior Lecturer by the court of examiners concerned.

21. A student who has passed the moderatorship examination but who has spent more than four years on his undergraduate course is described as a supplemental moderator, unless he has been specially permitted by the Senior Lecturer to extend the period of his course. A supplemental moderator is not eligible for a medal or a moderatorship prize.

22. A student who has graduated in general studies may be permitted to present himself for a supplemental moderatorship, on conditions laid down by the Senior Lecturer and the school committee concerned. A moderator in one subject may on the same basis be permitted to present himself for a supplemental moderatorship in another subject.

23. A student who has failed to obtain a moderatorship but has been allowed the B.A. degree, as provided in §20 above, may be per-

mitted to present himself for a supplemental moderatorship in a different subject, on conditions laid down by the Senior Lecturer and the school committee concerned.

Prizes

24. Various studentships, scholarships, exhibitions, and other prizes are awarded to honor students on the results of honor and other examinations, provided that sufficient merit is shown. For details see PRIZES AND OTHER AWARDS.

25. At examinations in Michaelmas term a prize of £4 is awarded to each candidate who obtains first rank honors, except in the following cases. In modern languages and literature a prize of £2 is awarded, in each language presented, to candidates obtaining first rank honors at the examinations in Michaelmas term. In economics, in the Junior Freshman year, the prize of £4 is awarded on the result of the examination held in Trinity term.

Successful candidates must select books at the university booksellers, and may have the college arms stamped on the covers provided that the total cost does not exceed the stated value of the prize; or, in the case of prizes in natural sciences, scientific instruments, with an inscription thereon, may, if approved by the Senior Lecturer, on a report of the professors concerned, be substituted for books.

HONOR COURSE IN MATHEMATICS[1]

Admission

1. A student wishing to take the course should apply to the Senior Tutor for admission to the School of Mathematics. Applicants must give evidence of mathematical ability greater than that required for matriculation.

Abridgement of course

2. A student may be admitted to the course as a Senior Freshman if, in the opinion of the School Committee, he is qualified by his knowledge and attainment to be so, or if he passes the Michaelmas Junior Freshman honor examination with sufficient merit. He must pay a fee before presenting himself for this examination. See COLLEGE CHARGES.

Description of course

3. The course covers basic topics in pure and applied mathematics, and in statistics. The Junior Freshman course is designed as a transition from school to university mathematics; provision is made for revision as well as for an unhurried introduction to the fundamental notions of contemporary mathematics. The bulk of the course is covered in the Senior Freshman and Junior Sophister years; in the Senior Sophister year students specialise in a number of advanced subjects chosen from a wide selection of topics, in consultation with the professors in the School.

Combined course

4. In addition to the honor course in mathematics described in §3, a student may study mathematics as a principal subject in the following combined honor course:

MATHEMATICS AND PHYSICS: the course comprises mathematics, additional mathematics and physics as its principal subjects, and is described in detail in the regulations governing the honor course in natural sciences.

Examinations

5. Examinations are held as stated in detail below. The moderatorship examination is in three parts. A student must take all examinations, unless exempted by the School Committee.

---

[1] For regulations and courses applying to students who entered in or before October, 1963, see *Calendar*, 1963-4, pp. 149-52.

Rowe Fund Library

6. Members of the Dublin University Mathematical Society have the use of a mathematical library in the society's rooms, 39 Trinity College, in addition to the College Library.

COURSES AND EXAMINATIONS

Parts of the courses marked with an asterisk are those prescribed in the Freshman years for additional mathematics as a subject on the honor course in natural sciences.

Junior Freshmen

Course

Pure Mathematics: Sets; algebraic structures; topology functions of one variable.

Applied Mathematics: Vector algebra; mechanics of particles and two-dimensional rigid bodies; waves in strings; introduction to statistical methods.

Examinations

MICHAELMAS TERM

An examination is held at the beginning of Michaelmas term on the course of the preceding three terms. Papers are set as follows:

1. Algebra
2. Analysis
3. Dynamics

An informal examination is usually held on the work of the first term in order to advise students on their suitability for the course.

Senior Freshmen

Course

Pure Mathematics: Vector spaces; ring theory; measure and Lebesgue integration; functions of several variables.

Applied Mathematics: Rigid body, Lagrangian and Hamiltonian dynamics; vector analysis; special functions; special relativity and tensors; statistics.

Examinations

TRINITY AND MICHAELMAS TERMS

Examinations are held at the beginning of Trinity term, and at the beginning of Michaelmas term. The Michaelmas examination, which is set on the course of both Freshman years, is part I of the moderatorship examination. At each examination four papers are set, two on pure mathematics and two on applied mathematics.

Honor courses
Junior Sophisters

Course

Pure Mathematics: Algebraic topology, topological groups; group representations; functional analysis; probability theory.

Applied Mathematics: Electromagnetic theory; statistical mechanics; perfect fluids; introduction to quantum theory.

Examination

MICHAELMAS TERM

The examination, which is set on the course of the Junior Sophister year, is part II of the moderatorship examination. Two papers are set on pure mathematics and two on applied mathematics.

Senior Sophisters

Course

Lectures are given on a number of advanced topics in pure and applied mathematics.

Examination

MICHAELMAS TERM

The examination, which is set on the course of the Senior Sophister year, is part III of the moderatorship examination. Candidates are examined in one paper in each of four advanced topics.

Moderatorship examination

Marks are apportioned to the three parts of the examination for moderatorship, as follows:

	Marks
part I	240
part II	400
part III	360
Total	1000

Ordinary degree of B.A. in Mathematics

A student who has passed parts I and II of the Moderatorship examination may have the ordinary B.A. degree conferred if he does not choose, or is not allowed, to proceed to part III of the Moderatorship. The court of examiners may allow the ordinary degree to be conferred on a student who has a small deficiency in one part of the Moderatorship examination but who has compensated by his answering in the other part. Except by permission of the University Council, on the recommendation of the School Committee, the ordinary degree of B.A. may be conferred only on candidates who have spent at least four years in the University.

HONOR COURSE IN CLASSICS

Admission

1. A student wishing to take the honor course in classics should apply through the Senior Tutor to the School of Classics Admission Committee. Places are allotted only to those who have qualified for admission to the University and who satisfy the committee that they have an adequate command of Greek and Latin.

Abridgement of course

2. A student may be admitted to the course as a Senior Freshman if, in the opinion of the Admission Committee, he is qualified by his knowledge and attainment to be so, or if he passes the Junior Freshman honor examination with sufficient merit. He must pay a fee before presenting himself for this examination. See COLLEGE CHARGES.

Subjects of study

3. During the four years of the honor course special lectures are provided on literary, linguistic and historical aspects of the authors listed below, together with general lectures on classical composition, ancient history, archaeology and comparative philology. Courses in ancient history and archaeology are given during the Senior Freshman and Junior Sophister years. As well as attending these lectures students are required to submit essays and exercises for tutorial discussion.

Examinations

4. Candidates are examined on the prescribed authors. They are expected to show a competent understanding of each author's literary and historical significance. Passages are also set for unseen translation and for Greek and Latin prose composition.[1]

The School Committee may refuse permission to a student to proceed with his course unless he answers satisfactorily at each honor examination, as well as performing the other exercises required by the School.

The moderatorship examination is in two parts. See below.

Recommended reading

5. The following books are specially recommended for literary history:

---

[1] Passages will also be set for verse composition, if notice is given to the School Committee not later than the end of arts lectures in the term preceding the examination.

Honor courses

H. J. Rose, *A handbook of Greek literature.*
J. Wight Duff, *A literary history of Rome.*
J. Wight Duff, *A literary history of Rome in the silver age.*

The following books are specially recommended to Junior Freshmen for general reading in Greek and Roman history:

J. B. Bury, *A history of Greece,* revised Russell Meiggs.
Max Cary, *A history of Rome.*
The Cambridge ancient history.

The following book is specially recommended for comparative philology:

A. Meillet, *Introduction à l'étude comparative des langues indo-européennes* (Hachette).

Library

6. Members of the College Classical Society may read in the society's rooms, 40 Trinity College, and borrow books from its library.

COURSES AND EXAMINATIONS

Special attention should be given to the texts prescribed, but a general knowledge of the authors and their period is also expected.

Junior Freshmen

Course

MICHAELMAS TERM
Homer, *Odyssey,* 6–12.
Horace, *Odes, Epodes, Carmen saeculare*; Ovid, *Fasti,* 3, 4.

HILARY TERM
Herodotus, 1–3.
Sallust, *Catiline*; Livy, 1, 2.

TRINITY TERM
Homer, *Iliad,* 13–24.
Virgil, *Aeneid,* 1, 2, 4, 6–8; Lucan, 1.

Examinations

HILARY AND MICHAELMAS TERMS
The Michaelmas examination is on the work of the previous two terms. A student must present himself at both examinations unless exempted by the School Committee. Exemption from the Hilary examination is normally granted only to those who are candidates for foundation scholarship in their Junior Freshman year.

The Hilary examination is arranged as follows:

	9.30 a.m. to 12.30 p.m.	2 p.m. to 5 p.m.
First day	Greek prescribed authors	Greek composition
Second day	Latin prescribed authors	Latin composition

154

The Michaelmas examination is arranged as follows:

	9.30 a.m. to 12.30 p.m.	2 p.m. to 5 p.m.
First day	Greek prescribed authors	Greek composition
Second day	Latin prescribed authors	Latin composition
	9.30 a.m. to 11.30 a.m.	2 p.m. to 4 p.m.
Third day	General essay paper	Unprepared Greek and Latin translation

Senior Freshmen

Course

MICHAELMAS TERM
  Euripides, *Medea, Troades, Bacchae.*
  Catullus; Lucretius, 1, 3, 5.

HILARY TERM
  Plato, *Phaedo, Symposium.*
  Horace, *Satires*; Juvenal, *Satires* 1, 3, 4, 7, 8, 10, 13, 14.

TRINITY TERM
  Aristophanes, *Frogs*; Theocritus.
  Seneca, *Selected letters*; Pliny, *Letters.*

Examination

MICHAELMAS TERM
The Michaelmas examination is on the work of the previous three terms, and is arranged as follows:

	9.30 a.m. to 12.30 p.m.	2 p.m. to 5 p.m.
First day	Greek prescribed authors	Greek composition
Second day	Latin prescribed authors	Latin composition
Third day	General paper	Unprepared Greek and Latin translation

Sophisters

Course

The course is spread over the two Sophister years, and Junior and Senior Sophisters attend lectures together.

1966-7 and alternate years

MICHAELMAS TERM
  Plato, *Republic* (selected topics); Aristotle, *Poetics.*
  Cicero, *In Verrem*, actio ii, 4, *Pro Caelio, Philippic* 2, *Selected letters.*

HILARY TERM
  Aeschylus, *Agamemnon, Eumenides, Prometheus vinctus.*
  Propertius.

TRINITY TERM
  Thucydides, 1, 2, 7.
  Tacitus, *Annals*, 13-16.

Honor courses

MICHAELMAS TERM

Lysias, *In Eratosthenem*; Demosthenes, *De Corona*; Aeschines, *In Ctesiphontem*.
Plautus, *Captivi*, *Miles Gloriosus*, *Rudens*; Terence, *Phormio*.

HILARY TERM

Sophocles, *Ajax*, *Antigone*, *Oedipus Tyrannus*.
Virgil, *Aeneid*, 9–12; Lucan, 7, 8.

TRINITY TERM

Pindar, *Odes*.
Cicero, *De Oratore*; Quintilian, 1, 10.

The course in ancient history for Senior Freshmen and Junior Sophisters is the history of Greece to the death of Alexander the Great, and the history of Rome to the death of Marcus Aurelius.

Examination

MICHAELMAS TERM: MODERATORSHIP EXAMINATION, PART I

All Junior Sophisters must present themselves at the Michaelmas Junior Sophister examination, which is part I of the moderatorship examination. A candidate must obtain at least third rank honors at this examination to be allowed to proceed with the honor course of the Senior Sophister year. At this examination Junior Sophisters are examined in the authors prescribed for the previous three terms. There are also papers on Greek and Latin prose composition[1], an essay paper, and a general paper containing questions on history, archaeology, literature, ancient thought, and philology. The marks obtained in the papers on Greek and Latin composition and the general paper are carried forward and added to the marks obtained in part II of the moderatorship examination. A student from Magee University College may postpone taking the general paper until the moderatorship examination, part II.

The moderatorship examination, part I, is arranged as follows:

	9.30 a.m. to 12.30 p.m.	From 2 p.m.
First day	Greek composition	Greek prescribed authors (3 hours)
Second day	Latin composition	Latin prescribed authors (3 hours)
Third day	General paper	Essay (2 hours)

MICHAELMAS TERM: MODERATORSHIP EXAMINATION, PART II

This examination is held in Michaelmas term at the end of the Senior Sophister year. Passages are set for translation, selected from the Greek and Latin classical authors generally. The prescribed books papers contain passages for translation and critical comment from the authors prescribed for the three terms preceding the examination. A candidate is required either to answer a special paper or to present a thesis. The special paper must be on *one* of the following: history, archaeology, literature, ancient thought, philology. A

[1] Passages will also be set for verse composition, if notice is given to the School Committee not later than the end of arts lectures in the term preceding the examination.

156

candidate must inform the appropriate professor or lecturer of his choice of special subject early in his Senior Sophister year. Instead of answering the special paper, a candidate who receives the permission of the appropriate professor may present a thesis to be written in his own time during the Senior Sophister year. A candidate who wishes to present a thesis should seek such permission, stating the subject of his choice, not later than the end of the third week of arts lectures in Michaelmas term. The thesis must be presented to the examiners not later than the end of Trinity term, and must be accompanied by an abstract of its contents.

The moderatorship examination, part II, is arranged as follows:

	9.30 a.m. to 12.30 p.m.	2 p.m. to 5 p.m.
First day	Greek translation (prose)	Prescribed authors (Greek)
Second day	Latin translation (prose)	Prescribed authors (Latin)
Third day	Special paper	Greek translation (verse)
Fourth day	Essay	Latin translation (verse)

The marks assigned to the various subjects of the moderatorship examination, part II (including those carried forward from the moderatorship examination, part I) are distributed as follows:

	Marks
Four papers of passages	400
Two compositions	100
Prescribed books (Greek)	100
Prescribed books (Latin)	100
General paper	100
Special paper or thesis	100
Essay	100
Total	1,000

HONOR COURSE IN MENTAL AND MORAL SCIENCE

Admission

1. A candidate for admission to the School of Mental and Moral Science must satisfy the general requirements for admission to the University. Preference will be given to an applicant who has matriculation qualifications in both mathematics and either Latin or Greek.

Abridgement of course

2. A student may be admitted to the course as a Senior Freshman if, in the opinion of the School Committee, he is qualified by his knowledge and attainment to be so, or if he passes the Junior Freshman honor examination with sufficient merit. He must pay a fee before presenting himself for this examination. See COLLEGE CHARGES.

Subjects of study

3. The course comprises mainly the study of metaphysics, problems in epistemology and moral philosophy. The history of philosophy in the Greek, medieval and modern periods is studied in outline, and some of the major systems of philosophy are studied in detail. The course includes also the study of logic, and an introduction to aesthetics.

Examinations

4. A student is required to take the Hilary Junior Freshman, and all three Michaelmas honor examinations, unless exempted by the School Committee, which may not allow him to proceed with the course if he fails to present himself at these examinations, or if his results are unsatisfactory. He is examined both in the course prescribed and in his general knowledge of the subject under consideration. The examinations are held at the beginning of the term referred to in each case.

Library and recommended books

5. Members of the Dublin University Metaphysical Society have the use of a philosophical library in 5 Trinity College, in addition to the College Library.

A list of books recommended to be read in connection with the prescribed courses may be obtained from the Admissions Office.

COURSES AND EXAMINATIONS

Junior Freshmen

Course

LOGIC

Some formal systems of propositional and predicate logic are studied. Some related questions in the philosophy of logic are treated.

The course is divided as follows:

(*a*) *Michaelmas term*: Introduction: the connection of logic and reasoning. The definition of validity; the notions of form, of variable, of logical constant. The connectives.

(*b*) *Hilary term*: Further development of propositional logic.

(*c*) *Trinity term*: First order predicate logic; the theory of relations.

METAPHYSICS AND THEORY OF KNOWLEDGE

(*a*) *Michaelmas term*: Introduction to philosophy.

The topics studied include the special nature of philosophical reasoning, the relations between philosophy and other studies, the divisions of philosophical subject-matter, the main contrasts in types of philosophical theory, philosophical terminology.

The topics are illustrated by reference to various philosophical authors, particularly to Descartes, whose *Metaphysical Meditations* is prescribed for reading during this term.

(*b*) *Hilary term*: Introduction to theory of knowledge.

The topics studied include knowledge and belief, the representative theory of perception, the perception of spatial relations, memory and imagination.

Special reference is made in treating the topics stated to the following works which are prescribed for reading: Locke, *An essay concerning human understanding*; Berkeley, *An essay towards a new theory of vision*.

(*c*) *Trinity term*: Metaphysics and theory of knowledge.

The topics studied include universals, sense-perception, cause, belief in an external world, the self, other minds.

Special reference is made in treating the topics stated to the following prescribed works: Berkeley, *A treatise concerning the principles of human knowledge*; Hume, *A treatise of human nature*, bk 1.

Examinations

Examinations are held at the beginning of Hilary term, on the course of the previous term, and at the beginning of Michaelmas term, on the course of the year.

In Hilary term two papers are set:

    I Logic

    II Introduction to philosophy

In Michaelmas term three papers are set: paper I relates to the logic course taken in all three terms, paper II relates mainly to the courses in introduction

Honor courses

to philosophy and theory of knowledge prescribed for Michaelmas and Hilary terms, paper III to the courses in metaphysics and theory of knowledge prescribed for Trinity term.

Senior Freshmen

Course

METAPHYSICS

(a) *Michaelmas term*: The topics studied include substance and attributes, determinism, space and time.

Special reference is made to the philosophies of Spinoza and Leibniz. Spinoza, *Ethics*, pts 1, 2 is prescribed for reading.

(b) *Hilary and Trinity terms*: The philosophy of Kant, with special reference to the following prescribed works: Kant, *Critique of pure reason*, and *Critique of judgment*, preface, introduction and pt 1.

Topics relevant to the prescribed reading are studied in tutorials.

ETHICS

In each term topics relevant to the prescribed reading are studied in tutorials.

(a) *Michaelmas term*: Greek ethics. Prescribed reading: Plato, *Republic*; Aristotle, *Nicomachean ethics*.

(b) *Hilary and Trinity terms*: Ethics. Prescribed reading: Hobbes, *Leviathan*, pt 1; Butler, *Dissertation on the nature of virtue, Sermons at the Rolls*, preface and sermons 1–3, 11; Hume, *An enquiry concerning the principles of morals, A treatise of human nature*, bk 2 (pt 1. xi, pt 2. vii, pt 3. iii), bk 3 (pt 1, pt 2. i, ii,v); Kant, *Fundamental principles of the metaphysic of morals, Dialectic of practical reason*, ch 2, pts 1–5; Mill, *Utilitarianism*; Sidgwick, *Methods of ethics*, bk 2, chs 1–3, bk 4.

HISTORY OF PHILOSOPHY

The Lecturer in the History of Philosophy gives a general course of lectures throughout the year. These lectures provide a broad survey of Greek, patristic, medieval and modern philosophy.

Examination

An examination is held in Michaelmas term on the course of the year. Six papers are set: paper I is set on Spinoza and the metaphysical problems treated in Michaelmas term, papers II and III are set on Kant's metaphysics and theory of aesthetic judgment, paper IV is set on Greek ethics, paper V on the ethics course prescribed for Hilary and Trinity terms, and paper VI on the history of philosophy course. A candidate is required to take *five* of these six papers.

Junior Sophisters

Course

METAPHYSICS

(a) *Michaelmas term*: The philosophy of Hegel, with special reference to Hegel, *The science of logic* (Part I of the *Encyclopaedia*, trans. W. Wallace) chs 1, 6–9.

(b) *Hilary term*: Hegel, as before.

(c) *Trinity term*: Problems in the philosophy of Plato. Prescribed reading: Plato, *Phaedo, Parmenides, Theaetetus, Sophist*.

LOGIC AND PHILOSOPHY OF SCIENCE
(a) *Michaelmas term*: Metalogic.
(b) *Hilary term*: Philosophy of logic.
(c) *Trinity term*: Philosophy of science.

MORAL AND POLITICAL PHILOSOPHY
(a) *Hilary term*: Ethics since 1900: the theories of Moore, Ross, Ayer and Hare
(b) *Trinity term*: Political philosophy.

The Berkeley Professor of Metaphysics delivers a course of lectures during Michaelmas and Hilary terms.

Examination

MODERATORSHIP EXAMINATION, PART I

The moderatorship examination, part I, is held at the beginning of Michaelmas term following the Junior Sophister year. A candidate takes papers I and II, and *two* of the papers III–VI.

I	Ethics
II	Hegel
III	Plato
IV	Logic
V	Political philosophy
VI	Philosophy of science

Paper I is set on the course in ethics prescribed for the Senior Freshman and Junior Sophister years, with special attention to the course of the Junior Sophister year. A candidate must give notice to the Senior Lecturer three weeks before the end of the preceding Trinity lecture term of the papers he intends to take.

A proportion of the marks obtained on the four papers is carried forward as part of the total moderatorship marks.

Senior Sophisters [1]

During this year the emphasis is on independent work by the student. He selects one of the special courses from those stated below. From the topics listed for his special course he chooses one, on which he writes a thesis, under supervision, in Michaelmas term. He may choose *either* to write a second thesis in Hilary term on a second topic from his special course, *or* to take an essay paper at part II of the moderatorship examination.

In addition to writing his thesis or theses, and reading for his special course, a student also attends seminars, during Michaelmas and Hilary terms, on recent topics and works in metaphysics and moral philosophy and prepares papers for them. During Trinity lecture term he attends one weekly seminar.

The following regulations apply to special courses and theses:

[1] Senior Sophisters during 1966-7 are subject to the regulations in the *Calendar*, 1965-6, pp. 159-161.

G

Honor courses

(a) A student may choose a special course only if there is a member of the teaching staff available to supervise his work. He must inform the Professor of Moral Philosophy of the course he proposes to take not later than 1 September at the end of his Junior Sophister year;

(b) In addition to writing a thesis or theses the student is examined on two special course papers at part II of the moderatorship examination;

(c) A thesis should be between 3000 and 4000 words in length or, in the case of logic, of comparable extent;

(d) A student normally visits his supervisor for three tutorials, relating to his thesis, in Michaelmas term; and similarly in Hilary term, if he is writing a second thesis;

(e) A supervisor may accept a topic in the area of a student's special course, even if this topic is not among those listed;

(f) A maximum of 100 marks is awarded to a thesis. Theses are examined by an internal examiner and by the external examiner;

(g) A student must complete and submit his Michaelmas term thesis not later than the first day of Hilary lecture term; a Hilary term thesis must be submitted by the first day of Trinity lecture term.

Special courses

A candidate chooses one of the following special courses for the moderatorship examination in accordance with the regulations stated above.

A

THE PHILOSOPHY OF PLATO

Topics: The theory of Forms; the one and the many; knowledge and opinion; pleasure and 'the Good'; appearance and reality; space, time and motion; methodology (hypothesis and division); doctrine of the soul.

The treatment and development of these topics is to be studied with special reference to the following dialogues:

Republic, bks 5–7, Phaedrus 244 a– 257 b, Parmenides, Theaetetus, Sophist, Philebus, Timaeus.

B

THE PHILOSOPHY OF ARISTOTLE

Topics: Eleatic monism; becoming; nature; causes and explanations; change; the infinite; time; substance; actuality and possibility; God; the soul-body relation; perception; knowledge; appetitive movement.

Reading: Aristotle, Physics, bks 1–4; Metaphysics Z,H,Θ,Λ; De anima.

C

THE PHILOSOPHY OF ST THOMAS AQUINAS

Topics: Substance; soul and body; theory of knowledge and will; natural law.

Reading: *De ente et essentia*; *De principiis naturae*; *Summa theologiae*, 1 qq. 75–88; Ia IIae qq.i, 90–4.

A general knowledge of medieval philosophy in the period 1100–1450 is expected.

D

SEVENTEENTH–CENTURY INTELLECTUALISM

Topics: Intuition and imagination; reason; substance and mode; space and time; freedom and determinism; the mind-body relation; relevant arguments for the existence of God; innate ideas; the representative theory of perception; philosophical method; error and evil.

Reading: Representative writings of Descartes, Spinoza, Leibniz and the Cambridge Platonists.

E

EMPIRICISM

Topics: Existence; perception; mind-body relation; personal identity; scientific law; time; space; the existence of God; substance and qualities; the nature of mathematics; knowledge and belief.

Reading: A selection from the major philosophical writings of Hobbes, Locke, Berkeley and Hume. Examination papers are set so that candidates can specialise in *two* of these four empiricists.

F

POST–HEGELIAN IDEALISM IN BRITAIN AND AMERICA

Topics: What idealism is; relations; the nature of truth; degrees of truth and reality; necessity; self; intelligibility of the Absolute; the Absolute and human experience; criticisms of empiricism.

Reading: Bradley, *Appearance and reality*, (especially on relations, the general nature of reality, the self)
Joachim, *The nature of truth*
Blanshard, *The nature of thought* (especially vol. II, chs 25–32)
Blanshard, *Reason and analysis* (especially chs 5, 6, 8–12)
G. Watts Cunningham, *The idealist argument* (on Bradley, Bosanquet, McTaggart, Royce, and critical chapters)

G

THE PHILOSOPHIES OF RUSSELL AND WITTGENSTEIN

Topics: Language; the nature of propositions; facts; existence; analysis; descriptions; logical laws; logicism; meaning; understanding; sensation; private language.

Reading: To be recommended by the supervisor from among the major philosophical writings of Russell and Wittgenstein but to include Russell: *Principles of mathematics, Our knowledge of the external world, An enquiry into meaning and truth, Logic and knowledge*; Wittgenstein:

Honor courses

Tractatus logico-philosophicus, Philosophical investigations. One examination paper is set on Russell and one on Wittgenstein. Questions may be set in either paper which pre-suppose a knowledge of both philosophers.

H

LOGIC

In paper I a candidate is examined on first order predicate logic with identity, elementary meta-theorems for propositional and predicate calculi, alternative logics, modal logic.

In paper II a candidate is examined on theories of truth, meaning and predication, of necessity and existence, of inference, proof and logical truth.

J

AESTHETICS

Topics: The nature of works of art; the relation of aesthetic to other kinds of activity; selected theories of aesthetics; aesthetic judgements; types of literature and literary uses of language.

Reading: To be recommended by the supervisor.

K

PHILOSOPHY OF RELIGION

Topics: Proofs of God's existence; the status of religious language; arguments from religious experience; the problem of evil; design and purpose in natural phenomena; the relation between religion and morality.

Reading: To be recommended by the supervisor.

L

PHILOSOPHY OF SCIENCE

Topics: Laws of nature; models; probability, causation, determinism, explanation and methodology in the physical and social sciences.

Reading: To be recommended by the supervisor.

Examination

MODERATORSHIP EXAMINATION, PART II

The moderatorship examination, part II, is held in Trinity term. A candidate is examined in two papers on his special course, and in two papers on problems in philosophy. A candidate not presenting a second thesis must take an essay paper. There is also a *viva voce* examination, at which the external examiner is present.

Mental and moral science

Marks are allotted as follows:

	Marks
Part I (carried forward)	300
Problems in metaphysics	150
Problems in moral philosophy	150
Special course, paper I	100
Special course, paper II	100
Thesis I	100
Thesis II *or* Essay paper	100
Total	1,000

HONOR COURSE IN PHILOSOPHY AND PSYCHOLOGY

Admission

1. A student wishing to take the honor course in philosophy and psychology should apply to the Senior Tutor for admission to the School of Mental and Moral Science. He must satisfy the general requirements for admission to the University. Preference will be given to an applicant who has matriculation qualifications in both mathematics and either Latin or Greek.

Abridgement of course

2. A student may be admitted to the course as a Senior Freshman if, in the opinion of the School Committee, he is qualified by his knowledge and attainment to be so, or if he passes the Junior Freshman honor examination with sufficient merit. He must pay a fee before presenting himself for this examination. See COLLEGE CHARGES.

Subjects of study

3. The course in philosophy comprises mainly the study of logic, metaphysics, problems in epistemology and moral philosophy. The course in psychology comprises the biological foundations of psychology, the main branches of experimental psychology, techniques of psychological measurement, personality theory, and social psychology; laboratory instruction is provided during each year.

Both subjects are studied during the first three years of the course. In the Senior Sophister year a student studies either philosophy or psychology. His choice of subject must have the approval of the School Committee.

Examinations

4. An examination in philosophy is held in Hilary term for Junior Freshmen. Examinations in both philosophy and psychology are held in Michaelmas term at the end of the Junior Freshman, Senior Freshman and Junior Sophister years. The School Committee may not allow a student to proceed with his course if he fails to present himself at these examinations, or if his results are unsatisfactory.

COURSES AND EXAMINATIONS

Junior Freshmen

Courses

PHILOSOPHY

As for students taking the honor course in Mental and Moral Science. A student taking philosophy and psychology is exempted from attending some of the seminars and tutorials.

PSYCHOLOGY

A. History of psychology

B. Learning and symbolic processes I

Laboratory classes are held on learning and remembering.

Examinations

Examinations are held at the beginning of Hilary term in philosophy, and at the beginning of Michaelmas term in both philosophy and psychology.

In Hilary term two papers are set:

I   Logic

II   Introduction to philosophy

In Michaelmas term a candidate takes two papers in philosophy, and two in psychology. In philosophy he takes paper I on logic, and *either* paper II *or* paper III as set for honor students in Mental and Moral Science. In psychology he takes a paper on learning and remembering, and a paper on the history of psychology.

Senior Freshmen

Courses

PHILOSOPHY

The courses in metaphysics and ethics as prescribed for students taking the honor course in Mental and Moral Science.

PSYCHOLOGY

C. Biological foundations I

D. Psychological measurement I

E. Perception

Laboratory classes are held in sensation and perception, and in animal behaviour.

Examination

An examination is held in Michaelmas term. In philosophy a candidate takes papers I, II and V as set for honor students in Mental and Moral Science. In psychology he takes a paper on biological foundations of psychology, and a paper on perception.

Honor courses

Junior Sophisters

Courses

PHILOSOPHY

A student attends each term at least one of the three courses of lectures provided for honor students in Mental and Moral Science.

PSYCHOLOGY

    C. Biological foundations II

    D. Psychological measurement II

    F. Intelligence and personality assessment

    G. Personality theory

    H. Developmental psychology

Laboratory classes are held in psychological testing.

Examination

An examination is held at the beginning of Michaelmas term. In philosophy a candidate takes two papers from among those set for honor students in Mental and Moral Science. He must choose as follows, and must inform the Senior Lecturer of his choice at least three weeks before the end of Trinity lecture term:

  I *Either* ethics *or* logic

  II *Either* Plato *or* Hegel *or* political philosophy *or* philosophy of science

In psychology a candidate takes two papers:

  I Personality theory and assessment

  II Biological foundations and developmental psychology

A student intending to specialise in psychology as a Senior Sophister must obtain at least third rank honors in his two philosophy papers (combined). The marks he obtains in the two psychology papers are carried forward to the moderatorship examination.

A student intending to specialise in philosophy as a Senior Sophister must obtain at least third rank honors in his two psychology papers (combined). The marks he obtains in his two philosophy papers are carried forward to the moderatorship examination.

Senior Sophisters

PHILOSOPHY

Courses

A student specialising in philosophy studies the Senior Sophister course as prescribed for students taking the honor course in Mental and Moral Science.

Moderatorship examination

The moderatorship examination is held in Trinity term. Marks are allotted as follows:

Philosophy marks carried forward	200
Problems in metaphysics	150
Problems in moral philosophy	150
Special course, paper I	100
Special course, paper II	100
Thesis I	100
Thesis II *or* Essay paper	100

	Total	900

PSYCHOLOGY

Courses

B.   Learning and symbolic processes II
D.   Psychological measurement III
J.   Abnormal psychology
K.   Social psychology
L.   Special topics

Laboratory classes are held in advanced experimental work and research projects.

Moderatorship examination

The moderatorship examination is held in Trinity term. A candidate takes the six papers numbered I to VI below. Marks are assigned to these, to the papers carried forward from the Junior Sophister examination, and to the work on projects during the year, as follows:

I	Learning and symbolic processes	100
II	Abnormal psychology	100
III	Social psychology	100
IV	Perception	100
V	Special course	100
VI	Essay	100
	Psychology marks carried forward	200
	Projects	200

	Total	1000

HONOR COURSE IN NATURAL SCIENCES

Admission

1. A student wishing to enter the School of Natural Sciences should apply through the Senior Tutor to the School Admission Committee.

2. Applicants must satisfy the admission requirements of the University. See ADMISSION REQUIREMENTS. The Admission Committee gives preference to applicants who have obtained honours at the Leaving Certificate examination, or passed with good marks at the matriculation examination, or with high grades at advanced level in a General Certificate of Education examination, in two of the following subjects: chemistry, physics, mathematics, additional mathematics, biology[1], botany, geography, geology or zoology. Applicants who do not have qualifications in scientific subjects, but have a high level of attainment in other subjects, may be considered, if places are available.

3. Applications from candidates resident in Ireland should reach the Senior Tutor before 1 January of the year in which they wish to enter, but applications may be accepted from them until 1 September. They are urged to apply as early as possible. Applications from candidates not resident in Ireland must reach the Senior Tutor before 1 January, *i.e.* completed application forms must reach the Senior Tutor by that date.

Abridgement of course

4. A student may be admitted to the course as a Senior Freshman if, in the opinion of the Admission Committee, he is qualified by his knowledge and attainment to be so, or if he passes the Junior Freshman honor examination with sufficient merit. He must pay a fee before presenting himself for this examination. See COLLEGE CHARGES.

Subjects of study

5. The subjects included in the natural sciences course are biochemistry, botany, chemistry, genetics, geography, geology, mathematics, additional mathematics, microbiology, physics and zoology. At least three of these are studied in the Freshman years, two subjects are studied in the Junior Sophister and one in the Senior Sophister year. Additional mathematics can be taken only in conjunction with physics (Course I) and mathematics. Students are urged to decide as early as possible in their course which subjects they wish to study in the Sophister years and to consult the professors concerned on the planning of their work.

Note. In certain departments the number of places for students of

[1] Biology may not be offered with botany or zoology.

each year is limited. While every effort is made to allow a student to study the subjects he wishes, it may be necessary to restrict the numbers in any year in these departments. The committee of the School of Natural Sciences reserves the right to allocate the available places.

JUNIOR FRESHMEN

6. The work of the Junior Freshman year is intended to provide both a training in general science and an introduction to the subjects which are to be studied in later years. Every student must attend courses in at least three subjects. The subjects available in the Junior Freshman year are: additional mathematics, biology, chemistry, mathematics, physics and physiography (which serves as an introduction to both geography and geology).

Alternative courses are available in chemistry and in physics. In chemistry there are three courses. Students who wish to specialize in chemistry should attend Course I. Students who intend to specialize in a biological subject should attend Course I or Course II. Students not proceeding in chemistry after the Junior Freshman year may attend Course III.

Two courses are available in physics. Students who wish to take physics in their Senior Freshman year must take Course I in physics and the course in mathematics; others take Course II in physics.

In selecting the subjects to be studied in the Junior Freshman year a student must remember that he will not normally be admitted to the Senior Freshman course in any subject in which he has not attended the appropriate course in the Junior Freshman year. Students wishing to proceed to biochemistry, botany, microbiology and/or zoology in the Senior Freshman year must take the course in biology in the Junior Freshman year.

A student who wishes to choose the subjects of his Senior Freshman year from biochemistry, botany, chemistry, microbiology and zoology takes biology, chemistry and physics in his Junior Freshman year.

A student who wishes to choose the subjects of his Senior Freshman year from botany, geography, geology and zoology takes biology, chemistry and physiography in his Junior Freshman year.

A student who intends to take chemistry, mathematics and physics in his Senior Freshman year must take chemistry, mathematics and physics in his Junior Freshman year.

A student who intends to take additional mathematics, mathematics and physics in his Senior Freshman year must take additional mathematics, chemistry, mathematics and physics in his Junior Freshman year.

Honor courses

A student who intends to take geology, mathematics and physics in his Senior Freshman year must take chemistry, mathematics, physics and physiography in the Junior Freshman year; he may be excused from the course in chemistry if in the opinions of the Chairman and Registrar of the School, he is qualified by his knowledge and attainment in chemistry to be so.

A student who intends to take chemistry, geology and physics in his Senior Freshman year must take chemistry, mathematics, physics and physiography in his Junior Freshman year; he may be excused from the course in mathematics if, in the opinions of the Chairman and the Registrar of the School, he is qualified by his knowledge and attainment in both pure and applied mathematics to be so.

A student must give notice to the Registrar of the School, not later than the end of the third week of Trinity lecture term, of his choice of subjects for the Senior Freshman year.

7. The School Committee may permit or may require a student to spend two years in studying the Junior Freshman courses. In the first of these years (known as the Junior Freshman preliminary science year) he studies Course III in chemistry and Course II in physics; he must also study a subject chosen from the Junior Freshman year of the course in general studies, but may not choose applied mathematics on that course. Such a student is not allowed to proceed to the courses of his second Junior Freshman year unless he passes an examination in these subjects at the end of Trinity term or a supplemental examination at the beginning of Michaelmas term. In his second Junior Freshman year he studies at least three subjects chosen from chemistry (Courses I or II), physics (Course I), biology, physiography, mathematics and additional mathematics.

SENIOR FRESHMEN

8. A Senior Freshman is required to study three subjects selected from biochemistry, botany, chemistry, geography, geology, mathematics, additional mathematics, microbiology, physics and zoology.

If microbiology be selected, the other two subjects must be chosen from biochemistry, botany, chemistry and zoology. A student who intends to study microbiology in the Junior Sophister year must obtain credit for the lectures in biochemistry of the Senior Freshman year.

If physics be selected as one of the subjects, the other two subjects must be chosen from mathematics, additional mathematics, geology and chemistry. If it is intended to take physics in the Junior Sophister year, mathematics must be taken in the Senior Freshman year.

A student who intends to study biochemistry in his Junior Sophister year should take chemistry as one of his subjects in the Senior Freshman year. Students who have not fulfilled this requirement will be admitted to the Junior Sophister year in biochemistry only in exceptional circumstances, and must satisfy the Professor of Biochemistry that their understanding of chemistry is sufficient to allow them to profit from the course.

If geography be selected, the other two subjects must be chosen from botany, chemistry and geology.

A student who intends to study geology in his Senior Sophister year must have obtained credit for the field-course in geological mapping which is held in the long vacation at the end of the Senior Freshman year. A Senior Freshman student of geology who thinks it probable that he will study this subject in his Senior Sophister year should take this field-course.

A student must give notice to the Registrar of the School, not later than the end of the third week of Trinity lecture term, of his choice of subjects for the Junior Sophister year.

JUNIOR SOPHISTERS

9. A Junior Sophister must select two subjects (not including mathematics, except in conjunction with physics) from those studied in his Senior Freshman year. Additional mathematics is not available as a subject in the Junior Sophister year.

If botany be selected, the other subject must be chosen from biochemistry, geography, geology, microbiology and zoology.

If geography be selected, the other subject must be chosen from botany or geology.

A student who intends to study physics in his Senior Sophister year must take mathematics as his second subject.

If chemistry be selected, the other subject must be chosen from biochemistry, geology or physics. A student taking physics and chemistry must attend additional practical classes in chemistry in lieu of the practical classes in physics.

A student who intends to study microbiology in his Senior Sophister year must take biochemistry as his second subject. A student who has not fulfilled this requirement will be admitted to the Senior Sophister year in microbiology only in exceptional circumstances and with the permission of the Professor of Bacteriology.

10. A student who intends to study chemistry, geography, geology or physics in his Senior Sophister year is required to give notice to the Registrar of the School not later than the first day of lectures of Michaelmas term of his Junior Sophister year (*i.e.* one year in advance).

Honor courses

A student who intends to study biochemistry, botany, genetics, microbiology or zoology in his Senior Sophister year is required to give notice to the Registrar of the School not later than the last day of lectures in the Hilary term of his Junior Sophister year. Requests for a transfer from the subject notified will be considered only in exceptional circumstances, and only if the necessary places are available.

SENIOR SOPHISTERS

11. A Senior Sophister must select one of the subjects studied in his Junior Sophister year for further study; mathematics is not available as a subject in the Senior Sophister year.

A student taking physics in his Senior Sophister year continues to study mathematics as part of his course; he may also take the Senior Sophister course in additional mathematics in lieu of attending practical classes in physics, provided he has taken additional mathematics in his Freshman years.

A student who has studied at least one of biochemistry, botany, microbiology, zoology in his Junior Sophister year may choose to study genetics in his Senior Sophister year.

Examinations

12. Annual examinations in all subjects except in mathematics are held at the beginning of Michaelmas term following the Junior Freshman, Senior Freshman and Junior Sophister years. Examinations in mathematics are held at the end of the Trinity term for these academic classes. An examination is held at the end of Trinity term for Junior Freshmen taking the preliminary science year: see §7 above.

Except with the special permission of the committee of the School of Natural Sciences, a student who fails to satisfy the examiners at any of these examinations is not allowed to proceed with the honor course. A student may be refused permission to proceed in any subject in which he has not maintained a satisfactory standard in the preceding year.

In order to proceed to the Senior Sophister year as a moderatorship candidate, a student must (a) pass in each of his two subjects at the Junior Sophister examination, except that a student taking physics and mathematics may be allowed to compensate for a small deficiency in either subject by his answering in the other, and (b) show sufficient promise of capacity for advanced work in the subject in which he wishes to proceed, to justify his acceptance as a moderatorship candidate.

13. *Moderatorship*. The moderatorship examination is held in Trinity term of the Senior Sophister year in biochemistry, chemistry, genetics

geography, geology and zoology, and at the beginning of Michaelmas term following the Senior Sophister year in botany, microbiology and physics.

14. If physics is studied in the Senior Sophister year, the marks awarded at the Junior Sophister examination count as 30 per cent of the total marks in moderatorship.

15. Formal lectures in subjects in which the moderatorship examinations are taken in Trinity term may be restricted to Michaelmas and Hilary terms and part only of Trinity term.

Moderatorship examination: scheme of marks

16. Papers and marks are in accordance with the following scheme:

BIOCHEMISTRY	Papers	600
	Practical work of the Senior Sophister year, research problem and practical examination	300
	Essays, seminars and special exercises	100
BOTANY	Papers	550
	Practical examination and *viva voce*	150
	Practical work of the Senior Sophister year	100
	Research problem	200
CHEMISTRY	Papers and essays	700
	Practical work of the Senior Sophister year and any special exercises	300
GENETICS	Papers	700
	Practical examination	150
	Practical work of the Senior Sophister year	150
GEOGRAPHY	Papers	400
	Essay	100
	Practical examination	200
	Special work	300
GEOLOGY	Papers and essay	550
	Practical examination	300
	Field mapping report	150
MATHEMATICS AND PHYSICS	Papers in physics	400
	Paper in theoretical physics	100
	Paper in additional mathematics	100
	S.F. mathematics and additional mathematics (carried forward)	150
	J.S. physics (carried forward)	150
	J.S. mathematics (carried forward)	100

Honor courses

MICROBIOLOGY	Papers	600
	Practical examination	200
	Special work of the Senior Sophister year	200
PHYSICS	Papers	500
	Practical examination and practical work of the Senior Sophister year	200
	J.S. examination (carried forward)	300
ZOOLOGY	Papers	500
	Practical examinations	300
	Special work and note-books	200

Ordinary degree of B.A. in natural sciences

17. A student who passes in both his subjects at the Junior Sophister annual examination may have the ordinary B.A. degree conferred if he does not choose, or is not allowed, to proceed as a candidate for moderatorship. The court of examiners may allow the ordinary degree to be conferred on a student who has a small deficiency in one subject at the Junior Sophister annual examination but who has compensated by his answering in the other subject. Except by special permission of the University Council, on the recommendation of the School Committee, the ordinary degree of B.A. may be conferred only on candidates who have spent at least three years in the school.

The names of candidates who pass the degree examination are published in three classes according to merit. Specially meritorious candidates are called respondents and receive honorary testimoniums.

COURSES
JUNIOR FRESHMEN
Biology

A comprehensive, introductory course of plant and animal biology, including a study of living organisms both at the structural and the cellular level; introduction to biochemistry, genetics and microbiology; plant and animal physiology; embryology; an introduction to evolutionary theory.

Chemistry

COURSE I is designed as the first of four successive courses leading to the honor degree with specialisation in chemistry. It consists of a general introduction to modern aspects of inorganic, physical and organic chemistry.

COURSE II is designed to meet the needs of students specialising in biology; honor students taking this course may be permitted to progress to the Senior Freshman course in chemistry. Weekly tutorials will be held.

COURSE III is a course designed to provide a broad-based review of modern inorganic, physical and organic chemistry suitable for students who require a basic knowledge of chemistry.

Natural sciences

An optional preliminary course for Junior Freshman students in chemistry will be given during the fortnight preceding Michaelmas lecture term. Students who have little previous knowledge of chemistry are advised to attend the preliminary course.

Physiography

The physical basis of geography, including landforms and climate with relevant practical work; the history of geography; general considerations regarding the origin, composition and structure of the earth; igneous rocks; movements of the earth's crust; the broad outlines of geological history; elementary knowledge of fossils and of organic evolution.

Mathematics

Pure Mathematics. Linear equations, determinants. Polynomials, algebraic equations, rational functions, partial fractions.

Differential calculus: functions of one variable. Elementary differential properties of plane curves. Maxima and minima. Mean value theorems.

Convergence and absolute convergence of infinite series, with simple tests; series of terms with alternating sign. Taylor expansions; expansions of binomial, exponential, logarithmic, circular and hyperbolic functions.

Integral calculus: technique for evaluating simple definite and indefinite integrals. Application to plane areas, arc lengths, areas and volumes of revolution.

Complex numbers: the Argand diagram, de Moivre's theorem. Definitions of exponential, logarithmic and circular functions of a complex variable.

Plane coordinate geometry.

Simple probability and statistics.

Applied mathematics. Vector algebra: geometrical applications.

Mechanics: particle statics, two- and three-dimensional particle motion (excluding inverse square law); energy, angular momentum. Two-dimensional rigid body kinematics; statics and dynamics.

Waves in strings.

Hydrostatics.

Additional Mathematics

Prescribed parts of the courses marked with an asterisk in the Junior Freshman honor course in mathematics.

Physics

Course I. Properties of matter; heat, wave motion and sound, elementary geometrical optics including simple optical instruments; velocity of light; photometry; introduction to magnetism and electricity including the laws of electromagnetic induction and their more elementary applications.

Course II. A general introductory course.

Honor courses
SENIOR FRESHMEN AND SOPHISTERS
Biochemistry
Senior Freshmen

Principles of biochemistry. Biological macromolecules and their monomers; enzymic catalysis; energy concepts; oxidation-reduction; intermediary metabolism of carbohydrates, lipids and proteins; control of metabolism.

Junior Sophisters[1]

A more detailed study of the work of the Senior Freshman year. The specialised aspects of biochemistry relating to mammals, lower animals, plants and micro-organisms.

Senior Sophisters

The course consists of lectures, tutorial classes, seminars and practical work in advanced biochemistry and biophysics and extends over Michaelmas, Hilary and Trinity terms. During Trinity term candidates must carry out research on a specific biochemical or biophysical problem and present a dissertation.

Botany

Field courses, each lasting about a week, at which attendance is compulsory, are organised for the Senior Freshman and Junior Sophister classes at the beginning of the long vacation. Students may be required to write a practical notebook to record the work of the course.

Senior Freshmen

The course is mainly devoted to the morphology of cryptogams, with some emphasis on their physiology and ecology, and to the morphology of higher vascular plants. There are elementary courses in higher plant ecology and physiology and in world vegetation.

Junior Sophisters[1]

There are courses in physiology of metabolism, growth and development, flora and vegetation of the British Isles, experimental taxonomy, plant pathology, and aspects of palaeobotany, ecology and morphology.

Senior Sophisters

More advanced work is carried out in plant physiology and biochemistry, ecology, mycology, taxonomy and morphology.

Each Senior Sophister is given a research problem on which to work during the year, and he must hand in at the Moderatorship examination a short thesis embodying the results of his investigations, discussed in the light of existing knowledge of the subject.

[1] See under GENETICS below.

Chemistry

The course extends over Michaelmas, Hilary and Trinity terms.

Inorganic chemistry. A more detailed study of the elements and their compounds, based upon atomic structure and position in the periodic classification, with particular emphasis on the comparative aspects of the subject.

Organic chemistry. A study of the chemistry of aliphatic and aromatic compounds.

Physical chemistry. A general course at intermediate level, including reaction kinetics, chemical thermodynamics and electrochemistry.

Practical work. Preparation of some inorganic compounds; qualitative and quantitative inorganic analysis; preparation of typical organic compounds, and the systematic analysis of organic compounds.

JUNIOR SOPHISTERS

The course extends over Michaelmas, Hilary and Trinity terms.

Inorganic chemistry. A course of lectures on the structure and stereochemistry of inorganic compounds.

Physical chemistry. A general course at a more advanced level, including molecular structure, reaction kinetics and mechanisms, chemical spectroscopy and the physics and chemistry of surfaces.

Organic chemistry. A more advanced course dealing with reaction mechanism, stereochemistry, aromaticity and heterocyclic chemistry.

Practical work. One term is allotted to experimental physical chemistry, one to inorganic and one to organic chemistry.

SENIOR SOPHISTERS

The course consists of lectures and practical work in organic chemistry, physical chemistry and inorganic chemistry, and extends over Michaelmas and Hilary terms and over the first fortnight of Trinity term.

Alternative courses A or B may be attended.

Organic chemistry	Reaction mechanisms	A, B
	Natural products based on heterocyclic systems	A, B
	Natural products based on alicyclic and acyclic systems	A
	Seminars	A
	Practical work	A
Inorganic chemistry	Special topics	A, B
	Solid state	B
Physical chemistry	Quantum chemistry	A, B
	Macromolecular chemistry	A, B
	Reaction rate theory	A, B
	Thermodynamics	B
	Modern topics	B
	Seminars	B
	Practical work	B

Honor courses

Genetics

A Junior Sophister student studying biochemistry, botany, microbiology or zoology attends a course in genetics during Michaelmas and Hilary terms. An examination is held immediately before the beginning of the Trinity arts lecture term. If one biological subject is taken in the Junior Sophister year the examination in genetics counts as 20 per cent of the examination in that subject. If two biological subjects are taken the genetics examination counts as 15 per cent of the examination in each of these two subjects.

Senior Sophisters

MICHAELMAS TERM

Cytogenetics of polyploids; spontaneous and induced mutation; nucleic acids; biochemistry of gene expression; genetics of bacteria; elementary statistics; analysis of genetic data; practical cytology.

HILARY TERM

Natural selection; sex, incompatibility and heterothallism; polygenic inheritance; cytology; genetics of viruses; analysis of genetic data; practical genetics.

TRINITY TERM

Human genetics; cytoplasmic inheritance; plant breeding; practical bacterial genetics.

Geography

Senior Freshmen

The course extends over Michaelmas, Hilary and Trinity terms.

Systematic geography. Climate, vegetation and soils.

Regional geography. Detailed study of two major natural regions.

Practical work. Map projections; methods of topographical survey; map construction, map reading and the cartographic representation of data.

A student should have some knowledge of the regional geography of the world, and especially of Europe, when he begins the Senior Freshman honor course. Special field work is allocated at the beginning of Trinity term and the resultant report must be presented before the Michaelmas honor examination of the Senior Freshman year.

All students attend a field course which is normally held during the Easter vacation.

Junior Sophisters

The lectures in Michaelmas, Hilary and Trinity terms include (*a*) a course in geomorphology with detailed study of topographical maps of various countries, and (*b*) studies in either human or historical geography, and in regional geography, with relevant practical work.

Field work is set during this year and students must write essays for discussion and criticism.

Senior Sophisters

The lectures consist mainly of detailed regional studies, together with map work, of various parts of the world, including some of the following: Ireland,

180

Great Britain, France, Scandinavia with Finland, North and South America. There are also lectures on either human or historical geography and some consideration of current writings in geographical literature.

A student must carry out a regional survey of some district in Ireland or Great Britain covering 50–100 square miles, and present a dissertation on the results of his investigations at least one month before the beginning of the moderatorship examination. The district selected must be approved by the Reader in Geography before the end of Trinity term in the Junior Sophister year, so that field work may be done during the summer vacation preceding the Senior Sophister year.

Geology

Senior Freshmen

Mineralogy. Crystal morphology, optics and structure; systematic mineralogy.

Palaeontology (invertebrate). Stratigraphical occurrence and skeletal morphology of major groups; nomenclature and principles of taxonomy.

Physical geology. Nature of the interior and crust of the earth; major features of the earth's surface; denudational processes and the resultant land forms; cycles of erosion.

Map work. Structural interpretation of geological maps.

Field classes. One week's field class during the Easter vacation. Two weeks' field mapping class at the beginning of the summer vacation for all students intending to take geology in their Senior Sophister year.

Junior Sophisters

Igneous petrology. Composition, characters and classification; physico-chemical development of mineral composition and rock texture.

Sedimentary petrology. Environments, sedimentation, and diagenesis; composition, classification; depositional and post-depositional features; heavy mineral suites.

Palaeontology (invertebrate). Functional morphology; methods of generic and specific identification; stratigraphical palaeontology including characteristic fossils and faunal assemblages; palaeoecology and faunal provinces; evolutionary palaeontology.

Stratigraphy. Principles of stratigraphy and palaeontology; Palaeozoic stratigraphy of British Isles and supplementary European areas.

Map work. Structural analysis of geological maps; isopachyte construction.

Field classes. Two weeks' field course during the Easter vacation.

Senior Sophisters

Stratigraphy. Mesozoic and Tertiary of British Isles and supplementary European areas; pre-Cambrian stratigraphy; regional studies of important extra-European areas; Quaternary geology.

Igneous and metamorphic petrology. Regional association and inter-relationships of igneous rocks (rock-suites); physico-chemical processes including crystallisation of silicate-melts; metamorphic rocks; metamorphic facies and grade.

Honor courses

Economic geology. Water-supply, ores, fuel (coal and petroleum) and constructional raw materials; site and foundation geology; geophysical methods.

Structural geology. Mechanics of rock deformation; folding and faulting; textural structures; regional crustal structures (geotectonics); map interpretations.

Surveying. Instrumental; photogrammetry; photogeology.

Palaeontology. Micropalaeontology; geological history and general morphological change of main groups of vertebrates; elementary palaeobotany including palynology and rock-forming algae.

Field classes. Senior Sophisters are expected to do a minimum of four weeks' independent mapping in the summer vacation preceding their Senior Sophister year. There will also be a two weeks' field class in the Easter vacation.

Mathematics

Senior Freshmen

Pure mathematics. Matrices; rank, latent roots. Reduction to canonical form. Quadratic forms.

Functions of several variables: partial differentiation. Taylor's theorem, superposition of small errors. Maxima and minima. Lagrange's method of undetermined multipliers. Jacobians.

Multiple integrals; change of variable.

Ordinary differential equations: simple linear first order equations. Linear equations with constant coefficients. Solution in series. Use of Laplace transform. Simultaneous systems of equations.

Partial differential equations: linear partial differential equations of first and second order in two variables, with applications.

Fourier series and Fourier analysis.

Applied mathematics. Mechanics: particle orbits under inverse square law. Rigid body kinematics. Three-dimensional statics; equivalence to force and couple. Motion of body with axis of symmetry; precession. General motion of rigid body; principal axes. Euler's equations.

Lagrange's equations; action principle. Small oscillations.

Waves in two and three dimensions.

Junior Sophisters

Pure mathematics. Elementary treatment of functions of a complex variable, residue theory and contour integration.

The basic properties of Legendre polynomials and Bessel functions. Formal expansion in Eigen functions. Application to various boundary value problems.

Calculus of variations: Euler's first condition. Isoperimetric problems.

Fourier transforms: application to the solution of boundary value problems.

Integral equations: solution of Fredholm equations with degenerate kernels.

Numerical methods: approximate numerical calculation of integrals. Interpolation. Numerical solution of equations.

Senior Sophisters[1]

Applied mathematics. Electrostatics and gravitation: inverse square law. Derivation of the Laplace and Poisson equations. The Dirac δ-function. Solution of Laplace's equations in different coordinates systems. Solution of simple problems, including use of Legendre polynomials. Applications to magnetostatics, dielectric and permeable materials. The vector potential.

Electromagnetism: magnetic induction. Maxwell's equations. Fourier analysis and the velocity of light. Relativistic form of equations; four-vector potential; field tensor. Lenard-Weichart potential.

Quantum theory: equivalence of waves and particles. Momentum and energy operators. The Schrödinger equation. One-dimensional problems; square well, harmonic oscillator. The hydrogen atom.

Statistical mechanics: ensemble averages. The partition function, energy, specific heats. Applications, including monatomic and diatomic gases. Grand partition function. Chemical equilibrium and the law of mass action. Fluctuations.

Additional mathematics

Senior Freshmen

Prescribed parts of the courses marked with an asterisk in the Senior Freshman honor course in mathematics.

Senior Sophisters

Any *one* of the advanced subjects offered in the Senior Sophister honor course in mathematics.

Microbiology

Junior Sophisters must attend and are examined in courses in general genetics (Michaelmas term) and biochemical genetics (Hilary term).

Senior Freshmen

Michaelmas term. Bacterial cytology. An introduction to soil microbiology.
Hilary term. Systematic bacteriology.
Trinity term. Serology and immunity.

Junior Sophisters[2]

Michaelmas term. Microbiology of water, food and dairy products. Bacteriophages.
Hilary term. Systematic bacteriology.
Trinity term. Microbial physiology and biochemistry. Industrial fermentations.

Senior Sophisters

Michaelmas term. Diagnostic medical microbiology. Virology. Microbial genetics.
Hilary term. Advanced microbiological chemistry.

[1] The course stated is prescribed for students taking physics in their Senior Sophister year; it is an integral part of the physics course.
[2] See under GENETICS above.

Honor courses

Physics

Senior Freshmen

More advanced treatment of properties of matter and of heat, including electrical methods of heat measurement; kinetic theory of gases; introduction to thermodynamics, including applications to thermoelectricity; simpler phenomena of polarisation, interference and diffraction; elementary discussion of thick lenses; a general introduction to atomic physics; electrical and magnetic measurements; electromagnetic induction; alternating currents; elementary theory of thermionic vacuum tubes and of photo-electric cells.

Junior Sophisters

Thermodynamics; elementary theory of spectra; determination of mobilities, charges and masses of ions and electrons; acceleration and focusing of charged particles; conduction of electricity in gases; collision processes; electrical oscillations and wireless; the study of crystalline structures by X-rays and by electron diffraction; nuclear physics; polarised light and geometrical optics; temperature radiation; specific heats at low temperatures; thermionic emission; low temperature work.

Senior Sophisters

The course consists mainly of a more advanced treatment of modern physics. The following subjects are included: interference and diffraction of light, quantum mechanics and statistics; nuclear physics; relativity; magnetism, electromagnetic theory; shortwave oscillations, transmission lines and waveguides; modern solid-state physics.

See also under MATHEMATICS above.

Zoology

Senior Freshmen and Junior Sophisters[1]

A course of vertebrate and invertebrate morphology in alternate years.

Special courses in biochemistry, cytology, embryology, experimental biology, genetics, histology, marine zoology and palaeontology.

Senior Sophisters

A student must study a particular branch of zoology at an advanced level. Special field work, practical work and seminars.

A student must choose a special subject from within the course and devote a proportion of his time to more advanced reading and to practical work in this subject.

[1] See under GENETICS above.

HONOR COURSE IN MODERN LANGUAGES AND LITERATURE

A student may take either courses in two languages, as provided in section A, or a course in English alone, as provided in section B.

A. COURSES IN TWO LANGUAGES

Subjects of study

1. Courses are taken in two of the following subjects: English, French, German, Irish, Italian and Spanish. (Any one of these may also be taken in combination with Latin: for this see HONOR COURSE IN ANCIENT AND MODERN LITERATURE.)

The two subjects are studied equally during the first three years of the course. In the fourth year studies are continued in one language only. The choice of the first language (*i.e.* the language studied in the Senior Sophister year) is made after the Senior Freshman examination and is subject to the approval of the School Committee.

Studies in departments other than English fall generally into three divisions: (1) practical exercises in the spoken and written language (phonetics, conversation, composition, translation); (2) history of the literature, with detailed study of selected literary periods and works; and (3) the historical development of the language, with detailed study of selected linguistic texts. Students are expected to acquaint themselves with the history and the social and political institutions of the country concerned, and they must spend not less than two months as undergraduates in the country of each language in order to fulfil the requirements of their course; students of Irish must spend at least the same length of time in the Gaeltacht. (This requirement can be waived only in exceptional circumstances and with the prior approval of the committee of the School of Modern Languages.)

Admission

2. Students wishing to enter the honor school of Modern Languages and Literature should apply through the Senior Tutor to the School Admission Committee. Applications are considered only from such students as have qualified for general admission and have passed the matriculation examination, or its recognised equivalent, in Latin. Students wishing to read French, German, and Irish must possess an

Honor courses

adequate knowledge of both the spoken and the written language. Italian and Spanish may be studied without previous knowledge of the language, but satisfactory evidence of general linguistic ability is required. In all departments applications are judged on evidence furnished of general intellectual ability and of aptitude for linguistic and literary studies.

Abridgement of course

3. A student may be admitted to the course as a Senior Freshman if, in the opinion of the Admission Committee, he is qualified by his knowledge and attainment to be so, or if he passes the Junior Freshman honor examination with sufficient merit. He must pay a fee before presenting himself for this examination. See COLLEGE CHARGES.

4.   *Examinations*

JUNIOR FRESHMEN

Examinations on the year's work are held in all six languages in Michaelmas term. In order to proceed to the Senior Freshman year in honors, a Junior Freshman must obtain at least third rank honors in both languages at this examination.

SENIOR FRESHMEN

Examinations on the year's work are held in all six languages in Michaelmas term. In order to proceed to the Junior Sophister year in honors, a Senior Freshman must obtain at least third rank honors in both languages at this examination.

JUNIOR SOPHISTERS

Examinations are held in Michaelmas term in all six languages. Candidates take part I of the moderatorship examination in their second language.

For details of papers and marks at moderatorship, part I, see below, under the courses for the various departments.

To proceed to moderatorship, part II, candidates must obtain at least a third class at moderatorship, part I, and perform satisfactorily the exercises prescribed in their first language.

SENIOR SOPHISTERS

Part II of the moderatorship examination is held in Michaelmas term at the end of the Senior Sophister year. Marks obtained for moderatorship, part I, in the second language (maximum 350) are added to those obtained for moderatorship, part II, in the first language (maximum 650). For details of papers and marks at moderatorship, see under the various languages.

186

5. No candidate at any honor or moderatorship examination who fails to satisfy the examiners in writing and speaking the language is allowed to pass.

Phonetics

6. A student attends a course in phonetics in the Junior Freshman year. Only at the discretion of the lecturer may this course be taken subsequently, or credit be obtained for it by examination. A student who has not satisfied this requirement is ineligible for the moderatorship examination.

The Regent House Library

7. Students of modern languages are eligible for membership of the Regent House Library, which contains books and periodicals in French, German, Italian, Spanish and English. Application for membership should be made to the supervisors.

8. The courses in the various departments are as follows:

English

Junior Freshmen

Shakespeare: a general survey, with a special study of *Richard II*, *A midsummer night's dream*, *Measure for measure*, *King Lear*, *Antony and Cleopatra*, *The winter's tale*.

Nineteenth-century poetry: selected poems (as directed) of Blake, Wordsworth, Coleridge, Byron, Shelley, Keats, Tennyson, Browning, Arnold.

Problems of criticism: an introduction to the theory of literature. Special attention is paid to Sidney, *An apology for poetry*; Johnson, *Preface to Shakespeare*; Wordsworth, *Preface to Lyrical ballads*; Coleridge, *Biographia literaria*; Shelley, *A defence of poetry*; M. H. Abrams, *The mirror and the lamp*.

Introduction to the modern novel; including selected novels by James, Joyce, Lawrence, Forster.

Senior Freshmen

Tudor and Stuart drama to 1642: special attention will be given to selected plays by Lyly, Greene, Peele, Kyd, Marlowe, Jonson, Heywood, Dekker, Marston, Chapman, Beaumont and Fletcher, Middleton, Webster, Tourneur, Massinger, Ford.

Poetry and prose, 1550–1640: special attention will be given to (*a*) Wyatt, Spenser, Sidney, Donne, Herbert, *The Oxford book of sixteenth-century verse*, *The metaphysical poets* (ed. H. Gardner); (*b*) Lodge, Nashe, Lyly, Greene, Deloney, Sidney, Bacon, Browne, Earle.

The novel: a study of the novel from Defoe to Hardy. Texts as prescribed by the lecturer.

Honor courses

Junior Sophisters

Poetry, 1640–1798: with special attention to Milton, Dryden, Pope, Thomson, Gray, Collins, Cowper, Crabbe, Burns.

Prose, 1640–1800: with special attention to Milton, Bunyan, Dryden, Swift, Addison, Johnson, Burke.

Restoration drama: with special attention to selected plays by Dryden, Otway, Etherege, Wycherley, Congreve, Farquhar.

Modern Anglo-Irish literature: (a) drama, especially Yeats, Synge, O'Casey; (b) poetry since 1900, including Yeats, Stephens, O'Sullivan, Clarke, Kavanagh; (c) prose, including Joyce, Moore, O'Flaherty, O'Faolain, O'Connor.

Moderatorship examination, part I, papers and marks

For students taking English as their second subject.
1. Poetry and drama, 1550–1642.
2. Poetry and prose: Milton, the Restoration and the eighteenth century.
3. Modern Anglo-Irish literature

All papers are of three hours' duration, are of equal weight, and together carry a maximum of 350 marks.

Moderatorship examination, part II, papers and marks

For students taking English as their first subject.
Papers 1, 2, 3 and any other two papers are to be taken. For courses see Section B below.
1. Shakespeare
2. General paper
3. English literature, 1380–1560.
4. The novel
5. Poetry since 1798
6. The drama since 1660
7. Discursive prose, 1550–1900
8. American literature
9. Old and Middle English philology
10. Old and Middle English literature to 1380

All papers are of three hours' duration and carry equal weight. The maximum mark for the five papers taken is 650.

French

Students beginning this course must possess a good French grammar; Roe and Lough, *French Prose Composition* (Longmans); a good French-English dictionary (the smaller edition of Mansion is especially recommended), and a good general history of French literature, such as L. Cazamian, *A history of French literature* (O.U.P.).

Modern languages and literature

Junior Freshmen

Seventeenth-century literature, with special reference to Molière, *L'école des femmes, Don Juan, Le misanthrope, L'avare, Tartuffe, Le malade imaginaire, Le bourgeois gentilhomme*; Corneille, *L'illusion comique, Le Cid, Horace, Polyeucte, Nicomède*; Racine, *Andromaque, Berénice, Bajazet, Phèdre, Esther, Athalie*; Descartes, *Discours de la méthode* (Manchester); Pascal, *Pensées* (Delmas, Paris); Madame de Sévigné, *Choix de Lettres* (Harrap); and readings from Boileau, La Fontaine, La Rochefoucauld, La Bruyère.

History of the language: Von Wartburg, *Évolution et structure de la langue française*, ch. 1.

Ritchie, *France, a companion to French studies*, ch. 1–4; G. Michaud, *Guide France, Manuel de civilisation française* (Hachette); Evans, *France, a geographical introduction*.

Senior Freshmen

Nineteenth-century poetry and drama, with special reference to *Twelve French poets* (Longmans); Hugo, *Hernani*; Musset, *Lorenzaccio, Un caprice* (Univ. London); Baudelaire, *Les fleurs du mal* (Blackwell); Verlaine, *Selections* (Manchester), *Sagesse* (Cambridge).

The novel, with special reference to Chateaubriand, *Atala*; Constant, *Adolphe*; Stendhal, *Le rouge et le noir*; Balzac, *Le père Goriot*; Flaubert, *Madame Bovary*; Fromentin, *Dominique* (Blackwell); Zola, *Germinal*.

Sixteenth-century literature, with special reference to *The Penguin Book of French verse*, vol. 2; Du Bellay, *Deffence et illustration de la langue françoyse* (Didier); Rabelais, *Pantagruel* (Droz, Geneva); Montaigne, *Selected essays* (Manchester, 3rd edition).

Medieval French: *La chanson de Roland*, vv. 703–1260; Von Wartburg, *op cit.*, ch. 2–4.

Phonetics: L. Armstrong, *The phonetics of French*.

Ritchie, *op. cit.*, ch. 5–8.

Junior Sophisters

Eighteenth-century prose, with special reference to Voltaire, *Zadig* (Oxford), *Candide* (Blackwell), *Lettres philosophiques* (Blackwell); Montesquieu, *Lettres persanes*; Rousseau, *Discours sur l'inégalité, Rêveries d'un promeneur solitaire* (Manchester).

Eighteenth-century comedy, with special reference to Le Sage, *Turcaret*; Marivaux, *Le jeu de l'amour et du hasard, Les fausses confidences*; Beaumarchais, *Le barbier de Séville* (Blackwell), *Le mariage de Figaro* (Blackwell).

The novel, with special reference to Madame de Lafayette, *La princesse de Clèves*; Prévost, *Manon Lescaut*; Diderot, *Le neveu de Rameau*; Rousseau, *La Nouvelle Héloïse*.

Twentieth-century literature, with special reference to Barrès, *Colette Baudoche*; Giraudoux, *Bella*; Mauriac, *Thérèse Desqueyroux* (Univ. London); Gide, *Les nourritures terrestres, Les nouvelles nourritures*; Martin du Gard, *Le*

Honor courses

cahier gris, Le pénitencier, La belle saison; Camus, *L'étranger, La peste*; N. Sarraute, *Le planétarium*.

Medieval French: *Le mystère d'Adam* (Manchester); Béroul, *Tristan* (Blackwell), vv. 1–1773; Villon, *Oeuvres* (CFMA); Von Wartburg, *op. cit.*, ch. 5–7.

Ritchie, *op. cit.*, ch. 8–11; Sayce, *Style in French prose. A method of analysis* (Oxford).

Moderatorship examination, part I, papers and marks

For students taking French as their second subject.

1. Prose composition	70
and unseen translation	30
2. History of the language	80
3. Literature	120
4. *Viva voce* examination	50

All papers are of three hours' duration. 350

Moderatorship examination, part II, papers and marks

For students taking French as their first subject.

1. Prose composition	100
2. Unseen translation	40
and essay in French	40
3. History of the language	75
4. Literature I (to 1600)	80
5. Literature II (1600–1800)	80
6. Literature III (1800 to the present)	100
7. Special subject	75
8. *Viva voce* examination	60

650

All papers are of three hours' duration. For paper 7, a number of alternative subjects are announced annually, covering the medieval, classical and modern periods; one of these subjects must be chosen, and approved, before the end of the Junior Sophister year.

The following subjects are set for 1966–7

The medieval religious drama in France.

The Troubadours.

Literary theory from the Pleiade to Boileau

The precursors of Corneille.

The eighteenth-century encyclopedists.

French comedy in the eighteenth century.

The personal novel in the nineteenth century.

The origin and evolution of free verse in nineteenth-century France.

The development of European pre-Romanticism in the eighteenth century.

Surrealism.

Modern languages and literature

Details of prescribed texts and a list of recommended books may be obtained from the Professor of French.

German

A student taking this course should possess and consult a good German grammar, *e.g.*, Jude, *Deutsche Grammatik* (Westermann), a suitable German-English and English-German dictionary such as *A German and English dictionary*, ed. Betteridge (Cassell), and J. G. Robertson, *A history of German literature* (new edition, revised by Edna Purdie).

Junior Freshmen

An anthology of German poetry 1730-1830, ed. Bithell; Novalis, *Heinrich von Ofterdingen, Hymnen an die Nacht* and *Geistliche Lieder* (Blackwell); Tieck, *Der blonde Eckbert*, and Brentano, *Geschichte vom braven Kasperl und dem schönen Annerl*, ed. Atkinson; Heine, *Poems*, ed. Webber; Heinrich von Kleist, *Prinz Friedrich von Homburg*, ed. Samuel; Grillparzer, *Sappho*, ed. Spalding; Halm, *Die Marzipan-Lise*, ed. Thomas; Mörike, *Mozart auf der Reise nach Prag*; Keller, *Two stories*, ed. Thomas; Meyer, *Die Versuchung des Pescara*, ed. Williams; *Germany, a companion to German studies*, ed. Bithell.

Senior Freshmen

Wright, *Middle High German primer*, 5th ed., pp. 1-83, 138-146, 163-178; Lessing, *Minna von Barnhelm, Nathan der Weise*; Goethe, *Götz von Berlichingen, Poems*, ed. Boyd; Schiller, *Wallenstein*, ed Witte, *Wilhelm Tell*; Lenz, *Die Soldaten* (Cambridge Plain Texts); Herder and Goethe, *Von deutscher Art und Kunst* (Oxford), ed. Purdie; H.v. Kleist, *Three stories*, ed. Garland (Manchester); Hebbel, *Maria Magdalena*.

Junior Sophisters

Barber, *Old High German reader*; Braune, *Abriss der althochdeutschen Grammatik*; *Das Nibelungenlied*, ed. Bartsch-de Boor; *Deutsche Barock-Lyrik*, ed. Cysarz (Reclam); Goethe, *Faust, Iphigenie auf Tauris, Torquato Tasso, Die Leiden des jungen Werthers*; Schiller, *Maria Stuart*; Storm, *Von Meer nud Heide* (Knaur); Keller, *Der Landvogt von Greifensee* (Blackwell), ed, Fairley; Mörike, *Poems*, ed. Thomas; G. Hauptmann, *Die Weber*; Hugo von Hofmannsthal, *Der Tor und der Tod*, ed. Gilbert; Kafka, *Das Urteil* (Fischer); Thomas Mann, *Der Tod in Venedig und andere Erzählungen* (Fischer); Gertrud von le Fort, *Am Tor des Himmels* (Insel): Bergengruen, *Der Grosstyrann und das Gericht*; Brecht, *Mutter Courage*; *Ergriffenes Dasein*, ed. Holthusen and Kemp (Wilhelm Langewiesche-Brandt); Frisch, *Andorra*.

Moderatorship examination, part I, papers and marks

For students taking German as their second subject.

1. Prose composition	100
2. Unseen translation	40

Honor courses

3. Literature	80
4. Old and Middle High German	80
5. *Viva voce* examination	50
	350

Papers 1, 3 and 4 are of three hours' duration. Paper 2 is of one and a half hours' duration.

Papers 3 and 4 are based on periods, authors and works studied in the three preceding years.

Moderatorship examination, part II, papers and marks

For students taking German as their first subject.

1. Prose composition	100
2. Unseen translation	40
3. Essay in German	40
4. Seventeenth and eighteenth-century literature	80
5. Nineteenth and twentieth-century literature	80
6. History of the language, Old High German and Middle High German	100
7. Medieval literature	80
8. Special subject	80
9. *Viva voce* examination	50
	650

All papers are of three hours' duration, except paper 2, which is of one and a half hours' duration.

For 1966-7 there will be a choice of special subjects (paper 8). Details of these and of prescribed texts may be obtained from the Professor of German.

Irish

Junior Freshmen

Ó Cadhain, *Idir shúgradh agus dáiríre*; Ó Flaithearta, *Dúil*; *Scothscéalta le Pádraic Ó Conaire*, *The Irish of Cois Fhairrge*, *Gaeilge Chois Fhairrge*, *an deilbhíocht*, ed. de Bhaldraithe; Bergin, *Stories from Keating*; *Cath Fionntrágha*, ed. O'Rahilly; Corkery, *The hidden Ireland*.

Senior Freshmen

Ó Laoghaire, *Séadna*; Ó Criomhthain, *An tOileánach*; *Caoine Airt Uí Laoghaire*, ed. Ó Tuama; Mac an tSaoi, *Margadh na saoire*; Ó Cuiv, *Párliament na mban*, *The Irish of West Muskerry*, *Irish dialects and Irish-speaking districts*; Knott, *Irish syllabic poetry*; Sjoestedt-Jonval, *Un parler irlandais de Kerry*.

Junior Sophisters

Knott, *The poems of Tadhg Dall Ó Huiginn*; O'Rahilly, *Dánta grádha*; Keating, *Trí biorghaoithe an bháis*; Ó Cuiv (ed.), *Seven centuries of Irish learning*. Máire, *Cioth is dealán*, *Caisleán óir*; Seosamh Mac Grianna, *Mo bhealach féin*; Ó Cadhain, *Cré na cille*; I. A. Macdhomhnuill, *Críochan Úra*.

Sommerfelt, *The dialect of Torr*; O'Rahilly, *Irish dialects past and present*; Jackson, *Common Gaelic*; Borgström, *Dialects of the Outer Hebrides*.

Moderatorship examination, part I, papers and marks

For students taking Irish as their second subject.

1. Classical Irish literature, 1200–1600	75
2. Modern Irish literature, 1850 to the present day	75
3. The modern dialects, including Scottish Gaelic	75
4. Composition and translation	75
5. *Viva voce* examination	50

All papers are of three hours' duration.   350

Moderatorship examination, part II, papers and marks

For students taking Irish as their first subject.

1. Prose composition	100
2. Unseen translation (from Irish and Scottish Gaelic)	100
3. Classical Irish language and literature, 1200–1600	100
4. Irish literature, 1600 to the present day	100
5. The modern dialects, including Scottish Gaelic and Manx	100
6. Special subject	100
7. *Viva voce* examination	50

All papers are of three hours' duration.   650

The alternative special subjects for paper 6 are (*a*) The history of the Irish language to 1200, (*b*) Scottish Gaelic literature from 1700 to the present day.

Students wishing to take moderatorship, part II, should apply to the Professor of Irish for a list of recommended books at the beginning of the Junior Sophister year.

Italian

Students beginning this course should possess copies of D. Lennie and M. Grego, *Italian for you*. They should also possess a good Italian dictionary: those by M. Hazon, G. Orlandi and N. Spinelli are particularly recommended. Students will also require a standard history of Italian literature, such as N. Sapegno, *Disegno storico della letteratura italiana*, or E. H. Wilkins, *A history of Italian literature*.

During their first year, students are expected to acquaint themselves with the broad features of Italian history and civilisation. Books especially recommended for this purpose are Jamison, Ady, Vernon and Terry, *Italy Medieval and Modern*; D. Pettoello, *An Outline of Italian Civilisation*; D. Mack Smith, *Italy*. A more detailed reading list is available on application to the Reader in Italian.

Junior Freshmen

Drama after 1880: Verga, *Teatro* (Mondadori); Pirandello, *Così è (se vi pare)*

193

H

Honor courses

(Mondadori), *Il berretto a sonagli, Il piacere dell'onestà, La giara* (Mondadori); Betti, *Two Plays* (Manchester University Press).

The novel after 1880: D'Annunzio, *Il piacere* (Mondadori); Svevo, *La coscienza di Zeno*.

Senior Freshmen

Italian literature of the eighteenth and nineteenth centuries, with special reference to the following texts: Parini, *Le odi* (BUR); Goldoni, *La locandiera, Il ventaglio, La vedova scaltra*; Alfieri, *Antologia alfieriana* (Soc. editrice Dante Alighieri); Leopardi, *Canti* (BUR); Manzoni, *I promessi sposi* (BUR); Carducci, *Antologia carducciana* (Zanichelli).

Camilli, *Pronuncia e grafia dell'italiano.*

Further lists of required reading, in connection with the introductory courses on Dante and the Renaissance held in Trinity term, will be issued by the lecturers concerned.

Sophisters

Course A and course B are given in alternate years. Junior and Senior Sophisters attend together.

Course A: 1966–7 and alternate years

Dante, *Inferno.*

Early literature, including a study of works by Iacopone, Guittone d'Arezzo, Compagni, Guinizelli, Dante, Cavalcanti, Cino da Pistoia, Petrarch, Boccaccio, and Sacchetti.

Literature from Tasso to Metastasio, including a study of works by Tasso, Marino, Galilei, Tassoni, Vico, Metastasio, and the Arcadian poets.

Course B: 1967–8 and alternate years

Dante, *Purgatorio.*

Renaissance literature, including a study of works by Poliziano, Lorenzo de' Medici, Pulci, Boiardo, Sannazaro, Ariosto, Machiavelli, Della Casa, Castiglione, Tasso, and Guarini.

Modern Italian literature, including a study of works by Parini, Foscolo, Manzoni, Leopardi, D'Annunzio, Verga, Pascoli and Pirandello.

Junior Sophisters reading Italian as their first subject, and Senior Sophisters, also attend courses on the history of the Italian language. Details of prescribed books may be obtained from the Reader in Italian.

Moderatorship examination, part I, papers and marks

For students taking Italian as their second subject.

1. Prose composition ⎱	100
2. Unseen translation ⎰	
3. Dante	50
4. Literature I	75
5. Literature II	75
6. *Viva voce*	50
	350

Papers 1 and 2 are of one and a half hours' duration, paper 3 of two hours' duration, and papers 4 and 5 of three hours' duration.

Moderatorship examination, part II, papers and marks
For students taking Italian as their first subject

1. Prose composition	75
2. Unseen translations	50
3. Dante	75
4. Literature I	100
5. Literature II	100
6. Essay in Italian	50
7. Special subject	75
8. History of the Italian language	75
9. *Viva voce*	50
	650

All papers are of three hours' duration, except papers 2 and 7, which are of two hours' duration.

The special subject (paper 7) for 1966–7 is 'Le commedie del primo Cinquecento'.

Spanish

Students beginning the study of Spanish require H. Ramsden, *An essential course in modern Spanish* (Harrap). All students require a good reference grammar, such as M. M. Ramsey, *A textbook of modern Spanish* (Revised Spaulding), or Harmer and Norton, *A manual of modern Spanish* (Univ. Tutorial Press); a suitable bilingual dictionary, such as E. B. Williams, *Holt's Spanish-English and English-Spanish dictionary*, or Martínez Amador, *English-Spanish and Spanish-English dictionary*; and a suitable Spanish dictionary, such as Vox, *Diccionario general ilustrado de la lengua española* (Madrid); a comprehensive history of literature, such as J. Hurtado and A. González Palencia, *Historia de la literatura española* (Madrid); W. C. Atkinson, *A history of Spain and Portugal* (Pelican); T. Navarro Tomás, *Arte del verso* (Mexico).

All students must obtain the list of required and recommended reading, available in the Department of Spanish on the first day of lectures in Michaelmas term.

Tuition in elementary Spanish is given to students without previous knowledge of the language during the first two terms of the Junior Freshman year. In their third term they join the other students in translation classes and in the study of advanced Spanish grammar.

Junior Freshmen

An introduction to modern Spanish literature, *c*. 1860–1960.

Poetry and drama: a general survey of development, with special attention to works by Darío, A. Machado, García Lorca, and poems in *Siete Poetas Españoles* (Taurus).

The novel and discursive prose: a general survey of development, with

Honor courses

special attention to works by Pérez Galdós, Unamuno, Pérez de Ayala, Cela. Outlines of Spanish history and culture.

Senior Freshmen and Junior Sophisters

Literature of the Golden Age. Versification.

Courses A and B are given in alternate years. Senior Freshmen and Junior Sophisters attend together.

Junior Sophisters reading Spanish as their first language also study the history of the language from Vulgar Latin to c. 1400, with selected *Textos lingüísticos del medioevo español*, ed. Gifford and Hodcroft (Dolphin).

Course A: 1967-8 and alternate years

Prose fiction, with special attention to Cervantes.

Drama, with special attention to Torres Naharro, Gil Vicente, Cervantes, Lope de Vega, Tirso de Molina, Ruiz de Alarcón, Moreto, Calderón.

Course B: 1966-7 and alternate years

Prose fiction, with special attention to *La Celestina*, *Lazarillo de Tormes* and works by Alemán, and Quevedo.

Poetry, with special attention to Garcilaso, Luis de León. San Juan de la Cruz, Góngora, Quevedo, and *Oxford Book of Spanish verse* pp. 59-74 and 443-460.

Moderatorship examination, part I, papers and marks

For students taking Spanish as their second subject.

1. Translation from and into Spanish	140
2. Modern literature: special authors	80
3. Literature of the Golden Age	100
4. *Viva voce* examination	30
	350

All papers are of three hours' duration.

The special authors for paper 2 are Pérez Galdós, Unamuno, A. Machado, García Lorca.

Senior Sophisters

Literature of the Golden Age: a more extensive study of works by authors studied in the Senior Freshman and Junior Sophister years, with, in addition, Menéndez Pidal, *Flor nueva de romances viejos* (Austral), and works by Gracián.

Medieval literature: a general survey of development, with special attention to the *Poema del Cid*, *Poema de Fernán González* (Clás. cast.), *Libro de buen amor*; works by Juan Manuel, Diego de San Pedro, Juan de Mena, Santillana, Jorge Manrique.

History of the language: late medieval and Golden-Age Spanish; modern Spanish dialects.

Special subject. There will be tutorial guidance but no lectures in the following subjects, one of which must be chosen at the commencement of the Senior Sophister year: (i) Cervantes, (ii) Pérez Galdós, (iii) American Spanish.

Moderatorship examination, part II, papers and marks

For students taking Spanish as their first subject.

1. Translation into Spanish	100
2. Translation from Spanish and Spanish essay	80
3. History of the language and versification	80
4. Modern literature: special authors	80
5. Literature of the Golden Age	100
6. Medieval literature	80
7. Special subject	80
8. *Viva voce* examination	50

All papers are of three hours' duration.   650

The special authors for paper 4 are Pérez Galdós, Unamuno, A. Machado, and García Lorca.

B. COURSE IN ENGLISH LITERATURE AND LANGUAGE

1. A student may take a course in English literature and language alone; he may also take English in combination with one of the languages, French, German, Irish, Italian, Spanish (see section A above), or with Latin (see ANCIENT AND MODERN LITERATURE).

Admission

2. To be considered for admission to take the course in English literature and language alone, a candidate must have qualified for general admission and have passed the matriculation examination, or its recognised equivalent, in Latin. He must also normally have obtained good passes in the matriculation examination (or an approved certificate examination at honor or advanced level) in English and in one of the languages French, German, Irish, Italian, Spanish, Latin, Greek.

Abridgement of course

3. A student may be admitted to the course as a Senior Freshman if, in the opinion of the Admission Committee, he is qualified by his knowledge and attainment to be so, or if he passes the Junior Freshman honor examination with sufficient merit. He must pay a fee before presenting himself for this examination. See COLLEGE CHARGES.

Subjects of study and examinations

4. The Junior Freshman year, introducing different periods and kinds of literature, provides a training in the methods of studying literature and language. The annual examination is held in Michaelmas term at the end of the Junior Freshman year. A student failing to reach a satisfactory standard is not allowed to continue the honor course.

Honor courses

The work of the Senior Freshman and Junior Sophister years forms the course for part I of the moderatorship examination, which is taken in Michaelmas term at the end of the Junior Sophister year. (An examination is also held in Michaelmas term at the end of the Senior Freshman year.)

The course of study for part II of the moderatorship examination offers opportunities of specialising. The examination papers are not confined to the subjects of the lecture courses given in the Senior Sophister year. All students must take a general paper.

In addition to attending the prescribed lectures, a student must write essays for discussion in class and also terminal essays.

COURSES AND EXAMINATIONS
Junior Freshmen
Courses

Shakespeare: a general survey, with a special study of *Richard II*, *A midsummer night's dream*, *Measure for measure*, *King Lear*, *Antony and Cleopatra*, *The winter's tale*.

Nineteenth-century poetry: selected poems (as directed) of Blake, Wordsworth, Coleridge, Byron, Shelley, Keats, Tennyson, Browning, Arnold.

Problems of criticism: an introduction to the theory of literature. Special attention is paid to Sidney, *An apology for poetry*; Johnson, *Preface to Shakespeare*; Wordsworth, *Preface to Lyrical ballads*; Coleridge, *Biographia literaria*; Shelley, *A defence of poetry*; M. H. Abrams, *The mirror and the lamp*.

Anglo-Irish literature, 1800–1900: a study of the prose, poetry and drama, including the beginning of the literary revival.

Introduction to the modern novel; including selected novels by James, Joyce, Lawrence, Forster.

Anglo-Saxon grammar and phonology, with a special study of selected passages from Sweet, *Anglo-Saxon primer*, and Sweet, *Anglo-Saxon reader*.

Examination

1. Shakespeare. 2. Romantic poetry. 3. English language. 4. Anglo-Irish literature. 5. Criticism.

Senior Freshmen
Courses

Tudor and Stuart drama to 1642: special attention will be given to selected plays by Lyly, Greene, Peele, Kyd, Marlowe, Jonson, Heywood, Dekker, Marston, Chapman, Beaumont and Fletcher, Middleton, Webster, Tourneur, Massinger, Ford.

Poetry and prose, 1550–1640: special attention will be given to (a) Wyatt, Spenser, Sidney, Donne, Herbert, *The Oxford book of sixteenth-century verse*, *The metaphysical poets* (ed. H. Gardner); (b) Lodge, Nashe, Lyly, Greene, Deloney, Sidney, Bacon, Browne, Earle.

The novel: a study of the novel from Defoe to Hardy, with special study of selected works.

Medieval literature: (a) Early English drama; (b) Chaucer and Langland, as directed by the lecturer.

Old English poetry, with a special study of *Beowulf, The Fight at Finnsburg, Widsith,* and *Deor's Lament.*

Examination

1. Prose and drama. 2. The novel. 3. Selected poems. 4. Medieval literature. 5. Old English poetry.

Junior Sophisters

Courses

Poetry, 1640-1798: with special attention to Milton, Dryden, Pope, Thomson, Gray, Collins, Cowper, Crabbe, Burns.

Prose, 1640-1800: with special attention to Milton, Bunyan, Dryden, Swift, Addison, Johnson, Burke.

Restoration drama: with special attention to selected plays by Dryden, Otway, Etherege, Wycherley, Congreve.

Modern Anglo-Irish literature: (a) drama, especially Yeats, Synge, O'Casey; (b) poetry since 1900, including Yeats, Stephens, O'Sullivan, Clarke, Kavanagh; (c) prose, including Joyce, Moore, O'Flaherty, O'Faolain, O'Connor.

The fourteenth century: with a special study of *Sir Orfeo; The Harley lyrics; Sir Gawain and the Green Knight; Pearl; The parlement of the three ages; Winner and Waster.*

Modern English philology: (a) development of the language from Chaucer to the present day, with a study of selected texts; (b) modern English structure.

Moderatorship examination, part I

A candidate takes six papers, as follows:

1. Poetry and drama, 1550-1642.
2. Poetry and prose: Milton, the Restoration and the eighteenth century.
3. Modern Anglo-Irish literature.
4. Old English.
5. Middle English.
6. Modern English.

All papers are of three hours duration. Forty per cent of the total moderatorship marks are allotted to part I of the examination.

Senior Sophisters

Courses

(Choice of courses is governed by the papers the candidate is taking at part II of the moderatorship examination.)

Honor courses

Shakespeare: a study of a selected group of plays, with a general survey of text, stage and sources.

Poetry since 1850.

The modern novel.

Nineteenth-century prose (excluding the novel).

Drama since 1700.

American literature.

Late medieval literature, from 1380 to 1560.

Old and Middle English philology.

Old and Middle English literature to 1380.

Moderatorship examination, part II

Papers are set as follows: papers 1, 2 and any other three papers are to be taken.

1. Shakespeare.
2. General paper.
3. English literature, 1380–1560.
4. The novel.
5. Poetry since 1798.
6. The drama from 1660.
7. Discursive prose, 1550–1900.
8. American literature.
9. Old and Middle English philology.
10. Old and Middle English literature to 1380.

All papers are of three hours' duration and carry equal weight. Sixty per cent of the total moderatorship marks are allotted to part II of the examination.

HONOR COURSE IN ANCIENT AND MODERN LITERATURE[1]

Admission

1. A student wishing to take the course in Ancient and Modern Literature must apply through the Senior Tutor to the Ancient and Modern Literature Admission Committee. He must have satisfied the requirements of the matriculation examination in Latin.

Abridgement of course

2. A student may be admitted to the course as a Senior Freshman if, in the opinion of the Admission Committee, he is qualified by his knowledge and attainment to be so, or if he passes the Junior Freshman honor examination with sufficient merit. He must pay a fee before presenting himself for this examination. See COLLEGE CHARGES.

Subjects of study

3. A student pursues a course in Latin and one language chosen from English, French, German, Irish, Italian or Spanish. He attends a course in comparative philology during the Freshman years. He attends a course in phonetics in the Junior Freshman year; only at the discretion of the lecturer may this course be taken subsequently, or credit be obtained for it by examination.

The languages are studied equally during the first three years of the course. In the fourth year studies are continued in one language only. The choice of the first language (*i.e.* the language studied in the Senior Sophister year) is made after the Senior Freshman examination and is subject to the approval of the School Committee.

Examinations

4. Honor examinations are held in Hilary term (in Latin) and Michaelmas term (in both languages) for Junior Freshmen and in Michaelmas term for Senior Freshmen.

In the Junior Sophister year examinations are held in Michaelmas term. Students take part I of the moderatorship examination in their second language. Part II of the moderatorship examination is held in the Michaelmas term following the Senior Sophister year. Marks obtained at moderatorship part I in the second language (maximum

[1] Regulations applying to students who entered in or before 1961 are as in the *Calendar* for 1961-2. pp. 189-91.

Honor courses

350) are added to those obtained at moderatorship part II in the first language (maximum 650).

A student cannot obtain honors or a moderatorship in both ancient and modern literature and classics, nor can he obtain honors or a moderatorship in both ancient and modern literature and modern languages and literature unless he offers different modern languages in each.

COURSES AND EXAMINATIONS

Freshmen

Courses

LATIN

As for students in the School of Classics. Students also attend a special course in medieval Latin.

MODERN LANGUAGE

As for students in the School of Modern Languages and Literature.

Examinations

Junior Freshmen are examined in Hilary term on the course of the preceding term in Latin. They are examined in Michaelmas term on the course of the three preceding terms in their modern language and in Latin.

To obtain credit for the Junior Freshman year a student must gain honors in both Latin and his modern language at the Michaelmas examination. Credit for the Senior Freshman year is obtained by gaining honors in the modern language and Latin in Michaelmas term.

Unless exempted by the School Committee a student must present himself at all the Freshman examinations.

Sophisters

Courses

LATIN

The course in Latin is spread over the two Sophister years, and Junior and Senior Sophisters attend lectures together. A special course in medieval Latin is given each year. For details apply to the lecturer.

1966–7 and alternate years

Michaelmas term. Latin oratory, with special attention to Cicero.
Hilary term. Latin elegy, with special attention to Propertius.
Trinity term. Roman historians, with special attention to Tacitus.

1967–8 and alternate years

Michaelmas term. Latin comedy, with special attention to Plautus.
Hilary term. Latin epic, with special attention to Virgil.
Trinity term. Roman education, with special attention to Quintilian.

MODERN LANGUAGE
As for students in the School of Modern Languages and Literature.

Examinations

A student taking Latin as his second language is examined in moderatorship part I on the course for the three preceding terms. Marks are distributed as follows:

Composition	50
Translation	100
Prescribed authors I	100
Prescribed authors II	100
	350

For the corresponding arrangements in the case of the modern language see HONOR COURSE IN MODERN LANGUAGES AND LITERATURE.

In moderatorship part II marks in Latin are allotted as follows:

Composition	50
Translation	100
Literature I	100
Literature II	100
Literature III	100
Special subject	100
General paper	50
Essay	50
	650

For the distribution of marks in the modern language see HONOR COURSE IN MODERN LANGUAGES AND LITERATURE.

Passages are set for unseen translation selected from Latin classical and medieval authors generally. Candidates are further examined in composition (prose composition being compulsory, verse composition optional), in grammar and textual criticism, and in literary history and appreciation. The general paper contains questions on history, literature, ancient thought and philology. The subjects for the essay emphasise the continuity of the classical tradition in modern life and letters.

Early in his Senior Sophister year a candidate for moderatorship part II in Latin must inform the appropriate professor or lecturer of his choice of special subject, which must be in one of the following fields: history, archaeology, literature, ancient thought, philology.

HONOR COURSES IN EARLY AND MODERN IRISH AND IN CELTIC LANGUAGES

Admission

1. A student intending to take the honor course in early and modern Irish or the honor course in Celtic languages must have a matriculation qualification in Latin, and must satisfy the general requirements for admission to the University.

Abridgement of course

2. A student may be admitted to the course as a Senior Freshman if, in the opinion of the School Committee, he is qualified by his knowledge and attainment to be so, or if he passes the Junior Freshman honor examination with sufficient merit. He must pay a fee before presenting himself for this examination. See COLLEGE CHARGES.

Subjects of study

3. In the two Freshman years the courses in early and modern Irish and in Celtic languages are the same. Old and middle Irish are studied, together with modern Irish. In the Junior Freshman year a student attends a course in phonetics.

4. In the Sophister years either the course in early and modern Irish or the course in Celtic languages may be taken.

A student of early and modern Irish takes, in his Junior Sophister year, a course in old and middle Irish and in history of the Irish language and literature to 1200 A.D., as prescribed below. In his Senior Sophister year he takes the course prescribed for Senior Sophister students in modern languages and literature taking Irish as their first language, but he must present Scottish Gaelic literature as his special subject at the moderatorship examination, part II.

A student of Celtic languages takes, in his Junior Sophister year, the course prescribed for Junior Sophister students in modern languages and literature taking Irish as their second language, but at the moderatorship examination, part I, he substitutes a paper in Welsh for the paper in modern Irish literature from 1850. In his Senior Sophister year he takes a course in old and middle Irish, Irish palaeography, medieval and modern Welsh texts, history, literature and comparative philology, as prescribed below.

Examinations

5. A student must pass an examination each year. The examinations

are held at the beginning of the Michaelmas term following the completion of the year. The examination held at the end of the Junior Sophister year is part I of the moderatorship examination; the examination held at the end of the Senior Sophister year is part II of the moderatorship examination.

In the Freshman years equal marks are assigned to early and to modern Irish, and students are required to satisfy the examiners in each. At all examinations on early Irish, questions are set on the manuscript sources of the Irish texts studied.

Phonetics

6. A course of lectures is given by the Lecturer in Phonetics and Linguistics, and should be attended in the Junior Freshman year. Only at the discretion of the lecturer may this course be taken subsequently, or credit be obtained for it by examination. A student who has not satisfied this requirement is ineligible for the moderatorship examination.

COURSES AND EXAMINATIONS
Junior Freshmen
Course

J. Strachan, *Old-Irish paradigms and selections from the old-Irish glosses*, 4th ed. (1949), *An old-Irish homily* (Ériu iii, 1–10), *Stories from the Táin*, 3rd ed. (1944); *Táin bó Fraích*; G. Murphy, *Early Irish lyrics*, poems 13–24.

E. C. Quiggin, 'Irish language and Irish literature', in article CELT, *Encyclopaedia Britannica*, 11th ed. (1910); *Early Irish society*, ed. M. Dillon (Cultural Relations Committee 1954); E. MacNeill, *Phases of Irish history*; J. Carney, *Studies in Irish literature and history*, chs 1–3.

Examination
Michaelmas term: Old and middle Irish, and modern Irish.

Senior Freshmen
Course

R. Thurneysen, *Old Irish reader*; *Bethu Patraic, pars prima*; *Serglige Con Culaind*; *Immram curaig Maíle Dúin* (including metrical version); *Echtra Chondla*; *Fís Adamnáin*; G. Murphy, *Early Irish lyrics*, poems 3–7, 9–12.

E. MacNeill, *Celtic Ireland*; T. F. O'Rahilly, *Early Irish history and mythology*, chs 1–5; C. S. Boswell, *An Irish precursor of Dante*; A. Nutt, *The happy other world*, in K. Meyer, *Imram Brain*, vol. 1.

Examination
Michaelmas term: Old and middle Irish, modern Irish.

Honor courses

EARLY AND MODERN IRISH

Junior Sophisters

Course

The Würzburg glosses on *Romans*, chs 1–8; *the old-Irish life of St. Brigit*; *Tochmarc Étaíne*; *Togail bruidne Da Dergae*; *Scéla muicce Meic Da Thó*; *Mesca Ulad*; G. Murphy, *Early Irish lyrics*, poems 25–37.

R. Thurneysen, *Die irische Helden- und Königsage*, pt 1; T. F. O'Rahilly, *Early Irish history and mythology*, ch 6; J. Carney, *Studies in Irish literature and history*, chs iv–vi, viii.

Moderatorship examination, part I

Papers are set as follows:

		Marks
1.	Old Irish	100
2.	Middle Irish	100
3.	History of the language	75
4.	History of literature	75
		350

Senior Sophisters

Course

A student intending to proceed to the Senior Sophister year in early and modern Irish should apply, at the beginning of his Junior Sophister year, to the Professor of Irish for a list of recommended books. See HONOR COURSE IN MODERN LANGUAGES AND LITERATURE, Irish.

Moderatorship examination, part II

For the papers set at this examination, and the marks assigned, see HONOR COURSE IN MODERN LANGUAGES AND LITERATURE, Irish. A student taking the course in early and modern Irish must take Scottish Gaelic literature as his special subject.

CELTIC LANGUAGES

Junior Sophisters

Course

The course is that prescribed in modern Irish for the Junior Sophister year of the honor course in modern languages and literature, substituting for literature from 1850 the following course in Welsh:

J. Strachan, *An introduction to early Welsh*, pp. 1–136; *Pwyll Pendeuic Dyfet*; C. O'Rahilly, *Ireland and Wales*.

Moderatorship examination, part I

For the papers set at this examination, and the marks assigned, see HONOR COURSE IN MODERN LANGUAGES AND LITERATURE, Irish. A student taking the course in Celtic languages takes a paper in Welsh in place of the paper in modern Irish literature, 1850 to the present day.

Senior Sophisters

Course

The Würzburg glosses on *Romans*, chs 9–16; the Milan glosses on the commentary on *Psalms* 1–8; *Táin bó Cúailnge*; *Fled Bricrend*; *Fingal Rónáin*; *Críth gablach*; *Félire Óengusso*, Prologue; J. Carney, *The Poems of Blathmacc son of Cú Brettan* (Irish Texts Society xlvii).

E. MacNeill, *Notes on the Irish Ogham inscriptions* (Proceedings of the Royal Irish Academy, 1909).

J. Strachan, *An introduction to early Welsh*, pp. 139–226, 237–42; *Pedeir Keinc y Mabinogi*; selected poems from T. Parry, *Oxford book of Welsh verse*.

Comparative philology, with special reference to the Celtic languages.

Elements of Irish palaeography.

T. F. O'Rahilly, *The Goidels and their predecessors, The two Patricks*; D. A. Binchy, *The linguistic value of the Irish law tracts*; E. MacNeill, *Early Irish laws and institutions*; T. Parry, *A history of Welsh literature*, with special reference to chs 1–4; I. Williams, *Lectures on early Welsh poetry*; P. Mac Cana, *Branwen daughter of LLyr*.

Moderatorship examination, part II

Papers are set as follows:

		Marks
1.	Old Irish I	100
2.	Old Irish II	100
3.	Middle Irish and metrics	75
4.	Philology and Ogham	100
5.	History and literature	75
6.	Welsh I	100
7.	Welsh II	100
		650

HONOR COURSE IN HEBREW AND SEMITIC LANGUAGES

Admission

1. Application for admission to the School of Hebrew and Semitic Languages should be made to the Senior Tutor. Applicants must satisfy the requirements for general admission to the university.

Subjects of study

2. Lectures are provided in Hebrew, Aramaic, Syriac and Arabic.

JUNIOR FRESHMAN YEAR. The lectures are devoted to the basic study of Hebrew grammar and the prescribed texts. Apart from the purely linguistic aspect of the language, instruction is given in the general history of ancient Israel.

Students entering the School of Hebrew and Semitic Languages without matriculation qualifications in Greek must attend the introductory course in either classical or Hellenistic Greek and pass a special examination arranged by the Professor.

SENIOR FRESHMAN YEAR. A student continues with the study of advanced Hebrew grammar and of the prescribed texts. In addition courses of lectures are given in Hebrew composition, in literary and textual criticism and in archaeology. A student begins the study of Aramaic in this year.

The student may begin the study of Syriac and Arabic in the Senior Freshman or Junior Sophister year. It is not advisable to postpone beginning the study of these languages till the Senior Sophister year, as some knowledge of them is required when entering on the moderatorship course.

JUNIOR SOPHISTER YEAR. In addition to the study of the prescribed course, which includes Rabbinic Hebrew, lectures are given in Hebrew composition and in biblical history and literature.

SENIOR SOPHISTER YEAR. In this year lectures are provided in the prescribed texts in Hebrew and the subsidiary language, as well as in advanced Hebrew prose and verse composition, comparative Semitic grammar, biblical archaeology and biblical history and literature.

Abridgement of course

3. A student may be admitted to the course as a Senior Freshman if, in the opinion of the School Committee, he is qualified by his

knowledge and attainment to be so, or if he passes the Junior Freshman honor examination with sufficient merit. He must pay a fee before presenting himself for this examination. See COLLEGE CHARGES.

Examinations

4. Honor examinations are held annually in October. A student who obtains a first or second rank honor may proceed to the following year; a student who obtains a third rank honor may be permitted to continue as an honor student at the discretion of the School Committee.

A student with no previous knowledge of Hebrew must present himself at a qualifying examination at the beginning of Trinity term in his Junior Freshman year. A candidate who in the opinion of the School Committee reaches a satisfactory standard is granted the status of an honor student.

Library and Museum

5. Students in the School have the use of a departmental library. See also MUSEUM OF BIBLICAL ANTIQUITIES.

COURSES AND EXAMINATIONS

Junior Freshmen

Course

MICHAELMAS TERM Hebrew grammar; *Genesis*, chs 1–4.
HILARY TERM Hebrew grammar; *Genesis*, chs 12–15.
TRINITY TERM Hebrew grammar; *Deuteronomy*, chs 4–6, *Joshua*, chs 1–5.
The history of Israel to the foundation of the monarchy, the Babylonian creation and flood stories and the archaeological background of the patriarchal society and the conquest of Canaan.

Examination

The annual examination is held in Michaelmas term.

Senior Freshmen

MICHAELMAS TERM Advanced Hebrew grammar; *1 Samuel*, chs 1–5.
Aramaic grammar; *Daniel*, chs 2–3.
Textual criticism.
HILARY TERM Advanced Hebrew grammar; *1 Samuel*, chs 6–11; *Amos*, chs 1–4.
Aramaic grammar; *Daniel*, chs 4–7.
Introduction to archaeology.
TRINITY TERM Advanced Hebrew grammar; *Exodus*, chs 13–21; *Psalms* 90–99.
Aramaic grammar; *Ezra*, chs 4–7.
Hebrew inscriptions.
The history of Israel to the fall of Jerusalem.

Honor courses

In each term a student also attends lectures in Hebrew composition, and in history and biblical criticism.

Examination

The annual examination is held in Michaelmas term.

Junior Sophisters

MICHAELMAS TERM *Pirķê ʾĀḅôṯ*, chs 1, 2; Targum on *Genesis*, chs 12–18.
HILARY TERM *Pirķê ʾĀḅôṯ*, chs 3, 4; Targum on *Numbers*, chs 20–25.
TRINITY TERM *Pirķê ʾĀḅôṯ*, chs 5, 6; Targum on *Isaiah*, chs 13–20.

In each term a student also attends lectures in Hebrew composition, and in literature and archaeology.

Junior and Senior Sophisters

1966-7 and alternate years

MICHAELMAS TERM 2 *Kings*, chs 1–13; *Isaiah*, chs 1–12, 28–31.
HILARY TERM 2 *Kings*, chs 14–25; *Isaiah*, chs 40–55.
TRINITY TERM *Hosea*; *Psalms* 100–106; *Proverbs*, chs 1–10.

1967-8 and alternate years

MICHAELMAS TERM 2 *Samuel*, chs 1–12; *Job*, chs 1–7.
HILARY TERM 2 *Samuel*, chs 13–22; *Amos*, chs 5–9; *Job*, chs 8–14, 27, 28.
TRINITY TERM *Jeremiah*, chs 1–8, 32, 36, 37; *Psalms* 120–140.

Senior Sophisters

MICHAELMAS TERM Ķimḥi on *Psalms* 1, 2; Targum on *Ruth*.
HILARY TERM Ķimḥi on *Psalms* 3–5; Aramaic inscriptions.
TRINITY TERM Selected chapters of *Mishna*; Aramaic Elephantine papyri. The history of Israel to the Maccabees.

Examinations

The annual Junior Sophister examination is held in Michaelmas term.

MODERATORSHIP EXAMINATION

A candidate for moderatorship in Hebrew and Semitic Languages is allowed to select one of two courses. These courses consist each of (A) a principal, and (B) a subsidiary language. These are

A PRINCIPAL LANGUAGE	B SUBSIDIARY LANGUAGE
I Hebrew	Arabic *or* Aramaic *or* Syriac
II Arabic[1]	Hebrew *or* Aramaic

The examination for the A. Hebrew moderatorship consists of two parts. The annual Junior Sophister honor examination is part I of the moderatorship examination and carries 250 marks. The final examination, held in June, is part II of the moderatorship examination and carries 750 marks.

[1] Subject to arrangement and adequate notice.

Hebrew and semitic languages

Candidates are examined by papers and orally. The tests consist of translation from and questions on prescribed texts, translation of passages from unprescribed texts, composition in the selected languages, questions on the history and literature of the different nations to whom those languages belong, questions on grammar and philology. For candidates taking Hebrew as the principal subject there is also a special paper. Candidates taking Arabic are expected to read an easy MS. letter.

For the different courses the following texts and special works on history, literature, philology, and grammar are prescribed:

I

Part II of the A. Hebrew moderatorship examination.

A. Hebrew

1966 and 1968: *2 Samuel*, chs 1–22, *Jeremiah*, chs 1–8, 32, 36, 37, *Amos*, chs 5–9, *Psalms* 120–140, *Job*, chs 1–14, 27, 28.

1967 and 1969: *2 Kings*, chs 1–25; *Isaiah*, chs 1–12, 28–55, *Hosea*, *Psalms* 100–106, *Proverbs*, chs 1–10.

Ḳimḥi on *Psalms* 1–5; selected chapters of *Mishna*.

G. A. Cooke, *North-Semitic inscriptions*, pp. 1–157; J. Bright, *A history of Israel*; M. Noth, *The history of Israel*; *A companion to the Bible*, ed. T. W. Manson, chs 6–8, 10, 11; W. Robertson Smith, *Religion of the Semites*; R. De Vaux, *Ancient Israel*; W. Wright, *Comparative grammar of the Semitic languages*; R. H. Pfeiffer, *An introduction to the Old Testament*, pts 1, 2 and the chapters dealing with the Old Testament books; G. W. Anderson, *A critical introduction to the Old Testament*.

Other recommended reading: A. Weiser, *Introduction to the Old Testament*; Y. Kaufmann, *The religion of Israel*; H. H. Rowley (ed.), *The Old Testament and modern study*, chs 3–7.

B. Arabic

Qu'rān, suras 3, 4; Yellin and Billig, *An Arabic reader* (Macmillan); Ibn Khaldūn, *Prolegomena*, a selection by MacDonald (Semitic Study Series IV).

Margoliouth, *Muhammad and the rise of Islam*; Nicholson, *A literary history of the Arabs*; Amir Ali, *A history of the Saracens*; Thatcher, *Arabic grammar*.

B. Aramaic

The Aramaic portions of the *Old Testament*; *Ruth* in the Targum.

Elephantine papyri, ed. Ungnad, nos 1–10; Cooke, *North-Semitic inscriptions*, Aramaic section, pp. 159–213.

Walker, 'Targums' in *A dictionary of the Bible*, ed. Hastings.

B. Syriac

The hymn of the soul, ed. Bevan; *St Matthew* in the Peschitta; J. Gwynn, *Remnants of the later Syriac versions*, introduction and pt 1.

Duval, *La littérature Syriaque*; Nestle, 'Syriac versions' in *A dictionary of the Bible*, ed. Hastings.

Honor courses

II

A. Arabic

Ibn Khaldūn, *Prolegomena*, bks 4, 5 (Beyrout, 1900); Yellin and Billig, *An Arabic reader* (Macmillan); Harīrī, *Mukamat*, ed. Reinaud and Derenbourg, nos 6, 11, 18, 49, 50; Saba' *Mu'allakat*, odes of Imrulkais and Labid, ed. Lyall; *Qu'rān*, suras 2, 7, 11, 18.

Muir, *Annals of the early Khalifat, Life of Muhammad*; Nicholson, *Literary history of the Arabs*; Wright, *Arabic grammar, Comparative grammar of the Semitic languages.*

Other editions of the Arabic texts specified may be used.

B. Hebrew

Exodus, chs 1–24; *Psalms* 90–106.

Wade, *Old Testament history*; Gray, *Critical introduction to the Old Testament*; Driver, *Introduction to notes on the Hebrew text of the book Samuel*, pp. 1–55.

The distribution of papers and allotment of marks is as follows:

	A. Hebrew	A. Arabic
FIRST AND SECOND DAYS (Principal language)		
Four papers on the prescribed texts	280	400
THIRD DAY		
Composition	100	125
History	70	100
FOURTH DAY (Subsidiary language)		
Two papers on the prescribed course	180	250
FIFTH DAY		
Special paper for A. Hebrew candidates	80	
General paper		75
Viva voce examination	40	50
Total	750	1,000

NOTE. In the case of each language unprescribed passages for translation are set along with those from the prescribed texts. The oral examination includes reading. In Hebrew, composition includes pointing unpointed passages.

Wall Biblical Scholarship and Hincks Memorial Prize

The attention of advanced students is drawn to the Wall Biblical Scholarship, value £20 a year for three years, and to the Hincks Memorial Prize, value £50. For details, see PRIZES AND OTHER AWARDS.

HONOR COURSE IN HISTORY AND POLITICAL SCIENCE

GENERAL REGULATIONS

Admission

1. A student intending to take the honor course in history and political science must, in addition to satisfying the ordinary conditions of admission, pass the matriculation examination, or its equivalent, in Latin and one of the languages, French, German, Irish, Italian, Spanish. Students from Africa or Asia whose mother tongue is not English are required to have a matriculation qualification in Latin, but not in one of the other languages.

Abridgement of course

2. A student may be admitted to the course as a Senior Freshman if, in the opinion of the School Committee, he is qualified by his knowledge and attainment to be so, or if he passes the Junior Freshman honor examination with sufficient merit. He must pay a fee before presenting himself for this examination. See COLLEGE CHARGES.

Subjects of study

3. The course is divided into two parts, the first part covering the Freshman years, the second part the Sophister years. Part I comprises (a) an introductory course in general history and on the nature, scope and methods of history, and (b) survey courses on European, British and Irish history from the fifth century (including courses on European economic, and on English constitutional, history) and on American history from the seventeenth century. Part II comprises the study of (a) the history of political thought, (b) contemporary political theories, and (c) one of two special courses.

4. Of the courses in Part I, those on general history and the history of Britain and Ireland are taken by all students. Of the other courses in Part I, Junior Freshmen choose any two of the following: general history of medieval Europe, economic history of medieval Europe, general history of modern Europe; and Senior Freshmen any three of the following: general history of modern Europe, economic history of modern Europe, constitutional history of medieval England, American history.

5. Of the courses in Part II, those on the history of political thought and on contemporary political theories are taken by all students, the

Honor courses

former in the Junior Sophister year, the latter in the Senior Sophister year. The four special subjects, of which two are taken in the Junior Sophister year and two in the Senior Sophister year, are chosen b students from two special courses, one mainly medieval, the other mainly modern, in content. A student's choice of special course and of special subjects within that course must be approved by the committee of the School of History and Political Science. See §§6–8 below.

6. Of the two special subjects taken in each of the Sophister years, one must be a subject on which teaching is given (see List I below and *Course* IXA) and one a subject to be studied independently, but under the supervision of the appropriate member of the teaching staff (see List II below and *Course* IXB).

7. Not later than the end of the second week of Trinity lectures in his Senior Freshman year, every student must submit to the secretary of the school committee a statement of his choice of special subjects for the Sophister years, giving one or two alternatives for each of the four subjects to be studied. Before the end of Trinity term the School Committee will approve, in relation to the preferences thus expressed and in accordance with §§5–6 above, a combination of special subjects to be taken by each student in his Sophister years. Subsequent changes of special subjects may be made only with the approval of the School Committee.

8. A student may present a thesis in place of a special subject in List II, in his Senior Sophister year. A student who wishes to do so must apply to the school committee, through its secretary, not later than the second week of Trinity lectures in his Junior Sophister year and must give particulars of the subject on which he proposes to write.

9. A student who has been permitted to present a thesis and whose subject has been approved is entitled to guidance from the appropriate professor or lecturer. The thesis must be based on a critical study of original sources. It should not exceed 12,000 words of text. It must include a table of contents, a classified bibliography, and systematic references to sources in the form of footnotes. It must be typewritten on quarto paper, on one side of the paper only, and must be securely bound. Two typed copies of the thesis must be handed in to the secretary of the school committee not later than the end of Trinity term.

Lectures and exercises

10. Freshmen must, in accordance with the general regulations for honor students, attend all the lectures and perform all the exercises prescribed for the course in history and political science. Sophisters

214

must perform all the prescribed exercises but attendance at lectures is optional for them.

Examinations

11. A student proceeding to a moderatorship in history and political science must pass a prescribed examination in the Michaelmas term following the completion of each of his undergraduate years. Particulars of these examinations are given below.

12. No one may pass any of the four examinations in history and political science who fails in more than one paper (or its equivalent). Moderatorships are awarded on the results of the final examination only.

Lecky Library

13. A student of history and political science is eligible to become a member of the Lecky Library, and as a member of that library may borrow books and use the reading-room in the Museum Building. Application for membership should be made to the Lecky Librarian.

Recommended books

14. A list of books recommended for the several parts of the course is issued every second year. Copies are obtainable in the Lecky Library.

COURSES AND EXAMINATIONS
FIRST PART
Courses

   I General history and the study of history

  II General history of Europe

        A 400–1494

        B 1494–1789 (in 1965–6 and alternate years)

        C 1789–1939 (in 1966–7 and alternate years)

 III Economic history of Europe

        A *c.* 450–*c.* 1500

        B *c.* 1500–1939

 IV History of Britain

        A 400–1485

        B 1485–1939

  V History of Ireland

        A 400–1494

        B 1494–1939

 VI Constitutional history of England to 1485

VII History of the U.S.A. to 1939

Honor courses

Junior Freshmen take courses I, IVA, VA, and any two of courses IIA, IIB or IIC, and IIIA. Senior Freshmen take courses IVB, VB, and any three of courses IIC or IIB, IIIB, VI, and VII.

Examinations

JUNIOR FRESHMAN EXAMINATION
>One paper on course IVA
>One paper on course VA
>
>Any two of the following papers:
>One paper on course IIA
>One paper on course IIB (in 1966) or course IIC (in 1967)
>One paper on course IIIA

SENIOR FRESHMAN EXAMINATION
>One paper on course IVB
>One paper on course VB
>
>Any three of the following papers:
>One paper on course IIC (in 1967) or course IIB (in 1968)
>One paper on course IIIB
>One paper on course VI
>One paper on course VII

SECOND PART
Courses

VIII Political science

Junior Sophister year
A History of political thought

Senior Sophister year
B Contemporary political theories

IX Medieval special course [1]

Junior Sophister year
A The changing society of the later middle ages.

B Students are required to pursue an intensive course of reading under supervision on one of the following aspects of the course:

The economic basis of society—population, agriculture, the classes of society, the towns, the rise of trade and industry.

The structure of the state—kingship, law, feudalism, military organization, governmental institutions, representative institutions, finance.

The church—the papacy, the religious orders, diocesan organization, the conciliar movement, canon law.

Intellectual life—the universities, art and architecture, the literary sources, science and technology, the beginnings of exploration.

---

[1] To take effect in 1967-8.

Senior Sophister year

C One subject from List I below, nos. 1–9

D One subject from List II below, nos. 1–15, or a thesis on an approved subject.

X Modern special course

Junior Sophister year

A One subject from List I below, nos. 4–9

B One subject from List II below, nos. 6–15.

Senior Sophister year

C One other subject from List I below, nos. 4–9

D One other subject from List II below, nos. 1–15, or a thesis on an approved subject.

Junior Sophisters take courses VIIIA and either IXA and IXB or XA and XB.

Senior Sophisters take courses VIIIB and either IXC and IXD or XC and XD.

Examinations

JUNIOR SOPHISTER EXAMINATION

One paper on VIIIA

and either

One paper on IXA
One paper on IXB

or

One paper on XA
One paper on XB

MODERATORSHIP EXAMINATION

A general paper
Two papers on VIIIA and VIIIB

and either

One paper on IXA
One paper on IXB and one paper on IXD; or a thesis
Two papers on IXC

or

One paper on XA
One paper on XB and one paper on XD; or a thesis
Two papers on XC

Honor courses

[1] 'The evolution of parliaments in western Europe' will continue to be available in 1966–7.

HONOR COURSE IN ECONOMICS
AND POLITICAL SCIENCE

Admission

1. Application for admission to the School of Economics and Political Science should be made to the Senior Tutor. A candidate for admission to the School must pass the matriculation examination, or have an equivalent qualification, in mathematics, and must satisfy the general requirements for admission to the University.

Abridgement of course

2. A student may be admitted to the course as a Senior Freshman if, in the opinion of the School Committee, he is qualified by his knowledge and attainment to be so, or if he passes the Junior Freshman honor examination with sufficient merit. He must pay a fee before presenting himself for this examination. See COLLEGE CHARGES.

Subjects of study

3. The studies of the Freshman years are designed to provide a general training in analytical and applied economics and cognate subjects. In the Sophister years a series of more advanced courses gives some opportunity for specialisation within the fields of statistics, mathematical economics, politics and business administration. In addition to the prescribed lectures, a student must attend seminars and practical classes and write essays on selected topics.

Honor examinations

4. To rise with his class, a student must (a) pass the Junior Freshman honor examination, (b) pass the Senior Freshman honor examination, (c) pass the Junior Sophister honor examination. In the Freshman examinations a candidate may be examined on all the preceding work. In the Junior Sophister examination a candidate is examined on the work of the Junior Sophister year.

Recommended books and Lecky Library

5. Detailed syllabuses and lists of books recommended for the several courses may be obtained, on application, from the Secretary of the School Committee.

An honor student in economics and political science is eligible for membership of the Lecky Library and, as a member of that library,

Honor courses

may borrow books and use the reading room (the Council Room) in the Museum Building. Application for membership should be made to the Lecky Librarian.

COURSES AND EXAMINATIONS

Junior Freshmen

Courses

Introduction to economics; political institutions I—the governments of Ireland and Great Britain; elementary statistics; economic history; mathematics for economists.

Examination

An honor student must take the Junior Freshman examination which is held after the end of Trinity lecture term. The examination consists of five three-hour papers:

      1, 2. Introduction to economics (including
            mathematics for economists)
        3. Political institutions I
        4. Elementary statistics
        5. Economic history

Senior Freshmen

Courses

Theories of value and distribution; the economy of Ireland; political institutions II—modern foreign governments; statistical method and sources; either economic history or mathematics.

A student intending to specialise in the Sophister years in statistics or mathematical economics must read mathematics in the Senior Freshman year.

Examination

The Senior Freshman examination is held in the Michaelmas term following the completion of the Senior Freshman year, and consists of five three-hour papers:

        1. Theories of value and distribution
        2. The economy of Ireland
        3. Political institutions II
        4. Statistical method and sources
  and 5. Economic history
   or 5. Mathematics

Junior Sophisters

Courses

Economics I; economics II; statistical theory and methods; econometrics I; mathematical economics I; development of political thought; international political institutions; organisation and management; industrial relations.

Economics and political science

Examination

The Junior Sophister examination is held in the Michaelmas term following the completion of the Junior Sophister year, and consists of four three-hour papers:

      1. Economics I
      2. Economics II
and 3. Statistical theory and methods
      4. Econometrics I
or 3. Mathematical economics I
      4. Econometrics I
or 3. History of political thought
      4. International political institutions
or 3. Organisation and management
      4. Industrial relations

Senior Sophisters

Courses

Economics III; economics IV; applied statistics; econometrics II; mathematical economics II; contemporary political theories; comparative government; law relating to business; industrial economics.

Examination

The moderatorship examination is held in the Michaelmas term following the completion of the Senior Sophister year on the course of the Sophister years, and consists of six three-hour papers:

      1. Economics I and II
      2. Economics III
      3. Economics IV
and 4. Statistical theory and methods
      5. Applied statistics
      6. Econometrics I and II
or 4. Mathematical economics I
      5. Mathematical economics II
      6. Econometrics I and II
or 4. Political theory I
      5. Political theory II
      6. Political institutions
or 4. Organisation and management
      5. Law relating to business
      6. Industrial economics and industrial relations.

HONOR COURSE IN LEGAL SCIENCE

Admission

1. All students wishing to read the honor course in legal science should apply through the Senior Tutor to the Legal Studies Admission Committee. All applicants must satisfy the admission requirements of the University and possess a matriculation qualification in Latin.

Applications from candidates whose home residences are outside Ireland (thirty-two counties) must reach the Senior Tutor on or before 31 December of the year previous to that in which the applicant desires to enter. Applications from Irish candidates will be received up to 1 September in the year of entry, but they are strongly urged to apply as early as possible.

Abridgement of course

2. A student may be admitted to the course as a Senior Freshman if, in the opinion of the Admission Committee, he is qualified by his knowledge and attainment to be so, or if he passes the Junior Freshman honor examination with sufficient merit. He must pay a fee before presenting himself for this examination. See COLLEGE CHARGES.

Subjects of study

3. The honor course in legal science normally requires four years of study. In the first three years an undergraduate studies the common law, roman law, international law and jurisprudence; in the fourth year he may have a choice of subjects in the fields of international law, common law and jurisprudence.

Examinations

4. Honor examinations are held at the beginning of Trinity and Michaelmas terms for Junior Freshmen, and at the beginning of Michaelmas term for Senior Freshmen.

The moderatorship examination is in two parts. Part I is taken at the end of the Junior Sophister year. Part II is taken at the end of the Senior Sophister year.

Recommended books and Lecky Library

5. Lists of books recommended for the honor course may be obtained on application at the Admissions Office or the Lecky Library.

An honor student in legal science who is a member of the Dublin

Legal science

University Law Society is eligible to become a member of the Lecky Library and as a member of that library may borrow books and use the reading-room in the Museum Building. Application for membership should be made to the Lecky Librarian.

COURSES AND EXAMINATIONS

The following regulations became effective as from the beginning of Michaelmas term 1963. Subject to the transitional provisions set out below, students who began their studies in legal science in or before Michaelmas term 1962 will complete their course in accordance with the regulations set out in the *Calendar* for 1962–3, pp. 205–209.

Junior Freshmen

Courses

HISTORICAL INTRODUCTION TO LAW

Michaelmas term. Introduction to the science of law; sources and literature of the common law; history of the courts in England and Ireland.

Hilary term. The history of procedure; history of criminal law; history of land law.

Trinity term. The history of the law of torts; history of the law of contracts; history of equity.

CONSTITUTIONAL LAW AND HISTORY

Michaelmas term. Introduction to constitutional law. Constitutional structure of Great Britain and Ireland; its history. Origins of Parliament. Legislatures and legislation.

Hilary term. The executive. Heads of State. History of royal prerogative. Cabinet. Civil Service. Police. Local government. The judiciary.

Trinity term. The citizen and the state. Fundamental rights. Judicial interpretation of written constitutions.

CRIMINAL LAW

Michaelmas term. General principles of criminal liability; offences against the person.

Hilary term. Offences against property; offences against the state; offences against public order.

Trinity term. Offences against the administration of justice; criminal jurisdiction of the courts; criminal procedure.

Examinations

Trinity term: three three-hour papers on historical introduction to law, constitutional law and criminal law. Candidates are examined on the work of the two previous terms.

Michaelmas term: three three-hour papers on historical introduction to law, constitutional law and criminal law. Candidates are examined on the work of the three previous terms.

Honor courses

The School Committee may refuse permission to a student to enter the Senior Freshman year unless he answers satisfactorily at each honor examination in the Junior Freshman year, as well as performing the other exercises required by the School.

Senior Freshmen

Courses

ROMAN LAW
Michaelmas term. History of roman law; law of persons.
Hilary term. Law of property and inheritance.
Trinity term. Law of obligations and actions.

ADMINISTRATIVE LAW
Michaelmas term. Introduction. Legislation; delegated legislation; doctrine of ultra vires. Administrative tribunals.
Hilary term. Judicial control. Organisation of executive; local government. Civil service.
Trinity term. Public corporations. Administrative law in America and Europe.

LAW OF CONTRACTS AND QUASI-CONTRACTS
Michaelmas term. Outline of the law of contracts; formation of contracts; contractual liability.
Hilary term. Circumstances which impair contractual obligations.
Trinity term. Possible parties to contracts. The law of quasi-contracts.

LAW OF EVIDENCE
Michaelmas term. General principles of evidence; matters which may be proved in evidence.
Hilary term. Matters which may be proved in evidence; matters which may not be proved in evidence.
Trinity term. Matters not requiring proof; practice and procedure in the courts in relation to evidence.

Examination

Michaelmas term: four three-hour papers on roman law, administrative law, contracts and quasi-contracts, and the law of evidence. Candidates are examined on the work of the three previous terms.

The School Committee may refuse permission to a student to enter the Junior Sophister year unless he answers satisfactorily at the honor examination in the Senior Freshman year, as well as performing the other exercises required by the School.

Junior Sophisters

Courses

JURISPRUDENCE I
Michaelmas term. Sources of law.
Hilary term. The purpose of law; the nature of law.
Trinity term. Legal concepts.

PUBLIC INTERNATIONAL LAW I

Michaelmas term. The history of the law of nations; elements of modern international law; administration of international law in international and municipal courts.

Hilary term. The main principles of international law.

Trinity term. The law of international institutions.

LAW OF PROPERTY I

Michaelmas term. The origin and development of the law of real property; tenure and estates; freehold and leasehold interests; co-ownership.

Hilary term. Uses and trusts; future interests; mortgages; transfer of ownership inter vivos and on death.

Trinity term. Involuntary alienation; incorporeal hereditaments; registration of deeds; registration of title.

TORTS

Michaelmas term. General outline of the law of torts.

Hilary term. Personal wrongs; wrongs to possession and property.

Trinity term. Wrongs to person, estate and property generally.

Examination

MODERATORSHIP EXAMINATION, PART I

The moderatorship examination, part I, is held at the beginning of Michaelmas term following the Junior Sophister year, and comprises the papers set out below; candidates must take all the papers numbered 1–4, and *either* paper number 5 *or* paper number 6. Two-fifths of the total moderatorship marks are assigned to part I.

> (1) Administrative law
> (2) Jurisprudence I
> (3) Public international law I
> (4) Torts
> (5) Criminal law
> (6) Roman law

To enter the Senior Sophister year, a student must have secured at least a third rank honor at this examination.

Senior Sophisters

Courses

Students in the Senior Sophister year must attend courses in equity, conflict of laws, and in *two* subjects selected from the following list: (1) Law of property II, (2) Jurisprudence II, (3) Public international law II, (4) Law of associations. A student must inform the Regius Professor of Laws of his choice not later than the end of the third week of lectures in Trinity term of his Junior Sophister year, and his selection is subject to the prior approval of the Regius Professor.

EQUITY

Michaelmas term. Origin and development of the court of chancery; maxims of equity; trusts, express, resulting and constructive; appointment of new

225

I

Honor courses

trustees; rights and duties of trustees; rights of the cestui que trust; breach of trust and the remedies therefor.

Hilary term. Charitable trusts in Ireland; persons under disability; equitable relief on ground of fraud, misrepresentation and mistake.

Trinity term. Satisfaction; performance; ademption; conversion; election; equitable remedies; administration of assets.

CONFLICT OF LAWS

Michaelmas term. Basic concepts and theory.

Hilary term. Jurisdiction; judgments; law of persons.

Trinity term. Obligations; property.

LAW OF PROPERTY II

Michaelmas term. Outline of the Irish Land Acts and Land Purchase Acts; law of landlord and tenant in Ireland.

Hilary term. Incorporeal hereditaments; choses in possession; choses in action.

Trinity term. Conditions of sale; requisitions on title; conveyances.

JURISPRUDENCE II

Michaelmas term. Theories of law and justice.

Hilary term. Basic principles of common law.

Trinity term. Contemporary legal problems; law reform.

PUBLIC INTERNATIONAL LAW II

Over the three terms not more than five topics to be appointed from the following:

Theory; international conflicts; United Nations; European institutions; state responsibility; state succession; treaties; law of the sea; law relating to individuals; contemporary problems.

LAW OF ASSOCIATIONS

Michaelmas term. Corporations aggregate.

Hilary term. Trade unions; other quasi-corporations.

Trinity term. Unincorporated associations.

Examination

MODERATORSHIP EXAMINATION, PART II

The moderatorship examination, part II, is held at the beginning of Michaelmas term following the Senior Sophister year, and comprises the papers set out below: candidates must take all the papers numbered 1–4, and *two* of those numbered 5–8. Three-fifths of the total moderatorship marks are assigned to part II.

(1) Contracts and quasi-contracts
(2) Law of property I
(3) Equity
(4) Conflict of laws
(5) Law of property II
(6) Jurisprudence II
(7) Public international law II
(8) Law of associations

Legal science

1. A student who began the honor course in legal science under the old regulations but who has not completed the Junior Freshman year under the old regulations shall, on the coming into force of the new regulations, be debarred from proceeding further under the old regulations.

2. The last moderatorship examinations under the old regulations will be

Part II—Michaelmas term, 1966.

3. A student who has by the beginning of Michaelmas term, 1965, failed to complete the Junior Sophister year under the old regulations shall, if permitted to do so, repeat his Junior Sophister year under the new regulations and pass the moderatorship examination part I under the new regulations in the subjects of jurisprudence I, public international law, criminal law and torts, at the end of that year.

4. A student who has by the beginning of Michaelmas term, 1966, failed to complete the Senior Sophister year under the old regulations shall, if permitted to do so, repeat his Senior Sophister year under the new regulations and pass the moderatorship examination part II under the new regulations at the end of that year.

5. A student who after the beginning of Michaelmas term, 1966, is permitted to present himself for a supplemental moderatorship in legal science, or is permitted to defer his examination for one year, shall present himself for that examination under the new regulations.

COURSES FOR
DIPLOMAS IN ARTS

HISTORY OF EUROPEAN PAINTING

SCHOLARSHIP AND DIPLOMA
IN THE
HISTORY OF EUROPEAN PAINTING

Regulations

1. In the year 1934 Miss Sarah Purser and Sir John Purser Griffith, desiring to encourage the study of the history of art, and to help to train persons who intend to take up this study as a career, gave £1,000 each to form two funds of equal amount, one to be administered by Trinity College, Dublin, and the other by University College, Dublin.

2. The income of the fund held by Trinity College is applied to provide a travelling scholarship and a prize, to be competed for at an examination in the history of European painting, held in Trinity term in every second year, beginning from 1935.

3. This examination is open to all persons, whether members of Trinity College or not, who can produce evidence (a) of having received a sound general education, and (b) of having an Irish domicile or of having resided for at least one year continuously in Ireland.

4. Notice of candidature and of the period selected in B (below), and evidence as to education and domicile, must be given to the Senior Lecturer before 1 May.

5. The first instalment is payable on the award of the scholarship. The second instalment is payable on receipt of a certificate from a responsible person in an approved institution to the effect that the holder has begun work there.

6. The scholarship and prize cannot be held at the same time by the same person, and neither can be awarded a second time to the same person unless a different special course is presented.

7. Diplomas are awarded to such candidates at the examination as may be judged to have shown high merit.

8. The fee for the examination is 10s. The fee for the diploma is £1.

Courses

9. The following courses have been appointed. (For a list of suitable books candidates should consult the Director of Studies in the Visual Arts.) Forty-five per cent of the marks are awarded for section A, thirty-five per cent for section B, and twenty per cent for section C.

A

The general history of European painting from 1200 to 1900.

B

One of the following periods or schools of painting is to be studied
in more detail. The candidate must give notice to the Senior Lecturer,
at least one month prior to the examination, of the period he intends
to select.

1. The Van Eycks and their immediate successors
2. The Venetian Cinquecento
3. Rembrandt and his school
4. French painting under Louis XIV and XV
5. The French Impressionists
6. Florentine painting in the fifteenth century
7. Velasquez and the School of Madrid
8. Rubens and Van Dyck
9. Eighteenth-century English portrait painters
10. Leonardo; Raphael; Michelangelo
11. Fresco painting in Italy
12. English landscape-painting
13. Dutch landscape-painting
14. The masters of still-life painting

C

A practical test in identifying period, author, technique, and condition
of particular paintings.

COURSES FOR PROFESSIONAL DEGREES AND DIPLOMAS

ARTS REQUIREMENTS FOR PROFESSIONAL STUDENTS

DIVINITY

LAW

PHYSIC

DENTAL SCIENCE

VETERINARY MEDICINE

ENGINEERING

AGRICULTURE

FORESTRY

MUSIC

EDUCATION

BUSINESS STUDIES

SOCIAL STUDIES

PHYSIOTHERAPY

Note

Students should also see GENERAL REGULATIONS FOR STUDENTS, Discipline and academic progress.

ARTS REQUIREMENTS FOR PROFESSIONAL STUDENTS

SCHOOL OF DIVINITY

1. Students reading for the testimonium in divinity must have obtained credit for the Freshman years in arts before being admitted to the preliminary divinity year; they must have obtained credit for the Junior Sophister year in arts before being admitted to the junior divinity year; and they must have passed the B.A. degree examination before being admitted to the senior divinity year. Having passed the final examination in divinity, they must have obtained the degree of B.A. before they can receive the divinity testimonium.

2. In the Freshman years a student intending to read divinity must take either an honor course or the full course in general studies. If he has chosen the latter alternative, he is required during his Sophister years to read only one of the following subjects: Latin, Greek, philosophy, Hebrew, provided that he has read the same subject during his Freshman years.

3. Candidates for the degree of B.D. must be graduates in arts of the University of Dublin, or of another recognised university, of at least three years' standing.

SCHOOL OF LAW

4. Students reading for the degree of LL.B. must have obtained credit for the Freshman years, and for at least one term of the Junior Sophister year, in arts, before presenting themselves for the intermediate examination in law. Having passed this examination, they must have obtained credit for the Junior Sophister year, and for at least one term of the Senior Sophister year, in arts, before presenting themselves for the final examination for the degree of LL.B. Having passed this examination, they must have obtained the degree of B.A. before the degree of LL.B. can be conferred on them. The arts course taken by such students is either the full course in general studies or an honor course.

SCHOOL OF MUSIC

5. Candidates for degrees in music are not required to take an arts course or to graduate in arts. If they wish to do so, they must take the full course in general studies or an honor course.

SCHOOL OF EDUCATION

6. Students reading for the higher diploma in education must have obtained the degree of B.A. of the University of Dublin or an equivalent qualification recognised by the Teachers' Registration Council of Ireland.

SCHOOLS OF PHYSIC, DENTAL SCIENCE, ENGINEERING, VETERINARY MEDICINE, AGRICULTURE, FORESTRY, BUSINESS STUDIES AND SOCIAL STUDIES

7. The arts subjects and courses available to students reading medicine, dental science, veterinary medicine, engineering, agriculture, forestry, business studies and social studies are selected from those prescribed for the course in general studies. The teaching in the selected subjects is given to these students in common with arts students, at hours that are left free from professional teaching. The arts examinations taken by them which are those prescribed for the course in general studies, are held each year in June, and there is a supplemental examination for Junior Freshmen in September/October. The rules relating to absence from lectures or examinations are the same for professional students reading arts as for arts students. The exercises of the Junior Freshman year include at least one English essay on a general subject, failure in which involves failure in the year as a whole. See COURSE IN GENERAL STUDIES, §§6-9.

The fee for a supplemental examination is £2, payable before 1 September.

8. To obtain credit for his year in arts a professional student in one of the enumerated schools must fulfil the same conditions in his arts subject as a student reading general studies must fulfil in each of his three subjects. See COURSE IN GENERAL STUDIES, §2.

9. A professional student reading for the B.A. degree must keep the same academic class in his arts and in his professional courses throughout the four undergraduate years.

10. A student may not repeat any academic year more than once and may not repeat more than two academic years except by special permission of the University Council (GENERAL REGULATIONS FOR STUDENTS, I, §14).

11. A professional student may change his arts subject during his Junior Freshman year, with the permission of the Senior Lecturer in

consultation with the head of the department to which the new subject relates. Any subsequent change of subject may be made only with the permission of the General Studies Committee.

Students reading Medicine, Dental Science or Engineering

12. Students reading for degrees in medicine, dental science, or engineering must study an arts subject, along with their professional course, in each of their four undergraduate years. Their arts subject must be chosen as provided in §§13 and 14. They must obtain credit for the course, and pass the examination, prescribed in their subject for each of the four years, as provided below. Having done so and having proceeded satisfactorily through the four corresponding years of their professional course, they receive the degree of B.A.

A Junior Freshman student in medicine, dental science or engineering who fails to obtain credit for his arts subject may not proceed to the courses of his Senior Freshman year either arts or professional unless he satisfactorily repeats the arts course of his Junior Freshman year and all or part of his professional course as required by the School Committee.

A student, other than a Junior Freshman, in medicine, dental science or engineering who has obtained credit for his year in his professional course, but who has failed to obtain credit for his year in arts may not proceed to the course of the following year, either arts or professional, unless he satisfactorily repeats the year in question. If however, his failure to obtain credit in his arts subject is due to failure in the annual examination, he may be permitted by the Senior Lecturer on the recommendation of the appropriate School Committee to proceed with the arts and the professional courses of the following year on condition that he must pass in that year the arts examination in which he was deficient.

A student who obtains credit for his arts subject but fails to obtain credit in his professional subjects is not required to repeat attendance in the course of his arts subject nor to present himself again for examination in it.

13. Students in medicine and dental science choose their arts subject from the following:

English
French
history; or history (Freshman years) and
    fine arts II (Sophister years)

14. Students in engineering choose their arts subject from the following:

Arts requirements for professional students

English; or English (Freshman years) and
   fine arts II (Sophister years)
French
Russian
economics
geography

Students reading Veterinary Medicine

15. Students reading for the degree in veterinary medicine must obtain credit for the general studies course of the Junior Freshman year in English, French or history and must pass the examination in their chosen subject in June or October of their pre-veterinary year. They may study one arts subject in each of their four undergraduate years and if they obtain credit for the course, and pass the examination prescribed in the subject for each of the four years, they receive the degree of B.A. If they choose not to read an arts course after their pre-veterinary year, or if they discontinue an arts course, they may none the less proceed to a degree in veterinary medicine.

A Junior Freshman student in veterinary medicine who fails to obtain credit for his arts subject may not proceed to the courses of his Senior Freshman year either arts or professional unless he satisfactorily repeats the arts course of his Junior Freshman year and all or part of his professional course as required by the School Committee.

A student in veterinary medicine, other than a Junior Freshman, who fails to obtain credit for his arts subject but who obtains credit in his professional course may either discontinue his arts course and proceed with his professional course only or, with the permission of the School Committee, he may repeat the courses both arts and professional of the year and if successful may then proceed with the courses of the following year.

A student who obtains credit for his arts subject but fails to obtain credit in his professional subjects is not required to repeat attendance in the course of his arts subject nor to present himself again for examination in it.

16. Students in veterinary medicine choose their arts subject from the following:

English
French
history; or history (Freshman years) and
   fine arts II (Sophister years)

Arts requirements for professional students

Students reading Agriculture, Forestry, Business Studies and
Social Studies

17. Students reading for degrees in agriculture, forestry, business studies or social studies may study one arts subject along with their professional course in each of their four undergraduate years. If they obtain credit for the course and pass the examination prescribed in the subject for each of the four years they receive the degree of B.A. If on the other hand they discontinue an arts course they may none the less proceed to a degree in their professional subject.

A student in agriculture, forestry, business studies or social studies who fails to obtain credit for his year in arts but who obtains credit in his professional course may either discontinue his arts course and proceed with the professional course only, or, with the permission of the School Committee, he may repeat the courses, both arts and professional, of the year and if successful may then proceed with the courses of the following year.

A student who obtains credit for his arts subject but fails to obtain credit in his professional subjects is not required to repeat attendance in the course of his arts subject nor to present himself again for examination in it.

18. Students in agriculture and in forestry may choose their arts subject from the following:

history; or history (Freshman years) and
fine arts II (Sophister years)
economics

19. Students in business studies and in social studies may choose their arts subject from the following:

English
French
history; or history (Freshman years) and
fine arts II (Sophister years)
pure mathematics
applied mathematics
philosophy

SCHOOL OF DIVINITY

TESTIMONIUM IN DIVINITY

GENERAL REGULATIONS

1. The Divinity Testimonium is awarded to students who attend satisfactorily the courses prescribed and pass the required examinations in biblical, dogmatic and historical theology.

2. A student who enters the School as a graduate may complete the requirements for the testimonium in two years, by being granted exemption from the Preliminary Year. An undergraduate in the University may enter the School when he is of Junior Sophister standing in arts, and may complete the requirements for the testimonium in three years. A student taking a moderatorship course is advised to postpone entry to the School until he has qualified for the B.A. degree.

3. Before beginning the last year of the course, *i.e.* the Senior Year, a student must have qualified for the degree of Bachelor in Arts or must be a graduate of a university approved by the Board of the College.

4. A student may enter on any year of the course only at the beginning of Michaelmas term.

Admission

5. Application for admission to the School must be made to the Archbishop King's Professor of Divinity before 1 July of the year in which admission is sought.

6. A candidate for admission must either have attended satisfactorily the catechetical lectures provided for the Freshman years, or pass an examination on the catechetical courses prescribed for those years. See CATECHETICAL COURSE.

Lectures and examinations

7. To obtain credit for any year, a student must (*a*) attend satisfactorily the courses prescribed, (*b*) perform satisfactorily the required exercises (essays, tutorial or practical work), and (*c*) pass the examinations of his year. A student prevented by illness from being present at lectures, other classes or examinations, must produce a medical certificate.

8 A student who fails to fulfil the requirements of his year must repeat attendance on the lectures and classes and pass the examinations of the year he is repeating, unless specially exempted by the Professors.

240

9. The examinations of each year are held normally at the end of Trinity lecture term, but certain papers may be set at the end of Hilary lecture term.

A student must satisfy the examiners in each subject. The examiners may allow a small deficiency in one subject to be compensated for by the answering in the other subjects. A student who fails to satisfy the examiners in not more than two subjects may be permitted to take a supplemental examination at the beginning of the following Michaelmas term in the subject or subjects in which he is deficient, and if unsuccessful at the supplemental examination may present himself again for examination in the same subject or subjects at the end of the following Trinity term.

A student who fails to satisfy the examiners in more than two subjects may be permitted to present himself again in all the subjects of his year at a supplemental examination at the beginning of the following Michaelmas term. If unsuccessful in not more than two subjects at the supplemental examination, he may repeat the examination in the subject or subjects in which he is deficient at the end of the following Trinity term. If unsuccessful in more than two subjects at the supplemental examination, he must repeat the year in full, unless specially exempted by the Professors in accordance with §8.

A student who, subsequent to the Michaelmas term supplemental examinations has not more than two subjects outstanding, if a member of the Junior Year, may rise from the Junior to the Senior Year though he will not receive the degree of Bachelor in Arts until he has completed in full the requirements of the Divinity Course for the Junior Year.

A student who has not passed in its entirety any examination within eighteen months from the date on which he first became eligible for it is reported to the Board as an unsatisfactory student.

Students taking the course in general studies

10. A student taking the course in general studies may replace two of the subjects of that course, in his Sophister years, by the course for the Divinity Testimonium, provided that the subject which he takes on the course in general studies is either Greek, Hebrew, Latin or philosophy, and that he has taken this subject in each of the Freshman years.

11. A student who opts to take one subject only of the general studies course in his Sophister years must satisfy in each year the requirements both of the course in general studies and of the divinity course. To obtain the degree of Bachelor in Arts such a student must

have completed the requirements of the Junior Year in divinity, and of his chosen subject in the general studies course.

12. In place of classical Greek, as prescribed on the course in general studies, an intending divinity student may take, during his Freshman years, the following course in Hellenistic Greek:

JUNIOR FRESHMEN. An introductory course.

SENIOR FRESHMEN. *The epistle to Diognetus*; *The martyrdom of Polycarp*; Ignatius, *Epistles*; Plutarch, *The life of Dion*.
Outlines of Hellenistic and Graeco-Roman history, 325 B.C.–193 A.D.

Fees

13. The fees payable by undergraduate and graduate divinity students are stated in COLLEGE CHARGES, §49.

Candidates preparing for ordination

14. Candidates for the Divinity Testimonium who seek ordination in the Church of Ireland or in a church in communion therewith are expected to reside in the Church of Ireland Divinity Hostel during the final two years of their course. They are subject to the authority of the Warden of the Hostel, and they must comply with regulations requiring their attendance at College Chapel. Instruction is given in various branches of pastoral theology under the direction of the Professor of Pastoral Theology, by whom a certificate is given to students who have attended satisfactorily.

The Church of Ireland Divinity Hostel is recognised by the Board of Trinity College as a registered place of residence for divinity students.

15. Candidates for ordination should note the regulations concerning health and the other requirements which must be satisfied before ordination.

COURSES AND EXAMINATIONS

Preliminary Year

Courses
I Introduction to the Old Testament
II Introduction to the New Testament
III Introduction to Christian doctrine
IV Liturgy
V The history of the Christian Church to 461 A.D.
VI A prescribed book of the New Testament
VII New Testament Greek

The work prescribed under VI above is *1 Peter*.

Testimonium in Divinity

Examination

The examination is held at the end of Trinity term. Papers are set on each of the courses. The marks awarded on courses IV and V are carried forward as part of the total marks for the testimonium.

Junior Year

Courses

    I   The history, literature and theology of the four Gospels
   II The history, literature and religion of Israel until the Exile
  III A specified portion of the New Testament in Greek
  IV A specified book of the Old Testament in English
   V The history of the Christian Church, a general course (two terms); the Church in Ireland from the earliest times (one term)
  VI Christian doctrine

A student entering the Junior Year as a graduate must also attend courses IV and V of the Preliminary Year. Such a student must attend special classes in New Testament Greek and pass a test at the end of his first term.

The following works are prescribed: under III above, *Gospel according to St Luke*, with chs 1-12 in Greek; under IV above, *Isaiah*, chs 1-39.

Examination

The examination is held at the end of Trinity term. Papers are set on each of the courses. A graduate attending courses IV and V of the Preliminary Year must also pass the papers set on these courses. The marks awarded on each of the papers are carried forward as part of the total marks for the testimonium.

An optional paper in translation from Latin and Hebrew into English may be taken at this examination. See also below, under 'Senior Year'.

Senior Year

Courses

    I   The history, literature and theology of the books of the New Testament excluding the Gospels
   II The history, literature and religion of the Jews from the Exile until 70 A.D.
  III A specified book of the New Testament in Greek
  IV A specified book of the Old Testament in English
   V The history of the Church: Reformation period (one term); from 1789 until the present day (one term)
  VI Philosophy of religion
 VII Moral theology
VIII Christian doctrine

The following works are prescribed: under III above, *Epistle to the Romans*; under IV above, *Isaiah*, chs 40-66.

Testimonium in Divinity

Examination

Papers are set on courses V and either on VI or on VII at the end of Hilary term. Papers are set on the remaining courses at the end of Trinity term, together with an optional paper in translation from Latin and Hebrew into English.

The Testimonium in Divinity is awarded on the marks obtained on all the papers set at the Junior Year and Senior Year examinations, together with those obtained on papers IV and V set at the Preliminary Year examination. The names of successful candidates are published in three classes. To obtain a first class testimonium a student must pass in both Latin and Hebrew in the optional paper in translation.

DEGREES IN DIVINITY

COURT FOR DIVINITY DEGREES

All exercises and examinations required for the obtaining of degrees in Divinity are under the control of the University Council.

All applicants for degrees in Divinity must apply for registration and information to the Dean of Graduate Studies.

DEGREE OF BACHELOR IN DIVINITY (B.D.)

A Bachelor in Divinity must

(1) be a graduate of at least three years standing of the University of Dublin, or of a University recognised by the Board of Trinity College on the recommendation of the Court for Divinity Degrees.

(2) have passed the examination prescribed for the B.D. degree, and

(3) have submitted a satisfactory thesis.

A candidate for this degree must show a general knowledge of the Bible, of ecclesiastical history, and of dogmatic theology, and must also have made a special study of particular branches of Divinity from amongst those specified below.

Those who seek to register as candidates for this degree must either hold the Divinity Testimonium or provide certificates or other satisfactory evidence of an equivalent knowledge of basic theology. This evidence must be submitted at least three months before the first examination. Where such evidence is not available a candidate may be expected to pass a qualifying test of a similar standard before being accepted.

Candidates will also be expected to provide evidence that they have reached a standard in Latin equivalent to that of Matriculation unless they hold a first class Divinity Testimonium or pass Division VII of this examination.

B.D. degree examination

Candidates are examined in the following course:

    I   Old Testament, including Hebrew,

    II   New Testament, including Greek,

    III Dogmatic theology,

    IV Ecclesiastical history

    and in any *two* of the following:

     V   The philosophy of religion
    VI   The comparative study of religion
   VII   Patristic study
 VIII   Liturgiology

A candidate must complete the examinations within three years of registration. An examination is held annually in March. A candidate may repeat at a supplemental examination in December those divisions in which he failed to pass in March, provided that he has shown sufficient merit.

The divisions may be presented in any order. A candidate's notice of examination must reach the Dean of Graduate Studies not later than 1 February and, in the case of a supplemental examination, not later than 1 November before the examination at which he proposes to present himself, stating the division or divisions in which he desires to be examined. With such notice he must send the receipt for the examination fee of £1 for each division specified in his notice; payment of the examination fees should be made to the Trinity College No. 2 Account at the Bank of Ireland, College Green, Dublin 2, and must be accompanied by the prescribed fee payment form.

Thesis

Candidates are required to submit two typewritten copies of a thesis (not returnable) accompanied by a receipt for the thesis examination fee to the Dean of Graduate Studies. The subject must be chosen by the candidate and approved by the School Committee for Divinity Studies. The thesis must contain references to the authors consulted in its composition. A thesis will only be accepted after successful completion of the examination and not later than twelve months from the date of completion of this examination.

DEGREE OF DOCTOR IN DIVINITY (D.D.)

A Doctor in Divinity must

(1) be a graduate of the University of Dublin of at least eight years' standing, and

(2) be a Bachelor in Divinity of a university recognised by the Board and the Council, and

(3) present a thesis.

The thesis must contain original work carried out independently by the candidate. Before submitting it the candidate must have the subject chosen approved by the Council.

He must present three copies of his thesis (which will not be returned), printed or typewritten in a form suitable for publication and securely bound, in which he has treated of and explained some portion of doctrine from the holy scriptures, or of the history of the Church, or of dogmatic theology, or of the philosophy of religion. The thesis must contain (*a*) a declaration that it has not been submitted as an exercise for a degree at any other university (*b*) that it is entirely the candidate's own work (*c*) all due acknowledgments, and (*d*) systematic references to sources and a classified list of all sources used.

This thesis must be submitted to the Dean of Graduate Studies with a receipt showing that the applicant has paid the thesis examination fee.

FEES

	£
B.D. DEGREE	
Matriculation fee, payable by candidates who are not graduates of the University	8
Qualifying examination fee	1
Examination fee (each division, and thesis)	1
Each supplementary examination	1
Degree fee	10
D.D. DEGREE	
Thesis examination fee	21
Degree fee	21

COURSE FOR THE B.D. DEGREE EXAMINATION

A candidate is required to present himself for examination in divisions I, II, III, IV and in any two of the divisions numbered V, VI, VII, VIII and IX.

The following is the course appointed.

I

Note. Two papers are set in this division. Candidates must pass in both A and B.

A

2 *Samuel* i-xx

A candidate is expected to be familiar with the readings of the *Septuagint*. A passage from the English Bible is set for re-translation into Hebrew.

B

A general knowledge of Judges, Ruth, 1 and 2 Samuel, 1 and 2 Kings.
H. B. Swete, *An introduction to the Old Testament in Greek*, pt 1, chs 1-4; pt 2, chs 3-5; pt 3, chs 3-6.

Degrees in Divinity

J. Bright, *A history of Israel*, chs 3–8.
J. Gray, *Archaeology and the Old Testament World*.
J. Barr, *The semantics of biblical language*.
H. H. Rowley (ed.) *The Old Testament and modern study*, Introduction and essays i, ii, iv, viii–xii.
H. W. Robinson, *Inspiration and revelation in the Old Testament*.
E. Jacob, *Theology of the Old Testament*.
M. Burrows, *More light on the Dead Sea scrolls*.

II

Note. Two papers are set in this division. Candidates must pass in both A and B

A.

Johannine Gospel and Epistles in Greek.

B

Questions will be asked concerning the history, literature, theology and criticism of the New Testament writings apart from those specified in section A of this division. See also list of recommended books.

The paper in the examination will always contain a question asking for comment on a series of texts from the New Testament which present special problems. This question will be compulsory.

III

(*a*) T. H. Bindley, *The ecumenical documents of the Faith* (4th edit. revised F. W. Green), pp 1–49 and 181–199.
J. N. D. Kelly, *Early Christian doctrines*, chs 6, 8–15.
J. Calvin, *Institutes of the Christian religion*, bk II, chs 12–17.
R. Hooker, *Laws of ecclesiastical polity*, bk III, chs 1–3, bk V, chs 1–10 and 50–56.
(*b*) Christology and ecclesiology (see recommended books).

IV

(*a*) General facts of Church History up to 461 A.D.
(*b*) The Reformation in the sixteenth century in Germany, Switzerland and France.

V

A general knowledge of the subject will be expected.

N. Smart, *Historical selections in the philosophy of religion*, pp 1–247.
John Macquarrie, *Twentieth-century religious thought*.
W. Temple, *Nature, man and God*.
J. Baillie, *The sense of the presence of God*.
H. D. Lewis, *Our experience of God*.

Special Work:

E. Gilson, *The Christian philosophy of St. Thomas Aquinas*.
Note. One-fourth of the total marks is assigned to the special work.

VI

COMPARATIVE RELIGION

A general knowledge will be expected:

Special Subject: Hinduism.

One-fourth of the total marks is assigned to the special subject. (For fuller details of this division see Recommended Books.)

VII

Augustine, *Confessions*, ed. Montgomery and Gibb.

Athanasius, *De Incarnatione* ed. F. L. Cross (text only).

Smith and Wace, *Dictionary of Christian Biography;* Articles; *Augustine* and *Athanasius.*

Oxford Dictionary of the Christian Church (ed. F. L. Cross); Articles; *Augustine* and *Athanasius.*

VIII

A

(*a*) The general facts of the history of Christian worship to the year 1000 A.D.

(*b*) The Armenian Rite.

B

The *Book of Common Prayer*, including the ordinal. A candidate is expected to be acquainted with (*a*) its sources (*b*) its history (*c*) its contents and also (*d*), as a subject of special study, the Scottish Rite.

C

Reformation and post-Reformation liturgies. Modern reformed rites other than Anglican.

Three fifths of the total marks are assigned to A. A candidate must, in addition to A, take either B or C and in giving notice to the Dean of Graduate Studies inform him of his choice.

The examination for the B.D. degree normally begins on the first Tuesday in March. The following order of examination will usually be observed:

Tues. 9.30 a.m. and 2 p.m., Division I
Wed. 9.30 a.m. and 2 p.m., Division II
Thurs. 9.30 a.m. Division III; 2 p.m., Division IV

The arrangements for the examination in the remaining divisions will be made known by the Regius Professor about ten days after he has received from the several candidates their notice of intention to present themselves.

Supplemental examinations for the B.D. degree granted to candidates repeating those divisions failed in the previous March will begin on the first Tuesday in December. The order of examination will depend on the subjects presented and will be made known about mid-November.

A new leaflet giving details for a further period will be published at least three months before the expiration of the current one.

LAW SCHOOL

I INTRODUCTION

The Law School of the University of Dublin provides part of the professional training of students of King's Inns and of solicitors' apprentices; it provides certain courses of lectures and examinations for the degree of Bachelor in Laws; and it examines candidates for the degree of Doctor in Laws.

The Law School is under the control of the Board of Trinity College, which acts in concurrence with the Benchers of King's Inns in matters which concern students of King's Inns.

The possession of a university degree in law does not entitle a person to practise law in Ireland or the United Kingdom as either barrister or solicitor. A student who seeks a professional qualification as a barrister should therefore consult *either* the Under-Treasurer, King's Inns, Henrietta Street, Dublin, *or* the Under-Treasurer, The Inn of Court of Northern Ireland, Royal Courts of Justice, Belfast, *or* the Secretary, The Council of Legal Education, Lincoln's Inn, London, W.C.2. A student who seeks a professional qualification as a solicitor should consult *either* the Secretary, The Incorporated Law Society of Ireland, Four Courts, Dublin, *or* the Secretary, The Incorporated Law Society of Northern Ireland, Royal Courts of Justice, Belfast, *or* the Secretary, The Incorporated Law Society, Chancery Lane, London, W.C.2.

For details of the four-year honor course in legal science see HONOR COURSE IN LEGAL SCIENCE.

II COURSES FOR STUDENTS OF KING'S INNS

1. Students who have been admitted to King's Inns may pursue part of their course of education in the Law School of the University of Dublin, in accordance with the Rules of the Honorable Society of King's Inns.

Admission and registration

2. To obtain admission to the Law School and thus to be entitled to attend lectures a student of King's Inns must (*a*) produce to the Registrar of the Law School a receipt for fees for admission to King's Inns, (*b*) produce a receipt for education fees for the current year issued by King's Inns, and (*c*) fill up a registration card each year and lodge

it with the Registrar of the Law School before the day on which university lectures begin in Michaelmas term.

Lectures

3. A student who is taking Course A under the Rules of King's Inns in his first year must attend the prescribed university lectures in (1) legal system and legal methods, (2) legal and constitutional history, (3) either economics or modern history, and (4) either Irish or English or Latin or Greek or French or German. A student who is taking Course B under the Rules of King's Inns in his first year, and a student who is taking Course A in his second year, must attend the prescribed university lectures in (1) law of real property, (2) law of torts, (3) constitutional law and (4) criminal law. A student who is taking Course B in his second year, and a student who is taking Course A in his third year, must attend the prescribed university lectures in (1) equity, (2) law of personal property, (3) jurisprudence, (4) law of contracts, (5) law of evidence, and (6) public international law. A timetable of these prescribed lectures is published on the Law School notice-board at the beginning of each term.

Examinations

4. A student who is taking Course A in his first year must present himself for the prescribed university annual examinations in all the subjects of the year's lectures. A student who is taking Course B in his second year, and a student who is taking Course A in his third year, must present himself for the prescribed Law School annual examinations in jurisprudence and public international law. To pass an annual examination, a candidate must secure 40 per cent of the marks. Supplemental examinations are held at the beginning of the Michaelmas Term for candidates who have failed in the annual examinations of the previous academic year. Further details of these examinations are published on the Law School notice-board. All other examinations for students taking either Course A or Course B are held at the King's Inns and the Rules of the King's Inns should be consulted in relation thereto.

Certificates

5. Only students who have attended the prescribed university lectures to the satisfaction of the lecturers and, in the case of subjects in which the prescribed examinations are conducted at the University, who have passed such annual or supplemental examinations will be given certificates of academic credit by the Registrar of the Law School.

Fees

6. A student producing evidence that he has been duly admitted as a student of King's Inns, and that he has paid such fees as may be there from time to time payable, is permitted to attend without further payment all lectures and annual examinations appropriate to his course. A student who proposes to repeat the lectures and examinations in a subject without repeating the year may do so on payment of a lecture and examination fee of £15. A candidate for any supplemental examination must pay a fee of £5 for each examination. This fee is payable to the Treasurer *before* the day of the examination, but will be collected by the Accountant. Fines at the rate of 1s. per week-day of default are imposed.

III COURSES FOR SOLICITORS' APPRENTICES

7. Solicitors' apprentices may pursue part of their course of education in the Law School, in accordance with the Regulations of the Incorporated Law Society of Ireland.

Registration

8. A solicitor's apprentice who wishes to take part of his course in Trinity College must fill up a registration card each year and lodge it with the Registrar of the Law School before the day on which lectures begin in Michaelmas term.

Lectures

9. To implement the Regulations of the Incorporated Law Society of Ireland a solicitor's apprentice must attend university lectures in (1) law of real and personal property, (2) law of contracts and quasi-contracts, (3) law of torts and (4) equity. A solicitor's apprentice may not attend lectures in equity until he has completed the course of lectures and passed the appointed examinations on the law of property. In addition a solicitor's apprentice may attend the Law School lectures in constitutional law, criminal law and the law of evidence at the discretion of the Registrar of the Law School. Details of the lectures which solicitor's apprentices are eligible to attend are published on the Law School notice-board before the first day of lectures in each term. Dates of lecture terms are set out in regulation 33.

Examinations

10. Term examinations may be held and annual examinations are held in all the subjects of the year's lectures. A solicitor's apprentice attending courses must present himself for these examinations. To pass

a term examination a candidate must secure at least 30 per cent of the marks and to pass an annual examination a candidate must secure at least 40 per cent of the marks. (Supplemental examinations are held at the beginning of each term for candidates who fail in the examinations of the previous term.) Further details of the examinations will be published on the Law School notice-board.

Certificates

11. Only students who have attended lectures in three consecutive terms to the satisfaction of the lecturers and who have passed the term and annual (or supplemental term and annual) examinations will be given certificates of academic credit by the Registrar of the Law School.

Fees

12. A solicitor's apprentice who proposes to attend the above lectures and to take the above examinations must pay, when registering for the first time, a registration fee of £3, and he must pay a lecture and examination fee of £15 for each of the courses numbered (1), (2), (3) and (4) in regulation 9, of £15 for the course on criminal law, of £10 for the course on constitutional law and of £5 for the course on the law of evidence. Students not resident in Ireland pay a surcharge of fifty per cent on the fees stated for the various courses. A candidate for a supplemental examination must pay a fee of £5 *before* the day of the examination. The above fees are payable to the Treasurer, but will be collected by the Accountant at the time specified on the Law School notice-board. Fines at the rate of 1s. per week-day of default will be imposed.

IV DEGREE OF BACHELOR IN LAWS (LL.B.)

13. The degree of LL.B. is conferred only on *graduates* in arts, science, letters or philosophy of the University of Dublin who have passed the intermediate examination in law and the final examination for the degree of LL.B. (and on certain graduates of the universities of Oxford or Cambridge: see regulation 24).

14. A person who wishes to read for the degree of LL.B. and who is not a graduate of one of these universities should first seek admission to the University of Dublin. For the regulations governing admission see ADMISSION REQUIREMENTS. All enquiries concerning admission should be addressed to the Admissions Office. The normal procedure is to enter the University as an undergraduate in arts and to read for the degree of B.A. for four years. Only when about to enter the Junior Sophister

year in arts should a candidate apply for admission to the Law School to read for the degree of LL.B.

15. The course and examinations for the degree of LL.B. are distinct from the *honor* course and moderatorship examination in legal science. The course in legal science is one of the four-year honor courses in arts. See HONOR COURSE IN LEGAL SCIENCE.

Admission

16. All students wishing to be admitted to the Law School for the purpose of attending lectures for the degree of LL.B. or taking the examinations for that degree should apply through the Registrar of the Law School to the Legal Studies Admission Committee. Applications will be considered only from those students who have completed the exercises for the Freshman years and who have a matriculation qualification in Latin. The number of places for overseas students is strictly limited. All applications for admission must reach the Registrar of the Law School on the appropriate form (to be obtained from the Secretary of the Law School) before 15 October of the academic year in which the applicant wishes to attend lectures or present himself for the intermediate examination in law.

Registration

17. Only students who propose to attend lectures on the subjects for the examinations for the degree of LL.B. are required to register with the Registrar of the Law School. They must do so before the first day of lectures in any term during which they intend to attend lectures. Any student failing to register before the first day of lectures will only be admitted to lectures at the discretion of the Registrar of the Law School. The dates of lecture terms in the current year are set out in regulation 33.

Syllabus

18. The subjects of the intermediate examination are
   (1) Roman law
   (2) Constitutional law and history
   (3) Criminal law and procedure
   (4) Law of property (real and personal)

The subjects of the final examination are
   (1) Law of torts
   (2) Law of contracts and quasi-contracts
   (3) Law of evidence

and *two* others to be chosen from the following:

   (4) Jurisprudence
   (5) Equity
   (6) Public international law
   (7) Administrative law.

A candidate who passed the intermediate examination in or before June 1962 must apply through the Registrar of the Law School to the Law School Committee for permission to present himself as a candidate for the final examination next following the date of his application. This application must be made at least six weeks prior to the date of the final examination in question.

ROMAN LAW

History of roman law; law of persons; law of property and inheritance; law of obligations and actions.

CONSTITUTIONAL LAW AND HISTORY

Growth of Parliament; Stuart conflict with Parliament; Magna Carta; Petition of Rights; Bill of Rights; rule of law; separation of powers; sovereignty; conventions of the constitution; composition and powers of legislative, executive and judiciary in Ireland and United Kingdom; judicial review of legislation in Ireland.

CRIMINAL LAW AND PROCEDURE

General principles of criminal liability; offences against the person; offences against property; offences against the state; offences against public order; offences against the administration of justice; criminal jurisdiction of the courts; criminal procedure.

LAW OF PROPERTY

The origin and development of the law of real property; tenures and estates; freehold and leasehold interests; co-ownership; uses and trusts; future interests; mortgages; the transfer of ownership of realty and personalty inter vivos and on death; involuntary alienation; incorporeal hereditaments; registration of deeds; registration of title.

LAW OF TORTS

General outline of the law of torts; personal wrongs; wrongs to possession and property; wrongs to person, estate and property generally.

LAW OF CONTRACTS AND QUASI-CONTRACTS

Formation of contracts; contractual liability; circumstances which impair contractual obligations; possible parties to contracts; quasi-contractual liability.

LAW OF EVIDENCE

General principles of the law of evidence; matters which may be proved in evidence; matters which may not be proved in evidence; matters not requiring proof; practice and procedure in the courts in relation to evidence.

JURISPRUDENCE

Sources of law; purpose of law; the nature of law. Rights and duties; legal

Law School

persons; legal relations; possession; ownership; obligations; principles of liability; classification of law.

EQUITY

Origin and development of the Court of Chancery; maxims of equity; trusts, express, resulting and constructive; charitable trusts in Ireland; appointment of new trustees; rights and duties of trustees; rights of the cestui que trust; breach of trust and remedies; persons under disability; satisfaction, performance and ademption; equitable relief on ground of fraud, misrepresentation and mistake; conversion; election; equitable remedies; administration of assets.

PUBLIC INTERNATIONAL LAW

History of international law; sources; subjects of international law; rights and duties of states; the individual in international law; the law of treaties; international organisations, in particular the United Nations and International Court of Justice.

ADMINISTRATIVE LAW

Definition of judicial, executive and legislative powers; legislative powers and their control; administrative tribunals; suits against the administration; judicial control of the administration; public corporations.

A booklet containing lists of the recommended books is issued annually by the Registrar of the Law School. Copies can be obtained from the Law School office. Students who propose to prepare for the examinations without attending lectures are recommended to read these books.

Lectures

19. A candidate for the degree of LL.B. is not required to attend lectures on the appointed subjects. But a student admitted to the Law School for the purpose of reading for the degree of LL.B. is eligible to attend (a) Law School lectures given by the Reid Professor in constitutional law and history, criminal law and procedure and the law of evidence, (b) honor lectures in legal science in the following subjects: roman law (Junior Freshman year), law of property (Junior Sophister year), law of torts (Junior Sophister year), law of contracts and quasi-contracts (Senior Freshman year), jurisprudence (Junior Sophister year), equity (Senior Sophister year), public international law (Junior Sophister year), and administrative law (Senior Freshman year). The dates of the lecture terms in the current year are set out in regulation 33. Details of the times and places of these lectures will be published before the first day of each lecture term on the Law School notice-board. Lecture fees payable for attendance at these lectures are set out in regulation 25.

The intermediate examination in law

20. This examination is open to all graduates (as limited by regulation 16). An undergraduate is eligible to enter for this examination provided that he has kept at least one term in arts in the Junior Sophister year, that his name is on the books of Trinity College, and that he has been admitted by the Legal Studies Admission Committee. A candidate must give at least fourteen days' notice in writing on the prescribed form to the Registrar of the Law School. A candidate who fails to give notice as prescribed will only be admitted to the examination at the discretion of the Registrar of the Law School, and then on payment of a fine at the rate of 1s. per week-day of default.

The intermediate examination consists of four papers: (1) roman law, (2) constitutional law and history, (3) criminal law and procedure and (4) law of property (real and personal). Equal weight is given to each paper. To pass the examination a candidate must satisfy the examiners in each paper. Successful candidates are placed in three classes according to merit. An unsuccessful candidate may present himself again at a succeeding intermediate examination, but if he fails a second time his place in the Law School is thereby forfeited.

The final examination for the degree of LL.B.

21. This examination is open to all graduates who have passed the intermediate examination. An undergraduate whose name is on the college books and who has passed the intermediate examination is eligible to enter for this examination provided that he has kept at least one term in arts in his Senior Sophister year. A candidate must give at least fourteen days' notice in writing on the prescribed form to the Registrar of the Law School. A candidate who fails to give notice as prescribed will be admitted to the examination only at the discretion of the Registrar of the Law School, and then on payment of a fine at the rate of 1s. per week-day of default.

Seven papers are set at this examination: (1) law of contracts and quasi-contracts, (2) law of torts, (3) law of evidence, (4) jurisprudence, (5) equity, (6) public international law, (7) administrative law. A candidate must take *five* of these papers including (1), (2) and (3), (except as qualified by regulation 18). Equal weight is given to each of these papers. To pass the final examination a candidate must satisfy the examiners in each of the five papers. Successful candidates are placed in three classes according to merit. An unsuccessful candidate may present himself again at another final examination, but if he fails a second time his place in the Law School is thereby forfeited.

Law School

A candidate who has passed the intermediate and final examinations is eligible for the degree of LL.B.

22. The dates of the examinations for the degree of LL.B. in the current academic year are set out in regulation 34. The times and places at which these examinations will be held are published on the Law School notice-board at least one month before the date of the examination.

Prize

23. The Julian prize is awarded to the candidate at the Michaelmas examination for the degree of LL.B., who (a) obtains the highest total of marks at the examination, (b) is placed by the examiners in the first class, and (c) is under M.A. standing at the date of the examination. This prize was established in 1923 pursuant to a bequest of Mrs. Margaret Julian and in memory of her son Ernest Lawrence Julian, B.A. (ex-Sch.), sometime Reid Professor. The current value of the prize is £20.

Graduates of Oxford or Cambridge Universities

24. A graduate in arts, science or letters of the University of Oxford or Cambridge wishing to present himself for the degree of LL.B. by examination should apply to the Senior Proctor for leave to take his arts, science or letters degree of the University of Dublin *ad eundem gradum*, pay the appropriate fee, and then send to the Registrar of the Law School notice of his intention to enter for the intermediate examination.

A graduate in arts, science or letters of the University of Oxford or Cambridge who has also received the Oxford degree of B.C.L. or the Cambridge degree of LL.B. may apply to the Board through the Senior Proctor for leave to take the degree of LL.B. *ad eundem gradum.*

Fees

25. (a) A student who proposes to attend lectures in the subjects for the degree of LL.B. must pay a lecture fee of £15 for a year's course of honor lectures in each subject, a fee of £15 for a course of Law School lectures in criminal law and procedure, a fee of £10 for a course of Law School lectures in constitutional law and history and a fee of £5 for a course of Law School lectures in the law of evidence. These fees must be paid before the first day of lectures. Legal science honor students, *i.e.*, those students who have obtained an honor in the Senior Freshman examination in legal science and who are attending satisfactorily lectures in legal science in the Sophister years, are exempt from payment of the above fees.

(*b*) A candidate for the intermediate examination in law must pay an examination fee of £12 (which is not returnable) fourteen days at least before the date of the examination.

(*c*) A candidate for the final examination for the degree of LL.B. must pay an examination fee of £12 (which is not returnable) fourteen days at least before the date of the examination.

(*d*) A student whose home residence is outside Ireland (thirty-two counties) pays a surcharge of fifty per cent on all annual college fees and on other tuition fees.

The above fees are to be paid to the Bank of Ireland, College Green, Dublin, to the credit of the TRINITY COLLEGE, DUBLIN, NO. 2 ACCOUNT. All payments must be accompanied by a properly completed fee-payment form (obtainable from the Accountant). The part of the form containing the bank's acknowledgment of payment must be presented to the Registrar of the Law School before the first day of lectures in the case of lecture fees, or when giving notice for examinations in the case of examination fees.

A student who fails to pay the fees at the appropriate times is liable for a fine of 1s. per week-day of default.

(*e*) The fee for the degree of LL.B. is £12 and is to be paid to the Accountant on or before the seventh day before Commencements. The fee for the degree of LL.B. *ad eundem gradum* as the degrees of B.C.L. of the University of Oxford and of LL.B. of the University of Cambridge is £20 and is likewise to be paid to the Accountant.

V DEGREE OF DOCTOR IN LAWS (LL.D.)

26. To obtain the degree of LL.D. a candidate must present an unpublished thesis or submit original published work on a subject connected with legal studies. This must show evidence of independent enquiry, and must either contain some substantial addition to knowledge or present a fresh interpretation of materials already used.

27. A candidate for the degree of LL.D. must be a Moderator in Legal Science or an LL.B. of the University of Dublin, or a B.C.L. or a B.A. (jurisprudence) of the University of Oxford, or an LL.B. or a B.A. (Law Tripos) of the University of Cambridge, of at least six years' standing.

28. A candidate may qualify for the degree in one of two ways:

(*a*) He may present an unpublished thesis of merit sufficient, in the judgment of the examiners, to entitle him to the degree. A candidate who proposes to adopt this method should submit to the Registrar of the Law School, for the consideration of the Law School Committee, the subject on which he proposes to write a thesis. He will then be informed whether in the opinion of the Law School Committee the subject proposed is suitable. Three printed or typewritten copies of the thesis (which will not be returned) should be sent to the Registrar of the Law School.

(*b*) He may submit original published work of merit sufficient, in the judgment of the examiners, to entitle him to the degree. A candidate who adopts this method should submit three copies of his published work (which will not be returned) to the Registrar of the Law School.

In each case the examiners have power, if they consider it necessary, to question the author personally on his work as well as on cognate subjects. In each case the candidate must declare in writing that the work is his own, and that it has not been submitted as an exercise for a degree at any other university.

The result of the examination will not be disclosed until at least three months after the submitted work has been received by the Registrar of the Law School.

29. The fee for the examination of work submitted for the degree of LL.D. is £20. This sum must be lodged with the Accountant when the candidate submits his work for examination. The fee for the degree of LL.D. is £25, and this fee is to be paid to the Accountant, on or before the seventh day before Commencements.

VI MISCELLANEOUS REGULATIONS

30. Besides those students who are reading for the degree of LL.B., other students may be admitted to Law School lectures at the discretion of the Registrar of the Law School. Such other students must pay a registration fee of £3 and a lecture fee of £5 per term for each course of lectures. These fees are payable to the Treasurer, but will be collected by the Accountant.

31. A small number of special lectures may be given on the Irish version of the Courts of Justice Acts if a sufficient number of students desire these lectures and satisfy the Professor of Irish that they are sufficiently expert in Irish to profit by them.

Prizes

32. At the end of Trinity term prizes amounting to £11 may be awarded by the professors and lecturers at their discretion in each of the following subjects: (1) law of property, (2) jurisprudence, (3) roman law and (4) constitutional law, criminal law and law of evidence. The merits of the candidates are determined by the marks obtained by them in the annual examination or, where term examinations have also been

held in any subject, by the aggregate of marks obtained in such term and annual examinations. Students reading for the degree of LL.B. as well as students of King's Inns and solicitors' apprentices are eligible to compete for these prizes.

VII ARRANGEMENTS FOR 1966-7
Lecture terms
33. The lecture terms begin on the following dates:

Michaelmas term 1966	24 October
Hilary term 1967	16 January
Trinity term 1967	10 April

Examinations for the degree of LL.B.
34. The final examination for the degree of LL.B. and the intermediate examination in law are held concurrently, and will begin on the following dates:

Monday 12 December 1966
Monday 19 June 1967
Monday 11 December 1967

SCHOOL OF PHYSIC

LECTURE AND EXAMINATION ARRANGEMENTS

Professional lectures and clinical instruction

Clinical instruction in the general hospitals commences on 1 October and continues throughout the year. Students in the clinical years are allowed one month's holiday during the long vacation, one week at Easter and approximately ten days at Christmas.

The lecture terms in the School are as follows:

MICHAELMAS TERM Monday 10 October to Saturday 10 December 1966
HILARY TERM Monday 9 January to Saturday 4 March 1967
TRINITY TERM Monday 3 April to Saturday 10 June 1967
See below, GENERAL REGULATIONS, *Entry for courses.*

The dates of commencement of pre-medical lectures are posted on the notice-boards of the laboratories concerned.

EXAMINATIONS

DATE OF EXAMINATION	LAST DAY FOR ENTRY

Pre-registration examination

Tuesday 20 September 1966	Monday 22 August 1966
Monday 12 June 1967	Tuesday 16 May 1967
Wednesday 20 September 1967	Tuesday 22 August 1967

First medical examination

Thursday 22 September 1966	Wednesday 24 August 1966
Thursday 2 March 1967	Wednesday 1 February 1967
Thursday 21 September 1967	Wednesday 23 August 1967

Second medical examination

Thursday 22 September 1966	Wednesday 24 August 1966
Friday 16 June 1967	Thursday 18 May 1967
Friday 22 September 1967	Thursday 24 August 1967

Final medical examination

PART I PATHOLOGY AND MICROBIOLOGY

Friday 2 December 1966	Thursday 3 November 1966
Friday 9 June 1967	Thursday 11 May 1967
Friday 1 December 1967	Thursday 2 November 1967

PART II   HYGIENE, SOCIAL MEDICINE AND PUBLIC HEALTH,
AND MEDICAL JURISPRUDENCE

Friday 13 January 1967	Thursday 15 December 1966
Friday 21 April 1967	Thursday 23 March 1967

PART III   MIDWIFERY AND GYNAECOLOGY

Friday 18 November 1966	Thursday 20 October 1966
Tuesday 23 May 1967	Monday 24 April 1967
Friday 17 November 1967	Thursday 19 October 1967

PART IV   MEDICINE AND PAEDIATRICS

Thursday 3 November 1966	Wednesday 5 October 1966
Wednesday 24 May 1967	Monday 24 April 1967
Thursday 2 November 1967	Wednesday 4 October 1967

PART V   SURGERY

Friday 11 November 1966	Thursday 13 October 1966
Friday 26 May 1967	Monday 24 April 1967
Friday 10 November 1967	Thursday 12 October 1967

ARTS LECTURE TERMS AND EXAMINATIONS

MICHAELMAS TERM	Monday 24 October to Saturday 10 December 1966
HILARY TERM	Monday 16 January to Saturday 4 March 1967
TRINITY TERM	Monday 10 April to Saturday 27 May 1967

JUNIOR FRESHMAN EXAMINATION	Wednesday 14 June 1967
	Thursday 28 September 1967 (supplemental)
SENIOR FRESHMAN EXAMINATION	Monday 19 June 1967
JUNIOR SOPHISTER EXAMINATION	Tuesday 6 June 1967
SENIOR SOPHISTER EXAMINATION	Thursday 1 June 1967
	Monday 2 October 1967 (supplemental)

GENERAL REGULATIONS
General requirements for primary medical degrees

In order to obtain the degrees of Bachelor in Medicine, Bachelor in Surgery and Bachelor in Obstetrics of the University of Dublin a student is required

(1) to fulfil the admission requirements of the University (see below),

(2) to attend, unless exempted, the full pre-medical course in Trinity College,

(3) to pass, unless exempted, the pre-registration examination of the University,

(4) to take an arts course and obtain the B.A. degree of the University, and

(5) to take the full medical course and pass all the medical examinations in the School of Physic.

Admission

Admission to the University of Dublin is a necessary condition of admission to the School, but does not carry any guarantee of a place in the School. Particulars of requirements for admission to the University may be obtained from the Admissions Office.

Places in the School are allocated by the Admission Committee, which considers only those applicants who have fulfilled the university admission requirements to the satisfaction of the Senior Tutor and have a matriculation qualification in mathematics or in physics[1].

Irish applicants should submit their application forms, duly completed, so as to reach Trinity College before 1 January of the year in which they wish to enter, but applications may be accepted from them until 1 September. Early application is strongly urged. Irish applicants are those whose home residences are within the thirty-two counties of Ireland, or who have received their full secondary education at Irish schools.

Other applicants must send in their application forms, duly completed, so as to reach Trinity College before 1 January of the year in which they wish to enter.

All candidates should note that their applications may be submitted before the examination requirements for admission have been fully satisfied.

No overseas applicant should come to Dublin unless he has been

[1] For admission to the University a candidate who holds a matriculation qualification in physics but not in mathematics must possess a matriculation qualification in Latin.

notified by the Senior Tutor that a place is available for him in the School.

Payment of first fees

A student accepted for admission before 1 August should pay his fees as soon as possible after acceptance but in any case not later than 1 September.

A student accepted for admission after 1 August must pay his fees within two weeks of receiving notification of his acceptance. Failure to comply with this regulation may lead to forfeiture of the place.

Exemption from the pre-medical year

Exemption from the pre-medical year may be granted to suitably qualified applicants. Applicants should apply to the Admissions Office for details of the qualifications required. They must also pass the Junior Freshman arts examination in any subject chosen from the general studies course, with the exception of applied mathematics. The Senior Tutor has discretion to accept alternative examination qualifications in arts subjects provided these are of a sufficiently high standard. Notice of candidature for the arts examination must be given to the Senior Lecturer at least one month in advance. For examination fee payable, see COLLEGE CHARGES.

Entry for courses

Entries for the courses of each year must be made on the appropriate entry forms, which are available in the School office. Entries are received in the office from 4 September until 2 October, both dates inclusive. A student leaving Dublin for the long vacation should obtain an entry form before he leaves at the end of Trinity term.

Attendance at courses

Students are required to attend regularly, and to the satisfaction of the professors and lecturers, the lectures, practical classes and demonstrations given in each of the courses of any year.

When a student is absent through illness, a medical certificate should be sent to the Dean at the time of the illness, or immediately afterwards.

A professor or lecturer may withhold credit from any student whose attendance he considers to have been unsatisfactory, or who has not attained a sufficient standard of knowledge as judged by examination.

Entry for examinations

Entries for pre-registration and professional examinations should reach the School office not later than 28 days before the date of commencement of the examination. Entries should be made on the appropriate entry forms, which can be obtained at the office. Late entries will be accepted up to 21 days before the commencing date, subject to payment of a tardy fee of 2s. 6d. for each working day in arrear. Tardy fees are payable at the office.

Credit for examinations

In assessing marks at any examination the examiners take into account the work done by the candidate throughout the course of study in the subject of the examination.

A candidate whose answering has been deficient in any subject may be required, on the recommendation of the examiners, to attend a further course of instruction in the subject before again presenting himself for examination.

Repetition of courses

A student who fails in any subject or subjects of the pre-registration examination may be permitted to repeat once only the courses in the subjects in which he has failed, *if sufficient places are available in the next pre-medical class*. If so permitted, he will not again be admitted to the examination unless he has credit for the courses repeated. A student who having repeated courses again fails to pass in any of the subjects of the pre-registration examination will not, unless in exceptional circumstances, be permitted to continue in the School.

A student who fails to obtain credit for the first or second medical years will be required to withdraw from the School. Only in exceptional circumstances will a student be permitted to repeat the year.

For the fees to be paid for repeated courses, see COLLEGE CHARGES, §8; for the fees to be paid for re-examination, see FEES below.

Applications for permission to repeat courses should be made through the Dean to the School of Physic Committee.

Exclusion of students

The School of Physic Committee may recommend to the University Council the exclusion from the School of any student whose progress is unsatisfactory or to the Board of Trinity College the exclusion of any student whose conduct is unsatisfactory.

A student who having been permitted to repeat courses again fails to obtain credit for the courses or to pass the required examinations will be reported to the University Council as having made unsatisfactory progress, and may be excluded from the School.

Change of address

A student is required to notify the School office of any change of home or Dublin address. He must also notify the Student Records Office within one week.

Health

All students are advised to avail themselves of the college scheme for regular examination by X-rays and tuberculin testing. Information about the scheme may be obtained from the School office. The Student Health Service is available in No. 11 where details may be obtained. Two doctors, one of whom attends daily, are available for consultation.

New regulations

New regulations are introduced only after due notice, but when introduced are binding upon all students.

PRE-MEDICAL YEAR

Subjects of study

The subjects for the pre-medical year are chemistry, physics and biology. The courses in chemistry and in physics extend through Michaelmas, Hilary and Trinity terms. The course in biology is given in Hilary and Trinity terms.

In addition to the above courses, a pre-medical student must obtain credit for a Junior Freshman general studies course in English, French or history before he can become a registered medical student. See ARTS REQUIREMENTS FOR PROFESSIONAL STUDENTS.

Pre-registration examination

Subjects. Chemistry, physics, biology.

The examination should be taken in Trinity term of the pre-medical year. A supplemental examination in each subject is held in September.

FIRST MEDICAL YEAR

Admission

In order to be registered as a medical student and admitted to the first medical year, a student must

(1) have passed the pre-registration examination, or have been exempted therefrom and

(2) have satisfied the arts requirements for the Junior Freshman year.

Subjects of study

Anatomy, including embryology; biochemistry; physiology; English, French or history on the Senior Freshman general studies course.

Examinations

Class examinations in anatomy, physiology and biochemistry are held during the year.

267

School of Physic

The Senior Freshman examination in general studies is held at the end of Trinity term.

SECOND MEDICAL YEAR
Admission

In order to enter the second medical year a student must have obtained credit for all the courses of the first year and have passed the class examinations in anatomy, biochemistry and physiology. He must also have satisfied the requirements of the Senior Freshman year in arts; see ARTS REQUIREMENTS FOR PROFESSIONAL STUDENTS.

Subjects of study: Michaelmas and Hilary terms

As for the first medical year, including English, French, history or fine arts II on the Junior Sophister general studies course.

First medical examination

Subjects. Anatomy, biochemistry, physiology.

This examination should be taken at the end of Hilary term in the second medical year. A supplemental examination is held before the commencement of Michaelmas lecture term.

Subjects of study: Trinity term

Pathology
Microbiology
Pharmacology and therapeutics
Applied anatomy
Applied physiology
Arts subject

A class examination in pharmacology is held at the end of Trinity term, and a supplemental examination is held before the commencement of Michaelmas lecture term.

The Junior Sophister examination in general studies is held at the end of Trinity term.

General hospital practice

In Trinity term of the second year, a student attends a course of elementary clinical instruction in one of the recognised hospitals. See below.

At the beginning of Trinity term a student should obtain from the office of the School a book containing vouchers which admit him to the general and special clinical courses. See FEES below.

At the beginning of this term a student should obtain from the School office a hospital attendance card which is to be initialled on the day of each attendance by a member of the teaching staff, and returned

268

to the office within seven days of the last day of the month to which it refers.

In order to obtain credit for the second medical year, a student must have credit for all the courses of the year, including hospital attendance, and must pass the first medical examination. He must also have satisfied the requirements of the Junior Sophister year in arts.

Clinical tutors

Clinical tutors have been appointed in the following hospitals: Sir Patrick Dun's, Royal City of Dublin, Meath, and Adelaide. The tutors in the respective hospitals report to the clinical professors at the end of each term, and at other times, if necessary, on the attendance and work of each student under their care. Credit for hospital attendance is withheld from any student unfavourably reported on by the clinical tutors.

At least three full academic years must have elapsed after obtaining credit for the second medical year before a student can be admitted to the final examinations in midwifery, medicine and surgery.

THIRD MEDICAL YEAR
Admission

In order to enter the third medical year, a student must have obtained credit for all the courses of the second year, including hospital attendance, have passed the first medical examination and have satisfied the requirements of the Junior Sophister year in arts.

Subjects of study

Pathology, together with
Microbiology, immunology and the epidemiology of infectious diseases
Pharmacology and therapeutics
Applied anatomy
Applied physiology
Psychological medicine
Anaesthetics
Genetics
Arts subject

General hospital practice

Hospital practice must be attended throughout the year. This includes clinical instruction in the wards, attendance at out-patient and specialist departments and at the almoner's department.

A student must obtain from the School office a hospital attendance card which is to be initialled on the day of each attendance by a

269

member of the teaching staff, and returned to the office within seven days of the last day of the month to which it refers. A student continues to work under the supervision of the clinical tutors.

During the third year, a student should begin the duties of clinical clerk and of surgical dresser. Special hospital cards are used for recording clerkships and dresserships. These are to be obtained from the office during the months in which these duties are being carried out. The cards should be returned to the office within seven days of the end of the period to which they refer. Each student acts as clinical clerk to the Professor of Clinical Medicine at the Meath Hospital for one month during this year.

During this year a student should also begin to write notes on post-mortem examinations.

Class examinations

Class examinations in pathology and in microbiology are held at the end of Hilary term, with supplemental examinations at the beginning of the following Michaelmas term. A student is required to pass class examinations in pathology and microbiology within a year of his completing the courses of instruction. If he fails to do so, he must repeat the courses.

B.A. degree examination

The B.A. degree examination is normally taken in June of the third medical year with a supplemental examination in October. A student who has not passed the examination by the end of his fourth medical year is not allowed to present himself for the examination again. He becomes ineligible for the medical degrees of the University but may, on completing the final examinations in medicine, surgery and obstetrics, obtain licences in those subjects. See LICENCES below.

Second medical examination

Subjects. Materia medica, pharmacology and therapeutics.

The examination is held at the end of Trinity term. A supplemental examination is held before the beginning of the following Michaelmas term.

Residence in general hospital

Students are required, after the end of Trinity term in the third medical year, to be resident students in their general hospital for a period of not less than three months. Charges for board and lodging during hospital residence must be paid directly to the hospital by the student.

FOURTH MEDICAL YEAR

Admission

A student who has obtained credit for the courses of the third medical year may enter the fourth year.

Subjects of study

Medicine
Obstetrics and gynaecology
Surgery
Paediatrics
Hygiene, social medicine and public health
Applied physiology
Applied pathology
Microbiology
Psychological medicine
Anaesthetics

General hospital practice

Attendance at the general hospitals must be continued throughout the year when not attending booked courses, and must be certified on hospital attendance cards, as in the third medical year. See above. During this year, a student should complete periods of six months as clinical clerk and as surgical dresser respectively and be resident in hospital for not less than three months. (See time-table arrangements below.)

Hygiene, social medicine and public health

The fourth-year course in these subjects consists of lectures on the organisation of public health services, bedside instruction concerning the influence of social factors on health and visits to centres under the control of local authorities and of voluntary organisations. These centres include child welfare clinics, school medical clinics and institutions for the care of handicapped children and of the aged.

Notes of medical cases

In the fourth year a student is required to deposit at the School office notes of at least two medical cases. The notes should be written during the time when the student is acting as clinical clerk or as medical resident, and should record his own observations. They are to be signed by the clinical teacher in charge of the case not later than fourteen days after the last recorded observation, and are to be left at the office not later than seven days after signature by the clinical teacher.

School of Physic

Notes of surgical cases

In the fourth year a student is required to deposit at the School office notes of at least three surgical cases. The notes should be written during the time when the student is acting as surgical dresser or as surgical resident, and should record his own observations. They are to be signed by the clinical teacher in charge of the case not later than fourteen days after the last recorded observation, and are to be left at the office not later than seven days after signature by the clinical teacher.

Pathology post-mortem examinations

A student must also present notes of six post-mortem examinations at which he has been present. The notes should contain the initials of the subject, the date of admission, a short account of the clinical history, the clinical diagnosis, the immediate manner, date and cause of death and the post-mortem findings. Any information derived from histological or bacteriological examination should be added, and the notes of each case should be signed within fourteen days by a recognised pathologist.

The notes must be handed in at the School office not later than the last day for entry for the final examination, part I.

A student is also expected to attend regularly at courses of instruction provided for students in hospital by the clinical tutors in pathology.

Clinicopathological conferences are held on Thursdays at noon in the School of Pathology. Details of these are displayed on the notice-board at the beginning of each term.

Special clinical courses

During the fourth year a student should complete some of the following courses, which are given in the special hospitals, or in special departments of the general hospitals. See below.

Paediatrics
Neo-natal paediatrics
Psychiatry
Infectious diseases
Surgery of the ear, nose and throat
Anaesthetics

Fourth Year time-table arrangements

The class will be divided into groups for special clinical courses and hospital residence for the mornings of this year. This system will be controlled at the Medical School Office and all bookings for these courses and for general hospital residence will be made from there. General hospital residence will commence for one quarter of the class at the end of Trinity Term of the Third Medical Year. All students will be booked for either residence or special clinical courses from 1 October.

PAEDIATRICS

A student must attend a course in paediatrics of one month in the fourth year and one month in the fifth year at the National Children's Hospital, where the Professorial Unit is situated. A student must also attend the neo-natal Paediatric Unit at the Rotunda Hospital for one month. In addition, he receives instruction on the work of the Child Welfare Centre and the School Medical Service, and must obtain credit for one attendance at a welfare centre and one attendance at a school medical clinic.

PSYCHIATRY

A student must attend a course in mental disease at St. Patrick's Hospital for a period of one month, and not less than six sessions of a recognised clinic for psychiatric out-patients. See below. A class examination in psychological medicine is held in Trinity term, and a supplemental examination is held in the following Michaelmas term.

INFECTIOUS DISEASES

A student must obtain credit for at least ten attendances at clinical instruction in infectious diseases at a recognised fever hospital. See below. A special course for Trinity College students is held at Cherry Orchard Hospital in the afternoons of Trinity Term. (See time-table.)

SURGERY OF THE EAR, NOSE AND THROAT

One month will be booked for attendance at an E.N.T. department of a general hospital. During this month a student may also attend teaching at other hospitals.

ANAESTHETICS

One month will be booked for instruction in anaesthetics and credit must be obtained for satisfactory attendance.

Maternity hospital practice

Apart from the preliminary attendance in Michaelmas term (see above), regular attendance at a maternity hospital may not be commenced until a student has acted for at least two months as clinical clerk and two months as surgical dresser in an approved general hospital. Regular attendance is required at the obstetrical, gynaecological, ante-natal and neo-natal departments of an approved maternity hospital for a period of not less than three months as a non-resident student, and two months as a resident student.

School of Physic

During the period of residence in the maternity hospital, a student is required to conduct personally, under official medical supervision, not less than twenty cases of labour.

Attendance at the maternity hospital is recorded on special hospital cards, to be obtained from, and returned to, the School office.

A student is also required to attend special classes in the Professorial Unit at the Rotunda Hospital during the fourth or fifth medical year.

Final medical examination, part I

The final examination, part I (pathology and microbiology), is held at the end of Trinity term of the fourth medical year, with a supplemental examination at the end of the following Michaelmas term. A student is not admitted to this or any other part of the final examination until he has passed the second medical examination. He must also have obtained credit for all the courses and class examinations in these subjects during the second, third and fourth years, and must hand in, not later than the last day of entry, notes of six post-mortem examinations at which he has been present. See above. Marks are given for these notes and count as part of the marks of the examination in pathology.

FIFTH MEDICAL YEAR
Admission

In order to begin the work of the fifth medical year, a student must have obtained credit for the courses of the fourth medical year, and have handed in notes of two medical and three surgical cases.

Subjects of study

Hygiene, social medicine and public health
Medical jurisprudence
Obstetrics and gynaecology (demonstrations)
Surgery lectures

OPHTHALMOLOGY
A student should attend a course of clinical instruction at the Royal Victoria Eye and Ear Hospital.

General hospital practice

Attendance at the general hospitals must be continued throughout the year, and must be certified on hospital attendance cards as in previous years.

Notes on medical and surgical cases

A student must hand in during the year notes of one medical, of one paediatric, and of three surgical cases, in addition to the notes of two medical and of three surgical cases given in during the fourth medical year. Notes on cases must be written during the time when the student is acting as clinical clerk or as surgical dresser or as a medical or surgical resident. All notes on cases must be given in at least one month before the date of commencement of the examination for which a student intends to enter.

Special clinical courses

During the fifth medical year a student must complete such of the following courses as were not taken during the fourth medical year: practical obstetrics and gynaecology, paediatrics, psychiatry, ophthalmology.

Final medical examination, parts II–V

Subjects

II   Hygiene, social medicine and public health, and medical jurisprudence
III Obstetrics and gynaecology
IV   Medicine (including paediatrics)
V   Surgery (including ophthalmology and surgery of the ear, nose and throat)

Admission

II. HYGIENE, SOCIAL MEDICINE AND PUBLIC HEALTH, AND MEDICAL JURISPRUDENCE

A student is admitted to the final medical examination in hygiene, social medicine and public health, and medical jurisprudence in Hilary term of the fifth medical year, provided that he has obtained credit for the lectures in these subjects.

PARTS III, IV AND V

A student is admitted to parts III, IV and V of the final examination only if he has passed in part I (pathology and microbiology) and part II (hygiene, social medicine and public health, and medical jurisprudence). Before entering for these parts a student must obtain from the office the entry form on which attendance upon the various necessary courses is to be certified.

At his first entry, a student must present himself for parts III, IV and V at the same time except by special permission of the School of Physic Committee.

III. OBSTETRICS AND GYNAECOLOGY

A student is admitted to the final medical examination in obstetrics in Trinity term of the fifth medical year on presenting certificates as follows:

School of Physic

(1) A certificate of having attended the practice of an approved general hospital or hospitals for not less than twenty-nine months after the completion of Trinity term of the second medical year.

(2) Certificates (*a*) of regular attendance at an approved maternity hospital for a period of three months, and as a resident student for a period of two months, (*b*) of having attended during the same three months the practice of the ante-natal clinics to the satisfaction of the hospital authorities, (*c*) of having personally conducted twenty cases of labour under official medical supervision, (*d*) of having attended a series of demonstrations in clinical gynaecology.

IV. MEDICINE (INCLUDING PAEDIATRICS)

A student is admitted to the final medical examination in medicine in Trinity term of the fifth medical year on presenting the following items:

(1) A certificate (*a*) of satisfactory attendance at a recognised general hospital for not less than thirty-three months after the completion of the second medical year, (*b*) of having acted as clinical clerk for not less than six months, (*c*) of having spent three months as a resident intern student.

(2) A certificate of having attended St. Patrick's Hospital for one month and a certificate of having attended six sessions at a recognised clinic for psychiatric out-patients.

(3) A certificate of satisfactory attendance at clinical instruction in infectious diseases.

(4) Certificates (*a*) of not less than two months' attendance at a course in paediatrics at the National Children's Hospital, and (*b*) of having received instruction in neo-natal paediatrics at the Rotunda Hospital.

(5) Notes of three medical cases and one paediatric case. These notes are marked and the marks awarded count as part of the marks of the final examination in medicine.

V. SURGERY (INCLUDING OPHTHALMOLOGY AND SURGERY OF THE EAR, NOSE AND THROAT)

A student is admitted to the final examination in surgery in Trinity term of the fifth medical year on presenting the following items:

(1) A certificate (*a*) of satisfactory attendance at a recognised general hospital for not less than thirty-three months after the completion of the second medical year, (*b*) of having acted as surgical dresser for not less than six months and (*c*) of having spent three months as a resident intern student.

(2) A certificate of proficiency after practical instruction in the administration of general anaesthetics. The certificate must be signed by the anaesthetist to the hospital attended by the student.

(3) Notes of six surgical cases as specified for the fourth and fifth year courses above.

Re-examination

A student who is remitted in parts IV or V of the final examination must, on entering for re-examination, present evidence of regular attendance at clinical instruction subsequent to the date of remission. A student remitted in, or absenting himself from, the final examination in medicine must present notes of four additional medical cases. A student remitted in surgery may, by special order of the examiners, be required to present notes of additional surgical cases.

DEGREES OF BACHELOR IN MEDICINE, BACHELOR IN SURGERY AND BACHELOR IN OBSTETRICS

To qualify for the degrees of Bachelor in Medicine (M.B.), Bachelor in Surgery (B.Ch.) and Bachelor in Obstetrics (B.A.O.), a student must have completed the prescribed courses of study in arts and medicine, and have passed the B.A. degree and final medical examinations. Before having his medical degrees conferred on him he must first have received the B.A. degree. Both the latter degree and the medical degrees may be conferred at the same Commencements. For degree fees see COLLEGE CHARGES.

Testimoniums of degrees are presented to candidates for degrees at Commencements, and are sent as soon as possible after Commencements to candidates who have received degrees *in absentia*.

LICENCES IN MEDICINE, SURGERY AND OBSTETRICS

A student who has satisfied the requirements of the courses in medicine, surgery and obstetrics, including the final medical examination, and who has completed the arts requirements for medical students, but has not passed the B.A. degree examination, may be granted licences in medicine, surgery and obstetrics.

INTERN YEAR

A student, on receiving his medical qualification, is required by law to spend one year of satisfactory service as resident house officer (intern) in an approved hospital or hospitals—six months in medicine and six months in surgery—before he can apply for full registration as a medical practitioner. Time spent in midwifery may be counted as, or reckoned towards, one or other of these periods.

Approved hospitals

A large number of hospitals in Ireland and in Great Britain are approved for the intern year. In addition, many overseas hospitals are suitable and either have been, or may be, approved. A student arranging to spend his intern year in any particular hospital should enquire whether it has been, or is likely to be, approved. The approving body for the purpose is the Medical Registration Council of the Republic of Ireland, to which all such enquiries should be addressed.

REGISTRATION AS A MEDICAL PRACTITIONER

Provisional registration

On receiving his medical qualification, a student must first register provisionally with the Medical Registration Council of the Republic of Ireland, 20 Fitzwilliam Square, Dublin. The fee is £9.

A student who wishes to spend his intern year in Great Britain, Northern Ireland, or overseas, must also register provisionally with the Irish Branch of the General Medical Council, 20 Fitzwilliam Square, Dublin. There is no fee for this registration.

Full registration

Having completed the intern year, the applicant must submit to the School office certificates of having satisfactorily carried out the required periods of service.

In order to obtain full registration with the Medical Registration Council of the Republic of Ireland a student should obtain from the School office a certificate of experience. This should be sent to the Registrar of the Medical Registration Council with the fee of £12.

In order to obtain full registration with the General Medical Council a student must obtain a form of application from the General Medical Council branch office on which the Dean, provided that he has received satisfactory certificates relating to the intern year, will sign the certificate of experience. The fee for full registration is £12.

HOSPITALS APPROVED BY THE BOARD OF TRINITY COLLEGE

The following Dublin hospitals are approved by the Board of Trinity College:

General hospitals
Sir Patrick Dun's Hospital

Adelaide Hospital
Royal City of Dublin Hospital
Dr Steevens' Hospital
Jervis Street Hospital
Mater Misericordiae Hospital

Meath Hospital
Mercer's Hospital
Richmond Hospital
St Vincent's Hospital

Ophthalmic Hospital
Royal Victoria Eye and Ear Hospital

Maternity hospitals

Rotunda Hospital
Coombe Hospital

National Maternity Hospital

The Professorial Unit (obstetrics and gynaecology) is at the Rotunda Hospital.

Children's hospitals

National Children's Hospital,
  Harcourt Street
Our Lady's Hospital for Sick Children,
  Crumlin

Children's Hospital,
  Temple Street

The Professorial Unit is at the National Children's Hospital, Harcourt Street.

Psychiatric hospitals

St Brendan's Hospital

St Patrick's Hospital

Hospitals for infectious diseases

Cherry Orchard Hospital,
  Ballyfermot

Vergemount Fever Hospital

The members of the clinical staffs of the above hospitals are approved as clinical teachers for students of Trinity College.

FEES

The annual fees, degree fees and other fees payable by medical students, and the regulations concerning payment of fees are stated in COLLEGE CHARGES.

Vouchers

At the beginning of Trinity term of the second medical year, a student should obtain from the School office a book containing vouchers which will admit him to the general and special clinical courses. The appropriate pages will be signed and stamped by the Secretary to the Dean and should then be presented to the hospital officer concerned. The officer then forwards the voucher to the Treasurer, Trinity College, for payment.

School of Physic

At the commencement of the third, fourth and fifth medical years, a student must submit at the School office his book of vouchers and receipt for the year's fees. The appropriate vouchers will then be signed and stamped for admission to the general and special clinical courses of the year.

If the book of vouchers is lost by a student, it will be replaced only on payment of a fee of five pounds (£5).

Re-examination fees

A student who, having entered for the pre-registration or any of the medical examinations, fails for any reason to obtain credit for it, must pay a fee of £5 for any subsequent entry. Re-examination fees should be paid to the Bank of Ireland, College Green, Dublin 2, accompanied by a fee-payment form duly completed. The receipt must be produced to the School office at the time of entry for the re-examination.

COURSE IN ARTS FOR MEDICAL AND DENTAL STUDENTS

1. Students who wish to obtain the degrees of M.B., B.Ch., and B.A.O., or B.Dent.Sc., must first have had conferred on them the degree of B.A. of the University of Dublin. They study one arts subject in each of four years, concurrently with their professional courses. For subjects and regulations, see ARTS REQUIREMENTS FOR PROFESSIONAL STUDENTS.

2. A medical student may present himself for a moderatorship in lieu of the degree examination prescribed for medical students. If he competes for a moderatorship in natural sciences, he need not attend arts lectures in the Senior Sophister year but must present evidence of satisfactory attendance at special work for moderatorship during his Senior Sophister year. If such a student has to drop one class in his Sophister years owing to the length of time required for preparation for a moderatorship in natural sciences, he will not, if successful, be called a supplemental moderator, and will be eligible for all the privileges granted to moderators, provided that satisfactory reports as to his work for moderatorship, during the year in which his name is off the books in arts, are supplied by his lecturers to the Senior Lecturer.

3. If at any time a student is reported by the Committee of the School of Physic to the Senior Lecturer, as having ceased to pursue his studies with diligence, he shall thereupon lose the privileges accorded to medical students, until such time as the Committee of the School of Physic report that he has resumed diligent attendance.

HIGHER DEGREES

Degree of Doctor in Medicine (M.D.)

1. To register for the degree of Doctor in Medicine a candidate must have had the degree of M.B. of the University of Dublin conferred upon him at least two years previously.

2. He must submit to the Dean of Graduate Studies a statement giving the subject of his research and outline of the work being done, the name of the hospital or department in which the work is being carried on and the names of collaborators, if any.

3. He must present a thesis for examination not less than twelve months after the date of registration, which is read by the Regius Professor of Physic (or a member of the staff of the School of Physic appointed by him) and an external examiner.

4. If his thesis is approved, he must pass an oral examination of an advanced standard on the subject of his thesis and on topics of general medicine.

Three bound copies of the thesis, typewritten or printed, must be sent so that they reach the School office not less than six weeks before the date of the Commencements at which the candidate wishes to have his degree conferred. Notice is given to the candidate of the date of the oral examination.

On presentation of a thesis a fee of £25 must be lodged for the credit of Trinity College, Dublin, No. 2 account, at the head office of the Bank of Ireland, College Green, Dublin 2, accompanied by a completed fee payment form which is obtainable from the Graduate Studies Office. The fee for the degree is £25, payable in the same way. This must reach the Bank of Ireland not less than seven days before the Commencements at which the degree is to be conferred.

Degree of Master in Surgery (M.Ch.)

1. To register for the degree of Master in Surgery a candidate must have had the degree of M.B. of the University of Dublin conferred upon him at least three years previously.

2. He must submit to the Dean of Graduate Studies a statement giving the subject of his research, an outline of the work being done, the name of the hospital or department in which the work is being carried on and the names of collaborators, if any.

3. After registration the candidate must pass an examination in general surgery, operative surgery and surgical pathology. This examination will be held at the time of the final examination in surgery.

4. If successful at the examination the candidate presents a thesis, not less than twelve months after the date of registration, which is read by

the Regius Professor of Surgery (or a member of the staff of the School of Physic appointed by him) and an external examiner.

Three bound copies of the thesis, typewritten or printed, must be sent so that they reach the School office not less than six weeks before the date of Commencements at which the candidate wishes to have his degree conferred.

Notice must be given to the School office two months before the date of the examination and at the same time the fee of £25 must be lodged for the credit of Trinity College, Dublin, No. 2 account, at the head office of the Bank of Ireland, College Green, Dublin 2, accompanied by a completed fee payment form which is obtainable from the Graduate Studies Office. The fee for the degree is £25, payable in the same way. This must reach the Bank of Ireland not less than seven days before the Commencements at which the degree is to be conferred.

Degree of Master in Obstetrics (M.A.O.)

The regulations for the degree of Master in Obstetrics are the same as those for the degree of Master in Surgery except: (1) that the subjects of the examination are as follows: practice of obstetrics, including antenatal care and infant hygiene; gynaecology, including gynaecological surgery, clinical obstetrics and gynaecology; anatomy of the female pelvis; elementary embryology, and that the examination will be held at the time of the final examination in obstetrics. (2) that the thesis is read by the Professor of Midwifery and Gynaecology (or a member of the staff of the School of Physic appointed by him) and an external examiner.

DIPLOMAS

Diploma in Gynaecology and Obstetrics

1. The Diploma in Gynaecology and Obstetrics is granted to registered medical practitioners who, having completed the requisite courses of instruction, have passed the examination for the diploma. This examination is of an advanced standard.

In order to be eligible for admission to the courses for the diploma, a candidate

(a) must have possessed for a period of not less than two calendar years a qualification which is registrable or temporarily registrable with the Medical Registration Council of the Republic of Ireland;

(b) must be actually registered as a medical practitioner; and

(c) should have a good knowledge of the English language.

Candidates accepted for admission to the course must obtain full or temporary registration with the Irish Medical Registration Council.

Applications should be addressed to the Registrar, Medical Registration Council, 20 Fitzwilliam Square, Dublin.

2. Application for admission to the courses should be made on a special form, which may be obtained from the Dean of the Faculty of Physic, to whom the completed application form should be returned. An application must be accompanied by a passport size photograph, certified on the back as being a true likeness of the applicant. *Original certificates should not be sent with the application form.* The completed form must be returned so as to reach the School office not later than 31 December.

The number of practitioners who can be admitted to the courses for the diploma is strictly limited.

No candidate should come to Dublin in the hope of studying for the diploma unless he has received a notification from Trinity College that a place is reserved for him.

Before the commencement of the course, each candidate is required to produce at the School office (a) his original certificate of qualification as a medical practitioner, (b) his original certificate of registration as a medical practitioner, and (c) a certificate of full or temporary registration in the Republic of Ireland.

3. The courses cover a period of six months (October to March) and are given as follows:

(A) INSTRUCTION IN TRINITY COLLEGE

This is given during the two winter terms (October to March) in anatomy of the female pelvis, embryology of the pelvic viscera, pathology of the female organs and the application of pathological methods to gynaecology and obstetrics.

Days and hours of instruction in Trinity College are announced at the beginning of the session in October, and only those members of the class who have regularly attended the courses of instruction provided are permitted to enter for the examination.

(B) INSTRUCTION AT THE MATERNITY HOSPITAL

This consists of six months' residence and clinical instruction in one of the following approved Dublin maternity hospitals: the Rotunda Hospital; the Coombe Lying-in Hospital; the National Maternity Hospital.

Clinical instruction is provided in obstetrics, gynaecology, ante-natal conditions, diseases of infants.

Certificates of satisfactory attendance at all the above courses are required.

4. The examination for the diploma is held by the University of

School of Physic

Dublin in March (at the conclusion of the course); a supplemental examination is held in June. The necessary entry form must be obtained from the School office, to which it must be returned, duly signed, not less than twenty-eight days before the date fixed for the examination to begin.

5. The following fees are payable to Trinity College:

(1) Registration fee	£30
(2) Fee for courses and examination	£60
	£90

Enquiries regarding fees for maintenance and instruction at the maternity hospital must be made to the Master of the maternity hospital[1].

Immediately on being notified that a place is provisionally reserved, a successful applicant must pay the registration fee. This fee is not refunded if the applicant fails to report for the course.

The receipt for the fee for courses and examination must be produced at the School office before a candidate can be admitted to the course.

A fee of £15 is charged for re-examination. The receipt for the re-examination fee must be produced at the School office at the time of entry.

Diploma in Psychological Medicine

The University grants a Diploma in Psychological Medicine which is open to registered medical practitioners. The examination for the diploma is in two parts. A candidate for part II of the examination must have graduated in medicine at least three years previously. At least six months before presenting himself for part II he must have passed the examination for part I conducted by the University unless exempted. In part I a candidate must pass in each section, (a) and (b). No courses are at present provided for this diploma.

The examination is held in Trinity term and in Michaelmas term. The two parts of the examination are as follows:

PART I

(a) The anatomy, physiology and histology of the nervous system. Importance is attached to the functional aspects of anatomy and to the physiological principles.

(b) Psychology. The following headings indicate the scope of the

[1] Each of the maternity hospitals mentioned above teaches and examines for a Licence in Midwifery (L.M.). Applications for particulars should be made to the Master of the appropriate hospital. The Dublin Diploma in Obstetrics (Dip. Obst. Dubl.) is granted by the Royal College of Physicians of Ireland; information is available from the Registrar of the College, 6 Kildare Street, Dublin.

examination: methods; typology; theories of consciousness and its functions; theories of the unconscious; mental energy; personality; temperament, character, with relevant theories and tests; contemporary schools of psychology; social psychology.

PART II

(*a*) Psychological medicine (2 papers)

(*b*) *Viva voce* examination

(*c*) Clinical examination

The examination covers all branches of psychological medicine, including child psychiatry, mental deficiency and, in particular, diagnosis and treatment of the psychoses and psychoneuroses.

On entering for part II of the examination a candidate must produce evidence of having held a whole-time appointment for at least one year in an approved mental hospital or hospitals.

Fees for the examination or for a re-examination:

PART I, £30.   PART II, £30.

Application for admission to either part of the examination must be received at the School of Physic, Trinity College, Dublin, by 31 March for the Trinity term examination, and by 31 October for the Michaelmas term examination. Candidates will be notified of the dates of the examination.

Exemption from part I of the examination may be granted to a candidate who has passed an examination recognised by the School of Physic Committee as equivalent thereto. Application for exemption should be addressed to the Dean of the Faculty of Physic and must be accompanied by the certificate by virtue of which the candidate claims exemption. A candidate to whom exemption is granted is required to pay an exemption fee of £10.

Diploma in Public Health

No course or examination is at present provided.

SPECIAL LECTURES

MARY LOUISA PRENTICE MONTGOMERY LECTURESHIP IN OPHTHALMOLOGY

This lectureship was founded in 1915 by the bequest of Robert John Montgomery, M.B., F.R.C.S.I. The conditions of tenure (which may be modified from time to time) are as follows:

The lecturer is appointed for one year, and is eligible for reappointment year by year for a period not to exceed five years.

The appointment rests, for alternating periods of five years, with

School of Physic

Trinity College and the Royal College of Surgeons in Ireland. (The right of appointment rests with Trinity College for the period 1966–70).

THE JOHN MALLET PURSER LECTURESHIP

In June, 1930, Miss Sarah H. Purser, R.H.A., presented to the Board of Trinity College a sum of £2,000 in order to establish an annual lecture, or lectures, on some scientific subject in which her brother, the late Dr John Mallet Purser, was interested. The Board accepted the benefaction with gratitude, and established the lectureship in accordance with the wishes expressed in Miss Purser's letter of 18 June, 1930.

THE FREDERICK PRICE LECTURESHIP

In 1946 Frederick W. Price, M.D. (EDIN.), F.R.C.P., presented the sum of £750 to establish a Frederick Price Lectureship in the School of Physic, Trinity College, with the object of promoting a closer association with the medical faculties of the other universities in Great Britain and Ireland.

A lecturer under this benefaction is appointed triennially. The next lecture will be given in Michaelmas term, 1966.

PRIZES

For further details see PRIZES AND OTHER AWARDS in the *Calendar*.

WILLIAM NUROCK PRIZE	
DR HENRY HUTCHINSON STEWART SCHOLARSHIPS	pre-medical and second medical years
ANDREW FRANCIS DIXON PRIZE	first year (anatomy)
JOHN MALLET PURSER MEDAL	first medical examination (physiology, biochemistry, histology)
DANIEL JOHN CUNNINGHAM MEDAL AND PRIZE	first medical examination (anatomy)
FOUNDATION SCHOLARSHIPS	first medical examination (advanced level)
WELLAND PRIZE	second medical year (pharmacology)
WALTER G. SMITH PRIZE	materia medica and therapeutics
AQUILLA SMITH PRIZE	final medical examination, part I
BEGLEY STUDENTSHIPS, J. W. BIGGER AND O'SULLIVAN SCHOLARSHIPS	awarded by committees
CONOLLY NORMAN MEDAL	fourth year (psychological medicine)
DE RENZY CENTENARY PRIZE	final examination (social and preventive medicine)
SIR JAMES CRAIG PRIZE	final examination (medicine)
ARTHUR BALL PRIZES	final medical examination (surgery)
BURTON PRIZE	final medical examination (surgery cases)
FITZ-PATRICK SCHOLARSHIP	highest aggregate mark in the five parts of the final medical examination
REUBEN HARVEY PRIZE	highest aggregate mark in final examinations in medicine, midwifery and surgery
RICHARD SMYTH PRIZES AND EXHIBITIONS	fifth year or postgraduate students (tropical medicine)

JOHN BANKS MEDAL AND PRIZE
EDWARD HALLARAN BENNETT PRIZE
BICENTENARY (1912) PRIZE
DR HENRY HUTCHINSON STEWART SCHOLARSHIP

} postgraduate prizes or scholarships (medicine, surgery and psychiatry)

SARAH PURSER MEDICAL RESEARCH	research in medical science
E. C. SMITH SCHOLARSHIP	research in pathology
ADRIAN STOKES FELLOWSHIP	postgraduate students (pathology or bacteriology)

SCHOOL OF DENTAL SCIENCE

Dates of terms

The dates of terms are the same as for medical students.

Dates of examinations

FIRST DENTAL EXAMINATION

Friday 30 September 1966	Thursday 1 September 1966
Friday 16 June 1967	Thursday 18 May 1967
Friday 29 September 1967	Thursday 31 August 1967

SECOND DENTAL EXAMINATION

Thursday 22 September 1966	Wednesday 24 August 1966
Thursday 23 February 1967	Wednesday 25 January 1967
Monday 25 September 1967	Monday 28 August 1967

FINAL DENTAL EXAMINATION

Thursday 3 November 1966	Wednesday 5 October 1966
Monday 19 June 1967	Monday 22 May 1967
Thursday 16 November 1967	Wednesday 18 October 1967

Admission

The conditions for admission to the Dental School are the same as for admission to the Medical School.

Degrees

The University of Dublin grants the degrees of Bachelor in Dental Science (B.Dent.Sc.) and Master in Dental Science (M.Dent.Sc.).

Arts

All students of dental science must, in addition to the dental curriculum, take an arts course, as for medical students, and must have the B.A. degree conferred before they can receive their dental degrees. See ARTS REQUIREMENTS FOR PROFESSIONAL STUDENTS.

Courses

Dental students take the same courses and examinations as medical students up to the end of Hilary term in the second medical year, and are required to pass the first medical examination. The regulations governing repetition of courses apply also to dental students. In Trinity term of the second year, they continue as follows:

SECOND DENTAL YEAR
Subjects of study: Trinity term

Dental anatomy and physiology
Pathology
Bacteriology
Pharmacology

General hospital practice

During this term, dental students attend general hospital practice as for medical students.

At the beginning of Trinity term of the second dental year and at the commencement of Michaelmas term in succeeding years, a student should obtain vouchers from the Medical School office which admit him to the clinical courses at a general hospital and at the Dental Hospital. See above.

First dental examination

This examination should be taken at the end of Trinity term of the second year. A supplemental examination is held in the following September or October.

A student who passes the first dental examination, but fails to pass the first medical examination in either Hilary term or Michaelmas term of the same year, may be permitted to repeat the second dental year. If so permitted, he must present himself for both examinations again.

A student who fails to pass the first dental examination is not permitted to proceed with the course in dental science.

THIRD DENTAL YEAR

A student cannot begin the work of the third dental year until he has passed the first medical and first dental examinations, and satisfied the requirements of the Junior Sophister year in arts.

Subjects of study

Pathology	Surgery
Practical bacteriology	Anaesthetics
Medicine	Applied dental anatomy

289

L

School of Dental Science

General hospital practice

A dental student attends general hospital practice for a period of six months during this year as for medical students.

Dental hospital practice

During this year a student attends the Dublin Dental Hospital as directed.

Second dental examination

This examination should be taken in Hilary term of the third dental year.

Subjects. Pathology, bacteriology, medicine, surgery.

FOURTH DENTAL YEAR

To be admitted to the fourth dental year, a student must have credit for the courses of the third dental year.

During the year a student attends the Dublin Dental Hospital as directed.

FIFTH DENTAL YEAR

To be admitted to the fifth dental year, a student must have credit for the courses of the fourth dental year.

During this year a student continues to attend the Dublin Dental Hospital as directed.

Final dental examination

At the conclusion of the fifth dental year, a student should enter for the final dental examination. The examination is divided into three parts.

SUBJECTS

    (*a*) Oral medicine and surgery,

    (*b*) Restorative dentistry,

    (*c*) Preventive dentistry.

The final examination is held in June, with a supplemental examination in November.

A candidate for the final examination must present certificates of regular attendance

    (1) at the practice of the Dental Hospital for a period of thirty calendar months,

    (2) at practical work in dental prosthetics at the Dental Hospital for a total of 800 hours.

All subjects should be taken and passed at the same time.

An unsuccessful candidate must submit a certificate of satisfactory clinical attendance at a Dental Hospital before being admitted to a re-examination.

DEGREE OF BACHELOR IN DENTAL SCIENCE

The degree of Bachelor in Dental Science (B.Dent.Sc.) is conferred on students who have obtained the B.A. degree, completed the above courses and passed the examinations.

FEES

The annual fees, degree fees and other fees payable by dental students, and the regulations concerning payment of fees are stated in COLLEGE CHARGES. The regulation concerning re-examination fees is the same as that for medical students.

PRIZE

For further details see PRIZES AND OTHER AWARDS in the *Calendar*.
SHELDON FRIEL PRIZE.   Final dental examination.

MASTER IN DENTAL SCIENCE

A candidate for the degree of Master in Dental Science (M.Dent.Sc.) must be a Bachelor in Dental Science of the University of Dublin of at least three years' standing. He must submit a thesis, and if the thesis be approved, undergo a *viva voce* examination.

An applicant must register with the Dean of Graduate Studies stating the subject on which he intends to present his thesis.

The thesis must be typewritten or printed, and suitably bound, and must also satisfy the examiners in its literary presentation. It must embody the results of original work by the candidate, and if the work of others is referred to should contain an adequate bibliography.

Three copies of the thesis (which will not be returned) must be sent so as to reach the Dean of the School of Dental Science at least three months before the date of a Commencements. The thesis will be read by such examiners as the Board may appoint. The examiners will fix a date for the *viva voce* examination, of which due notice will be given to the candidate. At the *viva voce* examination they will discuss with the candidate questions arising from the thesis, and may examine him in general dentistry.

The fee for the M.Dent.Sc. examination is £25, and the fee for the degree is £25.

SCHOOL OF VETERINARY MEDICINE

The University awards the degrees of Bachelor in Veterinary Medicine (M.V.B.) and Master in Veterinary Medicine (M.V.M.). A candidate for the degree of M.V.B. must take an arts course during the pre-veterinary year: see §5 below. If he wishes, he may take an arts course throughout four years, leading to the degree of Bachelor in Arts; for regulations applying to the arts course, see ARTS REQUIREMENTS FOR PROFESSIONAL STUDENTS[1].

DEGREE OF BACHELOR IN VETERINARY MEDICINE

1. In order to obtain the degree of Bachelor in Veterinary Medicine of the University of Dublin a student is required
   (1) to fulfil the admission requirements of the University,
   (2) to attend the full pre-veterinary course in Trinity College,
   (3) to pass the pre-registration examination of the University, and
   (4) to take the full veterinary course and pass all the veterinary examinations of the University.

Admission

2. Admission to the University is a necessary condition for admission to the School of Veterinary Medicine, but does not guarantee a place in the School. Particulars of requirements for admission to the University may be obtained from the Admissions Office, to which completed application forms should be returned.

Exemption from the pre-veterinary year

3. Subject to there being vacancies, exemption from the pre-veterinary year may be granted to suitably qualified applicants. Such applicants must satisfy special admission requirements, for details of which they should apply to the Admissions Office.

PRE-VETERINARY YEAR

4. In his first year a student takes the pre-veterinary subjects with pre-medical students in Trinity College, and attends an introductory course in mammalian anatomy at the Veterinary College.

---

[1] The regulations for students who entered the School in or before October 1961 are as in the *Calendar*, 1961–2, pp. 131–8.

For details of pre-veterinary subjects and examinations, see SCHOOL OF PHYSIC, regulations for pre-medical students.

5. During the pre-veterinary year a student must also obtain credit for the general studies course of the Junior Freshman year in English, French or history. He must pass the general studies examination in his chosen subject in June or October of his pre-veterinary year.

6. Because of the limited number of places available, admission to the first veterinary year depends upon a student's performance at the examinations of the pre-veterinary year. Candidates who satisfy the examiners in these examinations, both arts and pre-veterinary, are classed in order of merit according to their performance in pre-veterinary subjects. The first ten candidates are admitted to the first veterinary year.

FIRST VETERINARY YEAR
Subjects of study

7. The subjects of study are anatomy, physiology, histology, embryology, biochemistry, introductory animal husbandry.

The courses in physiology, biochemistry and histology are in part as for medical students, but special instruction is provided in aspects of these subjects important to veterinary students; these courses are given partly in Trinity College, and partly at the Veterinary College. The courses in anatomy, embryology and introductory animal husbandry are given at the Veterinary College.

Examinations

8. A College examination in introductory animal husbandry is held at the end of Hilary term.

First veterinary examination

9. *Subjects.* Anatomy, physiology, histology and embryology, biochemistry.

The examination should be taken at the end of Trinity term in the first veterinary year. Supplemental examinations are held at the beginning of Michaelmas term.

SECOND VETERINARY YEAR[1]

10. To enter the second veterinary year a student must have obtained credit for all the courses of the first veterinary year, have passed in all the subjects of the first veterinary examination and present certificates covering at least six weeks of practical farming experience working with livestock.

[1] See footnote on following page.

School of Veterinary Medicine

Subjects of study

11. The subjects of study are pathology, microbiology (including bacteriology, virology and mycology), parasitology (including helminthology, entomology and protozoology), pharmacology and, during Trinity term, an introductory course in clinical methods.

The courses in these subjects are taken partly in Trinity College, and partly at the Veterinary College.

Second veterinary examination

12. *Subjects.* Pathology, microbiology, parasitology, pharmacology.

The examination should be taken at the end of Trinity term in the second year. Supplemental examinations are held at the beginning of Michaelmas term.

THIRD VETERINARY YEAR [1]

13. To enter the third veterinary year a student must have obtained credit for all the courses of the second veterinary year, and have passed in all the subjects of the second veterinary examination.

Subjects of study

14. The subjects of study are medicine, surgery, therapeutics, preventive and state medicine, animal husbandry (including genetics and breeding, nutrition and dietetics, hygiene and sanitation, animal production and management).

Third veterinary examination

15. *Subject.* Animal husbandry.

The examination in animal husbandry should be taken at the end of Trinity term in the third year. A supplemental examination is held at the beginning of Michaelmas term.

FOURTH VETERINARY YEAR [1]

16. To enter the fourth veterinary year a student must have obtained credit for all the courses of the third veterinary year, and have passed the third veterinary examination.

[1] Students entering the third or fourth veterinary year in October 1966 take the courses prescribed in the *Calendar*, 1963-64, pp. 297-9, except that students in the third veterinary year, 1966-67, will take the degree examination in pharmacology at the end of Trinity term, 1967.

Subjects of study

17. The subjects of study are medicine, surgery, obstetrics and reproductive diseases, preventive and state medicine, public health (including food hygiene), veterinary jurisprudence and ethics, toxicology, therapeutics.

Fourth (final) veterinary examination

18. *Subjects.* Medicine, preventive and state medicine, surgery, obstetrics and reproductive diseases.

The examination should be taken at the end of Trinity term in the fourth veterinary year. A supplemental examination is held at the beginning of the following Michaelmas term. Before presenting themselves for the final examination students must have received at least six months of extra-mural instruction from approved practitioners in general veterinary practice. Attendance at an approved veterinary laboratory will be accepted as the equivalent of not more than one month of the total period of extra-mural instruction. Casebooks and other records kept during the period of extra-mural instruction, together with certificates covering the period, must be submitted before the final examination.

REGISTRATION

19. Students on whom the degree of Bachelor in Veterinary Medicine has been conferred must register with the Veterinary Council. The registration fee is £4 4s.

To practise in Great Britain and Northern Ireland graduates must be admitted to the General Veterinary Register of the Royal College of Veterinary Surgeons. The registration fee is £6 6s. Application for registration in the General Veterinary Register and payment of the prescribed fee should be made at the time of registration with the Veterinary Council.

ENTRY FOR COURSES

20. Entry for the courses of each year must be made in the School of Physic Office, Trinity College, on the appropriate form in October of each year.

ENTRY FOR EXAMINATIONS

21. Entry for examinations must be made on the appropriate forms which are obtainable in the School of Physic Office. The last date for giving notice for veterinary examinations is 28 days before the beginning of the examination. Late entries will be accepted subject to

payment of a tardy fee of 2s. 6d. for each working day in arrear. Tardy fees are payable at the office.

Foundation and non-foundation scholarships

22. A student taking the course in veterinary medicine is eligible for election to Scholarship. The examination for Scholarship consists of the papers prescribed for the annual examination of the first veterinary year together with additional papers. See FOUNDATION AND NON-FOUNDATION SCHOLARSHIPS.

FEES

23. The appropriate times and manner of paying fees to Trinity College are stated in COLLEGE CHARGES.

Supplemental examination fees are payable as follows: one subject £2; more than one subject, £5. Re-examination fees should be paid to the Bank of Ireland and the receipt must be produced at the time of entry.

DEGREE OF
MASTER IN VETERINARY MEDICINE (M.V.M.)

24. (1) To register for the degree of Master in Veterinary Medicine a candidate must have had the degree of Bachelor in Veterinary Science of the University or Bachelor in Veterinary Medicine of the University conferred upon him at least three years previously.

(2) He must submit to the Dean of Graduate Studies a statement giving the subject of his research and outline of the work being done, where the work is being carried out and the names of collaborators, if any.

(3) He must present a thesis for examination not less than twelve months after the date of registration, which is read by the Director of the School of Veterinary Medicine (or a member of staff in the School of Veterinary Medicine appointed by him) and an external examiner.

(4) If his thesis is approved, he must pass an oral examination of an advanced standard on the subject of his thesis and on related topics.

Three bound copies of the thesis, typewritten or printed, must be sent so that they reach the Director of the School not less than eight weeks before the date of the Commencements at which the candidate wishes to have his degree conferred. Notice is given to the candidate of the date of the oral examination.

On presentation of a thesis a fee of £25 must be lodged for the credit of Trinity College, Dublin, No. 2 account, at the head office of the Bank of Ireland, College Green, Dublin 2, accompanied by a completed fee payment form which is obtainable from the Graduate Studies Office. The fee for the degree is £25, payable in the same way. This must reach the Bank of Ireland not less than seven days before the Commencements at which the degree is to be conferred.

SCHOOL OF ENGINEERING

1. The University awards the degrees of Bachelor in Engineering (B.A.I.) and Master in Engineering (M.A.I.). A Licence in Engineering is also obtainable. A candidate for the degree of B.A.I. takes an arts course in addition to the course in engineering subjects. On the completion of his course in both arts and engineering, he is entitled to the degree of B.A. as well as the degree of B.A.I.

Holders of the B.A.I. awarded after 1961 are exempted from the appropriate parts of the professional examinations of the relevant engineering institutions.

I DEGREES OF BACHELOR IN ARTS AND BACHELOR IN ENGINEERING

2. The course for these degrees normally lasts four years, but there is provision for an abridgement of the course to three years. See below.

3. The greater part of the course is in general engineering, but after the first year a student may elect to study any one of the following four groups of subjects:

GROUP A. A course in which the emphasis is on civil engineering design and construction.

GROUP B. A course in which the emphasis is on mechanical and production engineering.

GROUP C. A course in which the emphasis is on electronic engineering.

GROUP D. A course in which the emphasis is on aerodynamics.

Admission

4. To qualify to be considered for admission to the School a candidate must have (*a*) satisfied the general admission requirements of the University and (*b*) passed not more than one year previously an entrance examination to the School or, being suitably qualified, having been granted exemption therefrom. The entrance examination is held in September or October. A student may enter on his course only at the beginning of Michaelmas term.

5. To qualify for admission to an entrance examination, an applicant must *either* (i) have passed the matriculation examination or been granted complete exemption from it, *or* (ii) have paid the matriculation fee with a view to fulfilling the matriculation requirements. See ADMISSION REQUIREMENTS, §§4, 5, 6, 12.

6. Notice of intention to take the entrance examination must reach

the Registrar of the School before 1 September. Forms for the purpose may be obtained from the Registrar of the School or from the Admissions Office.

A candidate may not attempt the examination more than twice, nor, in seeking to obtain exemption from it, may he submit the results of more than two other examinations and, except with the special approval of the University Council, all attempts to qualify for admission must have been made within a period of 18 months.

7. The entrance examination consists of one three-hour paper in arithmetic, algebra, geometry and trigonometry on the following course:

Arithmetic. Averages, percentages, square roots, calculation of areas and volumes, use of logarithmic tables.

Algebra. Remainder theorem, factorisation, fractions, equations in two or three unknowns, theory and solution of quadratic equations, theory of indices and logarithms, arithmetical, geometrical and arithmetico-geometrical progressions, graphs.

Calculus. The elements of calculus.

Geometry. The synthetic and analytic geometry of the straight line and circle.

Trigonometry. Trigonometrical identities, sine and cosine rules, formulae for the area of a triangle, circular measure and small angles, the addition formulae, transformation of sums and products, logarithmic solution of triangles, problems in heights and distances, trigonometrical equations.

Logarithmic tables are provided, but candidates should bring with them pencil compasses, set-square, protractor and a scale divided in centimetres.

Exemption from first year

8. In certain circumstances suitably qualified applicants may be exempted from the first year of the course. Such applicants must (*a*) satisfy the Senior Tutor as to matriculation requirements, (*b*) pass the first year supplemental engineering examination in physics, chemistry and mathematics[1], (*c*) attend an abbreviated course in September and pass an examination in geometrical drawing and elementary surveying, and (*d*) pass the Junior Freshman arts examination in June or October in any subject chosen from the general studies course with the exception of pure and applied mathematics. The Senior Tutor has discretion to accept alternative examination qualifications in arts subjects provided

[1] Suitably qualified applicants may be granted exemption from examination in the three subjects of this section. Applications to take the first year examinations in chemistry and physics are considered only if the applicants have followed an approved laboratory course in these subjects.

School of Engineering

these are of a sufficiently high standard. Notice of candidature for the arts examination must be given to the Senior Lecturer at least one month in advance. For the Junior Freshman arts examination fee, see COLLEGE CHARGES.

Course in arts

9. A student takes in each year one arts subject. For detailed regulations see ARTS REQUIREMENTS FOR PROFESSIONAL STUDENTS.

Duration and subjects of professional courses

10. The professional course continues for four years (except for those students granted exemption from the first year). During this time instruction is given, partly by lectures and partly in laboratories, in the field and in the drawing office, and is arranged as follows. The numbers in brackets after each course refer to the syllabus set out below.

First year

ALL GROUPS

Mathematics and mechanics (1) Drawing (5)
Physics (2) Surveying (6)
Chemistry (3)

Second year

GROUPS A, B AND D	GROUP C
Mathematics and mechanics (1)	Mathematics and mechanics (1)
Chemistry (4)	Physics (7)
Electrical engineering (8)	Electrical engineering (8)
Surveying (6)	Surveying (6)
Theory of structures (9)	Theory of structures (9)
Mechanical engineering (10)	Mechanical engineering (10)
Drawing (5)	Drawing (5)

Third year

GROUP A	GROUP B
Mathematics and mechanics (1)	Mathematics and mechanics (1)
Strength and properties of materials (13)	Strength and properties of materials (13)
Structures (11)	Control engineering (15)
Soil mechanics (14)	Production engineering (18)
Hydraulics (16)	Hydraulics (16)
Mechanical engineering (10)	Mechanical engineering (10)
Geology (17)	Surveying (6)
Surveying (6)	Theory of machines (21)
	Applied thermodynamics (24)

GROUP C
Mathematics and mechanics (1)
Strength and properties of
    materials (13)
Control engineering (15)
Electronic engineering (19)
Mechanical engineering (10)
Physics (7)

GROUP D
Mathematics and mechanics (1)
Strength and properties of
    materials (13)
Structures (11)
Mechanical engineering (10)
Aerodynamics (28)
Control engineering (15)
Electronic engineering (19)
Applied thermodynamics (24)

Fourth year

GROUP A
Strength and properties of
    materials (13)
Civil engineering structures (12a)
Hydraulic engineering (20)
Civil engineering design and
    quantities (22)
Soil mechanics (14)
Surveying (26)
Mathematics (optional) (25)
Town planning (optional) (27)

GROUP B
Strength and properties of
    materials (13)
Production engineering (18)
Theory of machines (21)
Statistics (23)
Control engineering
    (optional) (15)
Applied thermodynamics (24)
Mathematics (optional) (25)

GROUP C
Strength and properties of
    materials (13)
Electronic engineering (19)
Control engineering (15)
Statistics (23)
Mathematics (25)

GROUP D
Strength and properties of
    materials (13)
Control engineering (15)
Aircraft structures (12b)
Aerodynamics (28)
Mathematics (optional) (25)
Applied thermodynamics (24)

Examinations

11. Students are examined in the work of each year. The first year examination is held at the end of Trinity term. The second, third and final year examinations are held partly at the beginning and mainly at the end of Trinity term. A supplemental examination in all subjects for all years is held at the beginning of Michaelmas term.

12. A student whose name is not on the books of the School of Engineering must give notice to the Registrar of the School of his intention to present himself at any of these examinations at least a week before the first day of the examination.

School of Engineering

13. A student may not begin the second year course until he has completed the first year examination in *all* subjects, unless he has been completely exempted from the first year. It should be noted that there are no supplemental examinations in the general studies course in pure or applied mathematics.

14. A student in the second or third year who has not passed the regular or supplemental examination of his year in every subject is not, except at the discretion of the School Committee, allowed to proceed to the following year; if so allowed, he must present himself for re-examination in any subject in which he has not passed at the next opportunity if it is an arts subject or at either or both of the next two opportunities if it is a subject in the professional course, but may not do so thereafter. It should be noted that there are no supplemental examinations in the general studies course in either pure or applied mathematics or in the third arts subject in the second year and in the third arts subject only in the third year.

15. A student in the first, second or third year who does not obtain credit for the year owing to his failure either to attend the necessary lectures or practical classes, or to complete the required drawings, or to pass the regular or supplemental examination of his year, is not allowed to repeat the year except at the discretion of the Engineering School Committee. A student who is repeating any year except the fourth loses credit for having passed previously the examination in any of the subjects of that year; before being allowed to proceed, he must again attend the lectures, carry out the practical work and pass the examination in *all* subjects. A student who fails in more than two subjects in the regular examination for the degree of B.A.I. must present himself for re-examination in all subjects at the supplemental examination. A student who fails in more than two subjects at the supplemental examination will be required to present himself again for re-examination in all subjects. Students who fail to pass the supplemental examination in its entirety must, subject to the discretion of the School Committee, repeat the year in all subjects before being allowed to complete the examination; such students will be required to pay the full annual fee.

16. A student who has not passed in its entirety any examination within eighteen months from the date on which he first became eligible for it is reported to the Council as an unsatisfactory student, with a recommendation for his exclusion from the School.

17. Exemption from these requirements may be granted in exceptional circumstances after written application has been made by the student to the School Committee.

Credit for year

18. To complete the course for a year, a student must (*a*) attend satisfactorily the lectures in each subject of his course, both arts and engineering, (*b*) perform satisfactorily the prescribed exercises (essay, tutorial or practical work) and (*c*) satisfy the examiners at the annual or supplemental examination of the year. Failure to comply with conditions (*a*) and (*b*) may result in refusal of permission to take all or part of the annual examinations of the student's year.

Conferring of degrees

19. A student who has obtained credit for the four years' course is entitled to the degrees of B.A. and B.A.I. To have the B.A.I. degree conferred, he must first have had the B.A. degree conferred. Both degrees may be conferred at the same Commencements.

Licence in Engineering

20. A student who has passed the B.A.I. degree examination, but has failed to pass the B.A. degree examination, is entitled to receive a licence in engineering.

Honors and other awards

21. First and second class honors are awarded for superior merit shown in the examination for the degree of B.A.I. They are awarded on the total mark obtained in one of the four groups of principal subjects (Groups A, B, C or D) at this examination.

Except by special recommendation of the examiners, these honors are awarded only on the results of the regular B.A.I. degree examination of a student's year.

22. The following other awards are obtainable. For fuller details, see PRIZES AND OTHER AWARDS.

MARMADUKE BACKHOUSE PRIZE	On result of first year examination (value £48)
HANDCOCK MEMORIAL SCHOLARSHIP	At entrance (value £70 p.a. for three years)
FRANCIS SPRING PRIZE	On result of second year examination (value £40)
FOUNDATION SCHOLARSHIPS	Trinity term of third year
EDGE PRIZES	Third year examination in geology (value £10)
ALEXANDER PRIZE	At B.A.I. degree examination (value £22 10s.)
DAVID CLARK PRIZE	At B.A.I. degree examination (value £15)
CLARK MEMORIAL PRIZE	At B.A.I. degree examination (value £7 10s.)
JEFFCOTT PRIZE	At B.A.I. degree examination (value £10)
COLLEN PRIZE IN ARTS	At B.A. degree examination (value £25)
COLLEN PRIZES	Reports on current projects (value £15 each)
FITZGERALD PRIZE	Post B.A.I. degree (value c. £150)
EVERARD WILLIAM DIGBY FUND	Financial assistance: maximum £20

School of Engineering

D.U. Engineering Society
23. For details see SOCIETIES AND CLUBS.

Fees and charges
24. The annual fees, degree fees and other fees payable by students of engineering are stated in COLLEGE CHARGES.

25. A fee of £2 is payable for a supplemental examination in one subject, and a fee of £5 for a supplemental examination in more than one subject. The fee must be paid to the Bank of Ireland before 1 September for an examination in Michaelmas term, and before 1 April for a Trinity term examination, and must be accompanied by a duly-completed fee payment form.

26.

SYLLABUS

1. *Mathematics and mechanics*
The courses in pure mathematics and applied mathematics prescribed for the Senior Freshman, Junior Sophister and Senior Sophister years of the course in General Studies.

2. *Physics*
Junior Freshman honor course in physics (primary level), School of Natural Sciences.

3. *Chemistry*
A course of lectures extending over three terms covering elementary inorganic and physical chemistry, together with practical work on elementary analysis.

4. *Chemistry*
A course of lectures extending over three terms on special topics in chemistry as applied to engineering, together with practical work on more advanced and applied analysis.

5. *Drawing*
Use of drawing instruments and the planimeter; construction of scales; geometrical construction of plane curves; use of squared and logarithmic paper; orthographic, isometric and oblique projection; development of surfaces; graphical determination of moments; graphic statics; tracings and preparation of prints.

6. *Surveying*
Chain surveying; levelling; contours; plotting of plans and sections; ordnance survey maps; traverse surveying; plane table surveying; measurements of areas and volumes; mass haul diagrams.

Construction and adjustment of instruments; tacheometry; topographical and reconnaissance surveying; location and setting out of works; road and railway curves; hydrographical surveying; triangulation surveys; measurement of base lines.

7. *Physics*

Senior Freshman honor course in physics, School of Natural Sciences.

8. *Electrical engineering*

M.K.S. system of units, basic electromagnetic theory, basic theory of d.c. and a.c. circuits (single and three-phase); principles of d.c. and a.c. measurements with engineering applications; elementary treatment of the functioning and operation of d.c. and a.c. machines; simple electron devices; basic ideas of protective devices; illumination.

9. *Theory of structures*

Graphical and analytical determination of forces in framed structures; shearing force and bending moment diagrams for fixed and moving load systems; wind pressure; riveted joints; roof trusses; beams, simply supported and encastré; deflection of beams and frames.

10. *Mechanical engineering*

Drawing and design of machine parts; bolts, keys, shafts, couplings, bearings; belt, chain and gear drives; measurements and gauges; machine tool and engine parts.

Properties and thermodynamics of steam and the theory of the steam engine; temperature and heat-entropy diagrams; boilers and accessories; composition, analysis, combustion and calorific value of fuels; simple steam engines; valve gears and diagrams; testing of steam engines and boilers.

Thermodynamics and theory of gases; theory of heat engines; gas producers; gas and oil engines; indicators and indicator diagrams; oil fuels; testing of gas and oil engines; thermal efficiencies of engines and plant. Heavy oil, diesel and other internal-combustion engines; super-heated steam; compound steam engines; steam flow, nozzles and turbines; compressors, pumps and refrigerators.

Production of iron and steel and their properties; patterns, castings and foundry practice; methods of moulding, tools and appliances; operations of forging and smithing; drop forgings; rolling, bending and drawing; manufacture of wire, tubes and pipes; die castings; heat treatment of steels; pyrometry.

Testing of materials, iron, steel, timber, cement and concrete; testing machines for tension, compression, bending, hardness, impact and fatigue.

The courses provide for practical work in the drawing office, machine shop and laboratory, and include the following topics: the running and adjustment of engines; use of indicating apparatus; determination of brake horse-power and tests for mechanical and thermal efficiencies; consumption and boiler tests; the use of machine and bench tools and of testing machines for iron, steel, timber, cement and concrete.

11. *Structures*

Influence lines; indeterminate frames; moment distribution; elements of reinforced concrete; strain energy; Castigliano's theorems; principle of least work; pin-jointed three-dimensional frames; rings.

School of Engineering

12a. Civil engineering structures

Beams and plate girders; bridges and lattice girders; wind bracing; portals; arches; continuous girders; columns; reinforced concrete; pre-stressed concrete; column analogy; relaxation methods.

12b. Aircraft structures

Strain circle; electrical resistance strain gauge; Airy's stress function with elementary applications; torsion of non-circular sections; membrane analogy; torsion by relaxation methods; flexural centre of closed and open sections; types of failure of stringer reinforced panels; shear lag and axial constraint stresses; shear web theory; elastic instability of thin flat plates; vibration of uniform beams.

13. Strength and properties of materials

Working stresses; deflection; built-in and continuous beams; simple and compound stresses and strains; elastic constants; strain energy; springs; thin and thick cylinders; rotating cylinders and discs; torsion of circular and non-circular sections; curved beams; struts; stress concentration; fatigue; hardness; impact; atomic basis of the electric and magnetic properties of matter and plasma; measurement of these properties.

14. Soil mechanics

Classification of soils; methods of testing; stability of embankments and cuttings; earth pressure; retaining walls; foundation of roads and buildings; bearing and sheet piling; cement and concrete.

15. Control engineering

Introduction and background; differential equations of electrical, mechanical, hydraulic and thermal systems, and their solution by classical and the Laplace transform methods; transient analysis of servo-mechanisms, including block diagrams and transfer functions; frequency response; nyquist stability criterion; error detectors; root locus method of analysis; cascade and feedback compensation techniques; optimization; non-linearities; phase-plane and describing function techniques; treatment of Random signals; analogue computers; design studies on control problems in the following fields: nuclear reactor system, aircraft and rocket stability, industrial machine tools, chemical process control.

16. Hydraulics

Hydrostatics; stability of floating bodies; orifices, weirs and flumes; flow of water and oils in pipes and channels; turbines, pumps; hydraulic transmission of energy; viscosity, dimensional analysis; use of models.

17. Geology

General principles of geology, mineralogy, petrology, physical geology and stratigraphy; geological map-reading, engineering geology, the geology of engineering materials; water supplies; the geological background of soil mechanics; geophysical techniques.

A field tour lasting three days is held at the end of Hilary term and students are required to attend at least three local excursions during the year.

18. *Production engineering*

Analysis of workers' personality and biological characteristics; the man/machine combination; foremen, shop stewards, trade unions and employers' associations; wages, merit and motivation incentives; work study; causes and cure of disputes; personnel officer; employment, welfare, education, safety; employer/worker communications.

Analysis of organisation; line or management; functional or paperwork; specialist or advisory; feed-back or reporting; delegation and co-ordination.

Process design; production control; works engineer; inspection and statistical quality control; computer for planning, progressing, wages and costing.

Factory siting, lay-out, materials handling and stores; furnaces; hot forming, cold forming, heat treatment; metal cutting; lubrication, machining, metrology.

General characteristics of law in modern communities. Concept of the legal person—the present judicial system. Law and equity. The Law of Contract. The idea of property. General principles of law of tort (or private wrongs). Arbitration. Contracts. Agency. Sale of goods. The elements of industrial law, patents, trade marks, designs and copyrights.

19. *Electronic engineering*

Determination of electric and magnetic field distributions; electromagnetic waves; electron optics; electron devices including applications of semiconductors; analysis and general theory of the transient and steady state behaviour of electric networks; transmission lines; non-linear circuits; circuit synthesis; modulation, demodulation and frequency changing; advanced treatment of electrical measurements with particular reference to electronic equipment; generalised treatment of rotating machines with applications to control systems.

Application of these topics to the design and analysis of electronic equipment.

20. *Hydraulic engineering*

Sources of supply and quality of water; rainfall and run-off; river gauging; capacity of reservoirs; water treatment and distribution.

Design of sewers and sewerage schemes; treatment and purification of sewage.

21. *Theory of machines*

A continuation of the work in mechanical engineering (10) to a more advanced level and including the following topics: kinematics of machines; elements of mechanisms, rigid members and connecting pairs, inversion; velocity and acceleration diagrams; cams, gears, including epicyclic and worm gears; primary and secondary balancing of single and multi-cylinder in-line engines; vibrations; torsional oscillations of shafts, transverse vibrations of beams; whirling of shafts; forced vibrations with viscous damping; gyroscopes; tractive effort and performance curves for vehicles.

22. *Civil engineering design and quantities*

The design of civil engineering structures in steel and concrete.
Taking off quantities; preparation of bills of quantities.

23. *Statistics*

Basic statistical theory and method with applications.

24. *Applied thermodynamics*

Continuation of the work in mechanical engineering (10) and including the
following topics: cycles; Rankine, reheat, regenerative and binary vapour
cycles; constant volume, constant pressure and dual combustion cycles.

Heat transfer; conduction, convection and radiation.

Fuels, air supply, products of combustion.

Air compressors and motors. Multi-stage compressors; positive rotary
compressors.

Heat pumps and refrigeration, reversed cycles.

Steam. Flow of steam through nozzles. Impulse and reaction turbines. Gas
turbines.

Simple and regenerative cycles.

25. *Mathematics*

A continuation of the three-year course in mathematics with particular
reference to applications in the field of electrical engineering.

26. *Surveying*

Elements of geodesy; photogrammetry.

27. *Town and country planning*

A course of lectures in town and country planning is given to engineering
students of the fourth year.

An examination is held at the end of the course. Attendance at lectures and
examinations is optional.

Engineering graduates and architects may be admitted to the lectures, the
fee being one guinea for holders of the B.A.I. degree and two guineas for others.

28. *Aerodynamics*

Basic aerodynamic theory with applications.

Parsons Engineering Laboratories

27. The laboratories are equipped for testing, teaching and research
work in the fields of civil, mechanical and electrical engineering and
include workshops attached to the mechanical and electronic engineering sections.

Computer Laboratory

This laboratory is equipped with hand and electrical calculating
machines, analogue computers and an electronic digital computer.

II DEGREE OF MASTER IN ENGINEERING (M.A.I.)

28. Applications for the degree of M.A.I. should be addressed to the Dean of Graduate Studies. A candidate must have taken the degree of B.A.I. in the University of Dublin and must have practised for three years as an engineer after having obtained the degree of B.A.I. To qualify for the M.A.I. degree he must present a written thesis, which must take the form either of a report on a piece of engineering research carried out by the candidate himself individually or as one of a group, or else of a description of a substantial project in design, construction, development or production in an engineering field in which he has taken part.

29. A candidate must furnish evidence that the requirements stated above have been fulfilled and he must submit three bound copies of his thesis to the Professor of Engineering. On presentation of the thesis a fee of £25 must be lodged for the credit of TRINITY COLLEGE, DUBLIN, NO. 2 ACCOUNT at the head office of the Bank of Ireland, College Green, Dublin 2, accompanied by a completed fee payment form which can be obtained from the Graduate Studies Office. The degree fee of £25 is payable in the same way.

III GRADUATE SCHOOL OF ENGINEERING STUDIES

Courses are provided at postgraduate level for graduates and others and are designed for those who intend to follow a career in industry. The courses, which last for one academic year, lead to the degree of M.Sc. in the case of candidates already holding a primary degree of a recognised university, or to a diploma in the case of other candidates.

Admission requirements and procedure

Candidates for admission should be university graduates or should hold equivalent qualifications. Candidates who have not studied mathematics at a university are expected to hold a good honours degree.

All applicants must apply for registration to the Dean of Graduate Studies, but enquiries can be addressed, in the first instance, to the Registrar, Graduate School of Engineering Studies.

Courses available during 1966-7

Only one course will be provided starting in October, 1966. The subject of the course will be computer applications.

Syllabus

Basic principles of computers, principal systems used, input-output

School of Engineering

equipment, principles of programming and machine language and symbolic programming systems for both scientific and business applications, operations research, linear and dynamic programming, critical path scheduling, simulation, cybernetics, teaching machines, machine translation of languages.

Data processing, business programming systems, information retrieval, elementary numerical analysis with particular reference to matrix algebra, elementary statistics, stock control, payroll, organisation and methods.

Automatic programming systems suitable for scientific applications, numerical analysis and methods with practical applications.

Fees

For fees payable see COLLEGE CHARGES under heading SUMMARY OF FEES FOR HIGHER DEGREES.

Examination

There will be a written examination at the end of the course and, in addition, candidates must submit a dissertation on an individual project.

IV DATES OF EXAMINATIONS

Entrance examinations	20 September 1966
	20 September 1967
First year examinations	
supplemental	20 September 1966
regular	5 June 1967
supplemental	20 September 1967
Second year examinations	
supplemental	20 September 1966
regular	5 June 1967
supplemental	20 September 1967
Third year examinations	
supplemental	20 September 1966
regular, part 1	19 April 1967
regular, part 2	5 June 1967
supplemental	20 September 1967
B.A.I. degree examinations	
supplemental	20 September 1966
regular	29 May 1967
supplemental	20 September 1967
Foundation Scholarship examination	3 April 1967

All examinations begin at 9.30 a.m.

SCHOOLS OF AGRICULTURE
AND FORESTRY

TEACHING STAFF

Agriculture: The Farm Manager
Agricultural Microbiology: The Professors of Bacteriology and Botany
Biochemistry: The Professor of Biochemistry
Botany: The University Professor of Botany
Chemistry: The Professor of General Chemistry
Drawing and Surveying: The Lecturers in Civil Engineering
Economics: The Lecturers in Economics
Farm accountancy: [Vacant]
Farm management: The Farm Manager
Geography: The Reader in Geography
Geology: The Professor of Geology and Mineralogy
Mathematics: The Lecturers in Mathematics
Physics: Erasmus Smith's Professor of Natural and Experimental Philosophy
Physiography: The Professor of Geology and Mineralogy and the Reader in Geography
Statistics: The Lecturer in Statistics
Zoology: The Professor of Zoology and Comparative Anatomy

The Schools of Agriculture and Forestry aim to produce through their teaching and research a proper understanding of the husbandries and associated technologies within the economics of the agricultural industry. To this end the teaching is based on the fundamental natural sciences and on the economic and social sciences, and it extends to treating the farm or woodland as a business.

311

SCHOOL OF AGRICULTURE

Degrees obtainable

1. The University offers the following degrees in agriculture:

DEGREE OF BACHELOR IN AGRICULTURE (AGR.B.). A candidate pursues a four-year professional course, including two years at University College, Dublin.

DEGREE OF MASTER IN AGRICULTURE (AGR.M.). A candidate presents a thesis. See §§16-20.

DEGREE OF MASTER IN SCIENCE (M.SC.). A candidate presents a thesis following research as prescribed by the general regulations for the degree of M.Sc. See GRADUATE STUDIES AND HIGHER DEGREES.

A. DEGREE OF BACHELOR IN AGRICULTURE (AGR.B.)

Admission

2. A student wishing to enter the School of Agriculture should apply through the Senior Tutor to the School Admission Committee when he applies for general admission to the University.

Because of the limited number of places in the School applications can normally be considered only from candidates whose home residences are in Ireland (thirty-two counties). If places are available, applications may be considered from candidates one of whose parents is Irish or holds a degree from an Irish university.

Candidates resident in Ireland should send in their application forms, duly completed, before 1 January of the year in which they wish to enter, but applications may be accepted from them until 1 September. They are urged to apply as early as possible. Other candidates must send in their application forms, duly completed, before 1 January.

Applicants must satisfy the admission requirements of the University. See ADMISSION REQUIREMENTS. The Admission Committee gives preference to applicants who have obtained honours at the Leaving Certificate examination, or passed with good marks at the matriculation examination, or with high grades at advanced level in a General Certificate of Education examination, in two scientific subjects. One of these subjects must be chemistry, physics or mathematics; the other subject may also be from this group, or may be one of the following: additional mathematics, biology, botany, geography, geology, zoology. Applicants who do not have high qualifications in scientific subjects, but have a qualification in mathematics and a high level of attainment in other subjects, may be considered, if places are available.

312

Course

3. A student spends the Freshman years in Trinity College studying the general principles of the sciences which later find application in agriculture. At the end of the Junior Freshman year and at the end of the Senior Freshman year he must pass an examination in the professional subjects of the year. These annual examinations are held in Trinity College and are conducted by the examiners of the University. They are held at the end of Trinity term. Supplemental examinations for students who fail are held at the beginning of Michaelmas term. See §9 and §15.

4. At the end of Trinity term in the Senior Freshman year a student, to obtain admission to the courses of University College, must give evidence of a practical knowledge of agriculture or of an allied subject (forestry or horticulture). For this purpose he must pass a qualifying examination conducted by the Faculty of Agriculture of University College at its Experimental Farm in Glasnevin, Dublin. If he has not had adequate experience of practical agriculture, he may be required to obtain such experience before presenting himself for the qualifying examination.[1]

5. The Sophister years are spent at Glasnevin studying the husbandries, sciences and technologies of agriculture. A student at Glasnevin must attend the courses and perform the exercises satisfactorily which are prescribed by University College, and pass the third and fourth examinations in agricultural science of the National University of Ireland.

Final examination

6. The final examination in agriculture and agricultural science is conducted in University College, and mainly by the professors of that college. The University of Dublin is represented at the examination by an examiner appointed by Trinity College, and extern to University College.

Arts requirements

7. Students are not required to take an arts course, but they may, if they wish to obtain the degree of B.A., proceed according to the regulations stated under ARTS REQUIREMENTS FOR PROFESSIONAL STUDENTS[2].

[1] A student is considered to have had adequate experience if he has spent at least one year working full-time on a large general farm.
[2] Students who entered the school before October 1962 are subject to the regulations appearing in the Calendar for 1961-2.

School of Agriculture

Completion of year

8. A student is deemed to have completed the course for a year when he has (*a*) attended satisfactorily the lectures in each subject, (*b*) performed satisfactorily the prescribed exercises, essay, tutorials and/or practical work, and (*c*) satisfied the examiners at the examinations required.

Conditions (*a*) and (*b*) must be satisfied before a student is qualified to take the examinations of his year.

A Junior Freshman can proceed to the Senior Freshman year only if he has satisfied the examiners in all his subjects. A Senior Freshman or Junior Sophister who has not passed the regular or supplemental examination of his year in every subject is not, except at the discretion of the School Committee, allowed to proceed to the following year; if so allowed, he must present himself for re-examination in any subject in which he has not passed at either or both of the next two opportunities for examination in such subject, but may not do so thereafter.

Notice for examinations

9. Notice of intention to sit for the annual examination is not required. For the supplemental examination each candidate must complete an examination notice form and return it to the School Office by 1 September at the latest. Tardy notice may be accepted on payment of five shillings for each day in arrear up to seven days. If a notice more than seven days in arrear is accepted the fine is £2. Fines must be paid before the examination.

Conferring of degrees

10. A student who entered before October 1962 and who has completed the four years' course is entitled to receive the degrees of B.A. and Agr.B. To obtain the Agr.B. degree the B.A. degree must first be conferred. Both degrees may be conferred at the same Commencements.

A student entering the school in or after October 1962 may proceed to the Agr.B. degree without qualifying for the degree of B.A.

11.

SYLLABUS

JUNIOR FRESHMEN	SENIOR FRESHMEN
biology (J.F. natural science honor course)	agriculture (at the Kells Ingram Farm)
	agricultural microbiology
chemistry (J.F. natural science honor course II)	biochemistry (S.F. natural science honor course) or
physiography (J.F. natural science honor course)	chemistry (S.F. natural science honor course)
	drawing and surveying
physics (J.F. natural science honor course II)	soil geology
	statistics

JUNIOR SOPHISTERS	SENIOR SOPHISTERS
at University College Farm:	at University College Farm:
agriculture	agricultural economics II
agricultural botany	animal husbandry I
agricultural chemistry	animal husbandry II
agricultural economics I	crop husbandry
agricultural zoology	farm machinery and structures
genetics and plant breeding	farm management
soil science	plant pathology

Horticulture

In the Sophister years, professional students may substitute the following courses at U.C.D. for those in agriculture:

THIRD OR J.S. YEAR	FOURTH OR S.S. YEAR
genetics and plant breeding	arboriculture
horticultural botany	horticultural economics
horticultural chemistry	horticultural machinery and structures
horticultural zoology	horticulture I
horticulture I	horticulture II
horticulture II	plant pathology
soil science	

HONORS AND PRIZES

12. First and second class honors are awarded for superior merit in the final examination in agriculture in University College, provided that the candidate has obtained marks of an honor standard at the examination held at the end of the second year in Trinity College.

Edge Exhibition

13. One Edge Exhibition of £25 is offered at the end of the Senior Freshman year for merit in the professional course. The award is made by the Board of Trinity College on a report from the Registrar of the School of Agriculture.

FEES

14. The annual fees, degree fees and other fees payable by students of agriculture are stated in COLLEGE CHARGES.

A student of agriculture who, with the consent of the Senior Lecturer and the Registrar of the School of Agriculture, interrupts his academic course for a year in order to acquire practical experience of agriculture is not required to pay a replacement fee on resuming his academic course. See COLLEGE CHARGES, §16.

15. A Junior Freshman or Senior Freshman student taking the course for the Agr.B. degree and presenting himself for a supplemental exami-

School of Agriculture

nation in Michaelmas term must pay a fee of £2 for examination in one subject, and of £5 for examination in more than one subject. The fee must be paid to the Bank of Ireland, College Green, Dublin, and must be accompanied by a duly completed fee-payment form. The part of the fee-payment form which contains the bank's acknowledgement of payment must be sent to the School together with a properly completed examination notice form not later than 1 September.

B. DEGREE OF MASTER IN AGRICULTURE (AGR.M.)

16. An intending candidate for the Agr.M. degree must be a Bachelor in Agriculture of not less than three years' standing and have been engaged for two years at least in practical agriculture, or in advisory work, teaching or research connected with agriculture.

17. Applications to register for the Agr.M. degree should be sent to the Dean of Graduate Studies. The application must state the subject of study and the method of treatment proposed. If the applicant is accepted, he will be registered as a candidate if a graduate of the University.

18. The candidate must submit the results of his study in the form of a thesis not sooner than one year and not later than four years, except by permission of the School Committee, from the beginning of the academic year after registration. The thesis must be either printed or typewritten, and three securely bound and covered copies must be submitted. The examination fee, payable to the Treasurer, is £25.

19. The thesis is examined by two examiners who may require the candidate to present himself for a *viva voce* examination on the subject of his thesis.

20. The degree fee of £25 must be paid to the Accountant not later than the seventh day before the Commencements at which the degree is to be conferred.

SCHOOL OF FORESTRY

1. The regulations of the School of Agriculture regarding admission, arts requirements, completion of year, examinations, conferring of degrees and fees apply to the School of Forestry. See SCHOOL OF AGRICULTURE, §§2-10, 14-15.

2. The degrees obtainable in forestry are the degree of Bachelor in Agriculture (Forestry) and the degree of Master in Agriculture (Forestry).

A. DEGREE OF BACHELOR IN AGRICULTURE (FORESTRY)

Course

3. The course lasts four years. In the Freshman years a student follows the Freshman courses in the School of Agriculture for the degree of Agr.B.

4. To be admitted to the Junior Sophister course a student, if not exempted by reason of a previous test, must produce evidence of a practical knowledge of forestry.

5. In the Sophister years a student takes professional subjects at University College, Dublin.

Syllabus of course

6. Freshman years: as for students in the School of Agriculture.

7. Sophister years:

JUNIOR SOPHISTERS
at University College:
   forest botany
   forest chemistry
   forest zoology
   genetics and plant breeding
   forest mensuration
   silviculture
   soil science

SENIOR SOPHISTERS
at University College:
   forest economics and valuation
   forest machinery and structures
   forest management
   forest protection
   forest utilisation
   plant pathology

B. DEGREE OF MASTER IN AGRICULTURE
(FORESTRY)

8. The regulations for candidates seeking the degree of Agr.(Forest.)M. are as for candidates seeking the degree of Agr.M. with the difference that the intending candidate for the Agr.(Forest.)M. must be a Bachelor in Agriculture (Forestry) of not less than three years' standing and have been engaged for two years at least in practical forestry or in advisory work, teaching or research connected with forestry.

SCHOOL OF MUSIC

I DEGREE OF BACHELOR IN MUSIC (MUS.B.)

Admission

A candidate for the degree of Bachelor in Music must satisfy the general requirements for admission to the University and pay the matriculation fee, but he is not required to take a course in arts. Application should be made on forms obtainable from the Admissions Office. For fees see IV below.

Examinations

A candidate normally takes three examinations (Parts I, II and III as set out below).

A candidate who has an honours B.A. degree in music of the Universities of Oxford or Cambridge, will be exempted from Part I (Preliminary Examination) on applying to the Registrar of the School but he must pay an exemption fee of £10.

A candidate who holds the diploma of Fellowship of the Royal College of Organists (paper work) may not proceed to Part III of the examinations for Bachelor in Music on the strength of exemption claimed prior to 1967 unless he has already attempted the final examination before 1967.

Exemption from section (c) (performance) in Part II will be granted to a candidate with one of the following qualifications: F.R.C.O., L.R.A.M. (performers only—organ, piano), A.R.C.M. (performers only—organ, piano). The full examination fee of £10 must be paid for taking section (a) or (b) of Part II.

Part I, Preliminary Examination

Candidates will be examined in the following subjects:

(a) Harmony up to four parts (3-hour paper)

(b) Counterpoint in sixteenth century and baroque styles (3-hour paper)

(c) History of music from c.1400 up to c.1750 (3-hour paper)

(d) Ear tests, including musical dictation and the recognition of historical styles and instruments from excerpts played on the gramophone, or by other means (1 hour)

School of Music

(e) Candidates will also be examined *viva voce* on their general knowledge of music, including a critical knowledge of the works listed below. No candidate who fails to satisfy the examiners in section (e) will be given credit for the other parts of the Preliminary examination.

FOR 1967

(i) Byrd, *Mass for 5 voices*
(ii) Beethoven, *String Quartet in C minor Op. 18 No. 4*

Part II

Before entering for the final examination, a candidate must pass Part II of the examination, for which *two* out of the following three options must be chosen.

(a) Submit a composition of an extended nature, such as a String Quartet or Cantata for not less than three performers; or a folio consisting of a variety of smaller compositions.

The material should be sent to the Professor of Music not later than six months before a candidate intends to present himself for entry to the Final Examination, accompanied by a signed statement that the work is entirely of the candidate's own composition. The appropriate fee shall be paid to the Accountant before the exercise is submitted.

(b) Take a rehearsal of approximately one half hour of *one* of the following pieces:

FOR 1967

(i) *Sanctus, Benedictus* and *Agnus Dei* from Byrd, *4-part Mass for unaccompanied choir* (piano available)
(ii) Mozart, *Symphony No. 29 in A*, K.201. First two movements, with amateur orchestra
(iii) Mozart, *Clarinet Quintet*

N.B.—The choice will be decided by the availability of musicians, and not by the wish of the candidate.

(c) Undergo a practical test on an instrument of their own choosing. All keyboard players will be expected to sight-read, transpose, and *either* read from an open score in not more than 5 parts which may contain C clefs, *or* improvise on a given theme. Should the harpsichord be chosen, the ability to provide a continuo accompaniment from a figured bass will replace the previous alternatives. Players of other instruments will be given a sight-reading test, and will be expected to read a simple accompaniment on the pianoforte.

Every candidate in the practical test will be required to provide an extempore harmonisation of a simple melody, on the keyboard.

Each candidate must be prepared to play on the instrument of his choice a short programme of not less than 10 minutes duration, consisting of pieces of diploma standard covering a variety of styles.

In connection with Part II there will be a *viva voce* examination.

A candidate's achievement in one section of Part II will be assessed in relation to his ability in another.

The practical tests in Part II (sections (*b*) and (*c*)) will take place on the day before the final examination. A candidate who has qualified in Part II may enter for the final examination the following day.

Part III, Final Examination

Candidates will be examined in the following subjects:

(*a*) Harmony up to five parts (6-hour paper)

(*b*) Counterpoint in up to five parts, including canon in two parts with the addition of a free part. Candidates will be required to show a knowledge of the predominant styles and textures within the period 1650–1850 (3-hour paper)

(*c*) Fugue, up to four parts (3-hour paper)

(*d*) History of music from the period of C.P.E. Bach up to the present day. Questions may relate in a general way to music before this period (3-hour paper)

(*e*) Elementary acoustics (one obligatory question will be included in the History paper). (See footnote [1])

(*f*) Orchestration of given material (2½-hour paper)

(*g*) (*Viva voce*). General knowledge of music, including a critical knowledge of the following works:

FOR 1967

(i) Haydn, *The Creation* (*Die Schöpfung*) Part I (Full score)

(ii) Wagner, *Prelude & Liebestod from Tristan* (Orchestral version)

(iii) Bartok, *Music for Strings, percussion and celesta*

Tuition

Particulars concerning limited tuition leading to the degree of Bachelor

[1] A knowledge of the material covered in Alexander Wood's *The Physics of Music* will be sufficient for this question.

School of Music

in Music for members of the University reading other courses, and for other students resident in Dublin, can be obtained from the Professor of Music.

Candidates must normally make their own arrangements for tuition outside the University.

II DEGREE OF DOCTOR IN MUSIC (Mus.D.)

A Doctor in Music must be a Bachelor in Music of the University of Dublin. A candidate must submit an exercise and take an examination. The exercise, which must be submitted before the examination, may not be presented until four years after the candidate has qualified for the bachelor's degree.

The exercise may be either:

(a) A folio of musical compositions, at least one of which must be a major work for full orchestra with or without choir, or

(b) A musicological thesis of approximately 20,000 words, or

(c) A critical edition of one major work, or a group of smaller works (total performing time in either category, approximately 30 minutes)

The candidate is advised to consult the Professor of Music about the suitability of his exercise before submitting it for examination. It must be sent to the Professor of Music not later than six months before the date of the examination, with a signed statement that the material is the candidate's own unaided work. The appropriate fee shall be paid to the Accountant before the exercise is submitted.

Examination

Papers will be set in the following subjects:

(a) Technique of composition, showing a knowledge of the typical styles and textures of the great composers. Alternative questions will be offered (9 hours)

(b) History and critical knowledge of music (3 hours)

and *either*

(c) Composition: testing the candidate's originality and ability to provide satisfactory music for an occasion (6 hours), or

(d) The editing of a piece of music, which may be incomplete, in correct historical style. Alternatives will be offered (3 hours)

In addition to the set papers, the candidate will be interviewed.

GRADUATES OF OXFORD OR CAMBRIDGE UNIVERSITIES

Persons who hold the B.Mus. degree of Oxford or the Mus.B. degree of Cambridge may apply to the Board through the Senior Proctor for *ad eundem* status, and if this is granted may proceed to the examination for Mus.D. upon submitting the required exercise, provided that they have qualified for the B.Mus. or Mus.B. degree not less than four years previously. They must also pay to the Accountant the *ad eundem* Mus.B. fee of £20.

III ENTRY FOR EXAMINATIONS

Notice of intention to enter for any examination must be sent to the Registrar of the School of Music not later than two calendar months before the date of the examination. All fees which are due must have been paid to the Accountant by this date.

Timetable for Examinations 1967

Monday June 19	9.30—12.30 and 2.00—5.00	Mus.D. paper (*a*)
Tuesday June 20	9.30—12.30 2.30 p.m. 8.00 p.m.	Mus.D. paper (*a*) continued. Part II section (*c*) (performance) Part II section (*b*) (rehearsal technique) followed by *viva voce*.
Wednesday June 21	9.30—12.30 2.00—5.00	Part I Harmony, Part III Harmony, Mus.D. papers (*c*) or (*d*) Part I Counterpoint, Part III Harmony continued, Mus.D. paper (*c*) continued.
Thursday June 22	9.30—12.30 2.00—5.00	Part I History, Part III Counterpoint. Part I Ear test and *viva voce*, Part III History and acoustics, Mus.D. Critical and historical paper.
Friday June 23	9.30—12.30 2.00—5.00	Part III Fugue Mus.D. Interviews Part III Orchestration and *viva voce* examinations.

IV FEES

Students accepted into the School of Music for the purpose of proceeding to the degree of Bachelor in Music will be charged a registration fee of £5 per annum payable before the end of each Michael-

School of Music

mas term. The fee will entitle them to be registered for the ensuing year and is payable in the first instance before the end of the Michaelmas term after their acceptance has been notified. Only registered students whose registration fee has been paid may proceed to examinations.

	£	£
Matriculation fee		8
Bachelor in Music		
Part I: Preliminary examination (or exemption therefrom)	10	
Part II: Exercise and practical test	10	
Part III: Final examination	10	
Degree conferring fee	10	
		40
Bachelor in Music *ad eundem gradum*		20
Doctor in Music		
Exercise	10	
Examination	20	
Degree conferring fee	25	
		55

All fees must be paid to the Accountant. The fees are payable on each occasion that a candidate takes any part of the examinations. A candidate for the degree of Bachelor in Music must, when paying the preliminary examination fee (or the fee for exemption therefrom), send to the Accountant a statement of the date of matriculation.

If a candidate for the degree of Bachelor in Music is a Bachelor in Arts of the University, he pays a degree conferring fee of £10, and is not charged the examination fees nor the fee for the exercise and practical test. A candidate claiming this exemption must, when entering his name for the examination, state the year in which he graduated.

V PRIZES

Stewart and Prout prizes. Awarded at the Mus.D. and Mus.B. examinations. For details see PRIZES AND OTHER AWARDS.

Professor of Music and Registrar of the School of Music
Brian Boydell, B.A., MUS.D., L.R.I.A.M.

SCHOOL OF EDUCATION

1. The School of Education provides courses in education and educational psychology for graduate students who wish to qualify for the Higher Diploma in Education in order to become recognised secondary school teachers, and for students of the Church of Ireland Training College who are training to become primary school teachers.

The regulations for the Higher Diploma in Education are given below; details of the course for students of the Church of Ireland Training College will be found in the appropriate section of the *Calendar*.

DEPARTMENT FOR THE TRAINING OF SECONDARY TEACHERS
HIGHER DIPLOMA IN EDUCATION

2. The Department (which is under the control of the Professor of Education) provides theoretical and practical instruction for the HIGHER DIPLOMA IN THE HISTORY, THEORY AND PRACTICE OF EDUCATION.

Admission

3. Applicants for admission to the Department should be either teachers or students intending to become teachers, who hold university degrees or other equivalent qualifications recognised by the Teachers' Registration Council of Ireland. Applications are not normally considered from persons engaged in teaching at a school more than twelve miles from Trinity College. All applications should be made to the Professor of Education not later than 10 June of the year in which admission is sought.

Teaching practice

4. Candidate teachers obtain the necessary teaching practice in Dublin secondary schools, such practice being supervised by the staff of the School of Education under the direction of the Professor of Education. By arrangement with the school authorities concerned, similar supervision is exercised over the work of persons already engaged in teaching who join the course. All candidates must prepare, as required, lesson note-books, setting out in detail the content of lessons they will give. Overseas students, whose native language is not English, may be exempted from the requirements regarding teaching practice at the discretion of the Professor, provided that their training and experience in their own countries appears to justify this concession.

School of Education

5. Lectures, tutorial courses and seminars begin in October and end in June. They take place in the afternoon. The teaching practice extends throughout the secondary school year.

6. *Courses*

I The general theory of education

II Educational psychology A

III Educational psychology B
(In this course a completely written-up laboratory record is obligatory.)

IV The basic principles of teaching

V Comparative education

VI The history of education

VII Special methods of teaching school subjects
(Students must take method lectures in two subjects.)

VIII Individual study and investigation
(Students may be required to produce a short thesis or, alternatively, two or more essays during the training course, at the discretion of the Professor.)

Examination

7. At the examination for the Higher Diploma in Education five papers are set, one in each of the following: general theory of education; educational psychology A and basic principles of teaching; educational psychology B; history of education and comparative education; methods of teaching. A student must satisfy the examiners in each paper in order to qualify for the award of the diploma. Three hours are allowed for each paper.

A candidate may present himself for the diploma examination within one year of his completion of the lecture course, after which period a student is not allowed to present himself without the special permission of the Board. If permission is granted a replacement fee is payable.

Successful candidates for the diploma are divided into three classes according to merit. They are awarded first class honors, second class honors and pass respectively, the names in each class being arranged in alphabetical order. Candidates who fail in one subject only may be granted a supplemental examination in that subject, on the recommendation of the examiners, in Michaelmas term.

The examination in methods of teaching is usually held at the end of Hilary term. The examination in the other four papers is held in Trinity term: for dates, see ALMANACK.

Fees

8. The annual fee for the course is £55 (which includes the laboratory fee of £3), a third of the fee being payable in each term. Students whose home residences are not in Ireland pay a surcharge of fifty per cent. A registration fee of £5 is chargeable upon registration. This sum will be deducted from the course fee, but is not returnable to applicants who do not enter upon the course.

Fees should be paid before 30 October in Michaelmas term and before the first day of arts lectures in Hilary and Trinity terms. Payment should be made direct to the Bank of Ireland at its head office, College Green, Dublin. Cheques, etc., should be drawn payable to TRINITY COLLEGE, DUBLIN, NO. 2 ACCOUNT, and should be crossed. Each payment must be accompanied by a properly completed fee-payment form.

The fee for the diploma examination is £5, and should be paid not later than one week before the date of the examination. The fee for a supplemental examination in one subject is £2.

Higher Diploma in Education with Honors
(For students who obtained the Higher Diploma in Education before June 1958.)

9. Candidates for the higher diploma with honors must have passed in the first or second class at the ordinary higher diploma examination before June 1958. They may qualify for the higher diploma with honors by presenting a thesis, of merit sufficient to satisfy the examiners, on an approved subject connected with educational or psychological studies. The Professor of Education advises candidates on the selection of the subjects and supervises the preparation of their theses.

All theses are submitted to an external examiner.

Results are published twice yearly, in June and December.

The fee for the examination of the thesis is £6 for graduates of the University of Dublin, and £15 for other candidates.

The Registrar of the School of Education will supply any further information required.

SCHOOL OF BUSINESS AND SOCIAL STUDIES

1. The School of Commerce and the School of Social Studies were amalgamated in 1962 to form the School of Business and Social Studies. In the School of Business and Social Studies there are two departments: the Department of Business Studies and the Department of Social Studies.

2. The University awards the degrees of Bachelor in Business Studies (B.B.S.), Master in Administrative Studies (M.S.A.), and Bachelor in Social Studies (B.B.S.) and a Diploma in Social Studies. A candidate for the degree of B.B.S., or B.S.S., may, if he wishes, take a course in arts in addition to the course set out below. The course in arts leads to the degree of Bachelor in Arts (B.A.). For details of the arts course, see ARTS REQUIREMENTS FOR PROFESSIONAL STUDENTS.

I GRADUATE COURSE IN ADMINISTRATION

3. The graduate course in Administration is intended for those who are employed or will be employed in organised undertakings, and who need

(1) an understanding of the social, political and economic forces supporting, and constraining, productive activity;

(2) the analytical techniques and occupational skills needed to appreciate the value and limitations of specialist assistance;

(3) a balanced judgment when, as is usual in making decisions, conflicting interests have to be weighed.

4. The course is full-time. extending over one academic year. Provision is made whereby research assistants attached to the University's Administrative Research Bureau may spend two years on the course.

5. A graduate who has completed the course will be eligible for the degree of Master in Administrative Studies (M.S.A.). Other students who have completed the course will be awarded a Higher Diploma in Administration.

6. In addition to members of the University staff, there will be associate lecturers in specialist subjects from the staffs of institutes co-operating with the University in the teaching of administration and management.

328

Admission requirements

7. Applications for admission to the course may be received from

(*a*) graduates of the University of Dublin with first or second class moderatorships, or with first or second class honors in a professional degree course;

(*b*) graduates of other universities with first or second class honor degrees;

(*c*) employees of business undertakings (including state-sponsored undertakings), central or local government departments, trade unions, institutions or associations, provided they produce evidence of academic fitness as specified in §8 below;

8. Evidence of academic fitness is provided by a certificate showing the applicant to be the holder of

(1) a professional qualification in accountancy or in secretaryship recognized by the Department of Industry and Commerce;

(2) a professional qualification in engineering recognized by the Engineers Association of Ireland and the Institution of Civil Engineers of Ireland;

(3) a professional qualification in law;

(4) a professional qualification in marketing recognized by the Institute of Marketing and Sales Management;

(5) a professional qualification in medicine;

(6) a scientific qualification obtained through examination by a recognized college of technology, technical institute or school, or vocational school, following a minimum course of two years.

9. A candidate who cannot submit a certificate under §8 may apply for admission, provided he or she is thirty years of age or over, on the basis of work done in the field of business or administration which has been acknowledged by an award of merit, or by exceptional promotion in the employing body, or by publication.

10. An undergraduate in the University of Dublin, who is taking an honor or professional degree course but has yet to sit for the final moderatorship or professional degree examination, may be granted provisional admission if his performance throughout his undergraduate years has been at the level of second rank honors or higher.

11. The Admissions Committee reserves the right not to admit applicants who have graduated or obtained professional qualifications in a range of studies substantially similar to those on which the course is based.

Business and social studies

12. All applicants for admission must apply for registration to the Dean of Graduate Studies, to whom all enquiries should be addressed. Application forms, duly completed, must reach the Graduate Studies Office not later than 31 March, and must be accompanied by evidence of academic fitness (§§8, 9 above), and, in appropriate cases, by the registration fee (§§19, 20 below). Late applications from well qualified applicants may be considered.

Allocation of places

13. If the number of qualified candidates exceeds the number of places available, the Admissions Committee will allot places on the results of interviews and of such tests as the Committee may decide.

14. The Admissions Committee may (a) interview or test any or all of the candidates and may reject any candidate either before or after interview or test, (b) require a candidate applying under §9 to defend his work in oral examination.

COURSES AND EXERCISES

Courses

15. The courses are designed to present the knowledge and related techniques currently considered to be useful in business and administration within the following fields of study:

Administrative theory and practice, including behaviour, employment relations, management of work and organisation.

Economics, including the bases and structure of industry; international business, money and national income.

Environment of business, including employee and employer associations, financial institutions, law, and social and political institutions.

Operations analysis, including financial administration, information, marketing approach, operations research, planning and control, and work study.

Quantitative methods, including accounting, data processing, decision theory, managerial economics, and statistics.

Exercises

16. *Project assignments*. Each student must work on a project assignment. Those who have not had substantial experience in employment must work on a business project. Those with such experience must work on an academic project, but need not stay away from their places of employment during the summer vacation when the project is being written up.

17. To complete the course a student must (a) obtain satisfactory ratings each term on the tests prescribed by the teaching staff, (b) present by 1 September a satisfactory report on the project assignment. The prescribed tests include an examination at the end of Trinity term on the work of all three terms.

18. A student who, on the strength of his admission qualifications, is granted exemption from lectures or classwork, is nonetheless required to present himself for the examination in full and to satisfy the examiners in it.

FEES

19. The fees payable are:	A Student without a contract of employment	B Student with a contract of employment
Registration fee	nil	£10
Course fee	£130	£210
Annual capitation fee	£9	£9
Diploma or degree fee	£25	£25

20. The registration fee is payable when application is made for admission to the course. The fee will be refunded to candidates whose applications are unsuccessful.

21. The course fee is payable on or before 1 October. A student whose home residence is outside Ireland (thirty-two counties) pays a surcharge of fifty per cent on the course fee.

ADMINISTRATIVE RESEARCH BUREAU

The Bureau was established in 1965 as a complement to the graduate course:

(1) to provide an operating link between the University and the administrative and business sectors of the Irish economy;

and (2) to establish principles to improve, in the community interest, the practice of administration and the productivity of business.

Although closely associated with the Department of Business Studies, the Bureau has a separate Board of Directors.

Student Projects

As part of the graduate programme, students work on practical problems in undertakings and institutions outside the University. Although initiated for student development, the projects are intended to benefit the undertakings and institutions which co-operate with the University. In short, the aim is mutual benefit.

Business and social studies

The student projects are supervised by the staff teaching in the area to which the project relates. It is an essential and expected component of the exercise that there is a feed-back to teaching from the practical situation.

Faculty and Contract Research

The University can contribute effectively to the practice of administration, and productivity, if it has principles to teach which are applicable to practical situations. The establishment of such principles calls for research into a wide range of activities and calls for continuous co-operation between the University and outside bodies. Some research studies are initiated by the University and others by outside bodies for which the Bureau works on contract.

Finance

Because the Bureau is financed independently of the University, it depends on income from contract research and on financial support from business undertakings and institutions in the development of management and administration.

II DEGREE OF BACHELOR IN BUSINESS STUDIES

Admission

22. A student wishing to proceed to the degree of Bachelor in Business Studies should apply to the Senior Tutor not later than 1 January of the year in which he proposes to begin his studies. An applicant must satisfy (a) the general admission requirements of the University (see ADMISSION REQUIREMENTS) and (b) a selection committee as to his suitability for the course. Applications from Irish candidates received after 1 January and before 1 September will be considered.

General requirements

23. The course lasts four years. A student must begin the course at the beginning of Michaelmas term.

24. A student is deemed to have completed the course for a year when he has (a) attended satisfactorily the prescribed lectures and seminars, (b) performed satisfactorily the prescribed exercises (essay, tutorial and practical work), and (c) satisfied the court of examiners at the examinations of the year.

He is permitted to take the annual examination of the year only if he has attended the lectures and seminars and performed the prescribed exercises satisfactorily.

Examinations

25. Students are examined annually in the work of each year.

26. The annual examination is held in June.

27. The examinations in the Sophister years cover, where appropriate, the work of the earlier years.

28. A student must take all the papers prescribed for the annual examination of his year. If his performance is judged unsatisfactory, the School Committee may grant him a supplemental examination in the same year.

A student who is granted a supplemental examination must, if his performance at the annual examination was unsatisfactory in one subject only, present himself in that subject at the supplemental examination; if his performance was unsatisfactory in more than one subject, he must submit to supplemental examination in all subjects.

29. In all examinations, all papers carry equal weight.

30. *Honors.* The names of successful candidates at examinations are published in three classes according to merit: first class honors, second class honors (with two divisions, first and second), and pass.

31. *Degrees.* Degrees will be awarded in three classes according to merit: first class honors, second class honors (with two divisions, first and second) and pass. In determining merit, a student's performance throughout the course is taken into account.

32. The School Committee may recommend to the University Council that a student who does not satisfy the requirements of his year should be excluded from the school.

Foundation and non-foundation scholarships

33. A student reading the course in Business Studies is eligible for election to scholarship (see FOUNDATION AND NON-FOUNDATION SCHOLARSHIPS). The examination for scholarship will be held in April. It consists of the papers prescribed for the annual examination of the Junior Sophister year together with a paper on a prescribed subject and an essay paper. A course of reading for these general papers may be obtained from the head of the Department.

34.   **COURSES AND EXAMINATIONS**

Junior Freshmen
Courses

Economic geography; economic history; economics I; elements of law; elements of science—class; scientific method and elementary statistics.

Business and social studies

Examinations

Papers are set in the following subjects: economics; economic geography; economic history; elements of law; scientific method and elementary statistics.

Senior Freshmen

Courses

Accountancy I; administration I; economics II; law relating to business; political institutions; psychology; science and technology—class.

A student must spend at least one month, preferably during the long vacation, working in a business undertaking.

Examinations

Papers are set in the following subjects: accountancy; administration; economics; law relating to business; political institutions; psychology.

Junior Sophisters

Courses

Accountancy II; administration II; current affairs—seminar; economics III; employment relations; law relating to business; public finance.

Examinations

Papers are set in the following subjects: accountancy; administration; economics; employment relations; law relating to business; public finance.

Senior Sophisters

Courses

Accountancy III; administration III; current affairs—seminar; economics IV; government in the economy.

Examinations

Papers are set as follows: accountancy; administration (two papers); economics; government in the economy; essay.

The papers will require a knowledge of current affairs and of science and technology.

35. A syllabus booklet may be obtained from the Department of Business Studies. Reading lists are available to students only.

FEES

36. The annual fees, degree fee and other fees payable by a student taking the course for the B.B.S. degree are stated in COLLEGE CHARGES.

37. The fee for a supplemental examination in one subject is £2, the fee for a supplemental examination in all subjects is £5. Supplemental examination fees must be paid before 15 September. A student who has not paid the fee by the appropriate date is not permitted to present himself at the supplemental examination. The fee must be paid

at the head office of the Bank of Ireland, College Green, Dublin, and be accompanied by a properly completed fee-payment form.

III DEGREE OF BACHELOR IN SOCIAL STUDIES

The regulations which follow apply to students beginning the course in or after October 1964. The regulations which apply to students who began the course in or before October 1963 are as set out in the *Calendar* for 1965–66, pp. 326–9.

Admission

38. Students wishing to proceed to the degree of Bachelor in Social Studies should apply to the Senior Tutor not later than 1 January of the year in which they propose to enter, and should communicate at the same time with the Director of Practical Training in the Department of Social Studies. Applications from Irish candidates received after 1 January and before 1 September will be considered.

Applicants must (*a*) have reached the age of eighteen years before 15 October of the year in which they propose to begin the course, (*b*) satisfy the general admission requirements of the University (see ADMISSION REQUIREMENTS), and (*c*) satisfy a selection committee as to their suitability for the course. The selection committee will normally interview candidates.

General requirements

39. The course lasts four years. Students must begin the course at the beginning of Michaelmas term.

The course comprises both academic study and practical training, including periods of full-time work during vacations.

40. Students are deemed to have completed the course for a year when they have (*a*) attended satisfactorily the appointed courses of lectures and instruction, (*b*) performed satisfactorily the prescribed exercises and class work, (*c*) satisfied the court of examiners at the examinations of the year, and (*d*) completed the appointed practical training to the satisfaction of the School Committee.

The School Committee may recommend to the University Council that students who have not satisfied the requirements of their year should be excluded from the school.

Examinations

41. Students are examined annually in the work of each year.

The annual examination is held at the end of Trinity term in each year.

42. Unless excused by the School Committee, a student must take

the annual examination of the year. A student who fails in one subject may, at the discretion of the School Committee, take that subject again at a supplemental examination held at the beginning of Michaelmas term in each year. A student who fails in more than one subject may, at the discretion of the School Committee, take all subjects again at the supplemental examination.

43. *Honors.* The names of successful candidates at examinations are published in three classes according to merit as follows: first class honors, second class honors and pass. The names of candidates in the second class are further grouped in two divisions, first and second. In awarding honors a candidate's performance in practical training is taken into account.

Degrees

44. Degrees will be awarded in three classes as follows: first class honors, second class honors (with two divisions, first and second), and pass. In awarding degrees a student's examination results throughout the course and performance in practical training are taken into account.

Foundation and non-foundation scholarships

45. A student taking the course in Social Studies is eligible for election to scholarship. See FOUNDATION AND NON-FOUNDATION SCHOLARSHIPS.

46. COURSES AND EXAMINATIONS

Junior Freshmen

Courses

Lectures and tuition: social structure; political institutions; economics I; ethics; scientific method and elementary statistics.

Practical work: a student makes visits of observation and works with groups of children or does club work. Group meetings are held with the Director of Practical Training. Each student must write a report on the practical work of each term.

Examinations

Papers are set in the following subjects: social structure; political institutions; economics; ethics; scientific method and elementary statistics.

Senior Freshmen

Courses

Lectures and tuition: psychology I; economics II; social administration I; introductory science (Michaelmas term), medical studies I (Hilary and Trinity terms); principles of social work; history and philosophy of science.

Practical work: practical work will be arranged with groups of children or others in need of care. It must be performed satisfactorily. A student must attend a hospital out-patients department once weekly for one term, take part in visits of observation and attend lectures by extern lecturers. A written report on each term's practical work must be submitted to the Director of Practical Training.

During the summer vacation a student must carry out six weeks' supervised full-time practical work in a public authority, voluntary body or other organisation engaged in social or personnel work. The placement will be arranged by the Director of Practical Training.

Examinations

Papers are set in the following subjects: psychology; economics; social administration; medical studies; history and philosophy of science.

Junior Sophisters

Courses

Lectures and tuition: psychology II; social administration II; medical studies II; law; elementary casework; political theory.

Practical work: students work under supervision with medical or other social workers, and must take part in visits of observation and attend extern lectures. They must attend the children's court weekly for one term and visit each of the courts for adult persons. During the summer vacation each student must spend at least eight weeks continuously at full time work under the supervision of a fully qualified and experienced social worker in a public authority, voluntary body, or other organisation engaged in social or personnel work.

Examinations

Papers are set in the following subjects: psychology; social administration; medical studies; law; political theory.

Senior Sophisters

Courses

Lectures and tuition: social psychology; social administration III; elementary casework and two of the following: mental health; business administration; principles and methods of social surveys; criminology. Choice of subjects will be made in consultation between each individual student and the head of the department.

Practical work: a programme of practical work is drawn up for each student in the light of the special subjects chosen.

Examinations

Compulsory papers are set on: social administration; social psychology; elementary casework.

Optional papers, of which, a candidate takes the two corresponding to the lecture courses attended, are set on: mental health; business administration; principles and methods of social surveys; criminology.

Business and social studies

In addition a student must pass a *viva voce* examination in casework, in which an external examiner takes part.

FEES

47. The annual fees, degree and other fees payable by a student taking the course for the B.S.S. degree are stated in COLLEGE CHARGES.

48. The regulations concerning fees for supplemental examinations are as follows. The fee for a supplemental examination in one subject is £2, the fee for a supplemental examination in all subjects is £5. Supplemental examination fees must be paid before 15 September. A student who has not paid the fee by the appropriate date is not permitted to present himself at the supplemental examination. The fee must be paid at the head office of the Bank of Ireland, College Green, Dublin, and be accompanied by a properly completed fee-payment form.

IV DIPLOMA IN SOCIAL STUDIES

Admission

49. Students wishing to take the course for the Diploma in Social Studies should apply to the Senior Tutor not later than 1 January of the year in which they propose to begin their studies, and should communicate at the same time with the Director of Practical Training in the Department of Social Studies.

Applicants must (a) have reached the age of nineteen years before 1 October of the year in which they propose to begin the course, (b) satisfy the general admission requirements of the university (see ADMISSION REQUIREMENTS), and (c) satisfy a selection committee as to their suitability for the course.

General requirements

50. The course for the diploma lasts two years. Students must begin the course at the beginning of Michaelmas term.

The course comprises both academic study and practical training, including periods of full-time work during vacations.

51. To obtain credit for each year a student must (a) attend satisfactorily the appointed courses of lectures and instruction, (b) perform satisfactorily the prescribed exercises and class work, (c) satisfy the court of examiners at the examinations of the year, and (d) complete the appointed practical training to the satisfaction of the School Committee.

The School Committee may recommend to the University Council that students who have not satisfied the requirements of their year should be excluded from the department.

338

Examinations

52. Students are examined annually in the work of each year, at the end of Trinity term in each year.

53. A student who fails in one subject may, at the discretion of the School Committee, take that subject again at a supplemental examination held at the beginning of Michaelmas term. A student who fails in more than one subject may, at the discretion of the School Committee, take all subjects again at the supplemental examination.

COURSES AND EXAMINATIONS

54.

First year

Courses

Lectures and tuition: social structure; psychology; social administration I; introductory science (Michaelmas term), medical studies I (Hilary and Trinity terms); principles of social work.

Practical work: practical work will be arranged with groups of children or others in need of care. It must be performed satisfactorily. A student must attend a hospital out-patients department once weekly for one term, take part in visits of observation and attend lectures by extern lecturers. A written report on each term's practical work must be submitted to the Director of Practical Training.

During the summer vacation each student must carry out eight weeks' full-time practical work under the supervision of a fully qualified and experienced worker in a public authority, voluntary body or other organisation. The social work they must engage in shall be designated by the School Committee.

Examinations

Papers are set in the following subjects: social structure; social administration; psychology; medical studies.

Second year

Courses

Lectures and tuition: political institutions; social administration II; social psychology; medical studies II; law; elementary casework.

Practical work: students work under supervision with medical or other social workers, and must take part in visits of observation and attend extern lectures. They must attend the children's court weekly for one term and visit each of the courts for adult persons.

Examinations

Papers are set in the following subjects: political institutions; social administration; social psychology; medical studies; law; elementary casework.

Business and social studies

In addition a student must pass a *viva voce* examination in casework, in which an external examiner takes part.

FEES

55. The fees payable by a student taking the course for the Diploma in Social Studies are stated in COLLEGE CHARGES.

56. The regulations concerning fees for supplemental examinations are the same as apply to the course for the degree of Bachelor in Social Studies. See §48 above.

DIPLOMA IN PHYSIOTHERAPY

General requirements

1. Admission to the course for the diploma is granted only to candidates who have
   (a) been accepted for training by the Dublin School of Physiotherapy[1] and
   (b) passed the matriculation examination of the University of Dublin or an examination accepted by the University as equivalent.
2. Candidates for the diploma must further
   (a) attend the courses of lectures satisfactorily,
   (b) pass the necessary examinations, and
   (c) obtain the certificate of the Chartered Society of Physiotherapy.

Courses

3. The lectures and practical work for the diploma are intended to be completed in three academic years, commencing at the beginning of an academic year.

4. During the first and second years, the student attends lectures in physics, chemistry, physiology, anatomy and pathology, and receives theoretical and practical training in the Dublin School of Physiotherapy. During the third year the student continues to attend the courses in the Dublin School of Physiotherapy. Before entry for the final examination the student must produce a certificate of satisfactory progress issued by the Dublin School of Physiotherapy.

Examinations

5. Two examinations are held. The preliminary examination in chemistry and physics is held during the first year of training, and the second examination in anatomy and physiology, after not less than twelve months' training.

Fees

6. The fee for matriculation is £8.

7. Two annual fees of £5 each are payable, the first on registration and the second at the beginning of the second academic year[2]. These

---

[1] The Dublin School of Physiotherapy, 12 Hume Street, is approved by the Chartered Society of Physiotherapy as a training school for its examinations.
[2] Students whose home residences are outside Ireland (thirty-two counties) pay a surcharge of fifty per cent on the annual fees.

Diploma in Physiotherapy

fees should be paid on or before 1 November. Students who pay after that date will be fined one shilling for each week-day of default until the fine amounts to £1 after which their names may be removed from the roll. A diploma fee of £2 is payable on entry for the final examination.

8. Students who have to present themselves for a supplemental examination pay a fee of £1.

9. The above fees must be paid at the head office of the Bank of Ireland, College Green, Dublin. Payments must be made by crossed draft, cheque, money order or postal order drawn payable to TRINITY COLLEGE, NO. 2 ACCOUNT for the exact amount due, and accompanied by a duly completed fee-payment form.

10. In addition to these fees, fees for theoretical and practical training are payable to the Dublin School of Physiotherapy.

Admission

11. Application for admission to the course should be made to the Admissions Office, Trinity College, Dublin. The closing date is 1 September of the year of beginning the course in the Dublin School of Physiotherapy.

COURSES IN
RELIGIOUS KNOWLEDGE

CATECHETICAL COURSE

DIPLOMA IN BIBLICAL STUDIES

CATECHETICAL COURSE

I REGULATIONS

1. Catechetical lectures, providing courses of religious instruction, are given on Saturdays in arts lecture term at 9.30 a.m. in the Freshman years. Provision is also made for Sophisters. See §§9, 10.

2. Ordinary examinations are held at the beginning of each term, on a day stated in the ALMANACK. The examinations are conducted on the course prescribed for lectures. Certificates are awarded by the Catechist to students who have attended lectures satisfactorily and passed the ordinary examinations. A student who wishes to supplement omitted terms should apply beforehand to the Catechist.

3. Prize examinations are held on the same days as ordinary examinations. They are also held on the last day of lectures when they are open only to students who have credit for satisfactory lecture attendance.

A student who exhibits special merit at a prize examination is awarded a premium in books of value £2. Except in the Senior Freshman year, when a student who has obtained a premium in the earlier part of the year is eligible for a second premium at the examination held at the end of Trinity term or at the Michaelmas examination, a student can obtain only one premium in the year.

4. A candidate must give notice to the Catechist on the prescribed form of his intention to sit for an ordinary or a prize examination, not less than one fortnight and not more than one month before the date of the examination.

5. Parents and guardians who desire that students under their charge shall attend catechetical lectures or examinations should notify the Catechist, who will inform them what lectures or examinations have been attended.

6. A Presbyterian student who wishes to attend catechetical lectures must notify the Catechist not later than the morning of the second day before the lectures begin. He must state his class and his tutor.

7. Catechetical lectures and examinations are conducted by Fellows of the College, being members of the Church of Ireland, Professors or Lecturers in the Divinity School, the Dean of Residence for Church of Ireland students, ministers nominated by the Presbytery of Dublin whose names have been submitted to and approved by the Board, and any Presbyterian Fellow of the College appointed by the Catechist.

8. The Board of Trinity College is willing, on due application being

344

made by the heads of other religious denominations, to make similar arrangements for the religious instruction of students of such denominations.

9. Catechetical examinations are also provided in the two Sophister years, and the Catechist is authorised to grant a special certificate to students who have passed with credit four of these examinations, of which two at least must be in the Senior Sophister year, one being the Michaelmas examination of that year.

10. The Catechist is authorised to extend his premiums to the Sophister classes, the premiums to be awarded for merit shown either at an examination after lectures or at a term examination. Lectures for Sophisters will be arranged at suitable hours. Sophisters who wish to attend must notify the Catechist not later than the first day of arts lectures, and a class will be formed, if sufficient students give notice.

See §4 for the rule as to notice of intention to take a catechetical examination.

II COURSES

The books marked with an asterisk are prescribed for prize examinations and are not required for ordinary examinations. At each examination a candidate is examined on the course of the previous term.

Junior Freshmen
MICHAELMAS TERM. *Luke*. **Matthew*, **Mark*, **John*.
HILARY TERM. *Acts*. **1* and **2 Corinthians*.
TRINITY TERM. Church of Ireland students: A. W. Robinson, *The Church Catechism explained*; **Hebrews*. Presbyterian students: A. Whyte, *The Shorter Catechism*, questions 82–107; **H. Cook, *The prophets of the Bible*, introduction, pts 1, 2 (pp. 1–157).

Senior Freshmen
MICHAELMAS TERM. *Genesis, Exodus*, chs 1–20. **Exodus*, chs 20–end, **Leviticus*, chs 10, 14, 16, 23–25, **Numbers*, **Deuteronomy*.
HILARY TERM. *1* and *2 Samuel*, *1 Kings*, chs 1, 2. **Joshua*, **Judges*, **Ruth*.
TRINITY TERM. Church of Ireland students: *1 Kings*, chs 3–end, *2 Kings*; **T. H. Robinson, *Prophecy and the prophets in ancient Israel*. Presbyterian students: Lindsay, *The Reformation*, pts 2, 4; **J. S. Whale, *Christian doctrine*.

Junior Sophisters
MICHAELMAS TERM. *Ephesians, Colossians*, *1* and *2 Timothy, Philemon*. Church of Ireland students: J. Armitage Robinson, *The study of the Gospels*. Presbyterian students: H. A. A. Kennedy, *Theology of the Epistles*, introduction, pt 1, pp. 1–160.
HILARY TERM. *Romans, Galatians*. Church of Ireland students: B. F. Westcott, *The Bible in the Church*. Presbyterian students: C. H. Dodd, *The Epistle to the Romans*.

Catechetical course

TRINITY TERM. *1* and *2 Corinthians.* Church of Ireland students: A. R. Whitam, *The history of the Christian Church,* chs 1–13. Presbyterian students: W. Temple, *The faith and modern thought.*

Senior Sophisters

MICHAELMAS TERM. *Isaiah,* chs 1–33, (A.V. and R.V.). Church of Ireland students: Hooker, *Ecclesiastical polity,* bk 5, paras 1–68. Presbyterian students: Macpherson, *Westminster Confession of Faith,* introduction, chs 1, 2, 6, 8.

HILARY TERM. *Jeremiah,* chs 1–45, (A.V. and R.V.). Church of Ireland students: Perry, *A history of the Reformation in England.* Presbyterian students: J. Moffat, *The Presbyterian Churches.*

TRINITY TERM. *Hosea to Zephaniah,* (A.V. and R.V.). H. W. Robinson, *Religious ideas of the Old Testament.*

DIPLOMA IN BIBLICAL STUDIES

1. This diploma is granted for proficiency in biblical studies as tested by an examination following attendance on prescribed courses of lectures. Candidates must satisfy the matriculation requirements of the University, and pay the matriculation fee before beginning the courses. For the matriculation requirements and fee see ADMISSION REQUIRE-MENTS. Candidates may begin the courses only in Michaelmas term.

2. Two lectures, one on the Old Testament, and one on the New Testament, are delivered in successive hours on one day a week in arts term. Candidates may attend both courses of lectures in one year. If they wish to take the Old Testament course and the New Testament course in separate years, they are recommended to take them in that order.

3. The diploma is under the control of the Regius Professor of Divinity and of Archbishop King's Professor of Divinity. Those who wish to attend the lectures must send in their names to the Regius Professor of Divinity not later than 1 October in any year, specifying the course or courses they propose to take.

A candidate for the diploma must also register as a student in the College at the beginning of each academic year. Students entering the College for the first time must attend for registration in the Examination Hall on a stated day, or days, during the week preceding the beginning of arts lectures in Michaelmas term (GENERAL REGULATIONS FOR STUDENTS, §1).

4. The examination for the diploma consists of two parts, the subjects of which are (i) Old Testament, (ii) New Testament. These may be taken either separately or together. To take either part a candidate must first have attended satisfactorily the appropriate course of lectures throughout the whole year.

5. Candidates should normally present themselves for the examination immediately subsequent to the lecture course or courses which they have attended. The examination is held in the latter part of September. A supplemental examination may be taken one year later. Notice of intention to take an examination must reach the Regius Professor before 1 September (see also §6).

6. Candidates pay a fee of £9 per annum for each course of lectures attended, and a fee of £2 on presenting themselves for examination in any course. For the purposes of this rule, Old Testament and New Testament are regarded as two separate courses.

Diploma in Biblical Studies

The fees must be paid to the TRINITY COLLEGE, DUBLIN, NO. 2 ACCOUNT at the Bank of Ireland, College Green, Dublin 2, and must be accompanied by a duly completed fee-payment form, obtainable at the Bank or from the Accountant, Trinity College. The receipt for fees paid for lecture courses must be sent with the notice of intention to take a course of lectures. Fees for examinations must be paid at least one month before the date of the examination, and the receipt for payment must be sent to the Regius Professor of Divinity together with notice of intention to take the examination.

Candidates whose home residences are outside Ireland (thirty-two counties) pay a surcharge of fifty per cent on the fee for each course of lectures.

Magee University College students

7. A Magee University College student may be granted the Diploma in Biblical Studies on passing an examination which follows attendance on the prescribed courses of lectures.

8. Lectures given in Magee College, equivalent in number to those given in Trinity College (*i.e.* approximately 42) are recognised by Trinity College as preparation for the examination.

9. The examination is open only to those candidates who have credit for satisfactory attendance at lectures given in each year.

10. The examination is conducted by the lecturers on the course in Magee College, who are recognised by the Faculty of that college and approved by Trinity College; an examiner appointed by the Regius Professor and Archbishop King's Professor of Divinity acts as an extern examiner who must approve the standard attained by candidates and whose decision is final.

11. Candidates who for valid reasons cannot attend the prescribed courses of lectures during Michaelmas and Hilary terms may attend equivalent courses during vacations or in the Trinity term at Magee College.

COURSES AND EXAMINATIONS

12. The subjects which follow are prescribed for the examinations on the Old Testament course and the New Testament course. Lectures are given on the subjects prescribed, but do not necessarily cover the whole course appointed for examination.

Old Testament

I

The history of Israel and of Judaism to 70 A.D.; the literature of the Old Testament, including the formation of its canon.

II

The development of religious ideas, ethics and worship up to 70 A.D.

III

Portions of the Old Testament, in English, prescribed for detailed study, viz., *2 Samuel, Psalms 1–41, Isaiah*, chs 40–66.

New Testament

I

The Four Gospels, including their background and mutual relations.

II

The literature, history and religious thought of the apostolic age.

III

Portions of the New Testament prescribed for detailed study, viz. *Hebrews, Ephesians, 1 Peter*.

13. A general rather than a detailed knowledge of the subjects specified in sections I and II of the Old Testament and New Testament courses is required.

14. A list of recommended books may be obtained from the Regius Professor of Divinity.

SPECIAL AND PUBLIC LECTURES AND COURSES

SPECIAL LECTURES

PUBLIC LECTURES

INTERNATIONAL SUMMER SCHOOL

SPECIAL LECTURES

Elementary Irish

An introductory course in elementary Irish (three lectures per week) is given each year, confined to students on the college books and graduates of the University. Students on the college books pay no fees; graduates pay £5 per term.

Isotope techniques and measurements [1]

Short practical courses on isotope techniques and measurements are held in the Physical Laboratory in the vacations from time to time. They are intended to introduce graduates in science, medicine, engineering and allied subjects to the use and potentialities of radioactive isotopes.

Instruction is full time for one week, and the fee is £10.

Further information on the content of the courses may be obtained from Professor E. T. S. Walton, Physical Laboratory.

PUBLIC LECTURES

Hebrew

The Professor of Hebrew delivers public prelections from time to time as required by the rules of Erasmus Smith's Board.

The Donnellan Lectures

The Donnellan Lectures were founded by the Board on 22 February 1794, to carry out the intentions of Mrs Anne Donnellan, of the parish of St George, Hanover-square, Middlesex, spinster, who bequeathed £1,243 to the College 'for the encouragement of religion, learning, and good manners; the particular mode of application being left to the Provost and Senior Fellows'. The subject is presented in not less than two lectures.

The Godfrey Day Memorial Lectures

The Godfrey Day Memorial Lectureship was founded by the Board on 9 December 1939. The lecturer is appointed annually by the Board on the nomination of the Missionary Council of the Church of Ireland,

---

[1] These courses have been made possible through a grant for equipment from the Trinity College Dublin Trust.

and he delivers three lectures on subjects connected with missionary work.

The H. O. White Memorial Lectures

These lectures were founded in 1964 from funds provided by subscription to commemorate Herbert Martyn Oliver White, Professor of English Literature 1939-60. A public lecture is delivered every two or three years by a lecturer appointed by the Board and is followed by a seminar for senior students in English Literature.

The Joly Memorial Lectures

After the death of John Joly, F.T.C.D., SC.D., F.R.S., Professor of Geology and Mineralogy from 1897 to 1933, a number of his friends subscribed a sum of money to found a series of lectures in his memory. A lecturer is normally appointed every second year.

The O'Donnell Lectures in Celtic History and Literature

These lectures take their name from Charles James O'Donnell (1850–1934), who bequeathed a sum of money to found annual lectures in the universities of Oxford, Wales and Edinburgh, the National University of Ireland, and the University of Dublin. In the British universities the lectures are on the Celtic element in the English language and population; in the Irish universities they are on Irish history since Cromwell, with special reference to the history of ancient Irish families since 1641.

The first O'Donnell Lecture given in the University of Dublin was in 1957.

PUBLIC LECTURES IN THE SCHOOL OF PHYSIC
The Mary Louisa Prentice Montgomery Lectures in Ophthalmology
The John Mallett Purser Lectures
The Frederick Price Lectures

For details see SCHOOL OF PHYSIC.

N

DUBLIN UNIVERSITY
INTERNATIONAL SUMMER SCHOOL

The school is held each July under the authority of the Board of Trinity College, with financial assistance from the Cultural Relations Committee of Ireland and with the co-operation of students of Trinity College, especially members of the Dublin University Association for International Affairs.

Courses. Lectures are given by members of the university teaching staff and by guest lecturers. A general course (to be held 4–18 July 1967) presents a comprehensive view of Irish life and culture by means of lectures, tutorial classes and discussions, as well as excursions and visits to places of historical and artistic interest, including Dublin theatres. In association with the general course, during the period 4–29 July 1967, there will be held a residential course for a limited number of advanced students of English. It will comprise practical study of English language, and lectures and classes on Anglo-Irish literature.

Membership. Members should be students of universities or other institutions of higher education. Teachers of English as a foreign language are also eligible, and other applicants may be accepted if places are available.

Membership may be either resident or non-resident. Resident members are accommodated at Trinity Hall. Members of Dublin University may join as non-resident members paying a reduced fee.

Registration. Application should be made on a form which may be obtained from the registrar of the school. He will inform the applicant whether a place is available and register him as a member on payment of £3 (10s. in the case of members of the University). The balance of fees should be paid not later than the opening day of the school.

A limited number of scholarships are awarded by the Cultural Relations Committee of Ireland on the nomination of the committee of the school.

All enquiries about the summer school should be addressed to the registrar of the school.

GRADUATE STUDIES
AND HIGHER DEGREES

GRADUATE STUDIES AND HIGHER DEGREES

I GENERAL REGULATIONS

1. The regulations for higher degrees are administered by the Dean of Graduate Studies who acts in conjunction with the Graduate Studies Committee and committees of the various professional schools.

2. Applications and submissions for the degrees of Doctor in Letters (Litt.D.) and Doctor in Science (Sc.D.) and applications for registration for higher degrees in professional subjects (including applications for the degree of Master in Engineering, M.A.I.) are made to the Dean of Graduate Studies. For detailed regulations relating to higher degrees in professional subjects reference should be made to the section of the *Calendar* devoted to the school concerned.

3. Before entering upon research or a course of study leading to the degree of Master in Letters (M.Litt.), Master in Science (M.Sc.), Master in Administrative Studies (M.S.A.) or Doctor in Philosophy (Ph.D.) application for registration as a graduate student must be made to the Dean of Graduate Studies on the prescribed form.

4. In all cases where an applicant is required, upon registration, to state the subject of his research, the subject proposed must be approved by the head of the department to which it pertains who must also be satisfied that the applicant is qualified to undertake the research stated.

5. Registered graduate students are members of the University and are entitled to the same rights and privileges as undergraduate students. If they are not graduates of the University of Dublin, they are required to matriculate by paying the usual fee.

6. An applicant may not apply for two degrees at once, nor be on two registers in the University at the same time.

7. If a thesis is presented in fulfilment or partial fulfilment of the requirements for a higher degree it must be printed or typewritten, and must be securely bound. Three copies, which will not be returned, must be presented, accompanied by three copies of an abstract of the work (*not* exceeding 300 words). A thesis must contain (*a*) a declaration that it has not been submitted as an exercise for a degree at any other university, (*b*) a declaration that it is entirely the applicant's own work, or in the case of a scientific thesis, for which work has been carried out jointly, a statement of the extent to which it includes the work of others, (*c*) all due acknowledgments, and (*d*) systematic references to sources and a classified list of all sources used.

8. At least one copy of every thesis approved for a higher degree, except theses presented for a higher degree by examination and

dissertation, will be retained in the custody of the Librarian. A thesis so approved may be consulted or copied in the Library or through an inter-library loan. Borrowers must undertake not to use or reproduce material so obtained without the consent of the Librarian, and must acknowledge duly the source of such information. The writer of a thesis may withhold permission for the use of his work for a period not exceeding five years, after which it may be used as set out above.

9. Payment of fees should be made by crossed draft, cheque, money order or postal order, drawn payable to Trinity College, Dublin, No. 2 Account at the head office of the Bank of Ireland, College Green, Dublin 2, together with a duly completed fee payment form obtainable from the Graduate Studies Office.

II MASTER IN LETTERS (M.Litt.)

10. Graduates of the University of Dublin, or of any other university approved by the University Council, and persons holding qualifications from other institutions which are, in the opinion of the University Council, for this purpose equivalent to a university degree, may apply for registration as graduate students reading for the degree of Master in Letters (M.Litt.).

11. An applicant who is not a graduate of the University of Dublin may, at the discretion of the Dean of Graduate Studies and with the approval of the head of department concerned, be required to qualify for admission to the M.Litt. Register as follows:

(a) he may be required to enter the University as a One Year student (see ADMISSION REQUIREMENTS §21), read such parts of the honor course in the subject as the head of department may specify and, at the completion of one academic year, present himself at a qualifying examination. On the recommendation of the head of department the applicant's registration as a graduate student will then be confirmed and he may proceed to undertake a year of research as set out in §12 below. Admission of a One Year student is subject to the approval of the Senior Tutor; the fees payable by a One Year student are set out in COLLEGE CHARGES,

or (b) he may be required to spend a term working upon research, under supervision, as a probationary student. If his registration is confirmed it will be dated from the beginning of this period as a probationary student and the fees for this period will be those required of a student registered for the degree.

12. A student registered for the degree of M.Litt. is required to carry out research in literature, language, philosophy, history, politics, economics, social sciences, education or other cognate branch of learn-

ing. This research must be carried out under the direction of a supervisor approved by the Dean of Graduate Studies.

13. To qualify for the degree, students are required to carry out their research full-time within the University of Dublin for a period of not less than one year. Not later than three years from the date of registration they must submit three copies of a thesis (see §7 above) on the subject of their research to the Dean of Graduate Studies. Alternatively, honors graduates or graduates holding an equivalent professional qualification who are engaged upon research or teaching and are resident within thirty miles of the city of Dublin, will be permitted to register, provided that they can satisfy the Dean of Graduate Studies that they can attend in College for such periods of time as are necessary for adequate supervision of their research. In this case the minimum period of research before a thesis can be submitted will be two years from the date of registration and the maximum period, four years.

In exceptional cases an extension of the period within which the thesis can be presented may be obtained but only by special leave of the University Council on the recommendation of the supervisor.

14. The thesis must show evidence of independent inquiry and/or originality either in conclusions or in method.

15. The student may also be required to satisfy the examiners in a written or *viva voce* examination.

16. A student is permitted on completion of a year of research for the degree of M.Litt. to apply for transfer to the Ph.D. Register, provided that (*a*) he possesses the academic qualifications required of Ph.D. applicants, (*b*) he complies with the regulations for that degree and (*c*) his supervisor supports the application for transfer and certifies that the student has worked under his supervision for one academic year and has shown a marked aptitude for research. The work to be undertaken during the second year must be a continuation of, or in close connection with, that of the first.

17. As soon as an application for registration as an M.Litt. student is approved, the applicant must pay a fee of £80 for the first year. An applicant who is not a graduate of the University of Dublin must pay at the same time a matriculation fee of £8. After the first year has expired a graduate student pays an annual fee of £5 until he has obtained the degree or withdrawn as a registered student. This fee is due annually on the date on which the candidate first registered.

The examination fee of £10 must be paid when a thesis is presented. The degree fee is £15.

Full-time members of the University staff are exempt from all fees except the examination fee.

III MASTER IN SCIENCE (M.Sc.)

18. The regulations for the degree of M.Sc. are the same as those for the degree of M.Litt., but the subject of research must be in some branch of mathematical or natural sciences, pure or applied. Alternatively a registered student must spend at least one year in advanced study within an approved section of one of these sciences. A student who fulfils an approved course of graduate study (see section VII) may qualify for the degree by presenting himself for examination in the subject of his advanced study and by submission of a dissertation on some particular aspect of this study.

19. The fees payable are the same as for the degree of M.Litt., except that registered students working in a laboratory of the University also pay a laboratory fee of £30 for the first year, and of £10 per term for each subsequent term during which they continue to work in a laboratory of the University. Full-time members of the University staff are exempt from these fees.

IV DOCTOR IN PHILOSOPHY (Ph.D.)

20. The regulations for the degree of Ph.D. are the same as those for the degree of M.Litt. save that every registered student must spend at least two academic years in research full-time within the University in mathematical or natural sciences, pure or applied, or in literature, language, philosophy, history, politics, economics, social sciences, education, law or other cognate branch of learning. The period within which the thesis must be presented is five years from the date of registration unless an extension is obtained.

Exemption from the requirements of a period of full-time study will be granted only in exceptional circumstances and only to students previously registered for the degree of M.Litt. or M.Sc.

21. The thesis presented for the degree of Ph.D. must show evidence of independent inquiry and of originality either in conclusions or in method. More difficult or more extensive subjects and more extensive research are required for the degree of Ph.D. than for the degree of M.Litt. or M.Sc.

22. As soon as an application for registration is approved, an applicant must pay the fee of £80 for the first year. An applicant who is not a graduate of the University of Dublin must pay at the same time a matriculation fee of £8.

The fee of £80 for the second year is due one year after the date of registration.

Students working in a laboratory of the University also pay a laboratory fee of £30 for each of the first two years and of £10 per term for each subsequent term while so engaged.

After a period of two years has expired a student pays an annual fee of £5 until he has obtained the degree or has withdrawn as a registered graduate student. This fee is due annually on the date on which the student first registered. The examination fee of £15 must be paid when a thesis is presented, and the degree fee is £15. Full-time members of the University staff are exempt from all fees, except the examination fee.

V DOCTOR IN LETTERS (Litt.D.)

23. The degree of Litt.D. may be conferred on a Bachelor in Arts, a Master in Letters or a Doctor in Philosophy of the University of Dublin who has distinguished himself by original research in letters. Such a graduate must be of at least three years standing.

24. Application must be made in writing, through the Dean of Graduate Studies, to have the grace of the Board granted for the degree. An applicant must at the same time submit a statement of his published contributions to the study of literature, ancient or modern, philosophy, aesthetics, history, archaeology or other cognate branch of learning on which his claim to the degree is based. Three copies of any work cited in support of the application must also be submitted.

25. The application must be based wholly, or to a substantial extent, on original work carried out independently by the candidate. If additional work done in co-operation with others is also submitted, the candidate must make a written statement indicating precisely his share in the work.

A written declaration must also be made that the work has not been submitted as an exercise for a degree at another university.

26. The assessors appointed by the Board have power to question the candidate upon his work either in writing or *viva voce*.

27. The examination fee to be paid when application for the degree is made, is £20. The degree fee is £25. Full-time members of the University staff are exempt from the degree fee.

VI DOCTOR IN SCIENCE (Sc.D.)

28. The regulations for the degree of Sc.D. are the same as those for the degree of Litt.D., substituting science for letters.

VII GRADUATE COURSES

29. Full-time courses of instruction leading to the higher degrees of M.Sc. and M.S.A. are provided in approved subjects listed below.

Application for registration for these courses is made to the Dean of Graduate Studies.

30. Students registered for an M.Sc. course qualify for the degree by satisfactorily completing the work of the year, passing an examination held at the end of the Trinity term and submitting a dissertation on some particular aspect of the subject.

31. Students registered for the M.S.A. course qualify for the degree by satisfactorily completing the work of the year, passing an examination held at the end of the Trinity term and submitting a dissertation on some particular aspect of the subject.

32. A student may be required to present himself for a *viva voce* examination.

Mathematics (M.Sc. course)

33. The graduate course in mathematics extends over three terms. Currently the emphasis of the course is upon mathematical physics but it is intended that the syllabus will be flexible and enquiries relating to the syllabus should be addressed to the School of Mathematics. The degree examination consists of two papers.

Applicants for registration must have a good honors degree in a mathematical subject or an equivalent qualification.

Engineering (M.Sc. course)

34. For details of admission requirements and syllabus see GRADUATE SCHOOL OF ENGINEERING STUDIES.

All applicants must apply for registration to the Dean of Graduate Studies, but enquiries may be addressed, in the first instance, to the Registrar, Graduate School of Engineering Studies.

Administration (M.S.A. course)

35. For details of admission requirements and syllabus see SCHOOL OF BUSINESS AND SOCIAL STUDIES—Graduate course in Administration.

Entomology (Diploma course)

36. The course will be given in the Department of Zoology and will last three terms. Graduates in the natural sciences are eligible to attend the course; non graduates may be accepted depending upon their qualifications and experience.

The diploma will be awarded upon the results of an examination which will include written and practical exercises.

The fee for the course is £80.

Application forms may be obtained from the Graduate Studies Office, No. 2, Trinity College.

PRIZES AND OTHER AWARDS

ENTRANCE AWARDS

FOUNDATION AND NON-FOUNDATION SCHOLARSHIPS

PRIZES IN HONOR SUBJECTS

PRIZES IN PROFESSIONAL SUBJECTS

PRIZES IN THE ORDINARY COURSE IN ARTS

AWARDS FOR GENERAL DISTINCTION

RESEARCH AWARDS AND MODERATORSHIP PRIZES

MISCELLANEOUS AWARDS

FINANCIAL ASSISTANCE

SCHOLARSHIPS OFFERED BY LOCAL AUTHORITIES IN IRELAND

Note

All the awards stated are subject to the proviso that sufficient merit must be shown.

The awards whose titles include the names of persons are arranged in alphabetical order of surnames, *e.g.* Lloyd Exhibitions, Arthur Lyster Prize.

ENTRANCE AWARDS

Mode of entry

1. Candidates for these awards should in the first instance apply for information and the necessary forms to the Admissions Office.

I. ENTRANCE SCHOLARSHIPS AND EXHIBITIONS

Awards available

2. On the results of an examination held in Trinity term each year entrance scholarships and exhibitions are awarded as follows, provided that sufficient merit is shown:

(a) three entrance scholarships of £200 a year for two years;

(b) eight entrance exhibitions of £150 a year for two years[1];

(c) ten entrance exhibitions of £75 a year for two years[1].

Entrance scholars are entitled to occupy rooms in College or in Trinity Hall at the normal rent. Entrance scholars and exhibitioners of limited means may apply for sizarships. See section II below. Entrance scholars and exhibitioners are eligible for fee concessions. Candidates for entrance awards who wish to be considered for fee concessions must apply on the prescribed form before 1 June. See FINANCIAL ASSISTANCE, part I.

Entrance scholars and exhibitioners who are granted exemption from the Junior Freshman year[2] are entitled to receive, in lieu of their stipend for that year, one-half of the annual value of their scholarship or exhibition.

Foundation scholarship examination

3. Holders of entrance awards or matriculation awards (see section III below) normally present themselves at the examination for scholarships (foundation and non-foundation) in their Senior Freshman year, or, if they have entered a professional school, in their Junior Sophister year. They may present themselves at the scholarship examination as Junior Freshmen, but if elected foundation or non-foundation scholars

---

[1] The number of awards in this category may be increased if there is an exceptional number of meritorious candidates.

[2] See COURSE IN GENERAL STUDIES, regulations for the various honor courses, SCHOOL OF PHYSIC, SCHOOL OF VETERINARY MEDICINE, SCHOOL OF ENGINEERING.

365

Entrance awards

do not retain their entrance or matriculation awards for the Senior Freshman year.

Candidates distinguishing themselves at the examination for scholarships (foundation and non-foundation) are elected foundation or non-foundation scholars. Those not so elected, but awarded first rank or second rank honors on the marks obtained at the examination, are granted £75 a year for any two undergraduate academic years following the examination, save that these awards are not payable in any year during which they are in receipt of entrance scholarship, matriculation award, foundation scholarship or non-foundation scholarship. The awards are dependent on satisfactory lecture attendance and general progress, and are not payable in respect of a year which is being repeated.

Qualifications of candidates

4. Candidates must be under the age of nineteen on 1 May of the year of the examination. Forms of application to take the examination are obtainable from the Admissions Office. They must be completed and sent to the Admissions Office, together with a birth certificate, not later than 1 March. There is no special fee for taking the examination.

5. All entrance scholars and exhibitioners must have qualified for matriculation by the beginning of lectures in Michaelmas term; otherwise they forfeit their awards.

Conditions of tenure

6. A candidate awarded an entrance scholarship or exhibition, or any of the awards listed under section II below, must notify the Senior Tutor in writing, not later than 1 July of the year in which the award is made, that he intends to enter the College in the following October and that he has already paid his matriculation fee. If this is not done, his scholarship, exhibition or other award is re-allotted to the candidate next best qualified, provided that he has shown sufficient merit. Responsibility for ascertaining the result of the relevant examination rests with the candidate.

In special circumstances the Board may permit a successful candidate to defer his entrance to the College for one year. Applications for deferment must be made to the Senior Lecturer not later than 1 July of the year in which the award is made, and candidates to whom deferment is granted are not permitted to present themselves a second time for entrance scholarships and exhibitions.

7. A student who fails to make satisfactory progress or does not keep his name on the college books forfeits his entrance scholarship or exhibition, and the same penalty may be inflicted for any grave violation of college discipline.

8. Entrance scholarships and exhibitions are paid half-yearly in December and June. All payments except the first depend on the furnishing by the Senior Lecturer to the Treasurer of a certificate that the holder is making satisfactory progress.

Entrance scholars and exhibitioners are required normally to pay their first annual fee before 1 September, and subsequent fees on or before 1 October each year. To meet cases of hardship, the College has provided that fees may be deducted in whole or in part from awards gained in any one year; application for such deduction must be made each year to the Treasurer, through the student's tutor, before the date prescribed for payment of fees.

Examination subjects and marks

9. The subjects of examination and the allocation of marks are as follows:

(1)	English essay	150
(2)	General paper	150
(3)	One of the following: mathematics (pure and applied), classics, natural sciences, modern languages, Irish, ancient and modern literature, Hebrew, history	700

In addition to examination by written papers, candidates presenting themselves in natural sciences (excluding mathematics) are given a practical examination, and candidates in certain other subjects are examined *viva voce*. In modern languages (other than English) the *viva voce* examination is intended to test the candidates' ability in the use of the languages concerned; in other subjects the purpose of the *viva voce* examination is to test the candidates' quickness of apprehension and range of interests in their respective fields of study.

10. The courses for 1967 in the several subjects are as follows:

General paper

The general paper offers candidates a wide range of choice from the questions set, which include tests of the candidates' general knowledge of literature, art and music, of contemporary world history, and of recent scientific advances. Candidates are expected to translate into English a passage in Latin, French or German. (Candidates in classics and in Irish must translate a passage in French or German, candidates in modern languages must translate a passage in Latin. Candidates in ancient and modern literature must translate a passage

367

Entrance awards

in either French or German, with the proviso that candidates offering French in section (3) of the examination must take German on the general paper and *vice versa*.)

Mathematics (pure and applied)

The mathematics and additional mathematics A and B syllabuses for the matriculation examination.

Classics

>Unseen translation from Greek into English (3 hours)
>Unseen translation from Latin into English (3 hours)
>Greek prose composition ($1\frac{1}{2}$ hours)
>Latin prose composition ($1\frac{1}{2}$ hours)
>Greek history ($1\frac{1}{2}$ hours)
>Roman history ($1\frac{1}{2}$ hours)

Candidates are expected to know the principal facts in Greek history, and the outlines of Greek literature and art, down to 323 B.C.; and the principal facts in Roman history, and the outlines of Roman literature down to 37 A.D. The unseen papers include questions on grammar and metre.

An optional paper in Greek and Latin verse composition is also set: Greek and Latin dictionaries are made available to candidates. The candidates' performance in this paper is taken into consideration in assessing the final results, but no credit is given unless merit of a high order is shown.

There is also a *viva voce* examination.

Natural sciences

Candidates take any three of the following subjects: biology, botany, chemistry, geography, geology, mathematics, physics, zoology. Candidates offering biology may not offer botany or zoology. There is a practical as well as a theory examination in each subject except mathematics. The courses are as follows:

BIOLOGY

The course for matriculation, studied at a more advanced level, with the addition of the following:

Meiosis and its significance in life-cycles; elementary Mendelism, including the dihybrid ratio, and the concept of linkage.

The microscopic anatomy of the principal organs of a herbaceous flowering plant; osmosis, plasmolysis and turgor; the structure and life history of *Chlamydomonas, Volvox, Penicillium, Puccinia*, a moss and a fern; plant hormones.

The characteristic features of the following families: Cruciferae, Papilionaceae, Rosaceae, Umbelliferae, Compositae, Labiatae, Liliaceae, Iridaceae, Gramineae.

More detailed study of the functional anatomy of (a) an earthworm, (b) a dogfish, as revealed by dissection.

Parasitism, as exemplified by (a) a tapeworm, (b) the liver fluke. (Life cycles only.)

BOTANY

Morphology, anatomy and physiology of higher plants. Meiosis and its significance in life-cycles; elementary Mendelism, including the dihybrid ratio, the concept of linkage. Structure and life-cycle of *Chlamydomonas*, *Spirogyra*, *Mucor*, *Penicillium*, *Funaria* and *Dryopteris*. Candidates are expected to show familiarity with the native flora of the region in which their home or school is situated and with the interpretation of the structure and affinities of common garden plants. Recommended reading:

L. J. F. Brimble, *Intermediate Botany*, 4th ed. (Macmillan), chs 1–5, 10, 12–14, 18, 21, 22. G. E. Fogg, *The Growth of Plants* (Pelican Books). Detailed knowledge of chs 4 and 5 will not be required.

CHEMISTRY

The course is that prescribed for matriculation, treated at a more advanced level.

Practical examination. Preparation and identification of simple compounds; analysis of simple salts; acidimetry and alkalimetry, titrations with permanganate, and of iodine with thiosulphate.

GEOGRAPHY

The course is that prescribed for matriculation, treated at a more advanced level.

GEOLOGY

The course is that prescribed for matriculation, treated at a more advanced level.

Practical examination. The reasoned identification of hand specimens of common minerals and rocks, and the recognition of simple structural and textural criteria relating to the origin of such rocks. The structure and related topography of simple geological maps. The recognition of the geological age and major biological grouping of common fossils (a knowledge of biological structures not required).

MATHEMATICS

The mathematics and additional mathematics B syllabuses for the matriculation examination together with calculus, co-ordinate geometry, complex numbers and de Moivre's theorem of the A syllabus.

PHYSICS

The course is that prescribed for matriculation, treated at a more advanced level.

There is also a practical examination, in which candidates may be required to carry out experiments covered by any part of the course with the exception of 'Modern Physics'. An understanding of the limitations and errors of the methods used is expected.

ZOOLOGY

The mammal—structure and physiology as exemplified by the study and dissection of the rabbit or rat. Elements of structure and physiology of cells and tissues. The main features of the following organisms: *Amoeba*, *Paramoecium*, *Monocystis*, *Plasmodium*, *Hydra*, a turbellarian worm, a nematode, *Lumbricus*★,

369

the cockroach, the snail, the dogfish*, the frog*. Organisms marked * should be dissected or examined in sections. Parasites and vectors: the malarial parasite, the mosquito, a tapeworm, the liver fluke, the house fly. Embryology, as exemplified by *Amphioxus, Rana* and a bird. Elementary genetics. Evolution. Natural history, either of a common group of animals, or animals in well-defined habitat.

Modern languages

Candidates may choose any two of the following five languages: French, German, Irish, Italian, Spanish; or any one of these and English literature. In French, German, Italian and Spanish there are three three-hour papers, comprising (1) translation from English into the language and unseen passages of the language into English, (2) prescribed books, (3) an essay in the language and questions (in English) on history, geography or outlines of literature as specified below. In Irish there are three three-hour papers comprising (1) prescribed books, (2) translation from English into Irish, (3) translation of unseen passages into English. There is a *viva voce* examination—reading, conversation, practical phonetics—in all these languages. In English literature there are three three-hour papers, two dealing with the prescribed course, and one requiring comment on passages of unprescribed prose and verse.

The prescribed books are as follows:

FRENCH

Racine, *Bérénice*; Voltaire, *Lettres sur les Anglais* (Cambridge) or *Lettres philosophiques* (Blackwell); Flaubert, *Trois contes*; *Nine French poets, 1820–80*, ed. H. E. Berthon (Macmillan); Ledésert and Smith, *La France* (Harrap).

Candidates are expected to be familiar with the main events and authors in French literature of the 17th, 18th and 19th centuries. G. Brereton, *A short history of French literature* (Pelican books) is recommended.

GERMAN

Hebbel, *Agnes Bernauer*; Goethe, *Egmont*; Schiller, *Maria Stuart*; Annette von Droste-Hülshoff, *Poems*, ed. Atkinson (Clarendon); Kafka, *Short stories*, ed. J. M. S. Pasley (Clarendon); J. G. Robertson, *A history of German literature* (new and revised edition), candidates are required to read the whole of Robertson's book as background material, but questions on this text will be mainly concerned with the sections covering German literature in the 18th, 19th and 20th centuries.

IRISH

Peadar Chois Fhairrge, ed. Mac Giollarnáth; Ó Siochfhradha, *An baile seo gainne*; Mac Grianna, *Mo bhealach féin*; Ó Cuív, *Irish dialects and Irish-speaking districts*.

ITALIAN

G. Deledda, *Canne al vento* (Manchester); *Oxford book of Italian verse* (second edition, 1952), pp. 313–536; U. Betti, *Two plays* (Manchester); Gardner, *Companion to Italian studies* (Methuen), the chapters on the 14th, 16th and 19th centuries.

SPANISH

Cervantes, *La ilustre fregona*; the poems of Espronceda and Rubén Darío in *Oxford book of Spanish verse*; Ruiz de Alarcón, *La verdad sospechosa* (Harrap), *Cuentos de autores contemporáneos* (Harrap).

An outline of Spanish literature from 1500 to 1650.

An outline of Spanish history from 1500 to the present day.

ENGLISH LITERATURE

Shakespeare, *Twelfth night, Antony and Cleopatra*; Spenser, *Epithalamion, Prothalamion*; Milton, *Paradise lost*, bks 1, 2; Pope, *The rape of the lock*; Gray, *Elegy written in a country churchyard*; Goldsmith, *The deserted village*; Wordsworth, *Tintern Abbey, Michael*; Coleridge, *The ancient mariner*; Shelley, *Ode to the west wind, Adonais*; Keats, *The eve of St. Agnes, Odes*; Yeats, *The tower*, first four poems: 'Sailing to Byzantium', 'The tower', 'Meditations in time of civil war', 'Nineteen hundred and nineteen'; Eliot, *Selected poems* (Faber); Johnson, *The life of Pope*; Fielding, *Joseph Andrews*; Jane Austen, *Pride and prejudice, Mansfield Park*; Conrad, *Youth, Heart of darkness, The end of the tether*.

A general knowledge of the development of English literature from 1557 is required.

Irish

Irish may be taken either as one of the languages of the modern language group or as a special subject by itself. For candidates taking it as a special subject, the course is as prescribed for entrance scholarships and exhibitions in modern languages, with the following additions:

Measgra Dánta, pt I, ed. O'Rahilly; *Caoine Airt Uí Laoghaire*, ed. Ó Tuama; *Stories from Keating's History of Ireland*, ed. Bergin.

Irish essay.

Paper in Latin, unseen translation and prose composition.

The paper on the above prescribed books is entitled 'Prescribed books II'; the paper on the books given in the modern languages course is entitled 'Prescribed books I'.

Ancient and modern literature

Candidates take Latin and one of the following: English literature, French, German, Irish, Italian, Spanish. In Latin there are three three-hour papers comprising (1) essay and questions on Roman history and literature down to 37 A.D., (2) translation from English into Latin, (3) unseen translation from Latin into English. The unseen paper includes questions on grammar and metre. There is also an interview which is designed to test the candidates' intelligence and range of interests in languages. In French, German, Irish, Italian, Spanish and English literature the examination is identical with the examination in modern languages.

Hebrew

Candidates are examined in Hebrew on four papers, and in Greek on one paper. There is also a *viva voce* examination.

Entrance awards

The course in Hebrew is as follows: Hebrew grammar, composition, and pointing; *Exodus*, chs 1-14; *Micah*, chs 1-7; *Psalms*, 90-96; the history of Israel to the fall of Samaria; W. O. E. Oesterley, *A fresh approach to the psalms*, chs 3, 4, 7. Candidates are expected to have a knowledge of the main versions of the Old Testament and of the background of *Genesis*.

In the Greek paper candidates are examined on any one of the Greek texts prescribed for the matriculation examination in the same year.

The papers are as follows:

1. Hebrew grammar (1½ hours)
2. Hebrew prescribed texts (3 hours)
3. Hebrew composition, pointing, unseen (3 hours)
4. General paper (3 hours)
5. Greek prescribed text (1½ hours)

History

Candidates are examined on four papers and *viva voce*. The papers are as follows:

1. Essays in historical subjects
2. A paper in European history
3. A paper in British history
4. A paper in Irish history

Papers 2, 3 and 4 each cover the period 1494-1914, but are so set that candidates may specialise in any two centuries (1494-1598, 1598-1715, 1715-1815, 1815-1914). In these papers the emphasis is on general movements rather than on particular events, and a knowledge of economic and social trends is expected.

In addition, candidates must have a matriculation qualification in Latin and in one modern language other than English before being admitted.

JAMES PATRICK KIDD SCHOLARSHIP

This scholarship was founded in 1887 by a bequest from Mary Lang Kidd. The first entrance scholar in each year is known as the James Patrick Kidd Scholar.

LOUIS CLAUDE PURSER ENTRANCE SCHOLARSHIP

In 1933 the Board resolved to employ a portion of the income from the bequest made by Louis Claude Purser, Fellow 1881-1927, in founding an award in his name. The second entrance scholar in each year is known as the Louis Claude Purser Scholar.

II. OTHER AWARDS OFFERED TO CANDIDATES FOR ENTRANCE SCHOLARSHIPS AND EXHIBITIONS

SIZARSHIPS

Sizars are entrance scholars and exhibitioners of limited means who have their commons free. Women sizars receive £50 a year in lieu of commons.

The awards of sizarships are announced at the same time as the awards of entrance scholarships and exhibitions.

Candidates for entrance scholarships and exhibitions who wish to be considered for the award of sizarships should send to the Senior Lecturer on or before 31 March a statement on the prescribed form showing that they are qualified on the ground of limited means. Sizarships are awarded for two years in the first instance. This period runs from the first day of Michaelmas term following their election. Sizars normally present themselves at the examination for scholarships (foundation and non-foundation) in their Senior Freshman year. Those who are elected foundation or non-foundation scholars *ipso facto* vacate their sizarships. Those not so elected, but achieving an adequate standard of answering at the scholarship examination, have their sizarships renewed for a further two years, provided that their lecture attendance and general progress continue to be satisfactory. A sizar who fails to make satisfactory progress or does not keep his name on the college books forfeits his award, and the same penalty may be inflicted for any grave violation of college discipline.

The following exhibitions and prizes are awarded to qualified candidates subject to the condition that sufficient merit is shown. To qualify for an award candidates must place their names on the college books. Students holding awards tenable for two years who fail to make satisfactory progress or do not keep their names on the college books forfeit their awards, and the same penalty may be inflicted for any grave violation of college discipline.

REID ENTRANCE EXHIBITIONS
(formerly called Reid Sizarships)

In 1888 the sum of £6,200 was received under the will of the late Richard Tuohill Reid, to found additional sizarships, or exhibitions in the nature of sizarships. The awards, which do not exceed five in number, are open only to students of limited means, natives of the county of Kerry. Those who (i) are above the standing of rising Junior Freshman, or (ii) are graduates of any chartered university, or (iii) have completed their nineteenth year before the 1st of May of the year in which they compete, are not eligible.

Reid Entrance Exhibitions are granted to qualified candidates who, having competed at the annual examinations for entrance scholarships and exhibitions, are deemed to have shown sufficient merit. Candidates may, if they wish, present themselves for Reid awards only. Such candidates are not required to take the general paper, nor, if presenting themselves in Irish as their special subject, the associated Latin paper.

Reid Entrance Exhibitions are tenable for two years. Exhibitioners have their commons free, and receive a salary of not less than £75 per annum. Women exhibitioners receive £50 per annum in lieu of commons.

During the Senior Freshman year exhibitioners normally compete for scholarships (foundation and non-foundation). Those who fail to obtain such scholarships, but are deemed to have shown sufficient merit, have their exhibitions extended for two further years.

Entrance awards

WALTER WORMSER HARRIS PRIZE

This prize was founded in 1941 by a bequest from W. W. Harris. It is awarded annually to the best candidates among those who do not gain an entrance scholarship or exhibition. It is paid half-yearly and is subject to the same regulations as those which apply to the entrance scholarships and exhibitions. Value, £25 a year for two years.

CHARLES WILKINS MEMORIAL PRIZE

This prize was founded in 1879 by subscription in memory of Charles James Wilkins, Scholar 1877. It is awarded annually to the woman candidate at the examination for entrance scholarships and exhibitions who is next in merit after the Walter Wormser Harris awards. Value, £20.

For each of the following awards it is stipulated that candidates must have been pupils of certain specified schools. In each case, excepting that of the Erasmus Smith and Thompson Exhibitions, candidates must forward to the Senior Lecturer before 31 March evidence that they are qualified to compete.

ABBEY PRIZE

This prize is awarded annually to a candidate for entrance scholarships and exhibitions who does not obtain a scholarship or exhibition. Preference is given to a son or daughter of an old boy of the Abbey School, Tipperary. A candidate for entrance scholarships and exhibitions who claims to be qualified under this latter clause must apply to the Senior Lecturer before 31 March and provide the necessary evidence. If there is no such candidate, preference is given to candidates from schools in Munster and Connacht. Value, £5.

ANNIE ANDERSON MEMORIAL PRIZE

This prize was founded in 1926 by subscription in memory of Mrs William Anderson. It is awarded annually at the examination for entrance scholarships and exhibitions to the pupil of Mountjoy School who obtains the highest marks for English literature. Only those who have been pupils of Mountjoy School for at least two years are eligible to compete. Value, £9.

WILLIAM ANDERSON EXHIBITION

This exhibition was founded in 1941 by subscription to mark appreciation of the work of William Anderson as headmaster of Mountjoy School (1896–1939). It is awarded annually at the examination for entrance scholarships and exhibitions to the pupil of Mountjoy School who obtains the highest mark either in mathematics or in natural sciences. Only those who have been pupils of Mountjoy School for at least two years are eligible to compete. Value, £10.

BIGGS MEMORIAL PRIZE

This prize was founded in 1905 by subscription in memory of Richard Biggs. It is awarded annually at the examination for entrance scholarships and exhibitions to the best candidate of those who have been pupils for at least one year at Chesterfield School, Birr (or such other school at Birr as may

374

take its place), at Galway Grammar School, or at Portora Royal School. Value, £17 10s.

EDWARD JOHN FRENCH EXHIBITIONS

These exhibitions were founded in 1931 by a bequest from Edward John French. Two exhibitions are offered annually at the examination for entrance scholarships and exhibitions, one to the girl from Howell's School, Denbigh, who obtains the best marks in history, and the other to the boy from Shrewsbury School who obtains the best marks in classics. A candidate must have been a pupil at one of these schools for at least one year.

If in any year no deserving candidate from Howell's School presents herself, the exhibition is awarded in November to the student of most junior standing who obtained the exhibition at her entrance, has proceeded regularly with her class, and in the academic year then ending has obtained an honor or a scholarship or a moderatorship in history and political science. If no deserving candidate from Shrewsbury School presents himself, a similar award is made of the exhibition in classics. Value, £25 each exhibition.

HASLETT MEMORIAL SCHOLARSHIP

This scholarship was founded in 1907 by subscription in memory of William Woods Haslett. It is awarded annually to the best of those competitors for entrance scholarships and exhibitions who have been for the two preceding years pupils at St Andrew's College, Dublin. Value, £20.

ISABELLA MULVANY SCHOLARSHIP

This scholarship was founded in 1928 by subscription by the pupils and friends of Isabella Mulvany, to mark their appreciation of her labours on behalf of higher education, and particularly of her work as headmistress of Alexandra School (1881–1927). It is awarded annually at the examination for entrance scholarships and exhibitions to the best candidate who has spent at least two years between the ages of 12 and 16 at Alexandra School, Dublin. Value, £20 a year for two years.

ERASMUS SMITH AND THOMPSON EXHIBITIONS

In each year at the examination for entrance scholarships and exhibitions, two Erasmus Smith Exhibitions are offered, one to students who have been pupils of Galway Grammar School, or who normally reside in any of the counties Galway, Clare or Mayo and who have held or would have been eligible to compete for a scholarship offered by the Governors of the Erasmus Smith Schools, and one to pupils of the High School, Dublin. The Thompson Exhibition is offered at the same examination to a pupil of the High School, Dublin. Full particulars may be obtained from the Registrar of the Erasmus Smith Schools, 1–2 Leinster Street South, Dublin.

III. AWARDS OFFERED AT THE MIDSUMMER MATRICULATION EXAMINATION

The following awards are made on the results of the midsummer matriculation examination: one award of £150 a year for two years and three awards of £75 a year for two years.

Conditions of tenure are identical with those of entrance scholarships and exhibitions. These awards cannot be held simultaneously with entrance scholarships or awards. For courses see ADMISSION REQUIREMENTS.

A candidate who obtains an award at the midsummer matriculation examination may, in special circumstances, be permitted by the Board to defer his entrance to the College for one year. Such a candidate, if otherwise qualified to do so, may present himself in the following year at the examination for entrance scholarships. If successful at the latter competition, he will be allowed to choose between the awards, and, if unsuccessful, he will retain his original award.

ADMISSION REQUIREMENTS, §15, provides that a student may submit, if he so desires, seven or eight subjects instead of the required six at the matriculation examination. If a candidate does submit seven or eight subjects then his performance as a candidate for one of these awards is assessed by selecting the six subjects in which his answering is best, with the proviso that these six subjects include (a) English composition and either (b) Latin and a non-linguistic subject or (c) mathematics and a language.

PREMIUM IN IRISH

A premium of £10 is awarded to the best answerer in Irish at the midsummer matriculation examination who intends to enter the College. Payment is made after the first college fee has been received.

IV. HANDCOCK MEMORIAL SCHOLARSHIP

This scholarship was founded in 1964 by E. C. Handcock Ltd. It is awarded to a student reading for a degree in civil engineering or in mechanical and production engineering. Only candidates at the examination for entrance scholarships in mathematics or natural sciences are eligible, and their performance at this examination is taken into account. Competitors are interviewed in June by representatives of the School of Engineering and of Messrs Handcock Ltd.

The scholarship is tenable for three years, but continuance of the scholarship after the first year is dependent on sufficient merit being shown. A holder is expected to present himself at the examination for foundation scholarship in his Junior Sophister year; if he shows sufficient merit at this examination, but is not elected a scholar, his award will be renewed for a fourth year. Value, £70 per annum.

FOUNDATION AND NON-FOUNDATION SCHOLARSHIPS

FOUNDATION SCHOLARSHIPS

1. The College was founded as a corporation consisting of the Provost, the Fellows and the Scholars. Scholars who are members of the corporation are called *foundation scholars*, or *scholars of the house*, to distinguish them from the holders of other scholarships. Foundation scholarships are open to men only, and cannot exceed seventy in number.

2. Foundation scholars are elected annually in various subjects on the result of an examination held in Trinity term. The subjects are those of the honor courses in arts, and of the professional courses in physic, veterinary medicine, engineering, business studies and social studies. The courses for the examination in the various subjects are stated below, §19[1].

Mode of election

3. Elections are made by the Board on Trinity Monday.

4. The scholarship examination is held on such days in Trinity term before the beginning of lectures as the Board shall fix and promulgate at least six months beforehand.

5. Candidates must give notice to the Senior Lecturer at least three weeks before the end of arts lectures in Hilary term.

6. The previous conduct of candidates must have been satisfactory.

7. Candidates must have paid the current annual fee of their class.

8. No student can compete for a scholarship until after his name has been entered on the college books as a Junior Freshman, *i.e.* he cannot compete as a rising Junior Freshman.

9. On or before the day of election every candidate for scholarship must send to the Registrar his name and the name of the county in which he was born. The form in which this is generally done is as follows:

Ego, A. B. . . . . . filius, natus in comitatu N., sub ferula . . . . educatus, Discipulatum a te humillime peto.

Admission

10. Elected candidates must present themselves in the Theatre at

[1] For special awards open to entrance scholars and exhibitioners see ENTRANCE SCHOLARSHIPS AND EXHIBITIONS, §3.

Foundation scholarships

11 a.m. on the day following their election to be formally admitted as members of the corporation in accordance with the statutes of the College. Elected candidates who do not so present themselves may have their first quarter's salary forfeited.

Emoluments and privileges

11. Provided that they satisfy the requirements stated in §12–§15 below, foundation scholars

(a) have their commons free of charge,

(b) are entitled to rooms free of all rent, and

(c) receive a quarterly salary of £30 if resident in College, or of £45 if not so resident.

Tenure

12. Foundation scholars hold their scholarships normally either until the end of the June quarter following the date at which they become or might have become masters in arts, or until the end of the June quarter of the fifth year following their election, whichever of these two dates is the earlier.

13. Scholars must satisfy the requirements necessary for them to proceed with their class. Any scholar failing to do so forfeits his scholarship.

14. No scholar can have his name transferred to a lower class without the express permission of the Board.

15. Scholars who have passed, or might, according to their college standing, have passed the examination for the B.A. degree, and who do not continue an approved course of academic study, are entitled only to their dining rights for the duration of their scholarship.

Scholars of the same standing who pursue an approved course of further study in Dublin are entitled to continuation of the emoluments and privileges of scholarship, except that their quarterly salary will be £15.

Scholars of the same standing who undertake research under approved conditions are entitled to continuation of the emoluments and privileges of scholarship, except that their quarterly salary will be £15. They may apply to the Dean of Graduate Studies for an increase in their quarterly salary, up to a maximum of £45 (£30 for those resident in College), and such increase will be determined in accordance with the value of any salary, grants, exhibitions, or other scholarship which they may receive, and of the expenses which they are liable to incur.

Scholars of the same standing who continue their academic studies in a professional school in Dublin, making satisfactory progress with

378

their studies, are entitled to continuation of the full emoluments and privileges of scholarship.

Applications for continuation of scholarship privileges by graduate scholars, or scholars of Candidate Bachelor standing, must be made to the Dean of Graduate Studies, and the applicants must, if these privileges are to be continued, supply the Dean of Graduate Studies with evidence that they are satisfactorily continuing their studies. This evidence must be supplied not later than seven days before the end of each arts lecture term.

Waiterships

16. Ten scholars, or other students, are appointed annually to say grace before and after meat in the Dining Hall. They are called *waiters*. They receive a salary of £16, paid quarterly, provided that their duty has been satisfactorily discharged.

The waiters are selected by the Provost, in consultation with the Junior Dean, to whom applicants must send their names before the last day of June. Regard is had in the selection to the general character of the applicant.

The grace is repeated *memoriter* and in Latin, in a form prescribed by the statutes of the College.

NON-FOUNDATION SCHOLARSHIPS

17. As foundation scholarships are tenable only by men and are limited in number, non-foundation scholarships, open to men and women, are also provided by the College. These scholarships are awarded in the same subjects and at the same examination as foundation scholarships. Men elected to these scholarships enjoy the same emoluments and privileges as foundation scholars, subject to the same conditions.

Women elected to non-foundation scholarships (*a*) receive £50 per annum, paid quarterly, in lieu of commons, so long as they are undergraduates or continue an approved course of academic study, (*b*) are entitled to residence in Trinity Hall (during such times as the Hall is open to students) with a remission of 3 guineas a week from the standard charge for residence, and (*c*) receive a quarterly salary of £30 if resident in Trinity Hall, or of £45 if not so resident. Conditions of tenure are the same as for foundation scholarships.

18. Four non-foundation scholars, or other women students, are appointed annually to say grace at formal dinners in Trinity Hall. They receive a salary of £16, paid quarterly, provided that their duty has been satisfactorily discharged. Applicants must send their names to the Warden of Trinity Hall before the last day of June.

Foundation scholarships

19.   COURSES
Mathematics

Candidates are examined in all the pure and applied mathematics of the first five terms of the honor course in mathematics.

Classics

Candidates are examined in the work of the first five terms of the honor course. They are also examined in Greek and Latin prose composition[1], in Greek and Roman history and literature, in classical archaeology and in comparative philology.

The course in ancient history is as follows:

ODD YEARS

Roman history from the earliest times to 180 A.D.

EVEN YEARS

Greek history from the earliest times to 323 B.C.

The course in classical archaeology is as follows:

ODD YEARS

Greek and Roman sculpture and painting from 400 B.C. to 180 A.D.

EVEN YEARS

Greek sculpture and painting from the earliest times to 400 B.C.

Candidates are examined on the portions of the above courses covered by the lectures during the Michaelmas and Hilary terms immediately preceding the examination.

The course in comparative philology consists of the study of comparative phonetics and accidence of the Indo-European languages, with special reference to Greek and Latin. Reference should also be made to A. Meillet, *Introduction à l'étude comparative des langues indo-européennes.*

The course in literature is that prescribed for honor students during their first five terms. The literature paper contains essay questions on this course. The prescribed books papers contain passages for translation and critical comment on the following course:

ODD YEARS	EVEN YEARS
Homer, *Odyssey*, 9–12	Homer, *Iliad*, 22–24
Herodotus 1	Euripides, *Bacchae*
Euripides, *Medea*	Plato, *Symposium*
Demosthenes, *Philippic* 1	Demosthenes, *Philippic* 3
Cicero, *Pro lege Manilia*	Cicero, *In Pisonem*
Livy 1	Sallust, *Catiline*
Lucretius 3	Lucretius 1
Horace, *Odes*, 3, 4	Juvenal, *Satires*, 1, 3, 7, 10

---

[1] Passages will also be set for verse composition, if notice is given to the School Committee not later than the end of arts lectures in the term preceding the examination.

380

Marks are awarded as follows:

Four papers of unprescribed passages	400
Two composition papers	200
Literature paper	100
Two prescribed books papers	300
Paper on history and archaeology	200
Philology paper	100
Total	1,300

Mental and moral science

Candidates must answer six papers, the subjects of which are as follows:

1. Greek ethics: the course prescribed for Michaelmas term of the Senior Freshman year.

2. Logic: the honor course in logic to the end of the Senior Freshman Hilary term lectures.

3. Intellectualism: a text to be prescribed annually for detailed study, together with the other works of the author as read in the Freshman years.

4. Empiricism: a text to be prescribed annually for detailed study, together with the other works of the author as read in the Freshman years.

5. History of philosophy: the course covered in the Michaelmas and Hilary terms of the Senior Freshman year by the Lecturer in the History of Philosophy.

6. A special work: to be prescribed annually.

100 marks are allotted to each of the six papers.

Books prescribed for 1967

Intellectualism: Descartes, *The principles of philosophy*
Empiricism: Hume, *An enquiry concerning the human understanding*
Special work: J. L. Austin, *Sense and sensibilia*

Philosophy and psychology

Candidates are examined in three papers on philosophy, and three papers on psychology, each carrying 100 marks. The papers in philosophy are those set for the examination in Mental and Moral Science.

1. *Either* Greek ethics *or* logic
2. Intellectualism
3. Empiricism
4. Essay on a general psychological topic
5. Foundations of psychology: (A) biological, (B) historical
6. Learning and perception

Natural sciences

Candidates are examined in the three subjects of the Senior Freshman year. The scope of the examination in each subject is the course up to the end of the Hilary term of the Senior Freshman year, together with a course of reading to be obtained from the head of the department concerned.

Foundation scholarships

Modern languages and literature

Candidates are required to submit two of the languages English, French, German, Irish, Italian, Spanish *or* English language and literature alone.

Candidates are examined in the work of the first five terms of the honor course.

The scheme of papers and marks is as follows:

ENGLISH
(in combination with another language)

Literature I	175
Literature II	175
Literature III	150
Total	500

ENGLISH
(as sole subject)

Literature I	175
Literature II	175
Literature III	150
Literature IV	150
Language I	175
Language II	175
Total	1,000

	FRENCH	GERMAN	IRISH ITALIAN SPANISH
Translation and composition	120	120	100
Prescribed books I	100	100	100
Prescribed books II	100	100	100
Essay in the language	80	100	100
Viva voce	100	80	100
Total	500	500	500

Ancient and modern literature

Candidates are required to submit Latin and one of the six languages of the School of Modern Languages and Literature. The course in Latin is that prescribed for the first five terms of the honor course in Ancient and Modern Literature.

Candidates are also examined in Latin composition (prose composition being compulsory, verse composition optional), in unseen translation, in grammar and textual criticism, in literary history and appreciation, and in comparative philology. The course in comparative philology consists of the

382

lectures of the lecturer. The prescribed books I paper is set on the work of the Junior Freshman year; the prescribed books II paper is set on the work of the first two terms of the Senior Freshman year.

The marks assigned to the various subjects of examination are as follows:

Unseen translation	150
Composition	100
Philology paper	50
Prescribed books I	100
Prescribed books II	100
Total	500

The courses and scales of marks in each of the modern languages are those for scholarship in modern languages and literature.

Early and modern Irish

Candidates are examined on (a) the works prescribed for the Junior and Senior Freshman years of the honor course in Celtic languages, and (b) the works prescribed for the first five terms of the honor course in modern Irish. The scheme of papers and marks is as follows:

EARLY IRISH

Old Irish grammar and glosses	200
Middle Irish texts I	100
Middle Irish texts II	100
History, literature, etc.	100

MODERN IRISH

Translation and composition	100
Prescribed books I	100
Prescribed books II	100
Essay in Irish	100
Viva voce	100
Total	1,000

Hebrew and semitic languages

Candidates are examined *viva voce* on prescribed Hebrew and Aramaic texts of the first eight terms of the honor course as follows:

Viva voce:	*Genesis, Joshua, Judges*	50
	Samuel, Pirḳê 'Abôt	50
	Amos, Isaiah or *Job, Psalms*	50
	Daniel, Ezra	50
		200

383

Foundation scholarships

and papers are set as follows:

Hebrew prose composition	100
Hebrew verse composition	100
Unprescribed Hebrew passages (2 papers, prose and verse)	200
History	100
Archaeology	100
Literature (70), philology (30)	100
Unprescribed Aramaic passages	100
	—— 800
Total (including *viva voce* mark)	1,000

History and political science

Candidates will be examined on five papers, each carrying 100 marks, as follows:

1. A general paper
2. A paper on medieval English history: 'England in the fourteenth century'
3. A paper on medieval Irish history: 'Ireland in the thirteenth century'
4. A paper on a special field of modern British history: 'Great Britain and Europe, 1603–1763'
5. A paper on a special field of modern Irish history: 'Parliament in Ireland, 1660–1782'

Economics and political science

Candidates are examined in all subjects of the honor course up to and including the Trinity term of the Senior Freshman year.

The examination consists of five three-hour papers as follows:

1. Economic analysis
2. Applied economics
3. Political institutions
4. Statistical methods and sources
5. Economic history
or 5. Mathematical analysis

Legal science

Candidates are examined in all the subjects of the honor course from entrance up to and including the Hilary term of the Senior Freshman year. The examination comprises six papers, each carrying equal weight:

I Roman law
II Legal history
III Constitutional law and history
IV Administrative law
V Criminal law
VI Law of contracts

Medicine

The course is that for the first medical examination, but at an advanced level, with additional practical work in each subject, and with a course of reading as prescribed by the Professors of Anatomy, Biochemistry and Physiology.

Papers are set as follows:

1. Anatomy, including embryology and neuroanatomy (2 papers)
2. Physiology, including histology and neurophysiology (2 papers)
3. Biochemistry (2 papers)
4. An essay paper or papers on a special subject to be prescribed from time to time

There are practical and *viva voce* examinations in the subjects stated in 1, 2 and 3.

Veterinary medicine

The course is that for the first veterinary examination, but at an advanced level, with additional practical work in each subject, and with a course of reading as prescribed by the teachers of the several subjects.

Papers are set as follows:

1. Veterinary anatomy
2. Physiology and histology
3. Biochemistry
4. An essay paper or papers on a special subject or subjects to be prescribed from time to time

There are practical and *viva voce* examinations in the subjects stated in 1, 2 and 3.

Engineering

Papers are set as follows:

1. Structures *or* control engineering
2. Strength and properties of materials
3. Hydraulics *or* physics
4. Surveying *or* electrical and electronic engineering
5. Mathematics
6. Mechanics

The field covered by the examination in each subject embraces all the work in that subject up to the end of the Hilary term of the third year of the School of Engineering course, together with a course of reading to be obtained from the Professor of Engineering.

O

Foundation scholarships

Business studies

The examination consists of the papers prescribed for the annual examination of the Junior Sophister year together with a paper on a prescribed subject and an essay paper. Marks are assigned to the various papers as follows:

Accountancy	100
Economics	100
Political institutions	100
Law relating to business	100
Industrial relations	100
Prescribed subject	300
Essay	200
Total	1,000

The prescribed subject is decided each year by the School of Business and Social Studies and is studied independently by the candidates. Information about the subject and a reading list may be obtained from the Department of Business Studies.

Social studies

The examination consists of the papers prescribed for the annual examination of the Junior Sophister year together with a paper on a prescribed subject and an essay paper. Marks are assigned to the various papers as follows:

Psychology	100
Social administration	100
Medical studies	100
Law	100
Political theory	100
Prescribed subject	300
Essay	200
Total	1,000

The prescribed subject is decided each year by the School of Business and Social Studies and is studied independently by the candidates. Information about the subject and a reading list may be obtained from the Department of Social Studies.

PRIZES IN HONOR SUBJECTS

In addition to the prizes listed here, see the regulation concerning prizes awarded to students obtaining first rank honors in HONOR COURSES, General regulations. See also RESEARCH AWARDS AND MODERATORSHIP PRIZES.

Mathematics

LLOYD EXHIBITION

This exhibition was founded in 1839 by subscription in memory of Bartholomew Lloyd, Provost 1831-7. It is awarded to the candidate who obtains highest marks at the Junior Sophister Michaelmas honor examination in mathematics. No student may obtain the exhibition a second time. Value, £48.

ARTHUR LYSTER PRIZE

In 1951 a sum was received under the will of Miss Alice Lyster to found a prize in mathematics, and a further sum was added by her executors. The prize is awarded annually to the student who obtains the highest marks at the Junior Freshman Michaelmas honor examination in mathematics. Value, £45.

MICHAEL ROBERTS PRIZE

This prize was founded in 1883 in memory of Michael Roberts, Fellow 1843-82, by a gift from his widow. It is awarded annually on the results of part I of the moderatorship examination in mathematics. A student who has been awarded the Rowe Prize in full is not eligible for this prize. Value, £9.

ROWE PRIZE

This prize was founded in 1959 by a bequest from Mrs Olive Marjorie Rowe in memory of her husband, Charles Henry Rowe, Fellow 1920-43. It is awarded annually to the candidate obtaining highest marks at part I of the moderatorship examination in mathematics. Value, £50.

TOWNSEND MEMORIAL PRIZE

This prize was founded in 1885 by subscription in memory of Richard Townsend, Fellow 1845-84. It is awarded annually on the result of the Junior Freshman Michaelmas honor examination in mathematics. A candidate who has been awarded the Arthur Lyster Prize in full is not eligible for this prize.

Prizes in honor subjects

In making the award special consideration will be given to the answering on that part of the course related to geometrical studies. Value, £30.

Classics

JOHN ISAAC BEARE MEMORIAL PRIZE

This prize was founded in 1937 by a gift from Mrs Farran in memory of her father, John Isaac Beare, Fellow 1887–1918. It is awarded annually to the candidate for scholarship in classics who obtains the highest mark in the Greek translation and composition papers. Value, £5.

BISHOP BERKELEY'S GOLD MEDALS

These awards were founded in 1752 by a gift from George Berkeley, Fellow 1707–24. Two gold medals (first and second) are awarded on the results of an examination in Greek language and literature held annually in Hilary term, and open to all students under M.A. standing. No one can be a candidate more than three times, or obtain a medal more than once. Candidates are examined in composition, in the manner of the author or authors prescribed. The examination is conducted by the Regius Professor of Greek, the Professor of Latin, and a third examiner appointed by the Board. The course is announced annually by the Regius Professor of Greek. Candidates must notify the Senior Lecturer at least 21 days before the end of arts lectures in the previous Michaelmas term.

Course for 1967: Theognis

COMPOSITION PRIZES IN CLASSICS

A Junior Freshman and a Senior Freshman prize for composition are awarded each term to students attending the honor lectures in classics. Value, £1 10s each.

MULLINS CLASSICAL EXHIBITION

This exhibition was founded in 1898 by a bequest from John Mullins. It is awarded annually in Michaelmas term to the Junior Sophister student who obtains the highest aggregate of marks in the three classical honor examinations in Michaelmas term of the immediately preceding three academic years. Value, £40, payable in two instalments in December and June.

MARSHALL PORTER MEMORIAL PRIZE

This prize was founded in 1900 by a gift from A. M. Porter in memory of his son, Andrew Marshall Porter, Scholar 1895, who died of wounds received in action at Lindley, South Africa. It is awarded annually to the candidate for scholarship in classics next in merit to the last scholar elected. In case of equality of marks, preference is given to the candidate who has obtained the higher marks in classical composition. Value, £40, payable in June.

WILLIAM ROBERTS PRIZE

This prize was founded in 1884 in memory of William Roberts, Fellow 1841–83, by a gift from his widow. It is awarded annually to the student who obtains the highest marks at the Senior Freshman Michaelmas honor examination in classics and does not lose his class. Value, £9.

TYRRELL MEMORIAL MEDAL

This award was founded in 1877 by subscription in memory of William Gerald Tyrrell, Scholar 1871. A gold medal is awarded biennially for the best translations of passages into Greek prose, Latin prose, Greek verse and Latin verse. The passages set are announced in November each alternate year, and the compositions, with fictitious signatures, and accompanied by sealed envelopes containing the names of the candidates and of their tutors, must be sent to the Senior Lecturer on or before the first day of the following February. The competition is open to all students under the standing of M.A. having their names on the college books. The examiners are the Regius Professor of Greek and the Professor of Latin. Passages will be set in November 1967.

VICE-CHANCELLOR'S LATIN MEDALS

These awards were founded in 1869 by the Provost and Senior Fellows. Two gold medals are awarded on the result of an annual examination in Latin, similar to that for the Berkeley medals in Greek and subject to similar regulations. The examination is held in Michaelmas term on a day fixed at the end of the preceding Trinity term, after due notice has been received. The course is announced annually by the Professor of Latin.

Subject for 1966: Cicero, *Philippics*
Subject for 1967: *Appendix Vergiliana*, Virgil's *Eclogue* and *Georgics*

VICE-CHANCELLOR'S PRIZES

These prizes are awarded annually for the best compositions on proposed subjects in prose or verse in English, Greek, Irish and Latin. They are open to all students on the college books under M.A. standing, but a student cannot obtain a prize oftener than twice in succession, or more than three times in all. The examiners are the Professor of English Literature, the Regius Professor of Greek, the Professor of Irish and the Professor of Latin.

The subjects for compositions are announced before 1 June. Compositions, with fictitious signatures and accompanied by sealed envelopes containing the names of the essayists and of their tutors, must be sent to the Senior Lecturer before 1 December, the prizes being declared on 15 January following.

No prize is given of more than £20; prizes of less amount and more than one in each kind of composition, may be awarded on the recommendation of the examiners.

Subjects for the prizes to be awarded in January 1967
Greek or Latin prose: Cyprus
Greek or Latin verse: Selene

For subjects in English and Irish, see below under those headings.

Prizes in honor subjects
Mental and moral science

JOHN ISAAC BEARE PRIZE IN PHILOSOPHY

This prize was founded in 1953 by a bequest from W. E. P. Cotter in memory of John Isaac Beare, Fellow 1887–1918. It is divided into three parts and one part is awarded in each of the first three years of the honor course in mental and moral science. Part I is awarded at the end of the Trinity term in each year to the Junior Freshman student who has submitted the best essays on the subjects prescribed at tutorial or other lectures during the academic year. Similar regulations apply to parts II and III in the Senior Freshman and Junior Sophister years respectively. The prize-winners may select books, to the value of the prize awarded, at the University booksellers. Value, £4 10s. each part.

JOHN HENRY BERNARD PRIZES

These prizes were founded in 1929 by subscription in memory of John Henry Bernard, Provost 1919–27. A prize is awarded annually in each of the Freshman years and in the Junior Sophister year of the honor course in mental and moral science. In the Junior Freshman year it is awarded to the student who has obtained the highest aggregate of marks in the Hilary and Michaelmas term examinations; in the other two years, it is awarded to the student who has obtained the highest marks in the Michaelmas examination. Value of each prize, £15.

LILIAN MARY LUCE MEMORIAL PRIZE

This prize was founded in 1941 by a gift from the Rev. Arthur Aston Luce, Fellow, in memory of his wife, Lilian Mary Luce, gold medallist in mental and moral science. It is awarded on the result of a written examination held annually towards the end of Trinity term conducted by two examiners appointed from the honor examiners in mental and moral science. The course consists in the main of portions of Berkeley's philosophical works, preferably those not specified in the honor course. Works on the Berkeleian philosophy may be included. The course, which may be varied from year to year, is prescribed by the Professor of Moral Philosophy and announced in the *Calendar*. The examination is open only to Junior Freshmen students of mental and moral science. A month's notice of intention to compete must be sent to the Senior Lecturer. In the case of close answering the Board may divide the prize, on the recommendation of the examiners. Value, £20.

Course for 1967

Paper 1   *Philosophical commentaries* and *Three dialogues between Hylas and Philonous*

Paper 2   *Alciphron*, Dialogues 2, 3 and G. J. Warnock, *Berkeley*

HENRY STEWART MACRAN PRIZE

This prize was founded in 1941 by a bequest from Miss Eileen Frances Gertrude McCutchan in memory of Henry Stewart Macran, Fellow 1892–

1937. It is awarded annually to the candidate who gains the best aggregate of marks at a written examination on Hegel's system of philosophy and for an essay 'on a subject of a metaphysical or ethical and not merely psychological or logical character'.

A candidate must be under M.A. standing, and if an undergraduate, must have his name on the college books. No candidate may win the prize more than once, but an unsuccessful candidate may compete again.

The examination is held in Trinity term, before the beginning of arts lectures and, if possible, after the conclusion of the examination for scholarship in mental and moral science. The course consists of (1) a prescribed portion of Hegel's works (100 marks) and (2) a critical or expository work on Hegel (100 marks). Notice of intention to compete must be given to the Senior Lecturer at least three weeks before the last day of lectures in Hilary term.

The subject of the essay (200 marks) is one of a number of topics prescribed annually by the Professor of Moral Philosophy and two other examiners appointed by the Board, or else a topic proposed by the candidate at least three weeks before the end of Hilary term and approved by the examiners. It must be 8,000–9,000 words in length. It must be handed to the Professor on the morning of the first day of the examination, and must be signed by the candidate and accompanied by a list of authorities consulted, and by a statement that the essay is the candidate's own work. Value, £40.

Course for 1967

Paper 1	Hegel, *The philosophy of right*
Paper 2	J. N. Findlay, *Hegel: a re-examination*
Essay	'Propositions about the future' *or* 'The concept of art' or a subject proposed by the candidate

GEORGE McCUTCHAN PRIZE

This prize was founded in 1941 by a bequest from Miss Eileen Frances Gertrude McCutchan, in memory of her father, George McCutchan. It is awarded annually by the Board on the recommendation of the Professor of Moral Philosophy and the moderatorship examiners to the candidate for moderatorship in mental and moral science who obtains a first or second class moderatorship and shows the best knowledge of Hegel's system of philosophy on the course in Hegel prescribed for the compulsory portion of the moderatorship course. Value, £20.

WRAY PRIZE

This prize was founded in 1848 by a gift from Mrs Catherine Wray, widow of Henry Wray, Fellow 1800–47, to encourage metaphysical studies. It is awarded annually on the results of an examination held in Hilary term, on a day arranged at the end of the preceding Michaelmas term. Sophisters alone are eligible to compete. Candidates must give notice to the Senior Lecturer at least three weeks before the last day of lectures in Michaelmas term. In case of close answering the prize may be divided. No candidate may be awarded the prize or part of the prize more than once.

391

Prizes in honor subjects

The examination comprises
(1) a paper on the general history of philosophy (100 marks)
(2) a paper on a special theme (100 marks)
(3) a paper on a special work (100 marks)
(4) a *viva voce* examination (100 marks)

Value, £40.

Course for 1967   Theme: Change
Special work: L. J. Cohen, *The diversity of meaning*

Natural sciences

COCKER PRIZE IN ORGANIC CHEMISTRY

This prize was founded in 1949 by a gift from Sir William W. Cocker, LL.D.(*h.c.*). It is awarded annually by the Board on the recommendation of the Professor of Chemistry to the student who is pursuing a course in natural sciences and who shows the greatest manipulative skill in practical organic chemistry during his Senior Sophister year. If the income permits, additional prizes, or a prize of greater value, may be awarded. Value, £10 and a silver medal.

EDGE PRIZE IN BOTANY

This prize is awarded to the member of the Junior Sophister honor class who carries out the best practical work in botany during the year. The specimens, records and drawings illustrative of this work should be submitted to the Professor of Botany not later than the date of the Michaelmas Junior Sophister honor examination. Value, £10.

EDGE PRIZE IN GEOLOGY

This prize is awarded annually to the Junior Sophister who obtains the highest marks at the Junior Sophister honor examination in geology. Value, £10.

GOULDING SCHOLARSHIP IN CHEMISTRY

The scholarship was initiated in 1962 by Goulding Fertilisers, Ltd. of Dublin. A scholarship of £100 for one year is awarded annually, on the nomination of the Head of the Department of Chemistry, to a rising Senior Sophister student in chemistry who has reached first class rank in chemistry at the Junior Sophister annual examination. If in any year or years no student reaches the required standard, additional scholarships may be awarded in the following year or years.

HENLEY MEMORIAL PRIZE

This prize was founded in 1963 by a bequest from Miss Florence I. Henley in memory of her brothers, E. A. W. Henley, M.D., and F. L. Henley, M.A. The prize is awarded to the candidate who obtains the highest average mark at the Junior Freshman honor examination in natural sciences in Michaelmas term. Value, £5.

KINGSMILL JONES MEMORIAL PRIZE

This prize was founded in 1920 by subscription in memory of Captain Kingsmill Williams Jones, killed in action 2 August 1918. The prize is awarded on the result of the examination for foundation scholarship in natural sciences to the best unsuccessful candidate. Value, £20.

ADRIAN STOKES MEMORIAL FELLOWSHIP

See postgraduate awards in School of Physic below.

Modern languages and literature

DOMPIERRE-CHAUFEPIÉ PRIZE

This prize was founded in 1912 by a gift from Gerard Alston Exham, Fellow 1895–1920, in memory of Eugénie de Dompierre de Chaufepié, of The Hague. It is awarded annually on the results of an examination held in Hilary term of the Senior Freshman year. The examination consists of an essay in French and a *viva voce* examination to test the candidate's practical knowledge of French. A candidate must have attended three terms of honor lectures in French previous to the examination and must be approved by the Professor. Value, £10.

COMPOSITION PRIZES IN MODERN LANGUAGES

A Junior Freshman and a Senior Freshman prize for composition are awarded each term to students attending the honor lectures in English, in French, in German, in Irish and in Spanish. If sufficient merit is shown, two prizes may be awarded in English and in French. One prize for composition in English is awarded to Sophisters attending the Professor's lectures. Value, £1 10s. each.

COTTER PRIZE IN MODERN LANGUAGES

This prize was founded in 1953 by a bequest from W. E. P. Cotter. It is awarded annually to the most highly placed unsuccessful candidate for scholarship in modern languages and literature. Value, £14.

FERGUSON MEMORIAL PRIZE

This prize was founded in 1907 by subscription in memory of Sir Samuel and Lady Ferguson. It is awarded every third year. Work submitted for it may take the form of

(a) an investigation of some aspect or feature of Irish linguistic development, or

(b) a study of Irish literary sources, or

(c) an edition of an important text including translation, commentary and linguistic analysis

The prize is open to all undergraduates and to graduates of not more than seven years' standing.

The next award will be made in 1968 and exercises must reach the Senior Lecturer before 17 March 1968. Value, £100.

Prizes in honor subjects

FRENCH GOVERNMENT'S BRONZE MEDAL

This medal is awarded annually to the best candidate in French at the examination for moderatorship in modern languages and literature.

ROBERT WALLACE HENRY EXHIBITION

This exhibition was founded in 1946 by a gift from Mrs A. Wallace Henry. It is awarded to the student who gets the highest marks in English (papers 1 and 2) at the annual Junior Freshman honor examination. Value, £4.

RICHARD F. LITTLEDALE PRIZE

This prize was founded in 1892 by subscription in memory of Richard F. Littledale. It is awarded annually to the student who obtains the highest marks at the annual Senior Freshman honor examination in English literature and does not lose his class. Value, £10.

PRIZE IN OLD AND MIDDLE ENGLISH

This prize is awarded annually to the student obtaining the highest marks in English language at the Senior Freshman honor examination. Value, £10 10s.

REV. THADDEUS O'MAHONY, D.D. PRIZE

This prize was founded in 1931 by a bequest from Miss E. S. O'Mahony in memory of Thaddeus O'Mahony, Professor of Irish 1861–79. It is awarded annually on the results of the Michaelmas Junior Freshman honor examination in Irish. It must be expended on the purchase of Irish books under the supervision of the Professor of Irish. Value, £11.

PRIZES IN PROVENÇAL (INCLUDING CATALAN)

These prizes are temporarily suspended.

ERNST SCHEYER PRIZE

This prize was founded in 1960 by a gift in memory of Ernst Scheyer, lecturer in the Department of German 1947–58. It is awarded annually to the student obtaining the highest mark at the Junior Freshman honor examination in German. Value, £5.

SHERIDAN PRIZE

This prize was founded by a gift from an anonymous donor in 1961. It is awarded annually on the recommendation of the Professor of English Literature for an essay on some aspect of the English language after 1400, by a student below M.A. standing. Candidates are advised to consult the Professor of English Literature on the topics of their essays. Essays should reach the Registrar by 31 January. Value, about £8.

DR HENRY HUTCHINSON STEWART LITERARY SCHOLARSHIPS

These scholarships were founded in 1884 by a bequest from Henry Hutchinson Stewart. Two scholarships, each to be held for three years, are awarded annually in November to those students who have obtained the highest aggregate of marks in the annual honor examinations of the Junior Freshman, Senior Freshman and Junior Sophister years in modern languages and literature. Value, £50 and £30 a year, for three years.

VICE-CHANCELLOR'S PRIZES IN ENGLISH

For regulations, see prizes in classics above.

Subjects for the prizes to be awarded in January 1967
English prose: Drama at the present time
English verse: John Keats

VICE-CHANCELLOR'S PRIZES IN IRISH

For regulations see prizes in classics above.

Subjects for the prizes to be awarded in January 1967
Irish prose: Piaras Feiritéar
Irish verse: Diarmaid agus Gráinne

Hebrew and semitic languages

ARABIC PRIZES

Prizes for proficiency in Arabic are awarded annually on the results of examinations held in Trinity term open to students who have attended lectures in Arabic for at least three terms. Candidates must give notice to the Senior Lecturer at least twenty-one days before the end of Hilary term. Value: first year, £4; second year, £6.

Courses
FIRST YEAR. Elementary Arabic grammar (Thatcher, *Arabic grammar*); Yellin and Billig, *Arabic reader*, selected portions.
SECOND YEAR. Advanced Arabic grammar (Thatcher, *Arabic grammar*); Yellin and Billig, *Arabic reader*; Thornton and Nicholson, *First Arabic book*, selected portions; the *Qur'ân*, extracts.

PRIZES IN ARAMAIC AND SYRIAC

Two prizes are awarded each year at the end of Trinity term on the result of a special examination. Candidates must have passed the Junior Freshman honor examination in Hebrew. Notice of intention to compete must reach the Senior Lecturer at least three weeks before the last day of arts lectures in Hilary term. Value, £4 and £2.

Course
Aramaic and Syriac grammars
Aramaic: *Daniel*, chs 2, 3; *Ezra*, chs 5, 6
Syriac: *Colossians*; *Revelation*, chs 1–3

HINCKS MEMORIAL PRIZE

This prize was founded in 1944 by a gift from J. H. Magee in memory of Edward Hincks, Fellow 1813–20, and to encourage the study of the language,

Prizes in honor subjects

history, religion, literature, culture and ideas of the Hebrews in Old Testament times, and of Old Testament archaeology. It is awarded in Michaelmas term by a committee consisting of the Provost, the Senior Lecturer and the Professor of Hebrew. The committee may make an annual award, or, if it wishes to provide funds for study abroad, may award the prize for two or three years. It may award the prize either (*a*) to a student of the College who submits the best thesis written within one year of his obtaining the degree of B.A., on a subject of his own choice approved by the committee, or (*b*) to a student of the College, below M.A. standing, qualified and prepared to undertake a period of research work under suitable direction either in Palestine, Iraq or Egypt, or in a European university, and to embody the results of his research in a report.

Applications from candidates should reach the Senior Lecturer not later than 15 November. Value, £50.

JACK MORRISON MODERATORSHIP PRIZE

This prize was founded in 1963 by Jack Morrison, J.P. It is awarded annually to the student who answers best at the moderatorship examination in Hebrew and semitic languages. In the case of close answering the Board may divide the prize. Value, £25.

JACK MORRISON B'NAI B'RITH PRIZE

This prize was founded in 1963 by Jack Morrison, J.P. It is awarded annually to the student who answers best at the Senior Freshman honor examination in Hebrew and semitic languages. Value, £10.

WALL BIBLICAL SCHOLARSHIPS

These scholarships were founded in 1858 by a gift from Charles William Wall, Fellow 1805–62. One scholarship is awarded annually on the result of a special examination in Trinity term, in a portion of the *Pentateuch* as exhibited in Jewish and Samaritan editions of the Hebrew text, and translated in the *Septuagint*, Peshitta and Targum of Onkelos versions, together with such other work, dealing with the history and criticism of the text, and with the archaeological discoveries which throw light upon the *Pentateuch*, as may be prescribed each year. The examination includes translation of unprescribed passages, composition and pointing.

The names of undergraduate candidates must be on the college books, and their standing, reckoned from entrance, must be below that of M.A. Graduates of the University below the standing of M.A. may also be candidates. Candidates must give notice to the Senior Lecturer three weeks before the end of Hilary term. Value, £20 a year for three years, paid quarterly.

Course for 1967

Deuteronomy, chs 12–21, 29–34, in Hebrew; *Septuagint*, Targum (Onkelos) and Syriac (Peshitta) versions of the same. Candidates are also expected to be acquainted with the readings of the Samaritan *Pentateuch*.

Wright, *Lectures on the comparative grammar of the Semitic languages*; Buhl,

Canon and text of the Old Testament; Weir, *A short history of the Hebrew text of the Old Testament*; Abbott, *Essays on the text of the Old Testament*; Chwolson, *The quiescentes*; Chapman, *Introduction to the Pentateuch*; Caiger, *Bible and spade —an introduction to biblical archaeology*; Swete, *Introduction to the Old Testament in Greek*, chs 1–3; Duval, *La littérature syriaque*; Hastings, *A dictionary of the Bible*, articles on *Septuagint*, Syriac versions, Targums, Samaritan *Pentateuch* and the Code of Hammurabi.

Comparative philology and Sanskrit

PRIZE IN ELEMENTARY COMPARATIVE PHILOLOGY AND SANSKRIT

This prize is offered annually on the result of an examination held in Trinity term. Value, £10.

Course

The lectures of the Lecturer in Sanskrit and Comparative Philology. Descriptive and comparative grammar of classical Sanskrit. Lanman, *Sanskrit reader*, 'Nala', 'Hitopadesa', 'Mānavadharmasāstra'.

Students should use Macdonell, *Sanskrit grammar*, and Meillet, *Introduction à l'étude comparative des langues indo-européennes*.

FERRAR MEMORIAL PRIZE

This prize was founded in 1874 by subscription in memory of William Hugh Ferrar, Fellow 1859–71. It is awarded on the result of a special examination in a course of comparative philology held in Trinity term. The competition for the prize is open to all persons under M.A. standing except Fellows of the College, or Professors of the University, whose names are on the college books the day preceding the days of examination. No person who has won the prize can be admitted a second time as a candidate. Notice of intention to compete must be sent to the Senior Lecturer at least twenty-one days before the end of arts lectures in Hilary term. Value, £60.

Course

Comparative philology of the indo-european languages. (A higher standard is required than in the case of the prize in elementary comparative philology and Sanskrit.) Descriptive and comparative grammar of Vedic and classical Sanskrit.

Lanman, *Sanskrit reader*
Meillet, *Linguistique historique et linguistique générale*, tome I
    One of the following:
Meillet, *Aperçu d'une histoire de la langue grecque*
Meillet, *Esquisse d'une histoire de la langue latine*
Meillet, *Caractères généraux des langues germaniques*
Lewis and Pedersen, *A concise comparative Celtic grammar*
Grammont, *Traité de phonétique*
de Saussure, *Cours de linguistique générale*

Prizes in honor subjects
History and political science

BROWNE PRIZE

This prize was founded in 1966 by a bequest from Miss L. C. N. Browne. It is awarded annually to the candidate who obtains the highest marks at the Junior Freshman honor examination in history. The prize-winner may select books to the value of £7 at the University booksellers.

CLUFF MEMORIAL PRIZE

This prize was founded in 1870 by subscription in memory of James Stanton Cluff, Scholar 1858. A further endowment was provided by Mr. W. V. Cluff in 1965. It is awarded on the result of the Michaelmas Junior Sophister honor examination in history and political science. Value, £25.

CURTIS MEMORIAL PRIZE

This prize was founded in 1952 by subscription in memory of Edmund Curtis, Erasmus Smith's Professor of Modern History 1914–39 and Lecky Professor of Modern History 1939–43. The money subscribed having been entrusted to the Royal Irish Academy, the Council of the Academy has decided to use the income to award a prize of £50, or such sum as the Council may direct, for an essay on Irish history, based on original research, or a work of original interpretation. A candidate for the prize must be, or have been, a student of a university, and must not be more than 30 years of age on 1 January of the year in which an award is to be made.

A person wishing to become a candidate must apply for recognition to the Royal Irish Academy, 19 Dawson Street, Dublin 2, at any date up to 1 June of the previous year, giving particulars of the subject and scope of the proposed essay, and of progress made if work has already been begun upon it.

Essays, in typescript or print and securely bound, must be submitted not later than 1 January of the year in which an award is to be made. An essay must not normally exceed 40,000 words, and must contain a full bibliography.

The next award will be made in 1968.

DUNBAR INGRAM MEMORIAL PRIZE

This prize was founded in 1896 by a gift from John Kells Ingram, Fellow 1846–99, in memory of his son, T. Dunbar Ingram. It is awarded annually on the result of a special examination held in Michaelmas term before the beginning of the Junior Sophister lecture term. Only students in the School of History and Political Science who have proceeded satisfactorily in their Senior Freshman year are eligible for the prize. Value, £12.

Course: Ireland in the age of Swift

Recommended works: Swift, *Irish tracts*; *The Drapier's letters*.

Economics and political science

BASTABLE PRIZE

This prize was founded in 1933 by subscription in memory of Charles Francis Bastable, Professor of Political Economy 1908–32 and Regius Professor of Laws 1882–1932. It is awarded on the result of the Michaelmas Junior Sophister honor examination in economics and political science. Value, £5.

Legal science

HENRY HAMILTON HUNTER MEMORIAL PRIZE

This prize was founded in 1951 in memory of Henry Hamilton Hunter by a gift from his widow. It is awarded on the result of the Michaelmas Senior Freshman honor examination in legal science, providing the candidate obtains first rank honors, or second rank (first division). Value, £20.

PRIZES IN PROFESSIONAL SUBJECTS

Divinity

CARSON BIBLICAL PRIZE

This prize was founded in 1891 by a gift from Joseph Carson, Fellow 1837–98. It is awarded annually to the student obtaining the highest aggregate of marks in all the papers on the Bible at the junior divinity year and senior divinity year examinations combined. Value, £25.

CATECHETICAL PREMIUMS

See CATECHETICAL COURSE.

MONCRIEFF COX MEMORIAL PRIZE

This prize was founded in 1933 by subscription in memory of John Frank Moncrieff Cox. It is awarded annually by the Regius Professor of Divinity and the Professor of Pastoral Theology to that member of the senior divinity class who composes the best sermon on a subject set at the end of Hilary term by the Professor of Pastoral Theology. Consideration is given to the delivery of the sermon. Value, £5.

CHURCH FORMULARIES PRIZE AND RYAN PRIZE

The Church Formularies Prize was founded in 1868 by a gift from Robert R. Warren, M.P. for the University. The Ryan Prize was founded in 1812 by a gift from Edward Ryan. The joint prize is awarded annually to the student obtaining the highest aggregate of marks in the papers on Christian doctrine at the junior divinity year and senior divinity year examinations combined. Value, £8 10s.

DOWNES DIVINITY PREMIUMS

These prizes were founded in 1797 by a bequest from Dive Downes. They are open to any divinity student who has been a member of either the junior or senior class during the two terms antecedent to that in which the examinations are held.

WRITTEN COMPOSITION

The subject is announced in the last week of Hilary term by Archbishop King's Professor of Divinity, and on an appointed day the candidates deliver discourses on the subject, without hesitation, no discourse to exceed one-quarter of an hour in delivery. Two prizes are awarded, one to each of the two best candidates, regard being had to delivery as well as to matter. No candidate can obtain either prize in full more than once, nor can he obtain a second prize if he has already obtained a first prize. The examiners are the Regius Professor of Divinity, Archbishop King's Professor and the Professor of Oratory. Value, £20, £12.

ORATORY

The Professor of Pastoral Theology awards two prizes in Trinity term to the students who have profited most by his instruction in preaching and in the delivery of sermons. No candidate can obtain either prize a second time. Value, £14, £8.

READING THE LITURGY

Prizes are awarded each Trinity term to the two students who read in the best manner selected parts of the Liturgy. No candidate can obtain either prize a second time. Value, £8, £5.

ELRINGTON THEOLOGICAL PRIZE

This prize was founded in 1837 by subscription in memory of Thomas Elrington, Provost 1811-20. It is awarded for the best theological essay written by a graduate of not more than eight years' standing, on a subject announced two years in advance and changed annually. If sufficient merit is shown, a second prize may be awarded, but if sufficient merit is not shown, the prize may be withheld in whole or in part. A candidate who has obtained a first prize is thereby precluded from further competition and a second prize cannot be awarded more than once to any candidate.

The examiners are the Bishop of Ferns, the Provost and the Regius Professor of Divinity. Two copies of the essays, typewritten or printed, with fictitious signatures, accompanied by sealed envelopes containing the names of the essayists must reach the Regius Professor of Divinity before the first day of October in each year.

At least half of the amount of any prize awarded must be expended upon approved theological books.

Value, £80.

Subject for 1967: Episcopacy.

BISHOP FORSTER'S DIVINITY PREMIUM

This prize was founded in 1738 by a gift from Nicholas Forster, Fellow 1693-1714. It is awarded annually to the student obtaining the highest marks in the annual examination of the junior divinity year excluding papers IV and V of the preliminary year examination. Value, £33.

ARCHBISHOP KING'S DIVINITY PRIZE

This prize was founded in 1836 by the Board. It is awarded annually to the student obtaining the second highest marks in the annual examination of the junior divinity year excluding papers IV and V of the preliminary year examination. Value, £20.

ROBERT KING MEMORIAL PRIZE IN ECCLESIASTICAL HISTORY

This prize was founded in 1902 by subscription in memory of Robert King, Scholar 1835. It is awarded to the candidate who obtains the highest marks in ecclesiastical history at the final divinity examination either in Hilary or in Trinity term. Value, £6.

Prizes in professional subjects

KYLE IRISH PRIZE

This prize was founded in 1852 in memory of Samuel Kyle, Provost 1820–31. It is offered annually on the result of an examination in Irish for divinity students in Trinity term. It is competed for by candidates from dioceses in priority as follows: (1) Cork, Cloyne and Ross, (2) Limerick, Ardfert and Aghadoe, (3) Killaloe, Kilfenora, Clonfert and Kilmacduagh, (4) Tuam, Killala and Achonry, (5) Raphoe. Failing these, candidates are to be accepted from any other part of Ireland. A student may compete for this prize at any time during his divinity course, and if he obtains the prize may compete again the following year, but not oftener. He cannot hold it for more than two years. Notice should be given to the Senior Lecturer before the end of Hilary term. Value, £30.

Course

Irish grammar and composition
The four *Gospels, Acts, Romans, 1* and *2 Timothy, Hebrews*

LAMBERT PRIZE

This prize was founded in 1942 by a bequest from Richard A. Lambert. It is awarded annually to the student who obtains the highest aggregate of marks in (*a*) the paper set on a specified portion of the New Testament at the junior divinity year examination and (*b*) a special paper set on the *Acts of the Apostles.* Value, £9.

TOPLADY MEMORIAL SCRIPTURE PRIZE

This prize was founded in 1906 by a gift from William Batley, in memory of Augustus Montague Toplady. It is awarded annually to the student obtaining the second highest aggregate of marks in all the papers on the Bible at the junior divinity year and senior divinity year examinations combined. Value, £18.

WEIR PRIZE IN HOLY SCRIPTURE

This prize was founded in 1921 by a bequest from Edward Henry Weir. It is awarded to the student, completing the lectures of the junior year in Trinity term, who has shown most merit in the written examinations in Holy Scripture at a general examination of the junior class. Value, £5.

NEWPORT WHITE PRIZE IN GREEK TESTAMENT

This prize was founded in 1935 by a gift from N. J. D. White, Regius Professor of Divinity 1930–5. It is awarded annually to the candidate obtaining the highest marks in Greek Testament at the final divinity examination in Trinity term. Value, £7.

J. E. L. OULTON MEMORIAL FUND

This fund was formed in 1957 by subscription in memory of J. E. L. Oulton, Regius Professor of Divinity 1935–56. It is held by the Representative Body of the Church of Ireland, who distribute the income, at their discretion, for the purpose of helping clergymen of the Church of Ireland, or graduate ordinands, so that such person or persons may continue their studies, and/or for the purpose of the advancement of patristic study. Applications should reach the Secretary, Representative Church Body, 52 St Stephen's Green, Dublin 2, on or before 1 April each year. Applicants should give details of the work undertaken and expenditures incurred.

Law
ANNUAL PRIZES
At the end of Trinity term prizes amounting to £11 may be awarded by the professors and lecturers at their discretion in each of the following subjects: (1) law of property, (2) jurisprudence, (3) roman law and (4) constitutional law. The merits of the candidates are determined by the aggregate of marks obtained by them at the Michaelmas and Hilary term examinations and the Trinity annual examination. Students reading for the degree of LL.B. as well as students of King's Inns and solicitors' apprentices are eligible to compete for these prizes.

JULIAN PRIZE
This prize was founded in 1923 by a bequest from Mrs Margaret Julian in memory of her son, Ernest Lawrence Julian, Reid Professor of Penal Legislation 1909–14, who was killed in action at Suvla Bay in 1915. It is awarded annually to the first of the first class candidates at the Michaelmas LL.B. degree examination, provided that he is under M.A. standing at the date of the examination. Value, £20.

Medicine
ARTHUR BALL PRIZES
These prizes were founded in 1964 by a bequest from Lady Elizabeth Smyth Ball in memory of her late husband, Sir Charles Arthur Kinahan Ball, Bart., Regius Professor of Surgery 1933–46. They are awarded annually, provided sufficient merit is shown, to the candidates placed first and second at the Final Medical Examination, Part V (Surgery) at the Trinity Term examination. Value, about £30 and £15.

BURTON PRIZE
This prize was donated in the memory of Dr Norman A. Burton by his parents. It is awarded annually to the candidate who presents the best set of case histories for the final examination in surgery held in Trinity term of each year. The prize-winner may select books to the value of £4 at the University booksellers.

SIR JAMES CRAIG MEMORIAL PRIZE
This prize was founded in 1952 by a gift from James Wallace Craig in memory of his father, Sir James Craig, King's Professor of the Practice of Medicine 1910–33. It is awarded annually to the student gaining first place at the June final examination in medicine. Value, £7.

Prizes in professional subjects

DANIEL JOHN CUNNINGHAM MEMORIAL MEDAL AND PRIZE

This prize was founded in 1909 by subscription in memory of Daniel John Cunningham, University Professor of Anatomy 1883–1903. A bronze medal and a prize are awarded to the student who, having passed the first medical examination in March, obtains the highest marks in anatomy, provided he has been not longer than two years in the School of Physic at the time of the examination. Value, £7 10s.

DE RENZY CENTENARY PRIZE

This prize was founded in 1929 by a gift from Lady Martin to commemorate the centenary of the birth of her father, Surgeon-General Sir Annesley Charles Castriot de Renzy. It is awarded on the result of an examination in social and preventive medicine held in the fifth medical year. Value, £22 10s.

ANDREW FRANCIS DIXON PRIZE

This prize was founded in 1946 by a gift from a former student of the School of Physic in memory of Andrew Francis Dixon, University Professor of Anatomy 1903–36. It is awarded annually in July to the best student of anatomy in the first medical year. Value, £6.

FITZ-PATRICK SCHOLARSHIP

This prize was founded in 1901 by a gift from Mrs Fitz-Patrick in memory of her husband, Thomas Fitz-Patrick. It is awarded annually on the result of the five parts of the final medical examination. Value, £45.

REUBEN HARVEY PRIZES

These prizes are awarded by the Royal College of Physicians of Ireland. The conditions of award were changed in 1964. A prize is awarded annually, in each of the Dublin medical schools, to the candidate who obtains the highest aggregate of marks in the clinical subjects (medicine, midwifery, surgery) at the final medical examinations.

CONOLLY NORMAN MEDAL IN MENTAL DISEASES

This award was founded in 1934 by a bequest from Mrs Conolly Norman in memory of her husband. A medal is awarded on the result of an examination held in the fourth medical year by the lecturers in psychological medicine.

WILLIAM NUROCK PRIZE

This prize was founded in 1938 by a bequest from William Nurock. It is awarded annually in January to the medical student who obtained the highest mark in French at the examination in general studies for Junior Freshmen. Value, £6.

PROFESSORS' PRIZES IN THE SCHOOL OF PHYSIC

The Professors of Clinical Medicine and Materia Medica each award prizes of £5 at the end of their courses. Prizes are also awarded by the Professor of Clinical Surgery.

JOHN MALLET PURSER MEDAL

This award was founded in 1899 by subscription to mark the twenty-fifth year of tenure of the King's Professorship of the Institutes of Medicine by John Mallet Purser. A bronze medal is awarded annually to the student who, having passed the first medical examination in March, obtains the highest marks in physiology, biochemistry and histology, provided that he has been in the School of Physic at the time of the examination not longer than two years.

AQUILLA SMITH PRIZE

This prize was founded in 1932 in memory of Aquilla Smith, King's Professor of Materia Medica and Pharmacy 1864-81, by a bequest from his son, Walter G. Smith. It is awarded annually on the result of the final medical examination, part I (pathology and microbiology), held in Trinity term of the fourth medical year. Value, £10.

WALTER G. SMITH PRIZE

This prize was founded in 1932 by a bequest from Walter G. Smith, King's Professor of Materia Medica and Pharmacy 1881-1921. It is awarded annually on the result of the class examination held by the Professor at the end of his course in materia medica and therapeutics. Value, £10.

RICHARD SMYTH PRIZES IN TROPICAL BACTERIOLOGY, PARASITOLOGY AND HYGIENE

These prizes were founded in 1940 by a gift from Richard Smyth to encourage the study of tropical medicine. Three prizes are awarded annually on the result of an examination (written and practical) in bacteriology, parasitology and hygiene held in June. Special emphasis is placed on the causation and prevention of diseases prevalent in tropical countries, but candidates are not expected to have a practical knowledge of these diseases. A candidate must be in his final medical year or be a graduate in medicine of the University of Dublin of not more than three years' standing. A candidate who has been awarded the first prize may not compete again. Entries for the examination must reach the Dean of the Faculty of Physic not later than 1 May. Value: first prize, £20; second prize, £10; third prize, £5.

DR HENRY HUTCHINSON STEWART MEDICAL SCHOLARSHIPS

These scholarships were founded in 1884 by a bequest from Henry Hutchinson Stewart. The regulations were revised by the Board in 1961. One Henry Hutchinson Stewart Pre-medical Year Scholarship is awarded annually in June on the results of the pre-registration examination. Value, £10 per annum for three years.

One Dr Henry Hutchinson Stewart Scholarship is awarded annually to the best of the unsuccessful candidates at the examination for medical scholarships in the second medical year. Value, £30 per annum for three years. (In case of need the prizeman may apply to the Treasurer for the payment of all three instalments within the first year.)

WELLAND PRIZE

This prize was founded in 1938 by a bequest from Miss E. S. O'Mahony in memory of Joseph Rabiteau Welland. It is awarded annually on the result of the class examination in pharmacology at the end of the Trinity term of the second medical year. Value, £3 10s.

The following postgraduate awards are available:

POSTGRADUATE TRAVELLING SCHOLARSHIP IN MEDICINE OR SURGERY

One postgraduate scholarship is awarded annually in medicine and in surgery in alternate years. The award for 1966-7 will be in medicine. Value, £600.

The award is made on the recommendation of an interviewing committee. The successful candidate must engage in research for at least nine months. He will be paid £100 initially to cover the first month of the scholarship and £62 10s. each month for the following eight months. The candidate's supervisor will be asked for a report at the end of six months, and the final monthly payment will be made after a satisfactory report has been received.

This scholarship and the Dr Henry Hutchinson Stewart scholarship (*q.v.*) are awarded from a fund obtained by consolidating the following funds: the John Banks Fund, the Edward Hallaran Bennett Fund, the Bicentenary Fund, and the Dr Henry Hutchinson Stewart Fund.

For details of these funds see under the appropriate headings below.

JOHN BANKS FUND

This fund was established in 1907 by a gift from Sir John T. Banks, King's Professor of the Practice of Medicine 1849-69 and Regius Professor of Physic 1880-98. The income of the fund contributes to the provision of a postgraduate award in medicine. A John Banks Medal in bronze is given to the winner of the award. See above.

EDWARD HALLARAN BENNETT FUND

This fund was established in 1907 by past pupils in appreciation of E. H. Bennett, Professor of Surgery 1873-1906. The income of the fund contributes to the provision of a postgraduate award in surgery. An Edward Hallaran Bennett Medal in bronze is given to the winner of the award. See above.

BICENTENARY FUND

This fund was established in 1912 to mark the bicentenary of the School of Physic. The income of the fund contributes to the provision of postgraduate awards in medicine or surgery. See above.

SARAH PURSER MEDICAL RESEARCH FUND

Through the munificence of Miss Sarah H. Purser, R.H.A., a sum of £10,000 was given to Trinity College in 1942 to provide, from investment, an annual income to be devoted to the promotion of medical research in Ireland. The income from the fund pays the stipends of one or more investigators, who must be graduates of a university or hold diplomas in scientific subjects from recognised colleges. The investigators, when appointed, may carry out research in any branch of medical science in any institution in Ireland in which facilities for the investigation in hand for the time being can be made available. Investigators are appointed for periods of not more than two years by the Board of Trinity College on the nomination of the Professor of Experimental Medicine, from whom further particulars may be obtained.

E. C. SMITH SCHOLARSHIP IN PATHOLOGY

In 1956 a bequest was received under the will of the late Mrs J. A. Smith to found a scholarship for research in pathology in memory of her son, Edmund Cyril Smith, formerly assistant to the Professor of Pathology in the University.

The following regulations have been made by the Board:

1. The scholarship is offered triennially and is held for two years.

2. The scholar must carry out under the direction of a member of the staff of the medical school of Trinity College full-time research in pathology (including immunology, virology, and such aspects of microbiology as are relevant to disease in human beings).

3. The research must be carried on in Trinity College, or in a Dublin hospital, save that a Smith scholar who is a graduate of the University of Dublin may, if his supervisor considers it desirable, work elsewhere for a period of not more than twelve months.

4. The Professors of Bacteriology and of Pathology are invited in turn by the Graduate Studies Committee to nominate a candidate for the scholarship, with a statement of his qualifications and of his proposed course of research. If no nomination is received within three months, the Graduate Studies Committee advertises the post, and the successful candidate, if any, works in whatever department is most appropriate to his field of research.

5. The Graduate Studies Committee guarantees to augment the income of the fund from other sources sufficiently to pay the scholar a salary of £600 a year. The Professors of Pathology and Bacteriology are at liberty to augment further this salary with any funds they may have at their disposal, and if this source is adequately guaranteed, to advertise the post at a correspondingly higher salary.

6. The scholar is not permitted to undertake teaching or other work to a value of more than £50 a year, except with the permission of the Graduate Studies Committee; this permission is granted only in exceptional circumstances.

(The first scholar was appointed in 1959.)

SMITH, KLINE AND FRENCH SCHOLARSHIP IN PHARMACOLOGY

This scholarship was founded in 1964. It is awarded to a candidate registering for the degree of M.Sc., and proposing to carry out research in an approved subject in pharmacology. Value, £400.

Recipients of the award must be medical students in the University of Dublin who have passed the examination for the degree of B.A., or medical graduates of the University.

Application should be made to the Head of the Department of Pharmacology. The scholarship is awarded by the Board on the recommendation of a committee consisting of the Registrar, the Dean of the School of Physic, and the Head of the Department of Pharmacology.

The award is payable in four quarterly instalments.

RICHARD SMYTH EXHIBITION IN
TROPICAL MEDICINE

This prize was founded in 1940 by a gift from Richard Smyth to encourage the study of tropical medicine. It is offered biennially to the candidate who obtains the highest marks for (a) an essay on a tropical disease or on an aspect of tropical hygiene, and (b) reports on five cases of tropical disease personally studied by him either in the wards of a hospital for tropical diseases in Great Britain or Ireland, or in a tropical country. Equal marks are allotted to (a) and (b). A candidate must be a medical graduate of the University of not more than five years' standing, who has either been awarded a prize at the examination for the Richard Smyth Prizes, or been adjudged by the examiners to have attained a satisfactory mark.

A candidate who has been awarded the exhibition may not subsequently compete.

Essays and notes on cases must be dispatched so as to reach the Dean of the Faculty of Physic not later than 31 October in the year in which the exhibition is available. Value, £30.

DR HENRY HUTCHINSON STEWART
SCHOLARSHIP IN PSYCHIATRY

This scholarship was founded in 1884 by a bequest from Henry Hutchinson Stewart. For details application should be made to the Dean of the Faculty of Physic. Value, £350.

ADRIAN STOKES MEMORIAL FELLOWSHIP

This scholarship was founded in 1929 in memory of Adrian Stokes, Professor of Bacteriology and Preventive Medicine 1919–22. It is awarded biennially by the Board on the recommendation of a committee consisting of the Senior Lecturer, the Professor of Pathology and the Professor of Bacteriology.

A candidate for the fellowship must

(1) be a duly qualified medical practitioner, or a graduate in science in pathology or bacteriology,

(2) be not more than thirty years of age on 30 October of the year of the award, and

(3) wish to prosecute further the study of pathology or bacteriology in any of their branches.

A successful candidate must for a period of not less than six months during his year of tenure prosecute further the study of pathology or bacteriology in any of their branches at a university, school, hospital or institution (other than Trinity College, Dublin) to be approved by the Board. Value, £300.

EMILIE (MAFFETT) HARMSWORTH FUND
See RESEARCH AWARDS AND MODERATORSHIP PRIZES.

Dental science
SHELDON FRIEL PRIZE

This prize was founded in 1963 by subscription in appreciation of the work of Sheldon Friel, Professor of Orthodontics 1941–62. It is awarded annually to the student of dental science who, having proceeded regularly with his class, gains first place at the summer final examination. Value, £5.

Veterinary medicine
COMMONWEALTH BUREAU OF ANIMAL HEALTH PRIZE

This prize was instituted in 1962 by the Commonwealth Bureau of Animal Health. It is awarded annually to the student who passes the second veterinary examination in Trinity term at the first attempt, and who obtains the highest marks over 60 per cent in both the university and the class examinations in parasitology.

The prize consists of (a) one year's subscription to the Veterinary Bulletin, and (b) other books or periodicals selected by the winner from those published by the Commonwealth Agricultural Bureaux to the total value of £20.

EVANS MEDICAL VETERINARY STUDENTSHIP

A studentship is awarded annually by Evans Medical Ltd and Evans Medical (Ireland) Ltd to one student in each of the veterinary schools in Ireland and Great Britain. It is awarded to the student about to enter the final year of his veterinary course who is judged on the basis of his work during the previous years to be the most successful student. The candidate chosen is invited to visit the Evans Laboratories. The studentship is administered by the Animal Health Trust. Value, £25.

Engineering
ALEXANDER PRIZE

This prize was founded in 1922 by subscription in appreciation of the work of Thomas Alexander, Professor of Civil Engineering 1887–1921. It is awarded annually to the student who, having passed in all subjects at the regular examination for the degree of B.A.I., obtains the highest total of the marks allotted to the principal engineering subjects. Value, £22 10s.

Prizes in professional subjects

MARMADUKE BACKHOUSE PRIZE

This prize was founded in 1937 by a bequest from Mrs Alice Backhouse. It is awarded annually after the regular examination of the first year of the Engineering School to the student with the highest aggregate of marks at the first year examination, no mark below a pass mark being counted in computing the total.

The prize is paid in two equal instalments, the first in July following the award, and the second at the end of Hilary term of the following year. Payment of the second instalment is dependent on a satisfactory report from the Professor of Engineering on the student's work in the second year. Value £48.

DAVID CLARK PRIZE

This prize was founded by a bequest from David Clark, Professor of Civil Engineering 1921–33. It is awarded annually to the student who, having passed in all subjects at the regular examination for the degree of B.A.I., obtains the highest total of the marks allotted to the principal engineering subjects in Group A[1]. Value, £15.

JEFFCOTT PRIZE

This prize was founded in 1966 by a bequest from Mrs L. E. H. Jeffcott. It is awarded annually to the student who, having passed in all subjects at the regular examination for the degree of B.A.I., obtains the highest total of the marks allotted to the principal engineering subjects in Group B. Value, £10.

CLARK MEMORIAL PRIZE

This prize was founded in 1934 by subscription in memory of David Clark, Professor of Civil Engineering 1921–33. It is awarded annually to the student who, having passed in all subjects at the regular examination for the degree of B.A.I., obtains the highest[1] total of the marks allotted to the principal engineering subjects in Group C. Value, £7 10s.

COLLEN PRIZES

These prizes were founded in 1957 by a gift from L. D. G. Collen, M.A., M.A.I., to encourage interest in current engineering practice. One prize in civil engineering, one in mechanical/production engineering and one in electronic engineering are offered annually. No student can win more than one prize.

A student wishing to compete for one of these prizes must hand to the Professor of Engineering, on or before 31 December, a report of some engineering project, which should be illustrated by drawings or sketches, or, if desired, by a model or piece of handwork. Value, £15 each.

COLLEN PRIZE IN ARTS

This prize was founded in 1963 by a gift from L. D. G. Collen, M.A., M.A.I. The prize is awarded annually to the Senior Sophister engineering student who

---

[1] Second highest if the Alexander prizeman is from this group.

has most distinguished himself in the course leading to the B.A. degree. The prize is awarded on the recommendation of the Professor of Engineering in consultation with the Senior Lecturer. Value, £25.

EDGE ENGINEERING PRIZES

These prizes are awarded to the two students who obtain the highest and second highest marks in geology at the third year engineering examination. Value, first prize, £10; second prize, £5.

MAURICE F. FITZGERALD PRIZE

This prize was instituted in 1961 by a bequest from Anna Maria FitzGerald. It is awarded annually, where sufficient merit is shown, by the nomination of trustees on the result of the examination for the degree of B.A.I. Candidates must have achieved distinction during the engineering course and have made or be making satisfactory arrangements for the advancement of their knowledge of engineering and progress in the profession of engineer. Value about £150.

FRANCIS SPRING PRIZE

This prize was founded in 1935 by a bequest from Sir Francis Spring. It is awarded annually after the regular examination of the second year of the Engineering School to the student with the highest aggregate of marks at the second year examination, no mark below a pass mark being counted in computing the total.

The prize is paid in two equal instalments, the first in July following the award, and the second at the end of Hilary term of the following year. Payment of the second instalment is dependent on a satisfactory report from the Professor of Engineering on the student's work in the third year. Value, £40.

Agriculture

EDGE EXHIBITIONS IN AGRICULTURE

Two Edge Exhibitions are offered at the end of the Senior Freshman year. One is awarded for merit in the honor course and one for merit in the professional course to students on the college books or to graduates of the University of Dublin. The awards are made by the Board of Trinity College on a report from the Registrar of the School of Agriculture. Value, £15 each.

Music

PROUT PRIZE

This prize was founded in 1951 by a bequest from George Bell. It is awarded annually to the first candidate at the summer Mus.B. degree examination provided that more than one candidate sits for the examination. Value, £3 10s.

STEWART PRIZE

This prize was founded in 1951 by a bequest from George Bell. It is awarded annually to the first candidate at the summer Mus.D. degree examination provided that more than one candidate sits for the examination. Value, £3 10s.

Prizes in professional subjects

MAHAFFY MEMORIAL PRIZE

This prize was founded in 1951 by a bequest from George Bell. It is awarded every third year in Trinity term for either

(a) an essay on the theory or history of music, embodying some original research on the subject, or

(b) exceptionally meritorious performance in either the exercise or the examination for the degree of Doctor of Music during the current academic year.

Candidates must hold the degree of Bachelor in Music of the University of Dublin. Essays to be considered for the prize must be sent, in duplicate, to the Professor of Music not later than the last day of April of the year in which a prize is offered. The prize will next be awarded in 1968. Value, £25.

Business Studies

JOHN GOOD PRIZES

These prizes were founded in 1941 by a bequest from John Good. A prize of £25 is awarded to the student who obtains first place in the annual examination of the Senior Sophister year of the B.B.S. course, and a prize of £15 is awarded to the best student of the year in the M.S.A. course.

LECTURER IN ACCOUNTING PRIZE

This prize was founded in 1965 by a gift from Mostafa Hamdy Bahgat Abd El-Motaal, Lecturer in Accounting, to be awarded to the student who, at the first attempt, passes the annual examination with at least second class honors and gets the highest mark in Accounting Course I in the Department of Business Studies, the winner of the prize to select books to the value of £5 at the University booksellers.

MOSTAFA H.B. ABD EL-MOTAAL PRIZE FOR BEST GRADUATE IN ACCOUNTING

This prize was founded in 1963 by a gift from M. H. B. Abd El-Motaal, B.COM., M.COM., A.C.A. It is awarded annually to the candidate who, among those passing the B.B.S. degree examination as a whole at the first attempt, obtains the highest mark in accounting. In the event of a tie, past performance in accounting and performance in the degree examination as a whole are taken into account.

Social studies

ANNUAL PRIZES

The School Committee may recommend the award of prizes to the first and second students at each annual examination in the course for the Diploma in Social Studies, provided that such students obtain a satisfactory report from the Director of Practical Training in Social Studies. Value, first prize, £5 5s.; second prize, £3 3s.

PRIZES IN THE ORDINARY COURSE IN ARTS

KING EDWARD PRIZE

This prize was instituted by the Board in 1903 to commemorate the visit to the College of King Edward VII. It is awarded to the Respondent whom the Court of Examiners adjudges to have shown the greatest merit at the B.A. degree examination held in June. No student is eligible who has (*a*) been given any special concession or privilege, (*b*) dropped more than one class during his undergraduate course, (*c*) dropped a class after the annual Junior Sophister examination. Value, £10.

COSTELLO PRIZE IN ENGLISH LITERATURE

This prize was founded in 1954 by a bequest from Miss Louisa G. Costello. It is awarded annually to the woman student who passes the annual Senior Freshman examination in Trinity term and receives the highest marks in English. Value, £5.

COSTELLO PRIZE IN LATIN

This prize was founded in 1954 by a bequest from Miss Louisa G. Costello. It is awarded annually to the woman student who passes the annual Senior Freshman examination in Trinity term and receives the highest mark in Latin. Value, £5.

JELLETT PRIZES FOR GENERAL ANSWERING

These prizes were founded in 1889 by a gift from George Salmon, Provost 1888–1904, in memory of John Hewitt Jellett, Provost 1881–8, who had awarded prizes for general answering from 1884–7. They are awarded annually to the two students who obtain the highest aggregate of marks at the annnal Senior Freshman examination in Trinity term. To be eligible, a student must not (*a*) obtain less than 65 per cent of the total marks obtainable, (*b*) be a foundation or non-foundation scholar, (*c*) be a Kidd Scholar, entrance scholar or Erasmus Smith Exhibitioner, (*d*) have dropped a class since entering, or (*e*) have presented hellenistic in place of classical Greek at the examination. Value, £11 and £7. Where two students are of equal merit the Board may award £9 to each student.

PREMIUM IN IRISH

This prize is awarded to the student obtaining the highest marks in Irish at the annual Senior Freshman examination in Trinity term. Value, £10.

Awards for general distinction
EKENHEAD SCHOLARSHIP

This scholarship was founded in 1879 by a gift from Mrs Mary Dummett in memory of her brother, Thomas Ekenhead. It is confined to students from the county of Antrim.

A scholarship, tenable for three years, is awarded annually on the result of the Junior Freshman annual examination in the course in general studies. It may be awarded to a student in a professional school taking an arts course. A committee consisting of the Senior Lecturer and the Tutorial Committee nominates a candidate to the Board. Applications should be made to the Senior Lecturer not later than 1 June.

Students are considered to be from the county of Antrim if (a) they have been born in the county of Antrim, or (b) they have resided for not less than three years in the county of Antrim, or (c) they have attended a school in the county of Antrim for not less than three school years. Value, £15 a year for three years.

AWARDS FOR GENERAL DISTINCTION
LUCY GWYNN PRIZE

This prize was founded in 1948 by subscription in memory of Lucy Gwynn, first Lady Registrar. It is awarded annually in Michaelmas term to a Junior Sophister woman student for distinction in her college course. Professional as well as arts studies are taken into account. The award is made by the Dean of Women Students, another woman on the university staff nominated by the Board, and one of the tutors. Applications from candidates should be received by the Dean of Women Students not later than 15 November. Value, £10.

MINCHIN PRIZE

This prize was founded in 1921 in memory of George Minchin Minchin by a gift from his widow. It is awarded annually in Michaelmas term to a student from the outgoing Junior Sophister class chosen by a committee consisting of the Senior Lecturer, the Senior Dean, the Junior Dean, Erasmus Smith's Professor of Natural Philosophy and Erasmus Smith's Professor of Natural and Experimental Philosophy. In awarding the prize, regard is paid to character and academic proficiency, but in the case of equal merit preference is given to a student who shows proficiency in mathematics or physics.

Applications should reach the Senior Lecturer not later than 1 November. Value, £10.

ALICE OLDHAM MEMORIAL PRIZE

This prize was founded in 1908 by subscription in memory of Alice Oldham. It is awarded biennially in Michaelmas term in even years to the student judged to be the most distinguished of the women students completing their Junior Sophister year, and who attended classes at Alexandra College for at least one session. The award is made by a committee consisting of the Senior Lecturer, the Senior Dean and the Dean of Women Students. Value, £6.

RESEARCH AWARDS AND
MODERATORSHIP PRIZES

Research awards

Major exhibitions

1. A number of major research exhibitions (usually about six or seven) are awarded annually to graduates of the University if candidates of sufficient merit present themselves (see §5). The values of these exhibitions will be adjusted from time to time so that they remain comparable with research scholarships provided by other bodies. In making an award, fees and expenses will be taken into account as will the value of any other scholarship or grant the applicant may hold. In 1966-67 the value of each exhibition will not be less than the sum required to give the recipient a net income of £400 *per annum* after payment of fees.

2. Exhibitions are tenable for a year in the first instance but applications for renewal of an exhibition will be considered upon evidence being provided that the holder is making satisfactory progress. Travel grants may also be made either to recipients of these exhibitions or to graduates in receipt of awards from other bodies, if they propose to carry out research abroad. In certain circumstances postgraduate exhibitions or travel grants may be made on similar conditions for the purpose of advanced study instead of research, but preference will be given, other things being equal, to candidates proposing to undertake research.

Minor exhibitions

3. Minor research exhibitions will be awarded to graduates of the University of sufficient merit (see §5) who are registered for higher degrees in the University, provided they were permanently resident in Ireland during their undergraduate years and provided also that they are not otherwise in receipt of a substantial direct award. The value of these exhibitions will be at least equivalent to the fees payable each year for the higher degree for which the applicant is registered.

Applications

4. Applications for exhibitions must be made on the proper form, and must be accompanied by a recommendation from the proposed supervisor or head of department concerned. Forms can be obtained

Research awards and moderatorship prizes

from the Graduate Studies Office and completed forms must be returned to the Dean of Graduate Studies by 1 March.

5. Exhibitions will only be awarded to applicants who were placed in the first class or the first division of the second class at a moderatorship examination or obtained equivalent distinction at a final degree examination in a professional subject. Applicants must satisfy the Dean of Graduate Studies that they have applied for all other research scholarships open to them. They are advised to consult the head of department concerned and the Appointments Officer for information concerning other award-making bodies.

6. Candidates eligible to receive awards are informed before the end of the Trinity Term and in the case of an applicant who has not completed his moderatorship or other final examinations, such notification is made conditional upon the applicant reaching the standards laid down in the foregoing paragraph. The amounts of all awards are conditional upon the values of any scholarships or exhibitions received by the applicant from other sources (see §1). The receipt of any such awards must be notified immediately to the Graduate Studies Office. In the case of major exhibitions, payments are made quarterly in advance.

Conditions

7. The above research exhibitions are offered subject to the following conditions.

The holder must engage in full-time research or advanced study and normally is expected to register for a higher degree in the University of Dublin, although major exhibitions are also tenable at a university or institution approved by the Board. Awards made tenable at other institutions will not exceed in total value exhibitions held at the University of Dublin. The holder of a major exhibition must send to the Dean of Graduate Studies reports of satisfactory progress and attendance signed by his supervisor or other responsible officer which must reach the Graduate Studies Office by 15 December and 1 May. Quarterly payments will only be made on receipt of satisfactory reports. Unsatisfactory reports will be referred to the Graduate Studies Committee.

The holder of a research exhibition may earn by private tuition, demonstrating, etc., up to £75 in each year without any deduction, but work paid at a rate of more than £75 a year may only be undertaken by permission of the Dean of Graduate Studies, and a deduction may be made from his exhibition for earnings in excess of £75.

Research awards and moderatorship prizes

Research funds

8. Research exhibitions are payable from the following funds, subject to the limitations here shown. Fuller details of the several funds are given below.

Fund	Limitation
Blake	Irish History
Brooke	None, but preference for classics or mathematics
Burgess	None as to subject, but only for women
FitzGerald	Experimental physics
Hackett	Natural Sciences
Harmsworth	None, but preference for medicine, surgery, music, or a subject with a specifically Irish interest
Kells Ingram	None
Bishop Law	Mathematics
Ledoux	Medicine
Longfield	Modern literature
Lyster	None
McCullagh	Theoretical physics or applied mathematics
Madden	None
Lefroy Stein	None
Trinity College Trust	None (awards are made in concurrence with the Trinity College Trust)
Whately	Economics
Worrall	None as to subject, but only for men of limited means, sons of clergy of Dublin diocese or of citizens of Dublin

Research grants

9. Where permitted under the terms of the benefaction the residue of the annual income of the funds listed above after provision of the research exhibitions, is utilised to support research within the College in appropriate subjects. Applications for research grants should be addressed to the Dean of Graduate Studies and must reach him before 15 November or 15 May. They must be made or supported by the head of the department concerned and give full details of the proposed research.

P

Research awards and moderatorship prizes

Moderatorship prizes

A moderatorship prize of £20 is awarded each year, from the funds indicated, to the first moderator in each of the following subjects, provided that he obtains a first class moderatorship.

Subject	Fund
Mathematics	Bishop Law
Classics	Brooke
Natural sciences	Hackett
Modern literature	Longfield
History	Lyster
Economics	Whately

Research and moderatorship funds

Details of the funds referred to above in connection with research awards and moderatorship prizes are given below.

BLAKE NATIONAL HISTORY SCHOLARSHIP FUND

Established in 1884, by a bequest of Miss Helen Blake, to promote research in Irish history (£250)[1].

BROOKE FUND

Established in 1879, by a gift from the Misses Brooke (£185).

KATHLEEN BURGESS FUND

Established in 1929, by Mr and Mrs William R. Burgess, to provide prizes or exhibitions for women students, on graduating, in memory of their daughter Kathleen Burgess (£45).

FITZGERALD MEMORIAL FUND

Established in 1902 in memory of Professor George Francis FitzGerald, F.T.C.D., to promote research in experimental physics (£90).

JOHN WINTHROP HACKETT FUND

Established in 1926 by a bequest of Sir John Winthrop Hackett to provide a prize in applied science (£180).

EMILIE (MAFFETT) HARMSWORTH FUND

Established in 1943 by Lord Harmsworth of Egham to found exhibitions in memory of his wife. Preference is given to candidates proposing to carry out research in medicine, surgery, music or a subject with a specifically Irish interest (£260).

---

[1] The figure in brackets indicates in each case the approximate annual income of the fund.

Research awards and moderatorship prizes

BISHOP LAW FUND

Established in 1796, by a gift of John Law, Bishop of Elphin, to encourage the study of mathematics (£215).

MOUNTIFORT GEORGE LONGFIELD FUND

Established by a bequest in 1946 by Miss M. L. B. Longfield, to found a prize in modern languages (£50) and English language and literature (£20) in memory of her brother, Mountifort George Longfield.

THOMAS WILLIAM LYSTER FUND

Established by a bequest in 1946 by Mrs Jane Robinson Lyster, to found a prize in memory of her husband, Thomas William Lyster (£30).

McCULLAGH FUND

Established in 1854 by subscription in memory of James McCullagh, Fellow 1835-47, to encourage research in mathematics or theoretical physics (£55).

MADDEN FUND

Established in 1798 by a bequest of Samuel Molyneux Madden, originally with the primary purpose of providing a prize for the best unsuccessful candidate at the Fellowship examination. Half the income of the fund is now paid to the College's research funds and half to the College's publications fund. (Total £580).

LEFROY STEIN FUND

Established in 1935 by a bequest from Major Henry Seton Lefroy Stein to found scholarships or assist research. Part of the income of this fund is used to provide research exhibitions. The conditions of the award are determined from time to time by the Board on the advice of the Graduate Studies Committee (£550).

WHATELY MEMORIAL FUND

Established in 1871 by subscription in memory of Richard Whately, Archbishop of Dublin, to promote the study of political economy (£35).

WORRALL FUND

Established in 1753 by a bequest of John Worrall to provide exhibitions for poor scholars, the sons of clergymen of the diocese of Dublin, or in default of such, the sons of citizens of Dublin. Half the income of the fund is now paid to the College's research funds; the other half is available to provide exhibitions for undergraduates (Total £175).

*　*　*

Miscellaneous awards

THE IRISH SOCIETY'S SCHOLARSHIP

This scholarship is offered annually by the Hon. the Irish Society for research work to be carried out under the direction of the Director of the Research Institute, Lambeg, Co. Antrim, and to be embodied in a thesis to be submitted for the degree of M.Sc. A graduate of the University is eligible for this scholarship provided that he satisfies the conditions prescribed for the M.Sc. degree, and that he has received at least part of his education at one of the schools to which the Society contributes financial assistance. Applications should reach the secretary of the Institute before 2 August each year. Value, £120 a year for two years.

MISCELLANEOUS AWARDS

ABD EL-MOTAAL PRIZE IN ESSAY COMPETITION

This prize was founded in 1964 by Mr Mostafa H. B. Abd El-Motaal. The prize is offered for the best essay on Contemporary Egypt written by a student below M.A. standing. Arab students and students from the Middle East and North Africa are not eligible to compete. Value, £20.

Subject for 1966–7: to be announced.

BRONTË PRIZE

This prize was founded in 1921 by a bequest from Miss A. G. Woolson of Portland, U.S.A. It is awarded triennially by the Board on the recommendation of a committee for the best essay on either (i) an English author of Irish descent, or (ii) the seats of learning in Ireland prior to 900 A.D. The committee consists of the Regius Professor of Greek and the Professors of Latin and English Literature. A candidate must be of Irish birth or have been domiciled in Ireland for at least ten years. He must also be an undergraduate of the University or a graduate of not more than five years' standing. The next award will be made in 1967 and essays must reach the Registrar before 1 October 1967. Value, £45.

SCHOLARSHIP AND PRIZE IN THE HISTORY OF EUROPEAN PAINTING

These awards were founded in 1934 by gifts from Miss Sarah Purser and Sir John Purser. They are offered biennially at an examination held in Trinity term. See SCHOLARSHIP AND DIPLOMA IN THE HISTORY OF EUROPEAN PAINTING. The next examination will be held in 1967. Value: scholarship, £75; prize, £5.

420

FINANCIAL ASSISTANCE

I FEE CONCESSIONS

1. In addition to awards made under special conditions (see below) the College grants fee concessions to Irish students or remits the surcharge on fees of non-Irish students, one of whose parents is a graduate of the University of Dublin. The Board has made provision to meet cases of hardship as follows:

(*a*) permission to defer payment of one-half of the annual fee payable until 1 March (tardy payment of both instalments may be accepted subject to the same scale of fines as applies to payment of annual fees: see COLLEGE CHARGES, §13);

(*b*) fee concessions, in respect of the annual fee, varying from £30 to £60;

(*c*) in the case of students of limited means, who are not resident in Ireland but one of whose parents is a graduate of the University of Dublin, relief from the surcharge of fifty per cent on fees.

A student who is granted a fee concession under (*b*) and is resident in College rooms or in Trinity Hall may also be granted a reduction in room rent or in Hall fees.

2. Application for concessions under (*a*), (*b*) or (*c*) above, and also for grants from the Salmon and Culverwell funds (see below), must be made on the prescribed form, obtainable from the Senior Tutor, and must reach the Senior Tutor before 1 June. Towards the end of Trinity term the Fee Concessions Committee considers all such applications for the ensuing academic year.

Applications will be considered from prospective candidates for admission, as well as from students whose names are on the books of the College. Postgraduate students may also apply.

3. Applications are renewable each year.

4. A student who having been granted an award for the ensuing year fails to rise with his class, or to pay the balance of the fees due by the prescribed date for payment, thereby forfeits his right to the award. The rejection of an application or the forfeiture of a grant does not preclude a grant in a subsequent year.

II

The following exhibitions are awarded to students who satisfy the conditions specified. The exhibitions are paid quarterly provided that the holders (1) proceed regularly with their class, (2) have their names on the college books and (3) are under M.A. standing. Applications must be made on the prescribed forms and must reach the Senior Tutor before 1 November.

1963 BURSARY FUND

This fund was founded in 1963 by a gift of £12,000 from a donor who wished to remain anonymous. Bursaries up to a maximum of £100 each are awarded by the Board each year to deserving students of limited means, preference being given to sons and daughters of clergymen and to divinity students.

CROWE EXHIBITIONS

These exhibitions were founded in 1627 by a gift from William Crowe. Seven exhibitions are awarded annually by the Board to students of Irish birth. Preference is given to sons of clergy, especially those in the west of Ireland. Value, £30 each.

FIELD EXHIBITIONS

These exhibitions were founded in 1945 by a bequest from Charles Dickenson Field. Two exhibitions are awarded annually by the Board to deserving students of narrow means. Value, £14 each.

SPAN EXHIBITIONS

These exhibitions were founded in 1717 by a bequest from Benjamin Span. Two exhibitions are awarded annually by the Board to deserving students of narrow means. Value, £10 each.

STEARNE EXHIBITIONS

These exhibitions were founded in 1714 by a bequest from John Stearne, Vice-Chancellor 1721–43. Five exhibitions are awarded annually by the Board. In accordance with the wishes of the founder preference is given to students from the diocese of Clogher. Value, £10 each.

WORRALL EXHIBITIONS

These exhibitions were founded in 1753 by a bequest from John Worrall. The exhibitioners are chosen by the Board from scholars who have entered as sizars, the sons of clergymen in the diocese of Dublin, or, in default of these, the sons of citizens of the city of Dublin. An exhibition is awarded for one year only, but may be renewed on application. Value, £25 each.

WORTH EXHIBITIONS

These exhibitions were founded in 1699 by William Worth. Two exhibitions are awarded, the election being made by the Bishop of Cork, the Mayor of Cork, the heir-at-law of William Worth and the Provost of Trinity College. Preference is given to natives of the city and county of Cork. Exhibitioners are elected for not more than two years and are capable of re-election. Value, £10 a year each.

III

The following awards are attached to the subjects specified.

Divinity

The following exhibitions are awarded annually by special boards to divinity students of limited means who intend to take orders in the Church of Ireland. Regard is had to the student's character, ability, attainments and general fitness for the ministry of the Church. The exhibitions are tenable for one year and are paid quarterly, on condition that a holder proceeds with the divinity course.

CARSON MEMORIAL EXHIBITION

This exhibition was founded in 1898 by a gift from Miss Frances Anna Carson in memory of her father, Joseph Carson, Fellow 1837–98. It is awarded annually in Michaelmas term to a student beginning the senior year. The exhibitioner must promise that he will not receive holy orders until he has obtained the Divinity Testimonium. Payment each quarter is made on a certificate from the Regius Professor that the exhibitioner has satisfied the requirements for the preceding term. The board consists of the Provost, the Regius Professor and Archbishop King's Professor. Value, £30.

WALLACE EXHIBITIONS

These exhibitions were founded in 1899 by a gift from William Wallace. They are awarded annually in Michaelmas term, one to a student entering the junior year and the other to a student entering the senior year, on the same conditions as the Carson Memorial Exhibition.

The board consists of the Provost, if a member of the Church of Ireland (failing him, the senior of the Fellows who is a member of that Church), the Regius Professor and Archbishop King's Professor. Value, £30 each.

See also DOWNES EXHIBITIONS below.

The following exhibitions are also available:

BELSHAW, BEDDY, JOHN JACOB AND CHRISTIAN JACOB SCHOLARSHIPS

These four scholarships were founded in 1911 by Robert Redman Belshaw. One may be awarded each year to the best candidate at an examination held not more than once a year. They are tenable for two or three years, as the trustees may direct. A candidate must (1) be a student in divinity and in arts of Trinity College and (2) have been accepted by the Church Missionary Society as a fit person to be trained to become a missionary of the gospel in foreign parts. A woman who has provisionally been accepted as a missionary is eligible to compete. Applications containing lists of qualifications should reach Archbishop King's Professor as soon as possible after the beginning of the academic year in October. Value, £40 a year, each.

Financial assistance
BRADSHAW EXHIBITION
This exhibition was founded in 1949 by a bequest from Mrs G. W. Bradshaw. It is awarded annually to a divinity student of narrow means at the discretion of the Regius Professor. Applications should reach the Regius Professor before 1 December. Value, £12.

DOWNES EXHIBITIONS
Five exhibitions are awarded annually by the Board of Trinity College to divinity students of narrow means and academic merit. They are paid quarterly, provided that the holders proceed regularly with their class, have their names on the college books and are under Master's standing. An exhibitioner must vacate his exhibition if he ceases to be a member of the Divinity School, or if he accepts a stipend as a clerk in holy orders. Applications must be made on the prescribed form and must reach the Senior Tutor before 1 November. Value, £10 each.

Medicine
BEGLEY STUDENTSHIPS
These studentships were founded in 1905 by bequests from William Chapman Begley and his wife, Jane. One studentship, tenable for four years, is awarded annually by the Board on the recommendation of the Dean of the Faculty of Physic who shall have consulted the professors in whose schools the candidates have studied during the past academic year. It is open to all undergraduates who have completed their Senior Freshman year and who have entered, or are about to enter, the School of Physic. Where the qualifications and merits of the candidates are, in the opinion of the Board, otherwise equal, preference is given according to the seniority of their standing in arts at the time of their entering the School of Physic. Applications must be sent to the Dean before 1 November.

The studentships are paid half-yearly on 21 June and 23 December. If a holder obtains his medical qualification in Hilary or Trinity term of any year before the expiration of his four years' tenure, he must vacate the studentship after the June payment, and similarly after the December payment, if he qualifies in Michaelmas term. Another student may be elected for the unexpired portion of the studentship. Every student during his tenure must pursue his studies in the School to the satisfaction of the Board; if he fails to do so, or is guilty of any serious misconduct or breach of college discipline, he ceases to be entitled to the studentship, unless for special reasons the Board determines otherwise. Value, £45 a year for four years.

J. W. BIGGER MEMORIAL SCHOLARSHIP
This scholarship was founded in 1953 by a gift from Miss Florence Bigger in memory of her brother, Joseph Warwick Bigger, Professor of Bacteriology and Preventive Medicine 1924–51. It is awarded annually in November by the Board, on the nomination of the Committee of the School of Physic, to a medical student of not more than three years' standing who has passed the

first medical examination. In nominating a candidate, the Committee takes account of (1) his record in the School of Physic, (2) his general university record and (3) his financial circumstances. Preference is given to a candidate of Irish birth or parentage, whose financial means are limited.

A candidate must make application to the Dean of the Faculty of Physic on a special form (obtainable from the School office) before 1 November. Value, £50.

O'SULLIVAN MEMORIAL SCHOLARSHIP

This scholarship was founded in 1924 by subscription in memory of Alexander Charles O'Sullivan, Fellow 1886–1924 and Professor of Pathology 1895–1924. It is awarded annually in November by the Board, on the nomination of the Committee of the School of Physic, to a medical student of not more than four years' standing who has passed the first medical examination. In nominating a candidate the Committee takes account of (1) his record in the School of Physic, (2) his university career generally and (3) his financial circumstances.

Candidates must make application on a special form (which may be obtained from the School office) to the Dean of the Faculty of Physic before 1 November.

The scholarship is tenable for one year, but in exceptional circumstances a scholar may be re-elected for a second year. It is paid quarterly, provided that the holder is not struck off the books of the School of Physic before the first day of the month in which the quarter-day falls. Value, £45.

Engineering

EVERARD WILLIAM DIGBY MEMORIAL FUND

This fund was established in 1939 by a gift from Miss Alice Digby in memory of her brother. The income is available to assist deserving students in the School of Engineering, who may be in need of financial assistance. Applications, with full particulars, should be made to the Professor of Engineering. Income of fund, £20.

IV

Assistance is available, as indicated, from the following funds:

JOHN BENNETT FUND

This fund was established in 1957 by a bequest from Mrs C. P. Bennett in memory of her husband, formerly headmaster of the High School, Dublin. The accruing interest is paid annually to a deserving student, nominated by the Governors of the Erasmus Smith Schools, who must have been a pupil of the High School continuously for three years prior to entering the College. Value, £50 a year.

BOSTON FUND

This fund was established in 1926 by a gift from Miss Annie Elizabeth Boston for the benefit of women undergraduates of narrow means. Appli-

Financial assistance

cations for assistance from the fund should be made to the Dean of Women Students in Michaelmas term. Income, £20 a year.

ELLEN COTTER FUND

This fund was established in 1952 by a bequest from W. E. P. Cotter, in memory of his mother, for the benefit of women students of limited means. Applications for assistance from the fund should be made to the Dean of Women Students in Michaelmas term.

CULVERWELL FUND

This fund was established in 1929 by a gift from Edward Parnall Culverwell, Fellow 1883-1931. The income is used to make grants to students of limited means to assist them to pay their college fees. For mode of application see FEE CONCESSIONS above.

LUCY GWYNN FUND

This fund was established in 1948 by subscription in memory of the first Lady Registrar, the income to be used by the Dean of Women Students for the benefit of Senior Freshman women students in need of financial help.

JEAN MONTGOMERY FUND

This fund was established in 1950 by subscription in memory of Miss Jean Montgomery, Lady Superintendent of the Kitchen 1919-1948. Free commons for one undergraduate student of narrow means is provided throughout the year. The beneficiary is selected by the Senior and Junior Deans before the first day of Michaelmas term in each year from candidates proposed by the tutors.

FREDERICK PURSER UNDERGRADUATES' FUND

This fund was established in 1911 by gifts from John Purser Griffith and Mrs Griffith in memory of Frederick Purser, Fellow 1879-1910, with the object of helping some Sophister students of limited means who have shown promise in their previous course, so as to enable them to derive the most benefit possible from the teaching of the Sophister years, whether in arts or in the professional schools, and to save them as far as may be, from being compelled to divert their energies into other activities in order to obtain the necessary means of livelihood.

Application, accompanied by particulars as to the qualifications and prospects of the applicant, should be made to the trustees of the fund through his tutor; and the tutor and some of the teachers in the College with whom the applicant has been associated in his studies, are to be requested by him to send recommendations direct to the trustees. All communications are regarded as strictly confidential. They should be addressed to the Rev E. C. T. Perdue, Trinity College.

The trustees meet to consider applications on the last Thursday in November.

426

No application is considered unless it has reached the trustees at least three clear days before their day of meeting. Income, £100 a year.

FREDERICK PURSER GRADUATES' FUND

This fund was established in 1910 by gifts from Mr and Mrs John Purser Griffith in memory of Frederick Purser, Fellow 1879–1910. The object of the fund is to lend at nominal interest to graduates leaving the College sums of money which may assist them to attain at the outset of their several careers more readily than otherwise to permanent positions.

The qualifications which are principally taken into consideration in granting these loans are (1) the limited means of the applicant and of his parents or guardians and (2) such general distinction and character during his college course as will serve as a guarantee that the money lent will be applied to what is likely to prove of permanent benefit to the applicant.

Applications accompanied by particulars as to the qualifications of the applicant and as to the object and destination of the loan, should be made to the trustees of the fund through the applicant's tutor. The tutor and some of the professors or other teaching staff with whom the applicant has been associated in his studies, are to be requested by him to send recommendations direct to the trustees. All communications are regarded as strictly confidential. They should be addressed to the Rev E. C. T. Perdue, Trinity College.

It is only in exceptional circumstances that any single loan exceeds £100. Interest is charged at one per cent per annum, payable half-yearly. A recipient enters into an undertaking to keep the trustees acquainted with his residence, to pay the interest regularly, and, when remunerative employment is obtained, to repay the principal by instalments within a reasonable time, that time to be fixed by the trustees in each case according to the nature of the employment which has been obtained. If the principal is repaid within three years from the time the loan is made, the interest paid is refunded.

The trustees meet to consider applications on the last Thursday of each month during term. No application is considered unless it has reached the trustees at least three clear days before the day of meeting.

SALMON FUND

This fund was established in 1894 by George Salmon, Provost 1888–1904, to help poor students to pay their college fees, giving preference to sons of clergymen.

For mode of application see FEE CONCESSIONS above.

MACKAY WILSON FUND

This fund was established in 1913 by Robert Mackay Wilson and his wife Elizabeth Jackson Wilson for the benefit of women students of limited means resident at Trinity Hall. Grants are made to one student each year, and for one year only. A student may not receive a grant from this fund until she has completed the first year of her course in the University. The trustees of the fund must be satisfied as to the character and academic progress of the

427

applicant. Applications, which must be supported by a recommendation from the applicant's tutor, should be sent to the Dean of Women Students in Michaelmas term. Income, £25 a year.

V

GRANTS TO VISIT THE GAELTACHT

Special grants of £10 each may be made to Irish students to help to improve their knowledge of spoken Irish by vacation visits of at least three weeks to the Gaeltacht.

Applicants for grants must present themselves not later than three weeks before the end of arts lecture term to the Professor of Irish for an examination of an easy standard in spoken Irish, and the names of the successful candidates are sent by the Professor of Irish to the Senior Lecturer.

Students who have answered satisfactorily in Irish at the examination for entrance scholarships and exhibitions, or gained an honor in Irish at a term honor examination, are exempt from the examination.

Accepted students must send to the Professor of Irish not later than one week after the beginning of the following lecture term an account of their work in the Gaeltacht. The account should contain, *inter alia*, the dates of arrival and departure, the names of the townlands and parishes in which they were studying, and, as evidence of diligence in acquiring a knowledge of spoken Irish, material recorded by them from Irish speakers in the district, such as word-lists, phrases, folk-tales, folk-songs, etc. The grant is paid after the Professor of Irish has approved of the account.

SCHOLARSHIPS OFFERED BY LOCAL AUTHORITIES IN IRELAND

All the local authorities in Ireland avail themselves of the powers conferred on them by the Irish Universities Act, 1908, to offer scholarships for university education.

Scholarships offered by the following local authorities in the Republic of Ireland may be held in Trinity College: Cavan, Donegal, Dublin County, Kildare, Leitrim, Leix, Limerick City, Longford, Meath, Monaghan, Offaly, Roscommon, Tipperary North Riding, Westmeath and Wicklow. Subject to certain conditions being satisfied, scholarships from the following authorities may also be held: Carlow, Cork City, Dublin City, Kerry, Kilkenny, Louth, Mayo, Sligo, Waterford and Wexford. For various reasons (geographical restrictions, refusal, unacceptable conditions), scholarships offered by the other local authorities cannot be held in Trinity College[1].

Scholarships offered by all the local authorities in Northern Ireland (Antrim, Armagh, Down, Fermanagh, Londonderry, Tyrone, Belfast County Borough and Londonderry County Borough) may be held in Trinity College.

Enquiries should in all cases be addressed to the local county secretary.

---

[1] This represents the position for the scholarships offered for competition in 1967.

LIBRARIES, SOCIETIES AND OTHER INSTITUTIONS

COLLEGE LIBRARY

LECKY LIBRARY

MUSEUM OF BIBLICAL ANTIQUITIES

NORMAL CLIMATOLOGICAL STATION

BOTANIC GARDEN

KELLS INGRAM FARM

TRINITY HALL

HERMATHENA

COLLEGE GALLERY

RESEARCH STUDENTS COMMON ROOM

SOCIETIES AND CLUBS

TRINITY COLLEGE DUBLIN TRUST

UNIVERSITY OF DUBLIN FUND (U.S.A.)

APPOINTMENTS OFFICE

STUDENT HEALTH SERVICE

LIBRARY OF TRINITY COLLEGE

Curator: H. W. Parke, M.A., LITT.D.

Librarian: F. J. E. Hurst, M.A., A.L.A.

Long Room, Reading Rooms and Manuscript Room: hours of opening

LONG ROOM

The Long Room is normally open to visitors at the following times

Monday to Friday	10 a.m. to 4 p.m.
Saturday	10 a.m. to 1 p.m.

READING ROOMS

The Reading Rooms are normally open to readers at the following times

1 September to 30 June	10 a.m. to 10 p.m. (except Saturdays)
1 July to 31 August	10 a.m. to 6 p.m. (except Saturdays)
Saturdays	10 a.m. to 1 p.m.

The Long Room and Reading Rooms are closed on Christmas Eve from 1 p.m., on Christmas Day, and on the three week-days following; on Good Friday, Easter Eve, and Easter Monday; on St. Patrick's Day, Whit Monday and the first Monday in August. The Reading Rooms are closed for a fortnight in July at a date stated in the Almanack, but the Long Room remains open to visitors. Alterations to this programme may be made at the discretion of the Librarian.

MANUSCRIPT ROOM

The Manuscript Room is normally open to readers at the following times:

Monday to Friday	10 a.m. to 1 p.m.
	2 p.m. to 5 p.m.
Saturday	10 a.m. to 1 p.m.

Admission of readers

Life admission is granted only to graduates of the universities of Dublin, Oxford, and Cambridge, and to such other persons, engaged in research or eminent for learning, as may be approved by the Provost and Board.

The Librarian is empowered to issue tickets of admission to the Reading Rooms to undergraduates and, for periods of six months, to other persons approved by the Vice-Provost. The latter may have their tickets renewed on expiry by the Librarian at his discretion.

All readers, before admission, are required to make and sign the library declaration before the Vice-Provost.

Temporary permission to consult specified books is granted to visitors at the Librarian's discretion.

The Library is entitled to free copies of all books published in Great Britain or Ireland[1].

The Librarian is indebted to many universities, libraries, firms, societies and private persons in various parts of the world who presented material during the year, and also to members of the University staff who have presented off-prints and other versions of their own published works. It is impossible to mention all donors individually, but they include:

Mr A. E. Alimoff
American Academy of Political & Social Science
American Historical Society
American Psychological Association
Amsterdam, Koninklijk Instituut voor de Tropen
Mr G. Barrett
W. J. Barrow, Research Laboratory
Belfast Public Libraries
Belgian Embassy
Belgian Information & Documentation Institute
Mr W. C. Benni
Mr J. W. Boyle
Mr J. MacD. Broadhead
Buenos Aires, Fondo Nacional de Las Artes
Mr A. Burkhard
Dr R. A. Butlin
Camille Dreyfus Laboratory
Canadian Embassy
Mr E. M. Claspy
The Classical Association of Canada
William Nelson Cromwell Foundation

Mr R. V. Ely
Mr L. Fahey
Fisheries Research Board of Canada
Mr E. Flammarion
Dr B. Flodinn
Fondren Library, Rice University
French Embassy
Mr V. W. Graham
Mr J. E. Haffield
Halcyon-Commonwealth Foundation
Dr F. Hamilton
Hill Family Foundation
Indian Embassy
International Computation Centre
International Labour Office
Professor P. Isaac
Japanese Embassy
Mr A. C. John
University of Kansas
Mr A. Lerner
Library of Congress
Professor A. A. Luce
Dr P. D. McCormack
Miss C. C. Magenheimer
Mr G. Mistardis
Mr D. Molony

[1] The privilege was first given in the year 1801 (41 Geo. III, c. 107). By 5 and 6 Victoria, c. 45, the right of obtaining a copy of every book printed in the United Kingdom is confined to five libraries, *viz.* the British Museum, the Bodleian Library, the Public Library at Cambridge, the Library of the Faculty of Advocates at Edinburgh, and the Library of Trinity College. This privilege was extended by the Copyright Act 1911, to the National Library of Wales, Aberystwyth.

By the Industrial and Commercial Property (Protection) Act of the Irish Free State 1927, the copyright privilege of the Library was continued in respect of books published in Ireland, and a similar privilege was given to the libraries in Great Britain which had exercised it previously. This is now continued under the terms of the Copyright Act 1963.

Libraries, societies and other institutions

National Academy of Sciences
National Archives
Netherlands Embassy
Comdt. J. P. O'Keeffe
Rev. D. J. O'Kelly
Col. S. K. Oyrzynski
Pakistan High Commission
Pali Text Society
Mr G. E. Pangalos
Portuguese Legation
Mr J. Prescott
Professor A. J. Otway-Ruthven
Professor W. J. L. Ryan
Mr I. Senesi

Dr L. B. Somerville-Large
South African Embassy
Mr S. R. Speller
Mr F. & Mrs. M. P. Sullivan
Swedish Embassy
Thai Embassy
Professor G. D. Trotter
Venezuelan Embassy
Mr J. M. Ward
Miss H. Watson
Woods Hole Oceanographic Institution
World Health Organization
Mr A. B. Wright
Mr. L. M. Wright

FRIENDS OF THE LIBRARY

The society known as the Friends of the Library was founded in 1945 with the object of providing an income for the purchase of additional books and manuscripts, and also of promoting an interest in the general welfare of the Library. Exhibitions are held in the Long Room from time to time. The minimum subscription is 10s. per annum, or 10 guineas for life membership. Gifts and bequests of appropriate books or manuscripts are welcomed by the society.

> *President*: The Provost
>
> *Hon. Secretary*: R. B. McDowell, M.A., PH.D.
>
> *Hon. Treasurer*: F. J. E. Hurst, M.A., A.L.A.

LIBRARY EXTENSION FUND

A Fund for the construction of a new library was opened in October 1955. The Irish Government undertook to add one pound for every pound subscribed to the fund until the combined total of £640,900 was reached. Lists of subscribers have been published separately; see also BENEFACTORS OF TRINITY COLLEGE.

In 1961 the first prize in an international architectural competition for the new library building was won by Mr Paul Koralek. Construction began at the end of 1963 and will be completed early in 1967.

434

LECKY LIBRARY

Trustee and Chairman of the Lecky Library Committee:
T. W. Moody, M.A., PH.D., D.LIT.

Librarian and Secretary: Eileen M. I. Roche, B.A.

The library of William Edward Hartpole Lecky (1838-1903) was presented to the College by his widow in 1912 and housed in the Council Room. It covers a wide range of learning and is especially rich in history and cognate subjects. Under a scheme approved by the Board on 7 March 1951, a portion of this collection, consisting largely of pamphlets and foreign publications, was transferred to the College Library, and the remainder was combined with the collection previously known as the Economics, History and Law Joint Library to form a library in the Council Room for the special use of the schools of history and political science, economics and political science, and legal science. To this reconstituted Lecky Library was transferred the annual grant formerly made to the Joint Library.

In 1964, the School of Business and Social Studies also became associated with the Lecky Library. It is now administered by a Committee representing each of the Schools and the College Library, with the College Lending Librarian acting as secretary and librarian. The former law seminar room has been linked with the old Council Room to give more space, and the new library now contains about 8,000 volumes.

The former Economics, History and Law Joint Library originated in 1935 as a departmental lending library. In addition to the regular purchase of books for which the Board provided an annual grant, this library was enriched by private benefaction. In 1939 the late Walter Alison Phillips, on his retirement from the Lecky Professorship of Modern History, which he had held from 1914 to 1939, made a substantial donation of historical books to it from his library. In 1941 a portion of the income of the John Good Bequest was assigned to the purchase of books in economics and commerce. In 1945 the library of Charles Francis Bastable, Professor of Political Economy from 1882 to 1932, was presented to the College by Mrs Bastable, and the greater part of it, in accordance with Professor Bastable's wish that it should be made as accessible as possible to students, was added to the Joint Library, the remainder being included in the College Library. The new Lecky Library has also received generous grants from the Trinity

435

Libraries, societies and other institutions

College, Dublin, Trust and valuable gifts of American publications from the University of Dublin Fund (U.S.A.). Many books have also been presented by private donors.

The library is open to members between the hours of 10 a.m. and 5 p.m. during most of the year. Application for membership should be addressed to the Lecky Librarian.

MUSEUM OF BIBLICAL ANTIQUITIES

Director: J. Weingreen, M.A., PH.D.

The museum consists mainly of original, representative types of pottery of the Canaanite and Israelite periods, pottery figurines, stamped jar handles, small objects in bronze and iron and a variety of beads. In addition there are casts of inscriptions, ivories, painted pottery and seal impressions. The collection was started in 1952 with an important gift of pottery and small objects from the Wellcome Trust, while during the years 1953 to 1957 regular allocations were received from the Jericho archaeological expedition, to which the College had made annual contributions. Another substantial gift was received from the Wellcome Trust in 1956. A collection of Egyptian and Babylonian antiquities was added in 1957. In 1961 the late Lord Crookshank bequeathed a collection of Egyptian antiquities, Greek and Roman coins, Roman lamps, and leaves from seventeenth and eighteenth century Torch scrolls to the museum.

Though designed principally for teaching purposes, the museum is of general interest and may be visited by members of the public, by appointment, during lecture term. Applications should be made in writing to the Director of the Museum, School of Hebrew and Semitic Languages, Trinity College, Dublin.

NORMAL CLIMATOLOGICAL STATION

In January, 1904, the Provost and Senior Fellows established a normal climatological station within the precincts of Trinity College, at the instance of Sir John William Moore, M.D., D.SC. The station occupies an open space in the Fellows' Garden, and is fully equipped. It is now under the control of the School of Cosmic Physics in the Dublin Institute for Advanced Studies.

BOTANIC GARDEN

Director: W. A. Watts, M.A.

The garden is situated on Shelbourne Road, about one mile south-east of the College. The garden was acquired in 1806 on a lease of 175 years' duration.

Members of the academic staff, and students in the School of Botany are entitled to keys of the garden; other students may obtain a key on payment of a deposit. Visitors to Dublin are admitted to view the garden on an order signed by any Fellow or Professor.

KELLS INGRAM FARM

Farm and Woodland Committee: J. Johnston, M.A., G. F. Mitchell, M.A., M.SC., D. A. Webb, M.A., SC.D., F. C. W. Winkelmann, M.A., J. T. Baxter, M.A., PH.D., M.R.C.V.S., A. A. Pakenham-Walsh, M.A., N. W. K. Murray, B.A., AGR.(FOREST.)B., PH.D., L. G. Carr Lett, M.A., L. D. G. Collen, M.A., M.A.I., the Registrar of the School of Agriculture.

Farm Manager: Noel Hayes, B.A., AGR.B.

Forestry Supervisor: N. W. K. Murray, B.A., AGR. (FOREST.) B., PH.D.

Acting/Warden of Townley Hall: Lucy M. Mitchell, M.A.

The Trinity College farm, named after a former Senior Fellow of the College, is situated on the north bank of the river Boyne, four miles west of Drogheda. The farm was acquired by the College in 1957. It comprises 500 acres of farmland and 350 acres of woodland. The estate house, Townley Hall, was built by Francis Johnston at the beginning of the nineteenth century. The last resident owner, Mrs Townley Balfour, who died in 1955, was the daughter of John Kells Ingram, Fellow 1846–99.

The College purchased the farm in part from a legacy bequeathed in memory of his father, by the late Captain J. Kells Ingram, brother of Mrs Balfour, who died in 1956.

437

TRINITY HALL

In the year 1908 the house and grounds, now known as Trinity Hall, were acquired by the University and established as the official residence for those women students who do not reside with their parents or guardians. The adjoining house and grounds were purchased in 1910 by John Purser Griffith, M.I.C.E., and Mrs Griffith, and presented to the University, in memory of Frederick Purser, M.A., F.T.C.D. A further five acres were acquired in 1966. In the grounds the Dublin University Women's Hockey and Tennis Clubs have their fields and courts; and Trinity Hall thus serves as a centre for the use of all women students, whether resident or non-resident.

TRINITY HALL COMMITTEE: The Registrar, the Treasurer, Eileen Duncan, M.SC., Daphne D. Wormell, B.A., Anne E. R. Denard, M.A., the Warden (Secretary).

HERMATHENA

Editor: E. J. Furlong, M.A.

Editorial Committee: T. W. Moody, M.A., PH.D.,
D. E. W. Wormell, M.A., PH.D., F. G. A. Winder, M.A., M.SC., W. W. Dieneman, M.A., A.L.A., and the Editor.

Publishers: Dublin, Hodges Figgis & Co. Ltd.;
London, The Academic Press Ltd.

Hermathena, a Dublin University Review founded in 1873, publishes literary and scientific papers. As a general rule, contributions are accepted only from members of the University, including graduates. The periodical is published twice yearly, in the spring and in the autumn.

Back-numbers, if in print, may be obtained from the publishers, The Johnson Reprint Company is arranging to reprint back-numbers now unobtainable.

Subscriptions. Annual subscription (two numbers) 25s. ($4), post free. Single numbers 14s. ($2.25), post free. Forms for subscriptions and for bankers' orders may be obtained on application to the Editor.

Exchange arrangements. Enquiries concerning exchange of other periodicals for Hermathena should be made to the Librarian, Trinity College, Dublin 2.

COLLEGE GALLERY

The College Gallery is a collection of paintings and framed reproductions which can be hired by those students who live in college or in Trinity Hall. It was founded in 1959 with a grant from the Trinity Trusts and has since received substantial support from the Gulbenkian Foundation and from the Arts Council. Many individuals have given pictures. The collection includes about sixty paintings and fifty lithographs, among them works by Karel Appel, Alan Davie, Paul Henry, Evie Hone, Asger Jorn, Louis le Brocquy, William Scott and Jack Yeats, and over two hundred framed reproductions ranging from Etruscan painting to works by modern artists. The pictures are distributed by ballot at the beginning of each term. The hire charge for a term is 5s. or less for a reproduction and 7s. 6d. for a painting.

RESEARCH STUDENTS COMMON ROOM

President: T. B. H. McMurry, M.A., PH.D.

Hon. Secretary: D. P. Hanna, B.A.

Hon. Treasurer: J. F. Atkins, B.A.

The Research Students Common Room is situated in 7, College. Membership is open to any student registered for a higher degree, to all demonstrators and assistants in the College, and to persons engaged in post-doctoral or other research, on payment of an annual subscription of 10s.

SOCIETIES AND CLUBS

Clubs and Societies Committee

The Clubs and Societies Committee consists of the following members: chairman, the Provost; vice-chairman, the Senior Dean; secretary, Captain J. H. Shaw; the Dean of Women Students; representatives of the Board, the Scholars, the College Historical Society, the University Philosophical Society, the Dublin University Elizabethan Society, the faculty societies, the Dublin University Central Athletic Club and the Students' Representative Council. The committee administers the fees paid by students for the centralised support of student clubs and societies. See COLLEGE CHARGES III.

The Committee has approved certain rules for accountability and control over cash, which should be observed by officials of clubs and societies and, in particular, by treasurers. They should, when elected to office, make themselves familiar with these rules.

SOCIETIES

Of these societies, the College Historical Society, the University Philosophical Society, and the D.U. Elizabethan Society fulfil most of the functions of a students' union, the former two for men students, the last of the three for women students. For further information the notice boards of the various societies may be consulted, or enquiry may be made to the secretaries concerned.

The figure after the title of a society is the date of foundation.

COLLEGE HISTORICAL SOCIETY 1770
President. F. H. Boland, LL.D.,   *Librarian.* D. R. Hinds
  Chancellor of the University.   *Correspondence Secretary*
Auditor. R. B. Williamson   M. Ó Siadhail
Treasurer. A. J. Craig   *Censor.* E. Ó Murchú
Record Secretary. W. A. Stanford
The Society holds meetings on Wednesday nights.

UNIVERSITY PHILOSOPHICAL SOCIETY 1853
President. J. B. Trevaskis   *Librarian.* W. C. H. Ervine
Secretary. G. M. Goolnik   *Registrar.* A. D. Milliken
Treasurer. I. Larmour
The Society holds meetings on Thursday nights.

Libraries, societies and other institutions

DUBLIN UNIVERSITY ELIZABETHAN SOCIETY 1905
President. Janet L. Moody, Sch.
Treasurer. Cynthia E. Perdue
Librarian. Margaret E. C. Furlong

Correspondence Secretary.
  Melanie Nesbitt
Record Secretary. Jennifer M.
  Aikins, Sch.

The Society holds meetings once a week.

STUDENTS' REPRESENTATIVE COUNCIL (reconstituted 1957)
President. J. M. Adams
Deputy President. B. S. T. Vaughan
Treasurer. R. C. M. Wicklow

Secretary. Mary T. W. Bourke, Sch.
External Relations Officer.
  S. F. Morrow

COLLEGE THEOLOGICAL SOCIETY 1830
President. The Regius Professor of
  Divinity
Auditor. R. S. J. H. McKelvey, B.A.
  (Q.U.B.)

Secretary. D. R. A. Bacon
Treasurer. A. J. Parkhill
Librarian. W. J. Scott

The Society holds meetings on Monday evenings at 8 p.m. in the G.M.B.

AGRICULTURAL SOCIETY (D.U.) 1956
President. G. F. Mitchell, M.A., M.SC.
Auditor. D. Evans Tipping

Vice-Chairman, R. J. Gillespie
Secretary. D. N. H. Dagg

Meetings are held every week during Michaelmas and Hilary terms.

ARCHAEOLOGY AND FOLKLORE SOCIETY (T.C.D.) 1966
Auditor. J. Bradshaw
Treasurer. Lucy E. Mitchell

Secretary. Susan Gageby

ART SOCIETY (D.U.) 1960
President. J. White
Vice-President. Anne Crookshank, M.A.
Auditor. C. J. Benson

Secretary. J. W. ff. Young
Treasurer. C. Boydell
Publicity Officer. W. A. McComish

BIOLOGICAL ASSOCIATION (UNIV) 1873
President. B. Spencer, M.A., B.SC., PH.D.
Correspondence Secretary.
  G. R. Caird, B.A.
Treasurer. J. R. Bradshaw, B.A.

Record Secretary. Patricia Malone,
  B.A.
Librarian. W. R. Burnham

The Association holds meetings on Monday nights from November to April.

BRIDGE CLUB (D.U.) 1960
President. A. H. Davidson, M.D.,
  F.R.C.P.I.
Chairman. P. A. C. Stocken
Treasurer. N. Priestman

Secretary. R. T. R. Woods
Captain. J. F. Royds
Ladies' Captain. Dinah M. Stocken

Libraries, societies and other institutions

BUSINESS AND ECONOMICS SOCIETY (D.U.)   1930
President. W. J. L. Ryan, M.A., PH.D.   *Treasurer.* P. J. Ryan
Auditor. P. R. D. Walsh   *Assistant Secretary.* J. O. Brooks
Secretary. J. Micks   *Social Secretary.* Neville C.
    Priestman
Meetings are held weekly during lecture term.

CENTRAL MUSIC COMMITTEE (UNIV. OF D.)   1963
Chairman. B. P. Boydell, B.A., MUS.D.   *Concert Secretary and Treasurer.*
Secretary. D. D. Hill   Kit Musgrave
Librarian. P. Lambert
Delegates from the musical societies serve on the Committee, whose functions
include the coordination of musical activity and the arrangement and
presentation of concerts in College.

CHESS CLUB (D.U.)   1874
President. A. A. Luce, LITT.D., D.D.   *Librarian.* W. A. McComish
Secretary. B. S. Clarke   *Captain.* R. R. W. Devenney
Treasurer.
Meetings are held on Tuesday evenings.

CHORAL SOCIETY (UNIV. OF D.)   1837
President. The Provost   *Treasurer.* R. A. C. Lewis-Crosby
Conductor/Chairman. J. A. Groocock,   *Librarian.* D. T. Vigar
    B.A., MUS.B., F.R.C.O.   *Registrar.* Susan C. Grainger
Secretary. Camilla M. Neill   *Orchestral Registrar.* S. Stewart
Orchestra practice: Mondays at 7.30 p.m. Chorus practice: Tuesdays at 7.30
p.m. and Fridays at 4 p.m.

CHRISTIAN UNION (D.U.)   1955
President. A. Mills   *Prayer Secretary.* Sophie Shirley
Vice-President. Elizabeth Maguire   *Missionary Secretary.* Lois A. Nelson
Secretary. N. Hamilton   *Treasurer.* L. A. Batchelor
Assistant Secretary. J. W. Whitley
Meetings are held on Fridays at 1 p.m. and Saturdays at 8 p.m.

CLASSICAL SOCIETY (COLLEGE)   1906
President. H. W. Parke, M.A., LITT.D.   *Treasurer.* R. J. K. Gillespie
Auditor. Angela V. S. Durand   *Librarian.* A. Connolly
Secretary. L. J. Webb   *Assistant Secretary.* T. G. M. Graham
Meetings are held on Friday evenings.

ASSOCIATION INTERNATIONALE DES ÉTUDIANTS EN SCIENCES ÉCONOMIQUES ET
    COMMERCIALES (D.U. COMMITTEE)   1958
President. T. J. Jacobs   *Secretary.* Heather Rutledge
Treasurer. J. G. H. Chamney

Libraries, societies and other institutions

ENGINEERING SOCIETY (D.U.)   1895
President. W. Wright, M.A., PH.D.,   Correspondence Secretary.
  SC.D., F.R.S.E.   G. D. Browne
Auditor. D. R. M. Algeo   Record Secretary. M. M. R. Mitchell
Dance Secretary. A. R. Buchanin   Treasurer. M. W. Clapham
Meetings are held on Friday evenings at 8 p.m.

EXPERIMENTAL SCIENCE ASSOCIATION (D.U.)   1878
President. R. D. Goodhue, M.A.,   Record Secretary. Sylvia O'Brien
  B.SC., PH.D.   Treasurer. Gillian Stanley
Correspondence Secretary. A.H.Wynne-Jones
Sectional meetings of chemistry, physics, biology and microbiology are held
during term.

FABIAN SOCIETY (D.U.)   1952
President. J. Johnston, M.A.   Publicity Secretary. Ailsa Wortley
Chairman. R. F. Coghlan   Social Secretary. W. Moran
Secretary. W. H. Maxwell   Treasurer. P. E. Gillespie
Public meetings are held during term.

FAMINE RELIEF WEEK COMMITTEE (D.U.)   1966
Chairman. G. L. K. Stone   Treasurer. R. A. C. Verso

FAR EASTERN MISSION (D.U.)   1888
President. Archdeacon J. Tobias, B.D.   Secretary. Blanche Weekes, M.A.,
Chairman. Canon J. B. Neligan, M.A.   M.D., M.SC.
Treasurer. R. C. Cox, PH.D.

FILM SOCIETY (D.U.)
President. G. Thurley, B.A.   Secretary. P. McMaster
Chairman. S. A. Walmsley   Treasurer. G. Wynne Wilson
Meetings are held in the Dixon Hall on Tuesdays and Wednesdays at 8 p.m.

CUMANN GAELACH AN CHOLÁISTE   1907
Uachtarán. D. Ó hUaithne, M.A.   Cisteoir. E. Ó Murchu
Reachtaire. D. S. MacBhála   Bolscaire. Proinsias Nic Uait
Rúnaí. Lucy Ní Mhistéil   Stiúrthóir Drámaíochta. M. J. A.
                                           Lawless
Tionóltar cruinnithe in uimh 5 gach oiche aoine i rith an téarma.

GEOGRAPHICAL SOCIETY (D.U.)   1960
President. J. H. Andrews, M.A., PH.D.   Correspondence Secretary. A. A.
Chairman. M. A. M. Ryder   Horner
Treasurer. P. B. Smith   Record Secretary. Ann Reardon
Meetings are held on Monday evenings and field trips are arranged during term.

Libraries, societies and other institutions

GRAMOPHONE SOCIETY (D.U.)

President. Blanche Weekes, M.A.,   *Secretary.* Gillian M. Kingston
   M.D., M.SC.   *Treasurer.* M. C. C. Davie
Chairman. P. C. K. Lambert

The Society meets for concerts and talks on Friday evenings at 8 p.m. in No. 6.

HISTORY SOCIETY (D.U.) 1932

President. T. W. Moody, M.A., PH.D.   *Treasurer.* Deirdre Rogers
Auditor. S. H. B. Hewat   *Correspondence Secretary.*
Record Secretary. M. W. Heney   S. Morrow
Publicity Officer. D. Dickson

Meetings are held at 3.10 p.m. on Tuesdays in No. 4.

INTERNATIONAL AFFAIRS—UNITED NATIONS STUDENT ASSOCIATION, (D.U.),
   ASSOCIATION FOR 1949

President. D. W. Greene, M.A.   *Public Relations Officer.*
Chairman. M. A. Madha   L. A. Callendar
Secretary. Jennifer Simmons   *Editor.* R. W. Goslett
Treasurer. J. Dowling   *Social Works Officer.* J. F. Royle

Meetings are held on Tuesdays at 8 p.m.

JAZZ APPRECIATION SOCIETY (D.U.) 1959

Chairman. K. R. R. Donald   *Treasurer.* K. P. P. Fryer
Secretary. J. P. Nash

The Society meets on Monday nights in No. 6.

JOLY GEOLOGICAL SOCIETY 1960

President. C. J. Stillman, B.SC., PH.D.   *Secretary.* R. Smyth
Chairman. A. Senior   *Treasurer.* M. Pelling

The Society meets on alternate Mondays and Thursdays during term. Field
excursions are also arranged.

LAURENTIAN SOCIETY (D.U.) 1953

President. D. O'Sullivan, M.A., LITT.D.   *Secretary.* S. M. Scott-Hayward
Chairman. R. J. C. Hennessy   *Treasurer.* Nichola Whitaker

Meetings are held on Tuesdays at 8 p.m. and members and their friends meet
for coffee on Friday afternoons. The Society is a social society for Roman
Catholics.

LAW SOCIETY (D.U.)

President. C. B. McKenna, M.SC., LL.D.   *Secretary.* Elizabeth Wilson
Auditor. Mary T. W. Bourke, Sch.   *Publicity Officer.* A. M. O. Kirwan
Treasurer. H. J. Gibson

The Society holds six meetings a term in No. 4.

444

MATHEMATICAL SOCIETY (D.U.)
President. B. H. Murdoch, M.A., PH.D.   *Treasurer.* Charlotte H. T. Huang
Auditor J. K. Debenham, Sch.   *Librarian.* R. S. Cook
Secretary. D. P. Kennedy, Sch.
Meetings are held during term.

METAPHYSICAL SOCIETY (D.U.)   1929
President. E. J. Furlong, M.A.   *Treasurer.* R. G. Beresford-Evans
Auditor. R. Skelton   *Librarian.* M. Ryan
Secretary. B. M. Barfield
Meetings are held once a fortnight on Tuesdays at 3.15 p.m.

MISSION TO CHOTA NAGPUR (D.U.)   1890
Chairman. Ven. B. L. Handy, M.A.   *Treasurer.* J. J. Crawford, B.A.
Secretary. Rev. R. C. Armstrong,
    M.A., H.DIP.ED.
Meetings are held in the Precentor's Room on Tuesdays as need arises.

MODERN LANGUAGES SOCIETY (D.U.)   1924
President. E. J. F. Arnould, M.A.,   *Treasurer.* J. C. Brett
    PH.D., D.LITT., D.ÈS.LETTRES   *Secretary.* Susan Grainger
Chairman. J. C. C. Browne
Meetings are held once a week during term

MUSIC SOCIETY (D.U.)   1962
President. J. A. Groocock, B.A.,   *Librarian.* M. C. Boydell
    MUS.D., F.R.C.O.   *Treasurer.* J. Hall
Secretary. M. R. J. Pettigrew
Recitals are given on Wednesdays at 1.10 p.m. in No. 5.

ORIENTAL LANGUAGES SOCIETY (D.U.)   1961
President. J. Weingreen, M.A., PH.D.   *Treasurer.* D. J. Boden
Auditor. Ruth Gilbert   *Secretary.* L. D. A. Forrest
Librarian. J. Whitley
Meetings are held on Tuesdays in arts lecture term at 2 p.m.

PHOTOGRAPHIC ASSOCIATION (D.U.)   1948
President. G. F. Mitchell, M.A., M.SC.   *Treasurer.* D. Warren-Gash
Secretary. P. G. W. McMaster

PLAYERS (D.U.)
President. R. B. D. French, M.A.   *Treasurer.* F. Middleton
Chairman. D. C. Henderson   *Secretary.* Ruth M. Ludgate
Experimental play productions are held weekly during term in the Player's
Theatre.

Libraries, societies and other institutions

PSYCHOLOGICAL SOCIETY (D.U.) 1964

President. D. W. Forrest, M.A., PH.D.   *Treasurer.* Mary I. McCutchan
Chairman. J. D. Thompson   *Librarian.* Vivienne McDowell
Secretary. A. McCrea
The Society holds meetings four or five times each term.

REFUGEE COMMITTEE (D.U.) 1960   NOW FAMINE RELIEF WEEK COMMITTEE

SOCIETIES' CLUB 1964

Chairman. F. La T. Godfrey, M.A.   *Secretary.* Col. J. M. Walsh, M.A.
The Club exists for the purpose of providing social amenities in the College
Buttery. Membership is open to ladies and gentlemen who are at least eighteen
years of age, and are graduates or undergraduates on the books of the College,
or are members of the academic, administrative library or secretarial staff in the
University. The Club is managed by a Committee consisting of six members
ex officio and three elected members; the *ex officio* members are the Provost, the
Senior Dean, the Junior Dean, The Treasurer, the Dean of Women Students,
the Agent.

SOCIOLOGICAL SOCIETY (D.U.) 1956

President. J. H. Eustace, M.B., D.P.M.   *Treasurer.* Alison Gardner
Chairman. A. C. Logue   *Secretary.* Margery Stephens
The Society holds about five meetings each term.

STUDENT CHRISTIAN MOVEMENT (D.U. BRANCH)

President. J. N. R. Grainger, B.A.,   *Vice-Chairman.* S. P. Kerr
   M.SC., PH.D.   *Secretary.* Mary E. Deadman
Chairman. Stephanie M. Egan   *Treasurer.* P. Erskine
Meetings are held in No. 4 at 8 p.m. on Wednesdays.

TRINITY COLLEGE, DUBLIN, ASSOCIATION 1928

President. The Provost   *Treasurer.* J. C. Stronach, B.A.I.,
Secretary. W. F. Pyle, M.A., PH.D.   C.M.G.
The object of the Association is to keep past members of Trinity College in
touch with one another and with the College. Membership is open to graduates
of the University, to holders of certain diplomas, and to former undergraduates
who reached Senior Freshman standing or spent at least three terms in residence
in Trinity College or Trinity Hall. The life membership subscription is two
pounds. In the case of a graduate whose primary degree was conferred in or
after July 1955 and who applies for membership in due form the subscription
is paid by the College. The annual general meeting is held in Trinity College
on Trinity Monday. Members receive a copy of each issue of the register of
names and addresses of Trinity College men and women, are entitled to use the
rooms of the Association in 5 Trinity College, may wear the Trinity College
tie and the blazer of the Association, and may attend the dinner held annually
in Hall by the Association on the Saturday of Trinity Week, or on the Saturday
before.

446

Libraries, societies and other institutions

TRINITY COLLEGE, DUBLIN, ASSOCIATION OF NORTHERN IRELAND 1924

President. Beatrice K. Lawlor, B.A. *Treasurer.* Rosemary A. G.
Secretary. J. V. Hamilton, M.A., LL.B., Wallace, B.A.
  13 Lombard Street, Belfast 1.

All graduates of the University—men and women—resident in Northern Ireland are eligible to be considered for election to membership at an annual subscription of 5s. each. Life membership may be obtained by a single payment of two guineas. Subject to the discretion of the committee, persons who have entered the University and attended lectures, but who have not attained graduate standing, may also be elected to membership.

Members who have ceased to reside in Northern Ireland may continue their membership of the Association, if they so desire.

A dinner is held in October, a dance in January, and an informal supper before the annual general meeting in the spring.

TRINITY COLLEGE, DUBLIN, DINING CLUB, LONDON *c.* 1810

President. F. H. Boland, LL.D., Chancellor of the University.
Secretaries. G. W. E. Little, B.A., M.B., 448 Green Lane, Seven Kings, Ilford, Essex. T. J. C. Warriner, M.A., M.D., 207 Hook Road, Chessington, Surrey.
Treasurer. J. D. Gwynn, M.A.I., M.I.C.E.

The Club holds informal monthly dinners in London from November to April, evening parties, and an annual dinner in October. Graduates and undergraduates of the University may become members on payment of an annual subscription of 10s. or a life-membership subscription of five guineas.

UNIVERSITY OF DUBLIN GRADUATES' ASSOCIATION FOR THE NORTH OF ENGLAND *c.* 1893

Chairman. The Rt. Rev. W. D. L. Greer, D.D., Lord Bishop of Manchester.
Secretaries. Manchester section: J. G. Leather, B.A., M.B., 116 Green Lane, Bolton, Lancs. Liverpool section: G. F. Corbett, M.B., 'Sheilmartin', Red Lion Lane, Little Sutton, Wirral, Cheshire.

Membership is open to all graduates of the University residing in the North of England. There is no annual subscription. An annual dinner is held in Liverpool and Manchester in alternate years. Graduates who wish to receive notices of forthcoming dinners are invited to send their names and addresses to one of the secretaries.

VETERINARY SOCIETY 1962

President. L. R. Harper *Secretary-Treasurer.* Margaret Scott

VOLUNTARY SOCIAL WORK SOCIETY 1966

Chairman. M. King *Treasurer.* G. P. Strong
Secretary. Shirley Laird

Meetings are held once a week during term.

Libraries, societies and other institutions

WERNER CHEMICAL SOCIETY
President. W. Cocker, M.A., SC.D.,
  PH.D., D.SC.
Chairman. G. A. Lonergan, M.A., B.SC.,
  PH.D.

Treasurer. D. C. Pepper, M.A.,
  B.SC., PH.D.
Secretary. T. B. H. McMurry, M.A.,
  PH.D.

WOMEN GRADUATES' ASSOCIATION (D.U.)
President. Blanche Weekes, M.A., M.D.,
  M.SC.

Secretary. Gillian Share, M.A.
Treasurer. Tempe Parr, B.A.

WOMEN GRADUATES' ASSOCIATION (D.U.) IN BRITAIN
Chairman. Mrs. T. Tangney, B.A.
Vice-Chairman. Mrs. G. McCord
Secretary. Mrs. I. M. Whitehouse,
  126 Beaufort Mansions, Beaufort Street,
  London, S.W.3.

Assistant Secretary. Miss J. Hackett,
  13A Ennismore Mews, London,
  S.W.7.

This branch of the D.U.W.G.A. exists in London in order to provide a centre for women graduates living in, or visiting, Britain. An annual dinner is held in March, and there are other social gatherings throughout the year in conjunction with the T.C.D. Dining Club.

WORLD UNIVERSITY SERVICE (D.U. BRANCH) 1960
Chairman. J. N. R. Grainger,
  M.SC., PH.D.

Treasurer. G. Kelly
Secretary. C. J. T. Gould

CLUBS

DUBLIN UNIVERSITY CENTRAL ATHLETIC CLUB
Chairman. J. V. Luce, M.A.
Vice-Chairman. W. V. Denard,
  M.A., B.LITT.

Secretary. C. D. Anderson
Treasurer. S. S. Newman, B.A.

ASSOCIATION FOOTBALL CLUB (D.U.)
President. J. McKeever, M.A., M.D.
Captain. T. Nolan
Vice-Captain/Treasurer. C. D. Rae

Secretary. T. Mears
Junior Secretary. T. J. Sowerby

BASKETBALL CLUB (D.U.)
Captain. A. Tryfon
Secretary. P. D. Woods

Treasurer. B. Linnemann

BOAT CLUB (D.U.)
President. The Right Hon. the Earl of
  Iveagh, K.G., C.B., C.M.G., LL.D.
Captain. J. A. Gray

Secretary. B. J. Armstrong
Treasurer. A. C. Gibb

BOXING AND GYMNASTIC CLUB (D.U.)
President. D. A. Thornley, M.A., PH.D.   *Secretary.* M. Shortt
Captain. R. Condon   *Treasurer.* T. McCoy
Vice-Captain. C. Hamilton

CRICKET CLUB (D.U.)
President. J. V. Luce, M.A.   *Secretary.* T. V. Neill
Treasurer. A. Little

FOOTBALL CLUB (D.U.)
President. N. Falkiner, M.SC., M.D.   *Secretary.* J. S. Stubbings
Captain. D. F. Buchanan   *Treasurer.* R. Hutchinson
Vice-Captain. D. Spence   *Junior Secretary.* A. O'Sullivan

GAELIC FOOTBALL AND HURLING CLUB (D.U.)
President. E. R. Stuart, M.A., B.SC.   *Treasurer.* J. Connelly
   F.R.I.C.   *Captain of Football.* T. A. Hunt
Chairman. P. J. Doherty, B.A.   *Captain of Hurling.* M. Moran
Secretary. T. A. Hunt

GOLF CLUB (D.U.)
Captain. S. M. Black   *Treasurer.* R. K. M. Pollin
Secretary. D. Bishop

HOCKEY CLUB (D.U.)
President. J. V. Luce, M.A.   *Treasurer.* M. Fleming
Captain. M. S. McNulty   *Secretary.* J. Douglas
Vice-Captain. T. R. G. King

SQUASH RACQUETS CLUB (D.U.)
President. R. Sweetnam, B.A., B.COMM.   *Secretary.* D. Jardine
Captain. I. Angus   *Treasurer.* D. N. O. Budd, SCH.
Vice-Captain. W. B. A. Barr

SWIMMING CLUB (D.U.)
President. I. J. Dalrymple, M.B   *Secretary.* P. S. Scaife
Captain. R. H. Rice   *Treasurer.* A. Brophy
Vice-Captain. D. Scott

LAWN TENNIS CLUB (D.U.)
President. Col. J. M. Walsh, M.A.   *Secretary.* K. Fazel
Captain. A. S. Ashe   *Treasurer.* A. Donnelly

449

R

Libraries, societies and other institutions

MIXED CLUBS

BADMINTON CLUB (D.U.)
Captain. R. Carson
Treasurer. T. Jackson

Secretaries. V. Lambert and D. Beck

CLIMBING CLUB (T.C.D.)
President. K. E. Price
Secretary. I. M. Graham

Treasurer. T. K. Thorp
Hut Warden. P. Morris

FENCING CLUB (D.U.)
President. Blanche Weekes, M.A.,
   M.D., M.SC.
Men's Captain. P. Nicholson
Women's Captain. Sylvia O'Brien

Secretary. C. O'Brien
Treasurer. Dinah Barry-Tait
Armourer. M. Cochrane

HARRIERS AND ATHLETIC CLUB (D.U.)
President. W. G. Booker, M.A.
Captain. C. J. Butterworth
Vice-Captain. W. A. K. Warnock
Secretary. M. B. Nolan

Treasurer. M. S. Snaith
Captain of Harriers. K. Millington
Vice-Captain. T. E. Macey
Secretary. H. F. Gash

Women's Section

Captain. Janice Patterson
Vice-Captain. Olga Meagher

Secretary. Mary Kirby

JUDO CLUB (D.U.)
President. S. Kavanagh
Vice-President. G. Kelly, B.SC.
Captain. T. Morgan
Vice-Captain. G. Fenelon

Women's Captain. Jane Stewart
Instructor. A. J. Nolan
Secretary. R. A. Peilow
Treasurer. D. Sholdice

MOTOR CYCLE AND LIGHT CAR CLUB (D.U.)
President.
Captain.
Vice-Captain.

Secretary.
Treasurer.

RIFLE CLUB (D.U.)
Captain. M. J. D. Lewis
Treasurer. J. Martin

Secretaries. M. W. Clapham and
   B. J. Hope-Bell

SAILING CLUB (D.U.)
Commodore. D. O'Clery, M.A.I.,
   M.I.C.E.I.
Captain. B. J. Stacey

Secretary. J. A. Nixon
Treasurer. M. R. Mitchell

450

SKI CLUB (D.U.)
Captain. T. F. R. Schwartz

Secretary. Deborah M. T. Trenerry

TABLE TENNIS CLUB (D.U.)
Men's Captain. J. S. Armstrong
Women's Captain. Wilma Carey

Treasurer. M. Segal
Secretary. B. M. J. Orr

WOMEN'S CLUBS

WOMEN'S GOLF CLUB (D.U.)
Captain. Lesley Mathers
Secretary. Mary V. G. O'Connell

Treasurer. Jacqueline A. Nairn

WOMEN'S HOCKEY CLUB (D.U.)
Captain. Iris Morrison
Vice-Captain. Margaret Philp

Secretary. Mary Murphy
Treasurer. Cynthia Perdue

WOMEN'S LAWN TENNIS CLUB (D.U.)
Captain. Margaret P. Burns
Secretary. Pamela Thorp

Treasurer. Ann Reardon

WOMEN'S SQUASH RACQUETS CLUB (D.U.)
Captain. Gilda Emerson
Secretary. Elizabeth M. Sides

Treasurer. Iris Morrison

WOMEN'S SWIMMING CLUB (D.U.)
President. Rosemary Gibson, B.A.
Captain. Marilyn Casares
Vice-Captain. Sheila Greene

Secretary. Janet Mac Gregor
Treasurer. Patricia Aleers

TRINITY COLLEGE DUBLIN TRUST
(TRINITY COLLEGE (DUBLIN) EDUCATIONAL ENDOWMENT FUND

Trustees: The Hon. T. C. Kingsmill Moore, LL.D.
F. La Touche Godfrey, M.A.
G. F. Mitchell, M.A., M.SC.
Chairman: The Hon. T. C. Kingsmill Moore, LL.D.

Hon. Secretaries: R. R. Woods, M.B., F.R.C.S.I.

W. V. Denard, M.A., B.LITT.

Hon. Treasurer: T. B. H. McMurry, M.A., PH.D.

Secretary: Hazel D. Falkiner, B.A.

The Trinity College Dublin Trust was established in 1955 to continue and amplify the work of the Trinity College, Dublin, Educational Endowment Fund, which owed its inception to the initiative of the late Sir Robert Woods. The aim of the Trust is both to build up a capital sum large enough to augment substantially the existing endowments of the College, and to make grants to the College for the promotion of research or education in its widest sense.

A report on the progress of the Trust, together with a list of subscribers for the previous year, is sent annually to all graduates of the University.

Subscriptions and donations to the Trust may be sent to the secretary, at 5 Trinity College, Dublin.

Cheques should be made payable to the Trinity College, Dublin, Trust.

UNIVERSITY OF DUBLIN FUND (U. S. A.)

Trustees: F. C. Coulter, M.A., T. M. Dowling, B.A.,
S. J. S. McSharry, B.A., B.COMM., V. H. S. Mercier, B.A., PH.D.,
W. R. R. Watterson, B.COMM., C. W. Wolseley, B.A.

The University of Dublin Fund is a duly constituted fund in the U.S.A. with aims to promote education and research in the College.

Contributions by residents of the U.S.A. should be sent to Sean J. S. McSharry, c/o Morgan Guaranty Trust Co. of N.Y., 23 Wall St., New York, N.Y. 10015.

UNIVERSITY OF DUBLIN APPOINTMENTS OFFICE

In 1902 a University Appointments Association was formed to assist students and graduates of the University to obtain appointments and employment at home and abroad.

In 1953 the work was transferred to the Appointments Office, under the control of an executive committee and a full-time appointments staff.

Executive Committee: G. F. Mitchell, M.A. (chairman), D. A. Thornley, M.A., PHD.
W. A. Watts, M.A., Mary I. OBoyle
M.A., B.LITT., D. I. D. Howie, M.A., B.SC., PH.D.,
R. B. Henderson, B.A., R. S. Nesbitt, B.A.,
J. H. Sedgwick, B.COMM., S. S. O hEigeartaigh,
B.A., B.SC., R. W. Reynolds, M.A., PH.D.
B. K. P. Scaife, M.A., B.SC., PH.D.
J. F. M. Lydon, M.A., PH.D.

Appointments Officer: D. N. K. E. Montgomery, B.A.
1 Trinity College,
Telephone 72941, Ext. 321.

Assistant Appoint-
ments Officer: W. N. Keery, B.A., D.P.A.

Regulations

Any past or present member of the University may register, subject to the following regulations:

1. Candidates must obtain a registration form from the office, and complete, sign and return it to the Appointments Officer.

2. They should make an appointment to see him. He will, if necessary, ask for testimonials.

3. The Appointments Officer reserves the right, without giving reasons, to decline to register any candidate, to remove any candidate's name from the register, and to put forward or decline to put forward the name of any candidate for any given vacancy.

4. There is no registration fee for undergraduates or for graduates until after the second term from the date of their going off the books. All other candidates are required to pay a fee of £1 each time they come on the active list.

Notes

The best time for interview is nine to twelve months before the student's final examination. The recruitment of scientists usually starts in the January of the year in which they will be engaged, recruitment of arts graduates for business, etc., in the early spring. Candidates desiring September-October appointments in universities and schools should come for interview in the spring of that year, those requiring January or April appointments in the late summer of the preceding year.

There is no age limit to registration, but it should be understood that the office is mainly concerned with assisting young graduates and holders of diplomas to obtain a first appointment, and in the early years of their careers. The office does, however, receive notice of vacancies open to older and more experienced graduates, and it arranges vacation work for science and arts students who wish to gain useful industrial experience.

Parents and first year students may find it helpful to discuss with the Appointments Officer careers and prospects of employment in various fields.

STUDENT HEALTH SERVICE

The Student Health Service is available to all students who have paid the capitation fee. The nurse is in attendance at the consulting room in 11, Trinity College from 9.30 a.m. to 5 p.m. (excluding lunch time) from Monday to Friday and from 9.30 a.m. to 1 p.m. on Saturdays. One of the medical officers to the Service is at the consulting room to see patients at 2 p.m. on Monday, Wednesday and Friday and at 11.30 a.m. on Tuesday, Thursday and Saturday; appointments should be made with the nurse. The medical officer to Trinity Hall attends residents there on request.

A medical officer will attend a student at his or her place of residence in case of real need; calls should be arranged with the nurse. Visits are not possible to those resident beyond Clontarf, outside the city boundary to North, West and South or beyond Merrion Avenue.

Hospital treatment is as supplied under the National Health Scheme, students being treated as public ward patients; any charge demanded in excess by the Health Authority will be refunded by the College. Patients requiring psychiatric or gynaecological treatment are entitled to semi-private ward accommodation; others requesting special ward accommodation are responsible for charges and fees but the College will refund as much as would normally be paid for public ward accommodation. Some drugs and medicines are supplied free.

Certificates of disability will be issued only to those who have been seen by one of the medical officers to the Student Health Service. All medical information is confidential and will not be disclosed without the patient's permission. The following conditions are not covered by the Student Health Service: long standing surgical conditions, obstetric care, dental care, the provision of glasses for refraction errors.

Students who are taken to hospital in case of accident or emergency should inform the hospital that they are members of the University and are entitled to public ward treatment, and request the hospital to inform the medical officer here.

College telephone number of the Student Health Service: 556. Outside ordinary hours: Dublin 882648.

ASSOCIATED COLLEGES

CHURCH OF IRELAND TRAINING COLLEGE

MAGEE UNIVERSITY COLLEGE

RECOGNITION OF OTHER UNIVERSITIES

ARRANGEMENTS WITH THE CHURCH OF IRELAND TRAINING COLLEGE

1. The Training College pays to Trinity College two annual fees for all its students during the two years of their course.

2. Students of the Training College on payment to Trinity College of their first annual fee are recognised as students on the books of Trinity College, and are entitled to attend lectures; but they do not rank as fully matriculated students proceeding to degrees unless and until they satisfy the conditions specified in §9 below. They are subject to the usual college discipline.

COURSES AND EXAMINATIONS

Junior year

3. During their junior year students attend lectures in Irish, English, and the theory of education.

Courses

IRISH. The course in general studies as prescribed for Junior Freshmen. Students who satisfy the Professor of Irish that they have reached a sufficiently high standard may substitute the course in Irish prescribed for Junior Sophisters in general studies and take the Junior Sophister general studies examination.

ENGLISH. The course in general studies as prescribed for Junior Freshmen.

THEORY OF EDUCATION. The teacher's place in society; educational psychology; history of education.

Junior year examination

4. Students are required to pass an examination in June in Irish, English, and the theory of education. There is a supplemental examination in September/October.

Senior year

5. During their senior year students attend lectures in Irish, English, and the theory of education.

Courses

IRISH. The course in general studies as prescribed for Senior Freshmen. Students who passed the Junior Sophister examination in Irish in their

458

junior year may substitute the course in Irish prescribed for Senior Sophisters in general studies and take the Senior Sophister general studies examination.

ENGLISH. The course in general studies as prescribed for Senior Freshmen.

THEORY OF EDUCATION. Philosophical basis of educational theory; educational psychology; experimental education.

Senior year examination

6. Students are required to pass an examination in June in Irish, English, and the theory of education.

Further lectures

7. Students attend lectures, and take the requisite examinations in the remaining subjects of their programme (including religious knowledge and the art of teaching) at the Training College, and are tested in these subjects[1] (as well as in the theory of education) by the Inspectors of the Department of Education.

RECOGNITION AS NATIONAL TEACHERS

8. Students who pass the tests indicated in §§4-8 are provisionally recognized as national teachers by the Department of Education, which awards them a diploma when they have finished their probationary period of teaching.

STUDENTS PROCEEDING TO THE B.A. DEGREE

9. Those who wish to obtain the B.A. degree of the University, after they have passed the senior year examinations, should complete and return in duplicate to the Senior Tutor[2] a general admission form for Church of Ireland Training College students (obtainable from the Principal of that college). Provided they satisfy the Senior Tutor of their suitability to proceed further they may place their names on the college books as matriculated students of Junior Sophister standing on payment of the Junior Sophister fee. Save in exceptional circumstances such students must be resident within the city or in reasonable proximity of Dublin. They normally begin their Sophister course a year after completing their course at the Training College; they must complete the course for the B.A. degree within five years of completing the Training College course.

10. They are required to perform the same written exercises, and

---

[1] Excluding religious knowledge.
[2] This form must be lodged with the Senior Tutor not later than 1 September of the year in which the candidate is due to begin the Junior Sophister course.

to pass the same examinations as other students, but may be exempted in part from attendance at lectures. Partial exemption is granted by the Senior Lecturer having regard to their choice of subjects and to their performance at examinations already taken in Trinity College. They must attend at such times as may be required by their tutor, and by the lecturers in the courses they are studying.

11. During each Sophister year they must pursue courses in Irish, English, and *one* of the following: education[1], fine arts I, fine arts II, history.

12. Those who have completed satisfactorily the Sophister course in Irish, as provided in §§3, 5 above, are exempted from further examination in this subject; but students are not placed in a class at the B.A. examination unless they present themselves and pass in all three subjects.

REID EXHIBITIONS

13. Reid exhibitions of £75 per annum, tenable in Trinity College, may be awarded under certain conditions to Training College students from the County of Kerry. Particulars of these exhibitions may be obtained from the Principal of the Training College.

ARRANGEMENTS WITH MAGEE UNIVERSITY COLLEGE, LONDONDERRY

1. Students of Magee University College may proceed to the degree of B.A. in the University of Dublin, taking either an honor course or the course in general studies. They may also take the course for the B.B.S. degree.

HONOR COURSES
Courses permissible

2. The following of the university honor courses may be taken: mathematics, classics, mental and moral science, natural sciences, modern literature, ancient and modern literature, history and political science, economics and political science.

Lectures

3. During the first two years students attend lectures at Magee University College only. In the third year students are required to attend lectures at Trinity College during Trinity term. In the final

---

[1] This course is provided by the School of Education, the Registrar of which will supply particulars on request.

year they attend lectures at Trinity College in all three terms. Students in natural sciences attend Trinity College during the whole of the third and fourth years.

Examinations

4. Students present themselves for examinations in Trinity College in accordance with the regulations of their honor course.

COURSE IN GENERAL STUDIES

First and second years

5. During the first two years students attend lectures and take examinations at Magee University College.

Third and fourth years

6. In each of the third and fourth years, students of Magee University College are required to attend lectures for at least one term at Trinity College.

7. At the end of the third year students are required to take the Junior Sophister examination at Trinity College in June.

8. Students who intend to enter the ministry of the Presbyterian Church, if not attending lectures in Trinity College during either Michaelmas or Hilary term, are normally required to attend lectures in Magee University College. Such students attend the lectures of Trinity term in Trinity College[1].

9. Students of Magee University College who are reading the Magee Theological College course as well as the course in general studies may fulfil the requirements of the Senior Sophister year by satisfactory attendance at lectures, and by passing the B.A. degree examination, in one of the following subjects: Greek, Latin, philosophy.

10. Students are required to take the B.A. degree examination at Trinity College in June. There is a supplemental examination in October.

ORDINARY DEGREE IN NATURAL SCIENCES

11. During the first three years students attend lectures at Magee University College. In the final year they attend lectures at Trinity College in all three terms. See HONOR COURSE IN NATURAL SCIENCES, §§7, 17.

12. The examinations of all four years are those of Trinity College.

[1] This privilege is granted to Senior Sophister students attending divinity lectures in Magee Theological College. It may also be extended to Senior Sophister students in the Presbyterian Theological College, Belfast, subject to the consent of the Faculty of Arts at Magee University College.

Associated colleges

COURSE FOR THE B.B.S. DEGREE

13. The regulations are as for honor courses above.

STUDENTS INTENDING TO ENTER THE DIVINITY SCHOOL

14. Students who intend to enter the Divinity School in Trinity College may obtain special permission from the Regius and Archbishop King's Professors of Divinity to fulfil the requirements of the preliminary divinity year (other than the lectures on the Bible) while residing in Magee University College during Michaelmas and Hilary terms of their Junior Sophister year. Requests for such permission and for arrangement of their course must be made in writing to Archbishop King's Professor of Divinity at least one month before the beginning of their Junior Sophister year.

15. Students who have credit for attendance on the two years' catechetical course for members of the Church of Ireland in Magee Theological College are deemed to have fulfilled the requirements of the Divinity School in Trinity College in respect of catechetical terms, provided that the course which they studied at Magee Theological College was identical with the pass catechetical course prescribed for students in the Freshman years in Trinity College.

DIPLOMA IN BIBLICAL STUDIES

16. The regulations for Magee University College students are given under DIPLOMA IN BIBLICAL STUDIES.

FEES

Examination fees

17. An examination fee of £2 is charged for any honor examination taken before the Michaelmas Senior Freshman examination.

Annual fees

18. The names of Magee University College students are placed on the books of Trinity College when they pay the Junior Sophister annual fee. (They are not required to pay the matriculation fee.) They are then entitled to attend lectures at Trinity College. They also pay the Senior Sophister annual fee.

Capitation fee

19. If students attend lectures during only one term of an academic year they are not required to pay the capitation fee of £12. They may,

however, if they wish to join clubs and societies, become eligible to do so on paying a capitation fee of £6. See COLLEGE CHARGES III.

Fee concessions

20. Students may apply for fee concessions through the Bursar of Magee University College. See FINANCIAL ASSISTANCE.

RECOGNITION OF OTHER
UNIVERSITIES AND COLLEGES

I. ADMISSION OF STUDENTS WITH CREDIT FOR COURSES KEPT AT OTHER UNIVERSITIES AND COLLEGES

General regulations

1. Students seeking admission with credit from universities and colleges recognized by the Board and Council are subject to the regular admission requirements. Application must be made on forms obtainable from the Admissions Office.

2. Students from other recognized universities may be allowed credit for so much of the undergraduate course as the Senior Tutor may determine, taking account of the applicant's academic record in relation to the course he proposes to read.

3. A student granted admission with credit pays the matriculation fee, the fees for the class which he joins, and the capitation fee.

Oxford and Cambridge

4. Subject to §2, the amount of credit that may be allowed to students from the universities of Oxford and Cambridge depends on the number of terms they have kept by residence at their college.

The Royal College of Surgeons in Ireland

5. Students who have completed their course in the Royal College of Surgeons in Ireland may be allowed credit by the Senior Tutor for both the Freshman years.

Training colleges

6. Credit for the Junior Freshman year may be allowed by the Senior Tutor to students who have passed the final examination of one of the training colleges for teachers in elementary schools recognized by the Government of the Republic of Ireland, or of Northern Ireland, or of Great Britain. See also ARRANGEMENTS WITH THE CHURCH OF IRELAND TRAINING COLLEGE.

II. ATTENDANCE AT APPROVED COLLEGES

Under certain conditions the University regards attendance at approved courses, and the passing of approved examinations, at certain colleges in Ireland as partially fulfilling the exercises required for certain degrees of the University.

Colleges so recognized are as follows:

Magee University College, Londonderry, for certain approved courses and examinations in arts and science. See ARRANGEMENTS WITH MAGEE UNIVERSITY COLLEGE, LONDONDERRY.

University College, Dublin, for approved courses and examinations in agriculture and forestry. See SCHOOLS OF AGRICULTURE AND FORESTRY.

SENATUS ACADEMICUS

SENATUS ACADEMICUS

CANCELLARIUS: Fredericus Henricus Boland, LL.D.

PRO-CANCELLARII: Praehonorabilis Laurentius Michael Harvey Parsons, LL.D., Comes de Rosse.
Praehonorabilis Brianus Walterus Guinness, LL.D., Baro de Moyne.
Georgius Alexander Duncan, M.A.

PRÆPOSITUS: Albertus Joseph McConnell, SC.D.

VICE-PRÆPOSITUS: Herbertus Willelmus Parke, LITT.D.

MAGISTER SENIOR NON REGENS: Theodorus Willelmus Moody, M.A.

PROCURATORES: Senior—Ernestus Gordon Quin, M.A.
Junior—Jacobus Kirkwood Walton, M.A.

REGISTRARIUS: David Johannes Dickson Howie, M.A.

The undermentioned persons shall be members of the Senate, provided that in each case they are doctors or masters of the University:

1. Resident doctors or masters of the University, that is, doctors or masters who are not members of the College or University staff, but who hold rooms in College or are in attendance on lectures in arts or in the professional schools.

2. Doctors and masters of the University who have held a studentship of the University, or are moderators who have obtained a large gold medal, or moderators who have obtained a gold medal in or after 1935, or moderators who have obtained two moderatorships of a class higher than class III, and who have applied to the Registrar of the Senate to have their names entered permanently on the College books, as members of the Senate, without payment of fee;

3. Former fellows of the College;

4. Representatives and former representatives of the University in Seanad Éireann;

5. Members of the staff of the College or University, during their tenure of office;

6. Doctors or masters of the University who have applied to the Registrar of the Senate to have their names placed permanently on the College books, as members of the Senate, on payment of a fee of £5.

468

Aalen, Fredericus Arminius Andreasen, M.A. 1962

Abd-el-Motaal, Mostafa Hamdy Bahgat, M.A. 1965

Acheson, Roy Malcolmus, SC.D. 1962

Adams, Cinaethus Willelmus Johannes, M.A. 1964

Adams, Ricardus, M.A. 1935

Agnew, Alexander, M.A. 1948

Albin, Hugo Oliverius, M.A. 1944

Allen, Arturus Carolus, M.A. 1959

Armstrong, Claudius Blakeley, M.A. 1914

Arnould, Aemilius Julius Franciscus, M.A. 1948

Asmal, Abdul Kader, M.A. 1966

Auchmuty, Jacobus Johnston, PH.D. 1935

Aung, U Htin, PH.D. 1933

Baker, Cineathus Percivallus, PH.D. 1966

Baker, Joshua, PH.D. 1931

Ball, Nigellus Gresley, *Baronnetus*, M.A. 1921

Bathurst (*n.* McCormick), Georgina Campbell, M.A. 1917

Baxter, Jacobus Thomson, PH.D. 1966

Beckett, Samuel Barclay, LITT.D. 1959

Boggust, Willelmus Augustinus, PH.D. 1951

Boland, Carolus Ricardus, M.D. 1928

Boland, Fredericus Henricus, *Cancellarius*, LL.D. 1950

Booker, Willelmus Georgius, M.A. 1960

Boucher, Edgarus Willelmus Johannes, MUS.D. 1953

Bower, Bertha Gladys, M.A. 1961

Boyd, Hugo Alexander, M.LITT. 1960

Boyd, Malcolmus Ricardus, M.A. 1963

Boydell, Brianus Patricius, MUS.D. 1959

Boyle, Johannes Willelmus, M.A. 1942

Boyle, Petrus Huardus, PH.D. 1965

Brock, Catherine, M.A. 1964

Brown, Alanus, M.A. 1937

Brown, Giraldus Rodericus, PH.D. 1962

Brown, Johannes Simpson, M.A. 1949

Browne, Alanus Drury Harling, M.D. 1957

Browne, Percivallus Hugo, LL.D. 1919

Budd, Fredericus Gardner Orford, LL.D. 1928

Burrows, Georgius Henricus Jerram, M.A. 1937

Byrne, Johannes Gabriel, PH.D. 1961

Calcutt, Willelmus Edwinus Joseph Ricardus, M.A. 1946

Cantwell, Johannes Bosco, M.SC. 1964

Carroll, Michael Joseph, PH.D. 1965

Cathcart, Hektor Rex, PH.D. 1963

Chance, Arturus, M.D. 1912

Chapman, Terentius Telford, M.D. 1951

Chubb, Fredericus Basilius, M.A. 1950

Chubb (*n.* Rafther), Margaret Gertrude, M.A. 1965

Clarke, Aidanus, PH.D. 1959

Clarke, Michael Joseph, M.A. 1966

Coates (*n.* Renton), Janie Karolin, M.A. 1916

Cocker, Wesley, SC.D. 1948

Coffey, Victoria McCall, PH.D. 1965

Cole, Robertus Alanus, PH.D. 1948

Connolly, Thomas Franciscus, M.A. 1954

Coughlan, Johannes Antonius, M.A. 1964

Coutts, Johannes Archibaldus, M.A. 1937

Cox, Ranaldus Carolus, PH.D. 1962

Crane, Laurentius Johannes, M.A. 1964

Crawley (*n.* Leahy), Kathleen Elizabeth, M.A. 1926

Cronin, Michael Thomas Ignatius, PH.D. 1948

Cruickshank, Johannes, PH.D. 1952

Dahl, Thor, M.SC. 1962

Darling, Vivienne Honor, M.A. 1965

Darragh, Augustinus Sharpe, M.D. 1963

Davidson, Andreas Hope, M.D. 1920

Davies (*n.* Ffrench), Georgina Noelle Mary, M.A. 1926

Davies, Gordon Lesleius, M.A. 1957

Davis, Haraldus Percivallus Whitton, M.A. 1954

Davis (*n.* Alexander), Sybil Edith Doreen, M.A. 1940

Davis, Willelmus Johannes, M.A. 1958

Dawson, Georgius Willelmus Percivallus, M.A. 1953

Deane, Johannes Leonardus Barry, M.A. 1957

Delaney, Cyrillus Franciscus Georgius, PH.D. 1951

Denard (*n.* Brambell), Anne Elizabeth Rogers, M.A. 1954

Denard, Willelmus Vincentius, M.A. 1954

Dieneman, Willelmus Wolfgang, M.A. 1965

469

Senatus Academicus

Ditchburn, Robertus Willelmus, M.A. 1928
Dockrell, Rodney Beresford, M.DENT.SC 1954
Dowrick, Franciscus Ernestus, M.A. 1953
Duggan, Georgius Chester, LL.D. 1946
Duncan, Georgius Alexander, *Pro-Cancel-. larius*, M.A. 1926
Duncan, Lilian, M.A. 1917

Eccles, Willelmus, M.A. 1962
Edwards, Philippus Walterus, M.A. 1963
Edwards (*n.* Jones), Rosa Charlotte Pennick, M.SC. 1937
Erskine, Caecilius Alexander, PH.D. 1946
Evans, Johannes Ailba, M.A. 1964
Exshaw, Eldon Young, M.A. 1957

Falkiner, Ninianus McIntire, SC.D. 1932
Fegan, Willelmus Georgius, M.CH. 1952
Ferguson, Georgius Willelmus, M.A. 1961
Ferguson, Robertus Meruinus, M.A. 1928
FitzGibbon, Giraldus, M.A. 1941
Fleming, Johannes Browne, M.D. 1941
Florides, Petrus Serghiou, M.A. 1965
Frankl, Petrus Jeremias Lewinter, M.A. 1965
French, Robertus Butler Digby, M.A. 1931
Friel, Ernestus Sheldon, SC.D. 1928
Fuller, Alexander Ricardus Burnet, M.A. 1950
Furlong, Edmundus Jacobus Joseph, M.A. 1938

Gallaher, Michael Antonius, M.SC. 1947
Ganly, Andreas, M.A. 1960
Gardner, Giraldus Henricus Fraser, M.A. 1950
Garnett, Patricius Franciscus, M.A. 1946
Gatenby, Petrus Barry Brontë, M.D. 1949
Wade-Gery (*n.* Whitfield), Vivian, M.A. 1922
Gibson, Johannes Percivallus, M.A. 1923
Gill, Willelmus Daniel, M.A. 1955
Gillespie, Irene, M.A. 1926
Gillmor, Desmundus Alfredus, PH.D. 1966.
Giltrap, Giraldus Henricus Henzell, M.A 1950
Glen, Jacobus Alexander, M.A. 1919
Godfrey, Christabel Frances, M.A. 1919
Godfrey, Dionysius Rowley, PH.D. 1949

Godfrey, Franciscus La Touche, M.A. 1919
Goodhue, Reginaldus Theodoricus, M.A 1963
Graham, Duglasius Lesleius, M.A. 1934
Graham, Victor Willelmus, M.A. 1939
Grainger, Johannes Noellus Rowland, M.SC. 1949
Gray, Johannes, M.SC. 1945
Greene, David Willelmus, M.A. 1942
Gregg, Aleyn Hunter, M.A. 1942
Grene, Willelmus David, M.A. 1939
Griffith, Thomas Gwynfor, M.A. 1955

Hamill, Deirdre Enid Rosaleen, M.A. 1961
Hamilton, Cinaethus Maqueen, M.A. 1936
Hamilton, Jacobus Victor, M.A. 1954
Hanna, Merle Olivia, M.A. 1961
Hanson, Antonius Tyrrell, D.D. 1953
Hanson, Ricardus Patricius Crosland, D.D. 1950
Harmon, Hugo Joseph, M.A. 1942
Harris, Thomas Eduardus, M.A. 1937
Harte, Margaret, M.A. 1965
Hartin, Jacobus, M.A. 1960
Hatch, Carolus, M.A. 1962
Haughton, Joseph Pedlow, M.A. 1945
Hawthorne, Thomas Samuel Buller, M.A. 1942
Hewson, Georgius Henricus Phillips, MUS.D. 1914
Hill, Paulus McNeil, M.A. 1966
Hillis, Arturus Henricus Macnamara, M.A. 1947
Hinds, Alfredus Eduardus, M.A. 1957
Hornsby, Hazel Marie, PH.D. 1931
Howie, David Johannes Dickson, M.A. 1957
Hurst, Franciscus Johannes Embleton, M.A. 1959
Hyman (*antea* Tennenbaum), Nathan Ludovicus, M.A. 1944

Irfan, Muhammad, M.A. 1963

Jagoe, Willelmus Stanleius, M.D. 1964
Jaswon, Nicolas, M.D. 1965
Jeffares, Alexander Normanus, PH.D. 1945
Jenkins, Raimundus Gordon Finney, M.A. 1932
Jessop, Willelmus Johannes Eduardus, M.D. 1935

Johnston, Ericus Irvine, M.A. 1933
Johnston, Joseph, M.A. 1913
Johnston, Thomas Jacobus, M.A. 1927
Jones, Thomas Cedricus, M.A. 1966
Jordan, Patricius, M.A. 1957

Smith-Keary, Petrus Fredericus, PH.D. 1961
Keating, Justinus Pascal, M.A. 1962
Kelly, Michael Gerhardus Caecilius, M.A. 1966
Killingley, Frances Henrietta, M.A. 1959
Kennelly, Timotheus Brendanus, M.A. 1965
Kirwan, Reginaldus Willelmus, PH.D. 1964
Kyle, Johannes Andreas, M.A. 1918

Laidlaw, Willelmus Allison, LITT.D. 1933
Lane, Daniel Franciscus Victor, M.CH. 1954
Larminie, Margaret, M.A. 1959
Lewis, Maxwell Huardus Richards, PH.D. 1963
Lillie, Edwinus Willelmus, M.D. 1953
Little (n. Pope), Anita Carlotta, M.A. 1933
Lloyd, Robertus Oliverius Villiers, M.SC. 1942
Salvadori Lonergan, Corinna, M.A. 1962
Lonergan, Georgius Antonius, M.A. 1961
Lösel, Dorothy Margarita, M.A. 1962
Lösel, Franciscus Adolphus Gustavus, M.A. 1961
Luce, Arturus Aston, D.D. 1920
Luce, Johannes Victor, M.A. 1945
Lydon, Jacobus Franciscus Michael, M.A. 1962
Lynch, Mary Sinclair, M.A. 1962
Lyons, Franciscus Stewart Leland, LITT.D. 1966
Lyons, Willelmus Jacobus, M.A. 1952

McAdoo, Henricus Robertus, D.D. 1949
McAulay, Johannes Ross, PH.D. 1961
MacBride, Winifred Helen Baird, M.A. 1965
McCollum, Stanleius Thomas, M.A. 1960
McConnell, Adams Andreas, M.CH. 1946
McConnell, Albertus Joseph, Praepositus, SC.D. 1929
McCormack, Percivallus Davis, PH.D. 1956
McDonogh, Carolus Lewers, M.D. 1919
McDowell, Robertus Brendanus, PH.D. 1938

McGillycuddy, Dermitius, M.A. 1956
McGilvray, Jacobus Willelmus, M.A. 1963
McGuire, Robertus Ely, M.A. 1930
McHugh, Dorothy Alicia, M.SC. 1931
McIntosh, Maxwell Scott, M.A. 1934
Mack, Willelmus Henricus Bradshaw, Eques Auratus, LL.D. 1948
Mackey, Willelmus Elliott, M.A. 1954
McKeever, Joseph Theodoricus, M.D. 1949
McKenna, Carolus Beuno, LL.D. 1931
McManus, Margaret Eleanor, M.A. 1954
McMurry, Thomas Brianus Hamilton, PH.D. 1956
McNally, Patricius Aloysius, M.D. 1940
McVey, Hugo, M.D. 1955
McWilliam, Georgius Henricus, M.A. 1961
Madden, Robertus Willis, M.A. 1940
Magrath, Carolus Robertus Rich, M.A. 1933
Maguinness, Willelmus Stuart, M.A. 1929
Main, Dom Duglasius Willelmus Victor, M.A. 1958
Mansoor, Menahem, PH.D. 1944
Mercier, Vivianus Herbertus Samuel, PH.D. 1945
Micks, Eduardus Christophorus, M.A. 1961
Milliken, Jacobus Copeland, M.D. 1962
Milton, Johannes Alexander, M.A. 1965
Mills, Rosaleen Patricia Broughton, M.A. 1954
Milne, Cinaethus, M.A. 1960
Mitchell, David Michael, M.D. 1939
Mitchell, Georgius Franciscus, M.A. 1937
Mol, Willelmus Huyzer, M.A. 1937
Moody, Theodorus Willelmus, M.A. 1941
Moore, Johannes Normanus Parke, M.D. 1937
Moore, Honorabilis Theodorus Conyngham Kingsmill, LL.D. 1947
Morrow, Veronica Margaret Ruth, M.A. 1962
Moyne, Praehonorabilis Brianus Walterus Guinness, Baro de, Pro-Cancellarius, LL.D. 1958
Mullan, Carolus Seymour, M.A. 1919
Murdoch, Brianus Hughes, M.A. 1965

Nicholson, Ernestus Wilson, M.A. 1964
Nicholson, Johannes Armytage, M.A. 1949
North, Meta Evelyn, M.A. 1927
Nowlan, Georgius Samuel, M.A. 1931

471

Senatus Academicus

Nurock, Max, LL.D. 1962
Nunn, Willelmus Ricardus, M.A. 1963

O'Boyle, Mary Ita, M.A. 1962
OBrien, Brendanus Eduardus, M.D. 1950
O'Brien, Henricus Audoenus, M.A. 1939
Ó Cadhain, Martinus, M.A. 1958
O'Clery, Dermitius, M.A. 1943
O'Meara, Robertus Alanus Quain, M.D. 1931
O'Moore, Laurentius Butler, M.SC. 1946
O'Morchoe, Carolus Christophorus Creagh, M.D. 1961
O'Sullivan, Donaldus, LITT.D. 1951
O'Sullivan, Willelmus, M.A. 1961

Parke, Herbertus Willelmus, LITT.D. 1933
Pepper, David Carolus, M.A. 1947
Perdue, Ernestus Cope Todd, M.A. 1962
Pheifer, Joseph Donovan, M.A. 1963
Phillips, Willemus Eduardus Hadrianus, PH.D. 1966
Pollard, Mary, M.A. 1965
Pomeroy, Harriett Mary, M.A. 1958
Poole, Johannes Hewitt Jellett, SC.D. 1921
Powell, Brianus Leolinus, PH.D. 1962
Purser, Olive Constance, M.A. 1911
Pyle, Willelmus Fitzroy, PH.D. 1933

Quin, Ernestus Gordon, M.A. 1935
Quin, Jacobus Sinclair, M.D. 1925
Quinlan, Henricus Robertus, M.A. 1961

Raraty, Mauritius Michael, M.A. 1966
Reid, Duglasius Jacobus, M.SC. 1966
Reid, Thomas Bertrandus Wallace, M.A. 1927
Reiss, Johannes Siegbert, PH.D. 1944
Reynolds, Radulphus Wallace, M.A. 1951
Richardson, Leopoldus Johannes Dixon, M.A. 1920
Richardson, Thomas Normanus, M.SC. 1933
Riley, Eduardus Calverley, M.A. 1952
Risk, Henricus, PH.D. 1963 /
Risk (n. McHugh), May Haughton, PH.D. 1951
Roberts, Andreas Johannes Norton, M.A. 1942
Roberts, Willelmus Spence Lee, PH.D. 1963

Robinson, Huardus Waterhouse, PH.D. 1964
Rodgers, Edmundus Joseph, M.A. 1966
Rodgers, Valerie Ann Hilda, M.A. 1963
Rollin, Geneviève Julie Marie, M.A. 1966
Rosse, Praehonorabilis Laurentius Michael Harvey Parsons, Comes de, Pro-Cancellarius, LL.D. 1950
Roulston, Cinaethus Irwin, M.SC. 1941
Russell, Matthias, M.A. 1963
Russell, Robertus Eduinus, Eques Auratus, M.A. 1917
Otway-Ruthven, Annette Jocelyn, M.A. 1940
Ryan, Willelmus Jacobus Louden, PH.D. 1949

Scaife, Brendanus Coemgenus Patricius, M.A. 1964
Scaife, Willelmus Garrett Stanleius, M.A. 1964
Sevitt, Simon, M.SC. 1939
Sewell, Johannes Swindale Nanson, M.A. 1942
Shaw, Keith Meares, M.D. 1955
Shields, Hugo Eduinus, M.A. 1956
Shortt, Johannes Purser, M.A. 1918
Simms, David Johannes, M.A. 1959
Simms, Georgius Otto. Archiepiscopus Dublinensis, D.D. 1952
Simms, Johannes Giraldus, PH.D. 1952
Skeffington, Audoenus Lancelottus Sheehy, PH.D. 1935
Sloman, Albertus Eduardus, M.A. 1950
Smith, Lancelottus Upton, M.A. 1936
Smyly, Henricus Jocelinus, M.A. 1910
Smyth, Jacobus Desmundus, PH.D. 1942
Spaight, Jacobus Molony, LL.D. 1905
Spain, Barry, M.SC. 1938
Spencer, Brianus, M.A. 1963
Stanford, Willelmus Bedell, LITT.D. 1940
Star, Ellie Margaret, M.A. 1965
Starkie, Gualterus Fitzwilliam, LITT.D. 1924
Steen, Robertus Elsworth, M.D. 1927
Steinberg, Joshua Solly, M.A. 1952
Stewart, Fredericus Stanleius, M.D. 1944
Stokes, Albertus Eduardus, M.A. 1946
Stuart, Eduardus Robertson, M.A. 1949
Swenarton, Johannes Creighton, M.A. 1945
Synge, Johannes Lighton, SC.D. 1926

Synge, Victor Millington, M.D. 1919

Tait, Alanus Anderson, M.A. 1962
Tate, Herbertus, M.A. 1920
Temperley, Johannes Jesse, M.D. 1960
Temple, Mortimer, M.A. 1931
Thomas, Leonellus Hugo Christophorus, M.A. 1960
Thompson, Arturus Galfridus, M.D. 1932
Thornley, David Andrew, PH.D. 1959
Tomacelli, Eduardus, M.A. 1948
Torrens, David Smyth, M.A. 1932
Tucker (*n.* Daniels), Margaret Isabel, M.SC. 1936
Tunstead, Joseph, PH.D. 1942

Wallace, Betty Eileen, M.D. 1959
Pakenham-Walsh, Amory Allfrey, M.A. 1956
Walsh, Johannes Mainwaring, M.A. 1961
Walton, Ernestus Thomas Sinton, M.A. 1934
Walton, Jacobus Kirkwood, M.A. 1947
Warnock, Alanus Watson, M.A. 1941
Watson, Helen Middleton, M.A. 1934
Watts, Willelmus Arturus,. M.A. 1961
Webb, David Allardice, SC.D. 1961
Weekes, Blanche, M.D. 1956

Weingreen, Jacob, PH.D. 1931
Weir, Donaldus Georgius, M.D. 1962
West, Eduardus Percivallus, M.A. 1929
Grove-White, Carolus Willelmus, M.SC. 1942
Wilkins, Mauritius Arturus Carolus, M.A. 1911
Williams, Alfredus Caecilius, LL.D. 1962
Williams, Philippus Clivius, PH.D. 1966
Wilson, Robertus, M.D. 1940
Winder, Franciscus Gerhardus Augustinus, M.A. 1962
Winkelmann, Franciscus Carolus Gualterus, M.A. 1952
Wisdom, Johannes Oulton, PH.D. 1933
Woodhouse, Hugo Fredericus, D.D. 1952
Wormell, Donaldus Ernestus Wilson, M.A. 1939
Wright, Arturus Blackburn, M.LITT. 1960
Wright (*n.* Robinson), Barbara, M.A. 1960
Wright, Willelmus, SC.D. 1962
Wylie, Franciscus Verner, *Eques Auratus.* LL.D. 1923

Yasin, Said Ahmad, PH.D. 1943

Total 344

473

NAMES OF STUDENTS

SCHOLARS OF TRINITY COLLEGE

STUDENTS ON THE BOOKS

STUDENTS IN OTHER CATEGORIES

.

NUMBERS OF STUDENTS

SCHOLARS OF TRINITY COLLEGE[1]

(67 men + 17 women)

The names of women students, who are non-foundation scholars, are printed in italics. The letters N.F. are placed after the names of men students who are non-foundation scholars.

Armstrong, Michael John
Barklie, Robert Charles
Boal, Sydney John
Bond, Brian Lewis
Bourke, Marie Terese Winifred
Buckman, Rossly David
Budd, Declan Nicholas Orford
Butler, Walter John
Buttimore, Nigel Hugh
Byrn, Richard Francis MacDermot
Carson, Richard Mark
Cobbe, Hugh Michael Thomas
Cochran, David Samuel
Coulson, Shelagh
Craig, Alan James
Daunt, Stephen Paul Achilles
Debenham, John Keeys
Dinn, John Jared
Dobbs, Hugh Nevill
Dodd, George Henry
Donaldson, Alexander Ivan
Dowd, Doreen Elizabeth
England, Robert Gordon
Forrest, Robert William Edward
Frame, Robert Ferris
Gamble, Robert Bradley
Garber, Gwendoline
Gleasure, James William
Golding (née Elliott), Carole
Greenleaves, Susan Jennifer
Griffin, Alan Howard Foster
Hancock, Graham
Hansell, Michael Henry
Harris, Rosemary
Heelas, Ann Margaret

Henry, Mary Elizabeth Frances
Jackson, David Alexander
Jacques, William O'Donovan
Jones, Patrick Richard Lloyd
Kean, Charles James Coates
Kelly, Fergus Samuel
Kelly, John Stephen
Kelly, Patrick Hyde
Kennedy, Douglas Peter
Keppler, Robert Henry
Kevin, Anthony Charles Conwell
King, Ivan Brownlow
Lamki, Abdulla Mohammed Nasser
Lim, Hui Pin
McCartney, Agnes Elizabeth
McEvett, Allan William
Mackey, Desmond Alexander George
McNulty, Michael Stewart
MacWeeney, Susan Katherine
Mayes, Andrew David Hastings
Moody, Janet Lucy
Mullan, William Norman Boyd
Murtagh, Thomas Norman Francis
Neill, John Robert Winder
Newell, Alan Clive
Nixon, James Robert
Norris, David Patrick Bernard
Notley, Michael Garth
Ó hÉigeartaigh, Cian Sáirséal
Oldham, Elizabeth Evelyn
Porter, Christopher Michael
Pratt, Albert Creighton, N.F.
Pratt, Benjamin John, N.F.
Purcell, Derek Alan
Reynolds, Hilary Gaye

[1]As on 28 February 1966.

Reynolds, Julian Douglas
Roberts, Prudence Gabriel Nesfield
Rye (née Sarkies), Jennifer Helen
Ryle, Stephen Francis
Shaw, Alan Walter
Thompson, Christopher Lancelot
Walmsley, Charles Malcolm

Walton, Philip Wilson
Webb, Edward Timothy
White, Stephen Leonard
Williams, David Henry
Wilson, David Charles
Winterbottom, Robert
Withrington, John Knox

SCHOLARS ELECTED IN JUNE 1966
(10 *men*+1 *woman*)

Algeo, David Robert Murison
Aikins, Jennifer Mary
Bates, Ernest Timothy Brendan
Glass, Norman Jeffrey
Hartman, Mark Lawrence
Heaney, John Alan

Johnston, David Christopher
Keatinge, Terence Heber
Ó Siadhail, Micheál Lorcán
Saldanha, Loyola Furtunato Bernard
Stanford, William Aylmer Charles

STUDENTS ON THE BOOKS
ON 28 FEBRUARY 1966

1. In these lists the number placed *after* each name indicates the name of the student's tutor in accordance with the following table[1]:

2	Dr Gregg	34	Dr Powell
16	Mr French	35	Mr Exshaw
17	Mr Elliott	36	Miss O'Boyle
19	Dr Lösel	37	Miss Brock
20	Dr Lydon	38	Mr Coles
22	Mr FitzGibbon	39	Mr Coughlan
23	Mr Stuart	40	Dr Crane
24	Mr Denard	42	Mr Hinds
25	Dr Weekes	43	Dr Simms
26	Mr Winder	44	Dr Wright
27	Dr Andrews	45	Mr Nunn
28	Mr Davies	46	Mr Aalen
29	Dr Thornley	48	Mr Jones
30	Mrs Lynch	49	Mr Kennelly
32	Mr Tait	50	Mr Scaife

Where a student has been assigned to a new tutor for the academic year 1966–7, the latter and not his tutor on 28 February 1966 is indicated.

2. The number placed *before* each name indicates the student's college standing on 28 February 1966 in accordance with the following table:

1 = Junior Freshman   3 = Junior Sophister
2 = Senior Freshman   4 = Senior Sophister

3. The names of women students are printed in italics.

4. Although all foundation and non-foundation scholars are on the books in arts, the names of those who had graduated before March 1966 are omitted from the lists.

[1]The list of tutors is here repeated, with tutor's numbers in sequence.

45	Mr Aalen	16	Mr French	50	Mr Scaife
27	Dr Andrews	2	Dr Gregg	43	Dr Simms
37	Miss Brock	42	Mr Hinds	23	Mr Stuart
38	Mr Coles	48	Mr Jones	32	Mr Tait
39	Mr Coughlan	49	Mr Kennelly	29	Dr Thornley
40	Dr Crane	19	Dr Lösel	14	Mr Thornton
28	Mr Davies	20	Dr Lydon	25	Dr Weekes
24	Mr Denard	30	Mrs Lynch	26	Mr Winder
17	Mr Elliott	45	Mr Nunn	44	Dr Wright
35	Mr Exshaw	36	Miss O'Boyle		
22	Mr FitzGibbon	34	Dr Powell		

2	Aastorp, Borre	29
1	*Abbott, Judith Mary*	16
2	*Abbott, Pamela*	20
1	Abel, Robert Graham	2
1	*Abernethy, Alison Sara*	16
1	Abrahamson, David Michael	26
2	*Abrahamson, Marcia Grace*	24
1	*Acheson, Sara Fortune*	20
1	*Achilles, Edelgard Mathilde*	38
4	*Acunto, Eleanor Vera*	19
3	*Adair, Eileen Marianne*	27
1	*Adair, Lorna Deirdre*	45
1	*Adam, Elizabeth*	42
1	Adam, Ian Desmond	37
1	*Adam, Ruth Mary*	30
3	Adams, James Michael	20
1	Adams, Mark Browne	22
2	Adams, Thomas Declan	32
1	Adamson, Neil Thomas	17
3	Broughton-Adderley, Nicholas Randolph	28
3	Adler, Peter Lawrence	16
1	Agbaje, Adekola Raymond Arthur	26
1	Agnew, David Isaac Ferris	39
1	Ahern, Francis Timothy	25
4	*Ahern, Rosemary Ann*	17
3	*Aikins, Jennifer Mary* (Sch.)	16
1	Akerele, David Babatunde	37
3	*Akers, Clare Patricia*	34
4	Alakija, Olawole	23
1	Alexander, Angus George Allen	2
4	*Alexander, Marianne Mua*	27
3	Alford, David Graham	25
3	Algeo, David Robert Murison (Sch.)	22
1	Alkin, Edwin Randolph	37
2	Allan, Malcolm Warren Taylor	24
3	*Allberry, Elizabeth Anne*	19
4	Allen, Andrew Martin	22
4	Allen, Edward John Frederick	22
3	*Allen, Iris Lucinda*	28
1	*Allen, June Cherry Scott*	44
3	Allen, Thomas John Roy	28
3	Almeida, Oswald	26
1	*Almond, Julia Susan Felicity*	30
3	Altaras, David Maurice	35
2	Alvey, Michael Reid	26
1	Anarah, Ambrose Chukwuka	22
1	Anderson, Alan Myers	45
4	*Anderson, Elizabeth Mary*	25
4	*Anderson, Heather Emily*	25
3	*Anderson, Maureen Elizabeth*	20
1	Anderson, Robert Lynch	45
1	Anderson, Rodney Foster	2
1	Anderson, William Steen	27
1	*Andrew, Susan Mary*	16
1	*Andrews, Barbara Georgina*	19
2	Andrews, Charles James Morgan	39
2	Andrews, Paul Patrick	32
3	*Angus (née Best), Beatrice Elizabeth Lenore*	30
4	Angus, Ian Henderson	40
1	Anthony, Christopher Van Cleef	34
4	Archbold, James Alexander Allen	23
3	Archdall, Mervyn	29
1	*Archer, Jean Barbara*	27
1	Archer, Robin James	43
4	Ard, John	40
1	Ardis, Robert Alexander	40
2	Armstrong, Brian Joseph	22
2	Armstrong, Eric Douglas	32
1	*Armstrong, Jennifer Anne*	24
3	Armstrong, John Edward Norman	27
2	Armstrong, John Seamus	24
4	Armstrong, Michael John (Sch.)	22
3	Armstrong, William Harold	19
3	Arthurs, John Wilson	2
3	Asbury, Michael John	34

The number after a student's name indicates his tutor; the number before his name indicates his college standing as on 28 February 1966.

479

Students on the books in arts

4 Ashe, Alan Scott 29
1 Ashe, Francis St George 26
1 Ashe, Ian Thomas 30
4 *Ashmore, Sylvia Yvonne* 27
4 Aspinwall, John James 22
2 Aston, Richard Anthony
   Spicer 34
1 *Aston, Susan Margaret* 30
3 Atchia, Ahmad Ibrahim 25
3 Atiya, Kanaan Rayih 29
3 Atkinson, Joseph Giles Eyre 22
4 *Auckland, Rosalie Helen* 25
2 Aumeer, Peter Sewooduth 17
1 Aylward, James Gerard 23

3 Bacon, Derek Robert
   Alexander 17
  Bacon, Philip Andrew 29
  Bacon, Sheila Margaret 19
4 *Bailey, Marion Janet* 36
1 Bainbridge, John Gerald 45
4 Baine, George Shaun 35
4 *Baird, Eleanor Isobel* 29
4 Baker, Colin Edward 37
1 Baker, Richard John Ian 39
4 Baker, Thomas Evan Hindley 39
1 Baker, William Frederick 37
4 Baldry, Keith John 29
2 Ballagh, Brian Edward 2
4 Bamford, Christopher Guy
   Edward 16
3 Bamford, Michael Frederick 22
4 Banks, Alan Martin 17
2 Banks, Colin Nesbitt 29
2 Bannister, John Basil 19
3 *Baynard, Margaret Anne* 44
1 Barber, Graham Robert
   Lloyd 22
3 Barfield, Brian Michael 19
4 Barham, Richard
   Emfringham 25
4 *Barkley, Carys Rosemary Mills* 27

4 Barklie, Robert Charles (Sch.) 17
4 Barniston, Nathaniel Geoffrey 2
1 *Baron, Mary Patricia* 27
2 Barr, William Bruce
   Ainsworth 32
3 *Barrett, Jean Lambert* 30
3 *Barrie, Jean Valerie Stewart* 36
1 *Barrett, Linda Frances* 2
1 Barrett, Matthew Anthony 22
1 *Barry, Margaret Mary Teresa* 39
4 Bartnicki, Peter Mark 2
3 Basedow, Frederick Charles 22
2 *Bass, Rosemary Ann* 30
2 Batchelor, Leslie Alan 16
2 Bates, Ernest Timothy
   Brendan (Sch.) 35
1 Baudouy, Sylvain Jean Louis 34
3 Baxter, Stuart James 29
1 *Bayley, Angela Marine* 17
2 *Beacon, Eva* 24
3 *Beamish, Pamela Mary* 36
4 Beare, Brian Charles 2
3 Beattie, Derek Robert George 27
1 Beatty, Adrian Paul 29
3 Beck, Donald Lionel 33
3 Beddoe, Frederick Victor
   Robert Malcolm 28
3 Blankson-Beecham, George 17
3 *Beggs, Odette* 42
4 *Bell, Alison Mary* 39
3 Bell, Alistair Bruce 27
3 Hope-Bell, Beverley John 29
3 *Bell, Catherine Lois* 27
4 *Bell, Cecilia Elizabeth Mary* 35
4 Bell, Charles William 24
3 *Bell, Daphne Elizabeth Lamor* 19
4 *Bell, Deirdre Winifred Joy* 39
2 *Bell, Heather Elizabeth* 19
1 Bell, Henry 30
1 *Bell, Hilary* 34
4 *Bell, Honor Elizabeth* 20
3 *Bell, Janet Livingston* 30

The number after a student's name indicates his tutor; the number before his name indicates his college standing as on 28 February 1966.

4 Bell, Jeremy Nicholas	19	
3 Bell, Sydney John	2	
1 Bell, Thomas Douglas Samuel	2	
4 Benham, Martin Terence	37	
2 Bennett, John Hamilton	19	
4 *Bennett, Margaret Susan*	27	
1 Bennett, Paul Blake	32	
3 Bennett, Philip Andrew	44	
3 Bennett, Thomas Cyril	24	
3 Benson, Charles John	19	
2 Benson, John Christopher Mark	24	
3 Benson, Malcolm John	19	
2 *Pack-Beresford, Caroline Anne*	34	
2 Bevan, Michael Rodney Kinsella	27	
1 Bevan, Nicholas Charles David	40	
4 *Bevan, Phyllis Julia*	19	
3 Biddulph, Michael John Patrick	23	
3 Bingham, Richard Walker	34	
1 *Bingham, Rosemary Jill*	16	
3 *Binstead, Nancy Elizabeth*	30	
3 *Birch, Joan McGregor Graham*	26	
2 Bird, Richard Geoffrey	20	
1 *Birkett, Susan Mary*	36	
2 Bishop, David John	40	
1 Black, Anthony Gordon	39	
3 Black, James Alan Catherwood	26	
4 Black, Steven Morton	2	
4 Blackmore, Ian Henry	20	
1 *Blackwell, Hazel Anne*	38	
3 Blain, Sydney Thomas	27	
1 Blakeney, Hamilton Rowan Timothy	2	
1 Bleackley, Michael John	34	
4 Blick, William James	20	
1 Bloomfield, Frederick Jacob	17	
1 *Blount, Hilary*	26	
4 Boal, Sydney John (Sch.)	24	
1 Boase, Roger	19	

1 Boate, Alan Richard	23	
2 Boden, Derek John	24	
2 Boelens, Richard George Vincent	39	
2 Bolam, Robert John	25	
4 *Boland, Eavan*	16	
3 Boler, Simon Frederick Doubleday	37	
1 Boles, Derrick Alan	39	
2 Bonar, Donal Patrick	25	
4 Bond, Alastair Tom	27	
2 Bond, Ryan Edgar	22	
1 *Bonham, Eve*	24	
1 Bonner, Desmond	36	
3 Boothroyd, Michael John	17	
4 Borrett, George Frederick	2	
3 *Bouchard, Marie Ghiselaine Hilda*	28	
4 Boulting, Norris Chapman Roy	20	
1 Bourke, Adrian Patrick	35	
2 Bourke, Clive Mervyn	30	
4 Bourke, Edmund Francis	29	
2 Bourke, Henry Orme	35	
3 *Bourke, Mary Terese Winifred* (Sch.)	35	
2 Bourke, Michael Anthony Patrick	23	
1 *Bourke, Patricia Mary*	30	
2 Bourke, Terence Michael	23	
4 Bourne, James Raymond	39	
4 *Bourns, Patricia Ann*	35	
2 Bowder, William Maxwell	24	
1 Bowen, Anthony John	43	
4 *Bowen, Jacqueline Elizabeth*	20	
1 Bowers, Kevin John	40	
3 Bowie, Douglas Malcolm	34	
4 Bowles, Peter Francis	19	
2 Bowman, John Francis Xavier	20	
4 Boyce, Harold	40	
3 *Boyd, Elizabeth Anne*	39	
1 *Boyd, Janet Elizabeth*	17	
1 Boydell, Barra Ralph	19	

The number after a student's name indicates his tutor; the number before his name indicates his college standing as on 28 February 1966.

S

Students on the books in arts

The number after a student's name indicates his tutor; the number before his name indicate his college standing as on 28 February 1966.

The number after a student's name indicates his tutor; the number before his name indicates his college standing as on 28 February 1966.

Students on the books in arts

The number after a student's name indicates his tutor; the number before his name indicates his college standing as on 28 February 1966.

1	Collins, Henry Patrick	17
1	Collins, Patrick Anthony	2
4	Colville, James	2
1	Comiskey, Don	39
2	Concanon, John Patrick Nigel	35
3	Condon, Richard Anthony	23
3	*Conley, Mary*	16
4	Conlin, Maurice Arthur	35
3	Conn, Robert Alan	19
3	*Connell, Jennifer Margaret*	24
1	*Connelly, Alpha Margaret*	24
2	Connelly, John Pascal Martin	23
3	Connolly, Augustine Oliver	23
1	*Connolly, Philomena Mary*	20
1	*Connor, Sheelagh Patricia*	34
3	Conway, John	20
4	Conway, John Kenneth	29
1	Conway, Maurice	25
2	*Lenox-Conyngham, Eleanor Elizabeth Rita*	16
3	*Cook, Nora Marsali*	24
2	Cook, Robert Samuel	40
4	*Cooke, Alexandra Evelyn*	24
4	*Cooke, Jane Elizabeth*	20
2	*Cooper, Brigid Rosamund*	19
4	*Cooper, Dione Frances*	27
2	*Cooper, Jane Kathleen*	20
3	Cooper, Robert Kenneth Elliott	2
3	*Cooper, Sylvia Elizabeth Hamilton*	42
1	Cooper, Timothy Patrick	17
3	*Coote, Margaret Patricia*	19
4	*Copeland, Dorcas Averil*	36
3	*Copeland, Yvonne Patricia Melville*	28
3	*Corbett, Rosalind Anne*	30
2	Cordess, Christopher Charles	23
2	*Corran, Judith Ann*	20
3	Corran, Patrick Henry	26
3	Corrigan, Bernard John	42
2	Corrigan, Philip John	45
2	Corrigan, Richard Brian	45

1	Cosby, Ivan Patrick Sydney Godolphin	45
4	Cosgrove, Peter William	25
1	Coulter, Robert Philip	42
1	Coulter, Richard Percival	29
3	Coulter, Terence Stewart	22
4	Courtis, Ian Thomas	20
1	Courtney, Peter Ross	39
2	*Cox, Betty Anne*	25
3	*Cox, Catherine Olive*	26
4	*Cox, Jane Elizabeth*	22
1	Coy, John Hugh	17
3	Craig, Alan James (Sch.)	26
1	*Craig, Joanna Virginia*	34
1	Craig, John Lowry	45
1	Craig, Peter Joseph	37
1	*Craig, Sarah Elizabeth*	39
4	*Craig, Sarah Louisa*	39
3	Craig, Victor Frederick Jarman	22
4	Crampton, Derek Norman	29
3	Crane, Daniel Lionel	26
1	Crane, Michael David	25
1	Cranley, John James	45
3	Cranston, David Ambrose	28
1	Crawford, Brian Victor	16
1	*Crawford, Catherine Anne*	16
3	*Crawford, Hazel Rose Holmes*	28
2	Crawford, William Alan	23
4	*Crichton, Tania Frances*	39
4	Crickmay, Nicholas Hugh	20
1	*Croasdaile, Gillian Lindsey*	42
3	Crockett, Robin Geoffrey	16
4	Crockett, Trevor Burnside	23
1	Crofton, Jonathan	34
3	Fairfax-Crone, Charles Reginald	22
1	*Crook, Judith*	34
3	Crooks, John Anthony Irving, B.A.	24
1	*Crosby, Anne Geraldine Mary*	17
1	Lewis-Crosby, Robert Anthony Cornwall	45

The number after a student's name indicates his tutor; the number before his name indicates his college standing as on 28 February 1966.

Students on the books in arts

4 Cross, Thornton Dayton John 35
1 Crotty, Brian Patrick
  Anthony 20
1 Croughan, David Joseph 39
1 Crowe, Malcolm Kenneth 23
2 Crowe, Trevor Reginald 22
2 *Crozier, Irene June* 24
4 Crump, Anthony John 37
1 *Cubbidge, Sheena Maire Patricia* 39
4 Culbert, Brian Campbell 22
2 Cullen, Alan Fergus Francis 23
2 Cullen, Patrick Anthony 24
3 Cullen, Timothy William
  Brian 27
1 Culverwell, Geoffrey Tom 24
4 Cummings, Stanley Gordon 16
3 *Cunningham, Lilian Gail* 27
3 Curran, Arthur Joseph 23
1 *Curry, Catherine Jane* 2
4 Curtis, John Andrew Howard 37
1 Cusack, Paul Brefni Bethel
  Charles 16
3 Cushnie, Derek John 43

1 Dagg, Alan Harding Sidney 22
2 Dagg, David Nathanial
  Heuston 26
4 *Dahl, Astrid Mona Elisabeth* 25
4 Scott-Dalgleish, Moray Innes 17
1 *Dalley, Sonia Margaret* 44
4 Daly, Francis Gerard 26
1 Dalzell, James Ormonde 24
2 Dane, Brian Hubert 19
3 *Danefield, Ann Olivia* 25
4 *Daniel, Ruth Helen* 36
3 Daniels, David 29
1 D'Arcy, John Nicholas 24
2 Darling, Michael Roy
  Norman 2
1 *Daunt, Lucilla Rosemary* 44
3 Daunt, Stephen Paul Achilles
  (Sch.) 35

4 Daura, Mamman 20
2 D'Auria, Denis Andrew
  Primo 34
1 *David, Anastasia* 38
1 David, Philip Edmund 42
3 Davidson, Andrew James
  Lloyd 19
4 Davidson, Brian Andrew John 25
2 Davidson, Timothy
  Alexander 32
3 Davie, Mark Charles
  Christopher 27
1 Davies, Martin John 2
1 Davies, Robert 16
2 *Davies, Sarah Pritchard* 23
3 *Burdon Davies, Susan* 29
1 Davis, John Francis 40
1 *Davis, Paula* 32
4 Dawson, Christopher John 29
1 Day, Philip Maurice 42
3 Day, Stephen John William 42
3 *Deacon, Thelma Florence* 27
2 *Deadman, Mary Elizabeth* 19
2 *De Belleroche, Jacqueline Sarah* 34
3 Debenham, John Keeys (Sch.) 40
2 De Brommead, Jerome
  Andrew 17
4 *De Bunsen, Margaret Grenville* 16
1 De Cogan, Donard Maoliose 40
2 *Deeny, Carmel Mary
  Christina* 25
1 De Lacy, Walter Edward
  Peter 23
2 *Delaney, Lorna Mary* 30
1 Delaney, Owen Joseph 23
3 Delap, Charles Brian 16
1 *Delap, Deirdre Mary* 44
3 De Mille, Peter Noel 33
3 Denham, Brian Rishworth 23
1 Denham, Peter Edward 44
1 Dennehy, Patrick Joseph 28
1 *Dennison, Margaret Evelyn* 19
1 Desai, Ghanshyam Raojibhai 25

The number after a student's name indicates his tutor; the number before his name indicates his college standing as on 28 February 1966.

486

3	Develter, Herman Godfried Alfons Henri	2
1	Devenney, Raymond Robert Wilmont	42
2	Devlin, Declan Kieron	23
1	Dewar, Stephen	37
1	De Wit, Maarten Johan	17
3	*De Wolfe de Wytt, Carolyn Nora*	19
2	Dickey, Brien Thomas	35
3	*Dickey, Mary Elizabeth*	43
3	Dickson, Beverley	28
1	Dickson, Jocelyn Dickson	20
3	*Dickson, Eileen*	16
1	Dignam, Malcolm James	39
3	Digby, Robin Paul	22
1	Dinsmore, Robert John	26
1	*Disney, Anna Jane Wynn*	16
3	*Dobbin, Heather Susette*	1
4	Dobbin, Leonard Neill	20
3	Dobbin, Victor	28
3	Dobbs, Hugh Nevill (Sch.)	40
4	Dobree, Ronald Bonamy	25
3	Dockeray, Charles Julian	34
1	*Dockrell, Caroline Anne*	17
4	Dockrell, John Henry	35
3	Doherty, Modupe	25
3	Donaghy, Brian Charles Douglas	29
4	Donaghy, John Brendan	2
3	Donald, George Robert	2
3	Donald, Keith Raymond Russell	24
1	Donaldson, Francis Samuel Windsor	28
4	Donegan, David James	35
4	*Donelan, Maureen Sally O'Connor*	19
2	Donnelly, Andrew James Oliver	27
1	Donovan, David Patrick	2
2	*Donovan, Molly Deirdre*	34
3	*Donovan, Pauline Marjorie*	27

3	Doran, Kenneth Michael	26
1	Dorcey, Anthony Hugh Joseph	17
4	Dorman, David Eric	25
2	Dorman, Kerry Hobart	19
3	*Dougan, Heather Irene*	27
3	Dougan, Terence	30
1	*Douglas, Florence Noelle*	43
1	Douglas, John Alexander	27
1	Douglas, Richard John Charles Sholto	29
2	Dowling, John Declan	26
1	Dowling, Thomas Cormac	45
4	*Downes, Madeline Imelda Camille*	19
4	Dowse, Gerald Sinton	23
1	Dowse, John Marcus	23
4	*Doyle, Clare Frances*	23
3	*Doyle, Patricia Mary*	23
2	Drakeford, Robert Francis Etern	19
3	Dresser, Peter Quentin	39
1	Driscoll, Dennis John	35
2	*Drought, Judith Patricia Anne*	25
3	Duff, William George Turner	2
2	Dukes, George Clive	17
4	Duncan, William David	24
4	*Dunlop, Helen Florence Shaw*	16
1	Dunwoody, Eric William	35
3	*Durand, Angela Victoria Susan*	24
4	Durell, David Henry Dumaresq	16
2	Dutton, Charles John Gough	20
2	Duvivier, Hugh Michael	16
1	Dyer, Christopher Arthur Irwin	20
1	*Dykes, Margaret Agnes Elaine*	38
1	*Dworzak, Adelaide Elizabeth*	24
2	Eakins, George Alfred	39
1	Easby, John Richard	37
3	*East, Alison Ryder*	27

The number after a student's name indicates his tutor; the number before his name indicates his college standing as on 28 February 1966.

Students on the books in arts

The number after a student's name indicates his tutor; the number before his name indicates his college standing as on 28 February 1966.

3 FitzGibbon, Gerald Francis   35
2 Fitzsimons, Robert
    Barrington   25
2 *Flanagan, Caroline Mary*   36
4 Flanagan, Charles Edward
    Terence   25
3 Flanagan, Roderick   29
2 *Fleming, Caroline Mary*   16
1 Fleming, James Malcolm
    Stewart   23
4 *Fleming, Margaret Mary*   16
3 Fleming, Thomas John   29
3 *Fletcher, Janet Roselle*   16
3 Fletcher, Jeremy James   22
1 Fletcher, John Richard   37
4 Fletcher, Richard Evans   35
1 *Fletcher, Valerie Creeth*   44
4 Fleury, David Alexander   22
1 Foley, Thomas James   23
1 Foo, Shi-lan   25
3 Forbes, Christian   22
3 Forbes, Wellesley St Clair   2
2 Foreman, Robert Michael   30
2 Forrest, Leslie David Arthur   24
4 Forrest, Robert William
    Edward (Sch.)   24
4 Forshaw, John Derek   37
4 *Forster, Mary Villerius*   35
1 Forster, Timothy James   26
1 Fowler, Dudley Neal   28
4 Fox, Alan Dermod   22
1 Fox, Anthony John   2
4 Fox, Raymond Patrick   22
1 Fox, Ronald Frederick
    Walter   38
4 Frame, Robert Ferris (Sch.)   20
4 Frangopulos, George   37
1 *Frankland, Sara*   30
3 *Franklin, Mary*   25
1 Fraser, Alasdair Macleod   35
2 *Fraser, Kristine Irene*   17
2 Frayne, Edward James   45

4 *Freeburne, Sheila Ivy*   20
2 Freestone, Melvin Bernard   26
3 *French, Marilyn Jean*   30
4 Frewin, Nicholas Christopher
    Kenneth   26
2 Frost, Robert Alfred   40
4 Fry, William Oliver
    Houghton   41
3 *Funston, Lynda*   16
1 Furlong, Andrew William
    Ussher   40
1 *Furlong, Judy Mary*   30
3 *Furlong, Margaret Elizabeth
    Catherine*   24

2 *Gageby, Susan Jane*   35
1 Gahan, James Joseph   40
3 Galbraith, Brian John   30
2 *Galbraith, Edith Marjorie*   16
1 Gale, John Ralph   43
1 *Gallagher, Sara Elizabeth
    Juliette*   28
4 *Gallimore, Josephine Ann*   27
3 Galt, John Moore   16
3 Gamble, Robert Bradley
    (Sch.)   24
1 Ganly, Michael James   40
3 Gant, Nicholas John
    Greenwood   2
2 *Gardner, Alison Margaret*   30
4 Gardner, John Robert   37
1 Gargan, Edward Trevor   17
2 Garner, Henry William
    Yeames   20
1 *Garratt, Gillian Evelyn*   27
1 Garson, Bryan Philip Joseph   34
4 Garst, David Brackburn   35
2 Warren-Gash, David John   34
1 Gash, Hubert Fitzjohn   24
1 *Gates, Linda Patricia*   43
2 Gault, John William   17
4 *Gaw, Eleanor Sarah*   40

The number after a student's name indicates his tutor; the number before his name indicates his college standing as on 28 February 1966.

Students on the books in arts

2	*Gaynor, Clare Michaela*	20
4	Gbow, Mustapha Fama	25
1	Gelinas, Peter Joseph	2
1	George, Christopher John Davenport	2
1	George, Ronald Forsyth de Courcy	39
3	Gerrard, Peter Edward William Netterville	27
4	Getgood, William Trevor	19
4	Gibb, Andrew Craddock	19
1	*Gibbins, Philippa Margaret*	19
4	*Gibbon, Angela Clemency*	19
2	*Gibbons, Eileen Mary*	25
4	Laughlin-Gibson, Archibald Thomas	35
2	Gibson, Hugh John	35
1	*Gibson, Margaret Diana Hilary*	30
4	Gibson (née Frazer), Olive Mareline	27
2	Gilbert, Francis Humphrey	35
4	*Gilbert, Heather Emily*	17
1	Gilbert, Michael David	39
3	*Gilbert, Ruth Marilyn Joy*	25
1	Gilchrist, James Irwin	2
4	*Giles, Christine Nora*	20
3	*Gill, Rosemary Joy*	30
1	*Gill, Sarah Margaret*	16
1	Gillespie, Julian Thomas	44
4	Gillespie, John	2
3	Gillespie, Paul Edward	20
3	Gillespie, Richard John	39
1	Gillespie, Robert John Kneale	42
1	Gillespie, William James Killian	30
1	Gillman, Richard Morgan	23
2	Gilmartin, John Patrick Antony Maiben	39
2	*Given, Helen Margaret*	24
4	Glanville, Brian William Kingsmill	27
2	Glass, Norman Jeffrey (Sch.)	32
1	Glass, Roger John Francis	39
1	Godby, Michael Adrian Patrick	35
2	*Goddard, Geraldine Amelia Ayling*	30
3	Godfrey, Gordon Francis Morrison	35
1	Gofton, Edward Allan	34
1	Golding, Richard Peter	23
2	*Gomis, Annette*	16
1	Good, James Michael Barry	34
1	Goodbody, Richard Swithun Maxwell	16
3	Goode, John Walter Cyril	23
4	*Gooderson, Christine Stella*	20
4	Goodwillie, John Stoney	20
2	Goolnik, Geoffrey Morris	32
2	Goon, Liuyoon	25
2	Gordon, Donald Martin	17
2	Gordon, Robert Leslie	34
1	*Gordon, Susan Carol*	19
1	Gorman, Richard David	37
1	Goslett, Nicholas Stephen	30
1	Goslett, Roland William	30
2	*Gough, Coralie Mary Irwin*	19
3	Gough, William Harold Martin	22
4	Gould, Clifford John Thomason	45
1	Gould, John Christopher Colbert Knight	30
1	Goulding, Hamilton Paddy	22
1	Graham, Alan Thomas	37
2	*Graham, Carol*	19
2	Graham, David	19
2	Graham, Francis Stuart	17
3	Graham, Ian Maklim	34
2	*Graham, Lorna Patricia*	34
1	*Graham, Margaret Hazel*	19
1	Graham, Noel George	2
1	Graham, Timothy George Michael	24
2	*Grainger, Susan Christine*	24

The number after a student's name indicates his tutor; the number before his name indicates his college standing as on 28 February 1966.

4	Grange, Hugh	19
1	*Gray, Brigid Elizabeth*	19
3	*Gray, Deirdre Anne*	20
4	Gray, John Lindsay	29
3	Gray, Joseph Anthony	22
3	Gray, John Norman	22
3	*Gray, Lorna*	44
3	Gray, Patrick Julian Lawrence	40
2	Harwood-Grayson, David	2
3	*Harwood-Grayson, Evelyn Norma*	17
2	*Greatrex, Beth*	19
2	Greaves, Brian Hugh	34
3	Greaves, Nicholas Geoffrey	35
1	Green, James Joseph Michael	35
4	Green, Richard Anthony Bradbury	2
4	Greenaway, David Barry	20
1	*Greene, Daphne Margaret*	2
4	*Greene, Penelope Mary Johnston*	40
1	Greene, Richard Francis	26
2	*Greene, Sheila Mary*	27
2	Greenhalgh, David Robert	22
2	Greer, Howard John	22
2	Greer, Kenneth Ross McMaster	35
4	*Greer, Patricia Helen*	25
1	Greer, Stanley George Hobson	19
4	Greeves, Roger Derrick	24
2	Gregg, Richard Moore	2
1	Grene, Nicholas	16
2	*Grenham, Mary*	25
3	Greville, Nicholas Peter	29
4	Griffin, Alan Howard Foster (Sch.)	24
3	Griffin, John Francis Thomas	23
1	Griffin, Nigel Robert Foster	2
1	Grindle, Reginald John	37
3	Groom, David Eliot	17
3	*Groves, Elizabeth Margaret*	30
4	Grubb, Louis Michael	23
1	*Gunn, Mavis Anne Louis*	28
1	*Gusken, Andrea*	38
4	*Guthrie, Diana Ruth Thelma*	25
4	*Guthrie, Jill Veronica*	22
3	*Guy, Faith Alison*	28
1	*Gwynn, Sally Catherine*	42
3	Benson-Gyles, Richard Thomas	16
4	*Hadman, Mary Annabel Rose*	35
3	Hagenbach, Keith MacDonald	29
4	Haire, Thomas Alan	20
1	*Halahan, Anne Margaret*	30
2	Hale, John Rupert	16
3	Hale, Peter Stuart	19
1	*Hall, Catherine Elizabeth*	43
2	Hall, John	30
2	*Hall, Joyce Anne*	17
1	Hall, Kenneth Mervyn	39
2	Hall, Terence Gabriel	34
4	Halliday, Charles Francis Alexander Tollemache	39
1	Halliday, James Gordon Tollemache	16
2	Hamill, Roger	32
2	Hamill, William John	25
3	Hamilton, Hans Michael MacDougall	22
1	Hamilton, Richard Victor	22
2	Hamilton, Thomas Norman	24
4	Hammond, James Esuman	26
1	Hanaghan, David	22
1	Hancock, Christopher John	37
3	Hancock, Graham (Sch.)	17
4	Handy, Howard Peter George	24
2	Hanna, Alan John	22
3	*Hanna, Gillian Lavinia Cecile*	19
2	Hanna, John Robert	32
4	Hannigan, Barry Fitzgerald	2
3	Haran, Thomas Kevin	2
3	*Harbison, Joan Roberta*	30

The number after a student's name indicates his tutor; the number before his name indicates his college standing as on 28 February 1966.

491

Students on the books in arts

1 *Hard, Gaelynn Bridget* 44
4 Hardiman, Adam Veryan 22
4 Hardiman, Roger David 37
4 Hardwick, Roger Thomas 19
1 *Harman, Janet Valentine* 16
3 Harper, Leslie Robert 45
2 Harraher, Kevin 32
1 Harriman, William Paul 39
3 Harrington, Leo Anthony 22
4 Harrington, Daniel Edmund Peter 35
3 Harries, John Wyndham Nevill 37
4 Harris, Alan Stuart 2
1 Harris, Robert Lain Colquhoun 20
2 Harris, Steven Gill 35
4 Harrison, Alan James 24
4 Harrison, Brian Arnold 29
3 Harrison, David James 26
1 *Harrison, Eleanor Clare* 43
3 *Harrison, Pepeta Mary Theresa* 16
1 Harrison, Peter Seymour 35
2 Hart, Anthony Ronald 35
1 *Hart, Susanna Margaret* 25
1 Hartigan, Aubrey Spencer Gerald 37
4 Hartley, William James 45
3 Hartman, Mark Lawrence (Sch.) 17
1 Hartnell, Nigel Raymond 40
1 *Harvey, Audrey Mary* 2
2 Harvey, Christopher Sidney 17
4 *Harvey, Patricia Ann* 36
1 Hassard, Calvert Crawford 27
4 Haslett, Howard James 19
1 Hasson, Ian Thomas 27
1 Hatfield, Roger 24
3 Hautz, Paul Vincent 40
4 Hawkins, David Nicholas 29
1 Hawley, Henry Ashley Campbell 43

4 *Hawser, Gillian Margaret Greatrex* 29
1 *Hay, Heather Iveson Caley* 44
4 Hay, John Ronald 29
1 *Hayden, Geraldine Mary* 45
4 *Hayens, Anne Margaret* 20
4 Hayes, Edward George 45
1 Hayes, Denis Joseph 34
3 *Hayes, Meriel Constance* 16
4 *Hayward, Gillian Margaret* 45
1 Scott-Hayward, Sean Michael 39
4 Hazelton, Peter William Alexander 17
1 Healy, John Rowland 39
3 Healy, Liam O'Brien 20
3 Heaney, John Alan (Sch.) 2
4 Heaney, Michael Roger 23
1 *Hearnden, Margaret Ann* 40
4 Heaslett, Ian Henry David 25
4 Heaslip, William John 17
4 *Heelas, Ann Margaret* (Sch.) 25
1 Hellyer, Compton Graham 37
3 Helme, Donald Alastair 43
1 Henderson, Christopher John 39
3 Henderson, David Alastair 16
2 Henderson, David Victor Craigie 2
3 Henderson, Douglas Cameron 16
3 *Henderson, Frances Mary Elizabeth Margaret* 43
1 Henderson, Ian David 38
3 *Henderson, Lynda Mary* 16
3 *Henderson, Mary Isobel* 36
3 Henderson, Trevor David George 22
1 Hennessy, Richard Jeremy Christopher 42
1 Hennessy, Robert Patrick 23
3 Heney, Michael William 20
1 Henry, Norman William 45
1 *Henry, Veronica Joyce* 17
1 Herbert, David Anthony 37
1 Herman, Maurice John 17

The number after a student's name indicates his tutor; the number before his name indicates his college standing as on 28 February 1966.

Students on the books in arts

1	Haseltine, Peter	23
4	Heslop, Michael Latham	20
3	Hewat, Simon Henry Bingham	20
1	Hewitt, Colin Holt	38
3	Heywood, Douglas Scott	37
4	*Heyno, Ann Elizabeth*	35
2	Hickey, Garrett Michael	45
3	Hill, David Dorrien	19
1	Hill, Edward William Hawks	43
4	Hill, George Thomas Gary	35
1	Hill, James Desmond	39
4	*Hill, Jennifer Marianne*	35
4	*De Courcy-Hill (née Buswell), Susan Mary Sharland*	27
3	Hilliard, George Percival St John	24
1	Hilliard, Robert Martin	23
3	*Hillman, Patricia Burns*	36
3	Hillyard, Patrick Anthony Richard	30
3	Hinds, Desmond Ross	17
2	*Hirschfeld, Jacqueline Vera*	34
1	*Hitchman, Judith Anne*	44
2	*Hobbs, Elizabeth Kathleen*	25
4	*Hobson, Marjorie*	2
3	Hodder, Christopher	29
4	Vere-Hodge, Richard Anthony	25
2	Hogan, Daniel	26
2	Hogg, Edward William	45
2	*Hogg, Eileen*	36
1	Hogg, Henry George	23
1	Holder, Peter Jeremy	17
1	Holmes, David Salway	34
1	*Holmes, Jennifer*	16
2	*Holt, Valerie Margaret*	17
1	Holyland, Peter William	26
2	*Hopkins, Pamela Frances*	30
4	Hopkins, Richard Henry	29
1	Hornby, Keith Antony Delgado	35
2	Horner, Arnold Alexander	34

1	Hosford, Walter	17
3	Houlihan, John Brendan	23
1	*Houston, Margaret Patricia*	30
1	Houston, Niall Edward William	17
2	Howie, Michael Britchford	23
1	*Huang, Charlotte Hsiao Tet*	17
1	*Hudson, Stephanie Gay*	40
2	*Hubert, Helen Mary*	25
4	Huey, David Millar	2
4	Huff, Graham Jackson	35
1	Hughes, Alan James	22
4	*Hughes, Christine Margaret*	16
4	*Hughes, Christine Nora*	39
3	Hughes, Piers Heyworth	29
1	*Hughes, Susan Lesley*	19
4	Humfrey, Peter Edward	35
1	Humfrey, Peter Brian	19
2	Hunt, Thomas Alphonsus	39
4	*Hunter, Hilmary*	29
1	Hunter, Ian Stewart	45
3	Hunter, Samuel Graham	2
2	Hurley, Christopher Derek	17
4	Hurley, Roger Frederick	17
3	*Hutchinson, Elizabeth Alexandra*	43
4	*Hutchinson, Doreen Deirdre*	36
1	Hutchinson, John Anthony Michael	35
4	*Hutchinson, Olive Patricia*	29
1	Hutchinson, Peter Vivian	45
1	Hutchinson, Robert Charles	30
3	*Hutchinson, Roberta Anne*	43
3	Hutson, Julian James Elliott	35
1	*Hutton, Carol Mary*	45
2	Hyland, Paul Vincent	32
3	Idowu, Ademola	32
2	Ihenacho, Christopher Ndionyenma	17
2	*Impey, Richenda Margaret*	39
3	Ind, Peter Lewin Brodie	37

The number after a student's name indicates his tutor; the number before his name indicates his college standing as on 28 February 1966.

Students on the books in arts

The number after a student's name indicates his tutor; the number before his name indicates his college standing as on 28 February 1966.

The number after a student's name indicates his tutor; the number before his name indicates his college standing as on 28 February 1966.

Students on the books in arts

3	Kirwan, Anthony Michael Douglas	35
4	*Kirwan, Margaret Frances*	25
3	*Kissin, Evelyn Anne*	25
3	*Kitchin, Rosemary Deborah*	27
1	*Knapp, Ingrid Ormsby*	25
1	Knight, Martin David	37
4	Knight, Robert Ian Ensor	29
3	Knight, Roger John Beckett	20
3	Knox, Christopher	37
4	*Kohane, Judith Natasha*	16
4	Kraunsoe, Niels Anthony	22
1	*Kyle, Barbara Moore*	2
4	Kyle, Philip Kirkwood	35
1	Kynaston, Jeremy Robert	35
4	Kynaston, Roger Teesdale	20

3	*Laird, Carolyn Shirley*	35
1	Laird, David William	22
4	Laird, William Kenneth	20
4	*Lalani, Zinat Alinhai Premji*	25
1	*Lalor, Rosemary Jane*	44
2	Lam, Kai Ping	25
4	Lamb, David George	27
1	Lamb, Peter Wilfred	44
4	Lamb, Richard	39
2	Lambe, Patrick Eugene	30
4	Lambert, Michael Roderick Kirby, B.A.	17
2	*Lambert, Patricia Valerie*	34
3	Lambert, Patrick Charles Kirkley	17
4	Lamki, Abdulla Mohammed Nasser (Sch.)	17
4	*Lane, Alison Torrens*	17
3	Lane, Rupert Douglas	34
3	Langran, Colin Arthur	27
2	Lantos, Hugh William George	39
1	Larmour, Ian Francis	37
2	*Latham, Sara Jacqueline*	39
3	Laub, Peter Hieronymus	35

4	Lauriston, William James	22
1	Lavery, Michael Antony Waring	44
2	Lawless, Malacy John Andrew	39
2	Lawrence, Michael John Taite	24
2	*Lawson, Ann Margaret*	16
2	Lawson, Trevor John	19
4	*Layland, Janet Anne*	19
2	*Layang, Iris Hester*	19
3	*Leahy, Anne Christina*	30
1	Leahy, John Ralph	2
4	Learmond, Douglas William	22
1	Leathers, Jeremy Baxter	37
2	Leaver, Peter Lawrence Oppenheim	35
3	*Leckebusch, Hellgard Margarete*	19
3	*Le Clerc, Virginia Edith*	17
4	Ledbetter, David John	24
2	Ledbetter, Gordon Trevor	24
3	*Ledbetter, Patricia Henrietta*	20
3	Ledbetter, Peter George	2
2	Ledwich, William Delahoyde	35
2	*Lee, Diana Chee Fong*	17
2	Lee, Kee Ong	25
3	Lee, Kor Voon	25
3	Lee, Stanley Michael	25
3	*Le Fanu, Juliet Elizabeth*	16
3	*Le Geyt, Idina Prudence*	20
3	Lenaghan, David Ian	22
3	Lennie, David Timothy	17
4	Lentin, John Michael	29
3	*Leon, Susan Rosalind*	35
2	Leonard, Andre James	40
3	Lepp, William George Trevor	30
2	Lescher, Rupert	20
3	*Leslie, Leonie Deirdre Elise*	20
1	Levis, John Charles	23
3	Lewis, Charles Hylton	42
3	Lewis, Gordon Keith	22
1	Lewis, Henry Arthur	22
3	Lewis, Martyn John Dudley	27
1	Lewis, Trevor George	25
4	Lewis, William Gerald	24

The number after a student's name indicates his tutor; the number before his name indicates his college standing as on 28 February 1966.

1	*Lewis, Yvonne*	35
2	*Leyland, Ann Moreton*	16
3	*Lightfoot, Ann Margaret*	20
3	Lightwood, Max Carey	24
3	*Lilley, Yvonne Harriet*	27
1	Lillie, Edwin David	26
1	Lim, Elin Lin Neo	25
3	Lim, Kwee Keat	26
2	*Linde, Maret Kristina*	30
4	Delmar-Lindley, Charles Albert	35
1	*Lindner, Elizabeth Rose*	30
3	Lindsay, Derek Michael	2
2	Lindsay, Ronald Blenner Hassett	35
1	Ling, Ching Kok	17
2	*Linnane, Michelle Marguerite*	35
1	Linnemann, Bernard Maria	30
3	Lister, Paul Martin	23
1	Little, Alan John	27
4	*Livock, Ann Jennifer*	35
2	Lloyd, Brian Selwyn	34
1	Lloyd, Gerald Charles	26
2	*Lloyd, Sheelagh Scarff*	45
3	Lockton, Raymond Garfield	17
3	Logue, Andrew Cunningham	30
2	Loh, Hung Chey	22
4	*Loosley, Elizabeth Jill*	27
4	Loram, Roger Stile	2
1	Lord, Robin Charles	2
4	Lorenz, John Antonin	29
1	*Lorimer, Mary Ellen*	16
1	Lovegrove, David John	30
1	Lovesy, Hugh Owen	2
4	Lovett, Terence Edmund John	29
1	Lovitt, Anthony Alan	34
4	*Lowe, Joan Marion*	29
3	Lowes, Anthony Edward Ninian	22
3	Lowes, Marvin Langton	35
3	Lucas, Jeremy Robert	29
1	Lucas, Trevor Norman Henry	29
2	*Ludgate, Ruth Marion*	19
1	*Ludlow, Gillian Agnes*	27
1	Luke, David Anthony	26
4	Lukes, Heather Mary	36
1	*Lurring, Ruth Lesley*	44
2	*Lurring, Susan Mary*	16
4	Lutton, Joan Elizabeth	17
1	Lynch, Cyril Patrick Joseph	23
1	*Lynch, Geraldine Hazel*	28
2	*Lyons, Maureen Bernadette*	29
1	*Lysaght, Deborah Claire Royse*	25
1	*McAdoo, Lesley Gabrielle*	43
2	*McAleer, Katherine Mary*	2
4	McAllister, Eric Franklyn	24
3	McAlpine, William Roderick	27
1	MacAogain, Colm Michael Padraic	22
1	*McAuley, Mary Elizabeth*	19
2	McAvoy, William George	16
3	*McBratney, Sheelagh Norma*	40
2	McBryde, Charles Derek	22
2	McCabe, Alfred Marshall	17
4	*MacCafferty, Paula Christine*	16
2	McCahon, William Ernest	24
1	*McCall, Anne Marie*	23
3	*McCall, Bridget Gillian*	27
3	McCall, Simon Denis Montgomery	30
3	*McCandless, Norma Joan*	35
1	McCann, Alan Mervyn	17
3	*McCann, Grainne*	16
3	*McCann, Susan Gwendoline*	30
1	McCarter, William Thomas	37
1	McCartney, Alan Leonard McCrea	44
2	McCartney, Denis John	35
1	McCartney, William Christopher	38
4	*McCarthy, Kathleen Mary Patricia*	27
4	McClaughlin, Trevor	20
3	McClean, William Rentoul	40

The number after a sudent's name indicates his tutor; the number before his name indicates his college standing as on 28 February 1966.

497

Students on the books in arts

4 McClelland, Edward Murphy 22
1 *McClements, Joy Marguerite* 45
4 McClenaghan, Marcus Patrick 2
1 McClimond, Leonard
   Montgomery 20
2 McClinton, James Brian 24
4 *McCloskey, Aideen Mary* 25
2 *McComb, Mary Elizabeth*
   Helen 30
3 McComish, William Adams 27
1 *McConaghie, Anna Evelyn* 42
3 *McConaghie, Elizabeth Hazel* 42
4 *McConkey, Beryl Marguerite* 27
4 McConnell, Allan Benjamin
   Douglas 29
4 McConnell, David John 17
2 *McConnell, Mary Creaghan* 38
3 McConnell, William Thomas 22
1 McConway, Patrick Joseph 23
1 McCormack, John
   Christopher 39
1 McCormick, Christopher
   John 26
1 McCormick, David Paul
   Simon 37
4 *McCormick, Josephine Louise* 35
1 McCormick, Kenneth Pasley 42
1 McCormick, Samuel Graham 45
3 McCormick, Timothy Brian 29
1 McCorry, Francis Patrick
   Kevin 43
4 McCosh, James Michael
   William 22
3 *McCoubrey, Joan Wilson* 28
1 *McCourt, Pamela Mary* 44
2 McCoy, Terence Patrick 26
1 McCrea, Alan Donnelly 2
1 *McCulla, Rosemary Janet* 42
1 MacCullagh, Desmond
   George 37
2 McCullagh, John Eric 20
4 McCullagh, Mervyn
   Alexander 22

2 McCullough, Brian Henry 22
3 McCullough, John 36
1 McCurdy, John Derek 20
2 *McCutchan, Mary Isobel* 25
1 *McCutcheon, Rosalind Grace* 24
3 McDermot, Conor Victor 26
1 McDermott, Kerry 42
2 *MacDevitt, Loraine Patricia* 19
4 *McDonald, Fiona* 16
1 MacDonald, Ian Stewart 23
4 MacDonald, John Alan 35
1 MacDonald, Patrick George 42
2 MacDonald, Sam Adams
   Lewin 20
4 *McDonnell, Margaret Anne* 39
1 *MacDonnell, Moira Paolina* 16
4 *MacDonagh, Carolyn Park* 35
2 MacDougald, John Peter 34
3 *McDowall, Alice Joan* 30
1 MacDowall, Robert Oliver 35
1 *McDowall, Valerie Patricia* 38
1 *McDowell, Avril Patricia* 44
3 *McDowell, Daphne Vivienne* 30
3 *McDowell, Margaret Russell* 16
1 McDowell, Peter William
   Drewry 38
3 McElfatrick, Howard Victor
   Hayes 28
3 *McElwaine, Kenneth Corrie* 30
3 *McEntee, Kathleen Francis*
   Mary 42
3 *McEwan, Helen Margaret* 28
1 MacFarlane, Bruce Montague
   Erskine 35
2 *McFerran, Ann Patricia* 20
1 *McFerran, Lilian Sarah* 30
4 McFerran, Neil Vaughan 39
4 McGahey, Peter Richard 39
1 McGann, John Clement 22
1 McGarry, Michael Patrick 29
1 McGee, Thomas Vincent
   Peter 38
4 *McGirr, Idabell Josephine* 25

The number after a student's name indicates his tutor; the number before his name indicates his college standing as on 28 February 1966.

4 McGovern, Garrett Agustine
  Noel 2
1 *McGrath, Iris Bridget* 35
3 McGrath, Michael Patrick
  Colman 42
3 *MacGregor, Janet Cochrane* 17
4 *McGucken, Ida Vola Noella* 27
4 *McHarg, Susan Hilary* 36
3 McIlroy, James Alexander 19
2 McIlroy, Ronald Samuel 19
3 McIntosh, Ian Douglas 34
3 McKay, Ivan Alexander 42
4 MacKay, Neil Angus Martin 24
3 McKee, Colin William
  Robert 19
2 *McKee, Rebecca Jane* 36
1 *McKee, Ruth* 24
1 McKeever, Dennis George 22
4 McKenna, Terence John 35
1 *MacKenzie, Barbara Jean* 16
2 *McKerr, Felicity Anne* 17
1 MacKesy, David Poulter
  Thomas 23
1 *McKiddie, Madeline* 35
1 *MacKie, Christine* 25
2 McKillen, Terence Nigel 2
1 McKinley, Arthur Horace
  Nelson 42
3 McKinley, Ian Murdock 22
2 *McKinney, Maureen Ann
  Cameron* 25
3 *McLachlan, Elizabeth Jane* 30
4 McLachlan, Richard 20
2 *McLaughlin, Aileen Mary
  Frances* 16
1 McLaughlin, Niall James 38
1 McLay, James Alexander 22
3 *McLean, Norma Alexandra* 43
3 *McLeer, Diana Alison* 19
2 MacLean, Charles Andrew
  Bourke 29
1 Halford-MacLeod, Torcall
  Anthony Guy 16

3 McMahon, Hugh Campbell 39
4 *McManus, Kimberley Patricia* 36
1 *McManus, Susan Hilary* 16
3 McMaster, Philip Graham
  Wilson 17
2 *McMillan, Carol Ann* 36
2 *McMorran, Sheelagh Helen* 2
1 MacMullen, Bernard William 22
2 McMullen, Richard Anthony 19
3 *McMurray, Cecile Geraldine* 27
3 *McMurray, Moira Elizabeth* 30
2 *McMurray, Maura Jayne* 16
1 *MacNamara, Mary Margaret
  Anne* 30
4 McNamee, Martin John 27
3 McNeilly, Donald James 27
2 *McNiffe, Phyllis Kathleen* 39
1 McNulty, David Wilson 2
4 McNulty, Michael Stewart
  (Sch.) 26
2 *McQuillan, Angela* 19
2 *McQuillan, Deirdre Mary* 25
3 *MacQuillan, Hazel Ann* 34
3 McQuillan, Joseph David
  Alvin 16
4 McRae, Hamish Malcolm
  Donald 29
2 MacReady, Thomas Harper 30
3 McVeigh, John 38
1 *McVitty, June Helen* 34
3 *MacWeeney, Susan Katherine*
  (Sch.) 16
2 *McWhirter, Ilva Constance* 45
2 *McWilliam, Anne Heather* 27
2 McWilliams, Victor Francis 2

2 Macey, Timothy Ewon 35
2 *Madden, Joan Valerie* 16
3 Madill, William Robert 38
1 Madha, Michael Anthony 34
4 Madjd, Mohammad Hossein 22

The number after a student's name indicates his tutor; the number before his name indicates his college standing as on 28 February 1966.

Students on the books in arts

2 Magbadelo, Jonathan
  Adekunde — 17
1 Magee, Christopher John — 38
3 Magee, Frederick Isaac — 20
3 *Magowan, Helen Elizabeth* — 20
3 Magowan, Robert John — 43
3 *Maguire, Mary Elisabeth Ellen* — 30
3 *Maguire, Nuala Jane* — 20
1 *Maguire, Una Maire* — 38
1 *Mahoney, Mary Brigid* — 26
2 Majekodunmi, Koye Terence
  Marakinyo — 17
4 Malley, Arthur Dermod — 23
4 Mallinson, James Bernard — 29
4 *Mallory, Trina* — 27
1 *Malone, Adrienne Honor* — 26
4 Malone, James Anthony — 23
1 Malone, Leo John — 38
3 *Malone, Nuala Clare* — 26
3 *Malseed (née Mahood), Beryl*
  Eveline — 27
1 Manders, Barrington Seyhour — 20
3 *Manning, Anne Josephine* — 16
2 Maradufe, Asaph — 17
1 Marchant, John Bennett — 30
2 *Marcus, Margaret Ferguson*
  Maureen — 24
2 Markey, Patrick Owen — 29
1 Marks, Peter — 34
4 *Markus, Susan Irma* — 29
2 *Marlin, Elizabeth Willemien* — 34
1 Marr, Bruce Ogilvie — 39
3 Marr, Michael — 22
4 Marsh, Alan John — 25
1 Marshall, George Wilfred — 45
1 *Marshall, Pamela* — 34
1 Bannar-Martin, Brian
  Rawdon — 25
1 *Martin, Elizabeth* — 19
2 Martin, Eric — 23
2 Martin, James William — 22
4 Martin, John Scott — 24

2 Martin, John Stephen — 22
2 Martin, Patrick Fanshawe — 29
3 Martin, Robert Hans — 28
2 Martin, William Bryce — 45
2 *Masoliver, Chandra Sinclair* — 25
2 *Mason, Jill Marion* — 16
4 *Mason, Marguerite Jane* — 22
3 *Mathers, Joan Lesley* — 20
3 Mathew, Robert Knox — 29
4 *Mathias, Catherine Evelyn* — 27
2 Matkin, Christopher George — 35
2 *Matthews, Adeline Priscilla*
  Rosalind — 17
4 Matthews, Julian Richard
  Gadd — 27
3 *Matthews, Loveday* — 28
1 Boyd-Maunsell, Patrick
  Thomas — 24
1 Mawhinney, Alan Dales — 45
1 *Maxwell, Elizabeth May* — 38
2 Maxwell, Maurice Henry — 40
3 Maxwell, William Hewson — 20
3 May, James Garrett — 23
4 Mbwana, Frank — 24
3 *Meagher, Olga Eileen* — 17
1 Meaney, Frederick George — 22
3 Mears, William Thomas — 27
3 *Meiggs, Rosalind Jean* — 16
4 Melland, Charles Glencairn
  Beith — 19
1 Mellon, Richard Douglas — 17
1 *Mellors, Daphne Anne Claire* — 16
4 Mercer, John Phillip — 17
3 Mercer, Peter Crossley — 17
1 *Meredith, Mary Patricia* — 30
1 Merrick, William Brian — 24
3 *Messenger, Maire Josephine*
  Elizabeth — 16
4 Metcalf, Simon Railton — 20
4 Mew, Geoffrey — 17
1 Meyer, Harald Edward Karl — 19
1 Meyricke, Edward David — 24
1 Michael, Geoffrey Paul — 25

The number after a student's name indicates his tutor; the number before his name indicates his college standing as on 28 February 1966.

The number after a student's name indicates his tutor; the number before his name indicates his college standing as on 28 February 1966.

Students on the books in arts

The number after a student's name indicates his tutor; the number before his name indicates his college standing as on 28 February 1966.

2	Nixon, John Alexander	20
1	Nixon, John Frederick	22
1	Njoku, Sidney	23
4	Noble, Robert	35
3	Nolan, Anthony Joseph	17
1	Nolan, Martin Brian	23
3	Nolan, Thomas Ronald	23
3	Nono, Andrew Michael	28
2	Noran, Steven Frederick	34
4	Northridge, Robert Hamilton	22
3	Norris, David Patrick Bernard (Sch.)	35
3	Nayer-Nouri, Touradj	34
2	*Nunes, Jacina Ursula*	36

4	Oakley, Christopher Martin	29
4	*Oakley, Rosemary Clare Blathwayt*	36
3	*Oakman, Patricia Mary*	26
1	O'Brien, Anthony Derek	23
3	O'Brien, Brendan Thomas	27
1	O'Brien, Colm Murrough Vere	28
3	*Cruise-O'Brien, Fedelma Ann Lynd*	20
4	O'Brien, Martin	23
2	O'Brien, Paul Terence	32
3	*O'Brien, Sylvia Caroline*	26
3	O'Byrne, Neville Richard	20
1	O'Connell, John William	23
1	O'Connell, Julian Redmond	17
2	*O'Connell, Mary Veronica Gertrude*	30
2	*O'Connor, Catherine Margaret Mary*	36
2	O'Connor, Daniel Gerald Joseph	22
3	O'Connor, Richard Geoffrey	34
3	O'Connor, Richard James Anthony	23
3	*O'Connor, Sheila Mary*	23

4	O'Donnell, Hugh	37
2	O'Dwyer, Brendan Carew	23
4	Ó hÉigeartaigh, Cian Sáirséal (Sch.)	24
1	O'Ferrall, Conall John	16
1	O'Ferrall, Thomas Roderic Blacke	37
2	O'Farrell, William	26
1	Ogunyemi, Olajide Olugboyega Oresanyo	17
1	Okeke, Godfrey Chukwugozie	23
4	Okupe, Alaba Adegbo Yega	35
3	*O'Leary, Jacqueline Margaret*	23
4	Oliver, Julian Patrick Ritson	29
1	Olufunwa, Stephen Adefolarin	34
3	O'Mahony, Francis Joseph	30
1	O'Mahony, Paul Douglas	24
2	O'Meara, Michael Francis	22
1	O'Muirithe, Diarmaid	20
4	Onbowale, Babatunde Oladipo	23
2	O'Neill, Brian Clarke	22
1	*O'Neill, Ellen Robena Small*	19
4	O'Neill, Hugh John Louis David Samuel	2
2	*O'Neill, Margaret Mary*	39
4	*O'Neill, Marie Bernadine*	16
1	*O'Neill, Orla Kathleen*	28
2	O'Neill, Patrick Shaun	23
4	Ong, Tai Keng	23
3	Orchard, Peter Fleming	34
4	*O'Reilly, Clare Mary*	29
1	O'Reilly, Ian Rossa Christopher	40
3	*Ormsby, Janet Vaughan*	25
2	Orr, Brian Michael James	20
1	Orr, David Alexander	22
4	*Orr, June Audrey*	30
2	Osborne, Denis Henry	26
1	Osborne, William	38
2	O'Shea, Michael David	40

The number after a student's name indicates his tutor; the number before his name indicates his college standing as on 28 February 1966

Students on the books in arts

The number after a student's name indicates his tutor; the number before his name indicates his college standing as on 28 February 1966.

The number after a student's name indicates his tutor; the number before his name indicates his college standing as on 28 February 1966.

Students on the books in arts

2 Rietdyk, Denis Antony	22
1 *Riley, Maureen Catherine*	34
3 *Ring, Helen Patricia*	25
2 *Ritchie, Alison Iredale*	24
3 Ritchie, Ian	2
3 *Ritchie, Marie Alexandra*	44
4 Rix, Edward Martyn	39
2 Roberts, Ian Scott	22
1 *Roberts, Jane Morton McGregor*	43
3 Roberts, Norman Patrick	35
1 *Roberts, Susan*	20
2 Robertson, Garth Dundas	17
2 *Robertson, Jean*	36
3 Robertson, Malcolm Frank	27
3 Robinson, Alan Paul Seaton	30
1 Robinson, Charles Patrick	2
3 Robinson, Mervyn Oakman	43
3 Robinson, Michael Alexander	20
1 Robinson, Michael John Harold	34
3 Robinson, Nicholas Kenneth	29
1 Robinson, Peter Stewart Bruce	22
4 Robinson, Richard Anthony	29
1 Robson, Alastair Malcolm	34
3 Robson, James Johan	29
2 Roche, David Charles Henry	16
1 Roche, David O'Grady	23
4 Roche, Henry Gerard	26
1 Roddie, Alan Atkins	2
3 *Rodgers, Doris June*	16
1 Rodgers, Bruce Henry Arthur	38
3 *Rogers, Deirdre Irene Gwendoline*	20
2 *Rogerson, Clare Evelyn Mary Gerard*	25
1 Rokosu, Peter Ajibade Abayomi	26
2 *Root, Hilary Margaret*	19
2 Roper, John Paul	26
3 *Rose, Helen Josephine*	25
4 Rose, John Brian Loftus	20

4 *Rosen, Jutta Elizabeth Hedwig*	20
1 *Ross, Barbara Ann*	28
2 Ross, David Mabyn	40
3 *Ross, Elsie Jennifer Margaret*	27
1 Ross, John Derek Laying	22
2 Ross, Richard Ivan	2
3 Ross, William Cooper	19
1 Roundtree, Henry Edward John	39
2 Rowan, Edward Peter	27
1 *Rowe, Anna Phyllis*	27
4 Rowe, Clive Jocelyn	24
1 *Rowley, Rose Mary Teresa*	20
1 Maude-Roxby, Michael Leycester	16
2 Roycroft, Frederick Brian	22
2 Royds, John Formby	26
1 Royle, John Fanshawe	23
1 Rudd, Graham William	23
4 Ruddell, Michael Frith	22
3 *Rudnitzky, Anne Mary*	19
1 *Rudnitzky, Susan Emma*	19
2 Rushton, Kenneth John	35
1 Rusk, Derek Joseph	45
1 *Russell, Denise Howie*	43
4 *Russell, Judith Catherine*	19
1 Russell, Michael James	26
4 Russell, Roy Robert Baird	25
3 *Russell, Valerie Roberta*	19
3 Russell, William	17
3 Russell, William Michael	23
3 *Rutledge, Heather Elizabeth*	30
1 *Ryan, Andrea Mary*	39
2 *Ryan, Bronacha Frances*	44
3 Ryan, Michael Joseph	24
1 Ryan, Patrick Joseph	37
3 Ryder, Aidan Thomas Eugene	28
3 Ryder, Michael Antony Macleod	28
1 Rydning, Andreas	26
4 Rymer, Michael Vernon	29

The number after a student's name indicates his tutor; the number before his name indicates his college standing as on 28 February 1966.

The number after a student's name indicates his tutor; the number before his name indicates his college standing as on 28 February 1966.

Students on the books in arts

1 Simms, Christopher Michael 24
1 *Simms, Mary Katharine* 16
2 *Simons, Juliette Saskia* 19
4 *Muir-Simpson, Katherine Elizabeth* 40
3 *Simpson, Olive Elizabeth* 44
2 *Sinclair, Ailsa Mary Robertha* 26
4 Sinclair, Iain MacGregor 16
4 *Sinclair, Patricia Margaret* 36
1 Sinfield, Kenneth Desmond 39
3 *Singer, Ruth Elfreda* 19
2 Sinniah, Bharathalingam 23
1 Sinnott, John Brendan 39
3 Sheehy-Skeffington, Francis Eugene Denis 34
1 Sheehy-Skeffington, Richard Alan Louis 23
3 Skelton, Ross Murray 27
3 Slattery, Michael David 40
3 Slattery, Patrick Joseph John 35
4 Slowey, Gabriel Joseph 2
4 *Smale, Amy Louise* 29
2 Smiley, John Peter 30
2 Smith, David Alexander Caldwell 25
2 Baxter-Smith, David Cyril 2
1 Smith, David Patrick Alister 2
4 *Smith, Evelyn Hazel* 35
3 Smith, Howard Noel 23
4 *Smith, Jennifer Margaret* 36
3 Smith, Michael Aidan Paul 3
3 Smith, Peter Brandon 19
4 Smith, Peter Rowland 25
4 *Smith, Regina Mary* 2
2 Smith, Terence John Allfort 45
1 Smyth, Charles Francis 22
1 Smyth, Hugh Alexander 17
3 Smyth, Kenneth James 27
3 Smyth, Michael Thomas 2
4 *Smyth, Patricia* 20
4 *Smyth, Patricia Elizabeth* 29
2 *Smyth, Sharon Mary* 30
1 *Smyth, Victoria Ruth* 42

2 Smyth, Walter Ronald 17
2 Snaith, Martin Somerville 22
2 Snape, Clive 34
2 Snowdon, Thomas Patrick 22
1 *Soames, Evelyn Virginia* 43
2 Somerville, Julian John Fitzgerald 26
3 Soutar, Samuel Ian 19
2 *Southern, Susan* 25
2 Sowerby, Trevor John 16
1 Sowman, Francis Edward 35
3 Speers, James Neill 44
1 Speers, Samuel Hall 42
1 Spence, Derek Wilson 2
2 *Spence, Lucy Anne Kathleen* 35
4 *Spencer, Christine Anne* 24
4 *Spotswood, Anne Taylor* 24
3 Spratt, Henry Clifford 2
1 *Sproule, Heather* 42
4 Sproule, Thomas Albert 23
1 *Squire, Beryl Daphne* 17
4 Squires, Alan Goldsmith 29
2 *Stabb, Dinah Geraldine* 30
3 Stacey, Barry James 37
4 Stafford, John Dickinson 29
1 Stafford, Patrick Joseph David 29
4 Stainer, Thomas Frederick 29
3 Stamp, Richard John Morrell 35
2 Standen, Michael Robert 17
2 Stanford, William Alymer Charles (Sch.) 24
1 Stanley, Derek John Peter 26
4 *Stanley, Gillian Susan* 25
3 Stanley, James Derek 26
1 Stark, Michael Joseph 29
1 Starkey, James Harry 34
4 Steele, Norman John 35
1 *Steen, Anna Margaret* 42
4 *Steeples, Theresa Jill* 25
3 *Stephens, Margaret Evelyn* 27
2 Stephens, Richard Anthony Stuart 30
2 *Stephenson, Marjorie* 24

The number after a student's name indicates his tutor; the number before his name indicates his college standing as on 28 February 1966.

4	Stevenson, David	20
3	Stevenson, John Kennedy	28
3	*Stevenson, Linda Jane*	20
1	*Stevenson, Miranda Faye*	26
3	Stevenson, William Maurice	22
2	*Stewart, Helen Gilda*	16
2	*Stewart, Jane Elizabeth*	45
3	*Stewart, Kathryn Mary*	16
1	Stewart, Simon James	23
3	Stillwell, Robert John Taylor	35
3	*Stirling, Margaret Anne*	42
4	Stiven, Peter	20
4	Stock, David Christopher Livesley	16
3	Stocken, Peter Alfred Creswick	20
4	Stokes, Bruce Alister	22
2	Stokes, Daniel Patrick	29
1	Stokes, James Victor	19
4	Stokes, Patrick Francis Paul	25
2	Stokes, Simon Richard	39
3	*Storey, Jennifer Elizabeth*	22
2	Stone, Geoffrey Leonard Kirkpatrick	35
3	Stott, Michael Ann	17
3	Stoupe, Colin Archibald	29
4	Stout, Michael Oliver	16
3	*Street, Margaret Mary*	25
3	*Street, Paula Geraldine*	16
1	Strevens, Brian Edward	19
2	*Stringer, Caroline Ann*	24
2	*Strong, Elizabeth Anne*	35
3	Strong, Lieun Gerald Porter	24
4	Strong, Stephen Thomas	35
1	Stronge, Ronald James	37
2	*Stronge, Wendy Mary*	20
1	*Stuart, Rosemary Bliss*	42
3	*Stuart, Wendy Agnes Margaret*	30
2	Stuart, William Galland	26
2	Stubbings, John Simon	20
3	Stubbs, Peter John Morris	35
1	Sugars, John Colvin Richard	23
4	Sulzer, Dietlef Karl Ebenhard	22

1	Suter, David Andrew Izon	34
4	Sutton, John Stuart	23
2	*Swain, Mary Elizabeth*	19
1	Swan, Laurence Peter	28
3	Swan, Robert John Cockburn McKechnie	30
4	Swann, Edgar John	24
2	*Swarbrigg, Vivienne Eileen*	40
3	*Sweeney, Jennifer Anne*	44
4	*Sweetnam, Beatrice May*	27
1	Syme, Robert Graeme	28
2	Symes, Glascott Joseph Richard Mitchelbourne	17
2	Symmons, Edward Lockington	39
4	*Taggart, Diane Margaret*	24
2	*Barry-Tait, Dinah Amanda*	25
1	Talbot, Michael St John	35
4	Talbot, Richard Arthur	29
1	Tamanji, Ayonga	35
3	Tan, James Meng Kow	29
1	Tan, Siew Lay	34
2	Tan, Tee Juat	26
1	*Tanner, Susan Mary*	19
1	Tanner, William Arthur	26
1	Tansey, David Noel	38
4	Tarkang, Victor Ebai	40
2	Tate, George Denis	19
3	Taylor, Charles de Clare Studdhart	24
2	*Taylor, Christine Margery*	19
3	Taylor, David Robert	19
2	Taylor, Derek Keith	27
1	Taylor, Edmund John	17
3	Taylor, Ian Martin	37
3	*Taylor (née Aschenbrenner), Iris Margarethe*	19
1	*Taylor, Margaret*	19
2	Taylor, Rawdon Montgomerie	22

The number after a student's name indicates his tutor; the number before his name indicates his college standing as on 28 February 1966.

Students on the books in arts

1 Taylor, Philip John	25	
3 Taverner, Torquil Graham	22	
4 Teacher, Hugh Macdonald	27	
1 Teegan, Thomas Henry	16	
3 Telfer, Raymond Stuart	20	
2 Temple, Donald James	35	
1 Theumer, Markus Michael Christopher Rudolph	39	
1 Tho, Lai Fong	17	
2 Thomas, Roger Walwyn	17	
3 *Thomas, Sylvia Scott*	26	
3 Thompson, Andrew Edward Courtney	35	
2 *Thompson, Caroline Susan*	16	
4 Thompson, Francis Maurice	19	
1 Thompson, John Charles	20	
3 Thompson, John Daniel	27	
4 Thompson, Joseph Lefroy Courtenay	29	
3 *Thompson, Margaret Jean Fleming*	28	
2 Thompson, Martin George Henry	39	
3 Thompson, Michael Frederick	34	
3 Thompson, Robert William Harold	29	
4 Thompson, William George	23	
4 Thompson, William Warren	24	
2 Thorneloe, Michael Hugh	17	
1 Thorp, Nicholas Arthur	27	
3 *Thorp, Pamela Hilary Marian*	19	
3 Thorp, Terence Kingsmill	34	
4 *Thurley (née Felton), Wendy Elizabeth*	7	
1 *Tierney, Rhoda Margaret*	30	
3 Tighe, John Joseph	26	
4 *Timmons, Catherine Mary Therese*	23	
3 Timpson, James Patrick	23	
3 Evans-Tipping, David Gwynne	23	
1 Toft, David	26	
1 Tomkin, Giles	28	

2 Tomkin, Jocelyn	22	
1 Tomkins, Paul Stuart	39	
1 Tomkins, William	39	
3 Toms, Norman	17	
2 Toner, James Brian	40	
4 *Torrenslane, Alison*	17	
1 *Torrens, Phyllis Jean*	19	
1 Tosh, Joseph	2	
4 Towe, Robert Noel	29	
2 Tracey, John Patrick	26	
2 Tragett, Benjamin Richard Buchanan	36	
1 *Trenam, Petronella Maria*	44	
3 Trench, Brian Arthur Wilbraham	16	
4 *Trenerry, Deborah Margaret Tregarthen*	16	
2 Trevaskis, James Brian	20	
2 *Trohear, Patricia Martha*	16	
3 Tryfon, Andreas Stelios	37	
3 Tsotorvor, Emmanuel Kodzo	37	
1 Tucker, Charles Gordon John	2	
3 *Tucker, Dorothy Mary*	30	
1 *Tucker, Sheila Hannah Gordon*	16	
2 Tulett, Peter Alan	40	
1 *Tulitt, Philippa Mary*	30	
4 *Turbitt, Elizabeth Anne*	36	
4 *Turcan, Susan Lilias*	36	
1 Turkington, Geoffrey Albert	44	
3 *Turner, Jane*	16	
4 Twist, William John	26	
2 *O'Brien-Twohig, Brigid Mary*	16	
4 Twyble, James Kenneth	45	
1 Tyrrell, George Malcolm	22	
1 *Tyrrell, Susan Gay*	25	
4 Unwin, Roderic Maxwell	27	
3 Urch, Michael John	24	
4 Brock-Utne, John Gerhard	25	
1 Valk, William Edward	34	

The number after a student's name indicates his tutor; the number before his name indicates his college standing as on 28 February 1966.

1 *Adrian-Vallance, Elizabeth*
   Margaret   20
2 *Vance, Hilary Irving*   30
1 Vaughan, Beverley Seymour   16
3 Vaughan, William Edward   20
2 Veitch, Andrew David   30
4 Vernède, Robert Ian
   Cornellian   24
2 Verso, Robin Arthur Charles   32
1 *Veselsky, Katharina*   42
4 Vesey, Peter Lawrence   29
2 Vigar, David Thomas   2
3 *Vokes, Mary*   26

2 Waddell, William Derek   20
3 Wagstaff, David George   25
4 *Walker, Christine Mirabel*
   Charlotte Louis   36
1 Wallace, Arthur Vincent   39
4 Wallace, Christopher Brian   37
3 *Wallbank, Judith Phyllis*   16
1 Waller, Michael John   20
4 *Walmsley, Joanna Mary*   24
2 Walmsley, Sean Alasdair   20
1 *Walpole, Judith Carolyn*   27
2 Walsh, Aidan St Paul   29
1 *Walsh, Anne Margaret*   38
3 Walsh, Anthony Joseph   27
4 *Walsh, Caroline Wendy*
   Annabelle   27
4 Walsh, Gerald Walker   25
3 Walsh, Paul Roderick Dowse   29
3 Walshe, John Oliver   20
2 Walton, Derek Norman
   Travers   39
2 *Walton, Jean Margaret*   34
3 Ward, Richard John   26
1 *Wardlaw, Heather Hood*   38
1 Wardrop, Keith William
   Grange   39
1 Warner, Richard Anthony   44

2 Warnock, William Alan
   Keith   35
4 *Warwick, Patricia Ann*   27
1 Waterbury, Richard Colin   39
3 Waterman, Harold   35
4 Waterman, Stanley   2
1 Watson, David Craigmile   16
1 Watson, David Ronald   42
2 *Watson, Frances Patricia*   16
1 Watson, John David   23
2 *Watson, Kiera Louise*   27
4 *Watson, Maelissa Rose Mary*   35
3 *Watson, Valerie Gay*   29
3 Watt, Ronald Gordon Munro   29
2 Watt, Stephen Rupert   35
2 *Watters, Patricia Valerie*   24
4 Webb, Anthony John   29
2 Webb, Leslie John   24
4 Webb, Neale Thomas Justin   29
3 Weber, Jeremy   17
2 *Weir, Joan Alexandra*   20
3 Welch, David Michael
   Geoffrey   35
1 Welch, Peter Leonard
   McCurry   39
4 *Welland, Elizabeth Jane*   36
1 Went, David   35
4 Wesley, Paul Nolan   45
3 *West, Beatrice Elizabeth*
   Lenore   30
3 *West, Rosemary Norma*   19
2 *West, Sandra Margaret*   20
4 *Western, Caroline Clare*   27
3 Weston, Richard Guy
   Vaughan   16
4 Westwood, Clive Manne   24
4 Whelan, Howard Maurice   23
4 *Whidborne, Frances Anne*   35
1 Whisker, Francis Neville   20
1 Whiston, James Francis   44
4 Whitaker, John Christopher   24
1 *Whitaker, Nichola*   24
2 *White, Alison Barbara*   19

The number after a student's name indicates his tutor; the number before his name indicates his college standing as on 28 February 1966.

Students on the books in arts

The number after a student's name indicates his tutor; the number before his name indicates his college standing as on 28 February 1966.

T

STUDENTS IN OTHER CATEGORIES

The students included in these lists are mainly those whose names were not on the books on 28 February 1966. For convenience, however, some students whose names were on the books are included here. Their names are marked with an asterisk.

CANDIDATES FOR THE DIVINITY TESTIMONIUM NOT ON THE BOOKS IN ARTS
(21 men)

JUNIOR YEAR

*Bell, Charles William
Harman, Robert Desmond
Jardine, David John
McKelvey, Robert Samuel James Houston

*Mills, Hubert Cecil
*Parkhill, Alan John
*Semple, Studdart Patrick
*Sides, James Robert

SENIOR YEAR

Battye, John Noel
Black, Robert John Edward Francis Butler
Craig, Robert Joseph
*Crooks, John Anthony Irving
Dalton, Kevin
Dinnen, John Frederick

Ellis, John Wadsworth
Graham, Frederick Lawrence
McClatchie, Donald William
McKinley, Reginald Michael
Pike, Andrew Patrick
Pringle, Cecil Thomas
Sinnamon, William Desmond

CANDIDATES FOR THE DIPLOMA IN BIBLICAL STUDIES
(2 men + 1 woman)

*Collins, Henry Patrick
*Humfrey, Peter Edward

Phillips, Amy

STUDENTS IN LAW
(69 men + 9 women)

KING'S INNS STUDENTS

Appleby, Charles Mark
*Bourke, Henry Orme
Burke, Katherine Emilie Antoinette
Conneely, Michael Joseph
Doyle, Donald Francis Patrick
Govender, Oothamaseelan Candsamy
Henry, Leo Christopher

Hooper, Anson Garrett
Kennedy, Anthony
*Lindsay, Ronald Blennerhassett
Luykx, Hubert Francis Anton
Lynch, James Peter
McCluskey, Raymond Nicholas
Mall, Idris
Mayet, Ismail Ahmed

Students in other categories

*Mills, John Richard Patrick
Moores, Derek Charles
O'Leary, Michael
Omo, Michael Amuziam

Regan, Patrick
Staunton, Eoin Raymond Oliver
Timmons, Michael Finbarr
*Walsh, Anthony Joseph

SOLICITORS' APPRENTICES

Appelbe, Fergus Edward
Bolton, John Keith
Bradshaw, Eric Herbert Walshe
Brooks, Jonathan Philip Toppin
*Brunker, Eric Nicholas
*Crawford, Brian Victor
*Cullen, Patrick Anthony
*Donnelly, Andrew James Oliver
*Falkiner, Ninian Frederick David
Figgis, Thomas Fernsly
Foley, Felicity Mary
*Fray, William Oliver Houghton
Greenlee, Derek Hall
Hamilton, Blayney Chetwode
Hanahoe, Anthony Thomas
Hanahoe, Michael Ernest
Healy, Andrew William
*Kirwan, Anthony Michael Douglas
Linnane, Michelle Marguerite
Lovegrove, Richard Victor
McKenna, James Nugent Danial

*Macdowall, Robert Oliver
Magee, Brian Joseph Patrick
Maguire, Peter Martin
*Maxwell-FitzGerald, David
Molloy, Brian Godfrey
O'Connell, Mary Veronica Gertrude
*O'Donnell, Hugh Brian Joseph
O'Shea, John
*Potter, Dudley Alfred George
Quick, Simon Christopher
Kendrick
Reilly, Michael Christopher
*Robinson, Nicholas Kenneth
Smithwick, Paul Benedict
*Sowman, Francis Edward
de Lacy Staunton, Charles Cecil
Ronald Mary
*Strong, Stephen Thomas
Thompson, Jonathan Piers
*Waterman, Harold
*Williams, Robert Patrick Colin

LL.B. STUDENTS

Beamish, Pamela Mary
Bell, Celia Elizabeth Mary
Colhoun, Angela Freda
*Davidson, Andrew James Lloyd
*Farrall, John Robert
*Harries, John Wyndham Nevill
Henderson, Lynda Mary
*Ingram, Charles Frederick

*Mathew, Robert Knox
Maxwell, John Philip Barklie
*Morrogh, Peter
Ó hÉighneacháin, Padraig Seán
Raphael
Rice, Abraham
Turner, Jane
*Unwin, Roderic Maxwell

STUDENTS IN MUSIC

(31 men + 11 women)

*Bicker (née Bullock), Elizabeth
Margaret*
Bradshaw, Albert Harcourt
Calderhead, John Richard Wynne
Costigan, Marie Josephine

Dakin, Donald Hubert
Dobie, William Alexander
Draycott, Barry
Edmundson, John Charles
Ersu (née Jackson), Winifred Mavis

515

Students in other categories

Evans, Colin
Evans, John Glynn, M.A.
Greenway, Kenneth James
Grindle, Harry
Hallett, Frank Howard John
Hanley, Liam
Henshall, Arthur Edward
Hunter, James Malloch
Johnstone, Sandra Gillian
MacKenzie, Margaret Dolores
McGrath, Mary Colette
Moore, Frances Mary
Morris, David Hywel
Morrish, Donald James
Mulligan, Mary Margaret
O'Carroll, Fintan Patrick
Ormerod, David Herbert Abbott

O'Sullivan, John
Parker, Reginald Thomas Myles
Peffers, Audrey Marion
Rainey, Francis
Raynard, Alec Steele
Riley, Donald Henry
Roberts, Emlyn
Scarf, Christopher
Shillington, Eve Veronica Graham
Singh, Prabhu
Slader, Michael, M.A.
Slater, John Trevor
Stalker, William Hugh, M.A.
Weston, John Bernard
Wilkes, David John
Wilson, Pamela Margaret

STUDENTS IN MEDICINE, DENTAL SCIENCE AND VETERINARY MEDICINE NOT ON THE BOOKS IN ARTS
(92 men + 23 women)

Abbott, Bryan William
Addison, Assuman Ebenezer
Ahern, Michael Douglas
Angus, Charles William Gregor
Argyle, Geoffrey Malcolm Rose
Bacik, Edith Susan Milada
Bell, Donald William
Bickel, Jerome George
Blackman, Maurice
Boden, Michael Geoffrey
Bourke, Aubrey de Vere
Bradley, Anthony Michael
Bradshaw, John Richard
Braidwood, Michael Walter
Brown, John Ronald
Browne, Robert David
Burland, Jill
Chiu, John Wing Yee
Chiu, Jonathan Kai-Shun
Clements, John Marcus Murray
Cooper, Arthur Norman
Crawford, David Jamison
Crowdes, Robert Leslie
Cutler, Robin Stewart
Dane, Thomas Edward Brian

Danquah, Gloria Emily
Davidson, Brian Andrew John
Deane, Terence Horton Walker
Dick, Christopher Edward
Dickson, John Graham
Digges, Charles Nigel O'Neill
Dixon, Anthea Joly
Dowd, Doreen Elizabeth
Eakins, Sylvia Evelyn
Elmes, Roger John Robert
Eyers, John Gilbert
Fisher, John Melvyn
Fitzgerald, Raymond James
Floyd, Michael St John
Forson, Thomas Eugene
Fox, Michael John
Freedman, Derek Stuart
Gay, Raymond James
Geraghty, James Kieran
Gervais, Gordon Frazer
Graham, Catherine Margaret
Hackett, James Kevin William
Hafner, Daniel George
Hafner, Judith Abigail
Harris, Robert Standish Percy

Healy, Sara Louis
Hendron, Donal Patrick
Henry, James Ian
Hewitt, Thomas Leslie
Hodgins, George Adam
Huey, Kathleen Ann
Jeffares, Michael John
Keye, Richard Howard
Kilbey, Norman Albert William
Lall, Frank Ronald
Levine, Miles Rodney
Loh, Hung Soo
McCabe, Richard Peter
McElhinney, Mary Gertrude Bertha
McGinn, Brigid Jean
Macguire, John Dillon
McNeill, Harold George
Malone, Frances Patricia Marie
Martin, John Stirling
Michael, Philip Ernest
Middleton, Frederick Riach
   Ironside
Milliken, Alexander Donald
Milliken, Jacqueline Helen Jean
Montgomery, Gillian Joan
Moore, Robert Henry Stewart
Morrison, Cyril Charles Mitchell
Mowbray, Michael
Mulligan, Percy
Nairn, Jacqueline Ann
Newman, Hubert Neil
Nixon, George William Holmes
Nixon, James Robert
Ogunseinde, David Olatunji

O'Moore, Ruaidhri Roibeard
   Loaiseach de Valmont
Onadeko, Babatunde Owolabi
Otoo, John Christopher
Patel, Ramanlal Paragji
Peirce, Thomas Henry
Poots, Robert Victor
Raissian, Sayd Mohammad
Rattan, Carl Romesh
Robertson, Ranald Dundas
Rodale, Phillippa Ann
Rolfe, David Alun Huw
St George, Mary Alfred
Sarda, Kailashpati
Scott, Maeve
Seager, Stephen William James
Shanik, Donald Gregor
Shannon, Rosemary Susan
Simon, John Gerard
Slazenger, Cecil Ralph Michael
Smith, Teresa Victoria
Sundram, Felix Xavier
Taggart, David Alexander
Taylor, Ruth Viola
Thomas, David Edward
Thomson, Elizabeth Lesley
Thorpe, Richard Adrian Wells
Wan Min Kee, Wan Yew Khat
Wang, Wen-Shan
Watson, Ronald Gordon Kerr
Wilkinson, Julia Charlotte
William, John Rainsbury
Young, John Andrew

CANDIDATES FOR THE DIPLOMA IN GYNAECOLOGY AND OBSTETRICS

(9 men + 4 women)

Ahmed, Shaikh Mainuddin
Biblawi, Mahmoud Ezz-el-Din
   Ahmed Abdel Hafiz Fayad
Dharwar, Basavaraj Sangappa
El-Mansouri, Mahmoud Sadakah
Gogoi, Mahendra Nath
Hayat, Abu Muhammad Arizul

Holt, Betty Dora
Hossain, Altaf
Khamis, Foti Issa
Maqsoud, Widad Qasim
Naraine, Oudit
Siddiqi, Tahira
Sri-Hari, Vimala

Students in other categories

CANDIDATES FOR THE DIPLOMA IN
PSYCHOLOGICAL MEDICINE
(13 men+3 women)

Armed, Syed Anwar
Bennet, Edward Glin
Boyle, Neil Peter
Browne, Noel Christopher
Chaudhari, Gopal Rango
Cocks, Norman Martin
Collis, Robert John Maurice
Fennell, Michael John

Greene, Vincent Terence
Hynes, Mary Vivienne
Jackson, Edgar Basil Boggis
Mitchell, Ruth
Spencer, David John
Stack, Elizabeth Mary
Twomey, Michael Joseph
Whitty, Richard Joseph

CANDIDATES FOR THE HIGHER DIPLOMA IN
EDUCATION
(26 men+34 women)

Anderson, Christopher David
Benedikt, Helen
Benson, Kathleen Margaret
Berrill, Gerard James
Brett, Pamela Susan
Broderick, Daphne Margaret Agnes
Brown, Thomas Brendan
Bury, Mary Geraldine
Cannon, Conall Gerard
Chan, Janet Man Gay
Clancy, Christopher
Clarke, David William John
Cobbe, Joan Mervyn
Costello, Fintan Christopher
Craig, Aileen Mona
Crighton, Mary Joan
Crowe, Joy Margaret
Damji, Nizar Rajabali
Davis, Mary Catherine
Ellis, Olwen Densmere
Flack, Henry Holmes
Fryer, Kevin Peter Philip
Harper, Ruth Matilda
Henderson, Elspeth Anne
Hewitt, Abigail Stevenson
Hillis, Alice Daphne Esther
Hogan, Denise Mary
Holmes, Lorna Lilian Dorothy
Houston, Eleanor Jackson
Hughes, Rosamund Vivian Bourne

Johnston, Thomas Collis
Kerr, David James
Ledingham, George Milfull
Liddle, James Edward
McCarthy, Michael
McDonagh, James Daniel
McKeever, Denise Helena
McMahon, Dermot David
Macmillan, Rosemary Sara Doreen
Madden, Olive Elizabeth
Marsh, Kenneth Gilbert
Mew, Stella Gabrielle
Moinet, Marcella Marguerite
Murphy, Ann Theresa
Newman, Jennifer Florence
Rea, Michael Henry
Roche, Mary Sylvia
Russell, Wriothesley David Xavier
Ryall, Michael Richard
Sexton, Dermot Gerard
Shine, Michael Switzer
Skerrett, Alan Francis
Smith, June Elizabeth
Smith, Valerie Alison
Stanley, Kenneth James
Tinkler, Teresa
Toole, Susan Eileen
West, Derek Robert
Whitehead, Robin Harry
Wilson, Eva Helen

518

CANDIDATES FOR THE DIPLOMA IN SOCIAL STUDIES

(2 men + 16 women)

Angamia, Rashid Ahmed Suliman
Viner-Brady, Elizabeth Mary Joanna
Chow, Betty
Dawson, Mabel Winifred Joan
Dixon, Penelope
Garland, Olga Margaret Elizabeth
Harman, Gladys Almyra Jane
Hewetson, Susan Mary
Johnston, Patricia Elizabeth

Jones, George Thomas
Pinhard, Jane
Reid, Janet Elizabeth
Roberts, Diane Christine
Roberts, Diana Evelyn Rookherst
Sealy, Lucy Nuala
Timmins, Pauline Isobel
Tobin, Margaret Angela
Winter, Sheila Margaret

CANDIDATES FOR THE DIPLOMA IN PHYSIOTHERAPY

(45 women)

Abraham, Mary Yvonne
Ashraph, Marlene
Baxter, Jane
Boyce, Mavis Jessie
Buchanan, Desirée Avory Caroline
Chillingworth, Patricia Kate
Clarke, Fiona Sybil
Collier, Margaret Elizabeth Anne
Connell, Heather Patricia Du Quesne
Daly, Mary Patricia
Denham, Nuala Mary
Devereux, Philomena Anne Mary
Doyle, Johanna Mary
Faloon, Doris
Fox, Noneen Ethne
Harrington, Maeve Cabrini
Harvey, Elveen Myra Marsden
Hosford, Eleanor Jocelyn Anne
Jacob, Frances Ann
Jeffers, Heather Constance
Johnson, Ann Mary
Jones, Rowena Mary Mildred
Keatinge, Jacqueline Mary Wolseley

Killingley, Susan Edith Geraldine
King, Judith Marsena
Lamb, Catherine Marjorie
Lipscombe, Jane
McCauley, Helen Mary Emer
McKeown, Kathryn Jane
McNamara, Philomena Patricia Anne
Mackey, Dorothy Elizabeth
Mahon, Dympna Mary
Mitchell, Anne Hawthorne
Mullen, Sarah Winifred Diane
O'Herlihy, Brigid Mary Dympna
Pasley, Elizabeth Daphne
Perdue, Annette Edna
Reidy, Monica Anne Mary
Ridge, Joan Ethne
Seager, Elizabeth Anthea Dorothy Mary
Smyth, Eveline Valerie
Stephenson, Julia Gasteen
Tan, Eng-Siew
Tyrrell, Patricia Ann
Young, Helen Joan

Students in other categories

STUDENTS OF THE CHURCH OF IRELAND
TRAINING COLLEGE

(2 men + 50 women)

FIRST YEAR

Ailín, Prionséas Aléis Ní
(Allen, Frances Alicia)
Bháille, Eibhlineoir Coll Ní
(Bailey, Eleanor Hazel)
Bhorláin, Mairéad Eileana Ní
(Borland, Margaret Ellen)
Bhrádaigh, Jemima Eilís Ní
(Brady, Jemima Elizabeth)
Chesnutt, Sibéal Máire
(Chesnutt, Isabel May)
Chúipéir, Aidilín Ní
(Cooper, Adeline)
Corragán, Stiopháiní Noelle Máire
(Corrigan, Stephanie Noëlle Mary)
Fuireastail, Bhelda Áilis Ní
(Forster, Velda Alice)
Fhraoigh, Carilín Oilbhe Áine Ní
(Free, Caroleen Olive Anne)
Thomáis, Eibhlín Áine Ní
(Holmes, Eileen Anne)
Chiaráin, Bairbre Yvonne Ní
(Kearon, Barbara Yvonne)
Laoi, Córa Eibhlís Ní
(Lee, Cora Elizabeth)

Loingsigh, Áine Doireann Ní
(Lindsay, Anne Dorothy)
Leoin, Leislí Tomás Énrí
(Lyons, Leslie Thomas Henry)
Mhurchadha, Eilís Sinéad Ní
(Morrow, Elizabeth Jean)
Choinnigh, Déirdre Cláir Ní
(MacKenzie, Deirdre Claire)
Niocaill, Amy Mairéad Nic
(Nicholson, Amy Margaret)
Chaorthannáin, Míde Ní
(Rountree, Meta)
Ruiséal, Caitlín Padraigín Ní
(Russell, Kathleen Patricia)
Shearthain, Áine Eilís Ní
(Shorten, Annie Elizabeth)
Ghabhann, Helen Sorcha Ní
(Smith, Helen Sarah)
Stiofáin, Sinéad Mairéad Nic
(Stevenson, Jean Margaret)
Fuite, Eibhlín Máda de
(Whitten, Eileen Maude)

SECOND YEAR

Bairéad, Mairéid Goergina de
(Barrett, Myrtle Georgina)
Bhrattin, Ira Rebecca Ní
(Brattin, Ira Rebecca)
Chearra, Márta Eibhlín Ní
(Carson, Martha Evelyn)
Chothúun, Doris Thomásin Sara Ní
(Colhoun, Doris Thomasina Sara)
*Choiltealbhaigh, Eibhlíneoir
    Prionnseas Ní*
(Costello, Eleanor Frances)
Chorráin, Hilarí Eilís Ní
(Crean, Hilary Elizabeth)
Dhomhnaill, Nollaig Ainette Rebecca
(Daniels, Nowell Annette Rebecca)

Dhaibhidh, Robáirdín Eibhlín Nic
(Davidson, Roberta Eleanor
Dhochartaigh, Máiread Isibeal Ní
(Doherty, Margaret Isobel)
Éigear, Hilse Eiléana
(Eager, Hilda Helena)
Éimhín, Fraoch Clár Nic
(Evans, Heather Clare)
Ghilliard, Oibhe Eilis
(Gilliard, Olive Elizabeth)
Ghréacháin, Rae Silbhia Ní
(Graham, Rae Sylvia)
Hanbidge, Cristín Proinnseas
(Hanbidge, Christina Frances)

520

h-Íobard, Muirinn Eilis Audrey Ní
(Howard, Miriam Elizabeth
  Audrey)
Huston, Séarlait Áine
(Huston, Charlotte Anna)
Cheimmp, Síona Éilis de
(Kemp, Jacqueline Elizabeth)
Ghiolla Phádraig, Iréin Éilis Nic
(Kilpatrick, Irene Elizabeth)
Chinnseamháin, Vera Áine Ní
(Kingston, Vera Ann)
An Girr, Freda Liaimín Nic
(McGirr, Freda Wilamina)
Fhionnlaoich, Inez Eithne Nic
(McKinley, Inez Edith)
Fhionnlaoich, Rosabel Lidia Siobhán
  Nic
(McKinley, Rosabel Lydia Joan)

Students in other categories

Muilleora, Silbhia Sadhbh Sinéad Ní
(Millar, Sylvia Sophia Jane)
An Uasail, Leila Máire
(Noble, Leila Marion)
Poff, Eibhlín Griostain
(Poff, Eleanor Christina)
Shiaghail, Eithne Siobhán Ní
(Sheil, Edna Jane)
Seartan, Rós Jean
(Shorten, Rosemary Jean)
Bharren, Loftus Seósamh de
(Warren, Loftus Joseph)
Liam, Pearla Searlait Nic
(Williams, Pearl Charlotte)

ONE-YEAR STUDENTS
(13 men + 16 women)

Ash, Elizabeth Stanley
Aufochs, Hilde Marianne
Averill, Deborah Moore
Bowen, Kurt Derek
Burnham, Scott Joel
Caughron, Thomas Marshall
Christie, David Charles John
Declercq, Francoise Claude
Fergus, Elizabeth Blandyna
Ferris, William Reynolds
Flynn, Robert Allen
Frucht, Jamie Susan
Greite, Walter
Harsch, Jonathan Henry Hannum
Hudson, Jean Marie

Illig, Dale Walden
Johnson, Karen Bee
Kersch, Karen Sue
Leline, Leslie
McHugh, Fiona Blanaid
Mullikin, Kent Roberts
Norton, Lynne
Schoorel, Andriette Mathilde
Silberman, Renee Marcia
Stanton, Lynn Carol
Taft, Maria Herron
Wiksten, Judith Rae
Yarnall, Vanessa Montgomery
Graf Zu Dohna, Ruprecht
  Christoph

ONE-TERM STUDENTS
MICHAELMAS TERM 1965
(11 men + 18 women)

Aslund, Barbro Ingegard
Blennow, Kerstin Marie Louise
Bradshaw, Albert Harcourt
Bryson, Mary Elizabeth
Chambré, Rosaleen Aileen

Dollerup, Erik Cay Krebs
Erlingsson, David
Gronwall, Lena Maria
Hall, Tricia Leanna
Heroig, Carl Johann Georg

Students in other categories

Hogan, Sheila Mary Veronica
Hughes, Mary Jennifer Ann
Karlsson, Anita Elisabeth
Kilfeather, Hugh
MacKenzie, Margaret Dolores
Magnusson, Birgit Kristina
Markstrom, Sara Birgitta
Norman, Frederick Zircon Wilcox
Oskamp, Hans Pieter Atze
Korsgaard-Pedersen, Knud

Peffers, Audrey Marion
Shillington, Eve Veronica Graham
Staunton, Eoin Raymond Oliver
Sundgren, Bjorn Erik
Swisehr, Lina Thompson
Thomsen, Marianne Risbjerg
Von der Thusen, Joachim
Tui, Meeli
Wasen, Eva

HILARY TERM 1966
(5 men + 15 women)

Aslund, Barbro Ingegerd
Bjersö, Gunnel Katarina
Blennow, Kerstin Marie-Louise
Bryson, Mary Elizabeth
Chambré, Rosaleen Aileen
Cue, Beverlee Ann
Dicum, Henry Davinger
Dollerup, Erik Cay Krebs
Fernholm, Inger Margareta
FitzGibbon, Nicholas Kerr

Fulbright, Patricia Helene
Gentele, Jeanette Julia Elisabeth
Hall, Tricia Leanna
Hellbrand, Marie Louise
Iderot, Majken Agneta
Juneström, Eva Ingrid Margareta
Kelliher, Christine Mary
Norman, Frederick Zircon Wilcox
Sanders, Jocelyn Alvin Francis
Wunsch, Marianne

TRINITY TERM 1966
(4 men + 8 women)

Betinger, Pia Elisabeth
Chambré, Rosaleen Aileen
Cordova, Ronald Michael
Cue, Beverlee Ann
Fernholm, Inger Margareta
Finke, Behrend Klaus

Gentele, Jeanette Julia Elizabeth
Hall, Tricia Leanna
Juneström, Eva Ingrid Margareta
McIvor, James Stanley
Newman, Katherine Kincaid
O'Meara, Dominique John

CANDIDATES FOR HIGHER DEGREES
(223 men + 36 women)

PH.D.

Abd El-Motaal, Mohammed
    Hamdy Bahgat
Aboul'magd, Nadia Osman
    Mohammed
Ambrose, Thomas
Arnold, Lawrence James
Atkins, John Fuller
Baker, Kenneth Percy
Baxter, James Thomson

Bond, Brian Lewis
Bourke, Geoffrey Joseph
Boyle, Felix Paul
Brock, Catherine
Burns, Francis Walter
Butler, Christopher John
Byrne, Joan
Caldicott, Clive Edric John
Cantwell, John Bosco

Carson, James Frederick
Close, Anthony John
Cochran, David Samuel
Connor, John
Conry, Richard Joseph
Coughlan, Michael Patrick
Cox, John Winston
Crowley, John Patrick
Cummins, Derek Ormsby
Curtis, Robert
Dahl, Thor
Darcy, Laurence Edward
Davies, Gordon Leslie
Dooley, Michael John Thomas
Elliott, Ian
Empey, Clement Adrian
Evans, John Alba
Eze, Agom
Fekete, Antal Enore
Finch, Thomas Fraser
Flannery, James William
Francis, Neelamkavil Devassy
King-French, Iona
Fullerton, William Wardle
Gardiner, Peers Richard Rochfort
Gillmor, Desmond Alfred
Glynn, Thomas Edward
Greenwood, David Charles
Hall, Michael Amos
Hannigan, Finbarr Cornelius
Harkness, David William
Harris, Neville Robert
Harte, Francis Joseph
Hartin, James
Harvey, Dermot
Hatch, Charles
Hill, John Alan
Howe, Thomas Gilbert Barham
Hunter, Robert John
Hussey, Elinor Caroline
Hyde, Marlene Rosalind Mary
Jina, Abdulsultan Gulamali
Kaminski, Jan
Kavanagh, Patrick Joseph
Kazuno, Mitsuko
Keatinge, Neil Patrick

Kehoe, Constance de Muzio
Kennedy, Michael John
Kennelly, Timothy Brendan
Law, Therese
Lee, John
Lesi, Folorunso Ebun Akinboye
MacInerney, Mary Rhoda
McKillen, Michael Neil
McQuade, Eamonn
Mahmud, Kamal Raji
Martin, Graham Douglas
Megally, Fouad Hanna
Mitchell, Arthur Herbert
Mollan, Robert Charles
Moorhouse, Ellen Catherine
Moriarty, Christopher Ivor Dennis
Morley, Charles Trevor
Mulvey, Charles
Murphy, Catherine Alicia
Murphy, James Augustine
Murphy, Oliver
Murphy, Thomas
Murtagh, Thomas Norman
 Francis
Muthuswami, Sirugamani
 Vaidyanathan
O'Brien, Dermot John
O'Donoghue, Martin
*O'Donoghue, Siobhan Emily
 Fidelma*
O'Driscoll, Donal Joseph
O'Farrell, Patrick Neil
Ó Glaisne, Risteard Earnan
O'Hara, Charles Edward William
O'Morchoe, Charles Christopher
 Creagh
O'Neill, William
Oppong, E. N. W.
O'Sullivan, Denis Francis
Osuoji, Chibiko Iheanacho
Parker, William George
Phillips, William Edward Adrian
Pittion, Jean Paul
Pitts, Barry James Roger
Pollard, Walter Francis William
Pratt, Albert Creighton

Students in other categories

Pugh, David Michael
Reynolds, Christopher Graham
Richardson, Michael Thomas
Riyasaty, Shahla
Robins, Joseph Alphonsus
Rollin, Genevieve Julie Marie
Rooney, Seamus Augustine
Ryan, Dermot J. A.
Ryder, Rupert Joseph William
Sainsbury, Donald Marshall
Scaife, William Garrett Stanley
Scally, Bernard Gabriel
Scanlan, Paul Alexander
Schultz, Richard Wolfgang
Semple, David Leeson
Shah, Tara Prasad
Shields, Hugh Edwin
Kennedy-Skipton, Henry Kinmey
Smith, Joseph
Soulsby, John Allan
Staniland, Philip Anthony

Starr, Joseph Patric
Steinberg, Joshua Solly
Stevens, Richard John
Stilling, Roger James
Stuttard, Colin
Sweeney, Edward Joseph
Tait, Alan Anderson
Thompson, Alexander
Thornton, Edward Harold
Thurley, Geoffrey John
Greer Walker, Michael
Wallace, Michael Joseph
Walshe, Edward Thomas
Walton, Philip Wilson
White, Dean Guntner
Wilde, John Halahan
Wilson, Hill
Wilson, William Donald
Wingfield, Robert Talbot Rhys
Wisdom, George Brian

M.LITT.

Comer-Bruen, Marie
Carroll, Francis Martin
Condell, Jennifer
Corbalis, Bernard Charles
Fahey, Andrew Denis
Feeney, John Patrick
Ferris, William Reynolds
Finn, Kenneth Raymond
French, Frances Jane
Golding, Carole
Grantham, Mark
Greenleaves, Susan Jennifer Kelland
Chinery-Hesse, Mary
Hill, Colin Patrick Annesley Martin
Holmes, Robert Finlay
Holt, Jon Howard
Hull, Anne Bridget Georgina Mary
Kennedy, Raymond Thomas Christian
Lane, Stuart Nassau
Lewis, William Edward
Locke, Jeffrey Kethro
Lyons, Patrick Matthew David

McCaughey, James
McDonnell, Michael Francis
McGilvray, James William
Millen, Alan John
Ní Allurain, Eibhlin
O'Connor, Thomas Patrick
O'Donoghue, Maire Treasa
O'Donoghue, Patrick Joseph Thomas
O Dubhtaigh, Bearnard Ciaran
Patterson, Gertrude
Pike, Mary Edith
Pratt, Leighton
Salama, Fawzia Mahmoud
Saland, Arnold Gersow
Serumaga, Robert Ballarmine
Smythe, Colin Peter
Stock, Jonathan Curtis
Streather, John Godfrey
Thornley, Edward Price
Travis, Peter Warren
Weir, John Brian

Students in other categories

M.SC.

Abbott, Arthur John
Ahern, Thomas Francis Denis
Ahluwalia, Harmohinder Singh
Alcock, Ian
Baisya, Hira Lall
Browne, Michael James Pakenham
Bunbury, James St. Pierre
Burne, Geoffrey Christopher
  Stephen
Buttimore, Nigel Hugh
Carragher, James Paul
Cathcart, Robert Clive
Clark, Simon Crewe
Collery, Daphne
de Brit, Gerard John
Disit, Ramesh Chandra
Dockeray, Cynthia Joan
Doherty, John Joseph
Dundon, Edward Patrick
Fay, Charles William
Frayne, Robert Joseph
Griffith, David Herbert de
  Gorrequer
Guthrie, Graeme Stewart
Hallahan, Cornelius
Halligan, Ian David Franklin
Hammond, Robert Francis
Hanna, David Plunkett
Harrison, John
Hartigan, Patrick James
Harwood, John Andrew
Hatt, Thomas Lionel Patrick
Ibbetson, Rachel Mercia
Kirkham, Robert James Ronald

Langridge, David
Larkin, Barbara Sandra Claire
McCann, Eoin
McCarthy, Desmond Thomas
McCaughey, William John
Maynard, Haida
Moriarty, John James
Nathoo, Sadrudin Alibhai
  Rahemtulla
Noble, Noreen Joy
Nunn, William Richard
O'Connor, Gerald McCartian
O'Connor, Richard Michael
O'Neill, Frederick Rea
Peirce, Michael Alexander
Poole, Alfred Desmond
Raftery, Joan
Rawson, Alan Keith
Reid, John Charles
Reynolds, Patrick Edward
Roberts, Prudence Gabriel Nesfield
Robinson, John Alan
Seastopulo, George Demetrius
Sheridan, Donald Joseph Richard
Sheridan, James John Patrick
Stephen, Robert Charles
Thyer, Patrick Alan
Tobin, John
Tyrrell, Lynda Catherine
Vokes, Elizabeth
Millington-Ward, Athos
  Michaelides
Willoughby, Eileen Mary
Wright, George Brian

M.S.A.

Htun Aye, Maung
Browett, Eric Francis
Cooney, Seamus Liam
FitzGibbon, Finbarr Garbriel

Laydon, Dermot John
Lennon, Peter John
O'Canainn, Aodh
O'Dochartaigh, Breandan Antoine

NUMBERS OF STUDENTS IN
TRINITY COLLEGE ON 28 FEBRUARY 1966

I

Students on the books

	MEN	WOMEN	TOTAL
SCHOLARS OF THE HOUSE[1]	30	—	30
NON–FOUNDATION SCHOLARS[1]	—	5	5
PENSIONERS	1651	827	2478
	1681	832	2513

Students in other categories

	MEN	WOMEN	TOTAL
CANDIDATES FOR THE DIVINITY TESTIMONIUM	21	—	21
CANDIDATES FOR THE DIPLOMA IN BIBLICAL STUDIES	2	1	3
STUDENTS IN LAW	69	9	78
STUDENTS IN MUSIC	31	11	42
STUDENTS IN MEDICINE, DENTAL SCIENCE AND VETERINARY MEDICINE NOT ON THE BOOKS IN ARTS	92	23	115
CANDIDATES FOR THE DIPLOMA IN GYNAECOLOGY AND OBSTETRICS	9	4	13
CANDIDATES FOR THE DIPLOMA IN PSYCHOLOGICAL MEDICINE	13	3	16
CANDIDATES FOR THE HIGHER DIPLOMA IN EDUCATION	26	34	60
CANDIDATES FOR THE DIPLOMA IN SOCIAL STUDIES	2	16	18
CANDIDATES FOR THE DIPLOMA IN PHYSIOTHERAPY	—	45	45
STUDENTS OF THE CHURCH OF IRELAND TRAINING COLLEGE	2	50	52
ONE–YEAR STUDENTS	13	16	29
ONE–TERM STUDENTS	20	41	61
CANDIDATES FOR HIGHER DEGREES	223	36	259
Total	523	289	812
LESS STUDENTS IN MORE THAN ONE CATEGORY	35	8	43
	488	281	769
Grand Total	2169	1113	3282

[1]*Scholars not reckoned as on the books (see p. 478 above): 37 men (including 2 non-foundation scholars), 12 women.*

II

Students on the books arranged according to college standing

	MEN	WOMEN	TOTAL
SENIOR SOPHISTERS	373	194	567
JUNIOR SOPHISTERS	419	211	630
SENIOR FRESHMEN	357	197	554
JUNIOR FRESHMEN	532	230	762
Total	1681	832	2513

RECORDS

ELECTIONS TO FELLOWSHIP

ELECTIONS TO SCHOLARSHIP

ENTRANCE AWARDS

HONORARY DEGREES

HIGHER DEGREES CONFERRED

DEGREE EXAMINATION RESULTS

DIPLOMAS AWARDED

PRIZES AWARDED

PUBLIC LECTURES

RECENT PUBLICATIONS BY MEMBERS OF THE STAFF

RECENT PUBLICATIONS BY RESEARCH STUDENTS

THESES APPROVED FOR HIGHER DEGREES

BENEFACTORS OF THE COLLEGE

Note

A special supplemental volume is published from time to time as the Board may direct. It contains lists of Provosts, Fellows, Scholars, Professors, other officers of the University and College, and also lists of graduates and prizemen.

This volume was first published as volume 2 of the *Calendar* in 1901, and was published as volume 3 in 1906 and 1913. A further volume entitled *Trinity College record volume* was published in 1951.

ELECTIONS TO FELLOWSHIP 1966

*Elected to Fellowship in accordance with the
Consolidated Statutes, Chapter v, §7*
McCaughey, William Thomas Elliott

*Elected to Fellowship in accordance with the
Consolidated Statutes, chapter v, §6*
Smith-Keary, Peter Frederick
O'Morchoe, Charles Christopher Creagh
Simms, John Gerald

ELECTIONS TO SCHOLARSHIP 1966

CLASSICS
Stanford, William Aylmer Charles

NATURAL SCIENCES
Keatinge, Terence Heber

MODERN LANGUAGES AND LITERATURE
Aikins, Jennifer Mary

ENGLISH LITERATURE AND LANGUAGE
Bates, Ernest Timothy Brendan
Saldanha, Loyola Furtunato Bernard

EARLY AND MODERN IRISH
Ó Siadhail, Mícheál Lorcán

ECONOMICS AND POLITICAL SCIENCE
Glass, Norman Jeffrey

MEDICINE
Hartman, Mark Lawrence
Heaney, John Alan

ENGINEERING
Johnston, David Christopher
Algeo, David Robert Murison

ENTRANCE AWARDS 1966

The following candidates have been awarded these prizes subject to their entering College in 1966

AWARDS AT THE EXAMINATION FOR ENTRANCE SCHOLARSHIPS AND EXHIBITIONS

JAMES PATRICK KIDD SCHOLARSHIP
Mitchell, Rosamund Frances

LOUIS CLAUDE PURSER SCHOLARSHIP
Vipond, David Hugh

ENTRANCE SCHOLARSHIP
FitzGibbon, Nicholas Kerr

ENTRANCE EXHIBITIONS (CLASS I)

Saunders, Geoffrey Macaulay
Ford, David Frank
Thomas, Bernard Christopher
Grier, John

Walsh, David
Gray, Richard
Friel, Michael William

ENTRANCE EXHIBITIONS (CLASS II)

Lee, Ivan Victor
Tomkin, David Nevil Nelson
Allen, Norman Arthur
Talbot, Gordon Albert
Kingston, Irene Mary
Goodwillie, Roger North

Millar, John Minford
Pollak, Andrew John
Boyd, Robin McNeill
Kirkpatrick, Robert Wybrants
Johnston, Joan Hilary
Schloss, Barbara

WALTER WORMSER HARRIS PRIZE
Hamilton, James Henry
Martin, Patricia Helma
Matthews, Alan Henry

CHARLES WILKINS MEMORIAL PRIZE
Mayes, Brigid Anne

ANNIE ANDERSON MEMORIAL PRIZE
Corry, Geoffrey Alexander

WILLIAM ANDERSON EXHIBITION
Saunders, Geoffrey Macaulay

BIGGS MEMORIAL PRIZE
Friel, Michael William

ISABELLA MULVANY SCHOLARSHIP
Johnston, Joan Hilary

MATRICULATION EXAMINATION AWARDS

ENTRANCE EXHIBITIONS (CLASS I)
Reynolds, Richard Anthony

PREMIUM IN IRISH
Abbott, Henry James Joseph

HONORARY DEGREES 1965-6

DOCTORS IN LAWS
Andrews, Christopher Stephen
Masser, Alfred Henri

DOCTORS IN SCIENCE
Brambell, Francis William Rogers
Holroyd, Sir Ronald
Wright, Herbert Edgar Jr.

DOCTORS IN LETTERS
Clarke, Austin
Bruce-Mitford, Rupert Leo Scott

MASTERS IN ENGINEERING
Greer, Percy Howard
Gwynn, John David

HIGHER DEGREES CONFERRED 1965

Recipients of degrees honoris causa *are named separately on the preceding page. The names of graduates who received degrees* jure dignitatis *are marked with an asterisk.*

M.D.

Best, Frederick Ashley
Jaswon (*antea* Nathan), Nicholas
McCreery, William Cecil Charles
McCurdy, Alexander Matthew

Norman, Conolly Stewart
Pegum, John Michael
Scott, James Alexander
Storah, Peter Kenneth

Ph.D.

Attwood, Edwin Arthur
Boyle, Peter Howard
Carroll, Michael Joseph
Coffey, Victoria McCall
Davies, Peter Michael Cunliffe
Dawood, Marie Kamel
Downey, Nigel Edmund
Ekpo, Efiong Udo

Hurley, Finbarr Joseph
Khan, Mohammad Faheem
McCormick, John Hilgrove Cormac
McDonagh, Seán Patrick
Pinner Poole (*antea* Burton), Betty
Quraishy, Bibi Begum
Scott, John Martin
Simmons, Edward Roe
Yukawa, Takaaki

B.D.

Brown, John
Greer, John Edmund
Hall, William Norman
Hook, William John
Lowe, John Bethel
McGlaughlin, Basil Gordon Young

Rudd, Charles Robert Jordeson
Smith, Alexander Montgomery
Vaughan, Patrick Handley
Warner, Robert William
Wilkinson, James Noel Batthews

M.Ch.

Anderson, Patrick St George
Milliken, James Copeland

M.A.O.

Brennan, Robert Kenneth

M.A.I.

Harrison, Harold
McCabe, Richard Peter
Myles, Gordon Thomas

Higher degrees conferred

M.Sc.

Abrahams, John Roger
Browne, Alan Claude Henry
Victor-Byrne, Desmond Anthony
Caffrey, Maeve Frances Philomena
Ferguson, James Alexander
Hargaden, John Patrick
Harris, Anthony Barnard
Joyce, Cecilia Mary

Leith, Lewis
Madden, Robert Francis
Marwick, David Howie
Matthews, Peter Forbes Philip
O'Connor, Christopher Stephen
O'Neill, Eugene David
Reid, Brendan Patrick
Simmonds (*antea* Smyth),
    Eunice Dunbar

M.Litt.

Banerjee, Bholanath
Bowers, John Leslie
Chart, Charles Geoffrey
Combe, John Charles

d'Amico, Tommaso
Dooney Seán
Smith, Martin Ferguson

M.S.A.

Crawford, Thomas Henry
Kane, Alastair George
Moroney, William
Murphy, Patrick Joseph

Quinn, Frank
White, John Joesph
Wynne, Michael Brendan

DEGREE EXAMINATION RESULTS 1965

The results recorded are those of examinations held during the calendar year 1965. The names of successful candidates are arranged in alphabetical order within classes, except in the case of moderatorships where the names of successful candidates are arranged in order of merit within classes. The inclusion of a candidate's name does not imply that he has had the degree conferred upon him.

MODERATORSHIP EXAMINATIONS

Mathematics

FIRST CLASS
Oldham, Elizabeth Evelyn
Williams, David Henry
Roberts, Prudence Gabriel Nesfield

SECOND CLASS (FIRST DIVISION)
Winterbottom, Robert

THIRD CLASS
Hargrove, Marycita Jane

Classics

FIRST CLASS
Cobbe, Hugh Michael Thomas

SECOND CLASS (SECOND DIVISION)
Hodgson, John
Lavery, Peter Montgomery Graham
*Davies, George Mark Renshaw
*Pritchard, Arthur George Willman
*Stevenson, Christopher James
Hannon, Michael Stewart Moore

THIRD CLASS
Thompson, Paul Christopher

Mental and Moral Science

SECOND CLASS (SECOND DIVISION)
Alscher, Peter Jack
Mosesson, Michael Anthony
Rivett, John Graham Player
Burleton, Prudence Margaret
Kenrick, Judith Ann
*Turnbull, Geoffrey David
Tylor, John Edward

* *Indicates students placed equally with one another in each group.*

Degree examinations

THIRD CLASS

Newling, Michael Arthur
Dieneman, Marisa Louise
Schneider, Ann Morley

SUPPLEMENTAL MODERATORS

SECOND CLASS (SECOND DIVISION)

Anger, Patrick Christopher Stanley

ALLOWED B.A.

Hope, Ronald Alexander

Natural Sciences

BACTERIOLOGY

SECOND CLASS (FIRST DIVISION)

Tweedy, Jean Margaret
Burnett, John McNiven

SECOND CLASS (SECOND DIVISION)

Brookes, Jean Patricia

SUPPLEMENTAL MODERATORS

THIRD CLASS

Irwin, Margaret Helen

BIOCHEMISTRY

FIRST CLASS

Morgan, Michael James
McKillen, Michael Neil

SECOND CLASS (FIRST DIVISION)

*Hill, John Alan
* Tyrrell, Lynda Catherine*
Tinn, Richard Michael
Grene, Ruth
*Harvey, Dermot
*Wormell, Richard Oliver Wilson

SECOND CLASS (SECOND DIVISION)

Le Clerc, Cleome Susan
*Nesbitt, Samuel George Selby
Morgan, Leo Michael

SUPPLEMENTAL MODERATORS

SECOND CLASS (SECOND DIVISION)

Johnston, Elizabeth Anne

---

* *Indicates students placed equally with one another in each group.*

BOTANY
SECOND CLASS (SECOND DIVISION)
Lambert, Michael Roderick Kirkby

CHEMISTRY
FIRST CLASS
*Ronayne, Jarlath
*Dodd, George Henry
*Burns, Francis Walter

SECOND CLASS (FIRST DIVISION)
Louis, Charles Francis

SECOND CLASS (SECOND DIVISION)
O'Connor, Richard Michael
Hanna, David Plunkett
Mitchell, Teresa Helena

SUPPLEMENTAL MODERATORS

SECOND CLASS (SECOND DIVISION)
Hatt, Thomas Lionel Patrick

GENETICS
SECOND CLASS (FIRST DIVISION)
Atkins, John Fuller

GEOGRAPHY
THIRD CLASS
Osman, Patricia Margaret
Hughes, Helga Mary

SUPPLEMENTAL MODERATORS

SECOND CLASS (FIRST DIVISION)
Bloomer, Leslie Victor

GEOLOGY
FIRST CLASS
Chatterton, Brian Douglas Eyre

SECOND CLASS (FIRST DIVISION)
Meldrum, Andrea Herbert
Crow, Michael John

SUPPLEMENTAL MODERATORS

SECOND CLASS (FIRST DIVISION)
Marten, Brian Ernest

* *Indicates students placed equally with one another in each group.*

Degree examinations

PHYSICS

SECOND CLASS (FIRST DIVISION)

Townsend, Susan Jennifer Mary
O'Neill, Frederick Rea
Gough, Mark Christopher

SECOND CLASS (SECOND DIVISION)

Oliver, Michael Bernard

THIRD CLASS

*Bolton, David John
*Catty, Michael Anthony
*Clarke, David William John

SUPPLEMENTAL MODERATORS

SECOND CLASS (SECOND DIVISION)

Wafer, John Anthony

THIRD CLASS

Pettit, Alexander
Spearman, John Litting
Smith, John Michael Lawrence

ALLOWED B.A.

Pender, Francis Richard

ZOOLOGY

FIRST CLASS

Hinde, Francesca Rose D'Arcy
Okely, Elsine Frances
Neill, Caroline Helen

SECOND CLASS (FIRST DIVISION)

West, Alexander Brian

SECOND CLASS (SECOND DIVISION)

Fahy, Edward David
Everett, George Victor
*Jina, Abdulsultan Gulamali
*Spence, John Andrew

THIRD CLASS

Richardson, Alison Janet

★ *Indicates students placed equally with one another in each group.*

Modern Languages and Literature[1]

COURSE A

FIRST CLASS
Whitehead, Celia Felicity, FG
Pollen, Margaret Mary Clare, F IT

SECOND CLASS (FIRST DIVISION)
Lillie, Elisabeth Mary, FG
de Larrabeiti, Michael, EF
Mitchell, Hilary Mary, EF
English, Hugh Martin McDowell, FG
McDougall, Lorna McLaughlan, FG
Cubitt, Helen Mary Patricia, FG

SECOND CLASS (SECOND DIVISION)
Crawford, Ruth Victoria, FG
Wilson, Margaret Eleanor Elizabeth, FG
Cannon, Conall, FG
Morrow, Harold, EF
Stanbridge, Patricia Ann Eleanor, F IT
Ryan, Ann Elizabeth, FS
Cemlyn Jones, Michael Liam Patrick, FS
Reid, Margaret Anne, F IT
Webb, Susan, GS
Gardiner, Maureen Montgomery, EF
Titterington, Sheila Margaret Dawn, GS
Browne, Rosemary Margaret, F IT
Crawford, Wilbert, EF
Wilkinson, John Dirk, FG
Garner, Susan Elizabeth, EF
Sevenoaks, Jill, EF
Stanford, Melissa Dorothy, EF

THIRD CLASS
Logan, Elizabeth Isabella, FS
Green, Valerie Joan, EF
Doyle, Deirdre Anne, EF
Kennedy, William Torrens, EF
Kyle, Elizabeth Mary, FG
Bateman, Diana Mary, FS

SUPPLEMENTAL MODERATORS

FIRST CLASS
Hulton, Peter Richard, EF

[1] The languages taken by each candidate are indicated as follows: E English F French, G German, I Irish, It Italian, S Spanish.
    * *Indicates students placed equally with one another in each group.*

Degree examinations

SECOND CLASS (SECOND DIVISION)

Spence, William Lewis McCarroll, EF
Charmant, Eileen Elizabeth, F IT
Egan, Jennifer Margaret, FG

English Literature and Language

COURSE B

FIRST CLASS

Kelly, John Stephen
Graham, Ranald Ian Mackenzie

SECOND CLASS (FIRST DIVISION)

Swales, Mia Patricia

SECOND CLASS (SECOND DIVISION)

George, Vicki Anne
Gilliam, Beatrice Nina
Lowry, Deirdre Suzanne
Brodie, Elizabeth Juliet
Loxton, David Robert
Horlock, Wendy Jane
Weale, Anthony
Goldsmith, Angela Rosaleen
Whitehead, Ann Thornton
Stamp, Caroline Anne Morrell
Middleton, Meonetta Mary Tessimond
Christie, David Charles John
West, Derek Robert
Slattery, Anne Frances
★*Daybell, Patricia Jane*
★Kennedy, Malcolm Keith

THIRD CLASS

Maloney, Timothy John

Ancient and Modern Literature[1]

FIRST CLASS

de Vere White, Deborah, LE
Johnston, Jennifer Mary, LG
Jack, Margaret Elizabeth Jean, LG

SECOND CLASS (SECOND DIVISION)

Blackburn, Jean, LE
Whitehead, Robin Harry, LG

THIRD CLASS

Chapman, Valerie Jean, LF

[1] The symbol L after a name denotes Latin. The modern language taken is denoted as in Moderatorships in Modern Languages and Literature.

★ *Indicates students placed equally with one another in each group.*

Hebrew and Oriental Languages

SECOND CLASS (FIRST DIVISION)

Stark, Jurgen Kurt
Bates, Cecil Robert
Warner, Sean Michael

SECOND CLASS (SECOND DIVISION)

Aufochs, Helen Miriam

SUPPLEMENTAL MODERATORS

THIRD CLASS

Robinson, Cynthia
Harman, Robert Desmond

History and Political Science

FIRST CLASS

Kelly, Patrick Hyde

SECOND CLASS (FIRST DIVISION)

Redston, Colin Frank
*Bulford, Christopher Leonard
*Lewis, Jeremy Morley
*McBratney, Samuel
*MacKeown, Hugh Neil

SECOND CLASS (SECOND DIVISION)

Labbett, Beverley David Curtis
Craig, Jeremy Michael
Amangala, George Nakenayan
Bennett, Richard Lowry
MacGiffin, Kevin Henry Pratt
Bernard Smith, Marilyn
Irons, Peter Nicholas Lawrence
Blackley, Virginia Ethel Katherine
Shaw, David Carson
Fisher, Peter Hugh
Pilkington, Patricia Fiona
*Whitcomb, Ian Timothy
Wodehouse, Carolyn Persis
Jackson, Suzanne Cerise
*Liddle, James Edward
*Perrin, Donald Geoffrey
Saunders, Malcolm Jeffrey
Harris, Michael Maurice Grendon
Fehling, Christian Evan Anthony

★ *Indicates students placed equally with one another in each group.*

Degree examinations

Rahilly, *Christine Juliet*
McCloughan, William

THIRD CLASS
McCloskey, Leo Christopher

SUPPLEMENTAL MODERATORS
SECOND CLASS (SECOND DIVISION)
Moir, Martin James Gordon
Breen, Charles Winston

Economics and Political Science

SECOND CLASS (FIRST DIVISION)
Hutchinson, William Raymond
McDonald, Michael Brendan
Kendle, Roger James

SECOND CLASS (SECOND DIVISION)
Lowry, Eric Hamilton
Roche, Michael John
Ervine-Andrews, Robert Marcus
Whitehead, Paul Anthony
Horsley, Jefferson Andrew
Knott, Howard Boardman
*Halliday, Robert John Douglas
*Merrick, Robert Cecil
Robinson, John James Michael Laud
McMahon, Patrick Christopher
Simms, Nicholas Arthur Lewen
Duncan, Richard Howard
Williamson, Edythe Moira
Grant, Elspeth Parker
Stitt, John Lanktree

THIRD CLASS
Kemp, Richard John
Neil, Ronald George
O'Farrell, James Brendan
*Smith, Alan Huw
*Dunn, David John Hedley
Serumaga, Robert Bellamino
Deane, Brian Murrough
Campbell, Keith Charles
Charles, John Michael
Shillington, Anthony Drummond Graham
de Goguel, Constantine de Toulouse Lautrec

★ *Indicates students placed equally with one another in each group.*

Coker, John Baptist Hutchinson
Orr, Nigel Christopher

SUPPLEMENTAL MODERATORS

THIRD CLASS

Bolton, Gordon Sloan Bonner

Legal Science

SECOND CLASS (FIRST DIVISION)

Elliott, Fraser Caldwell

SECOND CLASS (SECOND DIVISION)

Milmo, John Boyle Martin
Swabey, Ian Martin Stephen
O'Connor, Trissa Garland
Orange, John Robert Wellwood
Stocken (née Wood), Dinah Maire
Pocock, Brian Leo
Cairns, Hugh Andrew David
Morrow, Clare Elizabeth
FitzHugh, Hugh William
Rankin, Peter James
Rountree, Robert James Stanley

THIRD CLASS

Moriarty, Bruce Henry
Sampson, Albert Agyin
Woodward, Richard Anthony

SUPPLEMENTAL MODERATORS

THIRD CLASS

Barnett, Ruby Shai Chan

U

Degree examinations

ORDINARY DEGREE OF B.A.

Medical students, and students in other professional schools, who qualify for the B.A. degree are omitted from these lists.

General Studies

June 1965

RESPONDENTS

Broderick, Daphne Margaret Agnes
Colhoun, Iris Alexandra
Laverty, Margaret
Marsh, Kenneth Gilbert
Percival, Ann Evelyn Rive
Poole, Alfred Desmond
Wayne, Arthur Westcott
West, Michael John

CLASS I

Beggs, Margaret Ann
Byrn, Rosamund Anne McDermot
Cobb, Patricia Anne
Ellis, Olwen Densmere
Mahon, Norman Derek
Merson, Elizabeth Ann

Mitchell, Janet Margaret
Mornin, Rosemary Eccles
Shaw, Paul George
Smith, Brian Eric
Turtle, Margaret Elizabeth

CLASS II

Adams, Irene Anne
Adams, Norman John
Aldridge, Patricia Mary
Al Kathiri, Ghalib Ali
Anderson, Christopher David
Austen, Stephen Conway
Benedikt, Helen Ann
Benson, Kathleen Margaret
Berry, Olive Elizabeth Margaret
Booth, Timothy Thomas
    Wentworth
Bridges, Lesley Frances
Stafford-Clark, Maxwell Robert
    Guthrie Stewart
Conlan, Beatrix Vance
Connolly, Stuart Malcolm
Cousley, Elizabeth Moira
Darley, John Edward
Dickson, Penelope Jayne
FitzGerald, Grania Mary Southwell

Fountaine, Richard Maurice
Fryer, Kevin Peter Philip
Galbraith, Ruby Heather
Gibson, Rosemary Elizabeth Jane
Gilmour, Michael Barton
Gittins, Margaret
Good, Donal Stanley Hamilton
Gordon, Alan Julyan Maitland
Grafton, Joseph Errol
Graham, Geoffrey
Graves, John Allan
Gray, June Elizabeth
Grimson, Brian
Halpin, Deborah Jane Teresa
Hamisi, Mgeni Musa
Harper, Ruth Matilda
Haslett, John Trevor
Henderson, Elspeth Anne
Hillis, Alice Daphne Esther
Holmes, Lorna Lilian Dorothy

546

Hope, Michael Edmund
Horlin, John Robert
James, Helen Margaret Glendon
Kee, Alicia Gertrude
Kilpatrick, David Edward George
Langfield, Paul Francis
Ledingham, George Milfull
Leitch, John Moore
Love, John Blackwood
McBratney, Maralyn
McBride, Moire Alexander
McCabe, James Francis
McDonald, Florence Roberta
Macfie, Sally Anne Stewart
McKeever, Denise Helena
Mackenzie, Michael Sydenham
McMahon, Patricia
Marshall, William Raymond
  Kennedy
Martin, Laetitia Mary Julia
Maxwell, Aileen Mary
Mew, Stella Gabrielle
Moody, Catherine Margaret
Mooney, Valerie June
El Mumayiz, Ibrahim
Nesbitt, Katherine
Noble, Noreen Joy

Parkinson, John Leslie
Porter, Arthur Gwyn
Pruden, Robert John
Read, Robert Frederick
Renwick, Daphne Margery
Rivington, Pamela Ann
Roberts, Thelma Frances
Ross, Gillian Mary
Russell, Wriothesley David Xavier
Shine, Michael Switzer
Smith, Valerie Alison
Snellgrove, Paul Nicholas
Speidel, Trevor Barton
Storry, Michael Francis
Suter, Rosemary Anne Izon
Theaker, Anthony Peter Frank
Valentine, Paul
Walker, Terence Arthur
Watson, Charles Alexander
Watson, Fiona Munro
Wauchope, Emily Elizabeth
West, William Henry
Whinney, Christopher Francis
  Colebrooke
Williams, George Maxwell Frazer
Wilson, Carol Patricia
Zakariya, Amjad Abdul-Kader

CLASS III

Ervine-Andrews, Felicity Mary
Barker, Elizabeth Winifred Ridley
Benson, Pamela Josephine
bin Salleh, Mohammad Radzi
Brinton, Sarah Ann
Broderick, Madeline Frances
Campbell, Helen Isobel
*Clotworthy, Suzanne Elizabeth
  Keller*
Conneely, Michael Joseph
Craig, Aileen Mona
Davis, Peter William
Dollin, Michael
Donovan, Nancy Gillian
Evans, Edwin Owen
Falls, David Wesley
Feldman, Samuel Stanley Barry
Flack, Henry Holmes

Ganly, Elizabeth Ruth
Heaton, Martin Christopher
  Crispin
Hennessy, Julian Michael Brendan
Jacobson, Laurence Walter
Stainton-James, Ian Charles
Jamina, Victor Francis
Jennings, Lesley Hope
Knight, Peter Richard Clifford
Lloyd, David John
Loughridge, Carol Madeline
Ludlow, Margaret Joyce
McCullagh, John Stuart
McMillan, Rosemary Sara Noreen
Abdel-Mutaal, Maamoun Abdel
  Mutaal Mohamed Abdulla
Nathoo, Sadrudin Alibhai
  Ramtulla

547

Degree examinations

More-Nisbett, Roger Hamilton
Potter, Dudley Alfred George
Pratt, James Alexander
Raghavan, Narasimha Vijaya
Rea, Michael Henry
Richards, Julia Rosemary Olivia
Shannon, John Bartley
Shepherd, Norma Frances Elizabeth
Sheppard, Susan Elizabeth
Skerrett, Alan Francis

Smith, George Edward Victor
Smith, Robert Alan
Tait, Frances Shirley
Tipping, Crawford Henry
Tyrrell, Eithne Mary
Tyrrell, James Stewart
Waldron, David John
Wheeler, Joyce Hill Elizabeth
Wilkinson, Clive Philip
Wilson, Eva Helen

October 1965

CLASS II

Black, Norman George William
Carroll, Justin Edward

Hughes, Anna Claire
Thal Larsen, Gilles

CLASS III

Alexander, Daphne Margaret
Armstrong, Vernon Walter Fowler
Broderick, Gladys Maureen Wilhelmina
Campbell, Elizabeth Sarah Frances
Carson, Eileen Jane
Corbett, Daniel Arthur Swan
Gyves, Michael

Johnston, Douglas Alexander
Lau, Pui Chuen Anthony
Love, Joan Lesley
Massey, Pauline Xenie Claudine
Naldrett, Monica Anne
Serumaga, Emmanuel Makaato
Tinkler, Teresa
Walker, Brian

Natural Sciences

June 1965

Barton, Anthony Arthur Royds
Blatchley, Simon Polwhele
Coates, Beverley Eden
Dormer, Terence Robert
Gordon, Brian Malcolm
Levinge, Susan Maureen
McDowell, June Charlotte

Onions, James Thomas Victor
Roberts, Christopher William
Scanlan, Terence John David Tennant
Shorland, Prudence Mary
Smiley, Samuel James Franklin

September 1965

Camier, John Edward Graham
Higgins, Michael John Robert
Lyndsay, David Erwin
Mackay, Michael Neil
Markham, Leslie Howard

O'Callaghan, Frederick Cornelius Westropp
Okoro, Ernest Ogbanno
Pearson, David Keith
Peel, Anthea

548

DEGREES IN PROFESSIONAL SCHOOLS

LL.B. EXAMINATION

Trinity term, 1965

CLASS II

Barnett, Ruby Sai Chan
Cairns, Hugh Andrew David
Dudley, James Nicholas Marshall
Hall, Julian
Milmo, John Boyle Martin
Robinson, Christopher James
Swabey, Ian Martin Stephen

UNCLASSED

McCaughey, Jayne Stewart

Michaelmas term, 1965

CLASS II

Pratt, Iain Robert Macdonald
Watson, Maelissa Rose Mary

M.B., B.CH., B.A.O. EXAMINATION

Trinity term, 1965

SECOND CLASS HONORS
Henry, Mary Elizabeth Frances

PASS

Akinsete, Valentine Omokehinde
Atkins, Maurice
Bowell, Roger Edward
Brattman, Richard Howard
Chen, Lena Ling Fen
Cosgrove, Ian Michael
Cudworth, George Hitchon
Dornan, John Dunwoodie
Fogarty, Anthony John
Frazer, Edith Valerie
Gibbons, Maeve Anne
Heaton, Juliet Mary
Heney, Niall Mercer
Inglis, Cecil Hammond
Kiesselbach, Nikolaus Hans Karl
Lai Fat Fur, Weng-Kun
Lavan, Stella Bebin
Lung, Charles Pak Chin
MacKeith, James Alexander Culvin
McKenna, Bridget Teresa
Mackey, Desmond Alexander George
Maingay, Christopher Hugh
Moore, Geoffrey Wescombe
Nash, William Norman Cecil
Prevatt, Francis Courtney
Pringle, Clare
Sinanan, Kenneth
Soiland, Henrik
Teh, Yew Yin
Trimble, William George Clements
Varian, John Patrick Werge
Whitney, Hugh Raymond Hatton
Williamson, Brian Richard James

Degree examinations

Michaelmas term, 1965

PASS

Bourke, Oliver Paget
Develter, Herman Godfried Alfons Henri
Hudson, Robert Basil Spencer

B.DENT.SC. EXAMINATION

Trinity term, 1965

PASS

Boursin, Charles Edward
Farrant, Robert Samuel
Ross, Peter John Scott

Michaelmas term, 1965
Kirwan, Miriam Ann

M.V.B. EXAMINATION

Trinity term, 1965

PASS

Dignam, George Leslie
Donaldson, Alexander Ivan
Donaldson, Robert Stewart
Thompson, Thomas Raymond

Michaelmas term, 1965

PASS

Bell, Peter David Montrose
Langley, Oliver Henry

B.A.I. EXAMINATION

Trinity term, 1965

FIRST CLASS HONORS

Plant, John Edward

SECOND CLASS HONORS

Alcock, Ian
Browne, Michael James Pakenham
Clarke, Geoffrey Richard
Clifford, Paul Geoffrey
Corbally, Bernard Humphreys
  Clement

Coulter, John Patrick
Gorman, Michael Charles
Guthrie, Ian Robert
Leeson, Alan William
Lloyd, Trevor Henry
Sides, John Patrick

PASS

Banks, Clayton Hatton
Blogh, Julian
Fleury, Richard Anthony
Kirkham, Robert James Ronald

McGloughlin, Alan James King
Pugh, Ean Griffith
Rudd, Ruary Nial

550

PASS

Adeosun, Adebowale
Behan, Patrick
Best, Edwin Allen
Bromwich, Brian John I'Anson
Bunbury, James St Pierre
Corrie, Brian Edward
Davies, Peter John
Dawson, Robert William
Doherty, Clive Brendan
Fisher, Jonathan Charles

Fleeton, Brian Richard
Haughton, Peter Benjamin Knox
Hudson, Alan Christopher Noble
Fox-Mills, John Barker
Park, Alan William Reginald
Shillington, Stephen Averell
  Carison
Tyrrell, Robert William Wavell
Williams, Edward Dickson
Williams, Francis Montague

AGR.B. EXAMINATION[1]

Michaelmas term, 1965

PASS

Harris, George Ion Eric
Hobson, John
Tisdall, Francis George Dowler

B.COMM. EXAMINATION

Trinity term, 1965

Carruthers, Robert Morris Liddell
Burne, Geoffrey Christopher
  Stephen
Coffey, Bartholomew Brendan
Coffey, Bartholomew Kevin
Corcoran, Timothy Patrick Eugene
Drummey, Michael James
Dyke, George Edward
Early, Hugh Barty
Fagan, Catherine Mary
Fahy, Michael Francis
Fox, Sean Broughan

Harkin, Niall Colman
Hirani, Aziz Din Suleman Kassan
Keatinge, Paul Fintan
Keenan, William Anthony
McAuley, Joseph Michael
McAuliffe, Thomas Finbar
Norman, Charles Anquetic
O'Byrne, Gerard Anthony
O'Donoghue, Maire Treasa
O'Donoghue, Patrick Joseph
  Dermot
Stanley, Laurence Joseph Dermot

Michaelmas term, 1965

Boylan, Brigid Mary
Burke, Eileen Noel
Falvey, John George
Grant, Campbell
Hanrahan, John

McGill, Norah Mary
McGreevy, Mary Teresa
Maher, John Patrick Joseph
Meldrum, John Albert Fife

MUS.B. EXAMINATION

Trinity term, 1965

Marsh, John Edward

Walker, Cyril Harold

[1] Final examination conducted by the National University of Ireland.

DIPLOMAS AWARDED 1965

DIVINITY TESTIMONIUM

FIRST CLASS
England, Robert Gordon, Sch.

SECOND CLASS (FIRST DIVISION)

Kerr, Andrew Henry Mayne — McCausland, Ivor Lawrence

SECOND CLASS (SECOND DIVISION)

Gordon, John Scott
McCamley, Gregor Alexander
Patterson, John Norton
Pickering, John Alexander

Sirr, John Maurice Glover
Swarbrigg, David Cecil
Whitty, Harold George

THIRD CLASS
Bayly, Samuel Niall Maurice

DIPLOMA IN BIBLICAL STUDIES

Knaggs, George
Lutton, John Arnold

Madden, Olive Elizabeth

DIPLOMA IN PSYCHOLOGICAL MEDICINE

Brennan, Kieran
Chaudhari, Gopal Rango
Collis, Robert John Maurice

Cocks, Norman Martin
Spencer, David John

DIPLOMA IN GYNAECOLOGY AND OBSTETRICS

Abdulla, Amira
Agrawal, Chandrakumar Babulal
Alamir, Ali Kassim
Baksh, Amina Rahim
El-Sherif, Ahmed Abdallah
  Mubarek
Hakeem, Iffat Rabia
Huneide, Mahmoud Ibrahim
Husain, Tahera
Jeawon, Sumanth Narain
Kattan, Faiza Daoud
Khan, Masroor Iraduth

Khan, Muhammed Azhar Ali
Morcos, Fawzy Helmy
Muntasser, Ibrahim Ahmed
Najeed, Azhar Amina
Patel, Vinodchandra Ambalal
Shirazi, Mohtaram
Talukder, Muhammed Abdul
  Goffar
Tapal, Sakina
Yassin Kassab, Abdulatif
Youssef, Amina Abdel Salaam
Zietzman, Hans Jurie

HIGHER DIPLOMA IN EDUCATION

FIRST CLASS HONORS

Hammond, Brighid Anne Chatterton
Johnston, Olga Muriel
Macey, Priscilla Ann

Somerfield, Adrian Edward
Treanor, James Stanley

Diplomas awarded

SECOND CLASS HONORS

Abbott, Arthur John
Brownlow, David Timothy
Fahey, Andrew Denis
Lucas, Dorothy Alison
McCaughey, Jayne Stewart
Molony, Margaret Josephine

Rotz, John Wayne
Rutherford, Andrew
Russell, James Robert Douglas
Taggart, Charles Scott Lindsay
Tyrrell, Mary Edith
Unoh, Solomon Ogbodum

PASS

Argyle, Frank Martin
Ashe, Ernest Thomas Eric
Bateman, Alan Julian Stuart
Cope, Malcolm Patrick
Doherty, Ruth Georgina Joan
Dormer, Hilary Sylvia May
Groocock, Doreen
Eka, Offiong Udo
Gault, Rosemary Mildred
Hall, Elizabeth Louise
Hallinan, Elizabeth Ann
Harte, Pamela Loraine
Jackson, Martha Elizabeth
Jones, Eric
Kelly, John
Ledbetter, Sheelagh
Leeson, Emily Francis
McWilliam, Michael Russell
Manning, Michael Patrick

Marshall, Rhona Heather
Micks, Fanny Geraldine Townsend
Mitchell, Robert Henry Stewart
Murphy, John Joseph
Needham, James Michael
O'Meara, Rebecca Mary
O'Sullivan, Anthony William
O'Sullivan, John Joseph
Snow, Adrian John
Streather, John Godfrey
Tilson, Harry Joseph
Uprichard, Joseph Edward
Wallace, Dorothy Elizabeth
Walsh, Anna Mary
Wheeler, Derek Arnold
Williams, Richard Jeremy Denis
Wilson, Robin Francis
White, Alicia

DIPLOMA IN SOCIAL STUDIES

Bain, Anne Evelyn
Birch, Elizabeth Carol
Davis, Frayda Lynn
Elworthy, Priscilla Mary
Fausset, Muriel June
Landale, Anne
McKnight, Margaret

Mason, Margaret Tennant
Morris, Mary Christiana Lucy
O'Connor, Roisin
Siggins, Elizabeth Villiers
Braddell-Smith, Hermione Elizabeth
Thompson, Janet Phyllida

DIPLOMA IN PHYSIOTHERAPY

Batchen, Diana Susan
Brooks, Elizabeth Joyce
Carroll, Maeve Anne
Doyle, Patricia Madeline Cecelia
FitzSimon, Sheelagh Constance
Furlong, Rosalie Anne
Hilton, Joan Ethne Frances

Judge, Maeve Kathleen
Lim, Vivien Poh Sim
McConnell, Hester Gillian
Swan, Margaret Ruth Elizabeth
Whitaker, Enid Ann
Whitten, Valerie Anne
Wright, Margaret Grace

PRIZES IN ARTS AND IN THE
PROFESSIONAL SCHOOLS 1965

ARTS

MODERATORSHIP PRIZES

Bishop Law Prize	Oldham, Elizabeth Evelyn
Brooke Prize in Classics	Cobbe, Hugh Michael Thomas
Hackett Fund Prize	*Chatterton, Brian Douglas
	*Morgan, Michael James
Jack Morrison Moderatorship Prize	Stark, Jurgen Kurt
Longfield Fund Prize	Whitehead, Celia Felicity
Lyster Prize	Kelly, Patrick Hyde

OTHER PRIZES IN ARTS

Abd El-Motaal Prize	Bulford, Christopher Leonard
Arabic, First Year Prize	Cathcart, Kevin James
Bastable Prize	Kevin, Anthony Charles Conwell
Cluff Memorial Prize	Frame, Robert Ferris
Cocker Prize and Medal	Hanna, David Plunkett
Costello Prize in English	Le Fanu, Juliet Elizabeth
Costello Prize in Latin	Bell, Catherine Lois
Cotter Prize in Modern Languages	Hanna, Gillian Lavinia Cecile
Dr Henry Hutchinson Stewart	Mullan, William Norman Boyd
Literary Scholarships	Bevan, Phyllis Julia
Dr John Bennett Fund	Scott, Derek
Edge Prize in Geology	Sutton, John Stewart
	Robinson, Keith Warren
Ernst Scheyer Memorial Prize	Graham, David
Ferrar Memorial Prize	Durand, Angela Victoria Susan
French Government's Bronze Medal	Pollen, Margaret Mary Clare
George McCutchan Prize	Mosessan, Michael Anthony
Henley Memorial Prize	Carson, Ronald Alfred James
Henry Hamilton Hunter Prize	Bourke, Mary Teresa Winifred
Henry Stewart Macran Prize	Alscher, Peter Jack
Irish Premium	Murphy, Michael
Jack Morrison B'nai B'rith Prize	Beattie, Derek Robert George
	Gilbert, Ruth Marilyn Joy
John Henry Bernard Prizes	
Junior Sophister:	Garst, David Blackburn
Senior Freshman:	Reynolds, Hilary Gaye
Junior Freshman:	Beresford-Evans, Robin Geoffrey

* *Indicates students placed equally.*

554

John Isaac Beare Memorial Prize	Boal, Sydney John
John Isaac Beare Prize in Philosophy	
Junior Sophisters:	Bowder, William Maxwell
	Beresford-Evans, Robin Geoffrey
Senior Freshmen:	Reynolds, Hilary Gaye
	Ryan, Michael Joseph
Junior Freshmen:	Bristow, Peter Edmund McGovern
	Steele, Norman John
King Edward Prize	West, Michael John
Kingsmill Jones Prize	Mercer, Peter Crossley
Lloyd Exhibition	Armstrong, Michael John
Marshall Porter Memorial Prize	Durand, Angela Victoria Susan
Michael Roberts Prize	Jackson, David Alexander
Mullins Classical Exhibition	Griffin, Alan Howard Foster
	King, Ivan Brownlow
Old and Middle English Prize	Stocken, Peter Alfred Creswick
Rev. Thaddeus O'Mahony Prize	O Siadhail, Michael Lorcan
Richard F. Littledale Prize	Stewart, Kathryn Mary
Robert Wallace Henry Exhibition	Bates, Ernest Timothy Brendan
Rowe Prize	Kennedy, Douglas Peter
Sarah Purser Scholarship in European Painting	Byrne, Donal
Sarah Purser Prize in European Painting	Richardson, Hilary
	Turpin, John
Townsend Memorial Prize	Carson, Ronald Alfred James
Vice-Chancellor's Prize in English Prose	Kelly, John Stephen
Vice-Chancellor's Prize in Greek Prose	Cobbe, Hugh Michael Thomas
Vice-Chancellor's Prize in Greek Verse	Pritchard, Arthur George William
William Roberts Prize	Gamble, Robert Bradley
Wray Prize	Alscher, Peter Jack

DIVINITY

Archbishop King's Divinity Prizes	*Battye, John Noel
	*Crooks, John Anthony Irving
	*Ellis, John Wadsworth
Bishop Forster's Divinity Premiums	*Battye, John Noel
	*Crooks, John Anthony Irving
	*Ellis, John Wadsworth
Church Formularies Prize	Kerr, Andrew Henry Mayne

* *Indicates students placed equally.*

555

Prizes awarded

Downes Divinity Premiums
 Oratory   1. England, Robert Gordon
            2. Swarbrigg, David Cecil
 Reading the Liturgy   1. Bayly, Samuel Niall Maurice
            2. Sinnamon, William Desmond
 Written Composition   *Sirr, John Maurice Glover
            *Swarbrigg, David Cecil
Kyle Irish Prize   Battye, John Noel
Lambert Prize   Crooks, John Anthony Irving
Moncrieff Cox Memorial Prize Kingston, Robert Kenneth
Newport White Prize   McCausland, Ivor Lawrence
Robert King Prize   Kerr, Andrew Henry Mayne
Ryan Prize   Kerr, Andrew Henry Mayne
Weir Prize   Battye, John Noel

LAW

Criminal Law, Law of Evidence,
 Constitutional Law and History Kilroy, Michael Gerard
Law of Property   1. Quick, Simon Christopher Kendrick
            2. Brunker, Eric Nicholas
            3. Figgis, Thomas Fernsly

PHYSIC

Andrew Francis Dixon Prize Hartman, Mark Lawrence
Aquilla Smith Prize   Patel, Ramanlal Paragji
Arthur Ball Prizes   1. Henry, Mary Elizabeth Frances
            2. Cudworth, George Hitchon
Begley Studentship   Hartman, Mark Lawrence
Conolly Norman Medal   Shannon, Rosemary Susan
Daniel John Cunningham Medal
 and Prize   Heelas, Ann Margaret
De Renzy Centenary Prize   Henry, Mary Elizabeth Frances
Dr Henry Hutchinson Stewart
 Medical Scholarship   Fine, Adrian
Dr Henry Hutchinson Stewart
 Pre-Medical Scholarship Thornloe, Michael Hugh
Fitz-Patrick Scholarship   Henry, Mary Elizabeth Frances
John Mallet Purser Medal   Kandiah, Sowntharaleela
J. W. Bigger Memorial Scholarship Carroll, Alan Michael
O'Sullivan Memorial Scholarship Caird, George Robert
Sir James Craig Memorial Prize Henry, Mary Elizabeth Frances
Walter G. Smith Prize   Martin, John Stirling
Welland Prize   Brock-Utne, John Gerhard

DENTAL SCIENCE

Sheldon Friel Prize   Farrant, Robert Samuel

* *Indicates students placed equally.*

ENGINEERING

Alexander Prize	Plant, John Edward
Clark Memorial Prize	Sides, John Patrick
Collen Prize in Civil Engineering	Sides, John Patrick
David Clark Prize	Browne, Michael John Patrick
Edge Prize	1. Lauriston, William James
	2. Kearon, Anthony Robin
Francis Spring Prize	Johnston, David Christopher
Marmaduke Backhouse Prize	Colin, Norman Edward Greer

COMMERCE

John Good Prizes
    Senior Sophister: Carruthers, Robert Morris Liddell
    D.P.A. Holders: ★Coffey, Bartholomew Kevin
                            ★Harkin, Niall Colman
                            ★O'Donoghue, Maire

Abd El-Motaal Prize   Archdall, Mervyn

•

★ *Indicates students placed equally.*

PUBLIC LECTURES 1965

TRINITY MONDAY DISCOURSE
R. B. D. French: 'Canon J. O. Hannay (George Birmingham), 1865–1950'

DONNELLAN LECTURES
T. R. Henn: 'The Bible in relation to the study of English literature today'

GODFREY DAY LECTURES
Rt. Rev. Joost de Blank: 'The Church's need today'

JOLY LECTURES
S. K. Runcorn: 'The evolution of the earth'
1. Palaeomagnetism and continental drift
2. Continental drift and the earth's evolution

O'DONNELL LECTURES
R. B. McDowell: 'The Irish convention, 1917–18'

RECENT PUBLICATIONS BY MEMBERS OF THE STAFF

Note. As far as possible the information given here is presented as supplied by the member of the staff under whose name it appears. A few items with joint authorship are listed more than once.

AALEN F. H. A., 'The evolution of the traditional house in western Ireland', *Journal of the Royal Society of Antiquaries of Ireland*, 96, 1 (1966).
Abstracts in *Geographical Abstracts: Social Geography*.

ABD EL-MOTAAL M. H. B., Review articles on 'Introduction to cost accountancy' and 'Management information and accountancy', R. W. Dobson in *A. T. M. Bulletin*, Birmingham, September 1965.
The textile and clothing industries in the Irish economy – Administrative Research Bureau, University of Dublin, July 1966.
Fourteen public companies – a comparative study – Administrative Research Bureau, University of Dublin, July 1966.

BAKER K. P., 'Skin disease in dogs', *Veterinary Record*, 78, 80 (1966).

BAXTER J. T., 'The chemotherapy of nematodirus disease in lambs', *Irish Veterinary Journal*, 19, 121–142 (1965).
'The winter housing of sheep', *Irish Veterinary Journal*, 20, 22–33 (1966) [with P. J. Kavanagh].

BOGGUST W. A., 'The thermolability of tissue thromboplastins', *Irish Journal of Medical Science*, No. 481, 11 (1966).

BOURKE G. J., 'The efficacy of car safety belts', *Journal of the Irish Medical Association*, 57, 110, October 1965.
'Tetanus prophylaxis', *Lancet*, 2, 1297, December 1965.
'Pregnancy and other contraindications to smallpox vaccination', Contribution to *Medical Letter* (New York), 7, No. 10, May 1965.
'Medical social worker', Part contribution to *Encyclopaedia Britannica* (1965).
'Smallpox vaccination and the obstetrician', *Obstetrics/Gynaecology Digest* (Illinois), August 1966.

BOYDELL B., '*A terrible beauty is born*', Cantata for soprano, contralto and baritone soloists, narrator, chorus and orchestra. Commissioned by Radio Eireann for the 1916 Jubilee celebrations, and recorded for the 'Italia' Prize (1966).

BOYLE P. H., 'Tetrahydromarrubiin', *Chemistry and Industry*, 33 (1966).

559

Recent publications

BROCK C., Chapter on Ireland, *Resale Price Maintenance*, ed. B. S. Yamey, Weidenfeld and Nicolson (London), 1966.

BROWNE A. D. H., 'Qualitative dietary survey on the diets of pregnant mothers, No. 2.' *Journal of the Irish Medical Association, 56*, 334, 110 (1965) [with Dorothy Callaghan].

'Vaginal delivery after previous Caesarean section', *Journal of Obstetrics and Gynaecology of the British Commonwealth, 72*, 557 (1965).

'Multiple repeat Caesarean section', *Journal of Obstetrics and Gynaecology of the British Commonwealth, 72*, 693 (1965).

'Difficult vaginal delivery', *Journal of Obstetrics and Gynaecology of the British Commonwealth, 72*, 866 (1965).

'Preparation for childbirth—a review', *Journal of the Irish Medical Association, 63*, 31 (1966).

'Clinical report of the Rotunda Hospital', *Irish Journal of Medical Science*, 6th Series, 482, February 1966.

CASTELL L., 'The quantization of fields with maximum spin $3/2$ and the application to SU_{12}', *Il Nuovo Cimento, 37*, 1236 (1965).

'The generalized Kemmer equation', *Il Nuovo Cimento, 39*, 344 (1965).

CHUBB F. B., *The Constitution*, Dublin (Institute of Public Administration), 2nd edition, 1966.

CLARKE A., 'The policies of the "old English" in parliament, 1640-41', *Historical Studies, V*, 85-102 (1965).

The Old English in Ireland, 1625-42, (MacGibbon and Kee) 1966.

CLARKE M. J., '*Orionastraea* in Ireland', *Irish Naturalists Journal* (1966)

'A new species of Fasciculate *Aulina* from Ireland', *Scientific Proceedings of the Royal Dublin Society, A,* 2 (1966)

'The palaeoecology of a Lower Viséan Crinoid Fauna from Feltrim, County Dublin', *R. G. S. Hudson Memorial Volume*: Royal Dublin Society [with R. G. S. Hudson and G. D. Sevastopulo].

'A detailed account of the Fauna and age of a waulsortian knoll-reef limestone and associated shales, Feltrim, County Dublin', *R. G. S. Hudson Memorial Volume*: Royal Dublin Society [with R. G. S. Hudson G. D. Sevastopulo].

'The Lower Carboniferous (Dinantian) stratigraphy of the Castleisland area, County Kerry', *R. G. S. Hudson Memorial Volume*: Royal Dublin Society [with R. G. S. Hudson and T. P. Brennand].

COCKER W., 'Dextrorotatory hardwickiic acid. An extractive of *Copaifera officinalis*', *Tetrahedron Letters, 24*, 1983 (1965) [with A. L. Moore and A. C. Pratt].

'A novel reaction of carene', *Chemical Communications, 12*, 254 (1965) [with P. V. R. Shannon and P. A. Staniland].

'The chemistry of terpenes, Part I. Hydrogenation of the pinenes and the carenes', *Journal of the Chemical Society*, *C1*, 41 (1966) [with P. V. R. Shannon and P. A. Staniland].

'Synthesis of 3-n-Butyltetrahydrophthalides', *Chemical Communications*, *20*, 479 (1965) [with D. M. Sainsbury].

'Oxidative hydroboronation of (+) car-3-ene', *Tetrahedron Letters*, 1409 (1966) [with P. V. R. Shannon and P. A. Staniland].

'The chemistry of terpenes, Part II. The physical properties of some *cis-trans* substituted cyclohexanes', *Journal of the Chemical Society*, *C*, 946 (1966) [with P. V. R. Shannon and P. A. Staniland].

COLES N., Reviews in *Hermathena* and *New Society*.

COLHOUN E. A., 'Recent bog flows and debris slides in the North of Ireland', *Scientific Proceedings of the Royal Dublin Society*, Ser. A, *2*, No. 10, 163–174 (1965) [with R. Common and M. M. Cruickshank].

'Observations on Pingos and other landforms in Schuchertdal, North-East Greenland', *Geographical Annaler*, Ser. A, *47*, 224–236 (1965) [with J. G. Cruickshank].

'Some examples of glacial drainage channels in the Sperrin Mountains, Northern Ireland', *Occasional Paper*, No. 3, 18–24 (British Geomorphological Research Group) 1966.

COUGHLAN J. A., *Aims of Social Policy: Reform in Ireland's Social Security and Health Services*, Tuairim pamphlet, 14 (1965).

'After the Dispensary: How to pay the general practitioner', *Irish Times*, 24th February 1966.

CRANE L. J., 'The effect of mechanical vibration on the break-up of a cylindrical water jet in air', *British Journal of Applied Physics*, *15*, 743–750 (1964) [with S. Birch and P. D. McCormack].

'An experimental and theoretical analysis of cylindrical liquid jets subject to vibration', *British Journal of Applied Physics*, *16*, 395–408 (1965) [with S. Birch and P. D. McCormack].

'Derivation of jet velocity modulation caused by injector vibration', *British Journal of Applied Physics*, *16*, 1911–1912 (1965) [with S. Birch and P. D. McCormack].

Contributions to *Mathematical Reviews* (American Mathematical Society).

CULLEN L. M., 'The Galway smuggling trade in the 1730's', *Journal of the Galway Archaeological* and *Historical Society* (forthcoming).

DAVIES G. L., 'Francis Bacon and continental drift', *Geological Magazine*, *102*, 347 (1965).

'The concept of denudation in seventeenth-century England', *Journal of the History of Ideas*, *27*, 278–284 (1966).

Recent publications

'Early British geomorphology, 1578-1705', *Geographical Journal*, 132 (1966).

'Cyclic surfaces in the Roundwood basin, County Wicklow', *Irish Geography*, 5 (1966).

Abstracts in *Geographical Abstracts*.

Book-reviews in *Irish Geography*.

DICKINSON C. H., 'Use of a selective cellulose agar for isolation of soil fungi', *Nature*, *207*, 440-441 (1965) [with G. J. F. Pugh].

'Studies on fungi in coastal soils. VI. *Gliocladium roseum* Bainier', *Transactions of the British Mycological Society*, *48*, 279-285 (1965) [with G. J. F. Pugh].

'The mycoflora associated with *Halimione portulacoides*. I. The establishment of the root surface flora of mature plants', *Transactions of the British Mycological Society*, *48*, 381-390 (1965) [with G. J. F. Pugh].

'The mycoflora associated with *Halimione portulacoides*. II. Root surface fungi of mature and excised plants', *Transactions of the British Mycological Society*, *48*, 595-602 (1965) [with G. J. F. Pugh].

'The mycoflora associated with *Halimione portulacoides*. III. Fungi on green and moribund leaves', *Transactions of the British Mycological Society*, *48*, 603-610 (1965).

'Nematode-trapping species of *Dactylella* and *Monacrosporium*', *Transactions of the British Mycological Society*, *48*, 621-629 (1965) [with R. C. Cooke].

'The mycoflora associated with *Halimione portulacoides*. IV. Observations on some species of Sphaeropsidales', *Transactions of the British Mycological Society*, *49*, 43-55 (1966) [with G. J. F. Pugh].

DRECHSLER F. S., 'Management and the laws of disorder', *Scientific Business*, Winter 1965.

Kilkenny Region, a pilot study [with R. B. Cadwell, W. Murray, A. A. Pakenham-Walsh and J. J. White].

EDWARDS P. W., *Thomas Kyd and Early Elizabethan Tragedy* (Longmans, Green & Co., for the British Council), 1966.

'Yeats and the Trinity Chair', *Hermathena*, *ci*, Autumn 1965.

ERSKINE C. A., 'Ancient greeting', *Science*, *148*, No. 3673 (Cover), 1965.

'Electronmicroscopy in the anatomy teaching programme', *Irish Journal of Medical Science*, *6*, 308 (1965).

'Anatomical science in teaching and research in the next decades', *WHO Medical Education Bulletin*, *1*, 13 (1966).

EVANS J. A., 'Haemoglobin typing of the Kerry breed of cattle', *Nature*, *209*, 309, January 1966 [with J. P. Crowley].

EXSHAW E. Y., 'Constitutional Rights', *Irish Law Times*, 100, 195.

FEENEY J. P., 'The changing role of the Labour Court in Ireland', *Business and Finance*.

FEGAN W. G., 'A histological assessment of continuous compression sclerotherapy', *Angiology*, *16*, 433 (1965) [with D. E. FitzGerald].

'A case of starch granuloma', *Irish Journal of Medical Science*, *475*, 335 (1965) [with W. H. Beesley].

'The abdominal venous pump', *Archives of Surgery*, *92*, 44 (1966) [with J. C. Milliken and D. E. FitzGerald].

'Compression sclerotherapy', *Current Therapy*, 181–183 (Saunders, Philadelphia) 1966.

'The influence of compression in sclerotherapy as a treatment for chronic venous insufficiency', *Modern Trends in Surgery*. In press.

'Influence of compression sclerotherapy in the treatment of chronic venous insufficiency', *The Journal of Cardiovascular Surgery*. In press.

'The diagnosis and treatment of venous insufficiency in pregnancy', *Journal of Obstetrics and Gynaecology of the British Commonwealth*, *73*, 2, 22, (1966) [with D. E. FitzGerald].

'The treatment of varicose veins in pregnancy', *Obstetrics/Gynaecology Digest* [with J. M. Pegum]. In press.

FLEMING J. B., Semmelweis Commemoration Meeting—Royal Society of Medicine, London. Invitation lecture delivered November 3rd, 1965.

'Puerperal fever: the historical development of its treatment', *Proceedings of the Royal Society of Medicine*, *59*, No. 4, 341–5, April 1966.

'Montgomery and the follicles of the areola as a sign of pregnancy (1837)', *Irish Journal of Medical Science*, 6th Series, No. 485, 169-182, May 1966.

FLORIDES P. S., 'Stationary gravitational fields due to symmetrical systems of bodies', *Proceedings of the Royal Society*, A, *284*, 32–9 (1965) [with J. L. Synge and T. Yukawa].

'Radiation coordinates in general relativity', *Proceedings of the Royal Society*, A, *292*, 1-13 (1966) [with J. L. Synge and Rev. J. McCrea].

'The foundation of the theory of relativity. 1. The special theory', *Kosmos*, *3*, 11–17 (1966).

FORREST D. W., 'Attitudes of undergraduate women to smoking', *Psychological Reports*, *19*, 83–87 (1966).

'Two types of set and the generalization of perceptual defence', *British Journal of Psychology* [with Ann Taylor]. In press.

FRENCH R. B. D., 'J. O. Hannay and the Gaelic League', *Hermathena*, cii, Spring 1966.

FURLONG E. J., 'Mrs George Berkeley and her washing machine', *Hermathena*, ci, Autumn 1965 [with I. C. Tipton].

'Berkeley and the tree in the quad', *Philosophy*, xli, 156, April 1966.

Recent publications

GATENBY P. B. B., 'Disorders of intestinal absorption', *Irish Journal of Medical Science*, November 1965.

'Vitamin B12 deficiency following partial gastrectomy', *Irish Journal of Medical Science*, March 1966 [with D. G. Weir and I. J. Temperley].

GILLMOR D. A., 'Foreign participation in Irish manufacturing', *Irish Geography*, 5 (1965).

Abstracts in *Geomorphological Abstracts* and *Geographical Abstracts*.

GRAINGER J. N. R., 'A model of a growing steady state system', *Journal of Theoretical Biology*, *10*, 387–398 (1966) [with L. Bass].

GREENE D. W., *Antologia shel ha-Shira ha-Gaelit*, Tel-Aviv, Am ha-Sefer, 1966 [with Pnina Navé].

'Fifty years of writing in Irish', *Studies*, Spring 1966.
'The prefix *in-*', *Ériu*, *xx*, 82–6 (1966).

HATCH C., 'The evaluation of anthelmintics in horses by field trials',

Proceedings of the First International Conference of the World Association for the Advancement of Veterinary Parasitology.

The Evaluation of Anthelmintics, 123–128 (1963).

HENCHY M. M., *Writings in Irish history, 1965* [with E. Semple].

'[Edward Kenealy], the Tichborne Claimant's defender', *Irish Times*, 19th January, 1966.

Public libraries in Ireland. Dublin, University College School of Librarianship (1966) [with M. Neylon].

HOWIE D. I. D., 'Problems relating to the site of secretion of the maturation hormone in the lugworm, *Arenicola marina* (L.)', *General and Comparative Endocrinology*, *5*, 686 (1965).

HUDSON the late R. G. S., 'A borehole section through the Lower Tournaisian, and Upper Old Red Sandstone, Ballyvergin, County Clare', *Scientific Proceedings of the Royal Dublin Society*. In press [with G. D. Sevastopulo].

JOHNSTON J., 'Irish economic headaches—a diagnosis', *Business and Finance* and *Commerce* (Aiste Eireannacha) 1966 (a pamphlet).

JONES T. C., 'Re Knox: conceptualism satisfied', *Irish Law Times*, 100, 25.

'Stone on lawyers' logic: twenty years on', *Irish Jurist*, 31, 21.

Book-reviews in *Northern Ireland Legal Quarterly*, *Irish Jurist* and *Irish Law Times*.

KEATINGE N. P., 'De Gaulle and Britain, 1940–1946', *International Relations*, *11*, No. 11, April 1965.

KENNELLY T. B., *The Florentines*. A novel; Dublin (Allen Figgis).

Up And At It. Poems; Dublin (New Square Publications).

'The heroic ideal in Yeats's Cuchulain plays', *Hermathena*, Autumn 1965.

'The poetry of Joseph Mary Plunkett', *The Dublin Magazine*, Easter 1966.

'Seán O'Casey—dramatist', *New Knowledge*, April 25th, 1966.

'The plays of J. M. Synge', *New Knowledge*, April 25th, 1966.

SOMERVILLE-LARGE L. B., 'William Daniel Moore 1813–1871', *Archives of Opthalmology*, *75*, March 1966.

LEONARD P. J., 'Plasma concentrations of free and protein-bound cortisol in hypoproteinaemia', *Journal of Endocrinology*, *34*, 265 (1966) [with P. G. D'Arbela].

'Total body water, extracellular fluid, plasma volume and red cell mass in healthy East Africans', *Clinical Science*, *29*, 427 (1965) [with V. Blackman and K. W. Jones].

'Serum proteins in African and Asian subjects in Kampala, Uganda', *East African Medical Journal*, *42*, 689 (1965) [with A. G. Shaper].

'Relationship between free and total cholesterol values in human serum', *American Journal of Clinical Nutrition*, *17*, 377 (1965) [with A. G. Shaper and K. W. Jones].

'The relationship between changes in plasma volume, plasma proteins and haemoglobin concentration during treatment in Kwashiorkor', *Transactions of the Royal Society of Tropical Medicine and Hygiene*, *59*, 582 (1965) [with K. M. MacWilliam and K. W. Jones].

'Some biochemical observations in the Wakalanga', *East African Medical Journal*, *42*, 692 (1965) [with J. P. Stanfield].

LUCE A. A., 'Berkeley's new principle completed', *New Studies in Berkeley's Philosophy* (New York), 1966.

LYONS P. M., 'Central Bank gives first clear directive', *Business and Finance*, December 1965.

'Ireland hits billion mark', *Business and Finance*, January 1966.

'Irish Banks face up to credit squeeze', *Business and Finance*, March 1966.

'Vital this year—incomes control', *Business and Finance*, March 1966.

'The dangers of too much State spending', *Business and Finance*, March 1966.

'Facing the crises of fifty years', *Business and Finance*, April 1966.

'Irish economy on the turn?', *Business and Finance*, May 1966.

McAULAY I. R., 'Byssinosis and other respiratory symptoms in flax workers in Northern Ireland', *British Journal of Industrial Medicine*, *22*, 27 (1965) [with P. C. Elwood, J. Pemberton, J. D. Merrett and G. C. R. Carey].

'A survey of dust concentrations in flax mills in Northern Ireland', *British Journal of Industrial Medicine*, *22*, 305 (1965) [with G. C. R. Carey, J. D. Merrett, R. H. McClarin, P. C. Elwood and J. Pemberton].

Recent publications

Byssinosis in Flax Workers in Northern Ireland, Her Majesty's Stationery Office (1965) [with G. C. R. Carey, P. C. Elwood, J. D. Merrett and J. Pemberton].

McCaughey W. T. E., 'Criteria for diagnosis of diffuse mesothelial tumours', *Annals of the New York Academy of Sciences*, *132*, 603 (1965).

'Hypertension due to subadventitial fibrosis of the renal artery', *British Heart Journal*, *28*, 382 (1966) [with J. Lyttle].

McCormack P. D., 'Derivation of jet velocity modulation caused by injector vibration', *British Journal of Applied Physics*, *16* (1965).

'Analysis and optimization of a multiple effect evaporator'. Third Congress of the International Federation of Automatic Control, London, June 1966.

'Periodic vorticity and its effect on jet mining', *Physics of Fluids*. In press.

'Mechanical vibration—a driving mechanism for combustion instability in rocket engines', Technical Report, Air Force Office of Scientific Research, AD 628920 (1966).

McKeever J. D., 'Buffered gluteraldehyde (cidex), a new disinfectant specially useful in Urology', *Journal of the Irish Medical Association*, *lviii*, 131, April 1966 [with V. Lane and M. Fallon].

McMurry T. B. H., 'A synthesis of $(\pm)$ otobain', *Tetrahedron Letters*, 975 (1966) [with H. K. Kennedy-Skipton].

'Keto-enol tautomerism in santonene and dihydrosantonene', *Chemical Communications*, 130 (1966) [with R. C. Mollan].

McWilliam G. H., 'The minor plays of Ugo Betti', *Italian Studies*, *xx*, 78–107 (1965).

'Some notes on the Irish contribution to the pre-Romantic rediscovery of Italian literature', *Italian Presence in Ireland* (Dublin, 1965), 51–78.

Reviews in *Italian Studies* and *The Modern Language Review*.

Martin E. A., 'Drugs as a hazard in neuro-psychiatric diagnosis', *Journal of the Irish Medical Association*, *lvi*, No. 334, 125 (1965).

'Alcoholic cerebellar degeneration: a report of three cases', *Journal of the Irish Medical Association*, *lvi*, No. 336, 172 (1965).

'Neurological books 1724–1894', *Irish Journal of Medical Science*. In press.

Milliken J. C., 'Technique of celiac blockade for relief of splanchnic ischemia', *Journal of the American Medical Association*, *7*, 192 (1965) [with R. Minton and J. Fine].

'A study of the factors involved in the development of peripheral vascular collapse following release of the occluded superior mesenteric artery', *The British Journal of Surgery*, *9*, 52 (1965) [with A. Nahor and J. Fine].

A case of acute thrombosis of the common femoral artery treated by emergency thrombo-endarterectomy', *Journal of the Irish Medical Association*, 342, 57 (1965).

'Effect of celiac blockade and dibenzyline on traumatic shock following release of occluded superior mesenteric artery', *Annals of Surgery*, 1, 163 (1966) [with A. Nahor and J. Fine].

'A clinical study of surgical shock', *Lancet*, 817, April 1966.

'The abdominal venous pump', *Archives of Surgery*, 92, 44 (1966) [with W. G. Fegan and D. E. FitzGerald].

MITCHELL D. M., 'Pituitary-adrenal recovery following long-term corticosteroid therapy', *Acta. Endocrin.*, 51, 1, 63 (1966) [with P. F. Roe and G. Pennington].

MITCHELL G. F., 'The quaternary deposits of the Ballaugh and Kirkmichael districts, Isle of Man', *Quarterly Journal of the Geological Society of London*, 121, 359–381 (1965).

'Littleton Bog, Tipperary: an Irish vegetational record', *Geological Society of America, Inc.*, Special Paper 84, 1–16 (1965).

'Littleton Bog, Tipperary: an Irish agricultural record', *Journal of the Royal Society of Antiquaries of Ireland*, 95, 121–132 (1965).

'The Henry Stopes lecture, 1965: the St. Erth Beds—an alternative explanation', *Proceedings of the Geologists' Association*, 76, 345–362 (1965).

'The pleistocene deposits of the Scilly Isles', *Proceedings of the Ussher Society*, 1, No. 95 (1965) [with A. R. Orme].

MURDOCH B. H., 'Some theorems on preharmonic functions', *Journal of the London Mathematical Society*, 40, 407–17 (1965).

'Rates of growth of preharmonic functions', *Journal of the London Mathematical Society*, 40, 605–18 (1965).

'A note on well distributed sequences', *Canadian Journal of Mathematics*, 808–10 (1965).

MURRAY W., 'The reality of management controls', *Management*, 12, Nos. 7, 8, 9 (one issue), 271–280, September 1965.

Contributor to the following publications by the Committee on Court practice and procedure.

'The preliminary investigation of indictment offences', Stationery Office, PR 7164 (1963).

'Jury service', Stationery Office, PR 8328 (1965)

'Jury trial in civil actions', and 'Jury challenges', Stationery Office, PR 8577 (1965).

'Kilkenny pilot study', (Kilkenny County Industrial Development Committee) 1965.

NICHOLSON E. W., 'Josiah's Reformation and Deuteronomy', *Transactions of the Glasgow University Oriental Society*, 20, 77–84 (1963–64).

Recent publications

O'DONOGHUE M., *Investment in Education*, Stationery Office [with P. Lynch, P. Nolan and W. Hyland].

'Cost-benefit and the analysis of Government expenditure', *Administration*, Winter 1965.

'Education and the theory of spillovers', *Public Finance*, March 1966.

'Regional planning in the Republic of Ireland', Supplement on Regional Planning to *Journal of Industrial Economics*, Spring 1965 [with W. J. L. Ryan].

O'MEARA R. A. Q., 'A screening test for substances inhibiting the cancer coagulative factor', *Nature*, *208*, 1009 (1965) [with E. M. Glaser and P. Spink].

'Some biological and biochemical aspects of human tumour growth'. International Symposium of Characterisation of Human Tumours. Summary: *European Journal of Cancer*, *1*, 319 (1965).

'The thermolability of tissue thromboplastins', *Irish Journal of Medical Science*, sixth series, No. 481, 11 (1966) [with W. A. Boggust].

O'MORCHOE C. C. C., 'Intrarenal distribution of nutrient blood flow in dogs during haemorrhagic hypotension', *Circulation Research 18*, 482 (1966) [with S. Carriere, G. D. Thorburn and A. C. Barger].

'Renal lymph flow in the anaesthetised dog', *Journal of Physiology*, *179*, 61 (1965) [with P. J. O'Morchoe].

'Collection and storage of urine for endocrine cytology', *Irish Journal of Medical Science*, *479*, 392 (1965) [with P. J. O'Morchoe].

'Endocrine cytology and basal body temperature recordings', *Irish Journal of Medical Science*, *479*, 389 (1965) [with P. J. O'Morchoe].

O'MORCHOE P. J., 'Renal lymph flow in the anaesthetised dog', *Journal of Physiology*, *179*, 61 (1965) [with C. C. C. O'Morchoe].

'Collection and storage of urine for endocrine cytology', *Irish Journal of Medical Science*, *479*, 392 (1965) [with C. C. C. O'Morchoe].

'Endocrine cytology and basal body temperature recordings', *Irish Journal of Medical Science*, *479*, 389 (1965) [with C. C. C. O'Morchoe].

PEPPER D. C., 'Factors limiting molecular weight in the cationic polymerisation of olefins', *Society of Chemical Industry Monograph*, No. 20, 115–122, London, 1966.

'Propagation reactions in the copolymerisation of styrene and p-Chloro styrene by perchloric acid', *Polymer*, *6*, 497–501 (1965) [with G. R. Brown].

'The polymerisation of styrene by perchloric acid', *Proceedings of the Royal Society*, *A*, *291*, 41–59 (1966) [with P. J. Reilly].

PHEIFER J. D., '*The Seafarer* 53–55', *Review of English Studies*, *xvi*, 282–4 (1965).

POWELL B. L., 'The control of the twenty-four hour rhythm of colour change in juvenile *Carcinus maenas* (L.), *Proceedings of the Royal Irish Academy*, *64B*, 379–399 (1966).

'The hormonal control of the tidal rhythm of locomotor activity in *Carcinus maenas* (L.), *General and Comparative Endocrinology*, 5, No. 6, 705–6 (1965).

'Biology at Trinity College, Dublin'. A paper in Welsh for *Y Gwyddonydd*, *3*, No. 4, 200–3 (1965).

PUGH D. M., 'The treatment of liver fluke infestation in sheep', *Irish Veterinary Journal*, *19*, No. 12 (1965).

'Some observations on the toxicity of hexachlorophane for sheep', *Veterinary Record*, *78*, No. 3, 88 (1966).

'Adrenal cortex insufficiency in ewes—its induction, recognition and treatment', *Irish Veterinary Journal*, *20*, No. 3, 46 (1966).

PYLE H., *Estella Solomons: portraits of patriots; with a biographical sketch of the artist*, Dublin (Allen Figgis) 1966.

Book-reviews in *Review of English Studies*, *Studies* and *Irish Times*.

RARATY M. M., 'The Chair of German at Trinity College, Dublin, 1774–1866', *Hermathena*, *102* (1966).

RICHARDSON L. J. D., Editor of *Studies in Mycenaean Inscriptions and Dialect*, *10*. London University Institute of Classical Studies (1965).

RILEY E. C., 'Sobre el arte de Sánchez Ferlosio: aspectos de *El Jarama*', *Filología*, Buenos Aires, IX (1963).

'Who's who in *Don Quixote*? Or an approach to the problem of identity', *Modern Language Notes*, 81 (1966).

OTWAY-RUTHVEN A. J., 'The character of Norman settlement in Ireland', *Historical Studies*, *V*, 75–84 (ed. J. L. McCracken).

'The chief governors of mediaeval Ireland', *Journal of the Royal Society of Antiquaries of Ireland*, *xcv*, 227–36.

SCAIFE B. K. P., 'Frequency dependence of the relative permittivity of polar substances', *Proceedings of the Physical Society*, *84*, 616–17 (1964).

'Frequency dependence of the relative permittivity of polar substances', *Electrical Research Association*, Report No. 5132/1017, 31pp. (1965).

'The role of dipole-dipole coupling in dielectric relaxation', *Molecular Relaxation Processes*, 15–19, Chemical Society, London (1966).

SCAIFE W. G., 'High pressure used in research into the properties of materials', *Bulletin of the Institution of Civil Engineers of Ireland*, *1*, No. 6, February 1966.

'Statistics of the Engineering profession—an analysis', *Engineers Journal*, *19*, No. 2, 3, February, March 1966.

Recent publications

SHANNON P. V. R., 'A novel reaction of carene', *Chemical Communications*, *12*, 254 (1965) [with W. Cocker and P. A. Staniland].

'The chemistry of terpenes, Part I. Hydrogenation of the pinenes and the carenes', *Journal of the Chemical Society*, C, 41 (1966) [with W. Cocker and P. A. Staniland].

'Natural acetylenes, Part XX. Tetraacetylenic and other metabolites from *Fistulina Hepatica* (*Huds*) Fr.', *Journal of the Chemical Society*, C, 139 (1966) [with Sir Ewart Jones and G. Lowe].

'Natural acetylenes, Part XXI. The biosynthesis and transformation of some polyacetylenic metabolites of *Merulins lachrymans Fr*. and *Clitocybe rhizophora* velen', *Journal of the Chemical Society*, C, 144 (1966) [with Sir Ewart Jones and G. Lowe].

'Oxidative hydroboronation of (+)-Car-3-ene', *Tetrahedron Letters*, No. 13, 1409 (1966) [with W. Cocker and P. A. Staniland].

'The chemistry of terpenes, Part II. The physical properties of some *cis-trans* substituted cyclohexanes', *Jounal of the Chemical Society*, C, 946 (1966) [with W. Cocker and P. A. Staniland].

SIMPSON W. B., 'Tin (II) acetates', *Journal of the Chemical Society*, 5942–7 (1964) [with J. D. Donaldson].

'Some notes on the applications of infrared spectroscopy to inorganic chemistry', *Education in Chemistry*, 58–64 (1966).

'Triphenyltin nitrate', *Chemistry and Industry*, 854 (1966).

SIMMS J. G., *The Jacobite parliament of 1689*, Dundalk, 1966.

'Dublin in 1685', *Irish Historical Studies*, 14, 212–26 (1965).

'Mayo landowners in the seventeenth century', *Journal of the Royal Society of Antiquaries of Ireland*, 95, 237–47 (1965).

'Sligo in the Jacobite war', *Irish Sword*, 7, 124–35 (1965).

SHEEHY SKEFFINGTON O., 'Parent teacher associations', *Irish Times*, January 1966.

'Francis Sheehy Skeffington', *Irish Times 1916 Supplement*, April 1966.

'James Connolly', *Irish Times 1916 Supplement*, April 1966.

'The 1916 ideals', *"T.C.D." 1916–1966 Supplement*, April 1966.

'Church and State', *"T.C.D." 1916–1966 Supplement*, April 1966.

'The McGahern case', *Censorship Quarterly* (London), Spring 1966.

SPENCER B., 'Vitamin A and sulphotransferases in foetal rat liver', *Biochemical Journal*, *96*, 78P (1965) [with J. Carroll].

'Sulphate activation and sulphotransferases in foetal guinea pigs and developing hen's eggs', *Biochemical Journal*, *99*, 35P (1966) [with J. Raftery].

'Sulphate transport in *Aspergillus nidulans*', *Biochemical Journal*, *96*, 78P (1965) [with J. M. Scott].

Recent publications

'The mechanism of choline sulphate utilization in fungi', *Nature*, 207, 632 (1965) [with C. Hussey, B. A. Orsi and J. Scott].

STEWART F. S., 'A red cell sensitising antigen of Group D streptococci', *Immunology*, 9, 319-326 [with M. McLoughlin].

STILLMAN C. J., 'The response to Lufilian folding of the basement complex around the northern edge of the Mpande Dome, Northern Rhodesia', *Journal of Geology*, 73, 131-141 (1965) [with A. M. J. de Swardt].

'The geology of the Musofu River and Mkushi areas; explanation of degree sheets 1329 NW and SW quarters', *Report of the Geological Survey of Zambia*, 12 (1965).

'The geology of the Nuanetsi Igneous Province', *Transactions of the Royal Society of London*, Series A, 257, 71-218 (1965) [with K. G. Cox, R. L. Johnson, L. J. Monkman, J. R. Vail and D. N. Wood].

'Absolute ages of some rocks and minerals from Northern Rhodesia', *Proceedings of the Central African Scientific and Medical Congress, 1963*, 129-140 (1965) [with A. R. Drysdall, E. Hamilton and N. J. Snelling].

TAIT A. A., 'The economic and legal interpretation of "Open Market Price" ', *British Tax Review*, 216-225, June-August 1965.

'Sales taxation in Eire, Denmark, and Finland', *National Tax Journal*, 18, 3, 386-96 [with J. F. Due].

'British Budgetary Policy 1964-65; the corporation tax and the taxation of capital gains', *Finanzarchiv*, N. F. 500-19. December 1965.

Book-review in *The Quarterly Review of Economics and Business*.

TEMPERLEY I. J., 'The significance of the serum vitamin B_{12} estimation in clinical practice', *Irish Journal of Medical Science*, 475, 317 (1965) [with D. Collery].

'Effect of ascorbic acid on the serum folic acid estimation', *Journal of Clinical Pathology*, 19, 43 (1966) [with N. Horner].

'Vitamin B_{12} deficiency following partial gastrectomy', *Irish Journal of Medical Science*, 483, 97 (1966) [with D. G. Weir and P. B. B. Gatenby].

THACKER C. J. C., ' "The theme of the present age": travellers' views of Pompey's Pillar', *English Miscellany*, 16, 297-319, Rome, 1965.

'The misplaced garden? Voltaire, Julian and *Candide*', *Studies on Voltaire and the Eighteenth Century*, 41, 189-202, Geneva, 1966.

Reviews in *French Studies, Yearbook of Comparative Literature*.

THOMAS L. H. C., *Two Stories. Frau Regel Amrain und ihr Jüngster* and *Regine* by Gottfried Keller. Edited with introduction and notes by Lionel Thomas (Oxford University Press), 1966.

'The prose fiction of Gottfried Keller', *Proceedings of the Leeds Philosophical and Literary Society* (Literary and Historical Section), 12, 1, 1-22 (1966).

Recent publications

Reviews in *Modern Language Review, German Life and Letters, Germanistik.*

THORNLEY D. A., 'Patrick Pearse—the evolution of a republican', *Studies*, Dublin, Spring 1966, and *Dublin 1916: leaders and men of the Easter Rising*, ed. F. X. Martin, O.SA., London (Methuen and Cornell University Press).

'The Blueshirts', *The years of the great test, 1926–36*, Cork (Mercier Press). In press.

'Eamon de Valera', *New Knowledge*, 6, London, No. 1.

'Irish identity', *Doctrine and Life*, Dublin, April 1966.

VASS J. D. R., 'The synthesis of 1H-Pyrazolo [3, 4–6] pyrioline', *Chemical Communications*, 293 (1966) [with T. L. P. Hatt].

VOKES F. E., 'Zeno of Verona, Apuleius and Africa', *Studia Patristica, VIII (Texte und Untersuchungen, XCIII)*, 135–9, Berlin, 1966.

'Montanism and the Ministry', *Studia Patristica, IX (Texte und Untersuchungen, XCIV)*, 298–307, Berlin, 1966.

Book-review in *Irish Times*.

PAKENHAM-WALSH A. A., 'Supervision', *International Handbook of Management*, ed. Karl E. Ettinger, New York (McGraw-Hill) 1965.

Export Finance, Dublin (Coras Trachtala) 1965.

Kilkenny Region—a pilot study, Dublin (Dublin University Administrative Research Bureau), February 1966 [with R. Cadwell, F. Dreschsler, W. Murray and J. White].

WALTON P. W. ' Measurement of the statistics of secondary electron emission' *I.E.E.E. Transactions on Nuclear Science*, NS-13, No. 1, 742 (1966) [with C. F. G. Delaney].

WATSON A. I., '*El pintor de su deshonra* and the Neo-Aristotelian theory of tragedy', reprinted in *Critical Essays on the Theatre of Calderón*, 203–223 (ed. B. W. Wardropper), New York (1965).

WATTS W. A., 'Late-Wisconsin pollen and seed analysis from the Nebraska Sandhills', *Ecology*, 47, 202–220 [with H. E. Wright Jr.].

WEBB D. A., 'Some difficulties in the establishment of phytogeographical divisions', *Revue Roumaine de Biologie (Série de Botanique)*, 10, 33 (1965).

'Chromosomes and plants', *Watsonia*, 6, 134 (1965).

'The flora of European Turkey', *Proceedings of the Royal Irish Academy*, 65B, 1 (1966).

WEIR D. G., 'Vitamin B_{12} deficiency following partial gastrectomy', *Irish Journal of Medical Science*, 97–103, March 1966 [with I. J. Temperley and, P. B. B. Gatenby].

'Acute Medical emergencies', *Dublin Medical Student's Journal*, 6, 11 (1965).

Recent publications

WERNER L. E. J., 'Le mode d'action de la Kératotomie délimitante dans le Fraitement de l'ulcère de Mooren', *Bulletins et Mémoires de la Société Française d'Ophtalmologie.*

WILSON C. W. M., 'Amphetamine', *Lancet*, 2, 496–7 (1965).

'The occurrence of circadian histamine rhythms in the rat', *International Archives Allergy*, 28, 32–34 (1965).

'Ponstan', *Drug and Therapeutics Bulletin*, 2, 61–2 (1964).

'The assessment of medical information—a consequence of the drug explosion', *Journal of the Irish Medical Association*, 57, 147–155 (1965).

'Pharmaceutical representatives: commercial or professional?', *Pharmaceutical Journal*, 196, 341–5 (1966) [with J. A. Banks].

' "Medical care" or "Social Medicine" ', *Lancet*, 1, 1038–9 (1966).

'Deliberate Aspirin intoxication', *British Medical Journal*, 1, 1090 (1966) [with J. S. Madden].

WILSON R., 'Respiratory function and clinical responses to Theophylline Guiaphenesin (Entair)', *Irish Journal of Medical Science*, Sixth Series, No. 485, 189–194, May 1966.

WINDER F. G. A., 'The accumulation of soluble carbohydrates in *Mycobacterium tuberculosis* during exposure to isoniazid: further studies', *Biochemical Journal*, 96, 77P (1965) [with I. Flynn].

'Effect of isoniazid on lipid metabolism in *Mycobacterium tuberculosis*,' *Biochemical Journal*, 96, 77P (1965) [with P. Brennan].

WOODS R. R., 'Soft tissue radiography in the diagnosis of hypopharyngeal tumours', *Journal of the Irish Medical Association*, LVII, No. 341, November 1965 [with O. Chance].

WRIGHT B., 'Un poème inédit de Fromentin: *La Fin du Rhamadan*', *French Review*, 38, 6, 777–780 (1965).

'*Valdieu*: a forgotten precursor of Fromentin's *Dominique*', *Modern Language Review*, 60, 4, 520–528 (1965).

Dominique, by Eugène Fromentin. Edited, with introduction and notes by Barbara Wright. Blackwell's French Texts, Basil Blackwell, Oxford (1965).

YASIN S. A., 'Projects for the development of the livestock industry in Trinidad'. *A Confidential F.A.O.—I.B.R.D. Report*, 145 (Rome), October 1965 [with R. A. Bishop, G. Ghouse and S. Galpin].

'Animal health and production in Trinidad'. *A Report to F.A.O.—I.B.R.D. Cooperative Program*, 45 (Rome), October 1965.

The following items were published by the Irish Medical Research Council

Recent publications

Laboratories under the direction of V. C. Barry, D.SC., Lecturer in Chemotherapy in the University of Dublin.

'Antitubercular substances XX synthesis of 4-nitrosopyrazoles and their derivatives', *Proceedings of the Royal Irish Academy*, *64B*, 187–193 (1965) [with C. O'Callaghan and D. Twomey].

Anticancer agents. I. Structure-activity relationships in a series of oxypolysaccharide-thiosmicarbazide derivatives', *Proceedings of the Royal Irish Academy*, *64B*, 335–354 (1966) [with M. L. Conalty, Joan E. McCormick, R. S. McElhinney and J. F. O'Sullivan].

'Characteristics of soluble carbohydrates which accumulate in *Mycobacterium tuberculosis* during exposure to isoniazid', *Federation of European Biochemical Societies, Vienna*, 75 (1965) [with P. Brennan and F. G. Winder].

'Biosynthesis of salicyclic acid by *Mycobacterium smegmatis*', *Federation of European Biochemical Societies, Vienna*, 257 (1965) [with C. Ratledge].

'Effect of isoniazid on lipid metabolism in *Mycobacterium tuberculosis*', *The Biochemical Journal*, *96*, 78P (1965) [with F. G. Winder and B. Brennan].

'The accumulation of soluble carbohydrates in *Mycobacterium tuberculosis* during exposure to isoniazid', *The Biochemical Journal*, *96*, 77P (1965) [with F. G. Winder and Irma Flynn].

'Derivatives of thiocarbamic acid. Part I. Preparation of 4-substituted thiosemicarbazides', *Journal of the Chemical Society*, 950–955 (1966) [with R. S. McElhinney].

RECENT PUBLICATIONS BY HIGHER DEGREE STUDENTS

Note. Where work is published in co-operation with a member of the staff, the title is given under the name of the member of staff.

ABRAHAMS J. R., 'Amplifier design with a digital computer', *Electronic Engineering*, November 1965.

BRENNAN P., See WINDER, F.G.A.

DAVIES P. M. C., 'The energy relations of *Carassius auratus* L. II. The effect of food, crowding and darkness on heat production', *Comparative Biochemistry & Physiology*, *17*, 983–995 (1966).

HATT T. L. P., See VASS, J. D. R.

NAYLOR D., 'The Upper Devonian and Carboniferous Geology of the Old Head of Kinsale, County Cork', *Scientific Proceedings of the Royal Dublin Society*, A, 2 (1966).

REILLY P. J., See PEPPER, D.C.

STANILAND P. A., See COCKER, W.

SWEENEY E. J., 'The aetiology of dysentery of swine', *Veterinary Record*, *78*, 372–375 (1966).

THESES APPROVED FOR
HIGHER DEGREES

M.D.

DRAPER, RONALD JOHN, 'Acute coronary heart disease, diagnosis and management in a General Practice'.

MCCREERY, WILLIAM CECIL CHARLES, 'The occurrence and treatment of El Tor cholera in Hong-Kong, 1961–1963'.

MEYNELL (*née* MCCLOY), ELINOR WRAY, 'Factors determining the virulence of Bacillus Anthracis. A genetical and physiological study using bacteriophage'.

TAYLOR, MERVYN RICHARD HAMILTON, 'Factors related to iron absorption'.

PH.D.

BAKER, KENNETH PERCY, 'An histological and histopathological study of the skin of the dog'.

BAXTER, JAMES THOMSON, 'Studies on *Nematodirus filicollis* and *Nematodirus battus* and their relationship to disease in sheep'.

BLAKE, PATRICK JOSEPH, 'Genetic analysis of unstable aromatic auxotrophs of *Salmonella typhimurium*'.

BOLT, ANTHONY JOHN NELSON, 'Studies on the chemistry of eudesmane lactones'.

BRENNAN, PATRICK JOSEPH, 'The effect of isoniazid on the composition and metabolism of mycobacteria'.

COFFEY, VICTORIA PHILOMENA, 'The incidence and aetiology of congenital defects in Ireland'.

CROWLEY, JOHN PATRICK, 'Some methods of increasing reproductive efficiency in cattle and sheep'.

DARLINGTON, OLIVER FRANKLIN, 'Reversions of a leucine auxotroph of *Salmonella typhimurium*'.

DAWOOD, MARIE KAMEL, 'John Galsworthy: a study of his plays'.

EKPO, EPIONG UDO, 'Growth and development in relation to food intake in eastern Nigeria'.

GILLMOR, DESMOND ALFRED, 'The cattle industry of the Republic of Ireland'.

KENNEDY, MICHAEL JOHN, 'The geology of North Achill Island, Co. Mayo. Ireland'.

MCCAUGHEY, WILLIAM JOHN, 'Changes in some constituents of blood and cervical mucus associated with oestrus in cattle'.

MCDONAGH, JOHN PATRICK, 'On some problems in the theory of numbers'.

MORLEY, CHARLES TREVOR, 'The geology of South Achill and Achill Beg, Co. Mayo, Ireland'.

576

Theses approved for higher degrees

O'BRIEN, HAROLD J., 'The representation of religion in the fiction of Liam O'Flaherty and Francis Stuart'.

O'SULLIVAN, DENIS FRANCIS, 'Production and decay of hypernuclei and interactions of low energy K^- mesons'.

PHILLIPS, WILLIAM EDWARD ADRIAN, 'The geology of Clare Island, Co. Mayo, Ireland'.

PINNER POOLE, BETTY BURTON, 'The endocrine glands in anencephaly'.

SAINSBURY, DONALD MARSHALL, 'Synthetic studies in the natural products field'.

SCALLY, BERNARD GABRIEL, 'A clinical and epidemiological study of the offspring of mental defectives'.

SCOTT, JOHN MARTIN, 'Studies on the uptake and storage of sulphate by *Aspergillus nidulans*'.

SHAH, TARA PRASAD, 'Emulsion studies of the interactions of K^- mesons with protons and the production and decay of hyperfragments'.

KENNEDY-SKIPTON, HENRY K., 'Studies in the lignan series and a total synthesis of $\pm$ otobain'.

TAIT, ALAN ANDERSON, 'The taxation of personal wealth'.

TAYLOR, MICHAEL CHRISTOPHER, 'Hydraulic model studies in a tidal river'.

WILKINSON, BRYAN ROBERT, 'The *Otia Imperilia* of Gervase of Tilbury'.

WILLIAMS, PHILIP CLIVE, 'Pestalozzi John, a study of the life and educational works of John Synge'.

WILSON, WILLIAM DONALD, 'The tragic situation of the individual as presented in the works of Roger Martin du Gard'.

YUKAWA, TAKAAKI, 'Spherically symmetric motion of energy in general relativity'.

B.D.

ADAMS, JOHN DAVID ANDREW, 'An investigation of the relationship between the Faith and Order Movement and the Life and Work Movement within the World Council of Churches'.

BAGNALL, ROBERT GEORGE, 'Christian education in a Secular Society'.

CHAMP, CYRIL BRUCE, 'The Doctrine of Original Sin'.

CLARKE, DANIEL, 'Development of religious ideas in children at school'.

DUNCAN, WILLIAM ALBERT, 'The Resurgence of the Ethnic Religions and the Mission of the Church'.

MACK, THOMAS HENRY, 'The "Ne Temere" decree and its background'.

POOTS, ROBERT FREDERICK SHANE, 'The Christian concept of marriage in contemporary society'.

SMITH, ALEXANDER MONTGOMERY, 'The Biblical concept of reward and punishment'.

VAUGHAN, PATRICK HANDLEY, 'The pre-exilic age: some aspects of its high places'.

WARNER, ROBERT WILLIAM, 'The social and Biblical setting of the pre-exilic prophets with particular reference to the eighth century, B.C.'.

V

Theses approved for higher degrees

WARREN, FREDERICK NOEL, 'The Eucharistic prayer, its Apostolic pattern and development up to the time of St. Cyril of Jerusalem'.

M.CH.

DEVLIN, HUGH BRENDAN, 'Intralymphatic radiotherapy'.

HENRY, ADRIAN NEEDHAM, 'Fibrous dysplasia of bone; a clinical study of 62 cases'.

MILLIKEN, JAMES COPELAND, 'Factors in the development and prevention of peripheral vascular collapse following the release of acute occlusions of the Superior Mesenteric Artery'.

M.SC.

BRIEN, TERENCE GEORGE, 'Plasma cortisol and insulin levels in normal and pathological subjects'.

GLEAVE, ALAN GORDON, 'The microwave radiation produced by sparking in a liquid'.

HARRIS, ANTHONY BARNARD, 'The kinetics and composition of *Mycobacterium smegmatis* culture with particular reference to nucleic acid zinc and iron metabolism'.

MCCARTHY, MARY PAMELA, 'The pharmacology of Sciadotenia toxifera'.

MACKEY, DESMOND ALEXANDER GEORGE, 'The accumulation of sulphate by isolated mitochondria'.

O'MOORE, RUAIDHRI ROIBEARD LAOISEACH DeVALMONT, 'Steroid hormone excretion in the urine during pregnancy'.

O'NEILL, EUGENE DAVID, 'Anionic polymerisation of 2,4,6–trimethyl styrene'.

REID, DOUGLAS JAMES, 'The deposition of thin films in high and ultra high vacuum'.

ROBINSON, JOHN ALAN, 'A test of Pavlov's cortical irradiation hypothesis'.

SMYTH, DYMPHNA CHRISTIANA, 'The administration, detection and effects on performance of five tranquilizing drugs'.

TOBIN, JOHN, 'A study of large scale co-operative pig production'.

Dissertations

AHERN, THOMAS FRANCIS DENIS, 'Filter syntheses on a digital computer'.

ALCOCK, IAN, 'Developments in man machine interaction'.

BOYLE, FELIX (PHELIM) PAUL, 'The unitary unimodular group in n dimensions'.

AVELLA BROSA, FREDERICK, 'The quantization of the electro-magnetic field with indefinite metric'.

BROWNE, MICHAEL JAMES PAKENHAM, 'Uses of matrix algebra in the analysis of electrical networks'.

BURNE, GEOFFREY CHRISTOPHER STEPHEN, 'Some analytical routines for inventory control'.

DUNDON, EDWARD PATRICK, 'Application of a digital computer to the calculations of complex equilibrium reactions'.

Theses approved for higher degrees

RAWSON, ALAN KEITH, 'The application of a digital computer to literary problems'.

REID, JOHN CHARLES, 'Applications of digital computers to the planning and control of contract work in the building and construction industry'.

M.LITT.

BROADBERRY, RICHARD ST. LAWRENCE, 'The christian doctrine of man and resurrection in the light of modern linguistic philosophy'.

COMBE, JOHN CHARLES, 'Jean-Baptiste Massillon (1663–1742)'.

DOONEY, SEAN, 'Training and its techniques for grades up to middle management in the Civil Service'.

MATSON, B. LESLIE, 'Problems of secondary education in Ireland'.

SMITH, MARTIN FERGUSON, 'Lucretius, the man and his mission'.

M.S.A.

Dissertations

CHANDRASEKERA, DEEPAL, 'Planning and control in a printing works'.

CRAWFORD, THOMAS HENRY, 'Feasibility of payment of Wages by Cheque'.

KANE, ALASTAIR GEORGE, 'Feasibility of payment of Wages by Cheque'.

KEHOE, MICHAEL ANTHONY, 'Planning and control in a printing works'.

MCCANN, MICHAEL THOMAS, 'Farm Accounting and Management'.

MORONEY, WILLIAM, 'Farm Accounting and Management'.

MURPHY, PATRICK JOSEPH, 'A comparative study of the reactions and attitudes of supervisors in two large undertakings to managerial planning and control'.

QUINN, FRANK, 'Management control in the College Works Department'.

WHITE, JOHN JOSEPH, 'Some aspects of communicating in the Building Industry'.

WYNNE, MICHAEL BRENDAN, 'Feasibility of payment of wages by cheque'.

BENEFACTORS OF TRINITY COLLEGE[1]

Austrian Institute: a gift of language records.

The late Mr. E. A. Barber: £50 for the Library Extension Fund.

The late Miss L. C. N. Browne: legacy of £100.

Deutsche Forschungsgemeinschaft: books for the Department of Psychology.

Mrs. R. C. P. Edwards: £50 for the purchase of books for the Italian Departmental Library.

German Research Association: books for the Department of German.

Mrs. K. G. Lefroy: gift of eight antique chairs for the Library.

The late Mr. C. J. Presho: £100 for the purchase of a substantial and permanent piece of laboratory equipment.

Professor and Mrs. G. O. Sayles: a silver sugar castor as an addition to the College Plate.

[1] See also the benefactors listed under LIBRARY OF TRINITY COLLEGE.

TRINITY TRUSTS:

£1,150 to purchase five petrological microscopes for the Department of Geology.

£1,000 to the Department of Biochemistry towards cost of equipment for the Animal Research Laboratory.

£800 to the D.U. Boat Club towards cost of new slipway.

£250 to the D.U. Elizabethan Society towards cost of carpets.

£250 Travel and Research grants.

Contributions for various research objects were received from the following (to July 1966):

Agricultural Institute
Albright & Wilson (Ireland) Ltd.
Allen & Hanburys Ltd.
American Chemical Society
Arthur Guinness Son & Co. (Dublin) Ltd.
Association for the aid of Crippled Children
Bord na Mona
Bristol Laboratories Inc., N.Y.
Chemical Services Ltd.
Conquer Cancer Campaign
Distillers Company Ltd.
Glaxo Laboratories
Henry Ford & Son Ltd.
Imperial Chemical Industries Ltd.

Irish National Productivity Committee
Lalor Foundation
Marie Curie Foundation
May & Baker Ltd.
Medical Research Council of Ireland
National Institutes of Health of the U.S. Public Health Service
Roche Products Ltd.
S.P.S. International
Tenovus
United States Air Force
United States Army
United States Navy
The Wellcome Trust

APPENDIX

GRANTS TO PENSIONERS

JEROME ALEXANDER FUND

This fund was established in 1670 by a bequest from Sir Jerome Alexander. The income is used to make grants to pensioners and needy dependants of former college servants. Annual income, £74.

CURTIS FUND

This fund was established in 1944 by a bequest from Edmund Curtis, Erasmus Smith's Professor of Modern History 1914–39 and Lecky Professor of Modern History 1939–43. The income is used to make grants to pensioners and needy dependants of former college servants. Annual income, £113.

★   ★   ★

ADDITIONAL GRADUATE SCHOLARSHIP

IBM Ireland Limited will offer a Bursary, value £350, in the session 1967-68 for graduate study in the fields of administration, data processing, engineering, marketing or mathematics. Further details and application forms will be available from the Graduate Studies Office. Completed applications should be submitted by 1 July 1967.

★   ★   ★

DIPLOMA COURSE IN ENGINEERING MATHEMATICS

This will be a part-time evening course leading to the award of a diploma. Details may be obtained from the Graduate School of Engineering Studies.

INDEXES

INDEX OF NEW REGULATIONS

GENERAL INDEX

INDEX OF OFFICERS

INDEX OF NEW REGULATIONS AND
OTHER CHANGES MADE IN 1965-6

Newly instituted

Abd El-Motaal Prize in Essay Competition 420.
Archaeology and Folklore Society 441.
Browne Prize 398.
Burton Prize 403.
Business and Economics Society 442.
Establishment of Chair of Experimental Physics 29.
Establishment of Chair of Geography 28.
Establishment of Chair of Quaternary Studies 29.
Establishment of Chair of Systematic Botany 27.
Famine Relief Week Committee 443.
Far Eastern Mission 443.
IBM Irish University Bursary 582.
Jeffcott Prize 410.
John Good Prizes 412.
Mission to Chota Nagpur 445.
Re-establishment of Chair of Pharmacology 36.
Voluntary Social Work Society 447.

Degrees, licences and diplomas

Conferring of degrees *jure officii* 78.
Diploma course in Engineering Mathematics 582.
Diploma course in Entomology 361.

Entrance

Application fee 85.
Entrance requirements for Business Studies 90.
Matriculation examination: German 93; Geography 93.

College charges

Increase on all annual college fees: see COLLEGE CHARGES.

General regulations for students

College chapel, times of services 114.
Changes in Commons arrangements 119.
Regulations concerning residence in Trinity Hall 121.

584

Index of new regulations

Ordinary course in arts

Course in general studies: Biblical Studies introduced as additional course 128; subjects of study: additional requirements 128; French 132; German 133; Hebrew 134; Irish 134; Spanish 136; Fine arts I 137; Fine arts II 138; Philosophy 141; Biblical Studies I: Old Testament 142; Biblical Studies II: New Testament 142.

Honor courses in arts

Mathematics: Junior Freshman examination 151.

Mental and Moral Science: courses 159–165.

Philosophy and Psychology: courses 167–169.

Natural Sciences: honor course in Bacteriology re-named Microbiology. Senior Freshman year 172; Junior Sophister year 173; Microbiology 176, 183; Botany 178; Zoology 184.

Modern Languages and Literature: English 187; French 188; German 191; Irish 192; Italian 193; Spanish 195; English Literature and Language 198–200.

Ancient and Modern Literature: Celtic Languages 207.

Hebrew and Oriental Languages: re-titled Hebrew and Semitic Languages. Legal Science 225–226.

Courses for professional degrees and diplomas

Testimonium in Divinity: preliminary and junior year courses 242–3.

Divinity: application and notice of examination 245–6; thesis 246.

Law: courses for students of King's Inns 246; courses for Solicitors' apprentices: examinations 252; Degree of Bachelor in Laws: syllabus 255–6.

Dental Science: final dental examination 290.

Engineering: examinations 302.

Agriculture: syllabus 314–5.

Music: examinations 319; fees 324; tuition 321.

Education: admission 325; teaching practice 325.

Business Studies: examinations 333; courses and examinations 333–4.

Social Studies: examinations 335; courses and examinations 336–7; diploma: courses and examinations 339.

Graduate Course in Administration: courses 330.

Physiotheraphy: admission 342.

Graduate Studies and higher degrees

Changes in regulations 356–359; diploma course in Entomology 361.

Prizes and other awards

Entrance scholarships and exhibitions: Botany 369; Geography 369; French 370; Irish 370.

Index of new regulations

GENERAL INDEX

A

ABBEY PRIZE 374
ABD EL-MOTAAL PRIZES 412, 420
ABRIDGEMENT OF COURSE
See EXEMPTION.
ABSENCE FROM LECTURES OR EXAMI-
NATIONS 128, 146
ACADEMICALS 73
ACADEMIC APPEALS COMMITTEE 61
ACADEMIC YEAR AND TERMS X, 71
ACCOUNTANT 45
ACCOUNTING, LECTURER 44
PRIZE 412
ADMINISTRATION, GRADUATE COURSE
328
ADMINISTRATIVE OFFICERS 11
ADMINISTRATIVE RESEARCH BUREAU
331
ADMISSION REQUIREMENTS 85
HIGHER DEGREES 99
HONOR COURSES 89
MATRICULATION 86
MUS.B. STUDENTS 319
ONE-TERM STUDENTS 98
ONE-YEAR STUDENTS 98
OVERSEAS STUDENTS 86, 87, 89
PROFESSIONAL COURSES 90
RE-ADMISSION 99
*See also the various professional
courses.*
ADRIAN STOKES FELLOWSHIP 393, 408
ADVISORY COMMITTEE ON
HONORARY DEGREES 61
AERODYNAMICS 298, 301
AGENT 49
AGRICULTURAL SOCIETY 441
AGRICULTURE, SCHOOL OF 311
ADMISSION 312
ARTS 236, 239, 313
COURSES 313, 314
DEGREES 312, 314, 316

AGRICULTURE, SCHOOL OF (*contd.*)
EXAMINATIONS 313, 314
FEES 105, 315
HONORS AND PRIZES 315, 411
KELLS INGRAM FARM 437
STAFF 43, 311
ALEXANDER PRIZE 437
ALICE OLDHAM PRIZE 414
ALL HALLOWS 2
ALLOWED DEGREE 148
ALMANACK ix
ALUMNI, RECORDER OF 49
ANAESTHETICS, LECTURER 39
ANATOMIST, UNIVERSITY 35
ANATOMY
STAFF 35, 41
UNIVERSITY PROFESSOR 10, 35
ANATOMY AND EMBRYOLOGY,
PROFESSOR 35
ANCIENT AND MODERN LITERATURE
ENTRANCE AWARDS 371
FOUNDATION SCHOLARSHIP 382
HONOR COURSE 201
ANCIENT HISTORY, LOUIS CLAUDE
PURSER PROFESSOR 26
ANDERSON EXHIBITION 374
ANDREW FRANCIS DIXON PRIZE 404
ANDREWS, PROVOST 3
ANIMAL HUSBANDRY, LECTURER 42
ANNIE ANDERSON PRIZE 374
APPLIED
ANATOMY, LECTURER 35
BACTERIOLOGY, LECTURER 37
ECONOMICS, PROFESSOR 33
MATHEMATICS, GENERAL
STUDIES 140
MATHEMATICS, LECTURER 26
PATHOLOGY, LECTURER 36
PHYSIOLOGY, LECTURER 35
APPOINTMENTS AND PROMOTIONS
COMMITTEE 61
APPOINTMENTS OFFICE 453

587

General index

General index

General index

General index

General index

I

General index

General index

General index

General index

General index

W

General index

INDEX OF UNIVERSITY AND COLLEGE OFFICERS

Details of degrees and offices will be found at the places indicated.

Index of officers

Index of officers

McCarthy, G. M. 36
McCartney, A. 51
McCaughey, T. P. 31
McCaughey, W. T. E. 25, 36
McClure, K. 51
McCollum, S. T. 39, 41
McConnell, A. A. 25
McConnell, A. J. 23
McConnell, G. B. G. 46, 48
McCormack, P. D. 25, 42, 43
McCracken, T. 38
McCutcheon, L. M. 48
McDonogh, C. L. 39
McDowell, R. B. 24, 32, 46, 49
McDowell, W. T. 46
McGillycuddy, D. 49
McGilvray, J. W. 33
McKeever, J. D. 37
McKenna, B. T. 35
McKenna, C. B. 34
McKenna, P. J. G. 50
McLoughlin, M. M. 37
McMackin, M. M. 32
Mackinnon, B. F. 51
MacMahon, C. H. 40
MacManus, M. E. 49
McMurry, T. B. H. 24, 28
McVey, H. 38
Mackey, W. E. 46
Magrath, J. 36
Moosai-Maharaj, C. S. 36
Martin, E. A. 40
Matthews, W. M. 45
Mayne, B. 40
Meek, C. E. 33
Melvin, M. C. 46
Miley, A. M. 50
Milliken, J. C. 39
Milton, J. A. 42
Mitchell, D. M. 38
Mitchell, G. F. 24, 29
Montgomery, D. N. K. E. 49
Montgomery, D. W. 40
Moody, T. W. 24, 32
Moore, J. N. P. 38

Moore, M. J. 50
Moore, T. C. Kingsmill 23
Morgan, P. 50
Moriarty, J. J. 43
Morris, V. B. 40
Morrow, V. M. R. 46
Moyne, Lord 23
Moyse, A. 50
Mulvey, C. 44
Murdoch, B. H. 25, 26
Murdock, J. M. 51
Murphy, D. 50
Murphy, T. G. 26
Murray, W. 44

Nally, F. 40
Newell, A. 50
Nicholson, E. W. 32
Nicholson, J. A. 41
Ní Chuilleanáin, E. 30
Noone, A. A. 50
North, M. E. 30
Nunn, W. R. 42, 47

O'Boyle, M. I. 31, 47
O Brien, B. E. 38, 41, 49
O'Brien, C. M. 38
Ó Cadhain, M. 31
O'Clery, D. 42
O'Doherty, A. A. 49
O'Doherty, T. 47
O'Donnell, C. 50
O'Donnell, M. J. 51
O'Donoghue, F. 36
O'Donoghue, M. 33
O'Farrell, J. E. 50
O'Flynn, J. D. 39
O'Meara, R. A. Q. 24, 37
O'Morchoe, C. C. C. 25, 35
O'Morchoe, P. J. 35
O'Neill, T. 39
O'Reilly, G. A. 50
Orsi, B. A. 35
O'Sullivan, W. 46

Index of officers

3

JENA GLASS ®

for science and technology

Our Programme

Laboratory Glassware	of the borosilicate glasses DURAN 50 and GERAETEGLAS 20: beakers, flasks, dishes, funnels, bottles, test tubes.
Filtering Apparatus	Loose glass filter discs, glass filter funnels and crucibles with pore-diameters of 200 μ - 0.6 μ for the filtration of liquids and gases as well as for biochemical work; gas washing bottles.
KPG	Cylindrical and conical precision glass tubes; precision at least 0.01 mm; KPG stirrers; KPG rotary and dosing pumps; cuvettes; syringe cylinders.
Capillary Viscometers	Ubbelohde viscometers, produced by the KPG precision method and ensuring highest degrees of accuracy; viscometers for the determination of molecular weights, and viscometers for dark liquids.
Glass Electrodes	as well as metal electrodes and supplementary equipment for pH-measurements.
High-vacuum Apparatus	Diffusion and vapour jet pumps for mercury and oil; ultrahigh-vacuum pumps; suction speeds from 4 to 100 litres per second; measuring apparatus and supplementary equipment.
Molecular Distillation	All glass apparatus of highest separation effect with film distributor; thin-layer evaporator.
Special Apparatus	for the production of mono- and bi-distilled water of utmost purity; vacuum circulation evaporator; determination apparatus.

JENA^{ER} GLASWERK SCHOTT & GEN., MAINZ
(WEST GERMANY)

Representative for Ireland: The Randall Optical Company Limited · One Lower Pembroke Street · Dublin, 2

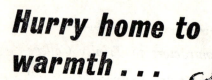

MONEY MATTERS..
..and CUSTOMERS

Nowadays the importance of expert and friendly

advice on financial affairs is widely appreciated but the

convenience of being able to call upon a complete

banking service is not always realised by those who do

not have a bank account. Such people are cordially

invited to visit any one of our 100 branches, when the

Agent will be glad to advise on any banking problems.

BANK OF IRELAND

Founded 1783

Head Office
College Green,
Dublin 2
and 100 branches
throughout
Ireland.

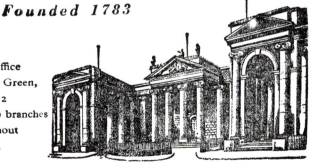

HODGES FIGGIS & CO. LTD.

*Booksellers and Publishers
to the University
New and second-hand textbooks*